Saved to Save
and
Saved to Serve

Saved to Save *and* Saved to Serve

Perspectives on Salvation Army History

HAROLD HILL
Foreword by John Larsson

RESOURCE *Publications* · Eugene, Oregon

SAVED TO SAVE AND SAVED TO SERVE
Perspectives on Salvation Army History

Copyright © 2017 Harold Hill. All rights reserved. Except for brief quotations in critical publications or reviews, no part of this book may be reproduced in any manner without prior written permission from the publisher. Write: Permissions, Wipf and Stock Publishers, 199 W. 8th Ave., Suite 3, Eugene, OR 97401.

Resource Publications
An Imprint of Wipf and Stock Publishers
199 W. 8th Ave., Suite 3
Eugene, OR 97401

www.wipfandstock.com

PAPERBACK ISBN: 978-1-5326-0167-5
HARDCOVER ISBN: 978-1-5326-0169-9
EBOOK ISBN: 978-1-5326-0168-2

Manufactured in the U.S.A.   JULY 5, 2017

First printed 2010 by Booth College, Sydney, as course notes for internal use of the Sydney College of Divinity. Course H7264, History of the Salvation Army.

"Stop.
Look back.
Often!"

Contents

Permissions and Disclaimer | *ix*
Foreword by John Larsson | *xi*
Preface | *xiii*
Abbreviations | *xvii*

Prologue	Victorian Britain	1
1	Overview of Salvation Army History	4
2	The Ecclesiology of the Salvation Army 1: Sect and Church	51
3	The Ecclesiology of The Salvation Army 2: Leadership	91
4	The Ecclesiology of The Salvation Army 3: The Role of Women	124
5	Salvation Army Theology 1: We Believe	157
6	Salvation Army Theology 2: Diversity	204
7	Salvation Army Theology 3: Worship	237
8	Social Work 1: In Darkest England	265
9	Social Work 2: Out of Darkest England	298
10	To the Ends of the Earth	331
Conclusion	Looking Back	377

Appendix One: Ranks of The Salvation Army 1878–2017 | *379*
Appendix Two: The Booth Dynasty | *381*
Appendix Three: Glossary | *382*
Bibliography | *385*

Permissions and Disclaimer

I am very grateful to Dr Roger Green for permission to quote in chapter 5 an extended passage from his work, *War on Two Fronts: The Redemptive Theology of William Booth* (1989). The General has kindly permitted the reprinting of two songs from the *Song Book of The Salvation Army* (2015), number 610 by Albert Orsborn, and number 467 by John Gowans. Wipf and Stock Publishers and Dr Grace Murdoch have allowed me to reproduce a graph from Dr Norman Murdoch's *Origins of The Salvation Army*. Wipf and Stock Publishers, and the copyright owner, the Territorial Commander for the Salvation Army in New Zealand, have also allowed me to use material from my earlier work, *Leadership in The Salvation Army: A Case Study in Clericalisation* (2007) in the chapters on Ecclesiology and Leadership; used by permission of Wipf and Stock Publishers. www.wipfandstock.com.

Every effort has been made to ensure the accuracy of quotations and to trace copyright holders and to obtain their permission for the use of copyright material. I apologize for any errors or omissions and would be grateful if notified of any corrections that should be incorporated in any future reprints or editions of this book.

Foreword

There are official histories of The Salvation Army, which describe its development—mostly in laudatory terms. There are interpretative histories, which seek to analyse and explain—sometimes critically. And then there is *Saved to Save and Saved to Serve* by Harold Hill, a book so original that it creates a new genre.

The author modestly describes his work as "a slightly eccentric collection of notes and quotes," but this refreshing volume is far more than that.

The book gives us an MRI scan of the Army. We go beneath the surface. We get the inside story. Taking a wide range of key issues of contemporary relevance, the author traces their history, and in so doing he often draws on internal sources not available to the general reader. As we watch the Salvationists of the past and present grappling with these issues against the backdrop of their day, their stories come alive.

The book is an extraordinary treasury of quoted material. For what must be the best part of a lifetime, the author has dug for gold nuggets in the most amazing locations outside and within the Army—including the Internet—and has stored them up in readiness for this book. And as he now holds them up to the light and shares them with us, we are enriched.

The book is prophetic—in the Old Testament sense of the prophets being the disturbers of Israel. The author, always an independent mind, at times dons his prophet robe and challenges our thinking, and he also gives a voice to outside critics of the Army and inside thinkers who differ from the official line.

The book furthermore introduces us to Harold Hill himself. Here is the born teacher who presents his material in a fascinating way and then invites us to reflect. His often witty and always discerning insights help us to interpret the images seen on the MRI scan of the Army. Like the teacher of the law of whom Jesus spoke, Harold Hill "brings out of his storeroom new treasures as well as old"—and does it superbly.

He concludes his book with these words: "The ability to stand back and see The Salvation Army in the context of its times, and a willingness to let the past inform the present can only enhance its capacity to do better in the future."

To that one can only say Yea and Amen.

John Larsson, General (Retired)
London, UK
May 2017

Preface

When he was a boy my friend Alan Condie's family emigrated from Scotland to New Zealand, settling in rural Southland. Looming above his new home ran the dark-green ridge of the aptly named Longwood forest. Fascinated, Alan asked, "What's that?" "The bush," he was told. "Can anyone go there?" "Yes." So he did—and promptly became lost. More than once. So he asked a friend's father, "How can I avoid getting lost in the bush?" "Three things," was the reply. "One, stop. Two, look back. Three, *often*." That seems good advice for the church as well, and in this case, for The Salvation Army.[1] For several years I have had the privilege of facilitating that process for external students of Booth College, Sydney, and these notes derive from teaching that course.

The Salvation Army has now been around for more than one hundred and fifty years, celebrating its sesquicentennial in 2015. Over the years the Army, and the world in which it appeared, have both changed beyond recognition. If we have not done too much of it before, this is a good time to stop and look back—not just to celebrate but to help us to see where we are now. The Army has not evolved in isolation from the world. Bringing its own history with it, it nevertheless belongs to the twenty-first century world as much as William Booth's little East End Mission belonged to nineteenth-century London. This book attempts to explore the inter-action between mission and world as it has impacted upon the Army's beliefs and practices as well as the place it now occupies in the wider world. This critical and analytical study may also be of interest to those beyond the Army's ranks who would like to learn more about this remarkable Movement.

This is an exciting time to be studying Salvation Army history, partly because there is a steady and deepening stream of new work on the Army's history and theology. It is becoming harder to keep up! General histories are rarer however; in fact the lack of a suitable text available for my course prompted me to provide these notes for the students. The official history by various authors, beginning with Robert Sandall's excellent three volumes published between 1947 and 1955, and with the tenth of the series now in

---

1. The principle is proverbial in many languages. In te reo Māori: *Inā kei te mohio koe ko wai koe, I anga mai koe i hea, kei te mohio koe. Kei te anga atu ki hea.* (If you know who you are and where you are from, then you will know where you are going.)

preparation, is comprehensive but uneven in quality. There is still a need for an up-to-date, general, critical history of the Movement.

This present work, however, is *not* it. This is, rather, a slightly eccentric collection of notes and quotes, if not of rags and patches, with not a few loose ends, and not concealing its origin as a composite of lecture notes, personal asides and resource material. Some parts of it have been seen before, in other contexts, but now largely out of print so I make no apology for resurrecting them here. It does not set out to inspire (the story does that without my help) though it might occasionally try to persuade. It may appear to gloss over screeds of worthy record while spending a disproportionate amount of time fossicking in odd historical corners. Institutional histories do not usually reflect Oliver Cromwell's preference for portraits to be painted "warts and all" but the odd wart or mole may be identified in this unofficial account. To that extent it may provide a counterpoint to the official histories.

Still, this is an attempt to place the Salvation Army in some sort of historical context, to direct attention to some of the more recent scholarship, and to deal fairly with some of the questions which might be asked about it. There will doubtless be errors of fact and probably some wrong-headed opinions, for which I crave readers' indulgence. I hope that this book may not only fill a gap but also encourage the writing of a more definitive work.

One of the challenges in a survey like this is whether to go about the task chronologically or thematically. It is helpful to have some overview of the whole sweep of the Movement's development in order to have some idea where the detail of topical "silos" fits into the whole picture. However, there are a number of the Salvation Army's distinctive features which repay particular examination and which may be lost sight of by being chopped up and distributed throughout a strictly chronological account. This account therefore begins with a chronological survey (with some asides on topical issues), and this is hung like a list on a simple time-line based on that provided in the Salvation Army's annual *Year Book*. This may appear an odd proceeding for such a book but suffices to cover the ground without resorting to pages of tedious prose. Subsequent chapters then pay attention to the details, examining the origins and development of some of the Salvation Army's distinctive characteristics—its ecclesiology, its beliefs and practices, its worship, its social work and its international expansion. These do not of course exhaust the possibilities but certainly fill the available space in this single volume.

Why the title, *Saved to Save and Saved to Serve*? The first phrase was a William Booth autograph, but by the time I was growing up that seemed largely forgotten and it was commonly supposed that the two S's on the Salvationist's uniform signified the second of these expressions. Initially the uniform badges were probably innocent of either intention and simply identified a "Salvationist." Nevertheless, the change in emphasis from saving to serving was in itself a significant marker of the Army's internal evolution. Recognizing that Booth's conception of salvation came to embrace both, and that his saving Army has also been shaped by, and may well have survived and thrived because of its commitment to service as well as salvation, my title incorporates both of these aims. Between them the two slogans also point to a third: "Heart to God and hand to man." That is as it should be.

NOTE ON STYLE

The Salvation Army's style guides for its publications stipulate the capitalisation of the initial 'T' in its legal name. This note acknowledges this practice but the usual conventions will be followed in this text except where quotations from sources require otherwise. Within the organisation's literature, references to the Founder tend to be similarly capitalised. This, for the sake of clarity, I have retained, along with the upper case M for "Movement," one of the Salvation Army's self-descriptions, and W for "the War," which is how it describes its mission. However, given the Army's enduring nineteenth-century tendency to capitalize almost any word that moves, I have attempted otherwise to mitigate the nuisance somewhat, except when quoting material.

Likewise, American spelling and punctuation have been employed except where the original sources of quotations did not.

In keeping with the provisions of Wipf and Stock Publisher's House Style, bibliographical footnotes are minimal and give only surnames of authors, referring the reader to the bibliography for details. An exception is that with so many Booths in print it has been thought helpful to footnote the Christian names of those other than William Booth, the Founder, as an aid to orienteering. His grand-daughter complicated things further by co-opting her father's Christian name with her surname after his death; she did not hyphenate these names when writing of her father, but *did* so when writing of her grandmother, whose Christian name she also shared! For clarity's sake the footnotes and bibliography therefore distinguish between Bramwell Booth and Bramwell-Booth, father and daughter.

ACKNOWLEDGEMENTS

My debt to many researchers and writers is obvious and acknowledged in the footnotes and bibliography. Not having been trained as a sociologist, I confess the influence of Roland Robertson, whose analysis of the Army's growth I first read some fifty years ago, and his more recent work on globalization has also helped give me a perspective on the Army in today's world. I acknowledge too Tor Wahlström ("Aristion"), whose articles in *The Officer* in 1974 pointed me in the same direction. Together they helped me find a place to stand and from which to look back.

Thanks include my gratitude to the late Philip Cairns, at whose invitation I spoke to the Booth College Association in Sydney in 2008 about my obsession with the clericalisation of the Salvation Army, and to Adam Couchman, who thereupon asked me to teach for Booth College in Sydney, and to Dr Glen O'Brien, who kept inviting me to do it again, and to the students for whom I have had to go on turning over my material. Archivists Susan Mitcham, Lindsay Cox, and Ross Wardle at the Salvation Army Archives in Washington, Melbourne, and Wellington, and Ruth MacDonald and others in Stephen Grinsted's team at the International Heritage Centre in London, have helpfully come up with material or information on request from time to time. Friends Graham Millar, Margaret and Laurence Hay, and Campbell Roberts have read various parts of the text and made very helpful suggestions for amendment and improvement, which I gratefully

PREFACE

acknowledge, along with Laurence's invaluable proof-reading. I am indebted to General John Larsson for his generous Foreword, and to Colonel Margaret Hay, and Professors Glen O'Brien, Peter Lineham, and Gordon Moyles for their kind cover commendations for this volume; and to Matt Wimer of Wipf and Stock for his guidance through the publishing process. The Salvation Army in New Zealand, on the initiative of Major Christina Tyson, Secretary for Communications and Editor-in-Chief, has provided much appreciated financial assistance with publishing expenses. And as always, the forbearance and encouragement of my wife, Pat, have enabled me to complete the task.

Harold Hill
Wellington, New Zealand

Abbreviations

CMG	Companion of the Order of St Michael and St George.
DC	Divisional Commander.
OECD	Organization for Economic Cooperation and Development.
OF	Order of the Founder.
SA	The Salvation Army.
The Army	The Salvation Army.
IHQ	International Headquarters.
TC	Territorial Commander.
THQ	Territorial Headquarters.
WC	*The War Cry.*
WCC	World Council of Churches.

Prologue

Victorian Britain

> Churches cannot be understood in solitude. They are open to the movements of the spirit and intelligence in the society which they share. While their call to love God and man gave Christian society its heart, they did not live behind a convent wall, but housed many citizens whose lungs breathed the economic or political or philosophical air of their age. If no one can understand a society without contemplating its religious forces, no one can understand a denomination without contemplating the secular society around.[1]
>
> —Owen Chadwick

The Booths were contemporaries of Queen Victoria; William and Catherine were eight years of age when Victoria, ten years their senior, acceded to the throne, and William died eleven years after the queen. They were truly "Victorians." Their Army quite soon became international in scope, but its characteristics were shaped in its British homeland from 1865 on. We need to note briefly what that looked like before considering how the movement has acclimatized in the almost 130 countries to which it spread in the succeeding 150 years.

During the first half of the nineteenth century huge changes were taking place in Britain. In the course of the previous century, an agrarian society had begun to industrialize; ancient crafts were being replaced by mechanized industries and this trend was accelerating. This led to the large-scale movement of people, from country to town and city, and to overseas colonies. As society became predominantly urban, a reducing death rate led to a steep increase in population. Britain's population (not including that of Ireland) was twenty-five million in the mid-1860s, and some three million emigrated between 1853 and 1880. London's population reached three million in the 1860s.

Britain industrialized and urbanized in advance of all other countries and its level of industrial production and overseas trade was greater than that of all rivals. By the end

---

1. Chadwick, *Victorian Church*, 1:569.

of the eighteenth century, a system of canals provided transport for goods and this was supplemented and eventually supplanted by a railway network which was established from the 1830s. The electric telegraph and penny postage brought a further communications revolution in the 1840s. To contemporary observers, the most impressive things about Britain were its commercial strength and its political stability compared with the revolution-prone countries of nineteenth-century Europe.

Nevertheless, these changes had affected the structure of British society, in that the closely integrated village hierarchy was breaking down. In the towns and cities, classes became more separated from each other, more sharply stratified and class-conscious. Rapid changes in technology and the economic cycles of "boom and bust" left many in poverty and squalor without the safety-nets of traditional society. Even in 1845 Benjamin Disraeli had written of the "two nations," the rich and the poor, "between whom there is no intercourse and no sympathy; who are as ignorant of each other's habits, thoughts and feelings, as if they were dwellers in different zones, or inhabitants of different planets; who are formed by different breeding, are fed by a different food, are ordered by different manners, and are not governed by the same laws."[2] The novels of Charles Dickens and the drawings of Gustave Doré graphically depict the condition of the poor. Cheap beer meant that alcohol consumption per head of population peaked in 1875 and public drunkenness was common. People began to look more to government—national and local—for remedies to grievances. There was a significant increase in government responsibility for education and public health in the last third of the nineteenth century.

New ideas and debates abounded. The new working class began to flex its muscles with Chartism (1840s), trades unions (a long history through the nineteenth century) and the Labor Party (late nineteenth and early twentieth centuries). The political structure was in transition toward democracy, with the property franchise progressively widening in 1830 (to urban middle-classes), 1867 (working class men in town), and 1884 (working class men in the country). But women were not included until 1919 and then not all of them; full adult suffrage did not come until 1928. The secret ballot was introduced in 1872; the powers of the House of Lords to delay legislation began to be restricted in 1911.

Natural science (geology, evolution) and historico-literary criticism began to undermine traditional religious beliefs. Religion was still central to the life of the people, but diminishing in significance. The eighteenth century Methodist revival had brought back evangelical religion and an emphasis on seriousness of life, but this revival had petered out. The "second evangelical awakening" in the 1850s and 1860s, in which the Booths played a notable part, gave some renewed impetus to evangelical religion, but the "lumpenproletariat," Marx's term for the unproductive urban poor, were untouched by and antagonistic to established religion and political movements alike.

Although the long Victorian Age is thought of as comparatively peaceful, there were many wars, some involving Britain, such as the Crimean War (1853 to 1856), the Indian "mutiny" (1857), the South African wars (1880 and 1881, and then 1899 to 1902), and a succession of colonial conflicts in places as widely spread as New Zealand, China and the Sudan. There were also other conflicts such as the American Civil War (1861 to

---

2. Disraeli, *Sybil*, 1:149.

1865), the Prussian attack on Denmark (1866), the Franco-Prussian War (1870), and the Russian war scare (1880s). All these, along with Paul's injunction to be good soldiers of Jesus Christ, provided the background to the Salvation Army's militarist persona.

This does not of course mean that the Salvation Army was merely a product of its times and place, simply reflecting the cultural and moral norms of its age and land. The movement was also counter-cultural, standing aside from or in some cases tackling society's values head on. The Booths joined with Josephine Butler, William T. Stead, and others in attacking the institution of child sex-slavery, notoriously ignored by polite society in the 1880s. Booth the pacifist was not the only Victorian to loathe the jingoism of the times—though pacifism may appear counter-intuitive in the founder of an Army. The key lay in his millennialist commitment to bringing about the Kingdom of Heaven on earth, for which reason he adopted, reinterpreted and reapplied in prophetic manner the forms and tropes supplied by the world around.

Having acknowledged, with this cursory account of Victorian Britain, one of Owen Chadwick's requirements for understanding church history, I conclude with a summary proposed by Herman Ausubel. He suggested that the two factors which really distinguished late Victorian England were firstly the progressive enfranchisement of the working class, and secondly the staying power of a baffling economic depression, which ran from the early 1870s to the late 1890s.[3] To the first of these, the Salvation Army's autocracy was counter-cultural: as Roland Robertson puts it, the Army's democracy was participatory but not decision-making.[4] The second aspect of the period provided the background to Booth's campaign to raise the condition of the poorest, both spiritually and physically.

---

3. Ausubel, *In Hard Times*, 1.
4. Robertson, "The Salvation Army," in Wilson, *Patterns of Sectarianism*, 82.

1

Overview of Salvation Army History

> The Army has only escaped from the old ruts in which it would have stuck fast and been incapable of accomplishing its great work by desperate fighting against itself . . . [It had succeeded] because the General has had, from the first, a single eye, and that single eye will enable us, if necessary, to emancipate ourselves further still, will make it as easy to abandon Army customs, as the custom which prevailed before The Army, whenever it may be proved to our satisfaction that, by so doing, we should more rapidly or completely attain the one great end in view.[1]
>
> —George Scott Railton

PROLOGUE

1829	Catherine Mumford (later Mrs Booth) born at Ashbourne, Derbyshire (17th January). William Booth born at Nottingham (10th April).
1842	William Booth apprenticed to a pawnbroker after his father's bankruptcy.
1843	Samuel Booth, William's father, died.
1844	William Booth began attending the Wesleyan chapel. Converted, he undertook freelance street-preaching as a teenager.
1846	Catherine Mumford converted.
1848–49	William completed his apprenticeship and was laid off work. After a year's unemployment, he shifted to London and was again employed by a pawnbroker.

---

1. Railton, *Twenty-one Years*, 93.

1851 William, a local preacher with Wesleyan Methodists, met Catherine Mumford at Methodist Reformed Chapel. Both were expelled from the Wesleyans for Reformist views.

1852 Funded by Edward Rabbits, William became a full-time preacher with the Methodist Reformers. Engaged to Catherine, he explored prospects of Congregational ministry, but rejected Calvinism. From November 1852 to February 1854 he was Methodist Reform minister at Spalding.

1854 Leaving the Reformers for the Methodist New Connexion and after brief training February to July, William was accepted on probation as minister and evangelist. He conducted evangelistic campaigns in many parts of England.

1855 William and Catherine were married at Stockwell New Chapel, London.

1856 William Bramwell Booth (the Booths' eldest son and second General of the Army) was born in Halifax.

1858 William Booth ordained as a Methodist minister in the New Connexion (27th May) and sent to Gateshead as minister.

1859 *Female Teaching*, Mrs Booth's first pamphlet, was published.

1860 Mrs Booth's first public address (Whit Sunday, 27th May) at Gateshead.

1861 The Booths left the Methodist New Connexion to become independent evangelists, a venture in faith when aged thirty-two and with four children. They were involved in revival campaigns in Cornwall and Wales, then Midlands. William was involved in the formation of the "Hallelujah Bands," free-lance working-class evangelists. Catherine increasingly took independent speaking commitments as well.

The Booths and the "Second Evangelical Awakening"

The "first" evangelical awakening was that associated with Wesley and others in the mid-eighteenth century. In 1858 there was a religious revival in the United States of America, spreading to the United Kingdom in 1859. J. Edwin Orr claimed that "the religious revival of 1859–65 equaled in magnitude the famed eighteenth century revival."[2] Significant converts and notable people influenced included Dr Tom Barnardo (founder of orphanages), James Chalmers (missionary to New Guinea), Hugh Price Hughes (Methodist leader), Evan Hopkins (founder of the Keswick Convention); Handley Moule and Francis Chavasse (both later Anglican bishops), and Alexander Whyte (Scottish preacher). The revival produced the Children's Special Service Mission, the East London Special Services Committee, the Salvation Army, the China Inland Mission and many other groups.

2. Orr, *Second Evangelical Awakening*, 6.

Orr reports the exploits of thirty-four-year-old William and Catherine Booth along with those of numerous other contemporary evangelists. For example, of a campaign in Hayle, Cornwall, in 1861, Orr writes that

> After-meetings for prayer followed each service, with much emotional demonstration and not a few conversions. Anglicans, Baptists and Methodists of three varieties were "delightfully united" in the work ... Great crowds could not gain entrance to the services, and were ministered to by other clergymen while William Booth was preaching. Two thousand people attended the final meetings, and six weeks' labour produced 500 conversions ... The total number [of converts] in all of Cornwall was 7,000 or so.[3]

> In the Spring of 1863 William and Catherine Booth, fresh from Revival meetings in Cornwall, began preaching in Cardiff, and won 500 people to the faith. Mrs Booth preached with great simplicity and modesty. So great was the interest in the Booth campaign that it became necessary to use a large circus building accommodating between 2,000 and 3,000 people. The effort was supported by Christians of every denomination.[4]

Orr considered that

> The most significant and fascinating home development of the 1859 Awakening was the birth of the Salvation Army ... Booth's experiences in Cornwall taught him the connection between holiness of Christian living and successful evangelism, for he preached one to achieve the other. His experience in the Black Country Revivals taught him that the masses could be most successfully reached by their own kind bearing witness. His frustrations at the hands of unsympathetic denominational directors must have determined him to shape an organization of his own. He was an inter-denominationalist, yet his Arminian convictions were strong; and so his brain-child, the Salvation Army, became inter-denominational in the support it commanded from all sorts of Christians, yet denominational enough to be considered a convinced Arminian fellowship, more Wesleyan than the modern Methodists ...
>
> The Salvation Army arose as a permanent expression of the 1859 Revival in its double ministry of evangelism and social uplift. Most of its activities today are those which were already begun by other workers of the Awakening—evangelism, indoor and outdoor, mission to fallen women, to criminals, social welfare work, missionary enterprise. Whilst the Salvation Army bears the indelible stamp of the personalities of William and Catherine Booth, it was cast by them in the mould of the 1859 Revival.[5]

1865   The Booths moved to London because Catherine had West End engagements. William began preaching in the East End.

---

3. Orr, Ibid., 113–16.
4. Orr, Ibid., 92.
5. Orr, Ibid., 215–16.

PHASES OF SALVATION ARMY HISTORY

As a framework for the chronological survey and to give some shape to Salvation Army history, I am using Roland Robertson's analysis of the Army's history in his essay, "The Salvation Army: the Persistence of Sectarianism," published in *Patterns of Sectarianism*, edited by Bryan R. Wilson in 1967.[6] Robertson, at that time a young sociologist, became a leading scholar in his field. This may be a dated approach now and does not offer a further framework for the interpretation of subsequent events, but Robertson's analysis makes good sense for the period it covers.

1. 1865–1878, the incipient phase.
2. 1878–1890, the phase of enthusiastic mobilization.
3. 1890–1931, the period of organization.
4. After 1931, the process of "terminal institutionalization."

Within these phases, to be teased out further in the process, we can place the events and dates adapted from the list provided in the Salvation Army's *Year Book*. Some particular events invite more commentary at this stage; others are discussed in later chapters.

1. 1865–1878 THE INCIPIENT PHASE

From para-church mission agency to autonomous entity

In 1859 the evangelical revival reached Britain. "Lord, I hear of showers of blessing" is a hymn inspired by, and descriptive of, the spirit of the time.[7] The "showers" spread to London and some church members cooperated in an effort to reach people in the East End with the Gospel. While retaining their own denominational affiliations, they formed the East London Special Services Committee in January 1861. Booth talked with them that year about the possibilities of his working in London. In 1864 the Committee erected a tent on a disused Quaker burial ground in Whitechapel and they were operating from this base during the summer of 1865 when William Booth met them on Mile End Waste.

In that year William Booth, an unemployed Methodist minister, shared in an open-air meeting outside "The Blind Beggar" public house. He readily accepted when invited to "have a word." The Committee's evangelist had fallen sick so Booth was engaged for one week. On Sunday 2nd July 1865 he conducted the first of his series of meetings in the tent. Three hundred people, gathered in a badly ventilated, canvas tent one "hot, sultry, July Sunday," gave birth to a vision which was to become the Salvation Army. The Committee asked him to stay on. In September, for Sundays only, they rented a dancing academy accommodating three hundred and fifty people.

In some ways this part of Booth's story is reminiscent of that of the camel who asked to be allowed to put his nose into the tent on a cold night. By morning, the whole camel was in the tent and the owner outside. Unlike the camel, Booth was invited in, but

---

6. Wilson, *Patterns of Sectarianism*, 1967.
7. Song 302, *Salvation Army Song Book*, 2015.

from being a temporary "hired help" in July 1865, by the end of the year he was running the mission.

The "East London Christian Revival Society" was founded. Various names were used: the "Christian Revival Association" in a magazine letter of 17th August 1865 and the "East London Revival Union" on a membership ticket dated September 1865. A later membership ticket for June 1866 refers to the "East London Revival Society."

A wool store accommodating one hundred and twenty was rented, and also Holywell Mount Chapel. Other preaching stations were a skittle alley (Alexandra Music Hall), a Victoria Park shop, the Effingham Theatre holding three thousand, the Union Temple Hall in Poplar, and a room behind a pigeon shop in Shoreditch. By now the group was called the "East London Christian Mission," and was mentioned in a press report.

Sandall describes 1867 as "the turning point," at which the Mission came to function as an independent and self-contained entity.[8] Catherine meanwhile had been preaching in the West End to fashionable crowds, and then in the popular south coast resorts where they went for the summer. She spoke in the East End for the first time in 1867.

In 1868 *The East London Evangelist* was published (renamed *The Christian Mission Magazine* in 1870 and *The Salvationist* in October 1879). The Mission's first venture outside East London was a temporary post in Upper Norwood in South London. In July 1869 the enterprise became known simply as "The Christian Mission."

The People's Market in Whitechapel Road was bought and reopened as the People's Mission Hall and Headquarters, proving to be a financial burden. An old plate factory was also used, and there was branch in Croydon (South London) The Mission entered into a temporary association with a mission in Edinburgh, given up in 1870 when it had to be subsidized from London funds. Support came from friends for the Booths; regular aid was received from the Evangelization Society (1865–68), and there were collections: £13.13s (13 guineas) in the second three months. In 1868 the Mission paid its way with £100 in hand.

The Mission expanded. Of the first fifteen stations, only Croydon was not in East London. The next four openings were to the south of London. Hastings was significant as there the first hall was built for the Christian Mission. Then followed three openings in Wales, then six stations in the Midlands, then seven openings in the North East of England.

In 1870 Booth was off sick from April to July, while Catherine ran the Mission. William evidently had a busy sick-leave; he published *How to Reach the Masses with the Gospel*. There was a debate current in Christian circles about the most suitable people to preach the gospel to the poor. Moody argued that eloquent people were required. William Booth disagreed and in a series of letters to *The Christian* magazine, he advocated the use of people who had been converted from the same condition. He also held that every outdoor meeting should be followed by an indoor meeting. Getting people away from distractions allowed them to hear the gospel more clearly and enabled prayer and appeals to follow Christ. Other practices he urged were advertising well (including billboards carried by people), holding meetings on week-nights as well as at weekends, and holding outdoor and indoor meetings all year round—not just in summer or "preaching season."

---

8. Sandall, *History*, I: 72.

During this time, Booth had run the Mission as his personal enterprise but with its expansion he felt a need to share the burden more widely. The first annual conference of the Christian Mission, in November 1870, established its first constitution on the model Booth knew best, that of the Methodist New Connexion. The annual conference was made the final authority.

In 1872 Booth had another bout of ill-health and Catherine ran the Mission again from April to October. The next year they recruited George Scott Railton, aged twenty-four, as secretary; William and Catherine were now forty-four and Bramwell, their eldest, was sixteen. In 1874 the Christian Mission work commenced in Wales.[9]

Having given away so much control, William found this did not suit him, nor his close associates. The first constitutional Deed Poll followed in 1875, giving the General Superintendent authority to over-rule decisions of the annual conference. This and subsequent constitutions are described in the chapter on ecclesiology.[10]

The *Rules and Doctrines of the Christian Mission* were published. Annie Davis was the first woman to be placed in charge of a station, at Barking. In 1876 *Revival Music* was published, and this time both Booths were off sick for three months after conference.

A review of ten years' growth shows that the Mission alternated between growth spurts and periods of stagnation and decline, but the overall trend was towards expansion.

1867–6 preaching places	1873–27
1868/9–16	1874–31
1870–18	1875–39
1871–22	1876–38
1872–19 (In 1871–72, no new stations were opened	1877–31
	1878–57

The slight set-back early in the decade can be seen, and the beginning of the boom at the end. This experimental phase, as it might be seen in retrospect, tested out the principles and some of the practices which would be carried forward and serve as the basis of the Salvation Army's exponential growth in the following decade. To these combustible raw materials the introduction of that distinctive name and style set a flame which blazed up into a fire which spread around the world.

---

9. Bernard Watson's splendid life of Railton, *Soldier Saint* (1970) was the first official Salvation Army biography not to be more in the nature of a hagiography.

10. A *deed poll* is a legal document signed by only one party. Its name originally indicated that the parchment has been "polled"—cut in half—so that there was no corresponding other half to be signed by another party. It is therefore not a contract because it binds only the signatory, and expresses an intention instead of a promise. Lodged with a Court ("Enrolled in Chancery") the Deed Poll became binding. The device is now used chiefly for changing a legal name but was earlier of more general application..

2. 1878–1890 THE PHASE OF ENTHUSIASTIC MOBILIZATION

The Christian Mission became the Salvation Army.

Gordon Moyles relates how several different versions of just how this change of name occurred were reported by participants and others but all involved the correction of a proof-copy of a report reading "The Christian Mission is a Volunteer Army" to read, "The Christian Mission is a Salvation Army."[11] There is also some debate about the reasons for this change in name and style at the end of the 1870s.

The Army's received tradition is of a steady progress, though not without set-backs and disappointments in the second half of the 1870s, such as

- The growing frustration of Booth and many of his supporters with the "government by committees" put in place in 1870.
- The slowing of evangelistic growth that seemed to accompany the securing of buildings with mortgages rather than rented halls.
- The abandonment of Sunday schools in 1877.
- The abandonment of relief work and feeding programs.
- The continuing financial struggle.
- The Booths' disappointment at not being able to persuade all their associates to adopt total abstinence as a requirement for membership.[12]

Some go further and speak of "failure in East London 1870–1877" as the primary reason for reorganization.[13] Norman Murdoch suggests that Booth's workers tended to be drawn from middle and working class people from outside the East End itself and that he had not in the end been able to engage successfully with his intended target group, the poorest of the poor. One of the reasons given for this is that such people were resistant to any form of organization—religious, political, or unionist—being so ground down by "near-starvation, chronic unemployment, the struggle for a day's wage at the dock gate, and erratic charity." They would take anything they were given, but would not buy into Booth's self-help ethic, *nor join up*. The other reason given is that the majority group in the East End were Irish Catholics (as well as Jews, Turks, Armenians, Russians, Chinese and others who tended as poor immigrants to settle in the poorest quarters), who resisted English, Protestant evangelism. The cultural gap was too great for Wesleyan revivalism to bridge. All of that may very well be the case.

Hugh McLeod says the characteristics of working class Londoners were "secularism and parochialism."

> The chief principle of this "secularism and parochialism" was the concentration of knowledge, responsibility and personal ties within a small area, and lack of interest in events outside; its corollaries included indifference to questions of abstract principle, a low valuation of education and non-participation in organizations. The

---

11. Moyles, *Exploring Salvation Army* History, 29–35.
12. Sandall, *History* I, 186–97.
13. Murdoch, *Origins of The Salvation Army*, 71–87.

features of working-class London that gave rise to this body of attitudes were the poverty of many, the insecurity of most, and, in relation to the social system as a whole, the lack of status and power that was universal. Working class parochialism was imposed by the exigencies of the struggle to scrape together a living; it was a form of physical self-defense against the threat of destitution and the workhouse; it was a form of escape from obligations which the gentry inherited together with their social position; above all, it was a form of psychic self-defense—the demarcation of a limited area within which those at the lower end of a highly stratified society could secure for themselves a degree of status and recognition.[14]

The Mission's membership inside London declined while it grew further afield, and its total membership also grew between 1871 and 1877. Booth's own statistics showed that there was minimal growth in the East End from 1865 to 1875, followed by stagnation and decline. Murdoch quotes Booth's address to the 1877 Conference: "In many of our old stations we appear, from the returns, to have had something very like stagnation during the year."[15] Roland Robertson also examines the class structure of the early Army and concludes that "the 'real' social constituency of the Salvation Army was lower middle class, initially conjoined with a substantial minority of diverse lower-class elements."[16] Glen Horridge comes to the same conclusion regarding officers. The majority of the East End population was of those yet lower still in the class league tables.

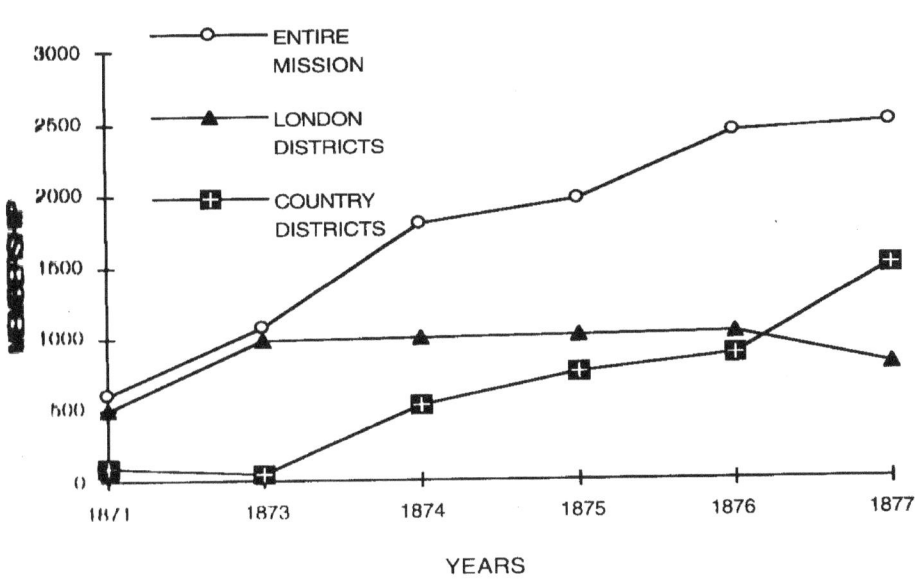

Christian Mission membership 1871–1877 (Norman Murdoch's graph)[17]

---

14. McLeod, *Class and Religion*, 42–43.
15. Murdoch, *Origins of the Salvation Army*, 87.
16. Robertson, "The Salvation Army," in Wilson, *Patterns of Sectarianism*, 98.
17. Murdoch, *Origins of the Salvation Army*, 83. Used by permission of Wipf and Stock Publishers. www.wipfandstock.com.

Murdoch's conclusion from these statistics is that, "Declines in London pointed to a need for organizational change."[18] While the statistics are convincing as far as the real state of the "war" was concerned, it is not clear that this entirely explains the way in which the Christian Mission morphed into the Salvation Army, or proves that Booth decided to counter decline in one part of his growing work specifically by this change in organizational style. Booth was already moving towards the exercise of greater control in order to ensure that his policies were adhered to; the new system "marshalled him in the way that he was going." There is ample evidence for the way the various threads—in structure, terminology and ethos—came together but less for the assertion that Booth was casting about for a silver bullet and happened to find this one. Sometimes, rather, as far as the "Army" style is concerned, he appears to have been a reluctant, even embarrassed participant: almost a case of the saying variously attributed to Ghandi and Ledru-Rollin amongst others, "There go my people. I must follow them, for I am their leader."

Stephen Grinsted, in an *Officer* article commenting on Murdoch's arguments, notes that "Cyril Barnes, Roger Green and [David] Bennett take the less radical view that the Salvation Army came into being as the result of an evolutionary process." He also quotes Green as saying: "The question is not really one of success and failure. The critical question is, in the great metropolis of London in general and East London in particular, how did this mission survive when countless others failed?"[19] The military style may well have provided Booth's silver bullet, but not because he had consciously chosen it as such.

Here were some of the ingredients in the mix:

- **Wars and rumors of wars** such as the 1876 Bulgarian uprising and Turkish atrocities. Russia championed the cause of Balkan Christians. The British felt Suez and Indian interests were threatened. In 1877 the possibility of a Russo-British war aroused excitement.

- **Militant Christianity** was a feature of 1860s and 1870s missions and hymns; in 1865 "Onward Christian Soldiers" was published.

- **Banners**. A Christian Mission banner surmounted its Eastern Star Headquarters in 1867. Bannerettes were used on the march and a flag discussed in 1874. In 1876, Booth said, "We are thinking of getting a flag, and if so, of crimson ground and blue border—the crimson signifying the atonement, the blue purity." Even in 1878, however, a report from Leicester mentioned that "the white flag of the Salvation Army is flying high in this wicked town."[20]

- **Disenchantment with government by conference and committee**. In 1876 a delegation of missioners told Booth, "We joined to serve under you, not one another." The 1877 Conference Committee decided that the annual conference would be a council of war, not a legislative assembly. At conference in June 1877, William Booth recommended adoption of the resolutions of the conference committee. These gave Booth the authority to accept and appoint evangelists. He anticipated

---

18. Murdoch, Ibid, 86.
19. Grinsted, "Christian Mission," 16.
20. *Christian Mission Magazine*, October 1878, 268.

imminent developments in his conference address when he said, "We have been called by the arrangement of Divine providence to be OFFICERS AND LEADERS IN HIS ARMY and we are met to consider how we can best advance the interests of THAT ARMY."

- **Adoption of military styles and terms**. Railton had called Booth "General" and described himself as Booth's "Lieutenant" from 1873. In 1875 Bramwell Booth wrote to a missioner encouraging him to be "in every way captain" to his station. In 1878 Elijah Cadman at Whitby called himself "Captain" and styled Booth as "General of the Hallelujah Army" on posters advertising his visit. The fashion caught on.

- **Change of name**. The printer's proof of the Mission's 1877 Annual Report said "the Christian Mission is a Volunteer Army". One account has Bramwell Booth objecting to being a volunteer—a part-time "territorial soldier"—because "we are always on duty." William Booth crossed out "Volunteer" and substituted "Salvation."[21] The name was thus at first descriptive of the Christian Mission, not a title in its own right. Booth referred to "the Salvation Army" in an address to the Christian Mission Conference in August 1877.[22]

1878   The Christian Mission became the Salvation Army, and the Reverend William Booth, General Superintendent, became known officially as the General, by which title he had been known unofficially in the family and the mission for several years. A new Deed-Poll, executed at the "war congress" in August 1877, set out the new constitution which consolidated his authority. Military terminology was adopted. The first corps flag was presented by Mrs Booth at Coventry (28th–30th September); *Orders and Regulations for The Salvation Army* were issued in October; brass band instruments were first used. The statistics for the growth accompanying all these changes are salutary:

	Officers	Corps
June 1878	88	50
December 1878	127	81

1879   The first corps were opened in **Scotland** and the **Channel Islands**; the first cadets were trained; uniform was introduced; the first corps band was formed in Consett; issue No 1 of *The War Cry* was published on 27th December.

1880   The first training home was opened, at Hackney, London; the first contingent of Salvation Army officers landed in the **United States of America**; Salvation Army work commenced in **Ireland**; children's meetings were commenced at

---

21. For the differing accounts, dates and places, given for this significant event, see Moyles, *Exploring Salvation Army History*, 29–35.
22. *Christian Mission Magazine*, August 1877, 194.

Blyth; work was extended to **Australia**. Catherine Booth published *Practical Religion* and began a series of meetings in the West End of London.

1881　Work began in **France**; *The Little Soldier* (subsequently *The Young Soldier*) was issued; *The Doctrines and Disciplines of The Salvation Army* prepared for use at training homes for Salvation Army officers, was published; Headquarters was moved to Queen Victoria Street.

1882　The Founder paid his first visit to France; the former London Orphan Asylum was opened as Clapton Congress Hall and National Training Barracks; work began in **Canada**, **India**, **Switzerland**, and **Sweden**.

1882–83　Negotiations were initiated by the Anglican Church to explore the possibility of incorporating the Salvation Army into the Church, but this did not eventuate.

Advances

The rapid expansion of the Salvation Army's work throughout the British Isles is a remarkable saga. Wordsworth's recollection of the excitement of the first years of the French Revolution—"Bliss it was in that dawn to be alive, But to be young was very heaven"—could have applied to the first decade of the Salvation Army.[23] Most of the officers were young, some very young, and threw themselves into the task with sacrificial abandon. Many burned out in short order. Many of them were women. Rachel and Louise Agar pioneered the Tyneside in 1878, raising twenty-two Stations, forty-seven officers and more than 3,000 members in the district within twelve months.[24] So many men were converted in Gateshead that the police charge-sheet was reported to have been reduced by fifty per cent.[25]

James Hay was converted at Patrick in Glasgow in 1881 aged sixteen, was a cadet in London at seventeen, and within months was Lieutenant at Aberdeen. Promoted to Captain at eighteen when his Captain fell by the wayside, he "was left in charge of two hundred soldiers and two Sunday congregations of about eight hundred each, besides the whole round of duty. Happily I was an early riser. Two hours on the Bible before breakfast, and full of spirit and prayer, I kept in humility and expectation with literally 'Every hour for souls and duty.'"[26]

Another Scot was seventeen-year-old William Murray, who joined the Army in Aberdeen in 1880 when it was pioneered by two women, Captain Mrs Smith and Lieutenant J. Gardner. Murray was treasurer there in Hay's time there, three years later, and was waiting

---

23. Wordsworth in "The Prelude," Book X, lines 693–94.
24. Sandall, *History*, II, 7.
25. Larsson, *My Best Men are Women*, 20.
26. Hay, *Aggressive Salvationism*, 17. A commissioner aged 44 and territorial commander for Australasia 1909–12, Australia 1912–21, British Commissioner briefly, then territorial commander in South Africa, and then in New Zealand 1926–29, Hay was president of the first High Council in 1929, retiring when TC in Canada in 1935.

to finish his apprenticeship before going to the training home. His diary-based memoirs reveal something of the early Salvationists' experiences from a soldier's perspective.

> Very soon our numbers swelled to a great extent, but in spite of the good work that was going on we were turned into the streets, by whom I know not, but out we were turned . . . my private opinion being "Holiness" was too much taught for them; next time we met was in the open-air we had with us Capt (now Colonel) Day & did we get kicked about I can tell you. However, we fought on, first in a small hall held 140 then another holding 250 then a larger 450 then a Sunday Hall for 1000 . . . The six months T[urner] and E[vans] were there was the hardest ever experienced & the least good done for eternity I believe, we went out many a night not knowing if we would come in alive again, but the Lord watched over us . . . In one fight J. Graham got about killed; A.J. got knocked down 3 or 4 times, there was swelled faces and blue legs, but what we did we did for eternity, & if we got pushed about, well we said we got almost killed for the devil many a time why should we not suffer for Christ's sake.[27]

Not all were young however, and some were unexpectedly pitched into leadership. Mrs Kate Shepherd was housekeeper and cook at the Whitechapel headquarters when she was sent with her four daughters to open fire in the Rhondda Valley in 1879 because she was Welsh-speaking. In the course of a few months, she saw 2,500 conversions and began a revival. Sandall notes that her success convinced the General that "just such lasses could with all propriety be sent out as leaders."[28] Louisa Lock, Kate Shepherd's successor in the Rhondda Valley, on the other hand was already a seasoned campaigner of eighteen in 1879, with three years' experience of leadership in the north of England. At Pentre in the Rhondda she became the first woman officer to be imprisoned (arrested with four men soldiers, receiving two days with hard labor for praying in the street and thereby allegedly obstructing the traffic) and was greeted by a crowd of twenty-thousand upon release. Contracting tuberculosis, perhaps in consequence of this experience amongst others, she was dead by twenty.[29]

The Army was recruited in the open air, where it presented all the razzmatazz of a circus come to town. Booth encouraged the unusual; even though he had private reservations. Writing to Bramwell in 1877 he said, "I wish we did not do so many silly things. I think I see a great difference between manly, natural, bold, daring action and weak, frivolous, childish comicality."[30] But he was no shrinking violet himself. Rudyard Kipling recalled seeing Booth come aboard ship in Bluff, New Zealand:

> I saw him walking backward in the dusk over the uneven wharf, his cloak blown upwards, tulip-fashion, over his grey head, while he beat a tambourine in the face of the singing, weeping, praying crowd who had come to see him off . . . I talked much with General Booth during that voyage. Like the young ass I was, I expressed my distaste at his appearance on Invercargill wharf. "Young feller," he

---

27. Smith *Fighting for God and* Eternity, 19–20.
28. Sandall, *History*, II, 13.
29. http://daibach-welldigger.blogspot.co.nz/2016/01/teenage-revivalists-in-rhondda-2-louisa.html. Accessed 27 May 2016.
30. Begbie, *William Booth*, I, 440.

replied, bending great brows at me, "if I thought I could win one more soul to the Lord by walking on my head [sic] and playing the tambourine with my toes, I'd—I'd learn how."[31]

So Bramwell Booth was carried through the streets in a coffin, and then preached from it.[32] One officer went every night during one winter week to lie down in the snow in one spot for forty-five minutes without speaking, and then, having drawn an expectant crowd by his last appearance, rose up to speak. Converts were advertised with all the subtlety of a freak show, given or giving themselves titles like "Cheap Jack," "the Hallelujah Pigeon-flyer," "Skelton the Thrasher," and "Wells the Converted Thief." As Bramwell Booth wrote, "We in the Army have learned to thank God for eccentricity and extravagance, and consecrate them to His service."[33] It paid off; the Army became the show to see.

As well as expansion of work in the United Kingdom, the decade of the eighties saw the Salvation Army tricolor planted in more than twenty other countries, beginning with the United States of America, pioneered informally by seventeen-year-old Lieutenant Eliza Shirley. Booth was not at first interested in overseas expansion; he felt he had enough on his hands at home. He tried to dissuade young Eliza Shirley from immigrating to the USA with her parents, and was unwilling that she should attempt to start the Army's work there.

> But if you are determined to go to America and you are determined to begin religious work there, you will do well to organize it along the line of the Army at home. If you do this, you have my permission to call it The Salvation Army; if it succeeds, and I believe it will, we may later see fit to take over the work you have started and continue it.[34]

Having begun two corps successfully in Philadelphia, Eliza and her parents wrote to William Booth asking for reinforcements. Booth commented:

> We were anxious to avoid this for a little longer, seeing how much remains to be done for the millions who remain in utter darkness even in this land of light . . . but we cannot blame the love and zeal which has driven them without waiting for us, to open the attack.[35]

George Scott Railton and seven "Hallelujah lassies" (Alice Coleman, Rachel Evans, Emma Elizabeth Florence Morris, Elizabeth Pearson, Clara Price, Annie Shaw, and Emma Westbrook, only the last of whom was a commissioned officer at the time) were farewelled from London in February 1880 to make the official attack on the United States. Despite reverses and schisms, the first of these as early as 1884, there were 238 corps and 569 officers, mostly American, in the Union when Booth paid his first visit in 1886.[36]

As in America, the Army was taken to Australia by immigrants from its homeland. John Gore and Edward Saunders, both converts of the Christian Mission in Britain, met

---

31. Kipling, *Something of Myself*, 61–62.
32. Nicol, *General Booth*, 290.
33. Booth, *Echoes and Memories*, 106–107.
34. Chesham, *Born to Battle*, 56.
35. Wisbey, *Soldiers without Swords*, 22.
36. Chesham, *Born to Battle*, 74.

in Adelaide and decided to form a Salvation Army corps. They held an open-air meeting in the Adelaide Botanic Gardens, allegedly "a notoriously wicked part of an otherwise respectable city," according to Manning Clark.[37] Gore's famous parting invitation was, "If there is any man here who hasn't had a decent meal today, let him come home to tea with me." They appealed to General Booth in London to send out an officer.

Captain and Mrs Thomas Sutherland were sent and arrived at Adelaide in February 1881. They were met by sixty-eight converts and Army followers. The first official Australian corps opened, Adelaide I. Sutherland was jailed for a street procession, and fined one shilling. During 1882 and 1883, twelve corps were opened. Within three years there were thirty-two officers and twelve corps, and on the third anniversary 3,600 soldiers mustered for the grand celebrations.[38]

Similar growth followed the invasion of New Zealand. In response to an invitation—and a draft for £200—from Miss Arabella Valpy of Dunedin, Booth dispatched nineteen-year-old George Pollard and twenty-year-old Edward Wright in 1883.[39] After nine months they held their first New Zealand congress with eleven corps represented and five brass bands and one drum and fife band on a march which comprised between five hundred and six hundred uniformed Salvationists. In his two and a half years in New Zealand, Pollard opened thirty-three corps, recruited over sixty officers, and enrolled nearly three thousand soldiers.[40]

India was invaded because Frederick Tucker, an assistant magistrate with the Indian Civil Service, had been sent a copy of the English *War Cry*, read it, and sailed to England to meet the Booths. Reluctantly accepted as an officer, he was commissioned a major and sent back to India with an invading force of four, arriving on the 19th September 1882. A series of confrontations followed with Imperial authorities anxious not to provoke inter-communal disturbances but the Salvationists were well-supported by all shades of Indian opinion. By the end of the decade there were one hundred and seventy officers in India, one hundred of them Indian, and fifty-seven corps. In Ceylon were a further thirty-three European officers and forty-seven nationals.[41]

So the work expanded. By 1890 the Army's flag also waved in Ireland, France, Canada, Switzerland, Sweden, South Africa, Newfoundland, Germany, Italy, Denmark, the Netherlands, Jamaica, Norway, Belgium, Finland, Argentina, and Uruguay. A.M. Nicol reported Booth's own explanation of the Army's spread:

> As he has frequently remarked: "The Salvation Army was not made to a plan. It was a growth, not a dream for a well-thought-out scheme. The life within it is largely responsible for its advance. I did not say 'Now is the time to go to Germany,' and then appoint men and women to seize a café and start preaching salvation in Stuttgart. The principle of what led us to begin operations in Germany has

---

37. Clark, *History of Australia*, IV, 369.

38. Historical research often uncovers a more complex back-story to the romantic legends of early days. See Hentzschel, "Hidden Turmoil."

39. £200 in 1882 was equivalent in value to about £22,200 in 2017. Booth did not give it all to Pollard and Wright!

40. Bradwell, *Fight the Good Fight*, 36.

41. Smith, *By Love Compelled*, 43.

prompted many other developments in the Salvation Army. A German strolled into a Salvation Army Hall in the Bowery of New York and gave his heart to God. He imbibed the spirit of the Army from the officer who dealt with him about his spiritual condition, and shortly afterwards he wrote to me that he felt that he ought to devote his life to the salvation of his Fatherland. I took that letter to indicate the line of Providence with respect to Germany, and ordered the German and his wife to Zurich and there learn more about the Army. He came, and in the course of time was commissioned to open Stuttgart and then Berlin. In that incident you have an illustration of the growth of the Salvation Army. It was not made to the plan of the General according to the whim of an ambitious fancy."[42]

Persecution and Opposition

Opposition began in Christian Mission days. In October 1874 William Booth wrote that in the previous month there had been

> Violent opposition encountered in the open-air, the police, the publicans, and lewd fellows of the baser sort having in turns, and in some instances all seemed to combine, to defeat and drive us from the ground . . . The public houses are the difficulty . . . drunken men are bribed with liquor to annoy and if possible break up the meetings.[43]

Cadman, at Hackney in 1876, reported:

> At our open-air services, publicans, policemen, butchers, and quite a number of "lewd fellows of the baser sort" have combined to drive us from the field . . . We were set upon by a band of ruffians shouting, howling and pilling us about. Some of the sisters were very roughly handled indeed. One man was knocked down and left with a black eye, but we stood our ground. They pelted us with all sorts of things, and flour in abundance. I was as white as a miller. We had a good meeting, and one man professed to be saved.[44]

Both Booth and Cadman evidently felt themselves in apostolic succession to Paul and Silas at Thessalonica in Acts 17:5.

Murdoch attributes some of the early opposition in the East End of London to the fact that the Mission was really invading Catholic Irish territory. Perhaps that is what lay behind the advice given in the 1881 *Doctrines and Discipline of The Salvation Army*, in the section concerned with "The Duty of An Officer" in respect of "Opposition and Persecution."

> Avoid those things which, though not essential to your success, yet provoke opposition. For instance, don't denounce particular *forms* of sin. Don't rail at Sabbath-breaking Shop-keepers, Publicans, Infidels, or Roman Catholics. Talk

---

42. Nicol, *General Booth*, 97.
43. Sandall, *History* I, 160.
44. Sandall, Ibid., I, 202.

against the Publicans, and you will soon have the police set upon you; or denounce the Papists, and you will soon get your head broke.[45]

It is certainly no coincidence that the period of the Salvation Army's most rapid growth was also the time of its fiercest persecution. It was newsworthy, it sought attention, it made enemies; it provoked determined and often brutal opposition. Public house and brothel owners were angered when former customers were converted in Booth's Army. Profits fell and business suffered. Many supported the "Skeleton Army" whose main ambition was to get rid of the Salvation Army at any cost. Glenn Horridge says that the opposition to the Salvation Army drew on an old English working class tradition of rough-musicing—riotous, mob-behavior—which could be good-humored but could also turn ugly and vicious.[46] Some Salvationists were killed because of their faith. Mrs Susannah Beatty became the Army's first martyr after being pelted with rocks, viciously kicked in the stomach and left for dead in a dark alleyway.

Since the Salvation Army was born in the open air, Salvationists continued to work to the maxim that if the sinful did not come to them then they must take the gospel message into the streets. The sight of Salvationist processions with flags waving often incited the protesters' anger and they took the opportunity for violent attack. All over the country Salvationists were faced with angry mobs which used ammunition in the form of dead rats and cats, tar, rocks, rotten vegetables and even burning coals and sulphur to show their hatred of the new movement. In 1882 alone, 669 Salvationists were assaulted, 251 of them women and twenty-three children under fifteen. Fifty-six buildings had been seriously damaged.

According to George Scott Railton, the original skeleton army was organized at Weston-super-Mare towards the end of 1881. The Christmas *War Cry* of that year states that "the chief officers of the Skeleton Army raised to oppose us at Exeter were converted." It was after that edition that the term skeleton army came into regular use.

An article about the organized opposition appeared in the *Bethnal Green Eastern Post* (November 1882):

> A genuine rabble of "roughs" pure and unadulterated has been infesting the district for several weeks past. These vagabonds style themselves the "Skeleton Army" . . . The "skeletons" have their collectors and their collecting sheets and one of them was thrust into my hands . . . it contained a number of shopkeepers' names . . . I found that publicans, beer-sellers and butchers are subscribing to this imposture . . . the collector told me that the object of the skeleton army was to put down the Salvationists by following them about everywhere, by beating a drum and burlesquing their songs, to render the conduct of their processions and services impossible . . . Amongst the skeleton rabble there is a large percentage of the most consummate loafers and unmitigated blackguards London can produce . . . worthy of the disreputable class of publicans who hate the London school

---

45. *Doctrines and Discipline of The Salvation Army*, Section 36.

46. Horridge, *Origins and Early Days*, 112, 192. "Rough music" is a form of English folklore, and refers to a centuries-old practice in which a humiliating punishment is inflicted upon people who have violated the standards of the rest of the community.

board, education and temperance, and who, seeing the beginning of the end of their immoral traffic, are prepared for the most desperate enterprise.[47]

The organization of skeleton armies in London and the publicity this received did much to spread trouble throughout the country. At first the Metropolitan Police turned a deaf ear to the appeals made for protection for Salvationists. Their then head, Sir Edmund Henderson, even denied that what was alleged was actually taking place. Serious fighting and conflicts with the police eventually turned the public against the Skeleton Army in London, resulting in drastic measures being introduced to deal with the rowdies, bringing organized trouble to an end.

The Skeleton Army however, thrived in other parts of the country until 1892. During those years the corps officer's wife at Guildford was kicked unconscious, not ten yards from the police station; a woman soldier was so injured that she died within a week; at Shoreham, a woman captain, Sarah Broadbent, died through being hit by a flying stone. Eastbourne's mayor declared that it was his intention to "put down this Salvation Army business," and if necessary the town council would call on the skeleton army to help them. This in fact happened, and many Salvationist were brutally assaulted, because they were denied the protection of the law and would not protect themselves.

Sometimes the tables were turned; Charles Jeffries, second-in-command of a skeleton army, who was converted along with thirty of his followers in Whitechapel in January 1882, eventually became a commissioner in the Salvation Army and was one of the leaders who requisitioned the first High Council in 1929.

In some places, an appeal to the mayor or magistrates brought police protection, as at Strood and Hastings. However, in many cases the police did very little to help. Brewers and publicans often served as councilors and Justices of the Peace, which stacked the odds against the Salvationists. In 1878 Captain Mrs Reynolds of Nottingham was sentenced to prison but friends paid her fine. In 1879 Captain Louisa Lock and four men of Pentre were imprisoned for praying in the roadway; she died eighteen months later of illness contracted in jail. In October 1879 Cadman was sentenced to imprisonment at Coventry but his fine was paid because the police feared a riot if he was jailed. Ballington Booth spent twenty-four hours in jail in Manchester for preaching in the street.

The policy of "peace at any price" adopted by the Home Office in October 1881 meant the police intervened as little as possible. The processions were not illegal, they were told, but if the peace of the town was endangered then they should try to prevent disturbances, preventing the Salvationists from marching. The result of this advice to magistrates is that Salvationists ended up being sent to jail because they had been attacked. Many found themselves in prison on trumped-up charges made by police and magistrates. By the end of 1884, 600 Salvationists had been jailed for such offences as "obstruction" and it was not until 1912 that the last officer was imprisoned for obstruction in England.

There was support as well as opposition. Even *The Times*, generally antagonistic to the Army, supported its right to march, regardless of the fact that it was "neither very judicious nor very conciliatory in its operations . . . all calculated to provoke opposition and antagonism . . . So long as it abides by the law, it is clearly entitled to the protection of

---

47. Sandall, *History* I, 193.

the law."⁴⁸ Some local bodies, such as that of Eastbourne, secured Local Acts with Anti-Salvation Army clauses which enabled them to "ambush" the Salvationists. However, the Queen's Bench of the High Court found for the Army on appeal, and eventually Parliament passed a Repeal Act which took effect from the beginning of September 1892. The Parliamentary Committee believed that "liberty of speech and liberty of procession" were the Englishman's basic right.⁴⁹ Other legislative protection followed: Shaw Clifton notes that even today, as a result of the Army's representations over the years, "there are over a hundred statutes in England which give a named exemption to marches organized by the Army."⁵⁰

Opposition was not confined to Britain of course; it happened wherever the Army went. In 1884 the officer at Prahan in Melbourne was sentenced to twenty-four hours imprisonment for leading a procession. When Major Barker led a procession to demand his release, Barker was sentenced to a month's imprisonment. Over a hundred Australian Salvationists were fined or imprisoned for street-preaching or marching, up to the last sentence for obstruction in 1907. In New Zealand, a skeleton army was actually formed in anticipation of the Salvation Army's arrival in the city of Wellington in 1883. There were many cases of prosecution for obstruction in New Zealand, the first being in Waimate in 1885, and many officers and soldiers were imprisoned in various towns. A protracted series of trials and disturbances at Milton in 1893 ended with the Borough Council in retreat, despite the defeat in the Upper House (Legislative Council) of a Government bill declaring council by-laws used against the Army as *ultra-vires* (beyond their legal power to make).⁵¹ The last case was in Christchurch in 1911.

In Switzerland Catherine Booth (eldest daughter of William and Catherine) and Captain Becquet were prosecuted and imprisoned in 1882. Frederick Tucker spent his thirtieth birthday in jail in Bombay. As territorial commander in Germany, Railton was deported from Prussia. In the 1880s and 90s in the United States, Captain Joseph Garabed (known as "Joe the Turk", though he was actually an Armenian) made a nationwide career of being thrown into jail for challenging anti-Army local legislation and usually being acquitted, bringing an end to the local difficulty. Stories of persecution could be told from many countries.

Opposition of Other Kinds

Words, rather than sticks and stones, were the weapons of choice of the more polite classes. Although some churches and clergy were supportive of the Army's work, criticism was common. A Wesleyan minister wrote a pamphlet complaining of the Army's lack of real religion, saying that "their services are frequently a travesty of music-hall entertainment."⁵² Perhaps Booth would have taken that as a compliment; it was what he aimed at.

48. Editorial in *The Times*, 14 June 1882, quoted by Rhemick, *New People of God*, 144.
49. Horridge, *Origins and Early Days*, 112.
50. Clifton, *Who Are These Salvationists?* 139.
51. Hay, "Onward Christian Soldiers," in Stenhouse and Thomson *Building God's Own Country*. 113–23.
52. Horridge, *Origins and Early Days*, 113.

The Army's teaching on holiness and the role of soldiers was also criticized:

> Egotism is of the very essence of the system. Each man and woman assumes to be a chosen vessel of the Holy Ghost, bound to look after the souls of others, and to lead them on by the aggressive manifestation of his or her own example. The advice of David, "Serve the Lord with fear, and rejoice unto Him with trembling," has no significance in their practice. They hold themselves to have that "perfect charity [which] casteth out fear," of which St. John speaks.[53]

Lack of reverence was offensive to many:

> [I]t indulges in a familiarity with holy things that is sometimes painful to Catholic ears. The Holy Name of Jesus is bandied about in songs which are profane, ribald, and almost blasphemous. It is shouted out in the "rollicking choruses" which General Booth speaks of with enthusiasm, in a way utterly at variance with the reverence due to the Name before which all in Heaven and on earth should bow. This . . . in itself, proves that it cannot be regarded as a work of the Holy Spirit of God. For true religion not only includes a spirit of reverence, but it is in itself an act of reverence.[54]

Charles Pratt said of Army worship:

> [T]here seems little real and deepening repentance and growing faith in the Lord Jesus Christ; there seems no room for real spiritual devotion, no recognition of the Christian sacraments, no culture of that truest Christian grace, humility.[55]

Another critic wrote of an Army poster:

> No one who has any reverence for Divine things can read this placard without being filled with a sense of shame, horror and disgust. Well might Lord Salisbury, in referring to it at a meeting on Saturday, remark that "the excesses of the Army were producing great irreverence of thought, of expression, and of action, turning religion into a play, and making it grotesque."[56]

John Price wrote:

> [L]et me call the knowing ones, the leaders and editors, the actors and actresses in this hateful caricature all that is sacred and holy, to a repentance which they need *far* more than the ignorant "masses" whom they compare with "the inhabitants of Sodom and Gomorrah!"[57]

The Editor of *The Month*:

> [T]he religion of The Salvation Army . . . certainly requires no internal obedience of heart and will. In order to "find Christ," to be "converted," to be "saved," there is no need of humility. There are no dogmas to be accepted. Salvationism is a

---

53. Chichester, "The Salvation Army," in *The Month: A Catholic Magazine and Review*, April 1882, 480, quoted by Rhemick, *New People of God*, 122–23.

54. Basom, *The New Theology*, 471, quoted by Rhemick, Ibid., 124.

55. Pratt, *The Salvation Army: A Sermon*, quoted by Rhemick, Ibid., 124.

56. *Truth, Religious Persecution, Sleeping Christianity. An Answer to "Behind the Scenes with The Salvation Army,"* quoted by Rhemick, Ibid., 145.

57. Price, *The Salvation Army Tested by their Works*, 21, quoted Rhemick, Ibid., 145.

religion without a theology, without ritual, and without sacraments, and such a religion cannot last. It has no backbone. It is a matter of feeling and sentiment. There is no subjection of the intellect . . . [58]

When negotiations with the Church of England were mooted, it was an opportune moment for the Bishop of Oxford to make sweeping allegations of immorality in the Salvation Army. Bramwell Booth circulated a questionnaire on "The Salvation Army and Charges of Immorality" to all corps officers in the United Kingdom, in response to which the returns showed that out of 449 corps there were twenty-eight cases of illegitimate children whose birth, it "might reasonably be thought . . . was due to the attendance of the Parents at our meetings." That may seem an astonishing admission but the Bishop of Oxford believed it to be a conservative estimate. Nevertheless, in Bramwell's words, he was "screwed up to the point of making a milk and water apology."[59] Such slanders were uttered elsewhere in the world: in Dunedin, New Zealand, the Reverend A. R. Fitchett warned readers of the *Otago Daily Times* that

> To the hundreds of young women who were present at the "Salvation Tea" in the Garrison Hall—factory girls, seamstresses, domestic servants—the Army meetings have brought nightly scenes of excitement, late hours, and a new code of easy and sympathetic relations with a corresponding number of young men. It is true that all this is supposed to be under the sanction and guardianship of religion, but no one acquainted with the history of religious excitements, and their tendency when not controlled to run into a particular form of immorality, will see much ground for reassurance in that.[60]

Fitchett was able to support his allegations by reference to the fact that "at the assembly of the Upper House of Convocation in England, the bishops had passed a nearly unanimous vote of condemnation of the Salvation Army on the grounds that its meetings promoted serious immorality." What has more recently been called "fake news" has a long shelf-life.

Bramwell Booth recalled long after that the Earl of Shaftsbury, great social reformer but bitter opponent of William Booth, had "solemnly stated that, as the result of much study, he had come to the conclusion that the Salvation Army was clearly the Anti-Christ; whereupon some silly admirer put the cap on his Lordship's absurdity by discovering that the letters in the name of William Booth made '666,' the mark of the beast!"[61]

Much of the "intellectual opposition" consisted of personal attacks on the character and probity of William Booth. Cartoonists exaggerated his Hebraic nose in order to offer Shylock-like depictions—although, despite his mother's maiden name being "Moss" and Evangeline Booth's claim to be of Jewish descent, no Jewish ancestry has actually been discovered for Booth.[62] Allegations that Booth amassed a fortune from donations and

---

58. Editorial, "The Salvation Army and Darkest England," *The Month* LXX, September–December, 1890, 470, quoted by Rhemick, Ibid., 146.

59. Horridge, *Origins*, 115, Booth, *Echoes and Memories*, 39.

60. *Otago Daily Times*, 2 June 1883, cited by Bradwell, *Fight the Good Fight*, 29–30.

61. Booth, *Echoes and Memories*, 40.

62. Green, *Life and Ministry of William Booth*, 7.

Salvation Army business were perhaps best answered by his will. His personal estate when he died in 1912 was worth £487 and nineteen shillings, in addition to which he was responsible for a trust fund worth £5,295, from the interest of which his salary had been paid. He had never drawn a salary from Salvation Army funds and this trust had been established by a friend in order to give him a small but regular independent income.[63]

Some critics were concerned that Booth aimed at establishing a secular power in the state, based on his authoritarian command of a militaristic organization. His most celebrated opponent of the Army was T. H. Huxley, the great zoologist. His attacks on Booth's probity were especially prompted by the Darkest England Scheme. By this time however, Booth enjoyed the defense of churchmen like Cardinal Manning.

Internal Opposition

Not all of Booth's critics were from without, as Booth's expectation of absolute obedience aroused resentment amongst some of his officers from time to time. In the late 1880s there was a "reforming spirit" amongst some, blamed on Colonel Henry Edmonds, once William Booth's ADC and later Territorial Commander for Scotland. Whereas some insubordinate persons were dismissed, or forced to resign, Edmonds was simply ignored—left with his rank but without any further appointment. Both the dispute and the character of his punishment may have been partly because he was a wealthy man and did not need to beg.

Bramwell Booth recalled that, "In the early days of the Army's expansion in the United Kingdom, one of the most anxious problems which concerned the Founder . . . was the unwillingness of a certain proportion of the first leaders to be moved from one place to another—from one appointment to another . . . Here was a serious question of principle . . ." Apparently the principle was the occasion of some disagreement in 1878, when Booth resumed autocratic powers and a minority of missioners parted company with him. "Twelve or fourteen years later the question again came to the front . . . Two men, both holding important positions . . . agitated for a change in the Army system." The Founder resisted the move. "His pronouncement was accepted throughout the then Army, to the immense gain of the movement. Several officers resigned . . . in particular the two men referred to promptly took their departure. They both came back a year or two later acknowledging their mistake."[64]

Edmonds, however, was not one of those who came back. In his unpublished memoirs he wrote of

> . . . the extent to which, at a certain period, the General and Headquarters carried their spying and persecuting propaganda against those whom they suspect of seeking reforms in the Army system, or criticizing any department of the Army, or any member of the Booth family, or their administration of their

---

63. Details of Booth's will are given in Moyles, *Farewell to the Founder*, 107–08. £487 in 1912 was apparently worth about £43,570 in 2016 terms. Booth was not a pauper but neither was he wealthy.

64. Booth, *These Fifty Years*, 142–48.

responsibilities, would be incredible but for the knowledge and experience of those who have suffered it.[65]

Some of the "spying" was inherent in the paperwork required, such as the forms to be filled in by incoming corps officers, exposing the failings of their predecessor's administration.[66] But Booth had other sources of information: he told the August 1878 conference of the Mission, the last such, that

> People who are not with me in purpose and plan must not complain if they do not have my confidence. If they keep secrets from me, they may be sure that I get to know it; little birds come to me in the midnight hour with such secrets, and they will be found out.[67]

It might have been his humor, but it had a threatening aspect. Edmonds was not a disinterested observer, but his account has to be reckoned with:

> Distrust and suspicion are the leading characteristics of its interior dealings, and a system of espionage and an elaborate secret service are at the disposal of its chiefs . . . Headquarters directly encourages this. It takes each officer into its interior confidence as regards his fellows, and on the other hand confides in every one of his comrades in reference to the officer himself. The officer is eagerly listened to in reference to his chief, and the chief examined in reference to the officer . . . The intelligence office at Headquarters is ever busy and though authorities are never given and accuser and accused are never brought face to face, yet reports are acted upon and people oft-times disciplined . . . This espionage obtains throughout the whole affair (and internationally), and from the highest to lowest all are more or less subject to its workings, indeed, those that are not and cannot be affected are only the General himself and his immediate entourage.[68]

Official histories understandably airbrushed out certain episodes. Murdoch reports:

> Increasingly, ex-officers, now growing in number, voiced their frustrations in public. Defections in 1886 by Colonel Day, the Southern Division commander, and Commissioner Corbridge, Booth's friend from Christian Mission days, pointed to dissension in the staff concerning Booth's arbitrary rule. Day later recanted his complaints; but Corbridge, whose charges had to do with financial reports sent him by army accountants, threatened to sue and contact the press. He had been the official fund-raiser. Day, Corbridge, and others held meetings to denounce the army. From 1886 to 1889, former staff officers brought court cases, all won by the army, which spawned negative press reports at a time when the army needed more income. Two of Booth's Aide-de-camps, Major Hodges and Colonel Edmunds [sic], resigned. These officers knew how to litigate and knew how much the army needed a good press. They also saw how little influence they had in an organization controlled by the Booth family. Thousands of lesser

---

65. Edmonds, unpublished memoirs, quoted by Horridge, *Origins and Early Days*, 88.
66. *Orders and Regulations*, 1878, Appendix, Form 1, 4. 1.
67. Murdoch, *Origins*, 96–97.
68. Horridge, *Origins and Early Days*, 89.

officers resigned due either to illness or to despair at their hard lot and the lack of influence they had in a system that profited from their labor.⁶⁹

Some former officers published books describing their experiences: J.J.R. Redstone's *An Ex-Captain's Experience of the Salvation Army* (1888); Abner Sumner's *The New Papacy* (1889); A. M. Nicol's *General Booth and The Salvation Army* (1911)—this last by a former commissioner—all embarrassed the Army's reputation, although Nicol's account was both fair and respectful of Booth. While the views of disaffected persons should not always be taken at face value, some of the charges made were manifestly correct, such as Nicol's statement that whereas field officers ("where the real work of the Army is carried on") frequently went without their allowance because other expenses had to be paid first, staff officers suffered no such privation—their income was guaranteed.⁷⁰ Set against well-publicized stories of officers broken down in health by over-work and poverty, and then discarded as failures, Bramwell Booth's smug comment to a newspaper editor that "We don't lose many that we want to keep" does not sit so well.⁷¹

Gordon Moyles recounts the impact of Boothian autocracy on the fledgling Army in Canada under the authority of Herbert Booth (whom he describes as "a martinet like [the Founder]."

> In 1892 a dissatisfaction with the rigidity—and lack of compassion—inherent in the Army system came to a boiling point . . . The chief spokesman for the dissident officers, Peter Philpott, was forced to resign and when he did so he took almost a hundred other officers and a few hundred soldiers with him . . . The newspapers labelled the affair "Boothism versus Philpottism," apprising the public in vivid detail of the "tyranny" under which Canadian officers worked.⁷²

Throughout this period Booth and his Army faced constant criticism, fueled by the revelations of former Salvationists. Newspapers loved to announce:

THE SALVATION ARMY MUTINY

CURIOUS REVELATIONS OF AN EX-CHIEF STATISTICIAN

> Some days have passed since the publication of the news of the revolt of the Camberwell and Nunhead corps of the Salvation Army, in consequence of the exactions, and the excessive financial charges of headquarters. Those reasons were given at the time, and the attention of those in authority at 101, Queen Victoria Street, was called to the matter; but the Army, which lives on the support of the public, has, so far, disdained to give the public any explanation, or to favour the world with any vindications of itself for the allegations made by its disaffected members . . .⁷³

The revelations which followed, that headquarters took 10 percent of all collections, and charged corps exorbitant rents on building schemes, were alleged by a Mr

---

69. Murdoch, *Origins*, 144.

70. Nicol, *General Booth*, 115. The system obtained until the mid-twentieth century.

71. "Bramwell Booth and the Future of his Movement," by the Editor of the *Daily News and Leader*, in *Salvation Army Year Book*, 1915, 2.

72. Moyles, *Exploring Salvation Army History*, 54.

73. *New Zealand Herald*, 7 July 1894, 2.

George Rapkins, "nearly twelve years an officer and ten years and a half on the staff of the General," who had resigned "in consequence of his failure to reconcile the business methods of the Army with their spiritual aims."

Such matters—relatively innocuous as they may appear today—were not considered proper to report or remark on for much of the Army's history, but their inclusion now is not intended to discount the heroism and devotion of the Army's workers, nor the vision and commitment of its founders and its leaders over the years. In Jungian psychology all personalities have a dark side, which must be acknowledged and embraced lest it grow more powerful in proportion to the extent to which its existence is denied. The consequence of not acknowledging and dealing with that dark side is that it continues to affect the person adversely, as a weakness rather than a strength. The same is true of organizations, which are in some measure the corporate projection of the individual personalities comprising them and in particular of those who most shape the corporate identity.[74]

I recall attending a Student Christian Movement camp, at which a guest speaker was a Catholic priest recently returned to New Zealand after spending seven years at the Vatican. He said that what he had seen and heard and experienced there [in pre-Vatican II days] had convinced him beyond all doubt that the church was divinely led, guided and protected by the Holy Spirit—he did not see how otherwise it could ever have survived. Despite such flaws and failings as have been noted, the early Salvation Army not only survived but thrived.

1883   Work began in **Sri Lanka**, **South Africa**, **New Zealand**, **Isle of Man**, and **Pakistan** (then a part of India); the first prison-gate home opened in Melbourne, Australia; *The Doctrines and Disciplines of The Salvation Army* was published in a public edition. The Salvation Army ceased to practice the sacraments of Baptism and the Lord's Supper.

1884   Women's Social Work was inaugurated; *The Soldier's Guide* for daily Bible reading published; work began in **St Helena**; *The Salvation Army Band Journal* was issued; *All the World*, a record of missionary enterprise, began publication.

1885   *Orders and Regulations for Divisional Officers* and *The Doctrines of The Salvation Army* were published; the Purity Agitation was launched; the Criminal Law Amendment Act became law on 14th August; the trial (began 23rd October) and acquittal of Bramwell Booth—charged, with W. T. Stead and Rebecca Jarrett, in connection with the "Maiden Tribute" campaign against child prostitution.

1886   Work began in **Newfoundland**; the first international congress was held in London; *The Musical Salvationist* first issued; first Self-Denial Week held; the first slum corps opened at Walworth, London, by 'Mother' Webb; work began in **Germany**; *Orders and Regulations for Field Officers* was published; the Founder first visited the United States and Canada.

---

74. Schaef and Fussell, *Addictive Organization* (1988) describes the relationship between the two.

	British		Overseas	
	Officers	Corps	Officers	Corps
1883	1,340	528	201	106
1886	2,260	1,006	1,932	746

1887   Work began in **Italy**, **Denmark**, **Netherlands**, and **Jamaica**; the Founder first visited Denmark, Sweden, and Norway. Young people's work was organized throughout Great Britain; a first food depot opened, in Limehouse, London; work began in **Norway**; Catherine Booth's last public address was given at the City Temple, London (21st June).

1889   Work began in **Belgium** and **Finland**; *The Deliverer* was first published.

Before we leave the 1880s and address the next stage of the Army's evolution, the phase of "routinization and institutionalization" which we somewhat arbitrarily date from 1890, we should note that the Army's onward march was not without reverses. We'll look at this again as background to the introduction of the Darkest England social scheme, but it is clear that the Army's life was not all big meetings, of the kind prescribed in the *Orders and Regulations* or described in Booth's visions. Perhaps Booth tended to think it was because when he was present the meetings tended to be big—and he became offended if they were not.[75] But in most corps the numbers were small and the graft hard.

There was also the difficulty of retaining converts. Nicol again described his disappointment on arriving at his second corps, Middlesborough:

> I was confronted with the failure of the Army to retain its converts. It was here that I received my first disappointment in "revival" work, to which I attached the utmost importance, and by which I hoped the world would eventually be introduced to a reign of peace and righteousness. Major James Dowdle and other successful officers of the Army had been stationed in Middlesbrough and had gained altogether 10,000 converts, but the strength of the three Corps in the town did not exceed 400, and many of the members belonging to the Corps wore no uniform, only attended meetings on Sundays, smoked tobacco, and were worldly in their attire.[76]

Hugh McLeod refers to the findings of a church attendance survey conducted by the *British Weekly* in 1887:

> Even at the time of the *British Weekly* census, when the reputation of the Army, then emerging from a period of persecution, was close to its highest point, attendance at Salvationist meetings in London was lower than was generally believed. When it was discovered that only 59,591 had attended Salvationist services at the mission hall census of 1887, Robinson Nicholl, the editor of the *British Weekly*, poured scorn on the Army's grand claims. Yet something had gone wrong with the Army's geography and the *British Weekly*'s arithmetic: the total which Nicholl derided had still been substantially inflated by the inclusion of returns from such

---

75. Nicol, *General Booth*, 10.
76. Nicol, Ibid., xi.

places as Hounslow and Canning Town and by a failure to add the figures correctly. The number attending Salvationist services in Inner London should have been 42,205; or 29,581 if, as in 1902–1903, afternoon services were excluded.[77]

Norman Murdoch cites the same survey:

> The Salvation Army's bleak situation was becoming apparent to a public audience by 1888. January's *British Weekly* survey indicated that London corps (the name for local Salvation Army mission halls) attracted only 7% of London's population to religious services. By comparison, an 1881 survey had shown that the Army had attracted 11.1% in provincial Scarborough, 7.4% in Hull, 6.8% in Barnsley, and 5.3% in Bristol. While the Army grew in working-class neighborhoods of the West End, the provinces, and overseas, it declined in East London. By late 1888, Church of England clergy were announcing in the secular press Booth's failure to win the "heathen masses" to the gospel. The phenomenal early growth of his newly-reorganized and renamed Salvation Army slowed dramatically and, after 1878, growth in cities stopped.
>
> The decline was particularly noticeable in London, headquarters of Booth's worldwide Christian imperium. In the Whitechapel and Bethnal Green districts of the East End, *British Weekly* surveyors could scarcely find a Salvationist. They found that the Army's main hall at Clapton was situated "among artisans and clerks," a class other Nonconformist groups were already reaching. Decline in East London, in spite of Booth's public denials, could be documented from his own *War Cry*, even though he stopped publishing statistics after 1886. On April 13th, 1889, District Officer Adjutant Morgan disclosed that the average East London corps' membership was 71.6, with a total number of about 1,000 in all East End corps. This was the same as the number at the East End Stations of Whitechapel, Limehouse, Poplar, and Shoreditch, fifteen years earlier when the Christian Mission reached its peak. The obvious conclusion was that the Army was not converting the "heathen masses" to the gospel.[78]

McLeod attempts to answer the question as to why the Army and other groups did not make headway in London, despite its being a home-grown London movement. The

> . . . interesting and difficult question is why working men did not respond to exclusion from the major denominations by forming their own sects, and why such bodies as the Primitive Methodists and the Salvation Army were even weaker in London than the Anglicans and the Wesleyans. It may be that the democratic sect makes greater demands on its members than most people are prepared to meet, but the fact remains that religion of this kind did attract a significant following in some parts of the country. [He cites such places as Hull, Bristol and Leicester in an end-note.]
>
> One possibly relevant factor was the working-class ethos of communal solidarity [in rural and industrial areas where] some form of Methodism (most commonly) was able to identify itself with the community as a whole . . . In London, however, the only parallel was within the Irish Roman Catholic community. Elsewhere, to join any sort of church was to mark yourself out as an individualist . . .

---

77. McLeod, *Class and Religion*, 38. The *British Weekly* figures were reported 5 November–17 December 1886 and 13–20 January 1888.

78. Murdoch, "William Booth's *In Darkest England*," 97–103.

> A second possible explanation for the religious indifference of so many members of the working and, to a lesser extent, of the lower middle class, who were committed to no anti-religious ideology, lies in sectarian parochialism, the source of which lay in hereditary subordination, and the consequent limitation of the area within which the individual was accustomed to knowledge, responsibility and power. Engels asserted that God was the personification of the mysterious forces controlling society, and the more men felt helpless, the readier they were to seek an explanation for their situation in the arbitrary will of God. According to my interpretation, the reverse was true: those who felt powerless in a world dominated by mysterious alien forces tended to respond by withdrawing into a more local world, within which their words and actions *were* of some consequence, and questions concerning the general nature of society, let alone of the universe, they tended to dismiss as irrelevant speculation; the arbitrary ruler of their world was not God but Fate.[79]

As Murdoch notes, Booth stopped publishing his field statistics when they ceased to reveal relentless progress. Nicol was still questioning this in 1911:

> Headquarters regularly publishes the number of staff and field officers, local officers, bandsmen, corps, outposts, shelters, rescue homes, training homes, with the number of cadets in each, prison-gate missions, the number of lodgers in shelters, and a mass of other minutiae. But for some mysterious reason, no mention is ever made in these statistical statements of the number of soldiers (or members). These figures remain a secret . . . I have not been able to discover a reasonable explanation for the singular silence.

Nicol went on to estimate the probable international soldier-strength of the Army from his knowledge of the various territories and came up with a total of 256,950.

> As nearly twenty thousand of these are in the pay of the Army as officers, it may be accepted that, in round numbers, there are a quarter of a million registered members of the Army in the world. That is the numerical result of forty years' evangelization throughout the world. Personally, I think the above statement the most astounding outcome of one man's consecration to the service of God that the world has ever seen or known, even when allowance is made for the number who are soldiers of the Army by mere profession, and the number is subtracted that have been won to the ranks from comfortable Christian homes . . . So that altogether the creation of a quarter of a million of people, sworn to conform to the vow of obedience and abstain from the luxuries and the pleasures of society, is an achievement that cannot be measured by a statistical table, although there is no earthly reason that I can conceive of for withholding the number so pledged from the knowledge of the public.[80]

The irony is that Booth need not have been bashful about his statistics; the hiatus of the 1880s over, the Army continued to grow, and continued to collect its statistics even if it did not reveal those of soldiers.

---

79. McLeod, *Class and Religion*, 282.
80. Nicol, *General Booth*, 212–20.

Year	Soldiers	Year	Soldiers	Year	Soldiers
1900	193,092	1940	563,991*	1980	661,526
1905	217,738	1945	580,912*	1985	735,063
1910	231,382	1950	505,532	1990	776,684
1915	256,214	1955	532,752	1995	834,379
1920	334,660*	1960	560,576	2000	1,019,137
1925	442,427*	1965	580,576	2005	1,045,253
1930	487,815*	1970	595,191	2010	1,123,048
1935	527,245*	1975	634,395	2013	1,174,238

Salvation Army, *Journey of Renewal*, 21. Years marked with asterisk combined numbers for soldiers and adherents. Inconsistent terms of reference for collection of data must be the bane of the statistician's life. The same could be said of occasional outbreaks of honesty (or discovery of clerical errors) and purges of rolls (42,000 removed from rolls in Kenya in 2002). This perhaps contributes to but not wholly explains, surely, a reported loss of 117,516 soldiers in recent years: the 2016 Salvation Army *Year Book* gave a 2015 figure of 1,056,722, down from 1,174,238 in 2013; back up to 1,130,400 in the 2017 *Year Book*.

Nevertheless, nearly a century elapsed before the *Yearbook* began reporting the number of soldiers in the Army; General Paul Rader instituted this practice in the 1990s.

3. 1890–1931 THE PERIOD OF ORGANIZATION AND "ROUTINIZATION"

The Movement becoming an Institution

In the terminology of sociology, "routinization of charisma" refers to the way whereby a movement originating in the vision of a charismatic individual passes into the control of the next generation of managers and practices originally innovative become routine. William Booth possessed the founding charisma, but his heir and successor, Bramwell, did not. Although Bramwell did not become General until 1912, he was, as Chief of the Staff, instrumental in the "institutionalization" of the movement. Roland Robertson takes 1890, the year of the publication of *In Darkest England*, as the hinge year of the transition from "enthusiastic mobilization" to an established institution. The change was not complete until the Salvation Army ceased to be the property of the Booth family and passed totally under the control of what John Coutts has described as a "self-perpetuating oligarchy," established in law by the Salvation Army Act of 1931.[81] Robertson's third period of the Army's history therefore encompasses this entire chain of events. It might be noted however that Salvationists have continued to this day to refer to the Army as "the Movement." What does that tell us about how the Salvation Army sees itself?

1890   Work began in **Argentina**; *Orders and Regulations for Soldiers of the Salvation Army* were issued; Catherine Booth was promoted to Glory (4th October);

---

81. Coutts, *Salvationists*, 26.

In Darkest England and the Way Out, by the Founder, was published and the "Social Wing" inaugurated; work began in **Uruguay**; the Banking Department opened (registered as The Salvation Army Bank, 1891, and Reliance Bank Ltd, 1900).

1891   The Founder publicly signed Darkest England (now The Salvation Army Social Work) Trust Deed; £108,000 was subscribed for Darkest England scheme; Land and Industrial Colony, Hadleigh, Essex, was established; the International Staff Band was formed; work began in **Rhodesia** (now Zimbabwe) and **Zululand**; the Founder made his first visits to South Africa, Australia, New Zealand, and India; the charter of the Methodist and General Assurance Society was acquired.

1892   The Band of Hope was inaugurated; the League of Mercy began in Canada.

1893   *The Officer* was first published.

1894   A second international congress took place; work began in the **Hawaiian Islands** and **Java** (now part of Indonesia); Naval and Military League (later Red Shield services) established; the Swiss Supreme Court granted rights to Salvation Army. The Assurance Society was launched; on which occasion Railton expressed public opposition to the dilution of the mission by social work and business enterprises.

1895   Work began in **British Guyana, Iceland, Japan,** and **Gibraltar** (until 1968).

1896   Young People's Legions and Corps Cadet Brigades were inaugurated; work began in **Bermuda** and **Malta** (until 1972).

1897   The first united young people's meetings held (later termed "councils"); and the first international social council; the Army's first hospital established at Nagercoil, India.

1898   *Orders and Regulations for Social Officers* were published; work began in **Barbados** and **Alaska**.

1901   Work began in **Trinidad**.

1902   Work began in **St Lucia** and **Grenada**.

1903   The Migration department inaugurated (became Reliance World Travel, 1981, closed 2001); work began in **Antigua**.

1904   A third international congress held. The Founder was received by Edward VII at Buckingham Palace, conducted his first motor campaign, and signed the Supplementary Deed Poll. Work began in **Panama**.

1905	The Founder campaigned in the Holy Land, Australia, and New Zealand; the first emigrant ship chartered by Salvation Army sailed for Canada; the International Staff Lodge (later College, now International College for Officers and Centre for Spiritual Life Development) was opened; work began in **St Vincent**.
1906	The *YP* (later *The Warrior*, then the *Vanguard*), and first *Salvation Army Year Book* were published.
1907	An Anti-Suicide Bureau was established; The Home League was inaugurated; *The Bandsman and Songster* (later *The Musician*) issued; an honorary degree of DCL, Oxford, was conferred on the Founder; work began in **Costa Rica**.
1908	Work began in **Korea**.
1909	Leprosy work began in **Java** (now part of Indonesia); and work began in **Chile**.
1910	Work began in **Peru**, **Paraguay**, and **Sumatra** (now part of Indonesia).
1912	The Founder made his last public appearance, in the Royal Albert Hall, London on 9th May, and was Promoted to Glory, 20th August; **William Bramwell Booth appointed General**.

The Booth family

William and Catherine Booth had a large family, and they all, apart from the invalid Marion, became fully engaged in the salvation war from an early age. From helping their parents they naturally became leading figures in what was a very young Army. Apart from Marion they were all gifted and there seemed no incongruity in their exercising roles of leadership at a young age when the majority of other officers were also in their twenties. The Booths also fostered a boy, George, who did not join the Salvation Army and was last known to have emigrated to the United States.

Incidentally, because so much we read of William Booth is in serious vein—his authoritarian style and irascibility, his bouts of depression, his passion for evangelism and single-minded drive to save the world—we tend to forget his other sides. There was the loving family man who delighted in and played with his children and grandchildren. There was his sense of humor—even if sometimes grim, as when he surveyed his battered troops after a riot at Sheffield and told them, "Now's the time to get your photographs taken!" And there was the public figure who made sometimes surprising interventions into public affairs, such as his joining forces with the non-conformist church leader, Dr John Clifford, to press the authorities—against the disapproval of most Free Churchmen—to bury the actor Henry Irving in Westminster Abbey in 1905.[82]

---

82. Pearson, *Bernard Shaw*, 163.

Bramwell was involved in helping his father from his early teenage years. He became second in command of the Army as Chief of the Staff from his early twenties when Railton went to the USA in 1880, although he had been "third ruler in the kingdom" as "travelling secretary" while Railton was "secretary" to the Mission until that year. Bramwell was the organizing genius behind the Army's expansion and kept a close hand on virtually everything. As responsibilities grew, he simply worked longer hours. For some years he doubled as Chief of the Staff and British Commissioner. Bramwell never held a rank until he became General; he was always "Mr Bramwell," as in a Victorian family business, or "the chief." (His siblings, apart from Marion and Lucy, chose their own ranks.)

Bramwell's need to control led to tensions with his younger siblings, apart from Lucy, the youngest. His succession by the sealed envelope nomination was seamless because he just continued doing as he had done, apart from no longer being able to discuss everything with his father. He served as General from 1912 to 1929.

Ballington, after some corps experience, took charge of officer-training at age twenty-three with the rank of colonel. He was appointed commander in Australasia aged twenty-seven in 1884–1886 and then in the USA 1886–1896, adopting the title of "Marshal." He and his able wife Maude resigned rather than accept a change of appointment, and attempted to lead a secession of the American forces. When thwarted by the intervention of Evangeline, he set up a new organization, the "Volunteers of America," which still exists and specializes in social work. He died in 1940.

Catherine pioneered the work in France and Switzerland in 1881 at the age of twenty-one, with the title of Maréchale (which honorific she retained after leaving the Salvation Army in 1902), and in 1887 married the brilliant but slightly unstable Arthur Clibborn who became Booth-Clibborn in the fashion adopted by all three Booth sons-in-law. They had eleven children. They resigned at the beginning of 1902 because of Arthur's theological views and partly because they had not wanted to be transferred from France. Catherine became an independent evangelist. She died in 1955.

Emma, aged twenty, ran the training of women officers (known as "the training home mother") until she married Frederick Tucker in 1888 and went out to India with him. His first wife had died there and Emma's ill-health necessitated their return to Britain within a few years. They were appointed to replace Ballington in USA in 1896, Emma taking the title of "Consul," and she was killed in a railway accident there in 1903 aged forty-three.

Herbert, was probably the most gifted of the Booth children, especially musically, and was thought of by his father as a future General—the General once suggested that Bramwell should name Herbert in *his* sealed envelope when the time came. He was responsible for training men officers at age twenty-one, then successively commander in Britain, Canada and then Australia in 1896 with the title of "Commandant."[83] From 1898 he fostered multi-media productions, including moving pictures produced by Joseph Perry. In 1902 he resigned after disputing with his brother and father over the closeness of IHQ control over territories. He became a travelling evangelist and died in 1926.

Marion, an invalid, lived at home and held the honorary rank of captain.

---

83. William Booth came to dislike these personal titles and wished his children would be content with conventional ranks.

Evangeline was a corps officer, then in charge of women's training in 1884, then London divisional commander aged twenty-three, then "field commissioner" for Britain, and then commander in Canada in 1896. Her father refused her permission to marry, saying she was too valuable single. In the USA with the title of "commander" from 1904 until 1934, she sent the "dough-nut girls" to the First World War and became an American citizen in 1923. She laid the foundations for the Army's American reputation. She resisted Bramwell's attempts to appoint her elsewhere and through the 1920s she led opposition to her brother's policies. Elected General in 1934, she retired in 1939 aged seventy-four, dying in 1950.

Lucy was the conformist child—content to be a "commissioner." She went to India when aged twenty-two, and became territorial commander there aged twenty-four. An early suitor, Colonel Lampard, who retracted with cold feet from the prospect of becoming a Booth, was labelled mentally unstable and resigned. Lucy eventually married the Swede Emanuel Hellborg, and they held joint territorial commands in India and Ceylon, France and Switzerland before he died in 1909 in Germany. As a widow she was principal of the international training college and territorial commander for Denmark, Norway, and South America. She died 1953.

There were accusations of nepotism about the treatment of the children as members of a Salvation Army "Royal Family." Henry Edmonds wrote that Bramwell's appointment as "Chief" over the heads of other senior men "led many officers of all ranks to resign." Horridge says officers feared they would not receive a fair hearing against rumors and in disagreements with members of the Booth family.[84] Nevertheless, even members of the family were also cut adrift if they disagreed with the General. The three who resigned became "un-persons" as far as the Army was concerned. As territorial commander in Australia, James Hay had Herbert's name chiseled off the foundation stones he had laid for buildings. In the *Year Book*s, their names were absent from lists of potted biographies of pioneer officers of the Army, even in 1940. William Booth always insisted that he was "the General of the Army, not of the Family." Relationships were almost entirely severed by desertion.

Bramwell also treated his family as a kind of "Royal Family." The *Year Book* always carried a special page about what the General's children were doing, as did other memorabilia like the brochure for the 1914 International Congress. A biography of his daughter Miriam, who died without having worked in an appointment, went to a second edition.[85] Bramwell's loyal Australian aide, George Carpenter, was banished back to Australia to an appointment he had held twenty years previously for having the courage to tackle him on the disquiet felt at his apparent favoring of his family for appointments and advice.

---

84. Edmonds, *My Adventures with General William Booth*, quoted by Horridge, *Origins and Early Days*, 88–89.

85. Carpenter, *Miriam Booth*.

Bramwell Booth's Generalship: 1912–1929.

William Booth was "Promoted to Glory" in 1912. In accordance with the Deed Poll of 1878, a sealed envelope was opened by the Army's solicitor and to no-one's surprise was found to contain the name of William Bramwell Booth. Then fifty-six years of age, he had in reality run the Army for the previous twenty years while his father had returned to his first love of peripatetic evangelism and made imperial progresses around his far-flung dominions. However, correspondence between father and son shows that William's hand remained firmly on the helm to almost the end of his life.

Bramwell had a prodigious capacity for work, and continued to control the day to day affairs of the organization.[86] The first part of his Generalship was overshadowed by the Great War, which almost overtook his international congress called for June 1914. He sought to preserve the Army's internationalism and maintain links with his forces amongst the central powers, setting himself against anti-German hysteria. He gave special attention to youth work and promoted missionary expansion—the flag was raised in twenty-three new countries between 1913 and 1928. Under his leadership the number of corps and outposts increased from 9,415 to 15,163, and the number of commissioned officers from 15,988 to 25,427.[87] It is interesting to compare these figures with the 14,389 corps and 24,888 officers reported in 2016.[88]

1913	Inauguration of the life-saving scouts; work began in **Celebes** (now part of Indonesia), and **Russia** (until 1923).
1914	Fourth international congress held (June).
1915	Work began in **British Honduras** (now Belize), and **Burma** (now Myanmar); life-saving guards were inaugurated
1916	Work began in **China** (until 1951), in **St Kitts**, and in **Portuguese East Africa** (now Mozambique) where it was officially recognized 1923.
1917	Work began in **Virgin Islands** (USA); The Order of the Founder was instituted.
1918	Work commenced in **Cuba**.
1919	Work began in **Czechoslovakia** (until 1950).
1920	Work began in **Nigeria** and **Bolivia**.
1921	Work began in **Kenya**; Sunbeams were inaugurated. A second international social conference was held.

---

86. Anecdotal evidence of Bramwell Booth's workaholism: a retired railway inspector told me of how the General would take over an empty compartment on his Hadley Wood to Kings Cross commuter train by laying out his paper-work on all the other seats to deter other would-be passengers from entering, so that he could work without interruption. H. Cooper to author, 14 February 1971.

87. Ervine, *God's Soldier*, II, 851.

88. *Salvation Army Yearbook*, 2017, 32.

1922	Work began in **Zambia** (then Northern Rhodesia), **Brazil**, and **Ghana** (then Gold Coast); a second *Handbook of Salvation Army Doctrine* was published.
1923	Work began in **Latvia** (until 1939).
1924	Work began in **Hungary** (until 1950), in **Surinam**, and **The Færoes**.
1927	Work began in **Austria**, **Estonia** (until 1940), and **Curaçao** (until 1980).
1928	General Bramwell Booth's last public appearance—the stone-laying of the International (William Booth Memorial) Training College, Denmark Hill, London (10th May).
1929	The **first High Council** (8th January—13th February) deposed General Bramwell Booth on grounds of ill-health; **Commissioner Edward J. Higgins was elected General**; General Bramwell Booth was promoted to Glory (16th June); Army work began in **Colombia** (until 1965).
1930	Work began in **Hong Kong**. A commissioners' conference was held in London.

Upward Mobility

> Fortunately I didn't go to any place of devotion, though I did get mixed up with a Salvation Army procession. It was quite interesting to be at close quarters with them, they're so absolutely different from what they used to be like when I first remember them in the eighties. They used to go about then unkempt and disheveled, in a sort of smiling rage with the world, and now they're spruce and jaunty and flamboyantly decorative, like a geranium bed with religious convictions. Laura Kettleway was going on about them in the lift in Dover Street Tube the other day, saying what a lot of good work they did, and what a loss it would have been if they'd never existed.[89]
>
> —"Saki" (H.H. Munro), in *Louise*.

This extract from a story by "Saki," dating from early in the twentieth century, reminds us that although the Army's conscious ecclesiology appeared to undergo little development in this period, sociological changes of significance for its future direction were inevitably taking place. Upward mobility had long been a feature of sectarian life in Britain. The oft-quoted judgement of the eighty-four-year-old John Wesley on Methodism could have been repeated of Salvationists by Bramwell Booth in his old age:

> The Methodists in every place grow diligent and frugal; consequently they increase in goods. Hence they proportionately increase in pride, in the desire of

---

89. Munro, *Short Stories of Saki*, 449. "Louise" was first published in *The Toys of Peace* in 1923. Hector Munro was killed on the Western Front in 1916.

the flesh, the desire of the eyes, and the pride of life. So although the form of religion remains, the spirit is swiftly vanishing away.[90]

Salvationists may not have risen to the same degree as the Methodists but the same process will have been taking place as for those earlier sectaries. While the social structures and class patterns differed from the British model, Salvationists in countries like New Zealand and Australia likewise participated in the general rise in the standard of living with increased opportunities for education and diversification of occupation. The proportion of unskilled workers in the ranks diminished and that of business and professional people increased. Some Salvationists sought the shelter of more respectable and less socially embarrassing religious groups and others drifted from any religious profession, but many took the Salvation Army with them as they rose. The Army therefore may be seen as conforming to many of the characteristics the sociologists attribute to a sect or movement in the process of consolidating or denominationalizing.

One of these is a change of focus from a mission to maintenance, from a crusade to change the world to a greater preoccupation with the interests, needs and desires of the existing members. The Salvation Army probably began this journey even before the period under consideration here.

This development did not necessarily involve a change in activities at first, but rather subtle changes in the way those activities were addressed. For example, brass bands were originally pressed into service within the Salvation Army in order to augment open-air witness—to support hymn singing, drown out the opposition and, because brass banding was a fashionable element in popular culture, to attract attention. The evangelical intention was gradually subsumed by the social and cultural needs of the bandsmen themselves, even though the ostensible rationale and rhetoric was unchanged. In time the actual music reflected this change of purpose; what William Booth called "soul-saving" music—inseparable from the words of the hymns and songs it accompanied—became music for the sake of the music. The musicians became much more presentable (as "Saki" observed) and the composers more inventive. The genre became in some sense decadent: the arrangement of themes from Tchaikovsky might appeal to brass band aficionados as music but was unlikely to touch people's consciences with the memory of words of hymns they had once learned in Sunday school.

Over this period the Army's practical theology also began to drift from its doctrinal moorings. Niebuhr says that "By its very nature the sectarian type of organization is valid for only one generation . . . Rarely does a second generation hold the convictions it has inherited with a fervor equal to that of its fathers, who fashioned these convictions in the heat of conflict and at the risk of martyrdom."[91] The children and grandchildren of those who had experienced the miracle of the changing of beer into furniture did not necessarily enjoy the same conversion experience themselves. They grew up within the world of the Salvation Army and it was their familiar sub-culture, but they may not have inherited the same passion for the lost. The fact that Salvationists have in general become less inclined or likely to be motivated to engage in personal evangelism probably indicates a slackening

90. Plumb, *England in the Eighteenth Century*, 97.
91. Niebuhr, *Social Sources of Denominationalism*, 20.

commitment to the doctrines underlying such activity. A diminished conviction that their neighbor is going to hell perhaps renders them less inclined to risk giving offence by trying to save him from it. Allen Satterlee also draws attention to disillusionment following the First World War as a factor contributing to loss of evangelical zeal.[92]

This doctrinal "cooling off" can also be seen in connection with the Army's characteristically sectarian "perfectionism." The Army had inherited the Wesleyan understanding of holiness, as mediated through the nineteenth century holiness revival and expounded by the Booths and notably by the American Commissioner S. L. Brengle (1860–1936). This held that the believer may be (indeed, *ought* to be) "sanctified," enjoying a "second blessing," a distinct and instantaneous work of grace subsequent to conversion, by which the tendency to sin is removed and power given for living a holy life. By mid-twentieth century a new generation of Salvationists found this doctrine difficult to reconcile with their experience and Brengle's books were being neglected. Frederick Coutts sought to reinterpret the doctrine in more accessible form, with greater emphasis on the "process" of sanctification than on the "crisis" entry experience.[93] This apparent diluting of perfectionist expectations was perhaps another sign of a denominationalizing tendency.

If one of the presenting characteristics of the sectarian ethos was the holding of the "world" at arms-length, the early Salvation Army certainly conformed to type in that respect, but the period from the Booths to the 1960s saw a steady, if slow, retreat from the ghetto. Early female converts had feathers snipped from their hats at the Mercy Seat. In 1929 a New Zealand officer, Ensign Bennett, so misguided as to mention in speaking at a youth meeting that she had attended a cinema found the rest of her remarks drowned out by energetic singing led by the Commissioner presiding.[94] In the 1930s it was still reprehensible to attend a football match—the participation of a Salvation Army rugby team in the local grades competition in Christchurch in the late 1930s greatly perturbed the Englishman serving as Chief Secretary in New Zealand. He tried, unsuccessfully, to ban it.[95] In the 1950s it was still daring to attend a dance. Today Salvationists still take the pledge to abstain from alcohol and gambling, but the "world" is now on their side as far as tobacco is concerned. Robertson sums it up in observing a shift "from abstention from worldly amusements and fashions to the injunction to be judicious and selective in such indulgences."[96]

It is instructive to review such changes described above in the light of Dean M. Kelly's 1972 survey and analysis of declining mainline churches and growing evangelical churches in the United States. Kelly concluded that "strict" churches (doctrinally and ethically), making significant demands on their members, were strong and grew, while declining churches asked less of their members.[97] The Salvation Army was tending towards

---

92. Satterlee, *Turning Points*, 76–80.

93. This is dealt with at greater length in a later section on the Salvation Army as a Holiness Movement.

94. Commissioner Hay, inveterate foe of the "movies," (he had disestablished the pioneering "Limelight" studio in Melbourne) was simply following an early Salvation Army tradition, known as "singing someone down," for curtailing over-long or tedious testimonies. See Moyles, *Come Join Our Army*, 17.

95. Bradwell, *Touched with Splendour*, 49–50.

96. Robertson, in Wilson, *Patterns of Sectarianism*, 74.

97. Kelly, *Why Conservative Churches are Growing*, 1972. Finke and Stark explain this in terms

the "declining main-line" profile in these years even though its rules and beliefs were still comparatively strict. The question remains as to whether churches decline because they are less demanding, or demand less as they decline, or whether both tendencies are part of the wider "denominationalizing" process, the one contributing to the other.

The Salvation Army has displayed a sectarian tendency to provide an all-embracing social milieu for its members. This period from the 1920s on saw a change from most activities being evangelical in intention (if not in achievement), and directed outward, to more activities being provided for the entertainment of the Salvationists themselves. This probably took place in two stages. At first the same activities, like brass banding, served both purposes, while later new activities which had no explicit evangelical rationale, such as "socials" (games, as an alternative to dancing) were introduced, along with youth groups, Baden Powell organizations and other recreational activities.[98] These served as points of entry for potential converts but they also served to hold the members together and make it unnecessary for them to seek diversion elsewhere. This was the nature of the "programmatic corps." Joan Hutson's engaging account of the Gisborne corps in the 1930s describes how "The Salvation Army buildings were also the centre of the corps' social life. Banquets, concerts, engagement parties, socials, twenty-first birthdays, wedding anniversaries, welcomes and farewells, all took place within these walls."[99]

The very smallness of the movement (for example, consistently about six and a half thousand soldiers in New Zealand from the 1920s until recent years), and the practice of holding regional and national meetings, congresses, band festivals and sports meetings, fostered a significant sense of community. These activities, plus the tendency for officers' children to leave home and marry into the local corps when their parents were appointed elsewhere, led to a situation where many Salvationists had relatives and friends, or at least acquaintances, throughout the country.

However, in terms of Wilson's observation that "sects have a totalitarian rather than segmental hold over their members,"[100] this hold was in the process of relaxing in the period under review. The tendency observed amongst Methodists in the nineteenth century, when "the 'Means of Grace' were fighting a losing battle to rival 'the social party, the secular concert, or the tennis club' as a claimant for the time and energy of members," was now to be found amongst Salvationists.[101] Werner Stark sees this as part of the sect's coming to terms with the fact that "the conflict of the sect with society must be solved somehow, for it is an acute crisis which cannot be turned into a lasting state . . . it must either withdraw from society or learn to live with it."[102]

A fear of being "led astray" by "worldly" education—an offer to pay for a university education for Bramwell Booth had been declined by his parents—might also have been a

---

of rational choice theory (that people do what serves their own interests) in *The Churching of America 1776–1990.*

98. Fookes, "Gymnastic Equipment," 322–24; Ware, "Saturday Afternoon Cinema Matinees," 243–46.

99. Hutson, *As for Me and My* House, 227.

100. Wilson, *Patterns of Sectarianism*, 24.

101. Gilbert, *Religion and Society in Industrial* England, 181, quoting Minutes of the Wesleyan Conference, 1890, 354–55.

102. Stark, *Sociology of Religion*, II, 235.

matter of class attitude amongst some New Zealand Salvationists before and even after the second world war. Another indicator of change might therefore be found in the increased number of Salvationists accessing higher education. From being rare, Salvationists obtaining tertiary education had become sufficiently numerous to be perceived to require some special pastoral support lest they be lost to the movement, and Salvation Army Students' Fellowships became established in countries like the United Kingdom and New Zealand in the 1950s. By the 1970s higher education was sufficiently common for this organization to have outlived its usefulness and fade away, in New Zealand at least.

Such observations need not be confined to the Army in Western countries. In countries with entrenched class or caste systems, upward mobility might also be observed, within limits. In India for example, the Army recruited chiefly amongst the lowest castes. Narayana Muthiah, a high caste Hindu, became a commissioner; more often the higher castes admired and supported the Army's work financially, much as the aristocracy did in Britain, but few of them were prepared to sign up. The Army itself, however, offered the means of rising in status; a "sweeper" could also become a commissioner. In many third world countries the Army, along with other churches, has undertaken to provide schools, and mission-school education has been the key to advancement. Conversely it has been suggested that the relative weakness of "corps life" in the some places in the United States territories today derives from a failure of the Army there to establish a strong middle-class presence, so that in some places the soldiery also double as a client base while the role of active "laity" in the "church" has devolved upon employees, who may not be Salvationists or even professing Christians, a growing trend in Western countries.[103]

The processes of institutionalization and clericalisation naturally affected the character of the Army's leadership as well; this will be looked at again in a chapter on Leadership. Ervine believed that "the success of the Army . . . was the cause of the change in the spirit of its officers. Formerly, they were men of God: now they were men of affairs . . . [Commissioner Elijah] Cadman did not care whether he was a corporal or a commissioner so long as he saved souls. His successors wanted to save souls, but they also wanted to be commissioners . . . "[104] Inevitably the second and third generations of leadership differed in attitude from the pioneers. George Bernard Shaw predicted in 1905 that

> its present staff of enthusiast-commanders shall be succeeded by a bureaucracy of men of business, who will be no better than bishops, and perhaps a good deal more unscrupulous. That has always happened sooner or later to great orders founded by saints; the order founded by William Booth is not exempt from the same danger.[105]

Shaw, as an observer of human nature, anticipated the sociologists here. Wilson says that,

> . . . the Churches have increasingly adopted the same style of operations and similar methods of organization as the large concerns of business, education and recreation in modern society . . . Administration has in some measure

---

103. *Salvation Army Year Book,* 2015, reported 84,539 soldiers and 60,559 employees nationally in the USA. In 2017 those figures were respectively 84,798 and 47,638, an interesting alteration.

104. Ervine, *God's Soldier*, II, 862–63.

105. Shaw, "Major Barbara" in *Complete Prefaces*, 126–27.

> superseded spirituality, and rational business organization has replaced the distribution of grace or the reception of divine inspiration . . . There can be few human activities on which rational planning, administrative co-ordination and the regulations of bureaucratic organization have such deleterious effects as religious movements.[106]

This is not to say that Salvation Army officers in administrative roles inevitably become less "spiritual" but particular spheres of responsibility shape the responses of the individual—we see from where we stand. The Army's early leaders tended to be out front leading the charge; their successors, the *apparatchiks*, became more cautious about counting the cost. Such loss of original verve and integrity did not affect just the higher echelons of command of course. Thomas O'Dea commented that when a professional pastorate emerges,

> there comes into existence a body of men for whom the clerical life offers not simply the "religious" satisfactions of the earlier charismatic period, but also prestige and respectability, power and influence . . . and satisfactions derived from the use of personal talents in teaching, leadership, etc. Moreover, the *maintenance* of the situation in which these rewards are forthcoming tends to become an element in the motivation of the group.[107]

It must be admitted that the demands of ministering to an established congregations naturally shape the role, outlook and expectations in ways quite different from those of the pioneer and itinerant evangelist—and may attract a different candidate.

It would be fair comment to say that rising standards of living, improved educational levels and the progressive secularization of western society, combined with the general diminution of evangelical zeal almost inevitable amongst the second and third generations of a movement, impacted upon the Salvation Army's self-understanding and behavior in the post-Boothian era. However, rhetoric often persists long after conviction has faded and we no longer walk the talk. The cinematic cartoon roadrunner character, charging well over the edge of the precipice before suddenly realizing that the void has opened below, might be analogous to the way the Army's sectarian persona was maintained long after many Salvationists had ceased to take it seriously, except for a niggling and ritualized sense of guilt. The sectarian mind-set enjoyed a long twilight. At the tail end of the period, however, many Salvationists would have struggled to recognize themselves in Robertson's mid-1960s summation:

> In essentials . . . the Army remains the same as in the early years of the present century—an authoritarian organization, demanding extensive commitment and obedience to its rules and regulations, which also extend to matters of private thought, conversation, socialization of children, work and leisure, financial expenditure, dress and physical health.[108]

It was no longer altogether true, even then. Gordon Moyles offers a critique of Robertson, suggesting that he had been misled by the traditional rhetoric of the Army's

---

106. Wilson, *Religion in Secular Society*, 138–140.
107. O'Dea, *Sociology of Religion*, 91.
108. Robertson, in Wilson, *Patterns of Sectarianism*, 89.

"stated policies and doctrines," and that "he ignores the beliefs of the Salvationists themselves, never acknowledging that there might be a vast difference between the formalized beliefs of the organization and of lay Salvationists."[109] Formal statements thus tend to be left behind in the wake of a sectarian community accommodating to the wider world. Werner Stark offers a similar reflection on Wilson's and Yinger's use of the term "established sect," terming it a "*contradictio in adjecto* . . . unjustified if the group's inner history is taken into account . . . A sect that ceases to be an elementary expression of passionate protest is a sect no more . . . It is in effect a denomination."[110] At the same time, the Army continued—as it still does—to retain *in some measure* such distinctively sectarian characteristics as "tests of merit on would-be members, . . . discipline, regulating the declared beliefs and the life habits of members, prescribing and operating sanctions for those who deviate, . . . demands . . . for commitment from its members."[111] Again, this will be discussed at greater length under the heading of the Army's ecclesiology.

In sum, then, during the forty or fifty years up to 1960, the Army's language and official line remained sectarian, while in practice its general tendency might be described as "denominationalizing."

4. 1931 AND AFTER: THE PROCESS OF "TERMINAL INSTITUTIONALIZATION"

An observation on the use of the word "institution" is in order at this point. James Pedlar points out that there is no agreed definition of this term in either sociology or theology, but it is often used in contrast to a more free-flowing, charismatic "movement." If institution is simply defined as "a stable pattern of social interaction, and is best conceived as existing on a continuum which includes everything from a recurring encounter between two persons to a large organization such as the United Nations," then of course the Salvation Army from its inception could be described as an institution.[112] However, for the purposes of our study I propose that "institutionalization" should refer to the process whereby a creative, radical, utopian movement becomes increasingly set in the forms, patterns and structures created by its rise and growth. The creation and maintenance of such structures is necessary for its survival, while at the same time they restrict its ability to continue adjusting to its changing circumstances and environment. "Terminal" implies the end result when this has taken place; it does not mean the outfit has died, although its "first, fine, careless rapture" usually has, even though a considerable amount of energy will be expended on trying to maintain or rediscover it.

In 1929 Edward Higgins, Bramwell's Chief of Staff for ten years, was elected to replace him, and secured the passage of the Salvation Army Act through the British Parliament in 1931, regularizing the election of successive Generals by high council and

---

109. Moyles, *Blood and Fire in Canada*, 228–44. By analogy, the Catholic Church's rules on birth-control and the extent to which those rules are actually observed by the laity.

110. Stark, *Sectarian Religion*, 266–67.

111. Wilson, "The Persistence of Sects." 2.

112. Pedlar, *Division, Diversity, and Unity*, 52.

vesting Salvation Army property in a trustee company instead of in the General as sole trustee. Evangeline Booth finally had her turn at the top from 1934 to 1939 but by this time the fire had gone out and the Army was in retreat in the land of its birth.

It was not only the Army in retreat in Britain in the 1930s; it was in the good company of non-conformist churches in general. While Anglicanism was getting its second wind, the Catholic Church was going from strength to strength and newer sects like the Pentecostals were beginning to assert themselves, the Methodists, Presbyterians, Baptists, and Congregationalists had entered upon steady decline. It was somewhat ironical that Evangeline Booth, having overseen the division of the United States Army into four territories in her thirty years of expansionist command there, chose this time to embark on a similar administrative reorganization in the United Kingdom, where the ranks were beginning to melt away. London and Southern, Northern, Scotland and Ireland, Wales and Western territories were created out of the British territory, each with a territorial commander and staff—though the British Commissioner looked after the London and Southern as well as the whole. The Scotland-Ireland axis, and later Scotland alone, survived as a separate territory until the 1990s but the rest of the grandiose project was allowed to lapse after Evangeline's departure.

An awareness of the Army's "loss of first love" was apparent towards the end of the 1930s, at any rate to some officers on international headquarters. Their concern would no doubt have been sharpened by the court martial and dismissal of the chief of the staff, Commissioner Henry Mapp, in 1937. *Time* magazine put that down to a power struggle between Evangeline and her Chief of Staff.[113] The details were not divulged to the public but it was alleged that Mapp had embezzled funds to support an inappropriate liaison.[114] A significant group of middle-ranked London officers wrote a circular letter to express their concerns to members of the high council assembling in London in 1939. Amongst the signatories were Majors Catherine Baird, William Cooper, Frederick L. Coutts, Frank Fairbank, Alfred J. Gilliard and Lt. Colonel Carvosso Gauntlett. No lightweights, these: Baird became a Colonel and all the others Commissioners, and Coutts became General. Their concern was "leadership" because "the power remains with the leaders and with the power, the responsibility to God and man." They wrote,

> . . . the Army must speedily face developments which are menacing its efficiency. We are driven to this conclusion by the apparent:
>
> —Loss of original simplicity in many methods
>
> —Decline in spiritual power
>
> —Grave loss in numerical strength
>
> —Disquieting financial position.
>
> These facts call for a frank approach to the rapidly changing conditions among the people for whose salvation the organization was brought into being. We feel that unless steps are taken without delay, it will soon be too late to rescue the Army from the worldliness and disintegration which attack and destroy all

---

113. TIME, 31 May, 1937, http://www.time.com/time/magazine/article/0,9171,847896,00.html, accessed 8 June 2016.

114. W.D. Wellman to author, May 1958. Wellman was the auditor who discovered the malfeasance.

Christian bodies which lose their vision and willingness for self-sacrifice . . . We wish to pledge ourselves to the giving of . . . support and to the following of a leader who, in making his or her own necessary sacrifices, will demand similar steps from others . . . We are deeply anxious that our new international leader, by his or her personal example in simplicity and devotion, and by the courageous facing of facts, will call forth from the Army of today its latent loyalties to Christ, and to the principles of the flag.

The writers were circumspect in proposing no specific agenda beyond "the facing of urgent problems, for the establishment of rallying points and above all, for a strengthening of that confidence in leadership which was so great a power to the Army in the past."[115] This could only be an expression of no-confidence in the existing leadership and direction of the Army at the end of the 1930s.

The times were however unpropitious for reforms. The Australian George Lyndon Carpenter (General 1939 to 1946) struggled to hold the international Army together in war time—it was progressively restricted or proscribed in nations under the Axis, money was in short supply and travel difficult—and Albert Orsborn (1946 to 1954) faced mounting tasks with diminishing resources in the post-war reconstruction period. In these years Europe especially was turning away from religion in general and the Army's well-tried methods no longer appeared to connect with an increasingly secularized society.

Depression, Recovery, War

1931   Work began in Uganda and the Bahamas; the Salvation Army Act 1931 was passed.

1932   Work began in **Namibia** (then South West Africa) (until 1939).

1933   Work began in **Yugoslavia** (until 1948), and on Devil's Island, **French Guiana** (until the closing of the penal settlement in 1952), and **Tanzania** (then Tanganyika).

1934   Work began in **Algeria** (until 1970); the **second High Council elected General Evangeline Booth**; work began in the (Belgian) **Congo (Kinshasa)**.

1935   Work began in **Singapore**.

1936   Work began in **Egypt** (until 1949).

1937   Work began in the (French) **Congo (Brazzaville)**, **the Philippines**, and **Mexico**.

1938   Torchbearer group movement was inaugurated (Jan); *All the World* was re-issued; work spread from Singapore to **Malaya** (now Malaysia).

1939   The **third High Council elected General George Lyndon Carpenter.**

115. Izzard, *Pen of Flame*, 57–58.

| 1941 | The Order of Distinguished Auxiliary Service was instituted; International Headquarters was destroyed in the London Blitz (10th May). |

The Brave New Post-War World: the Decline of the Homelands

1946	The **fourth High Council elected General Albert Orsborn**.
1948	The first worldwide Army broadcast was transmitted.
1950	Work began in **Haiti**; a first TV broadcast was made by a Salvation Army General, the Salvation Army Students' Fellowship received an official constitution; the first international youth congress was held in London; The Staff College (later International College for Officers) was re-opened.
1954	The **fifth High Council elected General Wilfred Kitching**.
1956	Work began in Port Moresby, **Papua New Guinea**; the first international corps cadet congress took place.
1959	Over-sixties clubs were inaugurated in Great Britain.

From the 1960s: Into the Second Century

1962	Work began in **Puerto Rico**.
1963	the **sixth High Council elected General Frederick Coutts**; Queen Elizabeth the Queen Mother opened the new International Headquarters.
1965	Queen Elizabeth II attended the international centenary commencement; a Founders' Day service was held in Westminster Abbey, London; work was re-established in **Taiwan** (originally pioneered 1928 but halted by the Second World War).
1967	Work began in **Malawi**.
1969	The **seventh High Council elected General Erik Wickberg**; new edition of *The Salvation Army Handbook of Doctrine* was published; work began in **Lesotho**.
1970	Cyclone relief operations in East Pakistan (later **Bangladesh**) led to start of work there in 1971.
1971	Work began in **Spain** and **Portugal**.
1972	Work began in **Venezuela**.

1973	Work began in **Fiji**.
1974	The **eighth High Council elected General Clarence Wiseman**.
1976	Work began in **Guatemala**; the Mexico, and Central America Territory (now Latin America North and Mexico Territories) was formed.
1977	The **ninth High Council elected General Arnold Brown**.
1978	The fifth international congress was held.
1980	The Salvation Army Act 1980 was passed; work recommenced in **French Guiana**.
1981	The **tenth High Council elected General Jarl Wahlström**.
1985	Work began in **Colombia**, **Marshall Islands**, **Angola** and **Ecuador**.
1986	Work began in **Tonga**; *The Salvationist* first issued (UK); **eleventh High Council elected General Eva Burrows**; Development Conference held at Sunbury Court, London.
1988	Work began in **Liberia**.
1989	Work began in **El Salvador**.
1990	Work re-commenced after fifty years in East Germany, Czechoslovakia, Hungary and re-established in Latvia; sixth international congress was held in London; United Kingdom territory established.
1991	International Headquarters was restructured as an entity separate from the United Kingdom territory; work re-opened in **Russia** after sixty-eight years.
1993	The **twelfth High Council elected General Bramwell H. Tillsley**; work began in **Micronesia**.
1994	A first international literary conference was held in Alexandria, Virginia, USA; General TilIsley retired due to ill-health; the **thirteenth High Council elected General Paul A. Rader**; work began in **Guam**.
1995	All married women officers were granted rank in their own right; work began in the **Dominican Republic**; work reopened in **Estonia**; work began in **Rwanda** following relief and development programs.
1996	Work began in Sabah (East Malaysia); initial meeting of the International Spiritual Life Commission was held.
1997	An international youth forum was held in Cape Town, South Africa; the first-ever congress met in Russia/Commonwealth of Independent States; Salvation Army leaders in Southern Africa acknowledged the Army's past failure to

stand against apartheid and signed a commitment to reconciliation; work began in **Botswana**.

1998 An international conference of leaders held in Melbourne, Australia, and received the report of International Spiritual Life Commission; a fourth *Handbook of Doctrine*, entitled *Salvation Story*, was published; the International Commission on Officership opened in London.

1999 An international education symposium met in London; work began in **Romania**; the **fourteenth High Council elected General John Gowans**.

2000 The International Commission on Officership completed its work and a survey of officer-opinion was carried out; work begun in **Macau**; the Salvation Army registered as a denomination in Sweden; a seventh international congress was held in Atlanta, Georgia, USA (first to be held outside the UK); work began in **Honduras**.

2001 An international theology and ethics symposium met in Winnipeg, Canada; an international music ministries forum was convened in London; an international poverty summit was held on the internet. The first "614 Corps" was opened in Toronto, Canada.

2002 The **fifteenth high council elected General John Larsson**.

2003 "The war college" opened in Vancouver, Canada.

2004 An international music and other creative ministries forum (MOSAIC) was held in Toronto, Canada; The new International Headquarters building at 101 Queen Victoria Street, London, was opened; IHQ Emergency Services coordinated disaster relief work after an Indian Ocean tsunami struck). "ALOVE" youth work was established in the UK.

2005 The Eastern Europe command was re-designated the Eastern Europe territory; Singapore, Malaysia and Myanmar command re-designated a territory; work in **Lithuania** was officially recognized by IHQ, and the Germany territory redesignated Germany and Lithuania territory; 'Project Warsaw' was launched to begin the Army's work in **Poland**; The East Africa territory re-designated Kenya territory, with the Uganda region given command status; the Salvation Army in Norway registered as a "Faith Community" outside the Lutheran Church.

2006 The **sixteenth High Council elected General Shaw Clifton**; a second international theology and ethics symposium met in Johannesburg, South Africa.

2007 The International Social Justice Commission was established, headed by an international director: work began in **Burundi** and **Greece**.

2008 The Kenya territory was divided into Kenya East and Kenya West territories; Tanzania became a territory. The Belgium command was divided and integrated into France and Netherlands territories. Work recommenced in **Namibia**, opened in **Mali**, and **Mongolia**; officers were appointed to **Kuwait**.

2009   Work began in **Nepal**.

2010   Work began in **Sierra Leone, Nicaragua,** and **United Arab Emirates**.

2011   **Linda Bond elected General by the seventeenth High Council.** Work began in the **Turks and Caicos Islands,** the **Solomon Islands,** and in **Togo.**

2012   Work in **Cambodia** commenced (on the initiative of a Korean local officer); and in **Greenland**.

2013   **André Cox elected General by the eighteenth High Council** after the early retirement of Linda Bond. **Spain** and **Portugal** commands were united.

2014   A fourth theology and ethics symposium met in London.

2015   The International Doctrine Council became the International Theological Council. The **Russia** Command and the **Eastern European** territory were separated. Work began in **Slovakia**. A 150th anniversary "Boundless" international congress met in London.

2016   The reform of governance and accountability project was launched. Work began in **Madagascar**.

The second half of the twentieth century has come to be seen as the period in which secularization began to determine more obviously the character of at least some of the developed world—Europe, the United Kingdom and Australasia in particular, although society in the United States of America has appeared to maintain a vigorously religious world-view for the time being.

What do we mean by secularization? Here is Peter Berger's definition:

> By secularization we mean the process by which sectors of society and culture are removed from the domination of religious institutions and symbols. When we speak of society and institutions in modern Western history, secularization manifests itself in the evacuation by the Christian Churches . . . in the separation of Church and state . . . or in the emancipation of education from ecclesiastical authority. When we speak of culture and symbols, however, we imply that secularization is more than a social-structural process. It affects the totality of cultural life and of ideation, and may be observed in the decline of religious contents in the arts, in philosophy, in literature and . . . in the rise of science as an autonomous, thoroughly secular perspective on the world. Moreover, it is implied here that secularization has a subjective side as well. As there is a secularization of society and culture, so there is a secularization of consciousness.[116]

---

116. Berger, *Social Reality of Religion*, 113, quoted by Jean-Daniel Plüs, "Globalization of Pentecostalism," in Dempster, Klaus, and Petersen (ed.), *Globalization of Pentecostalism*, 182.

Berger and others have revised their assessments and it is now commonly held that the persistence of spirituality and rise of fundamentalism of all kinds towards the end of twentieth century and the opening of the twenty-first have begun to throw back the secularist tide. In the West at least, this may be simply part of a reactive minority movement doomed to ebb again before gathering secularist ideological, sociological and economic forces. Even church attendance in the USA is now declining and parts of the developing world, hitherto bastionsof religious faithfulness, are showing signs of growing secularity and diversity, against which the hard line taken by some Nigerian Anglican Archbishops and Bangladeshi Islamic jihadists for example may be in the nature of protest votes rather than the expression of majority conviction. The sociologists' pendulum has certainly swung back to a recognition of the role of faith but it may be too soon to be sure. In any case, although more recent critics of the secularism thesis point out that "spirituality" of all kinds continues to flourish in the West, it is increasingly found *outside* the traditional religious institutions, which tend to have forfeited the public's confidence. With a turning away from traditional, institutionalized religion, and the tendency towards what Grace Davie termed "believing but not belonging," perhaps such a thoroughly organized and controlling body as the Salvation Army is not well-placed to take advantage of such a movement of spirituality unwilling to be confined to predetermined beliefs and structures.[117]

Against the background of this whole societal trend, we can review the internal life of the Army itself. Internationally, the numbers of Salvation Army corps and officers are now similar to those of 1929, but the number of soldiers has greatly increased. Robertson's analysis, which has provided the framework for our story, was of the Army in Britain, and because of cultural connections and similar development his categories could be used with reference to the former British Dominions, the "White" Commonwealth, and to some extent the USA. However, whereas in 1929 the majority of corps and officers were in UK, Europe, Australasia and North America, the numbers in the United Kingdom, the former "British Dominions" and Europe in particular have now fallen or are falling away.

"If you do what you've always done, you'll get what you always got," is a two-edged truth. If the right thing is being done, it will work and there will be good outcomes—until a tipping point is passed. You then cease to achieve the success you always had. Doing what you always did then becomes counter-productive. Clearly, in many territories that tipping point was passed long ago. There are no easy answers as to what changed at that point. Generalizations such as that the context changed but the Army did not, do not take us very far, nor is it clear what should be done to reverse the process—and it is not for want of trying. "Terminal institutionalization" becomes a more apt name for Robertson's fourth stage after all.

Numbers of Salvationists in the developing world on the other hand, particularly in Africa and Asia, have grown and now comprise well over 80 percent of Salvation Army forces. Can we say that they are continuing to do what they always did, and are still getting what they always got? A different kind of framework is required for the analysis of the twenty-first century Salvation Army. This will be looked at again in the final chapter.

---

117. Grace Davie, *Religion in Britain since 1945*, 93–117.

2

The Ecclesiology of the Salvation Army 1: Sect and Church

> No one could be more inclined towards the use of organization and system than he always was, and yet he always advocated an organization so open to all, and a system so elastic, that zeal might never be repressed, but only made the most of.[1]
>
> —George Scott Railton, on William Booth

Ecclesiology is the science of churches, or the study of the polity, the structure, of the church. It is a commonplace that Jesus came preaching the Kingdom of God, and what we got was the church. How did that happen?

There are at least two possible answers to that question:

1. *God planned it that way*. The church was the chicken always intended to hatch from that egg; its development has been overseen by the Holy Spirit. There are variations within this answer, about the amount of detailed planning God actually put into the proposal and the latitude he allows his servants. Cardinal Kasper asked:

> Has God given His Church a specific structure or has he left the Church to find its own concrete structure, in such a way that a pluralism of structures is possible; structures which are interchangeable and need only recognize each other mutually?[2]

William Booth preferred the second of Kasper's options. He wrote:

> No pattern for the government of the Kingdom of Christ on earth is authoritatively laid down in the New Testament. Those who think otherwise are in the most complete disagreement as to what that particular form of government was . . .[3]

---

1. Railton, *General Booth*, 16.
2. Kasper, "Still a place for optimism."
3. Booth, *Orders and Regulations* 1886, 161.

However, both Kasper and Booth assumed that church was what God had in mind. Even in the New Testament we find writers reading this view back into Jesus' ministry, and having him say things which made sense in a later, church, situation.[4] You might say he was being prophetic, or that he was laying down instructions for later use; or you might say those coming along later were legitimizing what they were doing by attributing their practices to Jesus' intentions. If you think the latter, you are more likely to believe the alternative answer, which is, not that God had it all mapped out for us, but that,

2. *People made it that way.* This is how groups of human beings function. All movements of the spirit either become more highly organized, a sociological process, or they die. Over the first few centuries, the church institutionalized and developed structures to organize for expansion, frame its message, and fend off unwelcome variations (heresies); and it accommodated to Roman society and to traditional religious expectations. By the fourth century, with Constantine and then Theodosius, the Empire was Christianized, and the church became imperial. The foundations of Christendom were poured and set.

So, was the church the design of God or work of men? The work of the Holy Spirit or the outcome of the fall? Maybe you can believe both at once, or some combination of the two. The Salvationist position was that enunciated by Wilfred Kitching, that the Army's history "bears striking witness to the guiding hand of the Lord."[5] In that, he stood in the mainstream of church tradition of course, as expressed for example by the then Cardinal Ratzinger, who rejected a merely sociological description: "Even with some theologians, the church appears to be a human construction, an instrument created by us . . . Without a view of the mystery of the church that is also supernatural and not only sociological, Christology itself loses its reference to the divine in favor of a purely human construct."[6]

However, I am approaching the subject of ecclesiology from the assumption that it is to some extent a human construct; though open to the assumption that God still had at least a (51 percent?) share-holding in the concern. God's connection with the church is perhaps rather like God's responsibility for the canon of scripture: revelation, but by fallible human means. Salvationists will have a range of views on the degree to which either God or humanity bears responsibility for either Bible or church.

Ideally the church should be in the world but not of it; in practice it became both in and of the world. From the very beginning there was a natural tension between its this-worldly and its other-worldly characteristics. So every so often some person or group of people would rise up and say, "We've lost the plot!" (Or more often, "*You've* lost the plot!") "We need to get back to basics, to the original teaching, to the apostolic pattern!" We might describe such people as "radical restorationists," calling, "Back to the roots!"

Of course they never succeed in getting back, because the past is inaccessible and we are able to see it only through the lens of the present; restorationists have striven to

---

4. For example, Matthew 18.17.
5. Kitching, Foreword to Wiggins, *History* IV, v.
6. Ratzinger, *Ratzinger* Report, 45–46.

recreate that which they understood to have been the apostolic situation.[7] Sometimes these reformers attempted to take the whole church with them—and sometimes they almost succeeded, for a time—and sometimes they struck out on their own so that we have a succession of splinter groups. Ronald Knox proposed that the essential characteristic of all such movements is "enthusiasm"; he gave that title to his classic historical survey of such groups from Montanists to Methodists.[8]

Sociology tries to find patterns and sequences in social activity. All these apparently so-different break-away and reformist groups follow a pattern. The life-cycles of organizations, including religious ones, follow a wave-like pattern or bell-curve; there are many variations on "man—movement—machine—monument—memory." General Bramwell Tillsley referred to a "Movement—Institution—Museum" sequence.[9] Organizations may plateau at the institutional stage and enter a period of decline, from which they may or may not recover. Commonly, with the onset of decline, some schismatic or renewal movement strikes out upon a new trajectory of growth before eventually repeating the pattern. So, in the Catholic church, various orders, institutes, and groups from monasticism in the second century to Opus Dei in the twentieth, as well as heretical fringe movements, have been the loci of such renewal. In Protestantism, itself such a movement in origin, sectarian groups have flourished. Sometimes, usually in response to the new offshoot, a large segment of the church experiences a measure of rejuvenation, as in the sixteenth century Counter-Reformation or with the charismatic renewal movement of the twentieth century.

Twentieth century sociologists of religion described and analyzed common characteristics of the sectarian groups descended from the Reformation by means of a "church-sect typology." Gordon Marshall summarizes as follows:

> As originally formulated by Max Weber (*The Sociology of Religion*, 1922) and Ernst Troeltsch (*The Social Teaching of the Christian Churches*, 1912), it was argued that the Church type attempted to embrace all members of society on a universalistic basis. The church, as a result, is a large, bureaucratic organization with a ministry or priesthood. It develops a formal orthodoxy, ritualistic patterns of worship, and recruits its members through socialization rather than evangelical conversion. The church is in political terms accommodated to the state and in social terms predominantly conservative in its beliefs and social standing. By contrast the sect is a small, evangelical group which recruits its members by conversion, and which adopts a radical stance towards the state and society. The medieval Roman Catholic Church was the principal example of a universalistic church; sects include Baptists, Quakers, Methodists.[10]

---

7. Lewis, in "De Descriptione Temporum," 4: "We can't get into the real forest of the past; that is part of what the word *past* means."

8. Knox, *Enthusiasm*.

9. Tillsley, *This Mind in You*, 31–32, and also in an undated pamphlet, "Focus on the Future," issued when he was General in 1993–94. A sharper, more cynical version was that of Eric Hoffer in *The Temper of Our Time*: "Every great cause begins as a movement, becomes a business and eventually degenerates into a racket."

10. Marshall, "Sect."

Later sociologists modified this typology by identifying the denomination as an organization which is mid-way between the sect and the church, and by defining various sub-types of the sect. Bryan Wilson defined four different sub-types in terms of the various ways in which they rejected social values or were indifferent to secular society.[11] These sub-types were the conversionist (such as the Salvation Army), the Adventist or revolutionary sects (for example Jehovah's Witnesses), the introversionist or pietistic sects (for instance Quakers), and the Gnostic sects (such as Christian Science and New Thought sects). These sub-types had different beliefs, methods of recruitment, and attitudes towards the world. The processes of social change within these sects were thus very different.

Wilson summarized the characteristics of the sect as:

> A voluntary association; membership is by proof to sect authorities of some claim to personal merit—such as knowledge of doctrine, affirmation of a conversion experience, or recommendation of members in good standing; exclusiveness is emphasized, and expulsion exercised against those who contravene doctrinal, moral or organizational precepts; its self-conception is of an elect, a gathered remnant, possessing special enlightenment; personal reflection is the expected standard of aspiration . . . it accepts, at least as an ideal, the priesthood of all believers; there is a high level of lay participation; there is opportunity for the member spontaneously to express his commitment; the sect is hostile or indifferent to the secular society and to the state.[12]

Which of these would describe the Salvation Army? Then? And now?

Roland Robertson, concurring with Wilson's view that sects do *not* evolve into denominations,[13] concluded that the Salvation Army had evolved rather into an "established sect"; one which had retained a sufficient number of its key pristine sectarian characteristics still to qualify in one sense as a sect, but had yet achieved a firm modus vivendi with the wider society, and become, in his infelicitous phrase, "terminally institutionalized."[14] That was in the 1960s; things may have moved on. Gordon Moyles's description and perceptive analysis of the Army in Canada showed the extent of the denominationalizing process which had taken place in the first two thirds of the twentieth century.[15]

These various "typological" descriptions of sects encounter the difficulty that very few religious bodies neatly fit the types, so that an ever more complex picture of mixed types and sub-types evolves. Benton Johnson drew attention to this difficulty, alternatively suggesting simply "rejection" of the world and "acceptance" of the social environment as the polarities of sects and denominational churches respectively.[16] Andrew Eason has pointed out that the sociologists' typecasting fails to take into account move-

---

11. Wilson, "Analysis of Sect Development," 4–6.

12. Wilson, Ibid., 1.

13. Wilson, "The Persistence of Sects."

14. Robertson, *Sociological Interpretation of Religion*, 127. See discussion in Taylor, *Like a Mighty Army*, 96, and Gates, *Altruism in the Context of Economic Ideologies*, 136–62.

15. Moyles, *Blood and Fire in Canada*, 228–44.

16. Johnson, "Critical Appraisal," 88–92; "Church and Sect," 539–49; "Church and Sect Revisited," 124–37.

ments like the Salvation Army which exhibit both sectarian and churchly characteristics. The Army has been sectarian in its theological objective of separation from the world, but churchly in its pragmatic accommodations to the world for the sake of mission and fund-raising.[17] Bruce Power has also judiciously reviewed the "sociology of Salvationism" in these terms, in papers published in *Word and Deed* in 1997 and most recently in 2016.[18]

Perhaps one of the underlying tensions in the life of the Salvation Army today is that between its being an "established sect" and its being a "denomination." This paradox still plays out in the movement's structure, beliefs and culture, the first of these modalities perhaps tending to resist change and the second to enable it, expressed in alternatively conservative or more flexible approaches to a range of issues.

As already suggested, the secular, sociological analysis is not the only way to describe the evolution of ecclesial bodies. An example of an alternative analysis taking into account the spiritual nature of the church is provided by James Pedlar in his work on charisms. His biblically and theologically-based analysis leads him to propose "a fourfold typology of ecclesial bodies . . . churches, movements, separated movements and movement-churches," within which schema the Salvation Army appears as a "movement-church."[19] Nevertheless, the tendencies observed and models proposed by secular writers in the Weberian tradition do provide helpful windows on the origins and development of the Salvation Army—however uncomfortable today's Salvationists may feel at Wilson's having typecast them as a "conversionist sect," or Robertson as an "established sect." Analysis of the movement's history in terms of the sect-church continuum still makes sense as an explanation or description of the Salvation Army's development and growth in the past.

However, the sociologists' analysis of institutionalism and decline needs to be re-examined in the light of the Army's international growth. The same processes no longer drive the evolution of the Army today, even in the secularized West, let alone in other cultures into which a Salvation Army already formed by those processes was transplanted holus-bolus. The Weberian thesis has been superseded by other explanations for social behavior, such as the phenomenological approach adopted by such sociologists as Peter Berger. I do not know of any investigation of the Salvation Army in these terms other than that in Elizabeth Milligan's 1982 Glasgow PhD thesis, "The Persistence of The Salvation Army."[20] As the title suggests, this was in part a critique of Wilson's and Robertson's analysis and conclusions. Perhaps these tools are better adapted to this postmodern era in that they are more interested in local characteristics and behaviors, with social order the result of every-day interactions, than in positing some meta-narrative by which the world might be described and interpreted.

It is over fifty years since Robertson outlined his framework and a century since sociologists began proposing their patterns of sects and types. In that time the Army in Britain and in other countries has moved on; it has long been a "denomination." The

17. Eason, "Salvation Army in Late-Victorian Britain, 3–27.
18. Power, "Towards a Sociology," 17–33; "Revisiting the Sociology," 47–69.
19. Pedlar, *Division, Diversity, and Unity*, 10.
20. Milligan, "Persistence of the Salvation Army."

applicability of his framework to the 80 percent of the Army in the developing world has yet to be discussed. Where does the Salvation Army fit now in Africa or India; as a denomination or a sect, or are those categories no longer relevant? Or are they "missions," like the early Salvation Army, or simply "religious communities?" When the cultures are so different, the framework provided by the "types" now serves mainly as a point of departure for discussion. In the meantime, we can still review the evolution of the Army's ecclesiology in terms of the "sect-church" continuum discussed above.

A SECT?

As befits that bell-shaped curve of the man—movement—machine—monument—memory continuum, the Salvation Army did indeed start with a man. "Booth led boldly," as Vachel Lindsay's poem declaims. Without him, Rider Haggard wrote in 1910, "the Salvation Army would not exist today, for it sprang from his brain like Minerva from the head of Jove, and has been driven to success by his single, forceful will."[21] At the same time, like Abraham, the bold leader was not always sure where he was going, and like Columbus, sometimes not sure where he had arrived when he got there. In a letter to *The Revival* dated the 17th August 1865, reporting on his East End activities, Booth informed readers that, "We have no very definite plans. We shall be guided by the Holy Spirit."

So, whence were they guided? What did they become? It was not the Booths' intention that the Salvation Army should become a church. In fact, Booth said, "From the first, I was strongly opposed to forming any separate organization."[22] Once he had, however unwillingly, an organization on his hands, William Booth still denied that it was a church or sect. "We are not and will not be made a Church. There are plenty for anyone who wishes to join them, to vote and to rest."[23] Thus he dismissed churches as characterized by democracy and a passive laity, neither of which he intended would have a place in his Army.

In an article in the *Contemporary Review* in August 1882, Booth expressed his hope that the Army would never grow into a sect. He felt that Wesley had been wrong to permit Methodism to become another denomination. This was unfair to Wesley, who unlike Booth had tried to prevent any such thing. Booth's armor-bearer, George Scott Railton, inveighed against sectarianism in *Heathen England*.

> "Shall we ever sink into a sectarian spirit of selfish care about our own, and cease to spend all our strength for the good of others?" Answering the hypothetical objection, "But this is making a new denomination—a new sect," he responded, "Well, and supposing that it is. Is there any harm in doing so? Is there not a need for just such a 'sect' in many cities? . . . But we deny that we are in any proper sense a sect . . . We are a corps of volunteers for Christ, organized as perfectly as we have been able to accomplish, seeking no Church status, avoiding as we

---

21. Rider Haggard, *Regeneration*, 212.
22. Booth, in Railton, *Twenty-one Years*, 22.
23. *Orders and Regulations*, 1878, 4.

would the plague every denominational rut, in order perpetually to reach more and more of those who lie outside every Church boundary."[24]

When interviewed by Sir Henry Lunn in 1895 on the Salvation Army position on the sacraments, Booth claimed, perhaps a little disingenuously, that "we came into this position originally by determining not to be a church. We did not wish to undertake the administration of the sacraments and thereby bring ourselves into collision with existing churches."[25] This glossed over the fact that the Christian Mission, and the Salvation Army until 1883, had in fact practiced the sacraments. Begbie also quotes Randall Davidson, later Archbishop of Canterbury, as saying of Booth (*a propos* negotiations between the Salvation Army and the Anglican Church in the early 1880s), "He certainly gave me to understand, and very emphatically, that he did not seek to establish a new sect."[26]

By "sect," Booth meant what we would today describe as a denomination. The sociologists had not yet taken responsibility for these terms. In the church-speak of the time, "Church" meant the Established church; "sect" meant a non-conformist church, but the words were used fairly loosely so these were also "small c" churches—and the Church of England was often lumped in with them. Sometimes "church" meant a larger, more respectable body and "sect" meant small, obscure, and peculiar.

Booth's use of the word "sect" suggests the pejorative sense, implying more than mere nonconformity. The fractured history of Methodism in the near century following Wesley's death and the arguments of the sectaries offended the Booths, not primarily because of the loss of unity and charity but because they meant distraction from the work of saving the lost. "The chief sorrow to me in connection with the sects of the past, had ever been their divisions on the subject of practical Godliness and immediate results . . . I constantly put from me the thought of attempting the formation of such a people."[27]

That the Army was not a church remained its official claim throughout the early years and well beyond. In a catechism-like pamphlet explaining the Army in the United States, one question asked, "Will not this movement result in the making of a new sect?" The answer: "Not in the sense in which a new sect is usually understood. It is not a Church, after the fashion of Churches, but an Army, that is aimed at—this is a force as real, as self-sacrificing, and as much under control for soul-saving purposes as the ordinary military armies are for slaughter and destruction. There is at present nothing after this model in existence; and if it be desirable and Scriptural, it does not matter much what it is called."[28] Maud Booth wrote, "There are sects and denominations enough. This is an Army, a band of aggressive men and women, whose work of saving and reclaiming the world must be done on entirely new lines . . . "[29]

Some recruits may have had the impression at a comparatively late date that the Salvation Army was intended to be only a kind of para-church organization. The Rev.

24. Railton, *Heathen England*, 143–44.
25. Begbie, *William Booth*, I, 468–69.
26. Begbie, Ibid., II, 29.
27. Railton, *Heathen England*, 22.
28. Smith, *All About the Salvation Army*, 20.
29. Booth, *Beneath Two Flags*, 271.

F.S. Webster describes how in "about 1877 or 1878," Wilson Carlile showed him his "soldier's certificate," "explaining that it was an Army and not a Church, that people could be banded together for the purposes of evangelization and soul-winning, as they were in connection with the Moody and Sankey missions, and yet remain, for the purposes of worship and edification, in connection with their own churches." Carlile's understanding of the situation would seem to have been anachronistic for as late as 1878 but he may well have received this impression from Booth's claims that the Army was not a "church." Webster also expressed his regret that, "Unfortunately—and, I think, most unwisely—General Booth deemed it necessary to make his Army into an independent Church."[30] From the course of events, however, it would be difficult to put a finger on any one place where it could be said that Booth had done that intentionally. Webster and Carlile went on to found the Church Army, in some respects an Anglican "Order."

Another even later witness to the Army's ambiguous ecclesiastical status was Brigadier Susan Swift, notable early American officer and close associate of the Booth family and later a Dominican nun. Writing about her second conversion, Swift looked back to her introduction to the Army in Glasgow in 1884. "The Army taught in those days that it was 'not a church but a mission' and placed no obstacle in the way of my receiving the 'sacraments' of my own or any other denomination."[31] An editorial in *The Field Officer* claimed that "A Corps is neither a Church nor a Mission," a negative version of having it both ways.[32]

In some European countries, where the "Christendom model" still functioned and membership of the state church was a corollary of citizenship, the fiction that the Army was not a "church" was longer maintained. Salvationists in Scandinavia were also Lutherans—members of the state church.[33] With his Swedish background, Colonel Karl Larsson, when Commander in Russia during the First World War, allowed Salvationist converts to remain in communion with the Orthodox Church.[34] Swiss Salvationist Victor Kunz, writing in 1947, stated that "the S.A. itself does not desire to be a church" and described himself as "a local officer of the Salvation Army and a convinced member of the Evangelical Swiss Church. All members of The Salvation Army, including Officers, without exception pay the Church tax . . ."[35] As the Nordic nations generally began to re-examine the relationship between their church and state, this ecclesiastical ambiguity was more recently found to involve legal complications. Only in 2000 was the Army registered as a "denomination" in Sweden, and in 2005 as a "Faith Community" in Norway.[36] Even today, "in Finland

---

30. Webster, "Personal Reminiscences," 168.

31. Swift, *The Conversion of Susan Swift*, 1897, 5. Quoted by Murdoch, *Soldiers of the Cross*, 101.

32. *Field Officer*, July 1901, 282.

33. See Krommenhoek, Kleman, and Puotiniemi, *Sacramental Army*. Jarl Wahlström, later General of the Salvation Army, served as a Finnish military chaplain in World War Two in his Lutheran capacity, by virtue of his having enrolled as a theological student, though he was also a Salvation Army officer at the time. See his *Autobiography*, 42–43.

34. Information courtesy of Aitken, author of *Blood and Fire, Tsar and Commissar*.

35. Kunz, "Salvation Army."

36. *Salvation Army Year Book*, 2010, 10; Lydholm, "Save souls, grow saints and serve suffering humanity."

the Salvation Army (Pelastusarmeija) is a society, not a denomination, so that most of its members continue to belong to the Lutheran Church."[37]

One of the ironies of Booth's history is that although he was determined that the Army would never become a sect, it did of course become just that. Cardinal Manning, noting Booth's protests on this point and giving him credit for his intention, commented that the Army did not have much choice: "Nevertheless we have a conviction that the Salvation Army will either become a sect or it will melt away. This world is not the abode of disembodied spirits."[38] As Ronald Knox remarks of Zinzendorf, "it is an old dream of the enthusiast that he can start a new religion without starting a new denomination."[39]

William Swatos notes of Methodism that it "is best understood as an order in origin, working firmly within the Church of England. Only after explicit schism is it properly treated as a sect or denomination. Likewise, the Salvation Army became sectarian, while the Episcopal Church's Church Army remained an order."[40] As late as the 1950s, General Albert Orsborn still denied emphatically that the Salvation Army was a "church," preferring to describe it as "a permanent mission to the unconverted."[41] General John Gowans recalled the Methodist Dr Gordon Rupp greeting Salvationist delegates at a British Council of Churches conference in the 1960s with, "You are our Franciscans. We Methodists began as a mission. We have become a Church. May the Army always remain a mission."[42]

However, the Army's founders were willing to think in terms of denomination when it suited their practical needs. Even in 1870 the Christian Mission had a rule that "Persons belonging to *other Churches* [my italics] seeking membership with us shall be admitted on presentation of their note of transfer if such can be obtained," which implies that the Mission already saw itself as a "church."[43] The Salvation Army soon began to claim denominational status when legal considerations suggested advantages. For example, the Salvation Army in Australia, presumably with the Founder's blessing, claimed legal status as a church as early as 1884.[44] Gordon Moyles notes that from 1892 Canadian Salvation Army officers could officiate at marriages, prior to which year the vows were administered by a clergyman of another denomination.[45] Salvation Army chaplains were gazetted for the New Zealand Defense Forces in 1913 on the assumption that the Salvation Army was a church like other churches.[46] More formally and famously, in 1917, the question of American officers' eligibility for military chaplaincy being at stake, the Judge Advocate General in Washington ruled that "The Salvation Army possesses all

---

37. http://evl.fi/EVLen.nsf/0/33BF84FA7709BE9BC22572CD002A4457?OpenDocument&lang=EN (Site maintained by the Evangelical Lutheran Church of Finland, downloaded 14 February 2012.)

38. Manning in *The Contemporary Review*, quoted by Begbie, *William Booth*, II, 31–32.

39. Knox, *Enthusiasm*, 403.

40. Swatos, "Church-Sect and Cult," 21.

41. *Officer*, March–April 1954, 74.

42. Hunter, *While the Light Lingers*, 36.

43. Minutes of the Christian Mission Conference, 1870, V: 17.

44. Hubbard, "The Army a Church?" 517.

45. Moyles, *Blood and Fire in Canada*, 289.

46. Bradwell, *Fight the Good Fight*, 100. In Britain this opportunity was not available until 1918.

the elements required for a religious denomination; and that its ministers are regularly ordained within the meaning of the statutes."[47]

Whatever its ambiguity about terminology, the Army had by that time become a church, or denomination, in the sense that its local congregations bore a resemblance to those of other non-conformist denominations, and its members had come to think of their leaders as the equivalent of clergy. One articulate soldier, John Hollins, was an early adopter. He wrote in the *Contemporary Review* in September 1898, "The Salvation Army is a religious denomination—nay, in what I believe to be a true sense of the word, a Church."[48] His leaders had not yet come to this conclusion.

We'll attempt to trace why and how that began to happen. The influences that chiefly shaped the Booths' ecclesiology were firstly Wesleyan and secondly "revivalist". In terms of the old question about the relative importance of nature or nurture, genes or upbringing, Booth's ecclesiology owed something to both.

Converted in the Methodist Church at the age of fifteen, Booth claimed in a speech on his sixtieth birthday that he "literally worshipped Methodism. To me there was one God and John Wesley was his prophet."[49] Wesley's example inspired Booth's evangelical zeal. Like Wesley, Booth took to the fields and the streets (and circuses, skating rinks and theatres) when the churches were closed to him. Like Wesley's, Booth's followers tended to be of the lower classes and they suffered similar persecution from mobs and vested interests. Wesley's Arminian faith and his teaching on "Christian perfection" or "holiness" were Booth's creed as well. The doctrines and conference polity of the Christian Mission were entirely Methodist.[50] The Salvation Army retained the doctrines but not the Conference.

Methodism carried forward into its church phase the ecclesiological ambiguities of its para-church ethos. Colonel Earl Robinson notes that "Our lack of precision in responding (to the question of to what extent is The Salvation Army an ecclesia) may be considered to be part of our Wesleyan heritage." He quotes David Smith's suggestion in *A Contemporary Wesleyan Theology* that Wesley did not think of his followers as being incorporated into a separate church, but rather forming a group of societies within the Anglican Church, an *ecclesiola in ecclesia*.[51] Robinson writes that the "same ambiguity existed in the early days of The Salvation Army, and to some extent exists still."[52]

Whatever that ambiguity, Booth shared Wesley's conviction that the laity was called to an active role in ministry. They were not merely pew fodder or spectators at religious ceremonies. The great strength of Methodism lay in the "classes" which were lay-led, and in the training and appointment of lay preachers. The Christian Mission, and in its turn the Salvation Army, also pressed every available man (and woman) into service.

---

47. The whole judgement is quoted in Clifton, *Who Are These Salvationists?* 16–17.
48. Hollins. "Note of Warning," 440.
49. Ervine, *God's Soldier*, II, 735.
50. Rhemick, *New People of God*; Green, *Life and Ministry*.
51. "A little church within a church," a term coined for small home groups by the Lutheran Pietist Philip Spener in his *Pia Desiderata* of 1675.
52. Robinson, "The Salvation Army—*Ecclesia?*" 9–42.

William Booth wrote that one of the "principles with which I believe my heart was inspired in the earliest days of my spiritual life" was "our employment of the people—out of which has grown our varied classes of officers, opportunities for testimony, and the open door and continued encouragement to every man, and every woman, and every child, to use and exercise whatever gifts they may have received from God for assisting Him in subduing and winning this rebellious world to Himself."[53] Catherine Booth's vigorous claim was, "Yes, thank God, we are teaching the Churches that others besides clergymen, ministers, deacons and elders can be used for the salvation of men. The multitudes have too long been left to these. As a clergyman said to me the other day, 'There are 35,000 souls in my parish, what can one do?' What indeed! Set the carpenters and the washerwomen on to them, saved and filled with the Spirit!"[54]

The Booths, then, wholeheartedly adopted the Wesleyan model of lay ministry. That was however only half the story. Wesley, for all his fostering of lay ministry, was less willing to share the government of the church with the laity. Booth, like Wesley, was an autocrat by temperament and conviction. Ervine puts the similarity strongly: "When Wesley, in his old age, surveyed his society and appraised his preachers, he realized that the whole organization was his, as the whole Salvation Army, more than a century after Wesley's death, was to be William Booth's: a foundation largely, if not entirely, the personal possession of its founder."[55]

Continuing power struggles between Methodist clergy and laity led to further schisms. William and Catherine had some brief involvement with the Methodist Reform movement. In that case, the pendulum had swung too far towards anti-clericalism for the Booths' taste, as Catherine explained in a letter. "The discipline of the Reform Society was very unsatisfactory to us both, in denying the minister his proper authority they went over to regard him as nothing, denying him every shadow of authority, and only allowing him to preside at their meetings when elected for the purpose, and speaking of him in public and in private as their 'hired' preacher . . . "[56] Ervine summed up Booth's attitude on the question of authority: " . . . his instincts were conservative, but he also had a natural hatred of committees and interfering laymen and a deep belief in the authority of the minister."[57] The shadow of the coming Army may be discerned in which the foot soldiers would certainly share the fighting but the officers would issue the orders.

There is another element in Methodism which we need to note as significant for the Army, and that is its "classes." The strength of the Methodist movement was in its small groups, which were not only for study but for personal accountability to the group. Unfortunately, this must be noted as one of the ways in which Booth's Army did not succeed in emulating that of his hero, Wesley. Roger Green has written:

> The genius of the class meeting was that it enhanced the disciplines of the inner life while at the same time allowing for the pastoral care of all members of the

---

53. Railton, *Heathen England*, 23.
54. Catherine Booth, *Salvation Army in Relation to Church & State*, 75.
55. Ervine, *God's Soldier*, I, 178.
56. Begbie, *William Booth*, I, 138.
57. Ervine, *God's Soldier*, I, 80.

community. Little wonder then that William Booth, early in the history of the Salvation Army, stated, "We must follow Wesley in this or we are a rope of sand."

Sadly, the Army was not able to sustain the commitment to the inner life that Booth obviously envisioned. The emphasis on large scale evangelistic meetings, the hectic pace of the weekly life of the officers and soldiers and the discipline required for all other programs in the life of the corps all served to drain the necessary energy for the most critical weekly commitment of The Salvation Army's soldiers—the class meeting.[58]

It is possible also that the Wesleyan class meetings, like Wesley's high view of the sacraments, had fallen into comparative formality and unimportance by the time Booth was active in the Methodist New Connexion, even though they were carried forward into the Christian Mission. The comment quoted by Green, Booth had written to his son, Bramwell, having been reading a life of Wesley while convalescing from illness in 1876; it sounded like a discovery rather than a recollection.[59] Booth's own account of the "class," remembering his days as a twenty-year-old in London, was unenthusiastic: "A Methodist sufficiently in earnest to get inside to a 'class' would find a handful of people reluctant to bear any witness to the power of God."[60]

In brief, then, the Wesleyan influence on the Booths can be seen in their emulation of Wesley himself and in parallels between the situation, ethos and doctrines of Methodism and Salvationism. It can also be traced in their conviction of the importance of lay-participation, and paradoxically, in their equally strong conviction of the value of authoritarian rule.

The other main influence on the Booths was the American Revivalist movement, itself the child of Methodism. This tended to be non-sectarian (what we would today call non-denominational) and lay-led and controlled. One of the best known nineteenth century evangelists, Dwight L. Moody, chose not to be ordained, even although he had in the course of his ministry, established and led more than one church congregation.[61] The influence of Charles Finney, James Caughey and Phoebe Palmer in particular, the latter two themselves children of Wesleyanism, helped shape the Booths' style of evangelism. All three visited Britain. Finney's books on theology and the revivals of religion were recommended; in 1899 the Salvation Army published an edition of his autobiography.

Caughey's British campaign from 1841 to 1846, organized largely without reference to the official structures of the church, led to a vigorous controversy within Methodism about revivalism and lay authority. As a fledgling teenage preacher, Booth was impressed by Caughey's "straightforward conversational way of putting the truth, and the common-sense method of pushing people up to decision, and the corresponding results that followed."[62] Caughey later gave the Booths counsel on a visit in 1858 when they stood at a crossroads in their career, and also baptized their son Ballington. It is interesting that Caughey, while

---

58. Green, "Call to the Inner Life," 5.

59. Begbie, *William Booth*, I, 397–97.

60. Green, *Life and Ministry of William Booth*, 6. Green sourced his quote from Railton's *Life of General Booth*, 27–28.

61. Pollock, *Moody Without Sankey*, 58–59.

62. Railton, *Twenty-one Years*, 8.

sympathizing with Booth's frustration at the reluctance of the New Connexion to give him liberty to work as an itinerant evangelist under their aegis, nevertheless urged caution. William should wait until he was ordained before leaving so as to resign "from a position of strength" as a fully accredited and recognized minister.[63] There were mixed messages there about the clerical-lay relationship and the significance of ordination.

Phoebe Palmer and her husband, both lay, evangelized together, but Mrs Palmer was the preacher and Dr Walter Palmer's was a support role. Catherine Booth took up cudgels in 1859 in defense of Phoebe Palmer's right, as a woman, to preach. This led towards Catherine's own destiny as an advocate and exemplar of female ministry and so to the Salvation Army's precept of the equality of the sexes in ministry.

The non-sectarian character of the revivalists' missions was important for the Booths. It must have seemed to them that most really effective evangelical work was happening outside the official church structures, while churches tended to be self-absorbed and complacent. Certainly the official bodies strongly rejected the revivalist movement of the late 1850s, though some Anglican and non-conformist clergy supported it. Describing their freelance work in the early 1860s, when the various Methodist Conferences had closed chapels against them on the ground that evangelistic movements were "unfavorable to church order," Booth recalled that, "undenominational work was just then coming into fashion. The theory was, save the people outside the churches and then send them to the churches to be trained and cared for."[64]

The "Hallelujah Band", a kind of prototype Salvation Army exercise in the Midlands, was a short-lived English lay-movement in 1862–1863. Through Booth's influence perhaps it could also be described as a child of American revivalism. Converts, especially those with colorful reputation as formerly notorious sinners or people of note amongst the working class—pugilists, former poachers and jailbirds who could draw a crowd to a salvation "freak show"—were set up as the preachers and open-air rallies were held. They attracted thousands of people. "Many of the most notorious characters in the district were converted."[65] Booth's presidential address to the 1877 Christian Mission Conference claimed that "with the origin of this movement I had something to do." He described how he had got together a "collection of people" for a Camp Meeting at Walsall. "Directly after this much the same set of brothers held meetings all through the Black Country . . . I never had the opportunity of taking part in it . . . "[66] The Hallelujah Band members wore Garibaldi-like red shirts which may have inspired the Salvationist red guernsey.[67]

At any rate the Hallelujah Band's example not only confirmed Booth's views on the mobilization of the laity. Their longer-term fate also confirmed his predilection for authority. "In course of time," he noted, "the leaders disagreed. Divisions crept in. There being no acknowledged authority, all did pretty much what was right in their own eyes.

---

63. Hattersley, *Blood & Fire*, 95–96.
64. Booth, in Railton, *Twenty-one Years*, 15.
65. Railton, Ibid., 16–17.
66. *Christian Mission Magazine*, July 1877, 182.
67. A "Guernsey" was a round-neck woolen jersey worn by fishermen from that Channel Isle, widely worn in Britain in the nineteenth century. It was adopted as uniform by Salvationists, usually with words "Salvation Army" or some Salvationist symbol woven on the chest.

The work gradually died out, or, at best, left only the monument of a few half-and-half Methodist societies behind."[68]

From the American revivalists, then, we see that Booth not only learned about evangelical methods and concluded that there was more freedom in their use outside the control of denominational structures, but also had confirmed his convictions about both the importance of lay-participation and the need for strong government.

We conclude from our sampling of these influences and experiences that ecclesiastical tradition and authority were not of great significance to the Booths. They took what they inherited, used what worked for them and discarded what did not. The key was the engagement of the laity. This, along with Booth's own disinclination to accept anyone else's authority, led them to work outside the existing denominational framework, and that led to their having to create an alternative framework, simply in order to organize what was happening and to secure its effectiveness and survival.

The period from 1865, when Booth began working in the East End of London, to 1878 when the Christian Mission became known as the Salvation Army, could be seen to encompass the transition from non-sectarian work to sect; from a parachurch agency to what was virtually a denominational church.

In a modern parachurch agency, working alongside the churches, the workers conventionally retain their membership of their original community of faith. Where the agency recruits individuals, rather than working with existing groups, and its main concern involves the holding of religious missions and services, the agency itself tends to become in practice a new and autonomous community of faith for its workers and their converts. It is not merely the vehicle for their work; it becomes the source of their own support and training, the locus of their fellowship and absorbing interest.

James Packer suggests that " . . . these agencies of God's kingdom draw interest, prayer, enthusiasm, and money away from the wider-ranging, slower-moving, less glamorous realities of congregational life, so that the parachurch body comes to have pride of place in supporters' affections and in effect to be their church."[69]

This certainly had happened with Methodism. This is also what happened with Booth's mission, whatever Booth's intention at first. William Booth's transition from a free-lance itinerant evangelist to his becoming established in the East End had involved much more than just a change of setting. Having spoken in meetings arranged by others, Booth now led his own workers. Instead of chapels, he hired all kinds of buildings. From exclusively indoor settings, he marched and spoke in the open air. Solo preaching was replaced by shared ministry, revival-seeking church congregations by people off the street. Previously his converts belonged to his campaign organizers, while now he had to figure out what to do with them. The solution changed a temporary mission into a permanent one.

> My first idea was simply to get people saved, and send them to the churches. This proved at the outset impracticable. 1st. They would not go when sent. 2nd. They were not wanted. And 3rd. We wanted some of them at least ourselves, to

---

68. Railton, *Twenty-one Years*, 16.
69. Packer, "Stunted Ecclesiology?"

help us in the business of saving others. We were thus driven to providing for the converts ourselves.[70]

Such provision marked the birth of a new faith community, although in his 1868 Report of the East London Christian Mission Booth informed its readers that "this is an unsectarian mission. Our creed is the Bible, our work is to publish the gospel, and we welcome as co-workers all who hold the Word of God as the standard of faith and practice, and whose hearts are in sympathy with revival work."

History is usually a seamless garment and the transition from one stage to another with such an organization is difficult to pin down. The Salvation Army has always regarded 1865 as its founding date—Railton published *Twenty-One Years Salvation Army* in 1886, even although that name was unheard of before 1877. However the point at which the Mission became the de facto community of faith for its adherents probably came earlier rather than later, probably in 1867, despite Booth's "unsectarian" claim of the following year.

The steps on the way are well documented by Sandall's official history. The Home Mission revival movement of the late 1850s spawned many small agencies and missions. Reginald Radcliffe formed the East London Special Services Committee in 1861 to try to co-ordinate their activities in London. Booth talked with representatives of this group in 1861 but it was not until 1865, after the Booths had moved to London for the sake of Catherine's speaking engagements that William became actively involved. His first regular engagement with the committee began in July 1865, with meetings held in a tent on a disused Quaker burial ground.

Pressed to continue his successful leadership of the "tent group," Booth informed the *Revival* (in the same number in which he denied having any definite plans), that, "In order to carry on this work we propose to establish a Christian Revival Association in which we think a hundred persons will enroll themselves at once. We shall also require some central building in which to hold our more private meetings, and in which to preach the gospel when not engaged in special work elsewhere." Nothing is plain sailing but after a year, there were sixty members.[71]

Sandall describes 1867 as "the turning point" as far as establishment of a distinct body is concerned. In that year the East London Christian Mission was named; acquired its first headquarters; hired a theatre for Sunday meetings and increased its number of "preaching stations" to six in the course of the year; began to hire workers (nine by the end of the year); established a system for processing converts (1st ensure a definite decision, 2nd give them instruction, 3rd train them and set them to work); printed its first document (combined Articles of Faith and Bond of Agreement, direct forbear of the "Soldier's Covenant" signed by Salvationists today); embarked on social relief for the hungry poor; organized its funds, issued its first financial statement and received a grant from the Evangelization Society.

Sandall mentions another significant development, a substantial change in membership. People left for various reasons, some perhaps because they did not like the way

---

70. Booth, in Railton, *Twenty-one Years*, 22.
71. Sandall, *History*, I, 42, 46–47.

things were going or the Booths' methods, and others because once the new mission was established they returned to their home churches which had loaned them. Booth set about building those who remained, and their converts, into a fighting force.[72] Significantly, for the first time a celebration of the Lord's Supper is recorded. The East London Christian Mission, like Methodism before it, was on its way to becoming a sect.

Out of the innovations of 1867, the hiring of staff marks the beginnings of the development of a full-time, paid ministry. The first paid helper, Mrs Eliza Collingridge, herself a convert, was described as a "Biblewoman." She later became Superintendent of the Shoreditch circuit when expansion required such organization and was therefore the first woman to hold office in the Christian Mission.

By 1868 *The Revival* recorded that "Twenty persons are wholly employed, assisted by a large band of devoted helpers." In the *East London Evangelist* of February that year, William Booth stated "not a single official salary is paid," perhaps meaning "office staff" as distinct from the Mission's field force. (Booth himself relied on support from friends and did not draw on the mission's funds.) "One hundred and twenty services outdoors and in are held weekly, at which the gospel is preached on an average to 14,000 people." Most of the "twenty persons" were presumably evangelists, though some were doubtless involved in relief work and one appears to have been responsible for a sewing class. At first the various preaching posts or "stations" (Salvation Army officers, like Methodists, are still described as "stationed" at their appointments today) were controlled centrally and evangelists rostered, like a Methodist circuit. James Dowdle was the first to be appointed to the charge of a particular center, though in a voluntary capacity; he became a full-time, employed evangelist in 1873. Fixed (though still very brief) appointments soon replaced itinerancy; by 1874 there were eight district superintendents.

After some stagnation the Mission was entering a period of rapid expansion and thereafter, in Bramwell Booth's phrase, was always "growing out of its clothes."[73] In 1874 there were ten "Districts."[74] The 1875 Report listed twenty-three stations and their District Superintendents.[75] The first issue of *The Salvationist* gave thirty stations and thirty-six evangelists for 1877, and eighty-one stations and one hundred and twenty-seven evangelists for 1878.[76] By the beginning of 1883 there were 442 Corps and 1067 officers operating in thirteen countries. Three years later, there were 1,749 Corps and 4,192 officers.[77]

With growth the Mission inevitably entered also a period of reorganization and constitution-making. The first Christian Mission Constitution, 1870, is described by Sandall—with a nod to the Long Parliament—as Booth's "Self-denying Ordinance" as by it he divested himself of much of his power.[78] Booth made Conference the final authority in the Mission's affairs, modelled on that of the Methodist New Connexion. The

---

72. Sandall, Ibid., I, 46–47.
73. Bramwell-Booth, *Bramwell Booth*, 90.
74. *Christian Mission Magazine,* August 1874, 226.
75. *Christian Mission Magazine,* July 1875, 191.
76. *Salvationist,* January 1879, 4.
77. Sandall, *History,* I, 170; 2, 338.
78. Sandall, Ibid., 1:178.

1876 Minutes instructed "That each district having a membership of 100 or upwards on 7th November next send their evangelist with one delegate if thought desirable to a meeting of the Conference Committee."[79] A major break from Methodist tradition was that women were admitted to full participation, in government as well as in ministry. Wesley had appointed women as local preachers, though the practice declined amongst the Wesleyans after his death and Conference prohibited it in 1803.

Conference rule proved too inhibiting for Booth, and for his band of enthusiasts, a delegation of whom asked him to assume more direct control. This led in 1875 to the first Constitutional Deed-Poll of the Christian Mission. This provided that the Mission should be "under the oversight direction and control of some one person." This reinforced the General Superintendent's role, giving power to over-ride decisions of Conference and also gave him power of appointment. He was to hold office for term of his natural life though he could be removed by unanimous vote of Conference. He could appoint his successor; failing which one could be elected by Conference. The General Superintendent would be the sole trustee for financial purposes. He could also amend the Deed-Poll if three quarters of the Conference agreed, and after five years, the Conference itself could amend constitution—*except for* doctrines; powers of General Superintendent; the elective character of Conference; the prohibition on the letting of halls; and the equality of role of women. It is not clear what else was left to do.

Endless talkfest and the unreality of trying to organize a rapidly expanding organization by annual decision-making and government by committees were still seen as inhibiting progress. A meeting of "Conference Committee" in January 1877 concurred with a motion to abolish Conference rule, this being ratified by the last Conference, styled a "Council of War," the following June. Thus by something like a palace *coup d'état*, Booth resumed full control of the Mission.

A new Deed-Poll executed at War Congress in August 1878, provided that:

- The Christian Mission should be always thereafter under the oversight, direction, and control of some one person who should be General Superintendent.
- That William Booth should continue to be, for the term of his natural life, the General Superintendent of The Christian Mission, unless he should resign.
- That William Booth and every General Superintendent who should succeed him should have power to appoint his successor to the office of General Superintendent, making a statement in writing, under seal, as to such successor or the means to be taken for the appointment of a successor.
- That the General Superintendent should have power to expend all monies contributed, but should annually publish a balance sheet.
- That he should have power to acquire or dispose of property and to set up or revoke trusts.
- The Deed-Poll established the doctrines and principles of the Salvation Army (August 1878) although the Deed-Poll is for The Christian Mission and nowhere refers

---

79. *Christian Mission Magazine*, July 1876, 171.

to "The Salvation Army." That name was not legally recorded until 1880 and finally "enrolled" as an "endorsement" to the Deed-Poll in 1906.

- Power to alter the Deed-Poll was not retained, so it would require Act of Parliament to do this.

We can see how the initial "band of brothers" (and sisters), mostly personally recruited by Booth himself, would happily endorse such powers. Later, Booth was popularly supposed to be claiming greater powers than the Pope, an accusation that dogged him all his life despite denials, such as Catherine's in an address on "The Probable Future of The Salvation Army" in 1883.[80] In 1889 a Canadian ex-staff-officer published a book entitled *The New Papacy: behind the Scenes in the Salvation Army*.[81] Booth himself had no illusions on this score. Announcing his position on the sacraments, he commented that any order he might give for the general administration of the sacraments would probably be ignored; hardly consistent with the absolute obedience to his orders generally thought to be exacted.[82] Of course, this was an order Booth may not in any case have wished to give. At the drawing up of the deed poll, the lawyer, Herbert Cozens-Hardy, later Master of the Rolls, protested, "Mr Booth, you want me to make you into a Pope, and I do not think it can be done!" To which Booth retorted, "Well, Mr Cozens-Hardy, I am sure that you will get as near to it as you suitably can!"[83] Not that he suffered delusions of grandeur; in some publications he put the military title *after* his name because he felt that "General William Booth" looked pretentious.[84] He was more interested in the substance of power than the shadow.

Between 1868 and 1878, then, the process took place whereby an independent mission staffed by volunteers from a variety of church backgrounds evolved into a highly centralized organization, a people with a distinct and common name and identity, and its own full-time, employed leaders, analogous to clergy.

It is significant that only the full-time, employed evangelists or missioners attended the Council of War in 1878, whereas "lay" delegates had attended earlier Conferences. The rank and file of the Salvation Army ceased to participate in the organization's government. At the same time as the Mission metamorphosed into the Salvation Army, it constitutionally reverted to Wesley's original Methodist model of benevolent dictatorship, but without his Conference.[85] There must have been some dissenting voices, for in an address on 18th June 1880, Booth complained,

> There is a growing spirit around us in favour of no government at all. All masters and no servants is the motto . . . the children don't want any authority; the workpeople don't want any authority; sinners don't want any authority; saints don't

---

80. Booth, *Church and State*, 66.
81. Accessible on http://www.archive.org/details/cihm_11259.
82. *War Cry*, 17 January 1883, 4.
83. Booth, *Echoes and Memories*, 2nd edn 1977, 184.
84. Booth, Ibid., 60–61. The title page of the 1910 *Year Book* said, "The Rev. William Booth, General."
85. Neely, *Origin and Development of Governing Conference*, 9–10, says, "Mr Wesley was the government; and, though he invited preachers to confer with him, he did not propose to abandon any of his original power."

want any authority. "There ought to be no submitting of one Corps to another," says one. A step further and there will be no submission of one man to another, and you will have, with individual independence, weakness, confusion, disorder, and destruction.[86]

Booth made no bones about the fact that he insisted that things would be done his way. He wrote to his son in 1877, that " . . . controversy is useless . . . I am determined that evangelists in this Mission must hold my views and work on my lines." Thirty-four years later his beliefs on this subject had not altered: "I feel as if I had a call from Heaven to make my officers and soldiers understand what I want in The S.A. and make them feel that they have got to work to my plans and not to ___'s or their own conceits."[87]

The government of the movement was clearly concentrated in the hands of a leading group, though always as a delegated authority derived in the end from the General himself. Only at the highest level in the Army, the High Council, by which the General is elected, was decision-making by majority vote. This autocratic model remained the norm for nearly 140 years, until very recently General André Cox began to initiate reforms instituting more participative government and distributed authority. However, for ordinary purposes, and for all of its history but the most recent, it may be seen that the role of an officer was to command, to direct the government of the organization at a particular level. The post-1877 polity certainly left the way open for the elevation of an "officer class" in the all-lay Army.

Railton defended the Army's "military order and system":

> The question is how men and women, hitherto averse to all religious control, and indeed, control of any kind, are induced to submit themselves without fee and reward to the orders of those who are often in every way their inferiors. Look at that young lad, not out of his teens, commanding a corps in some large city. His every sign is obeyed by men and women old enough to be his grandparents, by tradesmen who were accustomed to manage business affairs before he learned arithmetic (what little he knows of it), by sergeants and soldiers of the Army, who have served several years longer than himself in it, and some of whom know more of God and mankind, more of the work and literature of the Army, than he does . . . It is easy to explain all upon "the love of Christ constraineth" us principle, "submitting yourselves to one another in love;" but take that away, and what becomes of the Army's discipline?[88]

Some ecclesial bodies claim that they have maintained continuity with the original, apostolic church and have therefore preserved, or have developed its essence and form under the guidance of the Holy Spirit. As already noted, others claim that they have come into existence in order to recover the pattern and practice of that original. The varieties of expression presented under this rationale range from the communities of faithful laity under the guidance of and supported by the three-fold catholic ministry of bishop, priest and deacon, all belonging to a universal church at one extreme, to small, autonomous congregations without any designated, "separated" ministry at the other.

---

86. Coates, *Prophet of the Poor*, 133.
87. Bramwell-Booth, *Bramwell Booth*, 96, 217.
88. Railton, in Booth, *Popular Christianity*, 193.

The Salvation Army did not come about in either of these ways and has never claimed to re-institute any original pattern of what the church should look like. As already recalled, Booth wrote that

> . . . even if it could be shown what was the particular form of government practiced by the early Christians, it would still be impossible to show from the New Testament that because the apostles and first converts followed certain customs in the management of their religious assemblies, that we are under Divine obligation to adopt the same.[89]

Nevertheless, Salvationists were quite satisfied that the *spirit* of their operations was true to the original. Wyndham S. Heathcote had this impression of them in 1890:

> To a Salvationist, the birth of the Army in Whitechapel appeared to be a renewal of Pentecost. It was a genuine outpouring of spiritual enthusiasm. It was as though Christianity was thrown into its first simplicity and zeal in to the heart of the crowded metropolis, to shape and form itself once more.[90]

Or this, from the 1921 *Salvation Army Year Book*:

> The Salvation Army is, in a word, the modern manifestation of apostolic religion. For the first 200 years after the death of Jesus, the Christian Assemblies were very like Salvation Army meetings. The reading of the prophets or the Psalms, and copies of the manuscripts of the Gospels or Pauline letters, extempore prayers, testimonies—in which the women shared, and speaking generally, unconventional as against a set form of service."[91]

If we stand back and review what happened: a small, non-denominational mission grew to the point where it had all the marks of an independent sect. Its members were all "workers" in the mission. It multiplied "preaching stations," which with the adoption of quasi-military terminology became "corps," its members became soldiers and its full-time evangelists, officers. It was significant that the officers were not appointed to a corps but to a locality, as corps officers still are today. The earliest *Orders and Regulations* were emphatic: "You are sent to a place, not to a set of people."[92] Or as a later description put it: "No parish or parochial views of an Officer's life are allowed to rule; in fact, he is trained from his spiritual infancy to understand John Wesley's charter, "The World is my Parish."[93] Their role was missional, not pastoral; they were evangelists and leaders, not shepherds.

With the organization of the Army into divisions under divisional officers in 1880 a quasi-episcopal structure came into being.[94] International expansion soon brought about the three levels of command that still exist—territorial, divisional and corps. The Salvation Army was sometimes a bit hazy about the precise application of military terms

---

89. *Orders and Regulations*, 1886, 161.
90. Heathcote, *My Salvation Army Experience*, 59.
91. "Torchbearer," "Salvation Army and Sacerdotalism," 22.
92. *Orders and Regulations*, 1878, 13. This may have derived from the original Methodist idea that preachers were sent to a "Circuit" or "Round" rather than to a particular congregation.
93. Salvation Army, *Spiritual Conflict*, 9.
94. *War Cry*, 18 September, 1880.

and managed to make corps a subset of division rather than the reverse, probably in consequence of inventing the systems as they went along.[95] Not quite the traditional three-fold order of the Church, but it is interesting to compare this with Hans Küng's comment: "But even in non-episcopal missions in many cases an office corresponding to that of bishop, though bearing another name, has been established to meet the requirements of ecclesiastical life."[96]

With this history, early Salvation Army ecclesiology was not couched in traditional ecclesiastical terms. Rather it was motivational, descriptive and prescriptive of function. It encapsulated the dictum of Emil Brunner: "The Church exists by mission as fire exists by burning."[97] The Salvation Army movement was organized in the best way they could manage to facilitate that end. They didn't know they were doing ecclesiology. They did what seemed best to do next. Theory came later, as an explanation. Doctrine follows praxis.

Any subsequent theoretical justification they took from (1) Biblical models, such as First Testament patriarchy,[98] or the claim that General Booth occupied in respect of the Salvation Army a position analogous to that of Paul in the early church,[99] and (2) practical necessity—the exigencies of the war. "The power of a movement is in proportion to the force of its government," it claimed.[100] It was in no way interested in questions of authenticity and authority in relation to the historic ministry of the church. Questions of ecclesiology could be lived with, with a degree of imprecision and uncertainty that would not have been acceptable concerning matters considered more central to the Salvationists' faith.

The principles established in the time of the first two generations of Salvationists determined the nature of a tradition, of which some elements have been perpetuated as a cultural mythology (for example, the expectation of total obedience to superior officers) even when the reality has drifted from that ideal.

The most obvious thing about the Salvation Army is that it is an Army—an authoritarian religious organization structured on quasi-military lines and employing military terminology. This has implications for the status and function of officers within such a hierarchy.

Leadership, as the whole military metaphor would insist, would be the principal aspect of the officer's role. A vigorous note from William Booth to Bramwell in March 1877 encapsulates his theology of officership: "You must have a leader, and you must have a band of men who are 'alive.' Let us pour contempt on our 'ministerial helpers' and end them or mend them . . . Give me godly, go-ahead dare-devils and anybody may have

---

95. *Pace* John Read who suggests that such terminological solecisms were intentional: see his *Catherine Booth*, 137 n100. Ranks also ended up in curious order, with Colonel senior to Brigadier, unlike the British Army—though ranks did not always travel well; in some European countries, a Brigadier was a variety of NCO.

96. Küng, *Structures of the Church*, 134.

97. Brunner, *Word and World*, 11.

98. *Why and Wherefore of Salvation Army Rules and Regulations*, 3.

99. *Orders and Regulations*, 1886, 162.

100. Ibid., 1886, 159.

the preachers!"[101] His closest spirits shared his vision. Railton lauded the "superiority of a personal directorate over a divided management . . . By this means above all," he claimed, "can our members be preserved from the tendency to sectarianism and kept continually moving on to the fulfilment of the great evangelistic enterprise for which alone the Army exists. The supremacy of one who is pledged to an invariable and unalterable program is guarantee for the perpetual prosecution at every station of the same system, which has proved so blessedly successful hitherto."[102]

The *Orders and Regulations* spelled it out in Chapter VI, "The Government of the Army." Section 1 was about "Strong Government": "Where prompt, decided, forcible action is being continually required, there must be a form of government proportionately strong and determined." Section 2, on "Leadership," showed how such command, and corresponding obedience, was natural, scriptural, universal and effective. Section 3, "Description of the Government," claimed that "The Army has been modelled substantially after the fashion of the most powerful form of human government, a military one." Because, "to rise in the Army, a soldier has only to prove himself proportionately good and able . . . It is really the administration of government by the wisest and best . . . If the value and utility of a government be proved by its success in attaining the ends for which it is instituted, the unprecedented successes which have attended the career of The Army, taken alone, establish its claim to be considered not only wise and useful, but Divine."[103]

Commissioner Allister Smith, in opposing The Salvation Army Act of 1931, told a Parliamentary Select Committee that the General held office "by Divine Right."[104] Smith had voted against the deposition of Bramwell Booth in the 1929 High Council, and only echoed the views of the Founder, whose opinion, delivered to staff-officers in 1905, had been:

> The Staff Officer is the responsible governor under the Salvation Army system. It is to me, your General, as we have seen, and as you all knew before my mentioning it again, that God has delegated, by His grace, and in the order of His providence, certain responsibilities, authorities, and powers.[105]

Discipline has to be seen in the nineteenth-century context when even ordinary conditions of employment would be judged harsh by twenty-first century OECD-country expectations, and the Booths were leading a force many of whom were unused, as Railton noted, to discipline of any kind. An 1879 report announced that "Four officers were reduced to the ranks in December. 2 for light and frivolous conduct and conversation, 1 for contracting a matrimonial engagement immediately after appointment and without the consent of Headquarters. 1 for misbehaviour in the presence of the enemy."[106] To put the first fault in context, the second of John Wesley's four resolutions for daily living, was

---

101. Bramwell-Booth, *Bramwell Booth*, 90.
102. Railton, *Heathen England*, 180.
103. *Orders and Regulations*, 1886, 159–63.
104. Ervine, *God's Soldier*, II, 1007.
105. Nicol, *General Booth*, 120.
106. *War Cry*, 29 December 1879, 4.

"To labour after continual seriousness, not willingly indulging myself in any the least levity of behaviour, or in laughter; no, not for a moment."[107]

The earliest ecclesiology for Salvationists is found in the *Orders and Regulations*. Whereas most ecclesiologies, from the Second Vatican Council's "Lumen Gentium" to such expositions as J. Rodman Williams' "Renewal Theology," take their bearings from Scripture and the tradition of the church, Booth's mission was ordered entirely pragmatically.[108] Only later, when the Salvation Army wanted to claim some equivalent status to that held by the churches, or when in the course of ecumenical relationships it found it necessary to describe itself in terminology common to churches, did it start invoking Scripture and tradition for first principles rather than for explanatory comparisons.

At first all evangelists, and later all officers, were engaged by the Founder and heard from his own lips what character and duties he expected of them. As the organization grew, William Booth, Bramwell and Railton all spent much of their time on peripatetic inspections, encouraging and correcting the workers and their work. This proved increasingly unmanageable. Booth recalled that for a time he resorted to issuing "these instructions in the form of correspondence; but this also I soon found to be a task beyond my ability . . . I was therefore compelled to print such special directions as I had formerly issued in other forms."[109]

The Orders and Regulations of The Salvation Army, prepared by Railton under Booth's supervision and first published in October 1878, were the result. In it Booth claimed that "our system corresponds so closely to that of the Army and Navy of this country that we have been able to use even the very words of many of their regulations, and of Sir Garnet Wolseley's *Soldier's Pocket-book*."[110] This first edition majored on the practical issues to be addressed in seizing and holding posts for the Army and establishing corps. The much larger and more detailed *Orders and Regulations for Field Officers* appeared in 1886.[111] Additional volumes for the guidance of soldiers, secretaries and treasurers, staff officers, social officers, territorial commanders and chief secretaries, and anybody else appointed to do anything at all, followed. Their multifarious revisions continue to order the life of the Army today, providing cohesiveness and a legal framework.

Because they preceded any form of training—the most rudimentary form of which began in 1879—and because in Booth's words, "a very large proportion of my officers were uneducated and comparatively ill-trained,"[112] the "O's and R's" became very comprehensive. The 638 pages of the 1886 *Orders and Regulations for Field Officers* ranged over diverse matters from doctrine to book-keeping; "how to capture a town" and dealing with persecution; behavior on board ship and the "construction of the Army," how to talk with Mohammedans and how to march in formation; the need for fresh air in

---

107. Wesley, *Journal*, 62 (Entry for 28 March 1738).

108. Flannery, "Dogmatic Constitution on the Church" (Lumen Gentium) in *Vatican Council II*, 350–432; Williams, *Renewal Theology*, 15–285.

109. Booth, in Preface to Friederichs, *Romance*, 7–8.

110. *Orders and Regulations*, 1878, 9. The similarity between these texts is not immediately obvious.

111. Sandall, *History*, II, 33, 35.

112. Friederichs, *Romance*, 11.

bedrooms at night and the application of hydropathy to such illnesses as scarlet fever and "difficulties of the bladder and urine."

The Regulations prescribe the character and role of the officer. The expectations were high: "The F.O. [Field Officer], by virtue of his position, stands out before his Soldiers more prominently than any other man. To them he is the Ambassador and Representative of God. He is their Captain, their brother, and friend. Their eyes are on him night and day. They regard him as the pattern expressly set for them to copy, the leader who at all times it is their bounden duty to follow."[113] It is difficult to imagine a description of function more likely to inspire perceptions of status.

Chapter Two devotes twenty-seven pages to the officer's "War Qualifications," these being outlined under the headings of a Soldier's Spirit, Compassion for the Perishing, Intelligence, Improvement, Responsibility for Success, Humility in Prosperity, Perseverance in Adversity, Obedience, Manner, Loyalty and Business.

According to Bramwell, William Booth's "anxiety was to compile in that book a set of regulations which would perpetuate the Salvation Army, and preserve it from the mistakes and confusions which have befallen so many other societies in the religious sphere."[114] Against that, the elder Booth confessed that

> I have never placed too great a reliance upon either these laws or the methods of their application . . . I have ever been deeply impressed by a vivid sense of the utter powerlessness of any mere system, however wisely it may have been framed, which has not in its application that Spirit of Life which alone can impart that vital force without which no extensive or lasting good can be accomplished. God forbid that any regulations which I have issued, no matter how effective for their immediate purpose, should go to swell the number of dead forms and powerless systems already in existence.[115]

Well, the Army *is* still in existence, dead form or not, and probably owes that continued existence in some measure to those same Orders and Regulations. They have been the framework which has secured permanence and continuity; given the rapid changes of appointment for personnel, they have to some extent had to compensate for the constant attrition of institutional memory which has been one of the organization's problems. The regulations dwindled away from a comprehensive 638 pages in 1886 to a sparse 135 pages of "principles" in 1997. This loss of substance has been more than compensated for by the reams of constantly revised "Minutes" and "Policies" which now govern every aspect of the organization's life. The military model of the chain of command, albeit occasionally—even increasingly—consultative, but essentially with orders given and orders executed, nevertheless remained the Salvation Army modus operandi until well into the twenty-first century.

---

113. *Orders and Regulations*, 1886, Part I, Chapter I, Section 1, No. 4.
114. Begbie, *Booth*, II, 158.
115. Friederichs, *Romance*, 9.

A Road Not Taken

This is an appropriate point to consider another development in connection with the Salvation Army's ecclesiology; another direction which in the end was not taken. The national church, the Church of England, was divided in its view of the Army. Some elements of the church were interested in taking over the new religious movement that seemed to offer a means of rapprochement with the alienated working classes, while others regarded the Army with disgust because of its sensational and vulgar style. Dr William Thompson, the evangelical Archbishop of York, was keen on harnessing the Army's potential for the church, and, encouraged by Campbell Tait, Archbishop of Canterbury, initiated discussions with a letter to William Booth on 18th April 1882.

On the 10th of May the Lower House of Convocation requested the Upper House to " . . . ascertain the tenets and practices of this society . . . consider how far it is possible to attach it to the Church . . . [and] . . . generally to advise the clergy as to their duty with reference to it."[116]

The Upper House of Convocation, Canterbury, appointed a high-powered committee consisting of Dr Benson (Bishop of Truro, and shortly to become Archbishop of Canterbury) as Chairman, Dr Lightfoot (Bishop of Durham), Canon Westcott, Canon Wilkinson and Dr Randall Davidson (Dean of Windsor and Chaplain, and son-in-law, to Archbishop Tait, and himself Primate from 1903 to 1928), to negotiate with General Booth. Davidson and Benson attended a number of Salvation Army meetings. According to Bramwell Booth, Benson was very moved by a prayer meeting of some two hundred officers at Clapton Congress Hall, saying to him, "O, my dear brother, the Holy Spirit is with you."[117] Davidson was less impressed.

Sandall says the negotiations foundered on four issues: the role and authority of General Booth, with the associated matter of the doubtful status of Salvation Army officers as clergy and their likely subordination to each local vicar; the matter of female ministry (the most the church would concede was training as deaconesses); and the matter of the sacraments.[118] Of these, Randall Davidson viewed the first as the most serious. "Booth was determined to keep control, and a very autocratic control, of the Army . . . We could not get anything in the nature of control over the organization, and so we had to let it go."[119] Benson reported to the Upper House of Convocation in April 1883 that his impression was that the Army was in a state of transition and that they should continue to gather more information. Although informal discussions with General Booth had taken place, the committee *per se* had not actually met. However, because of "conflicting reports of the Army's teachings, the disdain of many churchmen for the Army's 'novel methods,' and suggestions of immorality," despite Benson's objections the committee was dissolved by nine votes to four on the 10th of May 1883.[120]

---

116. Horridge, *Origins and Early Days*, 114.

117. Booth, *Echoes and Memories* (1977) 84.

118. Sandall, *History*, II, 148; Horridge, *Origins and Early Days*, 114.

119. Begbie, *Booth*, II, 29.

120. Sandall, *History*, II, 148.

Booth had felt that there could be financial advantages in associating with the established church, given its great resources and the Army's frustrating poverty. On the other hand the Army's international expansion by this time offered difficulties of another sort; the Church of England was a national church so how would it relate to the Army's overseas and foreign territories? Note that the fourth impediment mentioned by Davidson, the administration of the sacraments, did not refer to Salvationists' non-observance because at that time they *did* observe. Rather, it was the validity of their observances that was at stake, and the question of who would preside over the administration. In the Anglican view, officers were not priests, and therefore ineligible.

For a brief period there had been signs that the Army might assume the character of an *ecclesiola*, a church within a church, rather as Wesley had thought of Methodism, because there are recorded instances of corps attending parish churches to take the sacrament. This was suggested by Canon Wilkinson as a way forward, and it was already happening in some places. The Nottingham corps attended St Mary's Church on 21st November 1881. The *Nottingham Express* recorded that "How Sweet the Name of Jesus Sounds" was sung to the tune "Auld Lang Syne" conducted by the Salvation Army captain standing on a seat and keeping time with his arms.[121]

Four hundred Salvationists attended communion at St Paul's Holgate in March 1882 at the invitation of Archbishop Thompson of York. The *War Cry* of 20th April 1882 reported a combined service at St. Mary's, Halifax, where over three hundred Salvationists participated in Holy Communion. The House seriously debated Wilkinson's proposal, to the indignation of the *Church Times*, and Bramwell Booth admitted that it "afterwards for a time bore some fruit."[122] Sandall records various instances of Salvation Army corps and Anglican parish churches participating in each other's services in the early 1880s.

The practice was not without difficulties; Booth later recalled that some clergymen "refused to administer the rite to our soldiers because they had not gone through the form of confirmation."[123] Some clergymen harangued the Salvationists about the need to be baptized and confirmed, or invited them to instruction classes. Booth did not want his soldiers divided at the church door, with those of non-conformist background or no church history at all, diverted to another table.[124] Wesley had refused to allow Methodist meetings to be held at the same time as parish church communion services, to avoid conflict and underline his view that followers were also faithful members of the Church of England, but his Methodists had often suffered similar rejection in their time.

In a 2009 article in *Fides et Historia*, Andrew Eason explores contemporary evidence of the connection between the Church of England's negotiations and the Army's discontinuance of the sacraments.[125] He shows from numerous examples that while some joint services worked happily, in other places the aggressive attitude of some Anglican clergy alienated Booth and caused him to fear that the Army would be drawn into

---

121. Booth, "The Salvation Army," in *Contemporary Review*, August 1882, 181, cited by Horridge, *Origins and Early Days*, 113.

122. Booth, *Echoes and Memories*, 77; Sandall, *History*, II, 147.

123. *Review of the Churches*, April 1895, quoted by Begbie, *William Booth*, I, 469.

124. *War Cry*, 17 January 1883, 4.

125. Eason, "Salvation Army and Sacraments," 51–71.

the Anglican controversies between High Churchmen and Evangelicals. It was these he regarded as the "poison of hell," likely to disrupt the Army's own unity. Eventually he forbade the practice of corps attending parish communion services. Eason thus credits the breakdown of these negotiations with being a major factor in Booth's decision to dispense with these observances.

It was not simply Booth who disengaged however; amongst other factors, the weight of Anglican opinion began to harden against the Army after Booth pulled a characteristic publicity stunt over a donation from Archbishop Tait towards to Army's purchase of the Eagle Tavern. Even the well-disposed Benson wrote to Westcott that "I'm afraid the Salvation Army is working nothing here but confusion, and the Report seems a hopeless task. They made me draft it—and I *can't* so far."[126] It was also held by some that the Army's vaunted success was exaggerated and its expansion beginning to tail off. Benson's own translation to Canterbury shortly thereafter gave him a good reason for being unable to see the project through.

It is interesting to compare the course of the Salvation Army's relationship with the Church of England with that of its Wesleyan original. Methodism grew out of the established church and the question was whether it could be contained. Salvationism was an independent entity and would need to have been grafted on to the Anglican stock—a more difficult exercise. With Methodism, the preachers, who had not hitherto been permitted to officiate at the sacraments, eventually assumed this role. Salvation Army evangelists and officers, who had enjoyed this privilege, relinquished it around this time.

In retrospect, it may be that the fundamental problem was that the Anglican church and the Salvation Army were too much alike—both were episcopal hierarchies and there seemed no possibility of their running in harness. One would need to have been absorbed by the other and as Booth realized, the Army would have ceased to function if every field officer was answerable primarily to the local vicar. Each party wanted to use the other for its own purposes, but was less open to being used. As very much the junior partner in any accommodation, the Salvation Army would have had much more to lose, and Booth probably came to believe that losses would outweigh gains. Randall Davidson was right; the central issue was one of control. No model of separate but equal hierarchies within the same structure was conceivable, let alone offered, in 1883.[127] It does say something for the Army's apparent success at the time that any kind of association was even contemplated by some in the church.

CONSTITUTIONAL DEVELOPMENT

After the 1880s, development of three kinds took place: firstly, the elaboration of headquarters structures to accommodate and administer ever-expanding fields of work;

---

126. E.W. Benson to B.F. Westcott, 14 December 1882, in Benson, *Life of Edward White Benson*, I, 540, quoted by Mews, "The General and the Bishops" 223. Booth evidently released a supportive extract from Tait's letter but did not mention the Archbishop's cautionary warnings contained in the same message.

127. A recent attempt at such an arrangement is that of the Anglican Church in New Zealand (1992 constitution); a "three tikanga" model whereby Pakeha (European), Maori and Pacifica churches have separate, parallel structures, with a General Synod presided over jointly by a trinity of Archbishops.

secondly, the elaboration of constitutional structures for dealing with the Generalship and managing the succession; thirdly, the development of consultative institutions.

The basic framework of the Army's polity was in place by the early 1880s. There was a four-tier hierarchy of command, with corps and corps Commanding Officers, grouped in divisions under the direction of Divisional Commanders (occasionally provinces under Provincial Commanders), making up territories under Territorial Commanders, and all answerable to International Headquarters, which existed to support and facilitate the office of the General as the international commander-in-chief. There was no consultative, representative or popularly responsible machinery, and no elective process; office was by appointment at all levels. There was also no institutionalized provision for the exchange and development of ideas or policies.

What soon became apparent was the burgeoning of bureaucracy. In 1894 Bramwell Booth wrote, "The Staff seems too numerous—in proportion to the number of Corps. They cost too much—but that they can't help if they are there . . . The duplication of work—tendency of untrained minds to think that because they are fully occupied they are usefully and remuneratively occupied . . . "[128] If only he had been able to envision the headquarters of the twenty-first century, where the largest departments are concerned with finance, HR compliance and IT management, he might have acted more decisively to mitigate the problem earlier in the Army's history.

One word which characterizes the outcome of hierarchy, quasi-militarism and bureaucracy, is centralization. But all centralizing, centripetal tendencies are in tension with and provoke centrifugal forces. In the late nineteenth century Salvation Army those forces seeking the devolution and dispersion of power were led by the Founder's own children. The Booths were the Army's "Royal Family," and were seen, and saw themselves, as the natural heirs to the thrones of this new Israel. They were part of the action from their earliest years and when quite young were given high command and imposing titles. However, their inheriting a generous portion of their father's headstrong and independent spirit made for difficulties with both William, the Army's Moses, and Bramwell, his Joshua.

Merely ordinary Salvationists, even colonels and commissioners, did not get to lead the troops up any hills but those chosen by the General (and the Chief). Some tried, and were seen off. Obedience was expected firstly in respect of the methods of evangelism espoused by Booth. In a letter dated 7th March 1877, he gave an account of his dealings with a missioner who preferred different tactics: "I wrote him very frankly and told him that the only way in which he could walk in harmony with me was in carrying out my wishes . . . I told him he must go in and do Mission work on Mission lines, or move off."[129]

And even his most faithful acolytes recognized that the need to control could lead to difficulties. Loyal as he was, Samuel Logan Brengle reflected in private on his concerns, in a 1912 letter to his wife:

> I think probably most of our difficulty at present in this country arises from this multiplicity of details and the infinite red tape with which we are tied up which

---

128. Bramwell-Booth, *Bramwell Booth*, 218.
129. Bramwell-Booth, *Bramwell Booth*, 90.

sap the strength and frustrate the piety of our people. If our officers had the spirit of the General when he refused to be tied up to a pastorate and broke away from the church, I am not sure that there are many of them who would remain with the present concern. To my mind it is one of the paradoxes of history how the General, with his free, large spirit which refuses to be bound by the mild rules of a Methodist conference, could have developed a system which binds men hand and foot with red tape, which is to Methodist rules what . . . calculus is to the multiplication table.[130]

Most irksome to some was the power of appointment, itinerancy by appointment being part of the Army's Methodist inheritance. It is ironical that Booth, who had left the Methodist New Connexion because he chose not to accept an appointment, was inflexible on this rule with his subordinates. As already noted, some of his earliest associates fell out with him on that score.

The Founder's daughter-in-law, Maud Booth wrote that

officers in the Army are liable to removal, promotion, or any other change of circumstances without a moment's warning or any reason assigned. This is quite true, and is known to every Candidate, and yet they multiply rapidly, even among those whose faces have been set like flint against it . . . Nothing human ever could do work such as this, and, if not human, its results being eminently Christian, what can it be but the Holy Spirit that can so change multitudes of human hearts, that they yield perfect obedience, that rarest of all fruits in this age, and especially in this land of self-assertion and independence.[131]

Ironically, it was in that land, the United States, that Maud and Ballington Booth themselves resigned rather than accept a change of appointment in 1896. While ordinary, non-family Salvationists tended to sink without trace after collision with authority, when resistance to the centralizing tendency was led by members of Booth's own family, the results were generally more spectacular, even if no more successful.

The centralizing process was seen by the younger Booths as the extension of elder brother Bramwell Booth's own authority as Chief of the Staff, so there was an element of sibling rivalry involved in the series of family-cum-constitutional crises between 1896 and 1929.

Ballington and Maud were the first to go. Their Volunteers of America still survives as a social agency in the States, but Evangeline Booth managed to rally the majority of the American troops behind the international flag, enabling the Booth-Tuckers to take over in 1896. Then came the departure of Booth's eldest daughter, Catherine, who had married Arthur Clibborn, with whom she jointly commanded the Army in France and Switzerland. Their re-assignment to the Netherlands in 1901 contributed to their resignation, though Clibborn's involvement in the Zionist sect of the prophet Alexander Dowie, who claimed to be the reincarnation of Elijah, would have made their position untenable and Catherine had no choice but to go with him. "I am your General before I am your father," wrote William to his daughter.[132]

---

130. Brengle, letter to his wife 22 July 1912, in Clark, *Dearest Lily*, 112.
131. Booth, *Under Two Flags*, 127–28.
132. Ervine, *God's Soldier*, II, 765.

Then came Herbert and Cornelie Booth's turn, in Australia later the following year. The straw that broke the camel's back for Herbert was the issuing of new regulations, setting up Territorial Boards and Councils, reducing territorial commanders' scope for independent action and engaging the role of the chief secretaries as a counterpoise to the territorial commanders by having them report directly to the Chief of the Staff in London. Herbert envisaged something more like a federal system, allowing greater local autonomy with more freedom of action for commanders, although not to their subordinates. He wrote to his father:

> The system which subjugates all the chief officers at the Army to the vote of their subordinates and yet leaves the supreme heads in absolute control seems to us *unjust, unreasonable* and *oppressive* . . . [133]

No dictator happily accepts another's dictatorship. Sadly, the differences were allowed to become matters of personality as well as of principle. William would have no more to do with those who had deserted him. When his daughter Emma Booth-Tucker was killed in a railway accident in the USA in 1903, Booth's journal mentions his receiving a letter from "Mrs Clibborn," giving no hint that this was his estranged eldest daughter. The renegades Ballington and Herbert were not permitted to attend Emma's funeral service. Much later, Bramwell and Herbert were both in Auckland in 1920 and some officers (who had fond memories of Herbert's Australasian command only twenty years earlier) suggested that Herbert be invited to sit on the platform at a meeting; Bramwell would not permit this and would not meet with Herbert.[134] Evangeline, to her credit, kept in touch with her erring siblings and spoke at Herbert's funeral in 1925.

The fourth act in this dynastic struggle was not played out in public until 1929, when the first High Council of the Salvation Army was called. By that time, Bramwell had been General for sixteen years, the next generation of younger Booths was now on the side of control and the opposition was now led by Bramwell's younger sister, Evangeline. The issue was no longer appointments, though that was an element in the mix, but the succession.

The background to this struggle went back to December 1896 when William Booth visited the eighty-seven year-old William Ewart Gladstone in his retirement. Gladstone asked what provision was made for a successor to the General. On being told of the sealed envelope arrangement, Gladstone thought it peculiar—as compared with, say, the election of the Pope by the College of Cardinals. He asked what would happen if the General died without appointing a successor, or if a General became insane, or criminal, or heretical. Booth was already concerned about this, and more so when a few days later he and Bramwell narrowly escaped an anarchist's bomb blast in London. But in drawing up the 1878 Deed Poll, he had failed to make provision for altering it, which meant this could be done only by Act of Parliament, to which he did not want to have recourse.

He consulted three lawyers: Herbert Asquith, Richard Haldane and Charles Sergeant, who suggested an "amending deed" which did not vary the original deed poll but only amplified or supplemented it. This was ready by late 1897, but Booth delayed

---

133. Ottman, *Herbert Booth*, 216.
134. Ottman, Ibid., 366.

because he feared the provision for removing a General could be misused; and that the deed might not be legally valid. Did removing a General change the original deed or merely amplify it?

The 1904 International Congress was due. Booth decided to get a final check on the Deed by three more constitutional lawyers. They advised executing the deed as it stood. Booth signed it at the Congress, saying, "I have just signed my death warrant."

The 1904 Supplementary Deed Poll supplemented only the sixth clause of the original, which dealt with the sealed envelope provision for nominating the General's successor. The original provided for the sealed envelope in case of General's death or "upon his ceasing to perform the duties of office." It did not explain under what circumstances this might happen. The provision now hinged on saying that one of the circumstances might be that the General has been removed from office.

The 1904 Deed Poll said that could happen if either

1. If four-fifths of commissioners in active service determine and write to say that the General is incapacitated mentally or physically from performing his duties, in which case the sealed envelope remains valid if it was signed earlier than a month before he was deemed mentally unsound.

2. If nine-tenths of commissioners in active service write to say the General is incompetent because of bankruptcy and insolvency, or dereliction of duty, or notorious misconduct or other circumstances making him unfit for office, in which case the sealed envelope becomes invalid.

    In these clauses the sole authority of the General is replaced in extreme circumstances by the collective authority of the commissioners. The third clause provided for cases where the unfitness of the General is not so clear cut and has to be established. It sets up the High Council as another authority.

3. If three-fourths of members present and voting in the High Council adjudicate the General unfit.

The High Council is then described and defined.

- Adjudicatory body to decide if General unfit for office.
- Summoned either by Chief of the Staff and four commissioners, or requisitioned by seven commissioners applying to the Chief of the Staff.
- The requisitioning invalidates any sealed envelope in existence. (Reactivated if the General found fit for office).
- High Council is to elect next General if it deposes the existing one, or if the General has failed to appoint a successor.
- High Council is to consist of all commissioners and all territorial commanders of any rank.
- Not a legislative or executive body; it is dissolved immediately after a General is elected.

Note there was no provision for resignation as a reason for ceasing to be General, but this was mentioned later in the Deed. The Deed could be altered by the General with consent of two-thirds of commissioners. All this was to be very important in 1929.

Through the 1920s, relations between Bramwell and Evangeline became increasingly strained. Firstly there was the old matter of appointments: Evangeline had been commander in the USA since 1904 and Bramwell wished to move her on but she resisted, and mobilizing such a body of American public opinion behind her that he did not dare proceed for fear of provoking another American breakaway. Secondly there was the matter of the succession. It was suspected that Bramwell had nominated his wife, Florence, to succeed him should he die in office, and she was unpopular. Later, it was feared that Bramwell was grooming his eldest daughter, Catherine, for the job, and she was if anything even less acceptable. An increasing number of senior commanders were also increasingly uncomfortable with the idea of the Generalship being tied to a dynastic succession. Evangeline concurred, with the proviso that her own case was different.

Bramwell had also instituted retirement ages for officers, including senior leadership—his brother-in-law Frederick Booth-Tucker was offended at having to retire at the age of seventy-two—but Bramwell himself intended to hold on to office as a sacred trust until death, like his father, or the Pope. The problem with this was that Bramwell was becoming regarded by senior commanders as increasingly arbitrary and despotic, and they resented the nepotism perceived in the advancement of his children. Bramwell's treatment of George Carpenter, a senior aide who tried to warn him of dissatisfaction, focused resentment. Some began to consider the need for curbs upon a General's authority. Through the later 1920s, unknown to the public or to the mass of Salvationists, a storm began to brew. The whole story is grippingly told by General John Larsson in his book, *1929: A Crisis that Shaped the Salvation Army's Future*. Larsson sums up the irony in the situation:

> Bramwell Booth had always taken his father as his role model, and what William Booth had done Bramwell Booth now did. Yet what was applauded in the father was criticized in the son. What was perfectly acceptable in the founder of a fledgling movement was unacceptable in his heir. The movement had moved on.
>
> William Booth was an absolute autocrat—and was lauded for it. Bramwell took the cue from his father—and was called a despot.
>
> William Booth relied greatly on his wife—and was hailed for making Catherine Booth co-founder of The Salvation Army. Bramwell Booth looked to his wife Florence for counsel—and was criticized for it. "Condemned over the eggs and bacon," it was said when he reversed some decision the next day.
>
> William Booth was applauded for appointing his son to be his Chief of the Staff. Bramwell Booth was berated for making Wycliffe his ADC.[135]
>
> William Booth appointed his other children straight to large commands and gave them extravagant titles such as *Maréchale*, Commander and Consul—and Salvationists were delighted. Bramwell Booth insisted that his seven children

---

135. Ironically, William and Bramwell had corresponded in 1908–9 about a situation in Canada, where the territorial commander had provoked complaints from senior officers by appointing his own son as his aide-de-camp. The Booths had speculated on whether there was need of a new regulation for territorial commanders to discourage nepotism. Correspondence in International Heritage Centre Archives. *PWB/1/45–PWB/1/59*.

must begin as cadets and work their way up to larger responsibilities—and was accused of nepotism.

William Booth decreed that he would be the sole trustee to expedite property and financial business, and the evangelists roared their approval. Bramwell Booth continued the system and was condemned for so doing.

William Booth was hailed for relying on a trust fund established by a benefactor so that he would not have to draw on Army funds for his personal needs. Bramwell Booth followed the same pattern through the Wisely Trust—and was censured for it.

William Booth, to universal approval, appointed his son to succeed him. When it was thought that Bramwell Booth might appoint a member of his family to follow him, he was accused of wanting to create a dynasty.

It was tough to be the son of a founder.[136]

Measures acceptable in and even appropriate to the initial, mobilizing phase of organizational life become less so once it has become more thoroughly institutionalized.

Bramwell resisted in particular the suggestion that he forgo the right to nominate his successor and allow election by senior commanders. "[William] Booth, after long consideration and constant seeking for the guidance of God," wrote Bramwell, had decided that the appointment of a General by his predecessor "was on the whole the safest and best."[137] "[The General] is not the maker or unmaker of the original Trust. He is the Trustee, the servant of the Trust. His great duty is to conform to its terms, preserve its integrity and spirit, to guard and fulfil it, and to hand it on in complete and unimpaired efficiency to his successor."[138]

Bramwell Booth's stubbornness on this point, claiming that he could not relinquish a sacred trust God had inspired the Founder to institute, is interesting in the light of Bryan Wilson's comment on the "absoluteness" of sectarian ideology. "Revealed truth, being God's will, cannot readily be countermanded . . . 'Reform' is not possible in a sectarian organization, since it must cast doubt on present and past arrangements which were ordained by God."[139] Was Bramwell still a "sectarian" while his subordinates were becoming more reformist? When he fell gravely ill in 1928 and was unable to discharge his duties for some months, fears that he was near death and that Catherine would succeed him prompted a number of commissioners to requisition a High Council in terms of the 1904 Deed Poll.

This was heading into uncharted waters, and the High Council, first meeting on 8th January 1929, had to face court action by Bramwell, or his advisors, contesting the validity of the 1904 Deed Poll under which the Council had been called, and under which he himself had taken office. His initial deposition on 17th January by a vote of fifty-five to eight was subject to a High Court challenge by his family, and it was not until 13th February that Bramwell was finally deposed by fifty-two votes to five. He was appointed a Companion of Honor by George V in April and died in June of that year.

136. Larsson, 1929, 60–61.

137. Ervine, *God's Soldier*, II, 908.

138. Letter from Bramwell Booth to Evangeline Booth, 24 November 1927, quoted by Bramwell-Booth, *Bramwell Booth*, 488.

139. Wilson, *Patterns of Sectarianism*, 10–11.

Edward Higgins, Bramwell's Chief of the Staff for ten years, was elected to replace him. A painful period ensued when it was found that Bramwell had lately altered his will so that instead of his successor becoming trustee upon his demise, the Army's property and funds were vested in his wife, his daughter Catherine and their solicitor. It took a year to sort that out.

That dealt with, Higgins asked Commissioner David Lamb to chair an Advisory Commission on reform and this met over the course of eight months. In April Higgins wrote to all commissioners and territorial commanders requesting their views on reform, and then in November 1930 he convened a conference of commissioners. This was a notable first. Such conferences subsequently became semi-regular events, usually called approximately mid-term of a General's tenure of office, but the 1930 meeting was the first occasion since the 1878 War Congress that the Army's senior leadership had been invited to discuss matters of moment to the Army.[140] Higgins further announced that he would abide by majority recommendations made by the Conference—which must say something both about Higgins and about the gravity of the situation. This voluntary limitation of prerogative was not repeated by later Generals at subsequent leaders' conferences. However, with greater opportunity for travel after the Second World War, consultative commissioners' conferences or international leaders' conferences were called by later Generals during their terms of office.

Some senior leaders, notably David Lamb, urged the creation of some further consultative structure so that leadership would be vested in a "General-in-Council." The Reforms Commission, chaired by Lamb, had touted this proposal, whereby the General would be chair of a permanent Council of seven Commissioners. Higgins would have none of it. The Conference narrowly rejected a proposal to modify the powers of the General.

One surprising action in the course of these events is that General Higgins wrote to all officers in the British Isles on 15th January 1931, polling their opinion on the proposed Salvation Army Act and asking them to return a form indicating Support or Not Support. The returns are no longer extant, but Higgins did later write another letter to officers indicating that the great majority had supported his move.[141] Such a consultation was unprecedented and not attempted again until General Gowans' international survey of 2000.

Higgins secured the passage of the Salvation Army Act through the British Parliament in July 1931, regularizing the election of successive Generals by High Council and vesting Salvation Army property in a Trustee Company instead of in the General as sole Trustee. Parliament deleted clauses relating to the retirement age of the General and the setting up of a panel to adjudicate differences of opinion between the General and senior officers, regarding these as matters for internal regulation. The retirement age was accordingly set at seventy-three by regulation but progressively modified in successive years. The adjudication panel was established but I do not know whether its provisions were ever invoked or when the provision was allowed to lapse.

---

140. The periodic calling of "staff councils" or "officers' councils" should not be taken as meaning that anyone's opinion had been asked about anything; they were occasions for listening rather than for discussing.

141. Copies of these letters are held in the Salvation Army Archives, New Zealand.

The extent to which Generals should consult, or have their powers curtailed, was debated in private amongst the Army's leadership before the passage of the Act, and continued to be discussed thereafter. The forces of devolution were no longer led by members of the Booth family: even Evangeline, having campaigned for democracy in opposition, was not disposed to further the cause of reform when in government. As General, she even discontinued her own former post of Commander-in-Chief, USA, and appointed Colonel Parker "National Secretary" to serve as her agent in the States until General Carpenter upgraded him to National Commander in the early 1940s.

Others continued to discuss further reforms. Lt. Commissioner Albert Orsborn circulated "Notes for discussion of proposed legislative and administrative arrangements" before the 1939 High Council and Commissioner David Lamb proposed a permanent council of five to seven senior Commissioners in continuous session as their sole appointments, to advise the General. Although the sole legal purpose of a High Council was to elect a General, the members of the 1939 body took nine days to achieve this because they sensibly spent some days outside their remit in discussing Lamb's proposal—without reaching agreement.[142] Nothing could be done during the war years. Lamb, by then retired, pressed on members of the 1946 High Council his memorandum, "Anent the idea of establishing a Council (of Commissioners) to advise and assist the General in all Army affairs and inter alia, showing how a Council can be set up and maintained without any legal alterations to our constitution or doing violence in any way to our foundation trust deeds."[143] Orsborn also circulated another paper.

Upon his election as General in 1946, Orsborn asked Catherine Bramwell-Booth to chair a commission on instituting an advisory council. The resulting Advisory Council first met in March 1947, "brought into being for the purpose of study, research and exploration, and to give guidance on matters on which the Army's supreme commander seeks to formulate a directive."[144] Seven London Commissioners, who had other appointments, would meet at first weekly to discuss an agenda provided by the General. Proposed senior appointments and promotions, revisions of Orders and Regulations, doctrinal matters, training policies, were amongst subjects discussed. Any officer could submit possible agenda items, through their territorial commander, for the General's consideration. The General did not participate in the discussions, but received written recommendations. With air travel possible, the procedure changed. Five London-based and five overseas commissioners would meet twice a year for several days at a time.

With the development of electronic communication, in 2001 General Gowans replaced the Advisory Council with the General's Consultative Council, to which all leaders eligible for the High Council would belong. Thrice-yearly meetings of about thirty members are attended by International Headquarters commissioners with the others serving in rotation, with all others monitoring and able to participate in proceedings by e-mail. Unlike the former Advisory Council, the Consultative Council is chaired by the General.

---

142. Coutts, *Better Fight*, 159–60.

143. Orsborn, *House of My Pilgrimage*, 152. One wonders what Council members made of Lamb's "Anent." The aging Scot used the archaic Scots word for "About."

144. *Salvation Army Year Book*, 1953, 36.

Some further restrictions of the Generals' prerogatives have been introduced over the years. General Wiseman instituted a five-year maximum term of office for General in 1975, and the age of retirement has been progressively brought down to sixty-eight. In 1986 General Wahlström made provision for a General's term to be extended for up to three years upon two thirds majority in a postal vote of those eligible for the High Council. General Eva Burrows served an extra two years under this arrangement, declining a third year (and still retired a year earlier than she would have had she not been elected General).

By the 1970s, with further modifications and amendments in 1965 and 1968, the Army's constitution had become hugely complex and unwieldy. The 1980 Salvation Army Act of the British Parliament revoked and annulled all earlier Salvation Army constitutional documents and started from scratch with a simplified document based on the realities of the Army's current situation. On the basis of this Act, General Burrows was able in 1990 to separate the British territory from International Headquarters, devolving some of the General's powers and 80 percent of the Army's United Kingdom assets to British appointees and a Trust Company. At the same time the creation of an International Management Council of all Commissioners serving on IHQ (now including the national leaders from the USA) came close to bringing into being David Lamb's "General-in-Council."

Some internal restructuring took place at IHQ and in most territories from the 1980s. The pattern inherited from the nineteenth century was that all responsibility flowed through the second-in-command, whether chief secretary or chief of the staff, from the leader, whether territorial commander or General. It was decided that this system overloaded the second-in-charge who became a bottle-neck in administration. Following an American business model, it was decided to distribute all departmental functions amongst three sections—Personnel, Program, and Business/Administration—under their own principals, each then reporting to the chief. In an age when flatter structures were becoming fashionable, the Salvation Army actually inserted another level into its hierarchy. At IHQ even this reformed model still leaves the Chief of the Staff carrying an unwieldy burden in that the zonal international secretaries largely channel decision-making upward rather than exercising any real authority in their respective spheres. None of these changes altered essentially the simple structure of the three-level chain of command, under the General, in place from 1880.

Such "consultative institutions" as have been referred to so far have involved only the upper echelons of leadership, and arose from the coup which wrested control of the Salvation Army from its founding family and devolved it upon an oligarchy of chief executives. A subsequent and wider catchment area for consultation will be explored in the next chapter, on "Leadership."

A CHURCH?

We began by tracing the Army's evolution from para-church agency to sect to de-facto denomination. While the organization's mission statement has recently described it as "an evangelical part of the universal Christian Church,"[145] it is also now sometimes described as "a worldwide evangelical Christian church."[146] General John Larsson, addressing a 2001 International Theology and Ethics Symposium in Winnipeg, Canada, stated that "A key question for us is how we make the transition from a movement to a church in such a way that we do not lose the original dynamic that brought the Army into being. Or if we have lost something of that dynamic, how do we regain it?"[147] Unfortunately "loss of original dynamic" may define an essential difference between "movement" and "church." Finke and Stark comment, "When successful sects are transformed into churches, that is, when their tension with the surrounding culture is greatly reduced, they soon cease to grow and eventually decline."[148]

In sum, for a century, Salvationists tended to resist any notion that they might be a church although they were happy to be counted a *part* of *the* church. At the same time the Army increasingly resembled a conventional church denomination, and eventually, as it entered the twenty-first century, it finally, unambiguously, described itself as "a church."[149] Colonel Earl Robinson plotted the course of this process in his paper for the Johannesburg Theological Symposium in 2006 through a series of quotes.[150] We can draw on these as follows:

- William Booth: "We are not a church. We are an army . . . " (1904) "The Army is part of the living Church of God . . . "

- Bramwell Booth: (1925) "Of this, the Great Church of the Living God, we claim . . . we of The Salvation Army are an integral part and element . . . "

- Albert Orsborn: (1954) "We are not a church—we are a permanent mission to the unconverted." "We are almost universally recognized as a religious denomination by governments . . . for convenience . . . That is as far as we wish to go in being known as a church." . . . "We are a part of the body of Christ called 'The Church Militant' . . . "

- Frederick Coutts: Not a church, but implies it. Didn't directly answer the question, saying, (1978) "Any definition of the Church must . . . be a New Testament definition—where it is set out not in terms of ecclesiastical structure but of a spiritual relationship."[151] (1967) In a sermon on Christian unity Coutts grouped together "Presbyterian, Congregationalist, Methodist, Anglican, Friend, Roman Catholic, Orthodox, Baptist, Salvationist . . . " implying denominational equivalence.[152]

---

145. *Salvation Army Year Book*, 2010, Title Page (International Mission Statement).

146. Ibid., 11. Until 2006, this page in the *Year Book*, under the heading, "What is the Salvation Army?" began with the words, "The Salvation Army is an integral part of the Christian Church, although distinctive in governance and practice." In 2007 this was changed to "a worldwide evangelical Christian church." The article was discontinued after 2012.

147. Quoted in background papers to the 2006 International Theology and Ethics Symposium, Johannesburg.

148. Finke and Stark, *Churching of America*, 148.

149. *Salvation Story*, 100.

150. Robinson, "People of God." 13–17, 28–31.

151. Coutts, *Salvation Army in relation to the Church*, 9.

152. Coutts, "Are We Great Enough?"

- The Eleven Points, the statement of Salvation Army belief, contain no doctrine of the Church. Salvationist doctrinal publications made few explicit references to the matter before 1969 when the new *Handbook of Doctrine* included the term "Church" for the first time in a sub-clause under "The Ministry of the Spirit": "The Holy Spirit called into being that fellowship of believers known in the New Testament as 'the Church.'"[153] This was not in earlier editions.

- Clarence Wiseman: (1976) "I believe the Salvation Army can truthfully be described as a 'church' in the more circumscribed, denominational sense of the word . . . We are both a church and a part of the universal Church."[154]

- Philip Needham: (1987) Needham's *Community in Mission* says that "The Salvation Army is as much an integral part of the one true catholic (universal) Christian church as is any other denomination or ecclesiastical tradition." His book "is not an ecclesiology of The Salvation Army, but a Salvationist ecclesiology . . . "[155] His argument is that the Church's ecclesiology ought to be shaped by its mission. "Other denomination" might imply the Army's claim to being *a* denomination but this is not claimed.

- *Salvation Story* (1998): Chapter 10, "People of God—the Doctrine of the Church," states the Army's belief in "the Church," and also refers to the denominational phenomenon known as "a church," saying "One very important change since the Eleven Articles were formulated and adopted is the evolution of the Movement from an agency for evangelism to a church, an evangelistic body of believers who worship, fellowship, minister and are in mission together."[156] We have already seen that this definition has been applicable since about 1867—ten years before the naming of the Salvation Army. However, *Salvation Story* does not offer any explanation for the claim to be "a church" or any defense of the concept of denominationalism. It confines its attention to "the Church" but implies that the non-Biblical denominational concept of "a church" is the same thing.

- John Larsson (2001) stated that the Army had reached "a watershed in its self-understanding . . . " and quoted John Rhemick's *New People of God* regarding "a period of transition towards a fuller understanding of ourselves as a church."[157] "A church" was now acceptable usage.

- Shaw Clifton (1999) stated the Army is "a church" rather than merely a part of the universal Christian Church, quoting *Salvation Story* and going on to justify the Army's claim to be "a church" in theological, sociological and legal terms.[158] This position is also now set out authoritatively in a statement published in 2008, *The Salvation Army in the Body of Christ: An Ecclesiological Statement*: "The Salva-

---

153. *Handbook of Doctrine*, 1969, 70.
154. Wiseman, "Are We a Church?" in Waldron, edited, *Salvation Army and the Churches*, 1–8.
155. Needham, *Community in Mission*, 2, 3.
156. *Salvation Story*, 100.
157. Larsson, "Salvationist Theology and Ethics for the New Millennium," 11, 13.
158. Clifton, *Who are These Salvationist?* 7–17.

tion Army ... belongs to and is an expression of the Body of Christ on earth, the Church universal, and is a Christian denomination in permanent mission to the unconverted, called into and sustained in being by God."[159]

I have offered my personal critique of this assumption of denominationalism:

> Sometimes the claim is advanced that the Salvation Army exhibits "the marks of the church," whether these are the traditional yardsticks of "one, holy, catholic and apostolic," or more involved criteria such as the no fewer than twenty adduced by Earl Robinson in his paper, and that therefore we are a church.[160] Certainly we should exhibit the marks of the church, if we really are a part of it. Praise God we do! But these are marks of *the* church, not of *a* church. We can't go from "these are the marks of *the* church" to "we exhibit these marks" to "therefore we are *a* church". The syllogism is flawed. We need to define what we mean by "the church," "a church" and "a part of the church."
>
> *Salvation Story* defines "*the* Church" as "the fellowship of all who are justified and sanctified by grace through faith in Christ." It goes on to define "*a* church" as "an evangelistic body of believers who worship, fellowship, minister, and are in mission together." It affirms that "Salvationists are members of the one body of Christ. We share common ground with the universal Church while manifesting our own characteristics ... [we are] one particular expression of the Church."
>
> *Salvation Story*'s definitions of *the* church and *a* church are good as far as they go, but they do not address the question of the relationship between the two except by implication. They leave unexamined the fact that there is in practice another level of entity between the two—that of separate associations or families of churches. We are on safe Biblical, theological and ecclesiological ground when we speak of *a* church as a local congregation and of *the* church as the whole church, but it is more difficult to justify the denominational entities except as the product of history. They are a concession to *realpolitik*, rather as Jesus spoke of Moses permitting divorce "because of your hardness of heart."
>
> Sometimes the view is expressed that the "real" church is spiritual, and quite independent of human, sociological structures, so it is unimportant how it is structured. I do not think the Army has ever subscribed to that theory; the body of Christ is clearly incarnate and has structure and organization. Further, the Army accepts that the church's unity is manifest in diversity ("with other Christian denominations and congregations," as *Salvation Story* puts it) rather than in uniformity, and Booth very early forbade criticism of any other body.[161]
>
> Since the Council of Jerusalem there have been rival factions of Christians: witness the great schisms which took place over discipline and doctrine, setting rival Donatist and Catholic, Arian and Catholic, Nestorian and Catholic, Celtic and Roman Catholic and eventually Orthodox and Roman churches squaring off against each other over the centuries. They could be compared with "denominations" in our modern sense in that they were rival associations of local churches,

---

159. *The Salvation Army in the Body of Christ*, 1. The International Mission Statement, reproduced on the title page of the annual *Year Book*, continues to describe the Salvation Army simply as "an evangelical part of the universal Christian Church."

160. Robinson, "People of God."

161. *Orders and Regulations*, 1886, Part XVI, Chap. 1.

in some cases occupying overlapping territory and each claiming to be more correct than the other—the *true* church.

Most of what we now call denominations are a comparatively recent phenomenon; the heirs of the Reformation. Although Pope Benedict XVI still claimed that all save the Roman Catholic Church were "defective" in some respect, these churches seldom anathematize one another today, being usually content with a slightly smug assumption of superiority.[162] Martin Palmer recalled that when putting together a historical chart of Christian traditions he asked the British Baptist media office for a founding date, and was informed that "the Baptist Church *per se* was founded by Jesus Christ c. AD 33."[163] It is difficult to generalize about the origins of these groups—personal disagreements, social and national interests, theological controversies have all played a part. In the now-ebbed high tide of ecumenism in the mid-twentieth century, it was held by many that the history of denominationalism in the church demonstrated the "scandal of disunity," a betrayal of Jesus' prayer "that they may all be one." To my mind that still is a dissuasive against it.[164]

Claiming to be a denomination consciously buys into that disunity. It attempts to sanctify that status quo. Our doctrine meekly follows our praxis. But we make no apology for not practicing the sacraments. We happily swim against the tide of general church doctrine and practice in positing our own spiritualized interpretations of baptism and the Lord's Supper, even on the grounds that they represent a valuable witness to the rest of the church. So why are we unable to hold the line on this no more peculiar but equally important distinctive mark, that we are not a "denomination?" Probably because it is the line of least resistance, and because there is some "secondary gain" or advantage in making the claim. We resist conforming to something arguably derived from the scripture but collude with something evolved in the era of the Enlightenment. In this we pass up the opportunity to maintain a witness to another great principle—the unity of *the* church, a refusal to accept the divisions of the church as final.

Obviously I am not claiming that our choice of vocabulary could heal the divisions amongst God's people; only that this take on the doctrine of the church gives us an opportunity to bear witness to something important. Have we ever claimed more than that for our stand on the sacraments?[165]

This is not intended as a criticism of the Salvation Army; it is about denominationalism as such. We are shaped by the discourse we choose to employ. Be that as it may, we have the situation that the Salvation Army, having long appeared as and behaved like a denominational church, is now describing itself as such. That is its official ecclesiology; like Methodism, it no longer aspires to be an *ecclesiola in ecclesia*, and is no longer satisfied to be simply "an Army."

---

162. Pope Benedict XVI, "Responses to Some Questions."

163. Palmer, *Sacred History*, 61. Even the Army's emphasis on its being "evangelical" sometimes conveys the impression that other denominations may be less so.

164. Admittedly this is tantamount to claiming that denominational distinctions are "contrary to God's will for His people," a proposition subsequently and expressly denied in *The Salvation Army in the Body of Christ*, 1, 5.

165. Hill, from "Four Anchors," 31–33.

3

The Ecclesiology of The Salvation Army 2: Leadership

> Ordination is about apostolic leadership, and you cannot have apostolic leadership in the church without the risk of clericalisation; and the key to overcoming the risk lies in the recovery of the servant (diaconal) nature of all ministry in the church, including the ministry of apostolic leadership.[1]
>
> —Ken Booth

CLERICALISATION

We have noted that sociological theories can suggest ways of explaining the development of the Salvation Army's ecclesial life. They can also tell us something about the history of its leadership, for example by looking at clericalisation, the process of maintaining or increasing the power of church leaders, or clerics. The following are some examples from the huge literature on this subject.

Robert Michels mentioned five factors encouraging the centralization of power in organizations.[2] These are the felt inadequacy of ordinary members, leading to limited participation and apathy; the experience of leadership enhancing leaders' knowledge, expertise and indispensability; the tendency of leaders to use their power to retain rewards of office; the tendency of organizations to become co-dependent with leadership, providing resources for their continued monopoly of power; the way in which tenure of leadership establishes a customary right to office. Michels said that these factors contributed to an "iron law of oligarchy." He was writing of politics but the concepts are transferable.

Role theory suggests how clergy come to be seen and to see themselves as a caste distinct from laity. Theodore Sarbin says the roles people play and narratives they tell

---

1. Ken Booth, "Something about Ordination," 2
2. Michels, *Political Parties*.

serve to construct their sense of identity.[3] Thomas O'Dea talked about "mixed motivation" as key to the clericalising process. Leadership in its earliest stages is characterized by single-mindedness but later other motivations creep in—the desire for prestige or power, the need for security within a professional structure.[4] Andrew Abbott saw clericalism as an example of professionalization, a profession defending its jurisdiction in a permanent state of turf war with the laity. What begins as a functional role seeks to establish a claim to spiritually legitimated status.[5] David Horrell says that clericalisation can be seen as struggle for power, associated with social conservatism, even in the early church.[6] Richard Schoenherr says that all religions have two opposite things going on. One derives from the need for authoritative structures to safeguard the original vision, and leads to elaboration of priestly hierarchies. The other emphasizes the individual's personal relationship with God so that the mediating role of structures is questioned.[7]

The early church was comparatively egalitarian. It had leaders but not priests. As it institutionalized over its first few centuries, it accommodated to traditional religious expectations, to hierarchical society and the Roman state.[8] Nearly all sectarian movements from and including the early church on—monasticism, the mendicant orders of friars, the Waldensians, the reformation churches and sects, the Methodists, the pentecostals, began as "lay" movements, acknowledging little distinction of status between leaders and led, and nearly all have ended up controlled by priestly hierarchies, whether so called or not. The more institutionalized the body becomes, the greater degree of clericalisation. Thus the waves of renewal are in their turn absorbed and new orthodoxies and hegemonies become established.

Having clerics does not necessarily involve clericalism. Not having clerics does not necessarily mean clericalism can be avoided. Office itself, formal or informal, inevitably confers power and power offers at least possibility of those who exercise it "tyrannizing over those allotted to [their] care."[9] Power, like steroids taken by an athlete, may enhance performance but exact a long-term cost.

Any human society needs some form of order to avoid falling into either anarchy or tyranny. A society called into being around some founding vision requires some means of maintaining what in the church is called "apostolicity"—authenticity derived from faithfulness to a founding vision. The danger with leadership, however, is that rather than being merely a means of maintaining authenticity, it can come to think of itself as central to it, the means becoming the end. That is clericalisation.

My argument is that the Salvation Army's development conforms to this general outline.

---

3. See for example: Sarbin and Allen, "Role Theory," and Sarbin (ed.), *Narrative Psychology*.
4. O'Dea, "Five Dilemmas," 33.
5. Abbott, *System of Professions*, 35–37.
6. Horrell, "Leadership Patterns," 323–41.
7. Schoenherr, "Power and Authority in Organised Religion," 52–71.
8. A comprehensive account of the process is found in Bulley, *Priesthood of Some Believers*.
9. 1 Peter 5:3.

OFFICERSHIP

Christian ministry is participation in Christ's ministry, and all such ministry is "vocational" because it is in response to Christ's calling. However, some people are paid to minister and so do not have the further responsibility of having to earn their living at the same time; this is how the Salvation Army differentiates the ministry of its officers from that of its soldiers. The *Orders and Regulations for Officers* says that "Officers of The Salvation Army are soldiers who have relinquished secular employment in response to a spiritual calling, so as to devote all their time and energies to the service of God and the people . . . " Or, as put more succinctly by Commissioner Wesley Harris, "Officership is availability,"[10] alternatively expressed as "Officership is *appointability.*" This also underlines that this commitment is within the framework of organizational obedience. Such conditions of service, expressed in an officers' "covenant" and "undertakings," are intended to help express and facilitate Christ's ministry in the world today.

Friends, supporters, employees and attendees at Salvation Army meetings, as well as Adherent Members, may all participate in the Army's, and Christ's, ministry. More narrowly, the basic constituent unit of the Salvation Army and therefore of its ministry, is the soldier. A soldier has signed the Soldier's Covenant, affirming Salvationist beliefs and committing to Salvationist lifestyle and disciplines, "the dedication of my life to His service for the salvation of the whole world." This encapsulates the Salvation Army's theology of ministry. Officers are soldiers first; it is not just officers but all soldiers who are expected "to love and serve Him supremely all my days," even though that phrase is drawn from the Officer's Covenant. The words do not support a theology of ministry distinct from that of any *non*-officer Salvationist. The difference is simply administrative; the Salvation Army does not have a priesthood theologically or ontologically distinct from that of all believers.

The situation is not so simple however, because sociology tends to trump theology in the evolution of ecclesiology. We might assume that we believe, and then act accordingly; that our theology shapes our practice. That is not necessarily so. The ways we behave in practice are sometimes at variance with what we think we believe. As Ray Anderson proposes: "Ministry precedes and produces theology, not the reverse."[11] Theology is not simply "faith seeking understanding"; it is the product of an on-going action-reflection process. That process has gradually altered the way the Salvation Army has thought about its leadership.

The institutional structure within which Salvation Army ministry is offered bears a superficial resemblance to that of the churches. The church has members; the Army has soldiers. Both the Army and the church have office-holders with pastoral and leadership roles. Both have units of corporate life; parishes or congregations or corps at the local level and most have collectives such as assemblies and presbyteries, synods or dioceses and provinces or divisions and territories to facilitate supervision.

However, the correspondence between these church and Salvation Army terms is not exact, because of their differing histories and the theologies arising from them. The

---

10. Harris, "Officership is Availability," 243.
11. Anderson, "Theology of Ministry," 7.

Scriptural call to share Christ's ministry is made to the whole people of God but inevitably the emergence of differing roles has led to gradations of status within the church. In the Catholic tradition, the calling to a separate vocational ministerial priesthood, essentially different from that of the laity, is believed to derive from the command of Christ himself. The Salvation Army, arising no earlier than 1865, holds no such doctrine of priestly character but its officership has also come to assume a similarly clerical ethos.

The theological underpinnings are different. For example, in the Catholic tradition the presidency of the Eucharist is central to the clerical role (or in the Reformed tradition, the ministry of both Word and Sacrament), rather than the "appointability" of the officer. Again, officers are still soldiers whereas clergy in the Catholic and most Reformation churches are by definition *not* laity. Clearly, the essence of officership as distinct from soldiership derives not from any theological rationale but lies in its practical convenience to the performance of the Army's mission. It arises from praxis; theologizing has followed. The Salvationist could argue that the same is true of Catholic priesthood or Reformed ministry. A different route has been taken to a similar destination: a clericalised vocational ministry.

Whereas the early Salvation Army used to rejoice that it differed from the churches, more recently it has come to assert its similarity, both formally (as with the introduction of the term "ordination") and informally (as in corps being described as churches and officers as pastors). Such claims obscure theological distinctions and promote an apparent convergence. This section explores the course of these developments, and the subsequent theologizing which has invested an originally functional role with a gloss of clerical identity.

The Salvation Army began as a "non-denominational" mission, the Christian Mission. It was not a "church" and its operatives were not clergy. William Booth, having been ordained in the Methodist New Connexion, always maintained his clerical distinction, but almost all of his associates in the new enterprise from the mid-1860s were *lay* evangelists.[12] Their assumption of military-style ranks from 1878 was not seen as a departure from that principle.

Nevertheless, the Salvation Army inherited Methodism's ambiguity about ministry—its officers were "lay," but like Wesley's lay-preachers before them, they increasingly adopted a clerical identity. As an originally focused evangelistic agency broadened to include a variety of functions including the discipling and pastoral care of its converts, its leaders adapted to new roles. Originally simply itinerant evangelists, with, in Wesley's words, "nothing to do but save souls,"[13] Salvation Army officers soon came to perform such clerical tasks as administration of sacraments, pastoring, preaching, teaching, and government.[14] In practice they soon became "clergy" even if it took several generations for the Army to make this claim. Reflection on this practical development has led to a

---

12. Occasional exceptions, such as Elwin Oliphant, in Anglican orders, brought their ordination with them.

13. Number 11 of John Wesley's 12 Rules for Preachers, quoted in Townsend, Workman, and Eayrs, *New History*, 1:296.

14. Including offering the sacraments of baptism and the Lord's Supper until a change of policy in 1883, and thereafter to be responsible for such quasi-sacramental equivalents as the Army devised.

changed form of belief. Doctrine has eventually followed praxis. Let us trace the process by which this came about.

On the one hand, William Booth wrote:

> I have lived, thank God, to witness the separation between layman and cleric become more and more obscured . . .[15]

> [There is] . . . no "exclusive order of preachers" nor ministry confined to a particular class of individuals who constitute a sacred order specially raised up and qualified . . . authorized to communicate the same power to their successors, who are, they again contend, empowered to pass on some special virtues to those who listen to their teaching . . . I honor the Order of Preachers; I belong to it myself . . . but as to his possessing any particular grace because of his having gone through any form of Ordination, or any other ceremonial whatever, I think that idea is a great mistake.
> And I want to say here, once and for all, that no such notion is taught in any authorized statement of Salvation Army doctrine or affirmed by any responsible officer in the organization . . . As Soldiers of Christ, the same duty places us all on one level.[16]

Not only were officers *not* "clergy" but soldiers in effect *were*. Booth in 1898 hoped that soldiers would not shirk their duty "by any talk of not being an officer."

> You cannot say you are not ordained. You were ordained when you signed Articles of War, under the blessed Flag. If not, I ordain every man, woman and child here present that has received the new life. . . . I ordain you with the breath of my mouth. I tell you what your true business in the world is, and in the name of the living God I authorize you to go and do it. Go into all the world and preach the gospel to every creature![17]

But along with such claims that the Army made no distinction between the "ordination" of officers and that of soldiers, we find a growing emphasis on the distinctive role of officers. Booth wrote in 1900:

> Indeed, the fact is ever before us—like Priest, like People; like Captain, like Corps.[18]

And in 1903:

> . . . it is the Officer upon whom all depends. It has always been so. If Moses had not made a priesthood, there would have been no Jewish nation. It was the priesthood of the Levites which kept them *alive*, saved them from their inherent rottenness . . . and perpetuated the law which made them.[19]

---

15. Railton, *General Booth*, 17.
16. Booth, in *Officer*, June 1899, 202–203.
17. *War Cry*, 22 January 1898, 9, col. 3.
18. Booth, *Letter to Commissioners*, 15.
19. Begbie, *William Booth*, II, 306.

Commenting on this statement, St. John Ervine considered that Booth's own views changing:

> This was a far different note from any that he had hitherto sounded. Priests had never previously been much esteemed by him who was more ready to admire prophets than priests . . . The Soldier-Prophet was about to leave his command to a Lawyer-Priest. A younger William Booth would have known that this was dangerous, but Booth was old and solitary and tired, and old men want priests more than they want warriors."[20]

Roland Robertson commented that William Booth had come "to the conclusion that the priesthood of all believers, although already effectively dropped in practice, had to be attenuated as an ideal."[21] This probably attributed to Booth a degree of intentionality for which there is insufficient evidence.

Bramwell Booth wrote in 1925:

> In this, we humbly but firmly claim that we are in no way inferior . . . We, no less than they, are called and chosen to sanctification of the Spirit and to the inheritance of eternal life. And our officers are, equally with them, ministers in the church of God . . .[22]

So, the Salvation Army had attempted to maintain a sectarian equality of believers, resisting the idea that its officers were clergy. At same time, it adopted a military, hierarchical structure which expedited the process of clericalisation. Conditions of officers' service would constitute their professional milieu in way not true of other Salvationists. The mystique of the call to officership, the intensive nature of officer-formation and sessional group bonding, the extent of personal commitment involved in the covenant and undertakings, the ranking and appointment systems, the expectations of the rank and file, the distinctive and all-absorbing work of officers, the sense of corporate identity and *esprit de corps*, together with the organizational advantages of claiming status as celebrants and chaplains, gave officership a character which was clerical compared with that of soldiers.

The end result: the Salvation Army became another denomination, its officers were regarded, and regarded themselves, as clergy, and its soldiers thought of themselves as laity. Despite a strong tradition of soldier-participation, officers became a professional religious class. The Army inherited and carried forward the ecclesiological contradictions of Methodism (and of most other sects). It has recapitulated, in its brief life, the history of the church as a whole. This denominationalizing tendency consolidated throughout the twentieth century even though the Army's official rhetoric long remained sectarian.

The usual pattern is that a period of consolidation and reflection ensues in a movement's second century as it adjusts to operating in different world from that of its origins. In the Army's case, this was evident from the 1960s in a debate over whether officership was simply a functional role or enjoyed a higher status. The same ambiguity or polarization became apparent in this debate as we have seen in the writings of the founders—it

20. Ervine, *God's Soldier*, II, 777–78.
21. Robertson, "The Salvation Army," 80.
22. Booth, *Echoes and Memories*, (1977) 82.

remained part of the Army's DNA. Commissioner Hubert Scotney, for example, resisted the drift to clericalisation:

> The distinction made today between clergy and laity does not exist in the New Testament . . . The terms layman and laity (in the current usage of those words) are completely out of character in a Salvation Army context . . . It is foreign to the entire concept of Salvationism to imagine two levels of involvement. Any distinction between officers and soldiers is one of function rather than status.[23]

Conversely, Colonel William Clark welcomed it:

> [By] a direct call from God into the ranks of Salvation Army officership, we have been given particular spiritual authority . . . Whatever our role . . . happens to be for the time being . . . we are primarily spiritual leaders . . . Our spiritual authority lies not only or chiefly in what we do, but in what we are . . . Our calling is to be a certain kind of person and not . . . to do a certain kind of job . . . The "ordained" ministry of the Church—to which body we belong by virtue of our calling, response, training and commissioning—is a distinctive ministry within the body of the whole people of God, different from that "general" ministry of the Church which is defined in the New Testament as "the priesthood of all believers."[24]

Inevitably the debate amongst Salvationists eventually found expression in official pronouncements, the first of which was General Arnold Brown's introduction of "ordination" in commissioning. The Chief of the Staff's 1978 letter to territorial commanders stated:

> It is the General's wish that a slight modification should be made to the wording of the Dedication Service during the Commissioning of cadets, in order to emphasize the fact that Salvation Army officers are ordained ministers of Christ and of His Gospel.
>
> After the cadets have made their Affirmation of Faith, the officer conducting the Commissioning should then say: "In accepting these pledges which you each have made, I commission you as officers of The Salvation Army and ordain you as ministers of His Gospel."[25]

General Brown's introduction of "ordination" provoked a new round of discussion. Captain Chick Yuill opposed this change:

> May I suggest that we need to re-emphasize the truth that there is no real distinction between officers and soldiers, that the difference is simply of function . . . If that little word "ordain" has crept in because of a subconscious desire that other Christians should realize that we are as "important" as the clergy of other denominations . . . in the end it matters not a jot where we stand in the estimation of any who would compile a league table of ecclesiastical importance.[26]

Brigadier Bramwell Darbyshire supported it:

23. Scotney, "Salvation Army," 452.
24. Clark, "Divinely Called," 289.
25. Letters in International Heritage Centre and Archives.
26. Yuill, "Matters Arising," 439–40.

> In spite of all the stuff about the priesthood of all believers, ordained and commissioned officers are different from non-officer Salvationists. They are not cleverer, wiser, more loved of God than their fellows, but they are special, set apart for Jesus . . . No one is more grateful for the Army's dedicated lay staff than this old warrior; but let's get it right. They may be as much involved as officers, but there is for an officer a sacramental dimension and if we lose sight of this the Army is finished.[27]

A pragmatic voice was that of Major Cecil Waters:

> We will go on looking for a definition of officership unless and until we recognize that officership exists firstly as a convenience by which we organize the Army and secondly as one function, among many, to which we feel called of God. [It is] impossible to define a concept of officership which is plainly and clearly distinct from that of soldiership. [He concluded] (a) That it would seem that the Army needs full time workers . . . Most, but by no means all, these workers are officers. (b) That we believe we may be called to be such workers—and this call may refer to officership (rather than employee or envoy status). (c) That to be so called and so engaged is sufficient to sustain our work, our spirit and our identity . . . we need look for nothing more special than this.[28]

Brown's decision did not command universal support even among the hierarchy. It was reviewed at leaders' conferences in 1988 and 1992, and in 2002 the rubric was amended by General John Gowans to read:

> The commissioning officer will say to each cadet in turn: "Cadet (name): Accepting your promises and recognizing that God has called, ordained and empowered you to be a minister of Christ and of his gospel, I commission you an officer of The Salvation Army."[29]

"Ordination" was now seen as something already done by God rather than in this ceremony by a representative of the organization. Commissioner Shaw Clifton was amongst those who disagreed with Gowans' initiative, resisted adopting it, and reversed it when he became General himself (2006–2011), although both rubrics may now be variously encountered in practice.

Meanwhile there had been other occasions for discussion. The 1982 World Council of Churches *Faith and Order Paper* 111 *on Baptism, Eucharist and Ministry* (the "Lima" document) was circulated amongst churches for comment. In its response, on the question of how Salvation Army ministry was perceived in relation to traditional Church belief about ordination, the Army missed significant areas of difference. It was vague about meaning of language of ordination and seemed to confuse the concept of indelible character of orders with Army's own expectation that officers had life-long ministry. It identified with the theology of "radical reformation" but also sought to be included in

---

27. *Salvationist*, 18 April 1998, 6.
28. Waters, "Us and Them!" 317.
29. International Heritage Centre and Archives.

the fold of "mainstream" ecclesiology by claiming to be just like everyone else but with different terminology. Or in the use of "ordination," the *same* terminology.[30]

Prepared at General Eva Burrow's request as a further response to "Lima," Major Philip Needham's *Community in Mission, A Salvationist Ecclesiology* was published 1987. Needham's basic premise was that "a Salvationist ecclesiology stands as a reminder to the Church that its mission in the world is primary, and that the life of the Church ought largely to be shaped by a basic commitment to mission."[31] His ecclesiology deals with ministry of the Army as a whole, and only incidentally with that of the officer corps in particular.

Needham "raised serious questions about interpretations of ordination that stress the conferring of a unique spiritual status." He claimed its significance was best expressed in the word "commissioning," used of both officers and soldiers taking up specific tasks, while "ordination" was commonly used in connection with "ministries that require theological training, specialized skills, pastoral leadership and a full-time vocation . . . the ordained ministry can only be understood as functional . . . "[32]

The Doctrine Council's 1998 edition of the *Handbook of Doctrine*, *Salvation Story*, summarized the evolution of the movement from an agency for evangelism to a denominational church. On ministry, it noted that all Christians are "ministers or servants of the gospel . . . share in the priestly ministry . . . In that sense there is no separated ministry." However:

> Within that common calling, some are called by Christ to be full-time officeholders within the Church. Their calling is affirmed by the gift of the Holy Spirit, the recognition of the Christian community and their commissioning—ordination—for service. Their function is to focus the mission and ministry of the whole Church so that its members are held faithful to their calling.[33]

Like *Community in Mission*, *Salvation Story* made clear the principle that ministry of particular persons arises out of the ministry of whole Christian community, and attempted to explain and justify how this happened in practice.

The Doctrine Council's later work *Servants Together* was prepared because the 1995 International Conference of Leaders' recommended that:

> The roles of officers and soldiers be defined and a theology of "the priesthood of all believers" be developed to encourage greater involvement in ministry (for example, spiritual leadership, leadership in general), worship, service and evangelism.[34]

Servants Together clearly stated that there was no distinction in status between soldiers and officers, although it then struggled to establish what was unique about the officer role, admitting that a variety of opinions were held on the subject. Such a concession

---

30. The Salvation Army's response was included in *Faith and Order Paper* 137 and also published separately as *One Faith, One Church*.
31. Needham, *Community in Mission*, 4, 5.
32. Needham, Ibid., 65.
33. *Salvation Story*, 108.
34. *Servants Together* (2002) 127.

to plurality of views was unusual for the Salvation Army. As an official response to the debate of the previous forty years, *Servants Together* entrenched the Army's traditional ambiguity about its "separated ministry"—although the 2008 edition, with its inclusion of the new *Minute* on Commissioning amongst other things, took the Army in a clericalising direction again. Nevertheless, we may still sum up the progression after the introduction of ordination in 1978 at least to *Servants Together* in 2002, by saying that to the 1970s the pendulum had swung steadily in direction of status for officers, while the Army's subsequent official publications tried to correct the imbalance and restore a functional view—while retaining the Movement's customary ambiguity about the question.

The late twentieth century saw more soldiers in ministry roles—as youth workers, pastoral workers, corps leaders, social workers and administrators—particularly in western countries with declining officer strength. As a kind of counterpoint to this debate on officership, discussion continued on the place of Salvationists who perform officer functions without officer status. These include non-commissioned and warranted ranks—Envoys, Auxiliary Captains, (and Lieutenants between 2001 and 2008, when that rank was not treated as an officer one)—and also soldiers.

In consequence, General Paul Rader, on the recommendation of the 1998 international conference of leaders, set up the International Commission on Officership, "to review all aspects of the concept of officership in the light of the contemporary situation and its challenges, with a view to introducing a greater measure of flexibility" into officer service.[35]

The Commission dealt with many important issues, but concerning the status of officership, the Commission was asked to do two things which did not sit easily together: to strengthen ideal of life-time service and to explore possibilities of short-term service. The first would shore up the "clerical" assumptions behind officership; the second would permit a greater degree of flexibility based on an "all-lay" ethos. The Commission offered ways of providing for both alternatives, but by making Lieutenancy a non-commissioned rank, replacing those of Envoy and Auxiliary Captain, General Gowans perpetuated the two-tier model, with two groups performing the same ministry roles but only one having the status of officership.

If General Gowans had bitten the bullet offered by the Commission on Officership and abolished the two-tier officership system, it would have mitigated an injustice and encouraged the variety of options of vocational service available. It would have been possible for all leaders in full-time paid employment to be called officers; the soldiers' covenant would have sufficed for all. Appointments could even have been held under employment contract rather than the anomalous "employed by God" fiction clung to for legal rather than theological reasons—a relic from a Christendom no longer inhabited. In that case the claim to ordination could have been dropped and the question of whether or not Salvation Army officers were as important as clergy need not have arisen. However, that is unlikely to happen; legal privileges are not lightly relinquished.

More recently, the Salvation Army has responded to another initiative by the World Council of Churches; Faith and Order Paper No. 214, *The Church: Towards a Common*

---

35. Howe, "International Commission," 19.

Vision.³⁶ In this response the Salvation Army has been unequivocal in defending its "functional" concept of church leadership.

> As in some other Christian denominations, ministry in the Salvation Army is essentially viewed as functional rather than as affording a particular status. Salvation Army officers are first of all soldiers—members of the church—and are marked by a calling from God to relinquish secular employment and be available to the organization for deployment. Despite the use of the word "ordination" in a Salvation Army officer commissioning ceremony, the ministry of *Salvation Army officership* does not support a theology of ministry that is essentially different from that of the committed non-officer Salvationist. The Salvation Army believes that all the people of God are called to ministry, exercised according to each individual's particular calling, gifts and graces.

As an outworking of the conviction that all people are equally created in God's image, equally redeemed by Christ, equally gifted by God, and equally called to use those gifts as God directs, all forms of Christian leadership in The Salvation Army, at any level of seniority, are open equally to men and women.

> The hierarchy of authority and governance in The Salvation Army is structural rather than ecclesial, practical rather than theological. This includes the ministry of oversight. However, the call to understand authority as "humble service, nourishing and building up the *koinonia* of the Church in faith, life and witness . . . a service of love without any domination or coercion" reflects closely the ecclesiological understanding and aspiration of The Salvation Army. The distinction between power and the pursuit of truth which leads to holiness and therefore "a greater authenticity in relationship with God, with others and with all creation" finds an echo in The Salvation Army's requirement that "by reason of the work to which they have committed themselves, and to which they declare themselves to be divinely called, it follows that officers must first of all live godly lives." Thus leadership is understood as spiritual leadership and any organizational authority is subservient to the spiritual authority which flows from a calling from God.³⁷

In my view the Salvation Army had three options regarding clerical status:

1. There *are* priests/clerics/people in orders in church, with status distinct from laity, but we *do not* have them in Salvation Army. That would mean the Army's acceptance of an "all lay" status for soldiers and officers, implying a second class clergy status for officers. The Army would be something like a lay "order" rather than a stand-alone entity like a "denomination." The negotiations with the Anglican church in 1882 might have opened the door to that possibility but they came to nothing, and Booth in effect rejected that option.

2. There *are* priests/clerics/people in orders in church, and we *do* have them as officers in Salvation Army. This is what General Brown claimed by adopting "ordination" and assuming that the Army's commissioning was always equivalent to ordination.

---

36. World Council of Churches, *The Church: Towards a Common Vision*.

37. Paper prepared by the International Theological Council in 2016: "A Response from the Salvation Army to *The Church: Towards a Common Vision*," 4, 5.

It endorsed officially what most Salvationists had already come to believe, partly in consequence of the ambiguity about church order inherited from Methodism, and partly from the desire to be accepted by other Christian denominations as one of them. *But* a claim to clerical status, even without necessarily claiming strictly clerical character in the Catholic sense, is a position difficult to hold without sliding into clericalism.

3. There are *no* priests/clerics/orders in church, and Salvation Army does *not* aspire to any. All Christians are "lay," all belong to the *laos*, the people of God, without distinction of status. This was Booth's theoretical position. However, the Army's ecclesiology was shaped instead by his autocratic temperament, the need for organization, the twin demons of militarism and bureaucracy, the susceptibility of human nature to pride and ambition, and historically conditioned expectations. So the Salvation Army became "clericalised." The difficulty lies in the tension between the hierarchical institutional structure and the more egalitarian "Priesthood of all Believers" ethos inherited from our more radical Protestant antecedents.

Clericalisation has had two related adverse effects on the church—and on the Salvation Army. Firstly, clericalism fosters a spirit incompatible with the "servanthood" Jesus modelled and undermines the kind of community Jesus calls together. Secondly, by concentrating power and influence in the hands of minority, clericalisation disempowers majority of members of church, thus diminishing its effectiveness in mission.

Of the first adverse effect, Bramwell Booth was aware. In 1894 he was complaining that "the D.O.'s [divisional officers] are often much more separate from their F.O.'s [field officers] than they ought to be. Class and caste grows with the growth of the military idea."[38] Thirty years later he was still anxious about divisional and territorial leaders in that "they are open to special dangers in that they rise and grow powerful and sink into a kind of opulence."[39] (Unfortunately captains are as susceptible as colonels to the tendency.) Dr Laura Petri of Sweden, in her thesis "Catherine Booth and Salvationism," regretted that "military persons easily become arrogant, unrestrained and tyrannical"— though in quoting her, Commissioner Tor Wahlström also noted that "Salvationist lack of humility is apt today to be more frequently seen in the anxiety of many a Jack to prove himself at least as good as his master!"[40]

General Albert Orsborn acknowledged to the 1949 Commissioners' Conference that

> dissatisfaction and decline . . . is blamed on our system of ranks, promotions, positions and differing salaries and retirements . . . that it has created envy and kindred evils and developed sycophancy, ingratiation, "wire-pulling," favoritism, etc . . . It is a sad reflection that we are in character, in spirituality, unable to meet the strain of our own system.[41]

---

38. Booth, letter of October 1894, in Bramwell-Booth, *Bramwell Booth*, 218.
39. Booth, letter of 17 April 1924, in Bramwell-Booth, Ibid., 437.
40. Wahlström, "The Gift of Humility," 413.
41. Quoted by Wickberg, in "Movements for Reform," Address at the 1971 International Conference of Leaders, Minutes, 9–10.

The Salvation Army's system is not alone in susceptibility to such weaknesses; it is in the nature of systems to undermine the reason they exist. Human nature will take its course, but a system which actually encourages it to do so requires extra vigilance.

And the second adverse effect, the disempowerment of the many by the exaltation of the few? The American Nazarene Kenneth E. Crow sums up: "Loyalty declines when ability to influence decision and policies declines. When institutionalization results in top-down management, one of the consequences is member apathy and withdrawal."[42]

It would be difficult to say whether clericalisation had led to a loss of zeal, or loss of zeal had been compensated for by a growing preoccupation with status, or whether each process fed the other. There is a paradox here: the military system, quite apart from the fact that it fitted Booth's autocratic temperament, was designed for rapid response, and is still officially justified in those terms.[43] The Army's first period of rapid growth followed its introduction. However the burgeoning of hierarchical and bureaucratic attitudes came to exert a counter-influence. The reason for success contained the seeds of failure. The longer-term effect of autocracy was to alienate many hitherto enthusiastic, and to deter subsequent generations, more habituated to free thought and democracy, from joining. Unfortunately clericalism is to clergy as water to fish. It is pervasive and taken for granted. We may find it encapsulated by the question of an incoming territorial commander, meeting for the first time with a group of youth officers and youth workers in a conference. As they were not in uniform, he asked, "Which of you are the *officers*? *You're* the ones I'm interested in!"

Clearly this argument refers to what we may loosely call the Western Army. In much of the "Third World" the Salvation Army is both expanding rapidly *and* also extremely rank-conscious. In a territory which shall remain nameless, a new toilet block erected at one corps featured three doors: one for men, one for women, and a third for officers.[44] One factor possibly contributing to the Army's current growth there is that those societies, less individualistic and with a stronger culture of "belonging" and traditional respect for authority, are more susceptible to the attractions of firm and decisive leadership. The cultures are different, but the long term results are yet to be seen. I find it difficult to believe that exaltation of status, so contrary to Jesus' own precept and practice, finally ensures good outcomes.

If clericalisation *is* a bad thing, how may its ill-effects be moderated? Leadership is indispensable to the effectiveness of any movement. Structure is necessary, and needs continuity, accountability and legitimacy to mitigate the effects of unrestrained personal power. But if institutionalization is inevitable, the prophetic critique, the Reformation's *ecclesia semper reformanda*, is essential.

There are two ways the problem can be approached: one is structural, the other attitudinal.

42. Crow, "The Church of the Nazarene."

43. "We are the 'special forces unit' of his Church on earth." Commissioner Israel Gaither, *Salvation Army Year Book*, 2004, 2.

44. By contrast, a story from a friend who once found himself standing next to General Orsborn at a urinal. He said, "I didn't expect to find the General here!" Orsborn responded, "Generals are but as other men."

The 2002 edition of *Servants Together* made the following suggestions for structural change "in order to facilitate servant leadership":

- Develop non-career-oriented leadership models.
- Dismantle as many forms of officer elitism as possible.
- Continue to find ways to expand participatory decision-making.[45]

Although these proposals, and the word "participatory," were deleted from the 2008 edition of the same book, the effect of reforms instigated more recently by General Cox could give the word renewed force. As a way of promoting transparency and accountability, and also in order to bring the Salvation Army into line with legislative requirements for charities in most legal jurisdictions internationally, these measures include a more rigorous demarcation between management and governance functions at all levels, distributed authority through a process of arriving at decisions by majority vote in all governance councils, and the inclusion of expert non-officers and non-Salvationists in many such councils. While not actually taking the Army's legislative and supervisory structures back to the pre-1877 Conference polity, this may amount to a revolution of equal significance to the changes instituted in that year. It involves an unprecedented devolution of power and responsibility within this hierarchical and hitherto autocratic organization. It runs counter to William Booth's, and the early Salvation Army's, exaltation of the virtues of autocracy. These will be very challenging concepts to implement; power is highly addictive and the prospect of its attenuation is very threatening to addicts.

However, no changes in structure will be effective without parallel attention to *attitudes*. The 2002 text of *Servants Together* made one other suggestion, also deleted from the 2008 edition, but one to which all can aspire:

- Teach leaders to be servants by modelling it.[46]

The mantra today is, "Servant Leadership." Too often, that is an oxymoron. Servant is as servant does. This is the only suggestion most can aspire to implement, but it is also the most important: to model servanthood. And where opportunity affords, to name and challenge its antithesis, its shadow, which is the abuse of power.

We have traced the gradual "clericalisation" of the Army's leadership, and noted at the more recent evolution of its governance from autocratic to consultative and even towards participative—a movement in the opposite direction. If praxis foreshadows and eventually determines doctrine, it may be interesting to see whether this latter trend towards participative governance has some eventual impact on the theoretical status of officers.

45. *Servants Together* (2002), 121.

46. *Servants Together* (2002), 121. The publication of the 2008 edition was marked by a circular to Territorial Commanders and Officers Commanding from the Chief of the Staff, dated 31 July 2008, requiring that "all copies of the previous edition be removed from Trade Department shelves, Training College libraries and any other resource centers . . . and destroyed . . . please encourage your officers and soldiers to purchase this latest edition and discard any copies they may have of the 2002 edition." This apparently draconian instruction was defended as a means to "avoid confusion." (The new edition also contained a revised rubric for commissioning of officers, amongst other matters.) Copy held by author.

OTHER RANKS

The ambiguity about the status of officers—the question of whether they are clerical or lay—brings us to consider the role of those who have clerical functions but are not accorded the status of clergy.

Many churches face declining vocations to the ordained ministry and expanding lay ministries. Comparison of *Year Book* figures show declining officer statistics in some Western territories and rising employee statistics, though even territories with increasing numbers of officers are employing more people as well.

	Year	Active Officers	Retired Officers	Employees
New Zealand	1984	403	168	569
	2006	346	195	2,552
	2016	296	250	2,741

	Year	Active Officers	Retired Officers	Employees
Norway	1984	387	266	451
	2004	199	247	1,357
	2016	154	219	1,364

Compare with

	Year	Active Officers	Retired Officers	Employees
Zimbabwe	1984	242	71	355
	2006	467	111	1,430
	2016	541	113	1,279

	Year	Active Officers	Retired Officers	Employees
Korea	1984	317	45	236
	2004	541	134	415
	2016	629	181	1,294

It is useful to explore the way in which these patterns have developed. At first the volunteer officials of the Mission, the elders, secretaries and the treasurers, became the "local officers,"[47] or "petty officers" as the 1878 *Orders and Regulations* called them.[48] The NCOs were the backbone of the corps, as distinct from those commissioned officers whose ministry was virtually itinerant in the early years.

Catherine Booth, in an address given at Cannon Street Hotel, March 20th 1883, announced "a new order of officers called 'Sergeants,' who come between the corps and the paid officers, and we hope soon to have a force of those who will systematically visit

---

47. Booth, *Echoes and Memories*, 177.
48. *Orders and Regulations*, 1878, iv.

every public house in the country . . ."[49] The 1886 *Orders and Regulations for Field Officers* listed seventeen varieties of sergeants in its index.[50]

The next development recorded was the introduction of "Envoys." From 1893 the Army began to set up "Circle Corps" to link together a number of village "societies" (a term inherited from Methodism). Meetings in these centers were led by "Local Specials" sent out from other corps—hence eventually the term "envoy." A supplementary book of regulations issued in 1896 stated, "Local Officers, who shall be known as Envoys, will assist in conducting the meetings at the different Societies composing the Circle."[51] *The Local Officer* explained that, "It is, in short, the old local-preacher system militarized and adapted to Army warfare."[52] This was a rare instance of a direct comparison being made between a "church" and an "Army" office, and an interesting assumption of the readers' familiarity with a Methodist model. It may also reveal the assumption that officers were now thought of as equivalent to ministers. "The Envoy will not require monetary support of any kind, seeing that like other Local Officers he either earns his own livelihood by the labour of his hands, or is possessed of some other means of subsistence."[53]

The next step in the evolution of this subsidiary order of officers was proposed by Bramwell Booth in 1927 with "The establishment of a new order of officers—to be known as "Auxiliary Officers"—to be enlisted for a term of years rather than for life; a thousand such for the U.K. and a thousand for other European countries."[54] This did not happen at that time—perhaps the onset of world-wide depression shortly thereafter made the timing financially unpropitious—but in the early 1930s another step in the deployment of envoys was made. These envoys, still unpaid volunteers, were permanently attached to a particular Society, in charge there, rather than peripatetic. In such a case, "Envoy" became a less apt description. Training was also made available, "The Envoy's Efficiency Course, consisting of twelve months' lessons."[55]

Two varieties of envoy evolved. Firstly, the unpaid, part-time, volunteer variety, who were engaged in evangelical work, either in charge of smaller corps or outposts, or available for "supply" in the Methodist lay-preacher tradition. In the case of these volunteers, the rank of envoy sometimes appeared to be awarded as a token of esteem for a senior local officer rather than for any specific envoy-like errand. Secondly, there were those in whole-time, paid employment in some branch of the Army's work, sometimes in a "ministry" role of spiritual leadership and sometimes in some ancillary support role in clerical or social work. Some envoys (of either volunteer or paid variety) were ex-officers who still felt a call to ministry. Some were younger people testing their vocation before becoming officers. Some were would-be officers who had not been accepted for training,

---

49. Booth, *Church and State*, 37. Wiseman (General, 1974–77) quoted this passage "to show that in the early days, there was no distinction of spiritual status between 'paid' officers and 'unpaid' voluntary speakers, soldiers and sergeants." Wiseman, "Coming of Age," 587.

50. *Orders and Regulations*, 1886, 635–36.

51. Salvation Army, *Why and Wherefore*, 93.

52. *Local Officer*, November 1897, 106.

53. *Local Officer*, January 1899, 161–64.

54. *Salvation Army Year Book*, 1927, 41.

55. *War Cry*, 7 January 1933, 15.

for whom this ministry was a consolation prize, which meant they were loosed upon the world without training to do work for which they had been adjudged unsuitable to be trained. Others again were people with a "late vocation," or who were not interested in becoming commissioned officers. From being a stopgap measure, envoys had become part of the regular forces. Additionally, from time to time over the years some full-time employees, usually in social institutions, were ranked as "sergeant," though in parts of Europe that rank may also be held by senior executives at territorial headquarters.

In the late 1950s Bramwell Booth's plan for the employment of a class of auxiliary officers resurfaced in a Minute from Chief of the Staff concerning "Auxiliary Captains."

> The General has decided that Salvationists unable for valid and acceptable reasons to enter a training college but desirous of giving full-time service to The Salvation Army, may, while undertaking responsibility of a Corps, or serving in a similar capacity in Social or comparable work, receive the designation of Auxiliary Captain, provided they have been soldiers for at least two years and are over thirty five years of age. The designation of Auxiliary Captain must not be introduced into any territory, nor exceptions made to the foregoing conditions without the approval of the Chief of the Staff, who will also give directions as to the conditions of acceptance and service.[56]

The draft of the "Employment Statement" was adapted from that for envoys and included: "I understand that although I may be required to perform duties of a religious nature, an Auxiliary Captain is not a Salvation Army Officer or a Minister of the Gospel of that branch of the Christian Church known as The Salvation Army, and that my appointment as an Auxiliary Captain does not entitle me to the rights and privileges of a Salvation Army officer."[57] In similar vein, a later but undated set of terms of reference includes the clause: "Although an Auxiliary-Captain is not a commissioned officer of The Salvation Army, I understand that, as an Auxiliary-Captain, I may be required to perform duties and accept responsibilities which are usually performed by a commissioned officer to the extent that they may be performed by a lay person."[58] The use of "lay" in this context also reveals an assumption about the clerical status of officers, who are assumed to be capable of performing unspecified duties beyond the scope of non-officers. What were they thinking of? It is sadly reminiscent of the Wizard of Oz, the little man with the megaphone, standing behind a curtain, and pretending to extraordinary powers while at the same time disclaiming them.

The "Memorandum of an Auxiliary Captain's Engagement with The Salvation Army" (1 January 1960) insists that Auxiliary Captaincy, "is an appointment, not a rank." It also described such persons as, "undertaking as VOLUNTARY WORKERS [sic] full-time responsibility for the oversight of a Corps, or serving in a similar capacity in social or comparable work . . . They . . . will be required to give full-time service to The Salvation Army and engage in no other occupation . . . both husband and wife will be

---

56. Minute signed by William J. Dray, Chief of the Staff, 23 May 1959.

57. Draft "Employment Statement" in Salvation Army International Heritage Centre Archives, EDL/7/6/1, 1959.

58. "Agreement between Applicant for Auxiliary-Captain and The Salvation Army", undated but including reference to Orders and Regulations Governing the Retirement of Auxiliary-Captains, 1963.

required to sign the form of application." They "will not be employed by the Army under a contract of service, and will have no legal rights to wages, their status as voluntary workers being in this respect the same as that of Officers." Sometimes they could apply for commissioning to substantive rank as Captains, provided they had completed certain in-service training requirements.

These conditions remained essentially unchanged for more than forty years. Auxiliary Captains were to enjoy all the disciplines, but were less certain of the "rights and privileges" (undefined) of Salvation Army Officers.

The rank was not intended for short-term service as envoyship could have been. The distinctive thing about auxiliary captains is that they wanted to be officers but were above the current age for acceptance into training. Ideally then, their equivalent training was in-service over five years, after which they could apply for commissioning. In practice the quality of training offered varied widely from place to place and from time to time.

Without these late-vocation candidates, the officer shortage would have been much more severe. In 1990, fifty-five cadets entered the UK officer training college; forty-five auxiliary captains, aged forty to forty-five, also began in-service training.[59]

A down side of this rank that was not a rank, for officers who were not officers, is that they, along with envoys, were sometimes made to feel second-class by their soldiers, and by comrade officers. Occasionally this surfaced in print. *The Salvationist* reported, "One of the group . . . had met a soldier who said, 'Oh, but you're not really an officer, are you?' The unthinking remark touched a sore spot."[60] Although the conditions varied from territory to territory, envoys and auxiliary captains also tended to be disadvantaged financially as compared with commissioned officers. For example, where pension arrangements depended upon years of service, disputes arose as to whether service as envoys counted towards the total, although given under "officer conditions."

At the same time, the idea of short-term commissions—for "real" officers rather than second-class officers—began to be mentioned. One of the earlier protagonists was Major John Gowans. In the 1970s he pointed out that many young people were willing to give service without tying themselves down to a lifetime commitment. He argued that shortage of candidates, the rate of resignation and the increasing dearth of officer-leadership in the United Kingdom all called for desperate measures. Further, given that two-thirds of British officers eventually resigned rather than retired from service, short-term commissions were already a reality.[61] Reaction was not encouraging but the question remained sufficiently live to be placed on the agenda of the International Commission on Officership in 1999. General John Gowans evidently felt unable thereafter to implement his earlier proposal.

It is interesting to compare the ambiguity of auxiliary officers' role with that of the permanent diaconate in the Roman Catholic Church. Frank DeRego and James Davidson draw attention to the tensions arising for the latter from the fact that their role is not adequately defined. "The problem is traceable to the definition of the office of deacon,

---

59. *Salvationist*, 1 February 1992, 8.

60. Ibid., 1 February 1992, 9.

61. Gowans, "Short Service Commissions."

which is stated in terms of a status, not in terms of a job to be done . . . Role conflict and ambiguity . . . adversely affect the actual relationships among deacons, priests and lay people."[62] For deacons, a key problem is their inability to perform sacramental functions; for auxiliary officers, the problems relate to status and working conditions. The ambiguity about their respective roles is however similar, suggesting again that the problem is as much sociological as theological.

This survey of auxiliary officership therefore raises questions about the connection between officer status and officer function. People enjoying a variety of status, as Envoys, Auxiliary Captains, Corps Leaders or soldiers without any conferment of rank, have discharged what appear to be the essential functions of officership. They have pastored, preached, taught, managed, led and acted as the focal bearers of the Salvation Army message, tradition and authority, either without rank or with a rank expressly designated as less than "clerical." At the same time, many commissioned officers have over the years served in back-office roles that did not include any of these activities. Their sole officer-distinction has been covenanted appointability.

SOLDIERS

An outline of the history of auxiliary officership, in which people who were soldiers rather than "real" officers, functioned as officers, leads us naturally to consider what the Salvation Army has said about its soldiers per se. How are they different from officers?

While we have approached this question as derivative from an investigation of "ordained" officer ministry within the Salvation Army, the last seventy years have seen a general reaction against this approach to the study of church order within the ecumenical context. The World Council of Churches' establishment of a Department of the Laity in the late 1940s and Vatican II's grounding all church office in the whole people of God were key markers.[63] The Salvation Army's pragmatic ecclesiology had always been premised on this understanding—officers remain soldiers. The territorial commander or General is still a soldier at some Corps.

We have seen that in the early Salvation Army, before growing institutionalization stratified the ranks and roles, there was a clearer recognition that all ranks were "laity." All were the people of God, all were soldiers called equally to the battlefront. While the Army's military structure enabled rapid deployment, it would be interesting to discover how much of its rapid early spread was independently soldier-led. Gordon Moyles says of Newfoundland that

> If one examines only the official records one sees what looks like an orderly, planned progression even in the invasion of the outports. But when one looks deeper, one sees that the spread of Salvationism throughout much of Newfoundland was a spontaneous, catalytic kind of phenomenon. [The growth of small corps, over 40 of which were opened in 1892–1902, were] after-the-fact

---

62. DeRego and Davidson, "Catholic Deacons," in Cousineau, *Religion in a Changing World*, 96.
63. *Lumen Gentium* Chapter II, in Flannery, *Vatican Council II*, 359.

affairs—the Army being forced to respond to impromptu, unplanned "glory-meetings" conducted by local fishermen who had been converted in the Army elsewhere.[64]

The history of the Salvation Army's expansion on the African continent has been marked by the same soldier-initiative. Lt. Colonel Ron Manning describes how, when he and his wife were working in retirement for World Vision with refugees in the Tete province of Mozambique in 1994–95, "a young Mozambican man, poorly dressed but with 'S's' on the lapels of his shirt, declared himself to be a Salvationist recently returned from Malawi and who had managed to commence an Outpost in the village."[65]

We have traced the gradual status-ization of the officers. What, during this process, was happening to the soldiers?

O'Dea writes that "the development of mixed motivation," while most significant in leadership roles, "is to be seen in the rank and file as well. As 'born members' replaced people who had been converted, a different kind of motivation and identification began to prevail in the church. As laity became a more passive element . . . lay people began to develop a different kind of identification, and their motives for participation changed as well."[66]

Firstly, they came to think of themselves as "laity," and they came to expect of the officers the same kind of pastoral ministry they understood to be incumbent upon the clergy of the churches. Secondly, they increasingly viewed the officers as the professionals who were paid to evangelize the unconverted. Unfortunately, many officers' time also tended to become wholly absorbed in looking after the soldiers and administering the organization. It became less clear that anyone was actually attending to the core business of evangelism except where individuals manifested a particular gift—although that expectation remained a burden upon all, whether so gifted or not.

Towards the end of the nineteenth century development of the Army's musical subculture began to contribute to the process. Bernard Watson argued that "the allocation of large groups of men and women into the musical sections within the Army tended to diminish independent, imaginative, versatile action by non-officer Salvationists."[67] The ascendancy of these excellent musical combinations in Britain and the "old Dominions"—Australia, New Zealand and Canada in particular—tended to relegate the congregation to an audience role, like the faithful at the Tridentine mass. For many Salvationists, "evangelism" came to mean the band playing hymn-tunes in the street.

What was true of the "field" (that is, the evangelical, church-oriented work of the Army) was also the case in social work. Amongst the pioneers of Salvation Army social work had been ordinary Salvationists who saw a need and did something. Inevitably such work grew too large to be undertaken by private individuals and was taken over by the organization, growing into an official and comprehensive social program, staffed mainly by officers, who became the professionals, paid to care for the needy.

64. Moyles, *Salvation Army in Newfoundland*, 21, 26.
65. Manning to author, 27 October 2011, quoted with permission.
66. O'Dea, *Sociology of Religion*, 92.
67. Watson, "The Contemporary Framework," 264.

The tradition of lay-initiative has never been entirely lost, as exemplified by Envoy David Ndoda OF of Bulawayo, Zimbabwe, who at his own volition and expense founded a home for orphans.[68] Some non-officer staff have always been employed in social work over the years. However it is only within the past twenty or so years that serious efforts have been made to reintegrate the differing expressions of the Army's ministry. Soldiers generally have only recently, in some places, begun to reassume interest in and ownership of social work in a voluntary capacity, or, increasingly, as paid employees.[69]

Nevertheless a century of widening gulf between the concerns and preoccupations of officers on the one hand and soldiers on the other also had consequences for the attitude of officers, perhaps especially corps officers, towards soldiers. A broad divide may be discerned between

- Seeing soldiers as "cannon-fodder," whose role is to be occupied so far as possible in Army activities, building the Salvation Army institution.
- Viewing soldiers as the front line of evangelism, beyond the organization's official structure and program, to be resourced and supported as well as led, in building the Kingdom of God.

These points of view represent a divide between the tendency to "clericalize" the "laity" and the recognition of a distinct "lay apostolate." Both have been strongly represented over the years.

The view that the soldiers should be fully engaged in the work of the Salvation Army grew out of two things. Firstly, converts from the kind of social milieu common to many early Salvationists lost their friends and interests with conversion, and had to replace them. The corps became their new way of life.[70] As they lost touch with the "world," they were absorbed into what became in time a semi-autonomous religious sub-culture.

Secondly, the expanding Army needed the manpower. Bramwell Booth wrote,

> Every soldier is expected to do something of the collecting, the cleaning, the visiting, the band playing, the caring for the children, the seeking after our lost sheep, and the score of other duties demanding attention. Tens of thousands of our soldiers devote every moment snatched from their daily labour to the work of their Corps. They delight that it should be so.[71]

A paradox may be seen at work, in that on the one hand the soldiers were to be set to work in ministry, while some also came to regard ministry as the exclusive responsibility of the officers. All of these are generalizations of course; both voices continued to be heard, and in recent years there has been a renewal of the understanding that pastoral care is a joint responsibility. The move towards lay pastoral care within corps has been

---

68. *Salvation Army Year Book,* 1999, 22.

69. An analysis, both scholarly and impassioned, of the way soldiers have been written out of Salvation Army history is found in Hein, "More Inspirational than Penetrating," 27–45.

70. The same principle lies behind the Alcoholics Anonymous recommendation to new members to attend "90 meetings in 90 days."

71. Booth, *Servants of All,* 23.

accompanied by complaints that the officer never visits—a complaint not restricted to Salvation Army congregations.

Quotes like that from Bramwell Booth, might give the impression that secular work was simply a means to the end of being able to devote the rest of one's time to the War, or at most provided further opportunities for witness to fellow-workers, rather than being a God-given vocation in its own right. Roy Terry, writing in *Magazine* in 1963, lamented that "Even our active laymen are mostly, to use Hendrik Kraemer's phrase, 'clericalised laity.' Most lay Salvationist activity is specifically 'religious' activity—keeping the organizational works going, and while there are Salvationists active in the world at large (whose lives do not revolve solely around the S.A. hall) they don't seem to receive much encouragement from officialdom, still less any constructive help."[72]

Admittedly William Booth wrote a series of letters about "work" in the *War Cry* and the *Social Gazette*, later collected in a volume on "Religion for Every Day." In these he encouraged Salvationists to think of work as of value in itself, "good and honest work, honorable in the sight of God, and serviceable to your fellow-men."[73] However it is true that the main focus on the workplace in Salvation Army writing has been related to the soldiers' witnessing. At least this acknowledged that soldiers' lives were not simply coextensive with the organized corps program.

Philip Needham, in a 1965 article, made an impassioned protest against clericalism in the Salvation Army and the systematic officer-recruitment of all the most promising soldiers. He felt it reflected an over-riding concern for the continuation of the institution rather than a commitment to its mission. "There is a sacred aura about officership, that is, the complete identification with the sacred institution. It is as though the Army were God's right hand. That we refer to officership as 'full-time service' is a gross perversion of the Christian faith. If there is any full-time Christian service, it is in the life of the laymen in the world. The particular and inherent weakness of a professional clergy—and this is particularly true of the Army—is that it is not full-time Christian service."[74]

Discussion has occasionally focused on the "them and us" aspect of officer-soldier relationships. A letter to *The Salvationist* from G. W. Lesworthy of Florida, drawing on fifty years' experience of soldiership in Britain and the USA, complained of the "shunting aside of the soldiers . . . You stress 'officership' so much that soldiers have no choice but to feel 'put down.'"[75] Editorial comment regretted any polarization, especially "since the Salvation Army advocates the priesthood of all believers and is essentially a lay movement seeking the evangelization of the people by the people."[76]

Soldiers have been employed by the Army (as distinct from volunteer activities) from the earliest days. Some spent a lifetime in the Army's service, filling very responsible

---

72. *Magazine*, Letter, October 1963, 13.

73. Booth, *Letters to Salvationists*, 29.

74. Needham, "Some Thoughts on Jeremiah's Editorial," 43. An example of what Needham protested against could be found on the front cover of the New Zealand *War Cry* for 7 February 1953, a "Commissioning" number: "Today the 'point of greatest impact' upon the future for any saved young person of ability is full-time service for Christ." (That meant, as an officer.)

75. *Salvationist*, 5 December 1987, 12.

76. *Salvationist*, 6 February 1988, 2.

roles, especially financial ones. More recently, soldiers (not just in the guise of Envoys or auxiliary officers) have been employed more often in ministry and administrative roles, hitherto reserved for commissioned or auxiliary officers. In New Zealand the trend probably began with the appointment of youth workers, attached to divisions or corps from the mid-1980s on and from the 1990s this was a growing phenomenon. Over the same period an increasing number of larger corps employed full-time non-officer pastoral workers or "corps assistants," usually second career, late-vocation people recruited from within the congregation. The growing shortage of commissioned officers has also meant that responsibility for the leadership of some corps has devolved upon full-time, employed soldier "corps leaders."

Not being subject to the appointability of officers, such non-officer pastoral ministers have tended to serve longer in the same appointments than officers do. Their pastoral relationship with people has also led to questions about how far they can exercise traditionally officer or clerical roles, such as the solemnization of marriages. Some denominations provide for the appointment of non-clergy, denominational-list marriage celebrants but strangely not usually the Salvation Army. Unranked soldiers therefore face in this respect the same discrimination we have met with in the case of envoys.

The same period has seen the appointment of more non-officer Salvationists to senior executive roles in the organization, especially in the sphere of social work. Gordon Bingham was appointed Social Services Secretary for the USA Western Territory in 1985 after years in various social work roles in the USA Central Territory. In New Zealand George Borthwick headed Employment Programs as National Manager from 1992 to 2008 directing some two hundred staff. Previously only officers had held such appointments.

Using soldiers in administration was urged particularly by Commissioner Kenneth Hodder, as territorial commander for the USA Southern territory and subsequently as National Commander. In the USA Southern territory the role of Territorial Sergeant Major was instituted around 1990, providing a full-time "lay" advisor to the territorial commander, and also serving as chairman of the Territorial Commission on Planning and Goals. In a farewell message to the Southern territory, Hodder commented that if he had his time over again, he would "have given greater significance to the place of the lay salvationists, our soldiery, on decision-making bodies." He wanted "to stimulate a recovery of the biblical teaching concerning the status of soldiers and officers as equal partners . . . and looked forward to the day when non-officer soldiers will serve on territorial boards of trustees, finance councils, property councils and other decision-making bodies."[77]

Addressing the 1995 International Conference of Leaders, Hodder lamented that

> the Army has yet to appreciate fully the need for the application of these principles to the governance, as well as the ministry, of our movement . . . beyond the scriptural, historical and philosophical dimensions of this issue, there is an additional reason for pursuing it . . .
>
> The expansion of the work and the small size of the officer corps demands that we take advantage of those Salvationists who, based on their giftedness,

---

77. Hodder, "Let's Use Soldiers," 435–36.

training and experience, are prepared and willing to undertake administrative responsibilities. Furthermore . . . that task of administration necessarily translates into decision-making, meaning that the incorporation of soldiery into our decision-making structure may simply be forced upon us by growth . . . I suggest that we should now place ourselves in a proactive, rather than a reactive, stance.

Hitherto the Army had tentatively tried some models for lay participation, such as the laymen's councils, but Hodder saw these as interim measures, in which the laity would soon lose interest.

> The failure of representative bodies to bring about effective lay participation in the governance of the Army is . . . traceable to the nature of our polity. As a hierarchical organization it simply is not possible to graft on a representative body of laypersons and expect that it will long endure.

Hodder therefore proposed a three-part action plan. Firstly, forums where soldiers and officers can express their views directly to each other. Secondly—anticipating General Cox's proposed reforms by more than twenty years—selection of qualified soldiers for service on boards of trustees, finance and property councils and similar decision-making bodies. Thirdly, "The Salvation Army must support organizational change initiatives that take place on a decentralized, localized basis." He concluded by quoting Pius X, who

> in his 1906 Encyclical entitled *Vehementer Nos*, said: "As for the masses, they have no other right than that of letting themselves be led, and of following their pastors as a docile flock." Despite many protestations to the contrary, this has sometimes been our functional view. In this we have simply been wrong.[78]

Anxiety about such proposals has been expressed, particularly by officers. One concern was that officers with professional qualifications were being squeezed out of roles that enabled them to use that training. The view that officers per se bring an added dimension to administrative tasks has also been expressed. Another concern was that the availability of non-officer work within Army service would adversely affect officer recruiting.

Yet another implication of the trend was spelt out by Commissioner Earle Maxwell, Chief of the Staff, in an address to the 1998 International Conference of Leaders. While the majority of governments still accepted the officer's relationship with the Army as being entirely "spiritual" and therefore not subject to employer/employee legislation, it was a different matter when the Army engaged an employee to do the same work as an officer. "Then it becomes very difficult—almost impossible—for the Army to claim that the officer performing this parallel function to that of the employee, should not be regarded as an employee! This relates particularly to administrative, financial, social service and public relations appointments."[79]

The tacit assumption in much of this material, that soldiers are "lay," with its concomitant implication that officers are "clergy," has not gone unchallenged. Gordon

---

78. Hodder. "The Development and Use of Lay Leaders." 7.
79. Maxwell, "Shaping the Army of the Future," 5.

Taylor asked in 1990, "Am I alone in disliking the increasing use of such terms as 'lay evangelists' or 'lay-personnel' when referring to non-officers? Is it appropriate to use such terminology when we do not have salvationist clergy or priests? Surely we are all salvationists with a divine commission."[80] The Army's theology of the laity, that all are laity, was not going to go away, but official usage became cemented in place.

John Cleary, Australian Salvation Army soldier, journalist and broadcaster has been concerned that in the "western" Army, the very institution of soldiership is withering away, with increasing numbers of both the "children of the regiment" and of new attenders at Army worship preferring some ambiguous membership status rather than making the lifestyle commitments incumbent on soldiers.

Cleary saw the crisis as resulting in part from the Army's inadequate ecclesiology, with its lack of clarity over the years about the connection between soldiership in the Army and membership of the church. His remedy for this trend was a revitalization of soldiership as special class of membership, with a higher commitment to the War than that of ordinary members. By analogy Cleary suggested soldiership might be the equivalent of the diaconate in the traditional three-fold order of the church.[81] He believed that this would attract the commitment of a new generation looking for "something to live for, something to die for." Certainly the decline of interest in soldiership in some western territories could, extrapolating present trends, eventually lead to it being merely a staging post on the way to officership, much as the "transitional" diaconate has been in the Catholic and Anglican churches until comparatively recently. Cleary's proposal resembles more closely the recovered Catholic institution of the "permanent diaconate."

Another analogy for soldiership apart from the diaconate might be the Third Orders of the Franciscans, Dominicans and Carmelites. These secular tertiaries are bound by promises to a distinctive life-style and have a special interest in the particular focus and charism of their order but pursue ordinary secular vocations and may marry. For Salvationists, evangelism and social service could be postulated as the particular callings of their "order"—although that would in fact be true now of only a minority of soldiers.

Analogies between traditional church categories and Salvation Army terms are at best only approximate, despite the similarities. While these analogies may or may not be entirely appropriate, and whether or not Cleary's proposal implicitly accepts the existence of "orders" of "status" or simply delineates roles within the movement, his solution appears to assume that officers are the equivalent of presbyters/priests.

The confusion between role and status affects soldiers as well as officers. The Salvation Army having inherited from Methodism the sectarian concept of membership, protected by commitments and covenants, there is always a tension between soldiership and simply being a Christian, which in a church setting would derive from baptism. In societies where people are increasingly reluctant to be tied down, such a concept is being questioned.

Quite apart from the officer-role, there are within membership of the Salvation Army degrees of association—Adherent Member, Recruit, Soldier, Local Officer—about

---

80. *Salvationist*, 12 May 1990.
81. Cleary, "Chosen to be a Soldier."

which questions of status arise. "Adherent" was a concept first mooted in 1886.[82] It provided for people to identify with the Salvation Army as their "church" without making any profession of faith, although there too there was local variation—in India profession of faith and abstinence from alcohol were required. Since 2003, people wishing to join the Salvation Army but not wanting to become soldiers can, upon profession of faith, be enrolled as "Adherent Members."[83]

The Salvation Army in the West now appears to be facing more acutely than hitherto the situation outlined by a Wesleyan preacher in 1907: "All the Christian Churches of England today have to deal with the question of their relation to numbers of people who join them in public worship, subscribe to their funds, live honorable lives, but decline to take the definite responsibilities of Church membership."[84] A crisis is faced when external recruitment tails off and endogenous growth is not providing replacement recruits. In the light of the tendency for sects to make less rigorous demands upon their members as they denominationalise, this change in the requirements for "Adherents" could be interpreted in more than one way. It raises the bar for adherents by requiring a profession of faith, but it lowers the bar for Salvationists who wish to belong without embracing the sectarian lifestyle of soldiership, leading some to question the future of soldiership: "Does it lower our standards? Will soldiership survive? Why become a soldier?"[85]

Major David Taylor proposed in 2004 a solution somewhat akin to Cleary's.

> Presently many types of ministry and leadership are only for soldiers [that is, excluding Adherents], deeply threatening the integrity of the "priesthood of all believers" which *Servants Together* seeks to uphold. The Army faces the spectacle of two tiers of membership, in which to be an adherent—a Christian and a member of God's church—is to be a second class member of The Salvation Army, with restricted access to ministry. If we want to work out the consequences of transitioning towards "a Church," it will be more authentic biblically to embrace adherents (with a more helpful name) as full members and to acknowledge soldiership as an order within this branch of the Church, in some ways akin to the Nazarites, with whom Paul identifies on several occasions for example. The only alternative would be to scrap Adherency and keep to being an Order within the Church, a decision that is no longer realistic for us at this stage of our development.[86]

Can a case still be made for seeing the Salvation Army as an "order" within the Church as a whole rather than of any existing denomination of it, as an alternative to the present acquiescence to "denominational" type-casting? David Martin draws attention to the fact that orders in the Catholic Church have provided a domain for Christian *virtuosi*, those with an exceptional vocation. Because Protestantism in theory rejected this

---

82. Paper prepared by Gordon Taylor for leaders at the request of General Larsson in 2003.

83. Larsson, Letter to Territorial Commanders, Officers Commanding, National Commander, International Secretaries and all other members of the General's Consultative Council, 12 September 2003; Minute 2004/IA/05.

84. Gilbert, *Religion and Society*, 198–89.

85. *Horizons*, May–June 2005, 11.

86. Taylor, "Army, Order or Church?" 15.

dual standard for Christians, "in Protestant cultures all men are called to be tertiaries."[87] By "denominationalizing," the process whereby a sect loses its zeal and its members accept for themselves an "ordinary" rather than an "exceptional" spirituality, the sect becomes like the Catholic Church from which it sought to distance itself, and a new elite has to emerge within it. Both Taylor's and Cleary's proposals tacitly acknowledge that this is what has happened to the Salvation Army.[88]

Some Salvationist voices have always been happy to claim the Army as an Order, if not in any formal ecclesiastical sense. Railton, in his life of General Booth, referred to the Salvation Army as "a great Christian Order of devotees out of every nation."[89] Half a century later, Alfred J. Gilliard likewise compared the *Orders and Regulations for Soldiers* with the *Rules for the Third Order of Saint Francis of Assisi*, and referred to the Salvation Army as "a great international Order, created by the Holy Spirit . . . "[90] And Tor Wahlström concluded in 1974 that "the Army is most fittingly to be regarded, not as a church nor as a sect . . . but as an order within the Church."[91]

That this is a live issue is evidenced by the formation in 2015–16 by a number of British and American Salvationists of a new group, "Infinitum," an association of soldiers espousing an exceptional vocation and enrolling its adherents as members of renewal communities rather than simply as individuals. Danielle Strickland's account of this is:

> Infinitum is the name of a community of communities, committed to exploring the depth and breadth of this life and supporting each other on that adventure. Early believers were first called "followers of The Way," such was the distinctiveness and power of their counter cultural lives. Infinitum communities seek to emulate that clarity of life and resultant impact in the places we live, work and worship.[92]

Another description, by Phil Wall, elaborates:

> Infinitum is an Invitation to a Rule of Life. Infinitum ("boundless" in Latin) exists to give expression to William Booth's captivating vision of extravagant grace and transformation around the world . . . In essence it is a global community of believers living a shared rule/way of life—seeking to maximize their individual and shared impact for the Kingdom of God. It weaves intentional discipleship and mission into the everyday rhythms of life, fostering a counter cultural movement of pilgrims, following Jesus in the place/sphere He has called us to live.

---

87. Martin, *Pacifism*, 163, quoted by Hill, *Religious Order*, 15.

88. The process whereby fresh "inner ring" groups are formed as the existing formations become too large and lose their initial purpose can also be seen for example in the British "Privy Council." This was originally the English King's inner circle of advisors, by contrast with the Great Council or Parliament. As membership of the "Privy Council" became wider and more formal, a new inner group described as a "Cabinet" took over its functions. Now that body is likely to be superseded by a "War Cabinet" (in times of war) or "kitchen cabinet," or some other inner circle of the Prime Minister's confidants, while some ministers are "outside cabinet." The Privy Council remains as an honorary distinction, unwieldy and largely ceremonial.

89. Railton, *Booth*, 25.

90. Gilliard, "Catching up with William Booth," 11.

91. Wahlström, "More Sociology of Salvationism," 556.

92. Strickland, http://www.daniellestrickland.com/projects/infinium/, downloaded 7 June 2016.

It has 1 Vision: Following Jesus. 2 Virtues: Loving God and Loving Others. 3. Vows: Surrender, Generosity and Mission.[93]

This model, virtually an Order within an Order, is still what Paul Hiebert describes as a "bounded set," where high thresholds protect the doctrine and mores of the ecclesial body, as against a "centered set," where attention is on message rather than the rules, and all-comers are equally valued.[94] Since that "bounded set" which is the Salvation Army already has officers who are not officers, it is only to be expected that it will have soldiers who are not soldiers!

In Rodney Stark's "religious economy" model, whereby sects which maintain a moderate to high tension with society, making greater demands upon their members but offering higher rewards (in terms of status in this life and felicity in the next), are likely to grow, while denominations which have relaxed that tension and no longer insist that their members "come out from among them" tend to lose market share.[95] The growing churches—tending to be fundamentalist or conservative—mop up those people still attracted by the "bounded set" culture. The comparison with newer conservative bodies suggests further that the growing preference for membership rather than soldiership, with less stringent personal commitments to the organization, can also be seen as indicative of a continuing denominationalizing tendency in the Salvation Army. Perhaps all this may argue that the Salvation Army is losing members in both directions or failing to gain many recruits from either—some preferring a more liberal approach and others gravitating to more conservative bodies.

Comparisons between the Salvation Army and the church lead to one further observation. In both the Salvation Army and the Catholic Church in particular a shortage of vocations to officership or priesthood has, as we have seen, been met by an increase in the number soldiers or laity involved in roles hitherto reserved for commissioned or ordained people. This expansion of ministries in the life of the church has been deplored as a distraction from the laity's real task of witness and service to the world. Pope John Paul II in *Christifideles Laici* n. 13, 1987, warned of the laity "being so strongly interested in Church services and tasks that some fail to become actively engaged in their responsibilities in the professional, social, cultural and political world."[96] This has become a theme, repeated in, for example, the Vatican's *Instruction on Certain Questions Regarding the Collaboration of the Non-Ordained Faithful in the Sacred Ministry of Priests* (15th August 1997).

Similar anxieties have been expressed about the "clericalisation of the laity" in the Salvation Army. The difference between the church and the Salvation Army lies in the fact that the Army does not in theory reserve spiritual ministry and leadership roles for a sacerdotal class. The similarity lies in the fact that in practice, because of its hierarchical structure and attribution of status to officers, the Army has tended to behave in the same way as the church, and change in this area therefore occasions similar tensions.

---

93. Wall, https://s]avn.tv/savn-chat/Infinitum, downloaded 7 June 2016.
94. Hiebert, *Mission and Renewal of the Church*.
95. Stark and Fink, *Acts of Faith*, 193–217.
96. Ormerod "Mission and Ministry in the Wake of Vatican II."

A VOICE IN COUNCIL

What part then do soldiers have in the direction of the war? Norman Murdoch observed that Booth's assumption of total control ran counter to the democratization of western society. Hattersley suggested the reason was to do with class—middle-class Methodism was becoming democratic while working-class Salvationism was still autocratic.[97] It can be argued that the Army's polity has not been able to respond so easily to subsequent social change, partly because of the absence of any formal representative mechanisms. Soldiers simply did not have any voice in council. This was remarked upon as early as 1898 by the perceptive Salvationist John Hollins:

> We have scarcely learned to use our own eyes, to examine and judge for ourselves, and have very little idea of the true proportions, the strength and weakness, the possibilities and dangers of the Salvation Army. What may be called "public opinion" has no existence amongst us. There is no open discussion of matters affecting the welfare of the organisation, such as we find in other religious bodies . . . The Salvation Army, like every other institution, is imperfect, but, under the domination of the military idea and in the name of loyalty, we appear to have all agreed to keep silence concerning the disquieting symptoms and weak places existing in it. This is unfortunate, and may in itself constitute one of our gravest perils . . . [T]he Salvation Army is sound enough and strong enough to profit by an honest exchange of opinion amongst its members in their councils and publications.[98]

From time to time other soldiers expressed concerns, though like Hollins they had to find "outside" platforms for their views, which meant that "honest exchange of opinion" was minimal. In a searching critique in 1967, Geoffrey Driver also reflected that

> Over the years a slow process of limited democratization has taken place, though it is clearly not radical enough to meet the needs of the present situation.
>
> There seem to be no signs yet of any radical reversal in the trend whereby orders come from above and innovations are reducible to perking up traditional Salvationist activities.[99]

An irony is that the first non-officers to be offered some structure for influence were also non-Salvationists. William Booth had engaged the assistance and advice of a small group of wealthy supporters in Christian Mission days but their role was phased out in a few years. In the late 1930s an Advisory Board was established in China, and this precedent was adopted with increasing enthusiasm in the United States in the 1940s and 50s, and spread then to other western countries.[100] The chief role of such boards was to give financial support and fund-raising help; they were strictly "advisory" so far as policy was concerned. Except for their occasional service on such boards when their social

---

97. Hattersley, *Blood & Fire*, 225.
98. Hollins, "Note of Warning," 436.
99. Driver, "Booth's Boots," 10.
100. The earliest to which I have found reference was set up in Nanking, China in the 1930s, chaired by Major Yin Hung Shun. Yee, *Good Morning China*, 174.

influence and financial status were considered commensurate with the role, soldiers were not invited to express an opinion at all.

Philip Needham suggested in 1965 that, "if the Army's soldiery were to become once more a truly Christian lay movement, the Army's official power structure would change accordingly . . . There is a danger, of course, that the Army's official leaders will have identified themselves so closely with the Army's power structures that reform would meet with misunderstanding and even active opposition."[101] Needham thus accurately foresaw a significant potential challenge to General Cox's reforms of more than fifty years' later.

Nevertheless, in the "Western world" Army, the second half of the twentieth century saw attempts to accommodate to the more democratic temper of the times with some consultative machinery on both local and territorial level. Corps Councils were the outcome, in the late 1950s.[102] These bodies consisted of the senior local officers of a corps, plus a few other soldiers or adherents or supporters, chaired by the corps officer. Personnel are not elected, but appointed by the corps officer, the names needing to be approved by the divisional commander. A council's role was advisory only; decision-making was the prerogative of the officer.[103] Decisions, or recommendations, were by consensus, not by voting. The system at least provided a statutory forum where matters concerning the corps could be discussed.

In New Zealand in the 1960s Commissioner A.J. Gilliard convened a successful series of local officers' residential councils—as Cyril Bradwell wrote, Gilliard was rare in believing that it might be important to discover what the rank and file was thinking.[104] However, his successors did not institutionalize this development, and the leading "laity" were left feeling that they could keep on saying the same things but that no one would do anything about them. In an article on "Laos—the Whole People of God," New Zealander Max Cresswell appealed against the attitude "which says, 'If you want to influence Army affairs, then you should become an officer.'" He urged that "soldiers should be enabled to make their views known on any subject or plan of action, and that existing boards and councils should be enlarged to include suitable lay Salvationists, including those bodies responsible for officer appointments."[105]

A Canadian initiative in 1966 was the Advisory Council of Salvation Army Laymen, or ACSAL, which operated on both regional and national levels. The territorial commander, Commissioner Clarence Wiseman, characterized this development in an *Officer* article as "Coming of Age—A study of Salvation Army Soldiership in the latter twentieth century."[106] Wiseman attributed ACSAL itself to "lay" initiative. It "grew out of the concern of a few soldiers who felt that some method should be developed so that the Army could benefit from the knowledge and experience of Salvationists hold-

---

101. Needham, *New Soldiers*, Spring 1965, 44.

102. *Orders and Regulations for Governing a Corps Council* were issued by IHQ, 21 January 1959.

103. Compare with Roman Catholic Canon 536, stipulating a consultative role only for parish councils.

104. Bradwell, *Touched with Splendour*, 149.

105. Cresswell, "Laos—The Whole People of God," 3.

106. Wiseman, "Coming of Age."

ing positions of responsibility in the secular world."[107] This example was followed in a number of other territories. In time Wiseman concluded that the separation of officers from non-officers "was in violation of a very important theological principle... To have segregated groupings is really in violation of the concept of the priesthood of all believers." He met with ACSAL groups in Canada and persuaded them that this was the case and "thereafter Officers came officially on to the ACSAL."

Some did not endure, however; their existence depended on whether a territorial commander valued or did not value their advice. Even in the land of its birth ACSAL was dispensed with after thirty years, although new consultative processes were developed subsequently.[108] Cyril Bradwell likewise referred to the abolition of the New Zealand ACSAL in the late 1990s, as "regrettable and somewhat arbitrary, with no clear rationale promulgated."[109] Such losses illustrate how vulnerable innovations might be when lacking any constitutional base. Peter Price refers to the same vulnerability in the Catholic Church: "The consultative structures of the Church are still only 'recommended' and 'advisory.' They do not necessarily facilitate Lay participation in real decision-making. Such participation as well as its authority are dependent on the individual Bishop or Parish Priest, and may be dismantled at will."[110]

In 1969, Commissioner Carey, USA national commander, announced that the National Layman's Commission was being disbanded; territorial and perhaps divisional commissions were being established instead to allow for broader representation and more frequent meetings. He noted that any recommendations of national import could be referred to the national Commissioners' Conference, "so that the lay voice will still be heard in the top policy body of the Salvation Army in the USA."[111] Perhaps the echo of a voice.

In 1978 the USA Western territory initiated a Territorial Laymen and Officers' Council. In 1989 a significant USA National Forum was held, with both officers and soldiers involved.[112] The British *Salvationist* reported in 1990 that an Advisory Council had been set up for the territory, mainly made up from soldiery chosen from each of the territory's twenty-one divisions. It described this as the "latest move in the territory's consultative process, which includes Corps Councils and Divisional Advisory Councils."[113] In more recent times the Canadian territory has been introducing wider consultative structures. The New Zealand territory held a series of consultative meetings in order to generate a new strategic mission plan in the early 2000s, but the experiment did not give rise to any permanent structures or protocols.

Another body involving both officer and non-officer representation was the Public Questions Board, set up in various territories from the mid-1950s.[114] This body, now

107. Wiseman, *Burning in My Bones*, 166.
108. Pedlar, *Horizons*, May–June 2005, 11.
109. Bradwell, *Touched with Splendour*, 319.
110. Price, "Vatican II: End of a Clerical Church (1)."
111. Proceedings of 1969 Commissioners' Conference, 27.
112. Gariepy, *History*, VIII, 184.
113. *Salvationist*, 20 January 1990, 1, 4.
114. Minutes in New Zealand Salvation Army Archives.

known as the Moral and Social Issues Council, was able to respond to requests by the territorial commander for comment on social issues and proposed legislative changes by government. An International MASIC was established by General Clifton in 2007, in association with an International Social Justice Unit based in New York. These ventures are described at greater length in Chapter 9.

Background study material circulated before the 1991 International Conference of Leaders included a section on "Making the Best Use of Soldiery." Recommendations were requested on, amongst other things, "The need for soldiers and local officers to have greater involvement in the decision-making processes of the Army." The paper also suggested that "the danger we are in today is that we are rapidly becoming an Army of, by, and for officers . . . Soldiers should be included in the consultative process at corps, divisional and territorial levels."[115] Nothing came of that at the time but shortly after his election as General in 1994, Paul Rader also expressed his support for consultative leadership. He expressed his intention to "encourage the active participation of lay Salvationists in the whole area of the Army's policy development and implementation of our mission."[116]

Some moves were forced upon the organization by outside pressures. Following a fraud case in 1992 when some funds of the Salvation Army in the United Kingdom were illegally invested offshore and disappeared from sight (fortunately to be wholly retrieved some years later after painstaking detective work), the Charity Commissioners insisted on some reforms in the territory's financial systems.[117] Qualified non-officer Salvationists and non-Salvationist experts were appointed along with officers as Directors of the Army's Trustee Company.[118] The territory may however have treated this as a formality to satisfy a legal requirement rather than permit it a true governance role.

Under General André Cox's reforms of governance, the principle is intended to be extended more widely. Cox referred to structural issues in a 2013 article shortly after taking office. He quoted Gary Hamel, author of *The Future of Management*, as writing, "Right now, your company has twenty-first century Internet-enabled business processes, mid-twentieth century management processes, all built atop nineteenth century management principles." The General commented, "I think we can all draw parallels for The Salvation Army from that statement."[119]

The autocratic model remained the norm for nearly 140 years, until in 2014 General Cox embarked upon the pursuit of a more focused and accountable structure, separating the roles of Governance and Management. His reforms, to be introduced over a number of years, do not provide for election to office (other than to the office of General, as has been the case since 1929), so the Salvation Army continues to be led by "a self-perpetuating oligarchy," in John Coutts's phrase.[120] As already mentioned, they do how-

---

115. 1991 International Conference of Leaders, Syndicated sessions background study material, 54–55. International Heritage Centre Archives, AD/5/1/14/3.

116. *War Cry* (USA) 21 January 1995, 7.

117. Gariepy, *History*, VIII, 278–79.

118. *Salvationist*, 2 November, 1996, 8–9.

119. Cox, "Immeasurably More," 5.

120. Coutts, *Salvationists*, 26.

ever envisage the determination of policy at all levels by majority vote in Governance Councils made up not only of commissioned officers but also including soldiers and independent non-salvationists co-opted for the sake of their particular expertise. Governance, impact measurement, finance and child-protection are the four main areas to be addressed by the project. These provisions are intended to bring the Army's processes within the legal requirements for charitable institutions in most jurisdictions, and also to promote transparency and accountability in the exercise of power within the organization. One caveat is that the successful implementation of such a plan really cannot be secured by autocratic fiat; only broadly-based buy-in and ownership at all levels, seen as indispensable by development agencies, will ultimately secure success. Such a process takes time; it must be hoped that time will be available. If successful, such measures ought to have far-reaching effects, representing the most significant modification of the Salvation Army's ecclesial structures since 1929, if not since 1878.

This does not exhaust the scope of the Accountability reforms; their extension to such matters as outcomes, key performance indicators, and impact measurement should enable the Salvation Army's assiduous collection of statistics to be invested in its mission as well as its fund-raising.[121] As always with such measures, the burden of compliance needs also to be monitored to ensure that it does not degenerate into a box-ticking exercise or stultify grass-roots effort. Every well-intentioned step forward comes with the risk of steps backward.

But in all this, the Salvation Army's ecclesiology nevertheless continues faithful to its founders' pragmatic principles. Rather than first establishing scriptural and traditional principles and precedents and then seeking to derive a structure from them, the founders simply did whatever it took to advance the War. As we have seen, the end result included the creation of an episcopal structure superficially resembling that of some other denominations which *do* claim to derive their first principles from Scripture and Tradition. Sociology often has the last word in the affairs of men. Even the most recent Salvationist essay in ecclesiology, the Accountability Movement, employs Scripture and tradition in support roles rather than deriving its schema from them. For example, the description of "Faith-Based Facilitation" proposed in the publication *Journey of Renewal*, appears indistinguishable from any other facilitative process, except that, presumably, those engaged in it will be people of faith.[122] This is intended as an observation, not as a criticism. The Army is possibly none the worse off for utilizing contemporary business concepts to ground its ecclesiology—after all, church creeds still employ categories derived from pre-Christian Greek philosophy to describe the nature of God.

---

121. Garland, "Impact Measurement," 8.
122. Salvation Army, *Journey of Renewal*, 74–80.

4

The Ecclesiology of The Salvation Army 3: The Role of Women

"Some of my best men are women"
—ATTRIBUTED TO WILLIAM BOOTH

Like many sayings attributed to public figures, this remark may be apocryphal, or part of the Army's oral tradition. Jenty Fairbank found a similar quote from Booth in *The War Cry* of 4th January 1887. When Booth was speaking in New York on 7th December 1886, "a gentleman enquired, 'Why do you have women leaders?' To this the General replied with a bland smile, 'Because they often lead better than men.'"[1]

It may seem odd to take one third of the space allotted to the Salvation Army's ecclesiology and devote it to the matter of gender equality. Nevertheless, that probably fairly apportions its significance; this is often seen as the most distinctive feature of the Army by non-Salvationist writers. The Army has usually explained its stand on gender equality in theological terms, but sociologists have seen its championing of women's rights as yet another aspect of sectarian protest of the disinherited. James A. Beckford, relating "the question of gender relations in religious communities" to "the dynamic between individuals and collectives," observes that "religious movements permit and encourage some dramatically extreme forms of gendered social relations and innovative approaches to sexuality among their members. [Some] seem to favour a heightened form of subordination of women to men. At the other extreme there are religious movements . . . that have aspired towards . . . unusually high degrees of equality between male and female followers in some respects."[2]

While the Army was not the first to accept the ministry of women on equal terms with that of men—the Quakers and Bible Christians were earlier, not to mention the primitive church of course—equality of the sexes has always been one of the Army's

---

1. *Salvationist*, 19 February 1994, 12.
2. Beckford, *Social Theory and Religion*, 181.

boasts. "In the Army," wrote Florence Booth, "we know no distinction, because of sex, which is calculated to limit either a woman's influence or her authority, or her opportunity to serve, by sacrifice, the Kingdom of God."[3]

Over many years, Salvationists regarded the struggles of other denominations over this question with assumed superiority. Bramwell Booth said, "Few things the Army stands for have been more bitterly assailed than this—that woman is on an equality with man. Even yet many of the civil laws in the West make differences against her, although many have been altered. Many of the churches still refuse to allow her to witness for Christ in their 'sacred' buildings and their privileged conventicles. But, in general, the western world has changed its views, and very soon the religious section of it will have to follow or be hopelessly left behind."[4] Of the furor following the ordination of eleven women by the American Protestant Episcopal Church in 1974, the editor of *The Officer* wrote, "Salvationists may be forgiven for asking, in response to such an item of news . . . What is all the fuss about? We settled the issue long ago."[5] In fact such smugness was not always justified, and on two grounds.

The first ground was theological, in that Salvation Army commentators did not always understand that the debate had moved on; by the twentieth century the point at issue was not whether women could exercise public ministry, but whether they could be priests. The Army's tendency to overlook the distinction probably arose from the sketchy nature of its own theology of ministry. A later editor acknowledged this point, noting that "in one sense it might seem that we are not concerned with such an argument. The Salvationist stands outside all controversies between sacramental Christians . . . "[6] (Although he did go on to make the point that any officer, of whatever sex, is competent to administer whatever means of grace Salvationists do practice.) Commenting on the 1992 decision of the Church of England General Synod to ordain women, *The Salvationist* editor noted that "We ought not to use the moment to boast . . . There are too many differences between Army officership and Anglican priesthood to make the comparison very useful."[7]

The second reason is that the Army's practice has not always matched its precepts. In fact, over much of its history the Army appeared to retreat from its early promise of gender equality, certainly relative to the general movement of Western society, and even by its own standards. This view was held by Mrs General Marie Wahlström, who referred to the equality of sexes in the Army's early days when speaking at the 1984 International Conference of Leaders. She went on to ask, "Would it not be correct to say that today this is rather the exception than the rule. If so, when and how was the development reversed? Has the development of the Army begun to move in the opposite direction to the general trend in society, where women are increasingly active in every field . . . ?"[8] Or Mrs Commissioner Marjorie Gauntlett, wife of the Chief of the Staff, who claimed

3. Florence Booth. "Place and Power of Women," 509–510.
4. Booth, *Talks with Officers*, 16.
5. *Officer*, November 1974, 527.
6. *Officer*, January 1979, 1–2.
7. *Salvationist*, 28 November 1992, 2.
8. Wahlström, "The Place and Position of the Woman Officer." 2.

in an interview in the same year that "The role of women in The Salvation Army seems to be going backwards—it's less now than when we started!"[9] Or Mrs Commissioner Marjorie Hodder, on her installation as National President of Women's Organizations in the United States in 1993, observed that "among the twenty-two officers holding the principal positions of leadership in the USA today, not one is a woman."[10]

Such concern was not new: Mrs General Bramwell Booth wrote in 1913 that

> Sometimes I am almost tempted to feel that the progress of woman's position in the SA might be described in the words of the Irishman who wrote to a friend from one of the battlefields of the American Civil War, "We are advancing backwards and the enemy is retreating on to us!"[11]

In 1930 Staff-Captain Mary MacFarlane of Australia had claimed that

> to many of the younger thinking women-Officers of The Army, this question of equality of treatment and opportunity for men and women in the Army is a burning one. Many of them work on Headquarters where they see and hear much that makes them ask—"ARE EQUAL STANDARDS MAINTAINED FOR MEN AND WOMEN OFFICERS ACCORDING TO THE ARMY'S CONSTITUTION?" And with no uncertain voice they are answering "No!"[12]

In some ways the experience of women officers parallels that of soldiers in the dynamic of Salvation Army history—beginning with a claim to equality, then experiencing a steady eclipse in role and respect, and then a slow and even tentative reassertion of significance. The cultural conditioning is about power and control, which is the shadow side of orders in the church. This is not any way to take away from the Army its significant achievement in gender equality. Women played a tremendous part in making and maintaining the Army, in a way that was truly counter-cultural for much of its history. At the same time we need to hear the voices of women who spoke of another version of its history.

There were precedents for the stand taken by the Salvation Army: John Wesley allowed women lay-preachers, though he did not give them a role in government and after his death the Methodist Conference forbade preaching by women. The Bible Christians, a Methodist revival movement in 1815 allowed women preachers but they eventually disallowed them as well. The Quakers had the principle of equality of sexes and some notable women preachers, but strictly speaking they had no clergy anyway. It was the independent American woman evangelist Phoebe Palmer who lit Catherine Booth's flame. From those antecedents we can trace the rise and fall and rise again of gender equality in the Salvation Army.

Catherine Booth was the leading example of the role of women in the Army, having been a freelance preacher of considerable reputation from the early 1860s. Although she never held a rank or an independent command in her own right, Catherine Booth was in the center of the Army's counsels as long as she lived and was known then and later as

---

9. *New Frontier*, 30 June 1984, 1.
10. *War Cry* (USA) 23 October 1993, 19.
11. *Field Officer*, March 1913, 84.
12. *Staff Review*, October 1930, 339.

the "Mother of the Salvation Army." The movement's ethos reflects not only the force of her influence but also her husband's support for her position.

Catherine's first essay on the rights of women, written at the age of 21, was a rebuttal of rather patronizing and derogatory words about woman as a moral being, in a sermon by the Reverend David Thomas in a Congregational Church.[13] The following year a connexional magazine article signed "C.M." (Catherine Mumford, her maiden name) claimed, "It is a significant fact that in the most cold, formal and worldly churches of the day we find the least female agency."[14]

Shortly before her marriage she addressed one of her long, instructional letters to her intended, about teetotalism (which he had adopted at her persuasion), and the equality of women with men in ministry. He responded briefly, "I would not stop a woman preaching on any account. I would not encourage one to begin. You should preach if you felt moved thereto; felt equal to the task. I would not stay you if I had the power to do so. Altho' I should not like it . . . "[15] This did not mean that Catherine saw herself in this preaching role at the time. As a young married woman when she was invited to address a Church leaders' meeting in the Circuit, "Of course I declined . . . I don't know what they can be thinking of."[16]

Her next step, ten years after her private rebuke to David Thomas, was more public. In 1859, Sunderland minister Arthur Rees attacked the preaching of Mrs Phoebe Palmer, then touring England, later publishing his sermon as a pamphlet. Catherine sprang to the lady's defense with a pamphlet of her own, the vigorous and erudite *Female Preaching*, which drew heavily on Mrs Palmer's own arguments.[17] It was not until the following year, however, that she herself told her husband, "I want to say a word," and preached at Gateshead's Bethesda Chapel on Whitsunday 1860. She continued to fill churches for the following twenty-eight years, and William *did* like it. In the early years of their freelance ministry, the family sometimes survived on Catherine's earnings from platform and pulpit.

Within weeks of Catherine's first sermon, William fell ill and for the following nine weeks Catherine filled his preaching engagements in the Circuit. In a letter to William, who was away recuperating at a health spa, she wrote, "Don't forget to pray for me. I have borne the weight of circuit matters to an extent I could not have believed possible and have been literally the 'Superintendent.'"[18] After the founding of the Christian Mission similar situations arose; in 1872 Catherine ran the Mission for six months while William was having a breakdown from over-work.[19] That the Booths were seen by others as equal in ministry is suggested by the foundation stone of Methodist Church at Ninfield East,

---

13. Letter to Rev. David Thomas, in 1850; Bramwell-Booth, *Catherine Booth*, 49–52.
14. Coutts, *In Good Company*, 64.
15. Bramwell-Booth, *Catherine Booth*, 143.
16. Catherine Booth, letter to her mother in 1858, quoted in Bramwell-Booth, *Catherine Booth*, 180–81.
17. Reprinted in various forms, including as a chapter in Catherine Booth's *Practical Religion*, 131–67. Later titled *Female Ministry*.
18. Bramwell-Booth, *Catherine Booth*, 190.
19. Sandall, *History*, I, 144–45.

Sussex, laid in July 1871 "... by Mrs. Booth, assisted by the Rev. Wm. Booth, Founders of the Christian Mission."[20]

Encouraged by Catherine's example others joined forces. In 1870 Mrs Collingridge, who in 1868 was the first person employed by the Mission, was superintendent of the Shoreditch Circuit and presided at meetings, becoming the first woman to hold office in the Mission as well. She was the usual preacher at the People's Mission Hall, Whitechapel Road, and when her health broke down, was replaced by Mrs Reynolds. In 1873 Miss Billups and Miss Funnell were supply evangelists while Miss Walker and Miss Sutton assisted at Whitechapel and Poplar respectively.[21] From 1874 however, evangelists were not merely on "supply" but stationed in charge of their local mission stations. Of the twenty-seven evangelists early in 1875, eight were women, but none of these were "in command."[22] However, there was a shortage of evangelists for the expanding work and, encouraged by Railton, Booth considered appointing more women, and in charge.

The 1875 Conference, over the reservations of some evangelists and even of Mrs Booth,[23] appointed Annie Davis in charge of the Barking station in what Railton described as a "daring experiment." Evangelist Abram Lamb resigned over this development.[24] Her success led to women evangelists being in the forefront of the great expansion by the end of the decade. Sisters Rachel and Louise Agar opened fire on Felling on Tyne in March 1878, the printer dubbing them "Hallelujah Lasses" on their posters. Booth or Railton wrote, "We have commenced operations on the Tyne at Felling, where a Mr Sharp . . . importuned us to send a sister. We sent two, and such has already been their success that we are sending two more, with whose help they will be able immediately to seize another town."[25] Within twelve months there were twenty-two stations, forty-seven officers and more than 3,000 members in the Tyne district.[26]

In Coventry Mrs Caroline Reynolds and Mrs Honor Burrell led the charge. While Mrs Burrell was a widow, Mrs Reynolds was accompanied by her husband, who was not employed by the Mission. At Salisbury, Mrs Sarah Sayers was assisted by sixteen-year-old Henry Edmonds.[27] Of ninety-one officers in the field in 1878, forty-one were women.[28] By 1880, women were in charge of forty-six out of one hundred and eighteen corps.[29]

Mrs Reynolds, now widowed, went on to open fire in Ireland in 1880, and in this appointment became first woman divisional officer.[30] Mrs Major Harriet Lawley served briefly as divisional officer for the Channel Islands in 1887 as a married woman (baby in arms) but had to give up that role for family reasons—her husband, John Lawley, worked

---

20. Harris, *Salvationist*, 20 May 2000, 24.
21. *Christian Mission Magazine*, September 1873, 136.
22. Boardman, "Officership—a Functional Ministry," 517.
23. Booth, *Echoes and Memories*, 178–79.
24. Bramwell-Booth, *Catherine Booth*, 263.
25. *Christian Mission Magazine*, May 1878, 122.
26. Sandall, *History*, II, 7.
27. Sandall, Ibid., I, 177, 214–15.
28. Larsson, *My Best Men Are Women*, 17.
29. Walker, "Proclaiming Women's Right to Preach," 22.
30. Sandall, *History*, II, 18–19.

in the Candidates Department but then became ADC to William Booth.[31] Captain Polly Ashton was appointed "England's first woman Divisional Officer" only in 1890.[32]

Bramwell Booth paid tribute to the examples of his sister Catherine as pioneer and leader of the Army in France and Switzerland from 1881 and of Hannah Ouchterlony as pioneer and leader in Sweden from 1883, as showing "that there was no adequate reason for withholding the higher Commands from women."[33]

The role of women was enshrined in the Constitution of the Christian Mission, Section XII of which stated,

> Female Preachers—As it is manifest from the Scripture of the Old and especially the New Testament that God has sanctioned the labours of Godly women in His Church; Godly women possessing the necessary gifts and qualifications, shall be employed as preachers itinerant or otherwise and class leaders and as such shall have appointments given to them on the preacher's plan; and they shall be eligible for any office, and to speak and vote at all official meetings.[34]

The Orders and Regulations for Salvation Army Staff Officers followed this up with,

> One of the leading principles upon which the Army is based is the right of women to have the right to an equal share with men in the great work of publishing Salvation to the world . . . She may hold any position of authority or power in the Army from that of a Local Officer to that of the General. Let it therefore be understood that women are eligible for the highest commands—indeed, no woman is to be kept back from any position of power or influence merely on account of her sex . . . Woman must be treated as equal with men in all the intellectual and social relationships of life.[35]

Although the reiterated gender-exclusive language of the Orders and Regulations strikes a discord in this age, for the nineteenth century the Army's stance was radical. An introductory note to the *Orders and Regulations for Field Officers* of 1886 and subsequently also safeguarded this commitment:

> In the Army men and women are alike eligible for all ranks authorities and duties, all positions being open to both alike. In these Orders, therefore, the words "man," "he," or "his" must be understood to refer to persons of either sex, unless otherwise indicated or evidently impossible.[36]

At intervals William Booth promoted the principle of equality. For example, in 1901 he wrote a "Letter to the Soldiers of the Salvation Army" on "Salvation Women," about the "Position and Opportunities possessed by Woman in the Army."

> Shall we tell them (young girls in the Army) that they are to grow up and settle down to the idea that the back-door drudgery of the Corps is all that lies before

31. Carpenter, *Lawley*, 96.
32. Fairbank, "Angles on Salvation Army History," 10.
33. Booth, *Echoes and Memories*, 181.
34. *Christian Mission Magazine*, July 1877, 182–83.
35. *Orders and Regulations for Staff Officers*, 16–17.
36. *Orders and Regulations for Field Officers*, 1886, [iv].

them?—that they can Give and Collect and do Tea Meetings and Harvest Festivals? That they can have Husbands and Children, and keep their Homes in order with a little singing, and a prayer, and a testimony or two thrown in now and then? Or shall we say to them, "Come along and take your stand by our side on the Salvation Army platform?"

Quoting from *The Orders and Regulations for Staff Officers* he reiterated

> Let it therefore be understood that no Woman is to be kept back from any position of power or influence merely on account of her sex.[37]

Booth returned to the subject in November with another letter, "More about Women's Rights," in which he urged women to take the initiative and claim their place.[38] In another letter on the subject, in 1908, to be read out in every corps on the 23rd of August that year, he stated that "woman is equal to man."[39]

Women went on to provide more than half of the officer strength of the Army, since over the years there have usually been more single women officers than single men, and in the case of married couples, both partners have usually been officers. In the earlier years the Army's ranks offered a greater opportunity for independence than most available for women. Horridge notes that "by the 1890s, more women Methodists and Anglicans were becoming officers, for the Army still offered a greater degree of equality than available elsewhere in religious societies."[40] In every part of the world women became the shock troops of salvation.

Some achieved some celebrity beyond the ranks; thousands of others have worked unsung for many years in hard and lonely places. Of single women officers Bramwell Booth wrote that, "Those women are worthy successors of the Apostles. Their devotion to the interests of others, their kindness, their patient toil, their enduring zeal, their humble following in the footsteps of their Master have done much to make The Salvation Army what it is." Booth, while not claiming any special virtue for the single life, noted with approbation that many single women officers chose to remain single rather than to "marry out of the work."[41] Reportedly pressure was sometimes put on women not to marry: William Booth forbade Evangeline to marry, saying to her suitor, "You and Eva are both too important to The Salvation Army as individual leaders to be tied up together."[42]

THE GLASS CEILING

There was another side to all this. Whatever the Army's aspirations to equality, women were not treated equally with their brethren in many respects. The phenomenon of the glass ceiling was painfully apparent to women officers long before Ann Morrison named

37. *Field Officer*, September 1901, 422–24.
38. *Field Officer*, November 1901, 513–14.
39. William Booth, in *Leeds Evening Post*, 24 August 1908. Quoted by Morris, "Female Ministry, Equality and the Salvation Army."
40. Horridge, *Origins*, 225.
41. Booth, *Servants of All*, 109.
42. Troutt, *General Was a Lady*, 78.

the problem in the American corporate world. Mary MacFarlane, already quoted, gave examples from Australia of women being given less significant appointments than men and deprived of opportunities, their relegation to tea-making and sandwich-serving while men junior to themselves were given recognition and authority, and the dearth of women in executive roles and on Boards.

Lt. Commissioner Mrs Povlsen, commenting on MacFarlane's article, quoted "a lady doctor who . . . declared her opinion that a woman officer would have to be practically abnormally gifted in order to get the same place in the ranks as an average man."[43] A similar comment was made in a 1948 radio lecture on "The woman officer of the Salvation Army" by Dr Laura Petrie of Sweden.[44] (Doubtless the same doctor.) Major Jenty Fairbank held the same view forty years later: "For a woman to be recognised as equal to a man she must show exceptional qualities—far surpassing his."[45]

Internationally, there has always been a tiny minority of senior women leaders, and this was true even in the days when there were far more women officers than at present. The 1908 *Year Book* listed only two women as territorial commanders, while Mrs Bramwell Booth was the executive head of women's social work, assisted by Commissioner Adelaide Cox. In 1920 there were three women territorial commanders—all of them Booths—and two other women commissioners. Soundings in the *Year Book* at ten year intervals between 1910 and 2000 reveal that the highest number of women commissioners, territorial commanders or officers commanding was six, in 1990; numbers mostly fluctuated between two and four.

An analysis of High Council membership provides the following figures:[46]

Year	Number attending	Number of women included
1929	63	7 (5 of them Booths)
1934	47	4 (3 of them Booths)
1939	55	2 (both Booths)
1946	50	3 (1 Booth remaining)
1954	48	3
1963	49	3
1969	45	2
1974	40	3
1977	41	3
1981	44	2
1986	46	5
1993	50	3

43. *Staff Review*, October, 1930, 348.
44. Larsson, *My Best Men*, 83.
45. Fairbank, "And Then There Were None," 408.
46. Coutts, *History* VI, 85–88, 123–26, 155–58, 283–86; Coutts, *History* VII, 70–72, 154–56, 241–43, 294–96, 324–26; Gariepy, *History*, VIII, 70–71, 134–35, 285–86, 300–02.

It may be noted that at most of the above High Councils the women representatives have included the leader of the women's social services in the Great Britain, plus a handful of women TCs of "missionary countries" and the occasional head of an IHQ department, but very rarely the TC of a "Western" territory. After 1994 the criteria for attendance were altered as commissioners' wives became commissioners in their own right and therefore eligible to be called to attend the High Council.

Only three out of the twenty Generals to date have been women: Evangeline Booth 1934–39, Eva Burrows 1986–93, and Linda Bond 2011–13. In the history of the Salvation Army in New Zealand, for example, there have been only three women divisional commanders: Lt. Colonel Edna Grice in 1955–58, Lt. Colonel Raeline Savage, a married woman, in 1995–98, and Major Heather Rodwell 2010–12.[47] There have been no women territorial commanders or chief secretaries in New Zealand—or in the majority of territories.

In most countries the number of single woman officers, once the backbone of both field (corps) and social work, has steadily diminished. This has been partly because of the "officers marry only officers" policy, and partly because of a decline in the number of unmarried candidates. In New Zealand, for example, analysis of appointments given in the annual *Disposition of Forces* shows that in 1918 there were 142 single women officers out of a total of 408, or 34.8 percent of the total. 80 out of 142 social officers were single women (25 were men, 25 were their wives, and 12 were single men.) Single women provided 54 out of 146 field officers (45 of these were men, with 45 wives, and there were two single men.) This means that about a third of all corps were led by single women, usually appointed in pairs, at that time. While single women have usually been appointed to smaller corps, especially in recent decades, a minority have held large field commands. Two women (Ellen Smith and Florence Birks) were leading the largest Auckland corps in 1918. By contrast, in 1998 there were sixteen single women amongst a total of 380 officers—4.2 percent. Of these, there were nine single women in social work out of a total of 95 officers, and seven out of a total of 191 field officers, leading about 6 percent of corps. In 2006, just four New Zealand corps were led by three single women, working on their own (one being responsible for two centers). In New Zealand in 2012, 26 out of 300 active officers were women on their own; that is, 8.6 percent of active officers.

Richard Pears gives the figure of 168 single women out of 1,184 field officers in the United Kingdom territory in 1996, with no women divisional commanders amongst the eighteen officers in that position.[48] The decline in the number of women officers in top leadership positions reflects the decline in the number of single women officers, as well as the Army's reluctance to give independent senior commands to married women. Single officers are always more "appointable" and the majority of single officers are women. Insecurity of tenure is a disincentive to both recruitment and retention.

Gender equality has probably always been resisted to some extent within the Army. Bramwell Booth recalled that this had been the case from the beginning. "Some of the men who had been converted in the Mission . . . as soon as they found themselves in office and with a certain influence in their own societies, demurred when women were

---

47. New Zealand *Disposition of Forces*, for the relevant years.
48. Pears, "Towards a Theology of Salvation Army Officership," 60.

placed beside them in similar positions . . . To place a woman in charge of one of these Societies . . . involved a new departure . . . Some of the leading Evangelists . . . were opposed to anything of this kind."[49] Catherine Bramwell-Booth believed that "many Salvation Army officers have accepted the Booths' ruling as to the position of women in the movement rather because it was their ruling than because the principle had been either understood or approved." She also suggested that Bramwell Booth was in the end deposed because his subordinates feared that he had nominated a woman to succeed him.[50] Alas, it was probably not because they feared women in general, but a *particular* woman—Bramwell's daughter, Catherine herself, whose name was believed to be in the sealed envelope. They did, after all, elect Evangeline Booth five years later. On the other hand, Evangeline was then sixty-nine years of age, and they knew they would not have her forever, whereas Catherine was only forty-six at the time. Had they known she would live to be one hundred and four, no doubt that would have strengthened their resolve.

Colonel Julius Nielsen of Czechoslovakia/Hungary, invited by the editor to comment on MacFarlane's article, questioned

> the wisdom of women-Officers being made Divisional Commanders, or being given similar positions . . . Take the highest positions in the Army—those of the General, and the Chief of the Staff: surely every one of us wishes to see only a strong man in those positions . . . Let me speak quite frankly. We all know . . . that there are times when a woman needs to be alone in quietness and certainly not on the public platform. Her whole mental outlook and ability are influenced by the condition in to which women come at such times.[51]

One can only imagine the feelings of the soon-to-be-General, Evangeline Booth, on reading this delicate allusion.

At grass roots level, male chauvinism has continued to be alive and well. When Captain Minnie Rowell was appointed to Fremantle, Australia, in the 1890s "the soldiers let her know; we don't want women officers. You can't manage our corps."[52] In his memoirs Cyril Bradwell records the diffidence of Adjutant Edna Grice when appointed as commanding officer of the Linwood corps in 1938, "in that male dominant decade," when "lassie officers had not commanded the corps since before the beginning of the century."[53] Richard Pears in his 1996 thesis says that "anecdotal evidence gathered from dialogue with soldiers over recent years coupled to the comments of the interview group (of officers) clearly suggests that Corps in fact do not really want single women officers as their leaders . . . it is not unreasonable to suggest that the autocratic structure of the Army, which enables the officer appointment system to function, has also been instrumental in maintaining women officers in ministry. Had there been a membership-based selection system it may well have been a different story."[54]

---

49. Booth, *Echoes and Memories*, 177–78.
50. Bramwell-Booth, *Bramwell Booth*, 198.
51. *Staff Officer*, October 1930, 346–47.
52. Carpenter, *Man of Peace in a World of War*, 63.
53. Bradwell, *Touched With Splendour*, 250.
54. Pears, Thesis, "Towards a theology," 64.

One American woman sued the Army in 1970 for discriminating against her in appointments on the basis of her sex. The Army won the case on the grounds that relations between a church and its ministers were exempt from the relevant provisions of the Civil Rights Act.[55]

The overlooking of the possibility of women's contributions is not confined to matters of appointment and promotion. A 1991 *Officer* editorial asked, "Where are the women?" and drew attention to the fact that at the 1989 International Strategy for Growth Conference, eighty out of ninety-six delegates were men.[56] Again, when two delegates were nominated by leadership from each of the three Australasian Territories to form a tri-territorial theological forum in 2003, members of the new body discovered that only men had been chosen. (Three women were appointed upon this being pointed out.)

In Western countries the retirement age for single women officers has until recently been set lower than that of men; sixty as compared with sixty-five. When men commissioners retired at seventy, women commissioners retired at sixty-five, until 1986, when a graduated lowering of the retirement age to sixty-five was instituted. In the 1970s Major Roy Lovatt of Great Britain suggested that this was one reason for the lack of women in the higher levels of leadership and proposed that "equal length of service is more likely to produce a more equal balance of leadership than any other single factor."[57] This was vigorously denied by Lt. Colonel Ruth Brewer of USA who believed such a change would only make "necessary a longer time for them to live with existing inequities!"[58]

Some of those inequities have been material. Financial differentials and discriminatory housing practices have in part derived from the English class system (inevitably echoed in the international but long British-centered Salvation Army hierarchy) and the application, until the last quarter of the twentieth century, of benefits for those higher up the pecking order. Such factors have perhaps impacted more on single women officers simply because fewer of them have risen high in the hierarchy.

For many years the rates of allowances (officers are not guaranteed wages or salary) discriminated against women. For example, when *The Officer* of February 1897 announced new allowances, single men captains were to receive 15/5 per week and lieutenants 12/-. Single women captains were to receive 12/-and lieutenants 9/-. A Minute of 1948 set the allowances of male and female probationary-lieutenants at £1.17.0d and £1.14.0d respectively.[59] Complaints about this sort of thing were not aired in print in the early days, whatever the private thoughts of the officers.

While Staff-Captain Mary MacFarlane, in the October 1930 *Staff Officer* article already cited, denied that equal standards were maintained "in the matter of salary and quarters," she did not allude so much to the discriminatory pay rates as to the living conditions. Field and social officers had quarters provided free, as did married staff officers, while single staff officers had to find their own accommodation and were allowed

55. McKinley, *Marching to Glory*, 203.
56. *Officer*, September 1991, 385.
57. *Officer*, January 1976, 37.
58. *Officer*, June 1976, 279.
59. *Salvationist*, 12 July 2003.

a mere 5/-extra for rent. She was supported in this complaint by Commissioner Johanna Van den Werken, to whom also the editor had referred the article for comment.[60] As a territorial commander in Netherlands East Indies in the 1920s, Van den Werken instituted official accommodation for single-women, and shared it herself. In New Zealand the building of an apartment building for single officers was initiated by Colonel A. Bramwell Cook, chief secretary, in the 1950s after he had found a senior woman officer in tears on the steps of the training college because she had been unable to find a place to board for the derisory allowance provided.

In fact it was the normal expectation of society that women could live more cheaply than men. Equality in Salvation Army single officer allowances was achieved after the Second World War, still putting the Army well in advance of secular salary structures. Finding a just balance between single officer and married couple allowances remains a vexed question, however.

A continuing sense of grievance is however evidenced by a letter from Major Fay Lewis (British Territory) who joined in a 1988 exchange on the plight of officer wives. "As I look at the role of female officers in our movement, I feel that in spite of the fact that our General is unmarried, the people who have suffered most are the single officers. I am becoming increasingly convinced that there will gradually be no place for us, unless it is to fulfil the 'demeaning roles.'" (An earlier correspondent had so characterized the work of "typist and filing clerk.")[61]

With concern mounting that the single woman leader was an endangered species, targeting or positive discrimination was floated by some as a solution. An *Officer* editorial in July 1984 suggested that "a positive bias towards female ministry is needed among those who make appointments and policy at every level, if the opposite tendency, which has to some extent developed, is to be addressed. And they need to make an honest assessment across the whole range of useful characteristics, and not just concentrate on those male-oriented qualities which have been traditionally regarded as essential to leadership and more or less exclusive to men."[62]

Eva Burrows, whose election as General some hoped would signal a move in this direction, actually opposed the appointment of any "statutory women" on boards and councils. Rather than tokenism she said that women "have to take their place by reason of their gifts and abilities."[63] Burrows was criticized by some for being insufficiently proactive on behalf of women. In relation to Burrows' role, Captain Christine Clement noted that "Mrs Thatcher has been Britain's Prime Minister for ten years, but is there a woman in the cabinet?"[64] Questioned on the subject, Burrows is reported as asking, "Where *are* the women?" Bishop Penny Jamieson's comment is apt, however: "The fundamental question for women in positions of power is whether the culture of these institutions is

---

60. *Staff Review*, October 1930, 340, 353.
61. *Officer*, October 1998, 422.
62. *Officer*, July 1984, 291.
63. Gariepy, *General of God's Army*, 204.
64. *Officer*, January, 1990, 32.

so intractable and seductive that they become themselves taken over and remade in an old likeness, taking on the characteristics of those who held that power before them."[65]

Nevertheless, Burrows directed territories to promote women to leadership and laid it down that each Territory should have at least one single woman lieutenant-colonel. Pears says that "Territories, however, rarely complied, or in some cases responded with token appointments or promotions."[66] Despite this, Captain Donna Ames, in a 1996 series of articles on "Changing Women's Roles," felt that Minutes issued in the previous year were beginning make a difference.[67] Her articles drew a mixed response, with Captain Allister du Plessis cautioning that cultural factors in some territories made the application of such policies difficult and Major Cecil Waters drawing attention to legal repercussions and counterproductive consequences of affirmative action for minorities in the USA.[68]

In recent times Commissioner Kay Rader challenged the prejudices of assembled Salvationist leaders:

> Perhaps even within this company of international leaders there are those who oppose this definite view held by The Salvation Army regarding its policy of equality between the sexes, married and single, in ministry and leadership.

She also stated that

> Although women in the Army enjoy the privilege of rank and, in most cases, an avenue of service, we must admit that they are working within a system which is for all intents and purposes, predominantly patriarchal. If women officers are to become equal partners in the business of running the Army, we may be called upon to remove what one author refers to as "patriarchal shackles."[69]

To balance these examples, it should be recognized that the Salvation Army's precept and practice of gender equality, however flawed, has been a significant factor in improving the respect accorded to women officers in patriarchal, third world countries. Sociologist Lorraine V. Aragon writes of Sulawesi in Indonesia that,

> European Protestant missionaries partly succeeded in their attempts to alter marriage patterns, household relations, and naming practices according to an idealized European model. While these transformations by the mission and colonial state might be said to generally undermine aspects of the indigenous status of women, the Salvation Army subsequently created a novel set of career opportunities that specifically favored women. Young girls no longer were destined exclusively to become dry rice farmers and mothers but some could aspire to be educated and trained as hospital aides, nurses, teachers, or even ministers—that is, Salvation Army officer wives.[70]

---

65. Jamieson, *Living at the Edge*, 32. In 1989 Jamieson became the first woman Anglican diocesan bishop in New Zealand, and in fact the first in the world to be elected to this role.
66. Pears, "Towards a Theology," 63.
67. Ames, *Officer*, December 1996, 549–50.
68. *Officer*, January 1997, 46–47; February 1997, 93.
69. Rader, "Women in Ministry," 5, 6.
70. Aragon, abstract of paper, "Making a Male God and Female Careers."

BEING EQUALLY YOKED

It is necessary to note at this point that quite soon officers were permitted to marry only other officers. In this, the Salvation Army had been anticipated by the Bible Christians, a West Country Methodist splinter group founded by William O'Bryan in 1815, whose female preachers could marry only other preachers.[71] With the decline in the number of single women officers in the course of the twentieth century, the role and situation of married women officers has become the focus of attention so far as gender equality in the Army is concerned. We need to step back and trace the history of this practice before going further.

In the early days of the Christian Mission, although we have seen that some married women took a leadership role, it was not expected that wives of evangelists would automatically join their husbands up front. "Mrs Garner, 'a sweet though mouse-like nature, was totally incapable of commanding anyone,' Mrs Beadle 'was little more than a domestic servant to her husband,' Mrs Clare was 'a good woman but entirely taken up with the affairs of her home.'"[72]

Later, in the transition period from Mission to Army, before the training system for married people or the commissioning procedure became formalized, it seems to have been the case that women married by men officers automatically became officers. (Or rather, "officers' wives.") When sergeant Marianne Parkyn of Torquay married George Scott Railton in 1884, she became Mrs Commissioner Railton.[73] Until the mid-1880s, wives of married entrants were given the choice of coming into training or remaining at home during the training period. Married men candidates were asked if they could, while away being trained, support their wife if she chose not to be trained.[74]

The 1886 *Orders and Regulations*, under the general heading of "The Social Relationships of the F.O.", included the following:

> Before being received as an Officer the following engagement is made by every F.O.:-
>
> (a) Not to marry anyone who is not a Soldier in The Army. (b) To abstain from courting for at least twelve months. (c) Not to do any courting with any Soldier in the Corps in which he may be stationed. (d) Not to make any engagement without first giving information to Headquarters.[75]

The argument then follows that since an officer's life is wholly given over to the work of the Army:

> It must be indispensable that he shall select a wife having the same convictions . . . especially in a path requiring so much self-sacrifice and toil . . . Further, to marry one outside The Army would probably mean leaving it . . . This must be

---

71. Coutts, *Salvationists*, 27 May 2000, 7.

72. Quoted by Boardman, "Officership—a Functional Ministry," 517–18. His source is not known to me.

73. Watson, *Soldier Saint*, 76.

74. Redstone, *Ex-Captain's Experience*, 8–9.

75. *Orders and Regulations for Field Officers*, 1886, 52.

seen to be most unfair and dishonorable. The Army cannot afford to pay the expenses and expend the labour and time of its Staff Officers in training men and women unless they agree to every arrangement which seems likely to secure them for its future service.[76]

The Orders and Regulations warned Female Officers particularly,

> to be very careful in this matter, seeing that to marry other than an Officer removes them from a position of great usefulness and honor, such as they will probably never have the opportunity of attaining again . . . lest . . . she should enter into relationships which would drag her down from this honourable and Christ-like career to spend the remainder of her life in looking back on what she has sacrificed, with bitter regret, if not with absolute despair.[77]

The paternalistic role of the organization is explicitly defended: "Many Officers are so young and inexperienced that they require some older person to give them counsel in such matters."[78] Salvation Army marriage practices, like everything else about the organization, were the subject of much speculation and rumor. Catherine Booth felt obliged to respond to

> the slanderous assertion that we are opposed to marriages amongst our officers! . . . In judging our instructions, however, on this point, please bear in mind that we have, I should think, 200 women officers not more than twenty, and perhaps as many men of the same age, and you will see the absolute necessity, for their own sakes, for some oversight with respect to engagements. I believe the Wesleyans refuse to accept a candidate for the ministry if he is engaged, and do not allow their young ministers to marry until their four years' probation has expired. How awful this must be in the eyes of our critics![79]

A revision to the Regulations, 2 August 1887, restricted both men and women to engagement either to other officers or to soldiers suitable for officership and willing to enter training.[80] In the words of Colonel Laurence Hay, "It seems likely that the reasons were administrative: changes of appointment could more easily be made if married officers had officer spouses. This administrative factor is still one of the major justifications given, yet, in the hierarchy of Christian values, administrative convenience must surely rank very near the bottom!"[81] The whole polity and history of the Salvation Army illustrates that practical measures soon become sacralized and fairly resistant to further adaptation.

A correspondent to *The Officer* in 1915 asked why officers had to marry officers. Why not let the men officers marry soldiers? (He was obviously indifferent to the plight of single women officers wanting husbands.) Colonel James Whiller, assistant field

---

76. Ibid., 53.
77. *Orders and Regulations for Field Officers*, 1886, 55.
78. Ibid., 54.
79. Booth, *Church and State*, 91.
80. *Orders and Regulations for Field Officers*, 1888, Supplement, 122.
81. *Officer*, October 1999, 26.

secretary, equally indifferent, gave the standard answer that the officer's partner was not only his wife but also his fellow leader.[82]

The *Appointments of Officers* 1883 list gives the names of 723 men and 746 women officers. As Horridge points out, there were many more women officers than acknowledged in this way, because a fifth of the men were married and although their wives were expected to work as officers in their corps, they were not listed separately.[83]

Until 1970 the New Zealand *Disposition of Forces*, the annual publication listing appointments and officers, gave only the husband's name. If he were married, this would be followed by an x, and a number denoting how many children "on strength"—that is, still living at home with their parents, who therefore received an additional allowance for their maintenance. In fact wives of THQ married men officers remained x's until 1976. When statistical summaries of officers were given in the *Disposition of Forces* (until 1974) by rank, wives were not included but enumerated at the end as "staff officers' wives" and "officers' wives." Advice of promotion, farewell orders and marching orders (to leave an appointment and proceed to another) were issued to the husband only.

Clearly the Army was not totally emancipated from the usual expectations of society; normally the husband's calling was presumed to have priority, and a woman officer, in marrying, lost her independent officer-status. In Horridge's words, "The loss of women officers' rights when marrying contradicts the constant statement regarding equality."[84] Commissioner Kay Rader, in an essay on the role of women in the Army, quotes Rebecca Merrill Groothuis as sourcing this practice in English common law as described by William Blackstone. In his 1765 commentary Blackstone upheld the "civil death" of women who married.

> By marriage, the husband and wife are one person in law: that is, the very being or legal existence of the woman is suspended during the marriage, or at least is incorporated and consolidated into that of the husband; under whose wing, protection, and cover, she performs everything . . .[85]

The Founder himself had expressed concern at this mindset, evident in his lifetime. In 1888, addressing a meeting in Exeter Hall, William Booth said, "We have a problem. When two officers marry, by some strange mistake in our organization, the woman doesn't count."[86] However Booth did nothing to ensure that it did not happen beyond exhorting his senior officers to value the work of married women officers. In his 1900 letter to senior leaders he urged,

> Let us maintain it with a jealous regard for the sacred rights of every woman, whether married or single, to the free and full exercise of all her gifts in the glorious work of the Salvation Army. To this end—Let women have the fullest opportunity to work. Let them be promoted in harmony with their ability and

---

82. *Officer*, July 1915, 445.
83. Horridge, *Origins*, 80.
84. Horridge, *Origins*, 81.
85. Blackstone, *Commentaries on the Laws of England*. 1, (1765), quoted by Rader, "Keeping the Dream Alive," 86.
86. *War Cry*, 12 May 1888. Quoted in *Salvationist*, 22 November 2003, 15.

worthiness. Let women be treated as equal with men in all the social relations of life. Let consideration be shown to the Mothers of young children. Bear in mind that after a few years, the circumstances of such women will allow them to come to the front with almost as much freedom as before marriage, and that they will likely take their places in the fight with greatly increased love and wisdom, and, consequently, with greatly enlarged influence and power.[87]

However, no structural provision was made to ensure this happened. Bramwell Booth in his turn struggled apparently in vain against the cultural norm. A letter to a territorial commander in 1924 instructs him,

> Do not fail me with the women. I look anxiously for the War Cry reports about their work . . . it is not only a principle with us, but it is a very strong personal desire on my own part that the women of the Army should be kept to the front; and that the married women should be made to feel that their responsibilities are not all dissolved in those of their husbands when they marry.[88]

Some notable exceptions still only tended to prove the rule. In the case of Captain Rachel Agar's betrothal to William Ebdon, and their joint appointment to open a corps at Northampton in 1879, William Booth agreed to the marriage only on the condition that Rachel should be first in the partnership so far as Salvation Army officership was concerned.[89] When Major and Mrs Simmonds "opened fire" in South Africa in 1883, it would appear that Mrs Simmonds, a talented evangelist, spearheaded the work, while her husband operated in a less prominent role.[90] Another example was that of Brigadier Hedwig Haartmann, a Finnish officer serving as provincial commander for German-speaking Switzerland when she married her ADC, Staff-Captain Franz von Tavel. They hyphenated their names but retained their ranks and roles. Alas the lady died soon afterwards, in 1892.[91] Most of Booth's own married daughters retained or assumed their own Ruritanian ranks and shared joint commands when they hyphenated their names with those of their husbands.[92]

The resolution of the tension between the assumptions behind the framework of officer marriage and the movement of societal expectations occupied the whole of the twentieth century, and the process is not by any means complete. Florence Booth claimed that "the work and influence of women in The Salvation Army is not confined to unmarried women . . . The work of married women, though often more indirect and unseen, has been of as great, and even of greater importance."[93] It had to be indirect because after marriage the actual appointment would be their husband's. Commissioner Karl Larsson cautioned women officers from running into marriage too soon because

87. Booth, *Letter to Commissioners and Territorial Commanders*, 25–26.
88. Bramwell-Booth, *Bramwell Booth*, 197.
89. Sandall, *History*, II, 37.
90. Escott, "Church Growth Theories," 53.
91. Duff, *Hedwig Von Haartman*.
92. Bramwell's wife, Florence, was content to be "Mrs Booth" until she became "Mrs General Booth," although William Booth had made her a Commissioner in 1888. *Salvation Army Year Book*, 1958, 7. She may have provided the inspiration for Commissioner Mrs Baines in Shaw's *Major Barbara* (1905).
93. *Field Officer*, March 1913, 122.

"Some of our best and most promising women, who have a good head and a good heart, and who as single officers would go far and occupy important positions, enter into marriages which hinder their development and circumscribe their sphere of work."[94]

Officers' wives' officership was merged with that of their husbands. The husband received the appointments and the promotions; the wife just tagged along. A Memorandum from the territorial commander in New Zealand as late as December 1963 on "Officer Commission and Promotion Certificate" reiterated the position (perhaps it was beginning to be questioned). "Husband to receive promotion certificate for each promotion up to and including the rank of Brigadier. Wife to receive no promotion certificate: she takes her husband's rank."[95] The regulations provided that when widowed, an officer-wife "if, or when, she has served the required number of years as an officer . . . will receive rank in her own right, except where the husband held the rank of Lt. Colonel or above, when the case will be reviewed by the Chief of the Staff."[96] The husband also received the allowance, augmented appropriately if he had a wife and family to support.

The system worked well for many people. Frederick Coutts described it in his memoirs as

> this unique form of service in which husband and wife work as one. Brigadier A. may be appointed divisional commander for the Cumbrian division, and Commissioner B. to be the territorial commander for Westralia, but Captain and Mrs C. will be sent to take charge of the corps at Middletown. This turns out to be not only for the good of the work but for the good of their marriage as well, insofar as they share not merely their leisure—which is all many husbands and wives can do—but their vocation also. Both have accepted the same calling. Both are trained for that calling. All that Captain does Mrs. Captain can do as well. She does not sit in the congregation but shares with her husband the Salvation Army equivalent of the pulpit—the platform. Captain will rejoice that Mrs. Captain is no cipher. Mrs. Captain will rejoice that she is no dumb piece of platform decoration . . .[97]

By the 1970s the relationship between officer husbands and wives was being described as a "joint covenant," although the actual term was not used in regulations. The *Orders and Regulations* were amended to this effect in 1981: "In marriage an officer's consecration is joined with that of the chosen partner and the united consecrations become one just as do husband and wife become 'one flesh' (Mark 10:8)."[98] Mrs Commissioner Hilda Cox, wife of the Chief of the Staff, in a 1990 article on "Married Women's Officer-role Within The Salvation Army," found the concept of a "joint covenant" "puzzling and unhelpful," and "only useful if we were able to envisage a complete and secure possibility of role-sharing or equality."

Mrs Cox, in the article referred to, admitted that "the equality policy within our midst has been . . . implemented with a mixture of success and failure," and that she had

---

94. *Officer's Review*, Sept–Oct 1939, 479.
95. Memorandum in New Zealand Salvation Army Archives.
96. Minute by The Chief of the Staff, 1977/IA/4.
97. Coutts, *No Continuing City*, 34–35.
98. Minute by The Chief of the Staff, 1981/IA/7.

been "bewildered, perplexed and not a little frustrated by its interpretation." She noted the danger of spiritual abuse: "The emphasis placed on a 'spiritual commitment' must never be used to force anyone into simply conforming to any situation, especially to one only partly understood, or to push anyone 'aside' into a non-existent channel." However, she also believed that women had to come to terms with the Army's administrative structure as a cultural given, and learn to work for equality within it.[99]

Mrs Major Margaret Hay (New Zealand) rejoined with the affirmation that "principles are sacred; structures and roles are not." She drew attention to the way in which the principle of equality had been eroded in successive editions of the *Orders and Regulations for Officers*. The 1900 edition had named gender equality as "one of the leading principles upon which the Army is based." The 1925 edition dropped the word "leading." The 1974 edition omitted the whole section on the position of women, "stressing instead the supportive role of the 'officer-wife.'" Hay also took up Cox's cue on "the exploitation of spiritual commitment to reinforce a reactionary social climate and bar women from the exercise of real authority." She believed that "given the will, structures can be transformed."[100]

The official assumption of male control continued to be reflected in *The Orders and Regulations for Officers* as late as the 1987 edition which, in the section devoted to "The officer and his wife" included the words, "In most appointments . . . an officer-wife should assist her husband. He is of course, responsible, but she should interest herself and, as opportunity permits, take her full share in every phase of the work under his direction . . . "[101] Major John Coutts commented on the 1974 edition,

> In seventh-century England, the blood-money for killing a churl was, of course, only half that payable for killing an earl. For a Welshman, of course, it was lower still. In seventeenth century Scotland, the children of miners were, of course, placed in life-long bondage to the pits at their baptism. In nineteenth-century America, Booker T. Washington was, of course, refused admission to College because he was black, while in Britain Catherine Booth came under fire for preaching. Of course—she was a woman.[102]

The offending phrase persisted until the 1997 edition.

The matter of the role and status of married women officers (including those widowed or divorced) generated a great deal of discussion in the final third of the twentieth century. Mrs General Marie Wahlström noted in 1984 that "there is a good deal of uncertainty and dissatisfaction among women officers, both married and single, with regard to their place and position in the Army."[103] There were fifty letters and articles on this subject in *The Officer* between 1972 and 1996 and fifteen in *The Salvationist* between 1990 and 1996. It seemed that the pressure on the traditional structure was steadily

---

99. Cox, "Married Women's Officer Role," 408–12, 415.

100. Hay, "Married Women-Officers," 70–71.

101. *Orders and Regulations for Officers*, 1974, 77.

102. *Officer*, December 1974, 562, 566.

103. Address to the International Conference of Leaders, Berlin 1984. International Heritage Centre file.

increasing and this no doubt contributed to the progressive modifications and reforms that have been instituted over the past few years.

Correspondents addressed a variety of themes. Some were concerned with the officer as a wife and mother, and juggling those responsibilities with ministry.[104] Some dealt with the nature of the officer husband-wife partnership.[105]

Some correspondents revisited the scriptural basis of Salvation Army practice. Major Howard Davies (Australia), for example, responded to Mrs Major Margaret Hay's argument from Salvation Army tradition and "sacrosanct principles" by expressing unease and suggesting that many officer-wives held back from exercising their ministry out of "scripturally-based reservations."[106] He evidently believed that the Bible mandated a subordinate role for women. He was supported by some correspondents and denounced by others.[107]

Other reactionary concerns were also referred to. Major Miriam Vinti (IHQ) asked how practical could a regulation be that allowed complete independence of career to man and wife? "How would a man accept the promotion of his wife to a commissioner and territorial commander, while he remained a major in his wife's Headquarters?"[108] Lt. Colonel Arthur Thompson believed that "if some husbands would find it intolerable to be in a lesser role than their wives, then lessons may have to be learned from the world, where this painful adjustment is taking place."[109]

For some, a serious problem in the existing structure was the waste of human resources, desperately needed by an Army stretched for personnel. Brigadier Lawrence Weggery (New Zealand) discovered from the *Orders and Regulations* that a wife "can in fact 'in certain circumstances' be entrusted by headquarters with some definite responsibility distinct from that of her husband," and urged that "ways will be found to encourage the officer-wife . . . to move out of her supernumerary position and undertake leadership in her own right."[110]

Lt. Colonel Arthur Thompson regretted that "whilst the autocratic command structure was designed to produce quicker decision-making our leaders at almost every level seemed to be locked in a kind of paralysis because of . . . prejudice and tradition . . . Without doubt, if we are not to be guilty of poor stewardship of our leadership resources, the time must soon come for the Army to move purposefully towards using our best talent most wisely, whether it be male or female, single or married."[111] Captain Geoffrey Parkin similarly condemned "the possible waste of a valuable resource, the loss of personal fulfilment and the potential strain between husband and wife."[112]

---

104. *Officer*, December 1981, 560–562, 555.
105. *Officer*, April 1993, 170–72.
106. *Officer*, February 1991, 70–71.
107. *Officer*, July 1991, 325; November 1991, 491–94; November 1996, 515–17.
108. *Officer*, February 1975, 78.
109. *Officer*, October 1984, 460.
110. *Officer*, January 1972, 36–37.
111. *Officer*, October 1984, 459–61.
112. *Officer*, June 1988, 268–69.

Against this, Major Patricia Yon discovered in the 1990s that 60 percent of married women officers surveyed in the UK "were to some degree satisfied to be appointed with their spouse . . . Some women would be vehemently opposed to the prospect of sacrificing this privilege."[113]

Others again expressed strong feelings about the situation of widowed and particularly separated or divorced officers. *The Orders and Regulations* confirmed that the "Officer's wife is herself an Officer . . . Should she become a widow, she is still an Officer . . . The widow of an officer may be appointed directly to another department or section of service and thereby be considered a widow on Active Service . . . She may be appointed as an employee . . . "[114] However this was all a matter of discretion and it had not been uncommon for widowed women officers to be given no option other than premature retirement. Mrs Major Harry Parkinson, whose husband died in his forties in 1942 while in command of Wellington City corps in New Zealand, brought up her family on a small pension and spent over fifty years in retirement. Some however were able to stick it out and IHQ allowed a few to reach or maintain executive roles. Mrs Colonel Violet Stobart, widowed in 1960, took over her late husband's role as territorial commander in Ceylon (perhaps inspired by Mrs Bandaranaike?) and retired from the command of Switzerland as a Lt. Commissioner. Commissioner Mary Rajakumari became territorial commander, Western India, upon the death of her husband, P.D. Krupa Das, in 2007.

The situation of officers who suffered the breakdown of their marriage was perhaps worse, as both parties had to resign their officership regardless of where the "fault," if any, lay. Those who chose could reapply for acceptance as officers at a later date. Captain Mrs Miriam Fredericksen (IHQ) described the dynamics of such service,[115] as did "Eunice", who wrote, "I know what it feels like to be made to feel 'second-class' because of something on which you had no influence . . . I know what it means to experience personal rejection and public humiliation."[116]

The administrative structure whereby the wives of corps, divisional and territorial leaders automatically assumed responsibility for the "women's work" and women's organizations, also came under fire. Mrs Lt. Colonel Emily Fritz (USA) believed that "the whole concept of the women's service department has outlived its usefulness . . . Salvation Army women may be better served if the women's service departments were absorbed into mainline administration. In the USA this would free a lot of officer-wives now stationed on divisional and territorial headquarters to be reassigned to appointments matching their special gifts."[117] Lt. Colonel Mary Elvin (Caribbean) also denounced this "Army within an Army." "To concentrate so much time, effort and personnel upon one aspect of the ministry will inevitably produce substantial results in that one aspect . . . but it often leads to a serious imbalance in both church attendance and in membership."[118]

---

113. Yon, "Areas of Stress and Conflict," 36.
114. *Orders and Regulations for Officers*, 1930, 486.
115. *Officer*, September 1981, 418–20, 426.
116. *Officer*, December 1991, 546–49.
117. *Officer*, December 1988, 496–97.
118. *Officer*, November 1996, 518–20.

To anticipate, the on-going reforms had left this women's "ghetto," to use Captain Danielle Strickland's term for it, untouched as yet. She explains,

> By women's ghetto I mean that part of the system of the Salvation Army that allows men to exercise leadership within the formal system while deploying their wives into corresponding positions over other women in a weird parallel universe. The end goal in this corporate structure is to be married to a Commissioner—and ultimately to be the wife of the General. It has no bearing on the election of a General whether or not his wife is even good at her job—as the position is not functional but positional . . . it is not a merited position and is not considered an appointment providing leadership experience to become a General . . . all the women's ghetto positions in the world cannot offer a reasonable opportunity for women to learn, cultivate or prove leadership qualities enough to get out of the ghetto . . . and any single woman General can add the job description of World President of Women's Organizations to her responsibility as international leader of the Salvation Army. Nice.[119]

The majority of correspondents however dealt with some aspect of the way in which married women officers felt that their ministry had been diminished or held in less regard once they married. The extent to which married women officers were able to maintain their ministry depended to some extent on the kind of work in which their husbands were engaged. In the case of married women corps officers, there was a pastoral role in which they could be fully absorbed along with their husbands. Responsibility for the pastoral care of women and children, often along with the leadership of particular women's groups, usually devolved upon officer-wives. The degree to which they shared public work, such as meeting leadership and preaching, depended on their individual capabilities, the dynamics of the marriage, family responsibilities and sometimes the expectations of the corps. "In one corps she is kept from the hall kitchen, it being unthinkable that she should leave the word of God and serve tables; in another . . . everyone goes home and leaves her with the dishes."[120]

The organization sometimes failed to recognize their work. A correspondent in 1919 took issue with the

> boast of The Salvation Army that women in its ranks are on an equality with men. I do not think that is wholly true . . . There are more women than men in our ranks, and many of them possess brains, education and godliness which qualifies them to occupy responsible positions. The married women officers might receive more recognition than they do. At the last Congress I attended not one married woman was asked to speak or pray. I know of one DC who sent out Christmas gifts to officers in his division, and in the case of a married couple who had a young lieutenant as an assistant, there was a remembrance to the lieutenant and to the officer in charge, but the letter conveying Christmas greetings was addressed to "Adjutant Blank and Lieutenant So-and-so." The poor wife was not even wished a happy Christmas. It was not the gift that mattered but the utter ignoring of a woman who did an equal part of the platform work, a fair share of the visitation and all of the clerical work, so as to free her husband

---

119. Strickland, "Married Women's Ghetto Rant," 5.
120. Editorial Comment, "Wife and Officer," *Officer*, September–October 1960, 358.

for the demands of outside corps work. I do not think an officer's wife should be treated as though she were a sort of upper servant . . .[121]

Such voices were not heard very often until much later in the century. When the debate then flared up, some expressed surprise. Retired officer, Mrs Major Ruth Saunders (UK) recalled that on her marriage "everyone . . . naturally expected that I would really share the platform ministry[122], the visitation, the census board meetings, etc, with total equality, and I, and the officer-wives of the previous generation as well as my own, did do that."[123] Some put the blame for loss of status on the wives themselves. Mrs Captain Katrina Thomas (British Territory) wrote that " . . . a great many female married officers have allowed their spouses to be the commanding officer . . . I regard myself as a commanding officer and I expect to be treated as such." She allowed that there were moments of frustration—"e.g. letters for my attention addressed to my husband, a divisional commander refusing to discuss corps business with 'Mrs Captain' . . . "[124]

On the other hand, some were happy to take a back seat. Mrs Captain Arvilla Hostetler (USA Eastern) explained, "He is the Captain, the pastor, of the Corps. A church has one pastor but there may be many ministers. Our people are not likely to introduce me as their Captain. I am the Captain's wife . . . My role is not secondary but complementary. My husband and I are a team . . . My pastoral duties may be different from my husband's but they are no less important."[125] Mrs Colonel May Holland (Retired, UK) admitted, "most of us accepted that when it came to marriage that our husbands were responsible for the decision making. There cannot be two commanding officers in one battalion. Personally that is how I wished it, and I was never brought into corps, divisional headquarters or territorial headquarters decision-making regarding any aspect of administration."[126] Mrs Captain Ruth Hampton (Australia) felt that "women in our corps need an example of true motherhood, the joy of being a wife and the responsibility of being a home-keeper, as well as being a servant of God."[127] Lt. Colonel John Gowans expressed regret that "some women officers have sold their birthright and retreated from any kind of public service altogether."[128]

In the case of social officers the wives' roles perhaps depended more on the nature of the appointment. In some cases there was more than enough to do—unremitting toil at laundry, cooking, sewing, cleaning and supervision as occasion required, and responsibility as matron for large numbers of people. On the other hand, Mrs Major Gladys Ford of New Zealand wrote of arriving at an appointment where her husband was to

---

121. *Officer*, April 1919, 357.
122. "Platform ministry": that is, Leading services and preaching.
123. *Officer*, June 1993, 287–88.
124. *Officer*, July 1989, 320–21.
125. *Officer*, December 1981, 457–58.
126. *Officer*, February 1975, 81.
127. *Officer*, December 1989, 567–68.
128. *Officer*, October 1984, 449.

be manager, only to be greeted by the non-Salvationist assistant manager with the comment, "There is no work here for you to do."[129] She found plenty to do however.

It was the problem of unemployed staff wives, whose husbands had positions on headquarters, which first attracted official notice however. Mrs Bramwell Booth, at the suggestion of Mrs Carpenter, decided in 1912 to set up what she called "The Bond of Service and Fellowship." This was partly to provide pastoral care for the wives of staff officers, and also to find work for wives of staff officers on IHQ. This labor-exchange directed such wives to the needs in corps, social institutions and hospital visitation.[130]

Perhaps this kind of thing was not to everyone's liking because from time to time chiding articles urged greater participation, noting "the danger of being the wife of a mandarin."[131] Another writer, having referred to the "humble and unobtrusive opportunities for work with Home Leagues, the YP Corps, League of Mercy, prison, hospital, common lodging house or saloon visitation," suggested that perhaps "such unobtrusive work does not attract them . . . ," they "want to preserve the freedom from official responsibilities of a soldier while retaining the position, the honour, and the prerogatives of a staff officer!"[132]

Such official responses missed the point, that married women officers were increasingly feeling devalued by the lack of respect shown for their calling as officers. Even in the early years this must have been felt: in 1899 Captain Minnie Rowell wrote to her intended husband, George Lyndon Carpenter, of her fear of being reduced to being a housewife upon marriage. "I am practically marrying out of the work. What am I to do? Keep my house nice and once a week visit a hospital?"[133]

While this frustration was contained or had little opportunity for expression in earlier years, the comparative freedom of the official publications towards the end of the twentieth century permitted a clear picture to emerge. Mrs Major Gwenyth Redhead (UK) described how, upon her husband's appointment to the staff of the officer training college, she sat through an interview in which the Principal explained at length her husband's duties. "Finally . . . I plucked up courage to ask, 'And my responsibilities?' Then came the sword-thrust deep into my heart, reducing my sense of self-worth to nil. 'It is not training college policy to provide officer-wives with official appointments.' I felt as if the word 'rejected' had been branded into my forehead for all the world to see."[134] Mrs Major Joy Emmons of South America West put it like this: "When we were brought to headquarters and I was not listed in the dispo I was crushed. I did what I was asked to do . . . but felt like excess baggage."[135]

The *Manual of Guidance for Staff Officers* included a short passage on "The Staff Officer's Wife".

---

129. *Officer,* February 1985, 81.
130. *Officer,* July 1917, 395–98; Carpenter, *Man of Peace,* 198.
131. *Officer*, June 1916, 419–22.
132. *Staff Review*, January 1922, 110–11.
133. Carpenter, *Man of Peace*, 102.
134. *Officer*, December 1991, 561.
135. *Officer*, October 1989, 436–37.

> It is not given to the wife of every Staff Officer to have specific or separate responsibilities. When such is the case, however, the husband will give encouragement to see that her duties are carried out without let or hindrance... Throughout the world, many Staff Officers' wives are a tower of strength to their husbands in a "behind the scenes" ministry, as well as exercising an independent influence in the districts where they live or in the Corps where they are soldiers.[136]

The wives of officers below staff rank serving on Headquarters presumably knew their place without being expressly instructed. Quite recently the *Orders and Regulations for Divisional Commanders* still advised that "A DC's wife needs to be especially careful not to intrude upon her husband's prerogatives of administration. She may not assume any of her husband's powers of authority."[137]

The Officer editorialized in 1984: "The crunch comes in specialist or headquarters appointments where the husband has a specific appointment which does not... include the wife, and where very often no effort is made to find her suitable and fulfilling work. She is often left to languish in a limbo of frustration and rejection in which she may (a) lose her sense of vocation... (b) Become satisfied with Martha tasks [by which the writer probably included the kind of work offered by the 'Bond of Service and Fellowship']. (c) Find some second-best fulfilment in agencies outside the Army, if such is available. None of these is a substitute for her officer vocation, and the organization has an obligation to find really fulfilling service for every officer."[138]

Personal experience of this situation led at least one senior officer to begin attending to the problem. Colonel Gordon Swansbury, appointed Staff Secretary at IHQ, found that his own wife had no designated assignment "and there was no peace in our house until her importuning secured an opening in another department in which she has found complete job satisfaction." Swansbury discovered that a study group had been commissioned to investigate the position of officer-wives and had made recommendations. Accordingly he initiated individual letters of appointment for all officer-wives serving on IHQ and also for officer-wives who had found roles elsewhere though their husbands worked on IHQ. He made it standard practice for wives of all in-coming officers to be interviewed as to their preferred service. As he stated, this did not mean that the ideal had been reached—the wives' appointments were still secondary to their husbands'—but it was a start.[139]

Major Patricia Yon, surveying married women officers in the UK in the early 1990s, learned that 23 percent of respondents to her questionnaire reported that "they have their own named appointment, which is separate from and independent of their spouse." She suggested that "this possibly reflects the fact that recently policy changes have occurred which support the provision of enhanced professional opportunities for married women. However, being appointed independently is no guarantee of being given a job

---

136. *Manual of Guidance for Staff Officers*, 16–17.

137. *Orders and Regulations for Divisional Commanders*, Chapter 1 Section 3 Para 5. Quoted in Salvation Army "Report and Recommendations of Gender Issues Commission, 2004," UK Territory, 16.

138. *Officer*, July 1984, 291.

139. *Officer*, September 1984, 414–15.

in any authentic sense."[140] Even in 2010, Lt. Colonel Lynda Watt of Canada—where she was at time of writing "Assistant to the Property Secretary"—noted that "nine years have passed since a territorial assignment was given to my spouse, and as we enter our tenth year I look back on six appointments at territorial headquarters which have taken me in a number of directions."[141]

John Coutts had warned some years earlier that, "No improvement will come by tinkering with the system or by 'finding little jobs for the ladies.' We need here, as in other matters, real openness about such sensitive matters as jobs and job satisfaction, rank and status and, lastly, money and allowances."[142]

So why was the general trend throughout most of the twentieth century towards a curtailment of woman's role in the Salvation Army?

Firstly, there could be unacknowledged but influential theological reasons. It could be that an alternative Salvation Army tradition, that of conservative evangelical theological reservations about gender equality, has become a significant factor for some people despite the official line. We have seen this for example in Major Howard Davies' letter earlier. Again, Major Karen Shakespeare drew attention to the untoward influence of the Genesis 2 account of creation, which presents woman as being essentially and intrinsically different in nature because of her gender, in contrast to Genesis 1 which describes male and female as created in the image of God.[143] Danielle Strickland notes that "a subtle yet increasing theological and systemic shift . . . has managed to render a huge section of the Army's leaders unusable . . . Now there are officers who believe that 'headship' is a scriptural principle and as a direct result keep married women in submissive positions as leaders. Married women officers themselves often have been taught and continue to believe this lie . . . Not only does the Army perpetuate it by its current system but has probably even established it by its current practice."[144]

Secondly, it could be argued that the situation did not actually deteriorate, but that women became more vocal in their objection to the status quo, and that this was made possible by more liberal opportunities for public debate. And it could also be pointed out that the gradual decline in the number of women in senior leadership was a consequence of the decline in the number of single women officers in general—the potential pool was smaller. That, however, does not explain why the organization was so reluctant to give married women independent commands as it sometimes had in the early days of the movement. And was the pool smaller because women were less willing to accept an inferior status?

Or had the patriarchy successfully turned back the feminist tide? Unfortunately the gradual changes noted by Margaret Hay in the *Orders and Regulations* suggest that the real reason was simply male chauvinism and the increasing conservatism of a movement institutionalizing and tending to be on the defensive. This touches on our clericalising theme as well. Whatever the Army's rhetoric, the men thought of themselves as clergy,

---

140. Yon, "Areas of Stress," 35.
141. *Officer*, January–February 2010, 7.
142. *Officer*, July 1975, 322.
143. Report and Recommendations of the Gender Issues Commission 2004, UK Territory, 5.
144. Strickland, "Married Women's Ghetto Rant," 6.

and in the world to which the Army was accommodating it was not yet trendy to think of the women as clergy as well. Salvationist men increasingly sought to represent themselves as clergy while in practice denying this status to most women officers. Inevitably, however, attempts to redress this inequity would further clericalize the women.

STEPS TO REFORM

The steps were somewhat leaden. The subject of gender equality was aired at successive conferences of commissioners and territorial leaders but action was tardy. The 1971 conference "recommended women being given a fuller representation in the top echelons of world leadership."[145] 1975 being International Woman's Year, wives of commissioners were invited for the first time to be present at the international conference. However they were not included in every session but held their own parallel sessions, bringing their report to the final plenary session. Commissioner Kathleen Kendrick (a single woman) hoped "that it might be but the beginning of wider participation of women in the central councils of the Army," and quoted a senior woman delegate as saying, "The idea that a woman's place is in the home and that there she must stay—I resent it!"[146]

In 1979 a similar arrangement obtained. Debating the equality of men and women officers, Mrs Commissioner Harry Williams (IHQ) asked why the longstanding passage on the principle of equality had been omitted from the 1974 *Orders and Regulations*. However Commissioner Ernest Holz (USA) "pointed out the difficulties in connection with the over-emphasis of equality, specific appointments and designation."[147] The Minutes did not record what difficulties he meant, but "it was pointed out that what a woman officer seeks is the satisfaction of using her best in the Master's Service." (Was it a man who pointed this out?) It was also mentioned that women officers' names were now included in the *Disposition of Forces* and in the *Official Gazette*.[148] Previously only their husbands had been named.

At the 1984 conference in Berlin, wives were for the first time invited to participate as full delegates, and the conference produced three recommendations affecting women in particular. (1) All gazetting should be for the couple and not for the husband alone—the 1979 claim must have been premature, (2) all correspondence concerning an officer couple should always be addressed to both, and (3) whenever possible the officer wife should be given her own appointment.[149] Such conferences could not enact decisions but only recommend to the General. However, under Burrows a further step was taken in that for the first time the wives of territorial commanders and chief secretaries were

---

145. *Officer*, January 1972, 36.

146. *Officer*, March 1976, 123–25.

147. Proceedings of 1979 International Conference of Leaders, 90. International Heritage Centre Archives, AD/5/1/11/4.

148. The *Official Gazette* is the publishing of appointments, promotions etc., usually in *The War Cry* or other periodicals.

149. Proceedings of the International Conference of Leaders, 1984. International Heritage Centre Archives AD/5/1/12/3.

invited to participate in zonal conferences, a step which had been urged in 1984 by Mrs General Wahlström.

The background study material for the 1991 conference, which asked if it "was time to speed up implementation of earlier recommendations," suggested that the recommendations had not got much further. The 1991 appointment of a married woman as principal of the training college in New Zealand (Mrs Major Margaret Hay), with her husband as a part-time member of her staff, was stated to have given impetus to the question. It was also asked whether the concept of a joint-covenant for married officers was still a live issue—apparently the 1988 conference had recommended that it remain in the expectation. The 1991 conference decided to propose an international commission to consider: (a) a review of the *Orders and Regulations*; (b) review of the position of territorial president of women's organizations; (c) separate appointments for married women; (d) the concept of joint-covenant; and (e) loss of officership in the event of marriage breakdown.[150] Such a commission was appointed by General Burrows, shortly before her retirement in 1993.

The fifteen-member commission chaired by Mrs Commissioner Rosemarie Fullarton presented its report in May 1994, with recommendations "based on the belief that men and women are equal in the sight of God, and that there is no theological conflict in the ministry of women in all spheres of service." The ten recommendations covered the following areas:

> (1) official encouragement for the enrichment of officer family life; (2) revisions of sections of Orders and Regulations for Officers; (3) recognizing all officers by rank, Christian name and surname regardless of marital status; (4) upgrading the role and duties of the territorial president of women's organizations; (5) equality of consideration to be given to the vocation of all officers at all levels of service, and in making appointments; (6) every woman officer, married/single, to be seen as a resource and developed to her full potential; (7) attention given to the full use of skills and gifts of women officers at all levels of service, including boards and councils; (8) a new system for calculating allowances replacing the tenure of married men officers as the basis; (9) single women officers to have appointments of opportunity according to their gifts and abilities; (10) child care and domestic support to be available where family duties may affect the ministry of married and single officers.[151]

General-elect Bramwell Tillsley, interviewed by *New Frontier*, admitted, "We haven't done very well in giving married women officers the opportunity to develop fully the gifts God has given them . . . Too often the assignments of wives have been dictated by the assignment of their husbands."[152] However Tillsley's term of office was cut short by illness in less than a year and it was left to his successor, Paul Rader, to implement some changes recommended by the commission. The new General's wife, Kay Rader, was a forceful personality and a vigorous campaigner on women's issues so

---

150. Proceedings of 1991 International Conference of Leaders. International Heritage Centre Archives *AD*/5/1/14/2.

151. Gariepy, *History*, VIII, 318–19.

152. *New Frontier*, 30 April 1993, 6.

her husband's election heralded major steps forward. Pears refers to her in his thesis as "a new champion."[153] Kay Rader's passion for reform arose from her own experience of injustice under a patriarchal system.[154]

New Minutes affecting women's service took effect in mid-1995. Most of the commission's proposals were actioned, although recommendations 8 and 10 were a matter for territorial discretion, according to local conditions, and some were expressions of principle rather than specific changes to practice. The most obvious and major change, able to be implemented at once, was the recognition that "in the case of active officers, up to and including the rank of Commissioner, each spouse holds their joint rank in his or her own right."[155] Mrs Captain Jones became Captain Mary Jones, or, if she preferred, Captain (Mrs) Mary Jones. Curiously, this does not seem to have been made much of in the Army's press, with no reference to the change in the British *Salvationist* or in the New Zealand or Australian editions of the *War Cry*. Perhaps it was thought unwise to call attention to the fact that it was only just happening in 1995—or perhaps it was not thought significant by those who determined editorial policy.

One of the downstream and apparently unanticipated implications of this change was that all commissioners/territorial commanders' wives, now commissioners in their own right, would become eligible for summons to the High Council and have a vote in the election of the next General. This increased female representation on that body at its next meeting from 10 percent to 37 percent. The male majority was maintained because the Territorial Commanders below the rank of Commissioner were nearly all men, whose wives were not eligible to attend. Another even-handed change was that whereas previously a woman officer marrying a man holding a rank lower than her own assumed the husband's rank, now whichever spouse had the lower rank would take the same rank as his or her new partner.

Other elements in this reform package included individual appointments, equality of consideration being given to both spouses' vocations in the making of appointments, appointments of both spouses being announced simultaneously (instead of the wife's being tacked on as a later afterthought), individual personnel reviews and service record cards, and appropriate assessment, orientation and on-going training for women whose family responsibilities or husband's appointments had restricted their own development. It was also provided that "a married woman officer may be given the leadership role in a joint appointment where this is appropriate and the stability of the marriage and family is not placed at risk."[156] Some cautious moves in this direction were made in a few territories. In the Philippines Major Noveminda Tanedo became divisional commander for Mindanao in 2000, with her husband as divisional secretary. In New Zealand Major Lynette Hutson became national manager for addictions services in 2003, and thus line manager for her husband, director of the Auckland Bridge Centre. In 2012 she was appointed secretary for business and administration, he then becoming a divisional commander.

153. Pears, "Towards a Theology", 66.
154. Hunt, *If Two Shall Agree*, 84.
155. Minute of the Chief of the Staff, 1995/IA/20, dated 7 July, 1995.
156. Minute by the Chief of the Staff, 1995/IA/15.

In 1997 Paul Rader took the further step of ruling that his wife would be ranked as a commissioner. Hitherto the General's wife had been known as, for example, Mrs General Rader. While not binding on his successors in office, this more than brought international leadership into line with the new provision for all wives to hold their rank in their own right; it also fueled "speculation that the time may come when other married officers will hold different ranks from their spouses."[157] And such in fact proved to be the case. Within a few years some corps were intrigued by the fact that their married officer couples now wore different insignia, dependent upon their individual length of service. In some countries cultural norms made this impracticable, and in territories embracing more than one country and culture the application of the new rule could cause puzzlement. Tonga for example is part of the New Zealand territory and subject to New Zealand regulation, but Tongan Salvationists were evidently surprised that their regional commander should be a captain while his wife was a major.

A marker of the changes over these years was the way in which the official form of address for married women officers changed from, for example, "Mrs Lieutenant Murray Flagg," to "Mrs Lieutenant Murray (Deborah) Flagg," to "Mrs Captain Deborah Flagg," to "Major Deborah Flagg."[158] The official designation changed from "officer-wife" (considered a great advance on "officer's wife")[159] to "married woman-officer"—although Captain Violet Smart wanted to know if men were now to be "married men-officers" as well. "No more labels, please!" she requested.[160]

Other anomalies remained in the new ranking system. Commissioned ranks of Lt. Colonel and above (once described as "staff ranks") are described as "conferred ranks" and go with certain senior administrative roles. The practice of individual ranks is only more recently being extended to this level, except in the case of the General's spouse. Major Vinti's 1975 vision of a woman commissioner with her spouse a major serving in her headquarters has not yet been realized.

Dr John Coutts, still campaigning for the principle of equality, rained on the Army's parade in 1998 by pointing out: "Now the wives of officers have gained their rank in their own right. This will certainly improve the gender balance at the High Council. But will the wives really be there in their own right? The new women Commissioners have in fact been appointed by virtue of being married to their husbands. A 'Mrs Major'—no matter how well qualified—will not progress until her other half is promoted."[161] Despite their new rank and status the women leaders may still be at a disadvantage in conference and council, without the necessary opportunities for real leadership over the years and experience that would give greater credibility to their views. That may take some years of "real" appointments to establish.

A piece of window-dressing in the *Yearbook* from 2003 was that the entry for each territory was now headed with the names of the territorial commander and spouse as "Territorial Leaders" but so that there should be no mistake this was immediately

---

157. *Salvationist*, 30 August 1997, 3.
158. Flagg, "Softly Eclipsed", *New Frontier*, 30 April 1997, 6–7; *Officer*, October 1997, 12–17.
159. *Officer*, September–October 1960, 358.
160. *Officer*, June 1992, 287–88.
161. *Salvationist*, 28 March 1998, 7.

followed by the name of the "territorial commander." At time of writing, the latter name is always that of the male partner. However, in 2013 the Commissioning of new officers in the New Zealand territory was undertaken by both Commissioners Robert and Janine Donaldson, who commissioned the lieutenants alternately. As they said, "Why not?"

The developments described above were taken further by the international commission on officership and subsequent changes in regulations. However at this point it is appropriate to pause and take stock.

The issue for women, and particularly for married women, has been whether they were really "officers." While the stand taken by the Booths was ground-breaking in the nineteenth century, they found it difficult to apply the principle of gender equality across the board, quite naturally because they were prisoners of their own times and assumptions. Theological principles are not easily imposed on resistant cultural norms. Andrew Mark Eason's *Women in God's Army* explores and analyzes:

> [T]he cultural and theological foundations upon which the organization was established. Reflecting views that were similar to those of their male counterparts, most Army women espoused beliefs and accepted roles that were incompatible with a principle of sexual equality. A female officer's moral and spiritual functions in the home, combined with her other domestic tasks, either called into question or placed constraints upon her public ministry . . . Within the public realm, a married or single female officer was usually confined to responsibilities consistent with the notion of sexual difference. She was encouraged to possess a femininity defined in terms of self-sacrifice, weakness, dependency and emotion. This construction of womanhood allowed women to challenge sinners publicly from the platform or engage in social work, but their overall ministry remained a modest one . . . Her ideal role was one of service and submission rather than leadership and authority.[162]

Lt. Colonel Barbara Robinson of Canada, reviewing Eason's book for *Word and Deed*, concluded, "The most disturbing aspect of this book . . . is that while Andrew Eason is a historian and *Women in God's Army* is a historical monograph, his book comes far too close to describing the contemporary Army practice for comfort. So read it—and shudder!"[163]

Major Karen Shakespeare also addressed the cultural factor in a theological reflection in the 2004 Report of the Gender Issues Commission in the United Kingdom.

> Historically the culture of British society has supported a patriarchal model for the theology of gender. The assumptions of modernity encouraged a gender separation in which men were seen to be logical, unemotional and suited to public life and leadership and women found their role in relational activities, most often in the home or in a 'caring' profession. The Salvation Army, whilst affirming the equality of all in doctrinal and policy statements, has in practice demonstrated a theology which privileges men and assumes an essentially different role for women, especially those who are married. In the post-modern world,

---

162. Eason, *Women in God's Army*, 152.
163. *Word and Deed*, November 2003, 90–93.

which no longer accepts the assumptions of modern culture, there is a need to re-assess and possibly re-think our theological understanding of gender.[164]

The principle of genuinely shared married leadership is however also enjoying a new lease of life. Major Richard Munn (USA), writing on "Married Officer Leadership," while noting that the Army is positioned "to speak with some authority on the subject of dual clergy couples" and so "effectively poised to engage a culture that is increasingly faced with the familial and marital ramifications of two employed parents," goes on to say that,

> While purporting egalitarian leadership . . . and advocating shared formal authority for men and women, the married officer leadership model often functions along quite traditional gender roles. Externally this is expressed through denominational polity with men consistently holding the dominant leadership positions. Internally it is expressed with the majority of officer couples indicating that the man is the "spiritual head of the family." Thus, while demonstrating much strength, the unique contribution of the married officer leadership model may not be fully maximized. The matter might be deficient theology.[165]

Munn takes Priscilla and Aquila as "the quintessential dual clergy couple" and explores the principles found in the six Bible references to them as appropriate for officer couples' ministry.[166] He suggests that the married officer leadership model is a unique strength of the Army and that "we seem unusually primed 'for such a time as this.'"

One of the commitments General Clifton made to the 2006 High Council was to "bring on more women leaders," and he had urged territorial leaders to appoint more women divisional commanders in order to provide a larger pool of potential senior women appointees to even more senior roles. A single woman was appointed Chief of the Staff. In the course of two years, three women had been appointed territorial commanders (two were already TCs but moved territories) and one as an international secretary, six as chief secretaries, fifteen to various cabinet roles and twenty as divisional commanders.[167] It is not clear how many of these were married women whose husbands held other appointments[168]—none of the territorial commanders or chief secretaries were. In 2011, a single woman was elected General (the third woman out of nineteen Generals in office to that point), and a married woman was appointed chief secretary in Germany, her husband being territorial youth secretary, a subordinate role.

In 2015 General Cox took a further step with the extension to "conferred ranks" (lieutenant colonel and above) of the principle of separate ranks for spouses. Hitherto the spouse of an officer promoted to lieut. colonel would take the same rank but it was announced that conferred ranks would be confined to those serving in specific senior roles, irrespective of gender. It is not clear how far such a practice may extend but it may

---

164. Shakespeare, quoted by Yuill in "Nettles and Wineskins," 15–16.
165. Munn, "Married Officer Leadership," *Officer*, July–August 2004, 11.
166. Acts 18:2, 18, 26; Romans 16:3; 2 Timothy 4:19; 1 Corinthians 16:19.
167. *Officer*, September–October 2009, 5–6.
168. From the 2010 *Year Book*: in the Australia Eastern, Canada, India Northern, Japan, Argentina and Sri Lanka territories at least one married woman whose husband held a separate appointment served as a Divisional Commander.

yet prove possible for a woman commissioner to be elected General while married to a major. General Cox's reforms of governance may also include significant changes in the roles of married senior leaders. Wives of male territorial commanders and chief secretaries need not find their sphere of service confined to "women's ministry" appointments, which will erode the "married women's ghetto" about which Major Danielle Strickland has written so passionately. At time of writing, the newly united Australian territory has committed to this reform.

It took a long time for the Christian ethic to bring about the cessation of gladiatorial contests and longer for it to achieve the abolition of slavery. It was only towards the end of the twentieth century that the mainstream protestant western church began to bring its understanding of ordained ministry into line with its belief that in Christ there is neither male nor female.[169] The Salvation Army, having in some senses pioneered this direction, evidently lost its momentum fairly early in its history, while continuing to believe its own rhetoric, and has only comparatively recently begun to address the issues again.

---

169. Galatians 3:28.

5

Salvation Army Theology 1: We Believe

> "The only thing we care to teach as to theological questions is,
> that they are to be avoided as much as possible."[1]
> —William Booth

Sir Paul Harvey in *The Oxford Dictionary of English Literature* brusquely dismissed William Booth as "entirely ignorant of theology."[2] Rather more generously, General Coutts wrote that "For the militant mission on which [the Army] set out . . . its doctrinal impedimenta had to go into the smallest of knapsacks."[3] The Salvation Army seldom referred to "theology" over the years. It had "doctrines": a handy summary of all that was needed to keep its preaching on the right track. Since the 1870s, it has subscribed to eleven statements of belief, or the "Eleven Points" of Doctrine.

1 **We believe** that the Scriptures of the Old and New Testaments were given by inspiration of God, and that they only constitute the Divine rule of Christian faith and practice.

2 **We believe** that there is only one God, who is infinitely perfect, the Creator, Preserver, and Governor of all things, and who is the only proper object of religious worship.

3 **We believe** that there are three persons in the Godhead—the Father, the Son, and the Holy Ghost, undivided in essence and co-equal in power and glory.

4 **We believe** that in the person of Jesus Christ the Divine and human natures are united, so that He is truly and properly God and truly and properly man.

5 **We believe** that our first parents were created in a state of innocency, but by their disobedience, they lost their purity and happiness, and that in consequence of their

---

1. Booth, in *Salvation War*, 165. (I am indebted to Gordon Cotterill for the quotation.)
2. Harvey, "Booth, William," 99.
3. Coutts, "Smallest of Knapsacks," 504.

fall, all men have become sinners, totally depraved, and as such are justly exposed to the wrath of God.

6 **We believe** that the Lord Jesus Christ has by His suffering and death made an atonement for the whole world so that whosoever will may be saved.

7 **We believe** that repentance toward God, faith in our Lord Jesus Christ and regeneration by the Holy Spirit are necessary to salvation.

8 **We believe** that we are justified by grace through faith in our Lord Jesus Christ and that he that believeth hath the witness in himself.

9 **We believe** that continuance in a state of salvation depends upon continued obedient faith in Christ.

10 **We believe** that it is the privilege of all believers to be wholly sanctified, and that their whole spirit and soul and body may be preserved blameless unto the coming of our Lord Jesus Christ.

11 **We believe** in the immortality of the soul, the resurrection of the body, in the general judgement at the end of the world, in the eternal happiness of the righteous, and in the endless punishment of the wicked.

These were not handed over on golden tablets by an angel, like the Book of Mormon. They had a pre-history, in the evangelical revival and Methodism, and a history, from the East London Christian Revival Society to the Christian Mission, to the Salvation Army; from a non-denominational group drawn from various traditions to a proto-denomination. In the earliest stages, the Christian Mission gives the impression of not being too fussy about them: the Rules of the Christian Mission (1875) read, "No person would be disqualified from membership on account of minor differences in doctrine, provided such did not cause dissension in the Society."[4] No example of such a "minor difference" was given, however.

Conversely, an example of a major difference was evidently Doctrine Nine, on Final Perseverance ("We believe that continuance in a state of salvation depends upon continued obedient faith in Christ"). This was in the Methodist New Connexion doctrines but had not figured in the Revival Society's doctrines—probably some members were from Calvinist-leaning churches—Congregationalists or Presbyterians; certainly some were Huguenots, belonging to "The Christian Community." There may have been some dissension about this, because Bramwell Booth moved at the 1873 Conference that "no person shall be allowed to teach in the Christian Mission the doctrine of Final Perseverance" (i.e. "once saved, always saved").[5] Such things are not said without cause. Perhaps, though there is no surviving evidence for this, Doctrine 9 was inserted into the Christian Mission's doctrines to ensure that evangelists maintained an Arminian account of free will.

So the Salvation Army *did* have a "theology;" it just didn't think of it as theology. Nor did anyone else until comparatively recently, and Salvationists are still likely to be

---

4. Sandall, *History*, I, 282.
5. Sandall, Ibid., I, 263–64.

informed loftily, as I was recently by a learned clergyman, that the Army is deficient in this respect. Only in 2015 was its "Doctrine Council" re-named a "Theology Council."

Our concern here is primarily historical rather than theological, so this study traces the evolution of Salvationist beliefs but does not attempt a detailed critique or evaluation of the various positions adopted and explanations offered. This chapter will look at the derivation of the Salvation Army's doctrinal position, its doctrinal development, its claim to be a holiness movement and its stance on sacraments.

DERIVATION AND DEVELOPMENT OF THE SALVATION ARMY'S DOCTRINAL POSITION

The Salvation Army's DNA is Methodist. Wesley's evangelicalism, Arminianism and teaching on "Christian perfection" or "holiness" were Booth's creed as well. The doctrines and conference polity of the Christian Mission were entirely Methodist.[6] The Salvation Army retained the doctrines but not the polity.

Having said that, Wesley, whose own opinions and methods changed and developed over a long life, had been in his grave thirty-eight years before William Booth's birth, and Methodism had not stood still in the intervening period. By the time Booth was ordained, over sixty years of evolution had produced a Methodist Church, or rather family of Wesleyan churches, which its founder might have struggled to recognize or own. Booth inherited an eroded Wesleyan theological landscape. Methodism's later ecclesiology would have been anathema to the churchman Wesley himself. An example of doctrinal divergence would be the varying emphasis on the sacraments: to Wesley a vital and objective means of grace, to some mid-nineteenth century Methodists more perfunctory and subjective, and by William Booth as an heir of Methodism, able to be dispensed with, apparently without any too severe a sense of loss.

Strictly speaking, Booth *was* ignorant of academic theology; he had little idea of the complex sources of Wesley's theology, of the English church tradition and the eastern mystics. He had had limited formal schooling, and minimal theological training on top of it. He spent a few months (July–October 1852) reading towards the Congregational Church's ministry, from which plan he withdrew upon discovering that they expected him to toe the Calvinist line on predestination. Then from February to July 1854 he studied for the Methodist New Connexion ministry in the home of Dr William Cooke, who soon saw that Booth found study frustrating and wanted to be out evangelizing, so he let him go and do that. That was it, as far as formal training was concerned. He wasn't proud of ignorance—Begbie says "he agonized more than was good for his health over intellectual deficiencies."[7]

Booth urged Bramwell to get a grounding in theology as he would need it in the role to which he would succeed. "You *must* have among other things a knowledge of systematic theology . . . You have lately felt your need here, and as a public man, probably a very public man, to hold your own with the preachers and with the public you must have

---

6. Rhemick, *New People of God*. Green; *Life and Ministry of William Booth*.
7. Begbie, *William Booth*, I, 206–07.

information and skill in controversial theology . . . *To go to College*—the difficulty would arise: *where?* . . . The effect of my son being at College would not be good, and *moreover*, I am sure there is no necessity, if you would set yourself and *adhere* to a moderate round of reading and study."[8]

Booth was not a systematic thinker and produced no systematic theology so any picture of his beliefs has to be pieced together from books and from articles in Army publications. Roger Green says that the task of researching Booth's theology is made difficult firstly by a lack of precision in Booth's own writing and in his seldom identifying his sources, and secondly by Booth's "lack of critical awareness of how theology is formulated or of how and why theology changes. He was not always aware of the forces which shaped his own theology or of the changes that were taking place in his theology."[9] None of this diminishes Booth's achievements; rather, it magnifies them. None of what he lacked stood in the way of his founding and leading a world-wide religious movement. He was so much the driving force behind the Salvation Army that it was his views and theological understanding which shaped the Army's theology. That also renders it the more necessary to understand him.

Booth saw Methodism through the lenses of the New England revivalism provided by Caughey, Finney and Palmer, to whose influence we have already referred.

James Caughey was an evangelist who visited and worked in Britain four times in the 1840s and 1850s, during which time the Booths met him, sought his counsel and observed his work. Norman Murdoch describes Caughey's legacy as "the idea of winning souls through mass meetings, house-to-house visitation, and personal witness."[10] A Methodist who worked independently from official church structures, Caughey also introduced Booth to the American practice of inviting penitents to come and kneel at the communion rail or mourners' bench during a prayer meeting after the sermon.

Charles Grandison Finney, who visited Britain twice, was a powerful evangelist, anti-slavery campaigner and advocate for women's rights (seekers at his meetings had to sign up for one or other cause or were not considered serious about their salvation). Like Caughey he called seekers to the altar rail and though a Presbyterian he did not hold strongly Calvinist views on election. Booth emulated his extemporary style of preaching. His *Lectures on Revivals and Religion* was a favorite book of the Booths and his autobiography was reprinted by the Army.

Phoebe Palmer was the third of this American triad who campaigned in Great Britain. She influenced the Booths for women's ministry—Catherine's pamphlet on "Female Preaching" was in Palmer's defense when she was criticized for speaking in public. Palmer was also a notable influence as far as the teaching of holiness was concerned. It has been argued that the Booths found Palmer's version of the Wesleyan doctrine of Christian Perfection to be entirely persuasive and adopted it holus-bolus as their standard, but John Read's recent study has shown that the sources of Catherine Booth's

---

8. Letter dated 27 August 1876, in Bramwell-Booth, *Bramwell Booth*, 70.

9. Green, *War on Two Fronts*, 15.

10. Murdoch, *Origins*, 8.

theology in particular were at the same time more authentically Wesleyan, more eclectic and more nuanced.[11]

The beliefs of the East London Christian Revival Society (or Union) were drawn up about 1866 with seven doctrines. The first printed document of the movement, issued in 1866 or 1867, included these seven "Articles of Faith" and a five-point "Bond of Agreement." This was to serve an "unsectarian mission," which co-workers who "hold the Word of God as the statement of faith and practice and whose hearts are in sympathy with revival work" were invited to join, without leaving their existing churches. In fact, this ushered in the phase when members *did* either leave their existing churches, or went back to them. With the gathering and retention of converts who belonged to no other church and would not go to them, other articles particularly concerned with the on-going Christian life after conversion were added. The seven articles evolved into ten by 1870 when they were listed in the new constitution of the Mission, and the eleventh was added around 1873–74.

The current *Handbook of Doctrine* says that Methodist derivation of Salvation Army doctrine is expressed particularly in "our strong emphasis on regeneration and sanctification, our conviction that the gospel is for the whosoever and our concern for humanity's free will . . . "[12]

John Rhemick produced a helpful comparison of the beliefs of Booth's former denomination the Methodist New Connexion (1838), the Revival Society and Salvation Army Doctrines in his book, *A New People of God*. He says:

> A casual reading of the doctrines of the Methodist New Connexion, The Salvation Army of 1878 (and the Christian Mission prior to this date), and the seven doctrines of the East London Christian Revival Society dating back to 1866 show that they contain essentially the same statements of faith. The New Connexion statement of faith contains one doctrine, no. 7, concerning free will in the statement of sin and damnation as well as redemption and salvation, which does not appear in either The Salvation Army or the Revival Society statements. The Revival Society statement contains no doctrine on justification by grace through faith or on sanctification as these were added later in the evolution of the Society to The Salvation Army. It is interesting to note that these later doctrinal statements of The Salvation Army (i.e. nos. 8 and 10) bear a close connection to their New Connexion counterpart, no. 6. Salvation Army doctrine 9, although similar in content to New Connexion 8, is quite different in wording.
>
> It is clear that Salvation Army doctrinal statements in the formative years of its growth were in no essential way different from the New Connexion statements and that . . . Salvation Army doctrine is a derivative of Methodist doctrine.[13]

Rhemick set out these doctrines in a table, adapted here:

---

11. Read, *Catherine Booth*, 85–118.
12. *Salvation Story*, 1998, 131.
13. Rhemick, *New People of God*, 30–34.

	Methodist New Connexion	East London Christian Revival Society	The Salvation Army
1	2. We believe that the scriptures of the Old and New Testaments are given by Divine inspiration, and form a complete rule of faith and practice.	1. We believe that the Scriptures of the Old and New Testaments were given by inspiration of God and are the only rule of Christian faith and practice.	1. We believe that the Scriptures of the Old and New Testaments were given by inspiration of God and that they only constitute the Divine rule of Christian faith and practice.
2	1. We believe in the existence and perfections of the Supreme Being.	3. We believe that there is one only living and true God—the Father, the Son, and the Holy Ghost—three persons in one God—equal in power and glory, and the only proper object of religious worship.	2. We believe that there is only one God who is infinitely perfect; the Creator, Preserver, and Governor of all things; and who is the only proper object of religious worship.
3	3. We believe in the Divinity of Christ, and in the Personality and Godhead of the Holy Spirit.	3. As above	3. We believe that there are three persons in the Godhead—the Father, the Son, and the Holy Ghost—undivided in essence and co-equal in power and glory.
4		3. We believe that in the person of Jesus Christ the Divine and human natures are united, so that He is truly and properly God, and truly and properly man.	4. We believe that in the person of Jesus Christ, the Divine and human natures are united, so that He is truly and properly God and truly and properly man
5	4. We believe that Adam, by his fall, involved all his posterity in guilt and depravity, and that Christ has made an atonement for the sins of all mankind; and that there is no other name given under heaven by which we can be saved.	4. We believe that all mankind, in consequence of the disobedience of Adam, are sinners, destitute of holiness, and justly exposed to the penalty of the divine law.	5. We believe that our first parents were created in a state of innocency but by their disobedience they lost their purity and happiness and that in consequence of their fall all men have become sinners totally depraved and as such are justly exposed to the wrath of God.
6	4. As above	5. We believe that the Lord Jesus Christ has, by His suffering and death made an atonement for the whole world, so that whosoever will may be saved.	6. We believe that the Lord Jesus Christ has by His suffering and death made an atonement for the whole world so that whosoever will may be saved.
7	5. We believe that repentance is absolutely necessary to salvation.	6. We believe that repentance towards God, faith in our Lord Jesus Christ, and regeneration by the Holy Spirit are necessary to salvation.	7. We believe that repentance toward God faith in our Lord Jesus Christ, and regeneration by the Holy Spirit are necessary to salvation.

	Methodist New Connexion	East London Christian Revival Society	The Salvation Army
	7. We believe that all our salvation is of God, and that man's damnation is all of himself. Nevertheless, we believe that in the gospel plan of redemption, men are treated as rational accountable creatures: that 'it is God that worketh in us to will and to do of his own good pleasure'; and that we are to 'work out our own salvation with fear and trembling.'		
8	6. We believe that justification is by grace through faith, and that he that believeth hath the witness in himself: that it is our privilege to be fully sanctified in the name of the Lord Jesus Christ, and by the Spirit of our God		8. We believe that we are justified by grace through faith in our Lord Jesus Christ and that he that believeth hath the witness in himself.
9	8. We believe that it is possible for man to fall finally from grace.		9. We believe that continuance in a state of salvation depends upon continued obedient faith in Christ.
10	Part of 6: . . . that it is our privilege to be fully sanctified in the name of the Lord Jesus Christ, and by the Spirit of our God.		10. We believe that it is the privilege of all believers to be 'wholly sanctified' and that their 'whole spirit and soul and body' may 'be preserved blameless unto the coming of our Lord Jesus Christ.' (I Thessalonians 5:23).
11	9. We believe the soul to be immortal, and that after death it immediately enters upon a state of happiness or misery.10. We believe in the general judgement at the last day, in the eternal happiness of the righteous and in the endless punishment of the wicked.	7. We believe in the immortality of the soul—in the resurrection of the body—in the general judgment at the end of the world—in the eternal happiness of the righteous—and in the endless punishment of the wicked.'	11. We believe in the immortality of the soul in the resurrection of the body in the general judgment at the end of the world in the eternal happiness of the righteous and in the endless punishment of the wicked.

The Salvation Army's belief concerning Scripture is set first because the Army, like all evangelical protestant bodies, regards the Bible as foundational. Although the New Connexion statement of faith gave this doctrine second rather than first place, the Revival Society, Booth's first essay at organization, followed the 1846 articles of the

Evangelical Alliance in beginning in this way. The Evangelical Alliance also included a separate article on the divine institution of Christian ministry and sacraments. These were evidently considered by Booth to be unnecessary in this context, even though he did at the time practice them, because his society was not, after all, intended to be a church. The New Connexion included these amongst Ordinances rather than Doctrines.

While the Army is sometimes regarded as "fundamentalist" in its view of the Bible, and some of its members today would claim to be fundamentalist, it never has been—it long pre-dated the emergence of modern biblical fundamentalism in the early twentieth century. Booth had a simple but not simplistic view of Scripture. Despite his thoroughly conservative, Protestant high view of the Bible, as enshrined in the Army's first doctrine, he believed that the Bible *contained* the Word of God rather than that it *was* the Word of God.[14] He did not subscribe to theories of verbal inspiration and inerrancy. He was fully alive to mistakes in preservation, translation and transmission of the text, and of commentary regarded as text.

> What is claimed for the Bible? Not that every word is inspired . . . Not that it is without mystery . . . Not that every passage is easily understood . . . Not that in its present form it is entirely free from errors . . . "[15]

This does not mean that he was familiar with or in agreement with all the emerging findings and fashions of the biblical scholarship of his time. None of that was very significant to him; as a pragmatist, his interest was that the books contained what God wanted people to know, that is:

1. The history of much of God's dealing with the race.
2. His view of human conduct, and the principles which ought to regulate it.
3. The redemption of mankind by Jesus Christ.
4. The possibility of our restoration to His favour.
5. The conditions of salvation.
6. The final future judgement.
7. The everlasting destiny of mankind.[16]

He also counselled that the Bible could be exalted too highly, and put in the place of God, and regretted that "the letter of it rather than its spirit has been held in chief regard." He said it was a mistake to regard it as God's only revelation: "It contains the fullest and highest but not the only, light He has given to men." While welcoming new translations, such as the *Revised Version* in 1885, he thought it would be better to "express it as nearly as we can, not in the stiff and ancient language used three hundred years ago, but in that

---

14. Theologically conservative Salvationists would prefer to express it otherwise: "It does not only *contain* the Word of God, but it *is* the Word of God." Agnew, *Manual of Salvationism*, 8.

15. Booth and Cunningham, *Bible*, 12. This was a brief collection from various sources. Booth's articles were from *War Cry* of 30 May, 1885, *Founder's Messages to Soldiers* 1907–08 (reprinted in 1921) Chapters XI and XII, and an article reprinted in *Staff Review* January 1927.

16. Booth and Cunningham, *Bible*, 13–14.

form of speech employed by people in the present day."[17] He accordingly distributed to English-speaking officers copies of the *Twentieth Century New Testament*, a contemporary translation which became available at the turn of the century.[18] He believed its most effective translation was into lives well lived. A useful account of this question is found in John Coutts' book, *The Salvationists*.[19] A collection of articles and chapters from books by a number of Salvationist writers was also published as *The Salvationist and the Scriptures*, edited by John D. Waldron.[20]

Alfred G. Cunningham spent years in literary work and retired as Chief of the Staff to General Carpenter in the 1940s. In the late 1920s, when biblical fundamentalism was gathering momentum in conservative evangelical circles, he published articles refuting such views.[21] Today, in the words of Gordon Moyles, "By most standards . . . the Salvation Army's approach to the Bible is firmly latitudinarian."[22]

The first handbook of Salvation Army beliefs was *The Doctrines and Discipline of The Salvation Army*, produced in 1881 "Prepared for the Training Homes" for Salvation Army officers. After allegations that this was a "secret book" containing the "real" beliefs and practices of the Army which he was supposedly unwilling to reveal to the general public, Booth published a public edition in 1883, identical apart from a more detailed explanation of the Army's teaching on holiness. Minus the "Disciplines" sections and called simply *Doctrines of The Salvation Army* after 1885, and subtitled "Prepared for the Use of Cadets Training for Officership" after 1900, this continued to be reprinted until 1917.[23] (The "Disciplines" were subsumed under a new edition of the *Orders and Regulations*, published in 1886.)

Philip Needham traced "the basic source for Booth's *Doctrines and Discipline* [to] the Rev. Benjamin Field's *The Student's Handbook of Christian Theology*, originally published in 1868." From this larger Methodist volume Booth selected and simplified the presentation of those doctrines he thought were necessary for the Army.[24] *Doctrines and Discipline* was set out as a catechism and its homely, colloquial aspect is illustrated in the scanned extract overleaf.

A new *Handbook of Salvation Army Doctrine* was published in 1922 as a "Training Garrison Edition" and then for general sale in 1923. This was prepared by Bramwell Booth, working with Alfred G. Cunningham. The new format, if not the theology, was more sophisticated and systematic rather than catechetical, and was based on the framework of the Eleven Points of Doctrine. This is also illustrated by a scanned extract.

---

17. Ibid., 13–14.
18. *The Twentieth Century New Testament* (London: Sunday School Union, 1904).
19. Coutts, *Salvationists*, 3–17.
20. Waldron, *Salvationist and Scriptures*, 1988.
21. Booth and Cunningham, *Bible*, 17–49. Cunningham's contribution was reprinted from *Staff Review*, October 1926, 393–401 and January 1927, 23–34.
22. Moyles, *Blood and Fire in Canada*, 236.
23. Waldron, *Salvationist and Scriptures*, 37.
24. Needham, "Redemption and Social Reformation," 1967, 126, cited by Green, *War on Two Fronts*, 43.

Section 4.—HOW WE BECAME SINNERS.

1. You say you have a soul. What do you mean by that?

That there is within man a spirit altogether separate from and independent of his body. A spirit which thinks, wills, knows, and feels, and by which he can distinguish good from evil.

2. Will this soul die with the body?

No; the soul is immortal; that is, it can never perish.

"Then shall the dust return to the earth as it was; and the spirit shall return unto God who gave it."—*Ecclesiastes* xii. 7.

"For what is a man profited, if he shall gain the whole world, and lose his own soul? or what shall a man give in exchange for his soul?"—*Matthew* xvi. 26.

3. You often say, when you are talking, that we are all sinners. How is this? Did God make men sinners?

Oh, dear, no. God made Adam and Eve, our first parents, *perfectly pure*, and pronounced them to be good. He also made every arrangement for them to keep on being *good and happy*, which had they done, the world would now have been full of holy, happy people.

"Lo, this only have I found, that God hath made man upright; but they have sought out many inventions."—*Ecclesiastes* vii. 29.

"O that thou hadst hearkened to my commandments! then had thy peace been as a river, and thy righteousness as the waves of the sea."—*Isaiah* xlviii. 18.

4. How then did they fall?

God gave Adam and Eve permission to eat of the fruit of every tree in the garden save one; if they ate of that

CHAPTER V

MAN

Sec. I.—The Nature of Man.
 ,, II.—The Origin of Man.
Sec. III.—The Fall of Man.
 ,, IV.—The Sinfulness of Man.

> 'We believe that our first parents were created in a state of innocence, but by their disobedience they lost their purity and happiness; and that, in consequence of their fall, all men have become sinners, totally depraved, and as such are justly exposed to the wrath of God.'

Section I.—THE NATURE OF MAN

1. Man, as we see and know him, is One Being, yet he has both a Body and a Soul, or a lower and a higher nature. This is clear from the fact that, at death, man's soul departs, leaving his body cold, lifeless, and decaying.

> 'Then shall the dust return to the earth as it was; and the spirit shall return unto God who gave it' (Ecclesiastes xii. 7).

(a) The *body* is the material part of man, that by which he is related to the natural world around him. The body is mortal; that is, it will die.

(b) The *soul* is the spirit within man, by which he is related to God and the unseen. The soul is immortal; that is, it will live after the death of the body (*see Chapter XI*).

The Bible does not clearly distinguish between 'soul' and 'spirit'; generally, however, man's higher nature is spoken of as 'soul' when considered in reference to the things of time and sense, as 'spirit' when considered in reference to the things of eternity.

We might compare the Salvation Army's practice with that of Pentecostalism. According to Macchia, "Pentecostals began [in the 1930s] to produce encyclopedic guides to 'Bible Doctrines.' These guides consisted of brief definitions of theological terms supported by clusters of proof texts. As guides to doctrine, they were written to define the essential beliefs of the Pentecostal churches. They were not theologies in the sense of being critically reflective on the church's belief and praxis in the light of the Scriptures and various contextual challenges."[25] That could have been said of the Salvation Army as well.

Revised editions of the Army's 1923 doctrine book were reprinted at intervals up until 1964. After many years' preparation a new *Handbook of Doctrine* was produced in 1969, followed by a simplified abridgement, *The Doctrine We Adorn*, in 1982. Both carried the Apostles Creed and the Nicene Creed as appendices—a first for Army publications. They were superseded in 1998 by *Salvation Story*, in colorful binding, with an accompanying *Study Guide* published the following year. A new edition, conflating these two books under the earlier name of *The Salvation Army Handbook of Doctrine*, and with a cover perhaps considered less frivolous, was published in 2010.

The doctrines themselves have remained unchanged since 1878. However, the preamble, "That the religious doctrines professed and believed and taught . . . are and shall for ever be as follows . . . " was changed in the 1980 Salvation Army Act which allowed that the schedule "may from time to time be extended or varied by deed executed by the General, such deed having the prior written approval of more than two-thirds of the Commissioners."[26]

As permitted by the Salvation Army Act 1980, the Doctrine Council constituted in 1992 asked if change could be recommended to the doctrines to correct omissions, the most significant of which is that of the resurrection of Christ. Such permission was initially granted. Later, on the advice of the Advisory Council to the General, the General instructed the Doctrine Council to make no changes . . . [27] However, in writing the 1998 Handbook of Doctrine, *Salvation Story*, the Council was able to include summary statements which dealt with doctrinal omissions, such as the Virgin Birth, the Resurrection and a doctrine of the Church.

Two other changes over the years, not to the doctrines themselves but to commentary on them, relate to additions to doctrines 9, on "final perseverance," and 10, on sanctification. At some point, possibly in 1876, the polemic against the Calvinist doctrine of election was emphasized by an addition to No. 9 indicating that it was "possible for those who have been truly converted to fall away and be eternally lost," drawing on the more negative expression in the New Connexion's doctrine 8. Also at the 1876 Christian Mission Conference Railton proposed an explanatory addition for No. 10, describing how after conversion "roots of bitterness" remained in the heart of the believer and that these could be totally removed with sanctification.[28]

25. Macchia, "Struggle for Global Witness," in Dempster, Klaus, and Petersen, *Globalization of Pentecostalism*, 9.

26. Salvation Army Act, 1980. cxxx, s14; quoted in Rivers, *Law of Organized Religion*, 85.

27. Robinson, "History of Salvation Army Doctrine," 34.

28. Sandall, *History*, I, 264.

While these additions were not incorporated in the doctrines as stated in the 1878 Foundation Deed Poll, they were commonly printed with them. In the 1886 *Orders and Regulations*, in the 1900 *Doctrines of The Salvation Army* and in the 1923 *Handbook of Doctrine* the two additions were printed with Doctrines 9 and 10 without any distinction from them. By the 1940 *Handbook* they were printed as footnotes or in parenthesis. General Coutts deleted both additions from the 1969 *Handbook*, being concerned that the scriptural "roots of bitterness" figure did not originally relate to this doctrine at all and could give a misleading impression, although the essence of the doctrines they were intended to elucidate remains unaltered.

Curiously, considering the subject's centrality for a movement called the Salvation Army, there appears to have been little debate on the nature of the atonement. Even although successive doctrine books have taken pains to outline a variety of imagery for explaining the inexplicable, anecdotal evidence from preaching suggests that "substitutionary" and "vicarious satisfaction" theories have usually been taken as the received orthodoxy.[29] When the Salvation Army in New Zealand was signing its first agreement with the theologically conservative Bible College of New Zealand (now Laidlaw College) for recognition of academic credentials, the Officer Training College education officer (dean of studies) queried the Army's position on this because penal substitutionary atonement was in the BCNZ statement of faith, to which the Army's college would have to adhere. He was told to go ahead and get it signed because substitutionary atonement was what the Army believed in.[30] On the other hand, John Read in his study of Catherine Booth's theology shows that she was uncomfortable with this theory.[31] One of Commissioner J. D. Waldron's numerous and valuable compilations of a century-worth of Salvationist writing on various topics deals with the question of atonement.[32]

Most writing about Salvation Army beliefs over the years has been exhortatory and inspirational, like Brengle's books on holiness, or else explanatory at a fairly simple level, like John Larsson's *Doctrine without Tears*, a booklet derived from a series of articles written for the youth magazine, *Vanguard*. There has been little analytical writing. A rare and all too brief general work was Harry Dean's *Reason to Believe*, described by William Barclay in his foreword as "the product of a full mind and an exploring intellect" and as "a valuable contribution to practical twentieth century Christian apologetic."[33]

While there may have been a number of academic theses on Salvation Army theology, I know of just two significant published works on the development of Salvation Army theology *in general*, though some other books have addressed particular areas

---

29. See the variety of interpretations made available for example in the most recent, *Salvation Army Handbook of Doctrine*, 2010, 134–41. I remember being taken to task after my first sermon ever, as a teenager, because I had drawn on the "moral influence" theory espoused by Augustine and Abelard.

30. Kingsley Sampson to author, email, 23 January 2017. The academic level at which Laidlaw operates is similar to that of the Salvation Army's Booth University College in Winnipeg. (Legally, the term "University" is restricted in New Zealand and private institutions do not have permission to use it, although their diploma and degree qualifications are accredited by the New Zealand Qualifications Authority.)

31. Read, *Catherine Booth*, 30–39.

32. Waldron, *Salvationist and the Atonement*.

33. Dean, *Reason to Believe*, [5].

of belief.[34] Both were derived from American PhD theses: Roger J. Green's *War on Two Fronts: the Redemptive Theology of William Booth*, published in 1989, and John R. Rhemick's *A New People of God: a Study in Salvationism*, published in 1993 though dating from 1984.

Both argue, in Rhemick's words, "that Army theology, and especially the expression of that theology, played a major role in establishing the Army as a religious and social institution . . . "[35] Secondly, both are concerned (again in Rhemick's words) with "one of the perennial theological problems of the Christian Church: how is the Church to combine faith and works in such a way as to treat the salvation of the soul with ultimate concern while not forsaking the equally demanding obligation of the Church to care for the physical well-being of the poor and destitute."[36] Thirdly, both see a renewal of Booth's theological insights as essential for the Army in finding its way in the present time. Rhemick again: "Unless this theology is again raised to pre-eminence in the hearts, minds and lives of the Army's people today, The Salvation Army will be left with a mission that defies its spiritual capacities."[37]

Rhemick's introduction proposes that his study would

> establish three positions with regard to the theology of The Salvation Army in its formative years: (1) that Salvation Army theology is a direct derivative of Methodist theological thought; (2) that the essence of the Army's theological constructs, namely its doctrines on salvation and sanctification, and its unwritten doctrine of the Church, met a critical social and cultural need, namely the disenfranchisement of the masses of poor people from societal provisions and possibilities; (3) that the nature of the Army's theological expression met a critical social and cultural need, namely the deprivation of feeling and faith, the emotive side of human nature, within the lives of the disenfranchised.[38]

The very "sensationalism" which earned Salvationists the contempt of the well-to-do and devout, guaranteed them the attention and response of the poor. Like the High Anglo-Catholic ritualism of the time, also popular with the working class, the Army provided theatre and color for otherwise drab lives. Salvationists were fully alive to this, and played up to it. Roger Green quotes a typical *War Cry* dispatch from the Corps at Hayle:

> Glory, glory, glory, glory to Jesus, to JESUS. We must conquer and win Hayle for Jesus. Good times all day on Sunday. Saints jumping, dancing, crying, shouting and rolling on the ground. We disgusted some people. Hallelujah.
>
> —Blood-washed Johnny.[39]

Salvation and holiness (to the second of which more attention will be given shortly) were the essential core of their message. These were distinct for the purposes

---

34. For example: Needham, *Community in Mission*; Waldron, *Creed and Deed*; *One Faith, One Church*.
35. Rhemick, *New People*, 5.
36. Rhemick, Ibid., 1–2.
37. Rhemick, Ibid., 224.
38. Rhemick, Ibid., 1.
39. Green, *Life and Ministry of William Booth*, 127.

of explanation, but constituted a continuum for living. Together they comprised "Full Salvation," the whole counsel of God for his people. Other doctrines were included in the framework perhaps because Booth and his followers took them for granted as the structure of Christian belief they had inherited. The Trinity was there, but it was largely without interest or nuance. Jesus was properly man and properly God, because that was a "given" for orthodox evangelicalism; they were not interested in splitting theological hairs over it. The essentials were sin; atonement for the "whosoever;" the holy life, which included the call to evangelism and service; heaven and hell. Introducing *The Salvationist* in 1879 Booth summed up the purpose of the Army as:

> We are a salvation people—this is our speciality—getting saved and keeping saved, and then getting somebody else saved, and then getting saved ourselves more and more until full salvation on earth makes the heaven within, which is finally perfected by the full salvation without, on the other side of the river.[40]

This was, as Coutts put it, doctrinal impedimenta for the smallest of knapsacks. In Gordon Moyles' words:

> The Salvation Army has tried to keep its doctrinal teaching simple and uncomplicated by what it considers needless intellectual enquiry. The nature of its early membership . . . meant that all doctrines except those deemed absolutely essential—salvation and sanctification—were underplayed.[41]

As for what "getting saved" consisted of, the *Doctrines of The Salvation Army* (1885–1916) expounded the standard nineteenth century orthodox evangelical beliefs in homely fashion. The distinctively Salvation Army thing about it was not the doctrine but that doctrine's presentation, which was "of the people, by the people and for the people." Middle-class respectability and rationality made no appeal to the lower working classes, who stayed away from the church in droves. They did however frequent the music hall and similar places of entertainment, so the Army's presentation of the gospel was couched in such terms and style as would appeal to them; in what Rhemick calls "the dramatic expression of [their] theological constructs."[42] Their preaching was vulgar and colorful, full of imagery, a sermon might consist simply of one extended simile; the Army's whole presentation was a metaphor. Booth, asked about people who "dislike your religion altogether?" responded,

> "Yes, they come in thinking they do. And we bide our time. They may get saved in the end; and they may not. But in the meantime—"
> "Yes, meantime?"
> "It cheers them up. They may laugh at it, but it makes the thing *go!* The music and the emotion stir them."[43]

---

40. *Salvationist*, January 1979, 1.

41. Moyles, *Blood and Fire in Canada*, 237.

42. Rhemick, *New People of God*, 6.

43. *Social Gazette*, 12 October 1893, 2, copied from *The Cape Times*, quoted in Fairbank, *Booth's Boots*, 142.

It was this facility to capture and stir the emotions which won the hearts of the poor. Lord Shaftesbury, who loathed Booth as much as he sought the same ends, wrote that "the devil, who having long tried to make Christianity odious, has now changed his hand, and endeavors to make it ridiculous."[44] But even he was on record as saying that "The working classes will never be reached but by an agency provided among themselves."[45] And that was what Booth was attempting to do.

John Rhemick's *New People of God* does not address changes in Booth's theology; he sees its social expression as inherent in its evangelical sources throughout. Green's *War on Two Fronts*, on the other hand, is structured around the *changes* in Booth's theology over the period of his ministry. The "Two Fronts" were not simply "spiritual" work contrasted with "social" work. They were firstly individual salvation and sanctification, and secondly corporate or social salvation and sanctification. As an evangelist Booth had concentrated on the former.

> The Bible and my own observation concurred in showing me that the highest service I could render to man was to rescue him from this position of antagonism to the Divine Government. Alongside this aspect of his condition, any temporary modification of his lot appeared trivial—nay, almost contemptible . . . the desire to persuade men to be reconciled to God became henceforth the main propelling purpose of my life.[46]

With the transition from itinerant evangelist to director of an organization, the leader of a religious community, Booth's view expanded to encompass a holy people as well as holy persons. In effect, that was his theology of the church. He often spoke of the Salvation Army as a modern Israel and compared it to the New Testament church. This was no sophisticated ecclesiological claim; all he meant by this was that here was a group of people filled with God's Spirit and united in obedience to the call of God to do God's work.

> If I did not think that the Lord was in this movement I would have nothing more to do with it, much less would I ask you to carry it on. I believe that The Salvation Army is as much of God as Israel was of God. . . . I believe Jesus has come again in this movement, and that not only in the Spirit, but in the manner of His coming [He referred to being of the poor and despised, being working men like the disciples, rejected by religious leaders etc at this point] . . . I believe this movement is of God . . .[47]

Then thirdly, with the development of social reform ministry in 1889–90, Booth envisaged a holy society. He wrote of how, having been preaching to individuals regarding their need for "spiritual" salvation, he came to realize that they also needed saving physically and socially.

> But as time wore on, the earthly miseries connected with the condition of the people, began to force themselves more particularly upon my notice . . . [described

---

44. Letter from Shaftesbury quoted by de Gasparin, *Read and Judge*, 55.

45. Sandall, *History*, I, illustration opposite 228.

46. Booth, "Salvation for Both Worlds," 1.

47. Booth, "The General's Address at Exeter Hall on Monday Evening," 9, cited by Green, *Life and Ministry of William Booth*, 56.

extensively at this point] I longed intensely to lend a hand to deliver the perishing; and should have been quite willing to have given myself up . . . to a life of hardship, if thereby I could have relieved or removed some of these woes that darkened the earthly lot of the children of my people. But at the outset I saw no remedy, and I said to myself, "If we cannot save them for time, we will save them for eternity!" . . .

But as I came to look more closely into things, and gathered more experience of the ways of God to man, I discovered that the miseries from which I sought to save man in the next world were substantially the same as those from which I everywhere found him suffering in this, and that they proceeded from the same cause—that is, from his alienation from, and his rebellion against God, and from his own disordered dispositions and appetites . . .

But with this discovery, there also came another . . . which was that I had two gospels of deliverance to preach—one for each world, or rather, I had one gospel which applied alike to both . . . Now I shouted, "I have found a remedy indeed!" Now I saw that this was the work that Jesus Christ came to accomplish—that he was manifested to dispossess all these fiends of evil for the souls of men, to destroy the works of the devil in the present time, and to set up in the soul the kingdom of heaven instead.[48]

Booth thus did not see his expansion of social work as a change of direction but as a natural extension of what he had already been doing. Roger Green, in his conclusion to *War on Two Fronts*, provides the following summary of his argument:

William Booth was first a nineteenth-century British revivalist, and his early theology reflected the context of his early ministry. He enjoyed a period of independent, revivalistic ministry first with New Connexion Methodism and, after 1861, apart from New Connexion Methodism. His early theology demonstrated little change through his founding in 1865, along with Catherine Booth, of what became known as The Christian Mission. This would remain true up to 1878 with the evolution of The Christian Mission into The Salvation Army.

His emphasis upon personalistic theological categories was evident and clear in his preaching and his writing during this stage in his life. He was an Evangelical revivalistic preacher, and along with the Evangelical community of nineteenth-century England, he stressed personal conversion from sin. However, he was not only an Evangelical, he was also Wesleyan. His theology included the Wesleyan doctrine of sanctification or perfect love. Booth applied the doctrines of salvation and sanctification to the individual, and he would continue to do so for the rest of his ministry. Although his theology changed, it would still embrace such individual categories as personal redemption and personal sanctification.

There are notable changes in Booth's theology after the naming of The Salvation Army in 1878. Within that context Booth added institutional categories and images to express his theology in order to include and incorporate the doctrinal changes which were taking place. Such extended theological language which accommodated his broadened theological views was common in much of Booth's theology after 1878, and this would continue to be true for the rest of his life.

This fact is clearest as Booth's theology reflected his loyalty to a growing institution. After 1878 he understood the doctrine of sanctification in a broader way to include institutional sanctification. Not only were individuals made holy

---

48. Booth, "Salvation for Both Worlds," 2.

by God, but groups were also sanctified by God, and he believed that this Salvation Army was especially blessed by the Holy Spirit.

For Booth the Salvation Army became an Army sanctified by God and divinely ordained for the work of ultimate redemption. Military language increasingly served as a vehicle of expression for his theology, and Christ became the model salvation soldier, the model redeemer, in the war against evil. Booth's final eschatological vision—providing hope, direction, and legitimation for his Army—was a fully redemptive vision in which sin and evil would ultimately be overcome. His eschatological goal embraced both spiritual and social redemption.

Many aspects of Booth's later redemptive theology provided a theological place of refuge for Booth and his followers, and the additions to his theology which he found so comforting and helpful would continue to be pressed home the rest of his life. In fact, these changes would lend support to and complement Booth's most critical change in his theology, a change which allowed him to see redemption in social as well as personal dimensions.

It is beyond doubt that his developed redemptive theology, which was evident after 1889, constituted the most dramatic change in the theology of William Booth. This change was articulated after The Salvation Army had increased its activity to reflect a dual mission that included social redemption. This climaxed between 1889 and 1890 with the establishment of the Social Reform Wing of The Salvation Army.

Characteristic of this change, the very meaning of the word salvation evolved in Booth's thinking to include social salvation as well as personal salvation. Those who have written about Booth in the past have often been seriously mistaken both theologically and historically in holding that what moved William Booth principally when he saw the plight of Londoners living in the East End in 1865 was their physical condition. What moved him was their spiritual condition—he saw them as sinners in rebellion against God. They affected his spiritual sensitivities, and he began his ministry among them as a revivalist and solely as a revivalist. At that time, salvation was personal and spiritual, and, convinced that people were sinners who needed such salvation, he called people to repentance, faith, and conversion.

But as a result of his long ministry among the poor and the destitute, and after many years of personal experience within the context of the Christian Mission and The Salvation Army's social involvement, Booth would come to realize that salvation had social dimensions as well, and in 1889 he struck a view of salvation which was sufficient to include both personal and spiritual dimensions. By 1889 the Army had already entered in many places upon a dual mission of saving sinners from their sin, and redeeming the world from the evils which so beset it. After 1889 the Army would engage in its dual mission on a much larger scale and in the context of an organization for that dual mission which it had not previously established. Beyond that, William Booth provided theological legitimacy for such a dual mission, while at the same time he continually attempted to strike a proper balance between the salvation of the soul and the salvation of the body. However, after 1889 the Army was encouraged to see itself as engaged in a war on two fronts—the war for souls, and the war for a rightly ordered society . . . [49]

---

49. Green, *War on Two Fronts*, 97–99. Passage reproduced by permission of Professor R.G. Green.

> . . . In the context of the Army's increasing redemptive mission, changes in Booth's theology evolved which both legitimated the existence of The Salvation Army and its work, and provided vision, guidance, and direction for its further work. In many ways the changes in Booth's theology provided structure for the continued redemptive work today of the Army. Booth provided the Army with a theology and with a desire consistently to act upon that theology—the waging of the salvation war on two fronts: the personal and the social.[50]

Neither Booth's nor the Salvation Army's theology changed in the sense of being influenced by contemporary theological debate or the impact of Higher Criticism, and did not become especially more theologically literate or "liberal" or stray from its Wesleyan and evangelical roots. However, we can see that the Salvation Army did change and develop in response to an enlarged vision and deeper insight into the nature of evil and the scope of redemption. This theological underpinning of its two-fold mission of proclamation and service has probably been significant for both its survival and its multi-faceted achievements as a community of faith. Failure to appreciate that may possibly have led to some polarization between the variations of theology espoused by "field" and "social" officers rather than an integrated approach.

It is interesting that this enlarged vision did not find expression in the "Officer's Covenant" (for which the earliest record of a "covenant service" dates only to 1922) until the mid-1990s, with the addition of the words in italics below:

> Called by God to proclaim the gospel of our Lord and Savior Jesus Christ as an officer of The Salvation Army, I bind myself to him in this solemn covenant: to love and serve him supremely all my days, to live to win souls and make their salvation the first purpose of my life, *to care for the poor, feed the hungry, clothe the naked, love the unlovable, and befriend those who have no friends,* to maintain the doctrines and principles of The Salvation Army, and, by God's grace, to prove myself a worthy officer.[51]

Matthew Seaman urges that a further expansion of Salvationists' conception of salvation should lead to the inclusion of care for the environment amongst these commitments.[52]

THE SALVATION ARMY AS A HOLINESS MOVEMENT

Through the Booths, the Army inherited not only Wesley's evangelicalism (which called for a definite "experience" of conversion) but also his doctrine of "Christian perfection." This did not mean what at first sight "perfection" might imply; it was not absolute perfection, or sinless perfection. Wesley nowhere taught that the Christian might in this life attain a state incapable of improvement or from which they might not fall. It was firstly an acknowledgement that while in "justification," a Christian was put right with God, enjoying the benefits of Christ's righteousness, the work of "perfection," of "making

---

50. Green, *War on Two Fronts*, 101–02.
51. *Conversations with the Catholic Church*, 35–36.
52. Seaman, "In Darkest Creation?" 194–234.

perfect," of transforming the character into the likeness of Christ, was still to come. We might say that this was "perfect" as a verb, not an adjective.

All Christians accepted that holiness, "without which no man would see God," was required. All believed that Christian disciplines should be embraced to that end. Traditional Catholicism, however rich in spiritual disciplines, had come to believe that only the refining fires of purgatory could finally prepare someone for that vision. Protestants, discarding purgatory, had fallen back on the hope that only the moment of death would finally release anyone, however justified, from sinful tendencies. Wesley dared to hope that God's power might enable victory over sin in *this* life.

How was it to be possible that a sinful, though forgiven, person might then begin to behave in a Christ-like way? Whereas many in the past had taught that a gradual process of obedience would transform the Christian's character, Wesley did not believe that "good works" would by themselves be any more efficacious in this respect than for justification. It would require further "grace." He came to posit a further experience, "event" or "crisis" (not his terms) as well as a "process" in the Christian life: "sanctification," which would transform the inner nature and enable Christ-like behavior. The combination of "event" and "process" perhaps points to the conflation of the twin sources of Wesley's spirituality, the Evangelical and the Catholic.

> Do you believe we are sanctified by faith? We know you believe that we are justified by faith; but do not you believe, and accordingly teach, that we are sanctified by our works?" So it has been roundly and vehemently affirmed for these five and twenty years: but I have constantly declared just the contrary; and that in all manner of ways. I have continually testified in private and in public, that we are sanctified as well as justified by faith. And indeed the one of those great truths does exceedingly illustrate the other. Exactly as we are justified by faith, so are we sanctified by faith. Faith is the condition, and the only condition, of sanctification, exactly as it is of justification. It is the *condition:* none is sanctified but he that believes; without faith no man is sanctified. And it is the *only condition*: this alone is sufficient for sanctification. Every one that believes is sanctified, whatever else he has or has not. In other words, no man is sanctified till he believes: every man when he believes is sanctified.[53]

Wesley's own thinking on this evolved. He evidently began by thinking that just a few people might attain the blessing—a little like Fowler's sixth stage of faith—and then probably late in life, or at the point of death. He progressively lowered the bar on this over the years, however.

1. Christian perfection is that love of God and our neighbor which implies deliverance from *all sin*;
2. that this is received merely *by faith*;
3. that it is given *instantaneously*, in one moment;
4. that we are to expect it, not at death, but *every moment*; that *now* is the accepted time, *now* is the day of this salvation.[54]

---

53. Wesley, Sermons: "The Scripture Way of Salvation."
54. Wesley, "Plain Account of Christian Perfection."

The question of whether Wesley personally laid claim to this blessing has been much debated. In 1762 he wrote to a correspondent (and recorded it in his diary) that "You have over and over denied instantaneous sanctification to me, but I have known and taught it these twenty years."[55] By "known," did Wesley mean "known about" or "experienced"? Surely the latter? Nine years later he wrote to another:

> Many years since I saw that "without holiness no man shall see the Lord." I began by following after it and inciting all with whom I had any intercourse to do the same. Ten years after, God gave me a clearer view than I had ever had before of the way how to obtain it, only by faith in the Son of God. And immediately I declared to all, "We are saved from sin. We are made holy by faith." This I testified to in private, in public, and in print, and God confirmed it by a thousand witnesses. I have continued to declare this for about thirty years and God has continued to affirm the work of grace.[56]

After Wesley's death, aspects of his theology became neglected. According to Catherine Bramwell-Booth, "as a doctrine, and still more as an experience, holiness, entire sanctification as Wesley called it, had almost died out in Methodist teaching when William Booth entered its ministry."[57] (Comparison with the Salvation Army in this respect is inevitable.) However, the teaching was given new life by mid-nineteenth century revivalists in the United States; Booth's mentors, Caughey, Finney and Palmer, were amongst its foremost exponents. The doctrine became progressively simplified and dogmatic.

For Phoebe Palmer, the analogy of the "altar" became her preferred way of explaining it. The holy altar in the Old Testament sanctified the gift laid upon it, so that it too became holy; likewise the life laid on the altar of consecration was to be regarded as instantly sanctified. This action removed what Railton, by a sleight of exegesis, called the "roots of bitterness," by which he meant the tendency to sin which remained in the human heart even after conversion.[58] Faith claimed the blessing, whether or not the individual felt anything had happened—though that internal "witness" could, indeed should, come later if not at once. Further, this was not to be an optional extra for those especially serious about their religion: this was an expectation of all Christians. Being a Christian was not a passive, formal, completed state but one requiring on-going growth in grace.

The common view has been that this "shorter way" as a version of Wesley's teaching was welcomed by William and Catherine Booth in the early 1860s and carried forward into the Salvation Army.[59] John Read's study of Catherine's writing has concluded otherwise, showing that John Fletcher, along with Wesley, Upham and Finney, was a greater influence on her understanding of holiness. Read says their affinity is apparent in a number of distinctive themes. (1) "A strong appreciation of moral law, as love of God and

---

55. Wesley, *Works*, 4, 140.
56. Wesley, *Works*, 7, 38.
57. Bramwell-Booth, *Bramwell Booth*, 141.
58. The metaphor, drawn from Deuteronomy 29.18 and used in Hebrews 12.15, originally referred to individuals disrupting the community of the people of God.
59. Green, *Catherine Booth*, 103–06.

humankind . . . their view is at root ethical and relational as well as deeply devotional." (2) "[T]hey each stress, against antinomianism, that human choice and action have a role to play in sanctification." (3) "Equally, each affirms that sanctification is God's work, impossible humanly speaking and only achievable through the full work of Christ and the Holy Spirit." (4) "It is the privilege of all believers to be sanctified . . . " (5) "The social character of holiness results in a strong eschatological hope . . . the manifestation of the Kingdom of God in human society."[60]

Whatever the derivation, holiness became an essential aspect of Salvation Army teaching. In 1877 William Booth said

> Holiness to the Lord is to us a fundamental truth; it stands to the forefront of our doctrines. We write it on our banners. It is in no shape or form an open debatable question as to whether God can sanctify wholly, whether Jesus does save his people from their sins. In the estimation of The Christian Mission that is settled for ever, and any evangelist who does not hold and proclaim the ability of Jesus Christ to save his people to the uttermost from sin and sinning I should consider out of place amongst us.[61]

This experience was variously and interchangeably called Entire Sanctification, the Second Blessing, Perfect Love, the Blessing of the Clean Heart, the Baptism of the Holy Ghost, Full Salvation or Holiness. The *War Cry* carried many articles on this doctrine. In 1883, a collection of *Holiness Readings* reprinted from *The War Cry* included papers by William and Catherine Booth, George S. Railton, W. Bramwell Booth, Rev. James Caughey, Dr Daniel Steele, Rev. J.A. Wood, Bishop Peck, Major Tucker and Miss Booth of Paris.[62] Besides innumerable articles, William Booth published a number of pamphlets and books on the subject, such as *Purity of Heart* (1902), *A Ladder to Holiness* (1903), and *Holy Living: or What The Salvation Army Teaches About Sanctification* (n.d.).

It was strongly held that as with salvation, sanctification should also be witnessed to at every opportunity, both to persuade others and to reinforce the speaker's own conviction. This vulgar revival of Wesleyan teaching on sanctification was one of many things held against the Salvation Army in its early days. Dean Farrar, later very supportive of the Army, expressed his disquiet thus:

> I would ask them how they can expect that ignorance should not be accompanied by egotism and self-assurance when they put forward men and women on platforms before thousands of people to claim sanctification as the result of a sudden conversion in that deplorable proceeding which they call "The Exhibition of Trophies," and, which seems even more shocking, "The Exhibition of Hallelujah Lasses?"[63]

60. Read, *Catherine Booth*, 115–16.

61. Booth, "Holiness. An Address at the Conference." 193. The same passage, with terminology changed from "Christian Mission" to "Salvation Army" and from "Evangelist" to "officer," is dated to 1880 in Robert Street's *Called to be God's People*, 64, and quoted by David Rightmire in his chapter on the Salvation Army's holiness theology in Metrustery, *Saved, Sanctified and Serving*," 75, though Rightmire still dates it to 1877.

62. Salvation Army (Booth and others), *Holiness Readings from the War Cry*.

63. *Sensation or Salvation*, 14, quoted by Rhemick, *New People*, 99.

Bramwell Booth conducted "Central Holiness Meetings" in Whitechapel for some years from 1879, a long table draped with a red cloth placed in the center of the hall becoming known as the Holiness Table, available as a place of prayer for those seeking the blessing.[64] It soon became customary for the less-well-attended morning meeting at corps, attended mainly by Salvationists, to be devoted to this teaching and called the "Holiness Meeting" while the evening meeting, with greater public attendance, was known as the "Salvation Meeting." In an age when there was "something on at the Army" every night of the week, one of these evening meetings would also be designated a "Holiness Meeting."[65] Increasingly, Salvation Army halls were furnished with a table, standing at the front below the platform, between the Mercy Seat or Penitent Form and the congregation. Inevitably the practice became ritualized and a "sacred space" established.

By the end of the nineteenth century, the American officer Samuel Logan Brengle had emerged as a leading Salvationist teacher, preacher and writer on this theme. Born in 1860, Brengle was a Methodist student pastor when he sought the experience of Holiness in 1885 under the influence of his teacher at Boston University, Daniel Steele, who also introduced him to the writings of Catherine Booth. At first he felt nothing had changed, but then within a few days underwent a powerful spiritual experience. Long after, he recalled it:

> It is over fifty years ago that I received the baptism and I loved and loved until it seemed to me that I would nearly die of love, and I wept and wept and wept and sorrowed to think that I had ever sinned against my blessed Lord. And that baptism has been an abiding blessing and has given me the power to continue to this day, loving and serving God and my fellow-men, and I do it gladly.[66]

Introduced to the Salvation Army, Brengle became an officer in 1887 and after serving in corps and divisional appointments was made "National Spiritual Special" in 1897. This was a remit to preach holiness throughout the United States and he eventually toured the world on the same errand. Besides numerous articles, Brengle wrote a score of books and pamphlets on holiness and his exposition of this doctrine became the standard Salvation Army teaching.[67] Brengle's books, some of them collections of previously-published articles, tended to be devotional and inspirational rather than expository and systematic.

Lilian Taiz relates Brengle's holiness teaching to a tendency for more educated, middle-class officers to be uncomfortable with the boisterous religious performances of

---

64. Bramwell-Booth, *Bramwell Booth*, 143–44.

65. Bramwell Booth, *Servants of All* (1899), 88–90, describes an officer's exhaustive weekly round of activities. Booth says he was given this by "an old Field Officer." The passage is also found in *Life and Labours of the People of London* (1885, page 329) by Charles Booth, who says he copied it from "a Salvation Army publication"—possibly Bramwell's own source. It gives the appearance of having been written originally "pour l'encouragement des autres," as Voltaire put it in another connection.

66. Brengle, quoted by Rightmire in *Sanctified Sanity*, 142.

67. Of these the chief, and still in print, were, *Helps to Holiness* (1896), *Heart Talks on Holiness* (1897), *Way of Holiness* (1902), *Soul-Winner's Secret* (1903), *When the Holy Ghost is Come* (1909), *Love Slaves* (1923), *Resurrection Life and Power* (1925), *Ancient Prophets* (1929), *Guest of the Soul* (1934).

the Army, thinking they "obscured the 'shallowness [and] spiritual ignorance' of many Salvationists."[68] She refers to Clarence Hall's biography of Brengle:

> [H]e saw in his soldiers' lack of the holiness experience both an explanation of the corps' present poverty and a certain prophecy of disaster to come. He determined therefore to make holiness the issue. Properly presented, it would operate sharply upon the soldiers' hearts, dividing the consecrated and sanctified from the holding-back and unsanctified, with the hope that the latter would either be driven on and up, or out and away. If they could not be mended, it would be better if their connection with the corps were ended.[69]

While Taiz does not report Brengle's own later reflection on this tactic in his first corps, ("I'm afraid I was not always wise in those early years,")[70] she does generalize from his experience to aver that

> What this young Captain failed to understand was that it was *precisely* the hallelujahs and tambourines and stirring appeals which "built up" many Salvation soldiers and made them feel emotionally committed to the Salvation Army and its religion . . . The Salvation Army attempted to mitigate tensions created by ecstatic experiential religious performance through its special application of the doctrine of Holiness.[71]

Just as John Wesley had held that the doctrine of holiness was the Methodist *raison d'être*, and that the movement would fall away if the teaching were neglected, the Booths believed the same of the Salvation Army. But as with the Methodists, and as happens with all renewal movements, the ardor of Salvationists also cooled over the generations. The doctrine had always been a little difficult. Even in Bramwell Booth's first published article he wrote:

> Holiness is looked upon in the Christian Mission as a state of grace greatly to be desired, by many as impossible to attain, by many as a standing duty which they fail to come up to, and they therefore are brought into a constant condemnation by reason of the fact that they have light but do not walk in it . . . They are enslaved within the reach of liberty, they hunger within full view of the heavenly table.[72]

Indeed, it would be interesting to know how far the doctrine was ever near universal experientially. Lilian Taiz alleges that "some Salvation Army soldiers failed to comprehend the full meaning of the second blessing, a fact that created tensions with officers more committed to asserting official Salvation Army theology. Many soldiers apparently preferred their own popular theology that encouraged the physical expression of religious feeling and saving the souls of sinners. One long-time field officer called

---

68. Taiz, *Hallelujah Lads & Lasses*, 93.
69. Hall, *Samuel Logan Brengle*, 81.
70. Hall, Ibid., 81.
71. Taize, *Hallelujah Lads& Lasses*, 93.
72. Bramwell-Booth, *Bramwell Booth*, 145.

holiness an 'impossible theory' and even suggested that by the 1890s few leaders actually preached the doctrine."[73]

As time went on, such a state of affairs probably became more rather than less general. Brengle was read by fewer people and the doctrine preached about less often and with less conviction.[74] There were always those blessed with saintly dispositions, but as an officer once said to me, "Those of us with more volcanic temperaments do not enjoy a head start to holiness!" Holiness was still regarded as a difficult subject, giving rise to unrealistic expectations, likely to lead to either an arid, doctrinaire insistence on formulae unrelated to real life by those who felt obliged to claim the blessing, or a sense of resignation over being relegated to second-class status amongst those more honest or more pessimistic about their spirituality.

To help address this situation Frederick Coutts in particular, in the middle decades of the twentieth century, sought to re-interpret the doctrine in terms which might recommend themselves to a newer generation of Salvationists. Following his years of backroom literary labors on *Company Orders* for Sunday Schools and *Corps Cadet Manuals*, such books as *The Call to Holiness* (1957), *Essentials of Christian Experience* (1969), *The Splendour of Holiness* (1983) and his slight volume of memoirs, *No Continuing City*, as well as many articles in periodicals, set a new benchmark for insightful and deeply spiritual writing on Salvation Army beliefs, both elegant and simple. Acknowledging his debt to contemporary writers such as Stephen Neill and C.H. Dodd, and quoting the latter's "We may fairly say that it is never safe to emphasize the call to holiness as part of Christian teaching, unless the idea of the Holy is understood by constant reference to the Jesus of the gospels, his example and teaching," he wrote

> Here was theological rock beneath my feet. The gifts of the Spirit are the virtues of Jesus and the virtues of Jesus are the gifts of the Spirit . . . Our highest spiritual goal—and what a goal it is—is to be increasingly conformed to his image.
>
> All in all it would be hard to improve upon Catherine Booth's earlier description of sanctification as "the simple reception of Christ as an all sufficient Saviour, dwelling in my heart and thus cleansing it from all sin." If we have once made Him welcome then, with our continued consent, He can be trusted to complete the good work which He has begun so that "when He shall appear, we shall be like Him."[75]

While Coutts's writing was no more systematic than Brengle's, some have characterized (even parodied, perhaps) their difference in presentation by saying that in Brengle the emphasis is on "process—CRISIS—process" as a description of the holy life, while Coutts would say, "PROCESS—crisis—PROCESS." Unhappily, some Salvationists have viewed his writing as a betrayal of Brengelian orthodoxy. Some even lobbied against his election as General on these grounds.[76] He has been criticized for effectively changing the basis of our holiness doctrine from a Wesleyan to a Reformed one. Coutts did

---

73. Price, "Random Reminiscences," quoted by Taize, *Hallelujah Lads& Lasses*, 99.

74. At the 1960 New Zealand Local Officers' Conference, for example, Bandmaster Bert Neeve asked why holiness was no longer being preached. Report in New Zealand Salvation Army Archives.

75. Coutts, *No Continuing City*, 61, 64–65.

76. About such matters the *odium theologicum* may even be found in Salvation Army microcosm.

however become General in 1963, and was able to leave his mark on systematic teaching by his final editing of the 1969 *Handbook of Doctrine* which had been largely prepared Colonel Gordon Mitchell and Lt-Colonel Cyril Barnes.[77]

General Paul Rader explained Brengle's and Coutts' differing emphases by asking whether

> Brengle was more the evangelist than the pastor, inclined by vocation and gifting to expect more immediate results? And that Coutts was more the pastor than the evangelist, inclined by experience and reflection to deal with the struggles of the faithful in quest of the holy heart and life? . . . In so far as the teaching of one can be set against the other, the particular gifts and ministries of these two advocates of the holy life may account in some measure for the emphases for which they have become known. The Army has learned and benefited immeasurably from the approaches of both Brengle and Coutts.[78]

Such later twentieth century Salvationist writers as Allister Smith, Milton Agnew, Bramwell Tillsley and Edward Read have also written extensively on holiness. More attention may have been paid to examining the holiness tradition than the evangelical fundamentals of the Army's faith, although probably more so in the United States than elsewhere, and then more along the lines of re-affirming the "faith once delivered to the saints," or at least to Brengle, than re-interpreting doctrine in a way accessible to post-moderns.[79] Most published material on the subject has been more devotional and exhortatory than theological. Chick Yuill in *We Need Saints* placed the Army's teaching in the context of the doctrinal history of the Church. Another active teacher and writer on the theme of Wesleyan holiness is Alan Harley.[80] In recent years there has been renewed official emphasis on the doctrine and new writers including Geoff and Katie Webb, Olivia Munn and Stephen Court have begun to publish on it.[81] It will be interesting to see if newer writers are able to instigate the revival of the holiness tradition within the Army's ranks.

SACRAMENTS

The Christian Mission and, until 1883, the Salvation Army, followed Methodist practice in infant baptism and celebration of the Lord's Supper and officials of the mission led these rites. We look firstly at evidence for these practices; secondly, at their discontinuance and reasons given at the time; thirdly, at further arguments subsequently advanced; and fourthly, at more recent discussion.

---

77. A helpful analysis of the Brengle-Coutts continuum is found in O'Brien, "Why Brengle? Why Coutts? Why Not?"

78. Rader, "Holiness and Mission," 8.

79. USA Eastern territory appoints an "Ambassador for Holiness," an itinerant "spiritual special," the role Brengle once filled.

80. See for example, Harley, "Wesleyan Understanding of Holiness of Life," and numerous papers in Court, edited, *Boston Common* (2010).

81. Webb, *Authentic "fair dinkum" Holiness*, (2007); Munn and Court, *The Uprising: a Holy Revolution*, (2007); Clifton and others, *New Love*, (2004).

Early Administration

The earliest reference to sacramental practices in the Mission is a printed report of the East London Christian Mission (c. Sept/Oct 1867). A list of meetings held at the Whitechapel Mission Hall, 188 Whitechapel Road included, "Sunday 3pm. Breaking of bread, or experience meeting, and service in the open air."

It is significant that this was the year in which, by Sandall's account, the Mission developed many signs of an independent existence. There was a significant change in membership, in that some who had supported the Mission as a parachurch agency returned to their own denominations. For those who remained, "breaking of bread" together could have been seen as part of their consciousness of belonging to a new entity.

Rule 39 of the Christian Mission in 1870 said that the Lord's Supper was to be observed once a month in each station unless two thirds of members desired it more often. Bramwell Booth's memoirs claim that when he "came on the scene as a responsible official of the Mission, in 1874, the Lord's Supper was administered monthly at all our stations to all members of the Mission and to such other Christian friends as were known to be in good standing and desired to join us."[82]

The 1878 *Orders and Regulations* refer to the sacraments only in passing, in connection with the "Formation of Corps," a subsection of "How to Capture a Town," which suggests that their occurrence was taken for granted but not considered of central importance. "The Sacrament should be administered during the latter part of this meeting, and if it can be prolonged to midnight or an unusually late hour, it will make all the deeper impression upon all."[83] Which seems a tad manipulative.

Reports of observances appear in the Mission's papers. At the conclusion of the "War Congress" of August 1878, "The usual unintoxicating wine having not been prepared for the sacrament, we managed uncommonly well with water . . . After the sacrament only a quarter of an hour remained for the love-feast, if we were to conclude, as intended, at six . . . "[84] *The Salvationist* reports an officers-only celebration when "at the house of Captain Broadbent . . . we took the sacrament together" after an all-night meeting in the hall ended at 5.00am.[85] Later, advertisements appeared in the *War Cry* for special meetings: "At Headquarters on the morning of Good Friday, at nine o'clock, there will be a workers' breakfast; and, at ten, a consecration and sacrament service. Miss Booth will speak."[86] A similar service was advertised in the *War Cry* for Easter 1881.

War Cry reports from various other parts of the world confirm the practice. An 1886 Wanganui, New Zealand, report on Christmas Day activities included, "11a.m., Sacrament service, when 50 or 60 partook of the emblems of the Savior's dying love. It was a heart-searching time."[87] This was nearly four years after the official cessation of such observances. Contemporary Australian editions of the *War Cry* carry similar

---

82. Booth, *Echoes and Memories*, 201.
83. *Orders and Regulations*, 1878, 72.
84. *Christian Mission Magazine*, September 1878, 252.
85. *Salvationist*, 1 December 1879, 325.
86. *War Cry*, 27 March, 1880, 3.
87. *War Cry* (New Zealand) 10 January 1886, 4, col. 2.

reports. Envoy George Hazell of Sydney suggested to me that movement of people between denominations would have been a factor. Primitive Methodists, relocating to an Australian outback town with no Methodist congregation but a Salvation Army corps in evidence, could have brought their sacramental practice with them without any sense of incongruity. A treasure in the Salvation Army's New Zealand Heritage Centre and Archives is a shapely glass flask, evidently for holding communion wine, decorated with an engraved Salvation Army crest, vine leaves and bunches of grapes. Its provenance is unknown: it was donated by a scrap merchant.

The 1881 *Doctrines and Discipline* catechism included a brief section on baptism, indicating that by "adult, or Believers baptism," "the person baptized declares that he wishes it to be known that he is converted." However, it is "DECIDEDLY NOT . . . a duty that must be performed . . . The Army considers only one baptism essential to salvation, and that is, THE BAPTISM OF THE HOLY GHOST." Likewise in response to the question, "What is the teaching of the Army on the subject of the Lord's Supper?" (all within the section on Baptism) the book says that "When such an ordinance is helpful to the faith of our Soldiers, we recommend its adoption." This passage remained in subsequent editions of the book until 1885, two years after the Army had ceased to practice the sacraments. But it was made clear that it was "certainly not . . . essential to membership of the Army, or to salvation."[88]

Horridge says that by mid–1882 barely two dozen stations still continued the practice. He quotes Henry Edmonds to the effect that those that did gave it no consecration but "break bread and pass it round with a cup of currant jelly-water in Remembrance."[89]

In 1881 we also have a reported explanation by William Booth to an Anglican clergyman (who wrote of the conversation to the Archbishop of Canterbury) "that some of his people on their own responsibility had had a very simple 'breaking of bread' together but that this was no part of the 'Army'—as an evangelistic agency."[90] This seems a little disingenuous, given the official regulation, but is consistent with their sitting lightly to the sacraments.

The issue probably came to a head in 1882 at the same time as discussions with the Anglican Church and perhaps because of them. That church was divided in its view of the Army. Some elements of the church were interested in taking over the new religious movement that seemed to offer a means of rapprochement with the alienated working classes—while others regarded the Army with disgust because of its sensational and vulgar style. As recounted earlier, in May 1882 the Upper House of Convocation, Canterbury, appointed a committee to negotiate with General Booth.

According to Sandall, and Randall Davidson, the negotiations foundered on four issues (as already discussed in the chapter on Ecclesiology), and these included the matter of the sacraments.[91] Note that the "administration of the sacraments" did not refer to Salvationists' non-observance because at that time they *did* observe. Rather, it was the

---

88. *Doctrines and Discipline*, 1881, Section 26.

89. Edmonds, *My Adventures with General William Booth*, 442, quoted by Horridge, *Origins and Early Days*, 116.

90. Begbie, *Booth*, II, 26.

91. Sandall, *History*, II, 148.

validity of their observances that was at stake, and the question of who would preside over the administration. In the Anglican view, officers were not priests, and therefore ineligible to preside.

As we have seen, there are recorded instances of corps attending parish churches to take the sacrament. But Booth later recalled that some clergymen "refused to administer the rite to our soldiers because they had not gone through the form of confirmation."[92] He did not want his soldiers divided at the church door, with those of non-conformist background or no church history at all, diverted to another table.[93] Andrew Eason's 2009 article in *Fides et Historia*, exploring contemporary evidence of the connection between the Church of England's negotiations and the Army's discontinuance of the sacraments, has already been mentioned.[94] He credits this aspect of these negotiations with being a major factor in Booth's decision to dispense with these observances. This was not an explanation Booth offered in public however.

Discontinuance, and reasons given at the time

William Booth announced the Salvation Army's abandonment of the sacraments at a council of London officers on 2 January 1883 and his statement was printed in the *War Cry* two weeks later. He prefaced his remarks: "Here we will make one statement which will help to dismiss any serious anxiety from your minds very considerably, I have no doubt, as it has done with us, and this is one in which I think you will all agree." Such an opening suggests that (1) there had been on-going discussion of the subject, and that (2) some harbored "serious anxiety"—presumably, Booth assumed, about observance rather than non-observance, or perhaps it was simply about the damaging controversies which had arisen.

The main points he went on to make were that, (1) "The 'Sacraments' must not, nay, they cannot, rightly be regarded as conditions of Salvation"; (2) that any order he gave for their observance "would be likely to produce grave dissensions" on account of the wide variety of practices followed amongst the churches; (3) that "we are not professing to be a church, nor aiming at becoming one"; (4) that it is wise for us "to postpone any settlement of the question, to leave it over to some future day, when we shall have more light, and see more clearly the way before us."

In the meanwhile, (5) "we do not prohibit our own people . . . from taking the Sacraments . . . if this is a matter of conscience . . . the churches and chapels around will welcome you for this." (6) He also urged Salvationists to "remember His love every hour of our lives, and continually feed on Him—not on Sundays only . . . " and that they all agree on "one baptism—that is the Baptism of the Holy Ghost." (7) Finally, having also announced the introduction of a new "formal service for the Dedication of Children," he

---

92. *Review of the Churches*, April 1895, quoted by Begbie, *Booth*, I, 469.
93. *War Cry*, 17 January 1883, 4.
94. Eason, "Salvation Army and the Sacraments," 53.

concluded, "Let us keep off all mere forms, and do nothing in which, as far as possible, the hearts of our Soldiers do not go with us."[95]

Sandall quotes Booth as saying on this occasion, "I cannot accept any obligation as binding upon my conscience, neither will I seek to bind any upon yours, to do, or believe, or teach anything for which authority cannot be furnished from the Word of God, or which God Himself does not reveal to us by His Spirit, as our present duty."[96]

Some disapproval must have been expressed, whether from within or without, because Booth responded in an Exeter Hall meeting on 16 April 1883. "The great charge against us is that we depreciate the sacraments because we say that baptism with water and the taking of bread and wine at the Lord's Supper are not conditions of salvation. If it were proved that they were so, you would shut out from heaven some of the best and holiest that ever walked the face of the earth . . . "[97]

Was the fear of "grave dissensions" because of the variety of possible practice a present danger or a hypothetical one? Did Booth have evidence that "the hearts of our soldiers" did not support the continuance of the practices? There is now no strong evidence that existing practices were causing strife within the Army or that many deserted the ranks in consequence of the change. However, Eason's research casts new light on the nature of the strife Booth feared; it may have been other groups' strife with which Booth wished to avoid entanglement. A few senior officers, resigning for various reasons, mentioned the sacraments as contributory factors—Major Thomas Moore, when setting up his short-lived secessionist Salvation Army in the USA in 1884, re-instituted sacraments, as did Ballington Booth when he set up his "Volunteers of America" in 1896.

This was in the period of the Army's very rapid expansion, particularly amongst people with little or no previous church experience. The sacraments had no meaning for them, and the majority of Salvationists were, if not all illiterate, then certainly theologically illiterate; they were not going to argue with Booth about anything so apparently inconsequential. Schillebeeckx makes the point that throughout the history of the church whenever there has been any significant change, "on each occasion official documents sanction a church practice which has grown up from the grass roots."[98] Perhaps Booth's apprehension that any general order he might give enforcing sacramental observances would probably be ignored also indicated an instinctive reading of his times and people, and Schillebeeckx's rule may be observed here in a Salvationist context.[99]

Most of those Salvationists who did have a church background—and they may have been a majority of recruits—probably brought with them from their previous denominations a "low" view of the Sacraments, with little or no emphasis on their being objectively a "means of grace." For example, the understanding of the Methodist New Connexion, from which the Booths came, was as follows:

---

95. *War Cry*, 17 January 1883, 4, col. 2.
96. Sandall, History, II, 130.
97. *War Cry*, 25 April 1883, 2, col. 2.
98. Schillebeeckx, *Ministry*, 3.
99. *War Cry*, 17 January 1883, 4.

Baptism

> Baptism is that Ordinance in which children are dedicated to the Lord, and by which, they are recognized as included in the covenant of redemption, and as belonging to the Kingdom of God . . .

The Lord's Supper

> In this Ordinance believers commemorate the death of the Lord Jesus Christ, at His table. The bread, and the wine, are received as emblems of His body which was wounded, and of His blood which was shed, for the remission of sins . . . [100]

On this basis the sacraments might come to be seen as church customs of no more significance than any other (and to be discarded as the movement sought non-churchly ways of presenting the Gospel to the un-churched masses); as a simple "memorial," a scriptural event recalled and re-enacted rather than a command given by the Lord (as Booth put it, on par with foot-washing); as a means of grace only in so far as the recipient subjectively entered into a state of spiritual communion and not dependent on any objective reality attributed to the elements. Presumably even clerical officer-recruits like Brengle (a Methodist student-minister) and Oliphant (an Anglican priest)—both later commissioners—held or adopted similar views.[101]

Such a position naturally made the abandonment of the practices much easier in due course. It suggests that while the Army's formerly-Methodist leaders accepted the practice of the sacraments as a church custom, the Methodist tradition they had inherited had drifted far from Wesley's strongly sacramental theology.

Lest a lack of emphasis on sacramental observances be thought a free church characteristic alone, it may be remembered that until the rise of Anglo-Catholicism in the second half of the nineteenth century, even Anglican churches did not practice communion frequently; no more than quarterly celebration was the norm. In 1853 only twelve English cathedrals (out of about forty) had a weekly celebration.[102] Adrian Hastings comments on "a steady tendency to diminish both the significance and frequency of communion."

> This happened in the Church of England as well as the Free Churches, but the centrality for Anglican practice of the Book of Common Prayer restrained the tendency to some extent . . . The Free Churches, on the other hand, had not only long been satisfied with a rather thin Zwinglian doctrine of the sacrament (many did not care even to use the word 'sacrament'); in the nineteenth century they had been irritated, rather than stimulated, by Tractarianism so that they had moved by and large in a still more anti-sacramentalist direction.[103]

---

100. Baggaly, *Digest of the Minutes*, 230.

101. Oliphant's Salvation Army biography was entitled "The Curate of Onslow Square." Holy Trinity Brompton, Onslow Square, London SW7, is still a leading evangelical Anglican church.

102. Hastings, *History of English Christianity*, 77.

103. Hastings, Ibid., 110.

Great numbers of Anglicans, especially country and working class people who had not had the opportunity of confirmation, did not take the sacrament at all.[104] Many of Booth's converts did not miss what they had never had.

Later explanations

In April 1895, in response to questioning by Henry Lunn, and published in *The Review of the Churches*, Booth gave further reasons for his decision, some of them different from those in his 1883 announcement:

> In the first place, we do not consider that the Sacraments are essentials of salvation . . .
>
> Secondly. With reference to the question as to our Lord's intention to institute these as permanent ceremonies in the Church, we reply that there are other ordinances that are apparently commands of a similar character which the Church has universally agreed in not observing. The most striking example of that is the command to wash one another's feet.
>
> Thirdly. We came into this position originally by determining not to be a Church. We did not wish to undertake the administration of the Sacraments and thereby bring ourselves into collision with the existing churches.
>
> Fourthly. We were further driven to take up our present position by clergymen of the Church of England refusing to administer the rite to our soldiers because they had not gone through the form of confirmation. This created difficulties which seemed to me only to be solved by the declaration of my own conviction that these Sacraments were not essential to salvation.
>
> Fifthly. We have found the existing notions with reference to these ordinances seriously interfering with the right views of penitence and holy living. Men and women are constantly in danger of putting their trust in ordinances, and thinking that baptised communicants must be in a secure position, no matter how inconsistently they are living . . .
>
> Sixthly. Moreover I should like to emphasize the fact that this with us is not a settled question. We never declaim against the Sacraments. We are anxious not to destroy the confidence of Christian people in institutions which are helpful to them.[105]

Comments on some of these points follow.

It might be agreed by many Christians that sacraments were not essential to salvation, but this in itself would not be a reason for non-observance. Nevertheless, this was a necessary point of departure in that unless this point were conceded, no other arguments could be persuasive.

As for their not being intended as a permanent institution, Booth would not have recognized the expression "traditioning the text," but this would not be far off his view of the way the Church had come to adopt sacramental practices. That is, rather than the text being seen as lying behind and giving rise to church tradition, the text, and its received interpretation and application, is, by what Bruggemann calls a process of

---

104. Hastings, Ibid., 67.
105. Lunn, *Review of the Churches*, April 1895, quoted in Begbie, *Booth*, I, 468–69.

"imaginative remembering," a construct arising from church tradition. Thus the church had come to believe that Jesus intended to establish a permanent institution of sacramental observances, because the church had, on the basis of the Gospel record of Jesus' words and actions instituted such observances. Booth's view would have been consistent with that of Emil Brunner for example, that sacraments as practiced today are, like the priesthood, a "misunderstanding of the Church," arising from traditional practice.[106] Major Ray Harris of Canada offered support for this critique of traditional sacramental practice in an article on "Sacramental Living" in 2006, quoting the New Testament scholar Luke Timothy Johnson:

> The account of Jesus' last meal with his disciples has had such an obvious and overwhelming importance for the Christian community . . . [However,] Christian liturgical practice is not based on this text but rather on a complex development of ritual traditions that look back to the Gospels only for legitimation after the fact.[107]

Philip Layton appears to have been the first Salvationist apologist to draw attention to the actual words of institution and attempt to place them in a Passover context.[108] The words, "When you do this, as often as you do it, remember me," could be seen as those of an observant Jew speaking to other observant Jews, who might be expected to continue to be observant Jews (as they did, at first). Whereas in the past, it is suggested, they would have remembered Moses on such occasions, they would now remember Jesus and the new "exodus" he would lead (the word is used by Luke in his transfiguration account in Luke 9.31), when they celebrated his "new covenant" (Luke 22. 14–20).

The irony is that whereas Booth instinctively grasped that church practice had "traditioned the text," and therefore felt free to dispense with church practice, his Army of more than a hundred years later probably now tends to tradition the text as well—to see the text through the lens of the new tradition established by William Booth and the early Salvation Army.

If anything were to refute accusations that the Army is literalist and "fundamentalist" in its view of Scripture, it would be Booth's own writings on the subject.[109] Despite the uncompromising appearance of the Army's first doctrine, the Army pre-dated the advent of modern fundamentalism and sits uncomfortably with it. While the Army appears to adopt the conservative Protestant stance of "Scripture first" and "tradition later," in *practice* its view of the relationship between Scripture and tradition is not that far removed from that of the Catholic Church—that the tradition produced Scripture. Both the church and the modern Salvation Army "tradition the text." That is, their views on the biblical provenance of the sacraments are conditioned by their respective traditions rather than the other way round. They come to different conclusions about the text because of their different traditions of praxis.

---

106. Brunner, *Dogmatics* III, *Christian Doctrine of the Church*, 52–66.
107. Harris, in http://www.salvationist.ca/2006/sacramental-living/, downloaded 6 June 2006.
108. Layton, *Sacraments and the Bible*, 43–47.
109. See Booth and Cunningham, *Bible: Its Divine Revelation*.

Booth claimed that the Army was not a church, and not wanting to be "in collision" with churches by setting up an alternative sacramental usage. Bramwell Booth recalled that while Dean Farrar "made a great effort to persuade me to ask for the reintroduction amongst us of the supper," Dr Westcott had said "they approved of the stand we took . . . as this meant a refusal to embark on what was, in their view, a 'schismatic procedure.'"[110] Westcott's view would have been that the only legitimate church would be one whose ministry was in the apostolic succession of orders and whose administration of the sacraments would therefore be valid. Farrar on the other hand thought "You ought to give the sacraments, even though there may be questions about the effectiveness of your agents."[111] After all, an Anglican would have been equally dubious about the credentials of any other non-conformist clergy. Today of course the Army *is* choosing to describe itself as "a church" but the concomitant implications for sacramental observances are not followed through.

Booth's fifth Point, concerning the tendency to trust in outward observances to the neglect of disciplined living, reflects particularly the views of Railton and of Catherine Booth. They were probably most influential in persuading William Booth to make the break with sacramental practice. Catherine's strongest statement is found in a lecture reprinted in her *Popular Christianity*, where she attacks four "mock salvations"—theory, ceremony, mere belief and unbelief.

> Another mock salvation is presented in the shape of ceremonies and sacraments. These were only intended as outward signs of an inward spiritual reality, whereas men are taught that by going through them or partaking of them, they are to be saved. Amongst these may be classed Baptism, the Last Supper, and the ceremonials of ancient or modern Churches . . . What an inveterate tendency there is in the human heart to trust in outward forms, instead of seeking inward grace! And where this is the case, what a hindrance, rather than help, have these forms proved to the growth, nay, to the very existence, of that spiritual life which constitutes the real and only force of Christian experience![112]

Bramwell Booth was less willing to change at first. He described himself as possibly the last officer to officiate at the Lord's Supper, his father having given him "a freedom in this matter which, so far as I am aware, he gave to no one else, and which he gave me on no other subject of importance on which our views were for the time out of accord. But gradually I, too, realized how prone the human mind is to lean upon the outward."[113]

In his 1895 interview, Lunn put two other questions to Booth about the sacraments: firstly whether anything was substituted for the sacraments, and secondly whether Salvationists would still be free to be baptized and take communion if they so desired. To the first, Booth suggested that every meal was an occasion to remember Christ's sacrifice, and to the second, "the General gave an unqualified answer in the affirmative."

---

110. Bramwell Booth, *Echoes and Memories*, 207.
111. Bramwell Booth, Ibid., 209.
112. Catherine Booth, *Popular Christianity*, 42–43.
113. Bramwell Booth, *Echoes and Memories*, 204.

Substitutes for sacraments

It is curious that Booth's suggestion that every meal might be the occasion of sacramental remembering was not subsequently made more of. Given the Passover meal context of the Gospel institution, a case might have been made for appropriate words to have become the regular "grace before meat" practice of Salvationists. Did he judge it too difficult to persuade his followers to implement this practice, which he appeared to support?

Nevertheless, the history of the Salvation Army actually illustrates the maxim that if the sacraments did not exist, it would be necessary (to adapt Voltaire) to invent them.[114] Forms and ceremonies have been substituted. The *Directory* or catechism for children included the question:

> What are the FIVE ORDINANCES of the Army?
>
> The Army's Five Ordinances are:
> The Dedication of Children to God and the Army.
> The Mercy Seat.
> Enrolment under the Army Flag.
> Commissioning of Officers.
> Marriage according to Army rules.[115]

The very term "ordinances" implies sacramental usage.

It could be argued that if officers only rather than soldiers administer these ceremonies, they make of the officers a priesthood in the sacerdotal sense. Soldiers sometimes dedicate infants but officers would always conduct the enrolment of soldiers. For a while it seems that this function may have been reserved for divisional officers, rather like an episcopal confirmation rite. A contemporary witness claimed there was a rule that "All soldiers must be SWORN IN PUBLICLY by the Divisional Officer, the Officer in charge of the corps having previously, at the soldiers' roll-call, read and explained the doctrines and the articles of war."[116] The commissioning of officers likewise became, once the practice was established, the prerogative of the General, or in his stead, a commissioner or territorial commander as his representative.

It is curious that the list of "ordinances" did not include the wearing of uniform, which certainly serves as an "outward and visible sign of an inward and spiritual grace," as the catechism in the *Book of Common Prayer* described the sacraments. By 1923 the new *Handbook of Doctrine* had an appendix on the sacraments, and "uniform-wearing" was listed as one of the "outward signs" by which "the Ends which the Advocates of Water Baptism claim to be fulfilled by this Ceremony are otherwise provided for in The Army."[117] It also provides the medium for the nearest the Salvation Army comes to a form of excommunication. For such lapses as immorality (sex out of wedlock), smoking

---

114. Voltaire's "Si Dieu n'existait pas, il faudrait l'inventer" (If God did not exist, it would be necessary to invent him) is from his 1768 response to an atheist text.
115. *Salvation Army Directory, No II*, 62.
116. [Abner Sumner] *New Papacy*, 63.
117. *Handbook of Doctrine* (1923) 172.

tobacco (since 1975) or drinking alcohol, incurring a criminal conviction or suffering a marriage break-down, a soldier might be "stood down"—relieved of duties and temporarily suspended from the soldiers' roll for a period of amendment of life, and so obliged to refrain from wearing uniform.

Also absent from the "ordinances" was the "Love Feast," a Moravian Brethren and Primitive Methodist practice at times, though not widely, employed in the Salvation Army, and presumably in that case presided over by the corps officer.

It would have to be said that although after 1883 the officers did not have a sacramental role in the conventional sense, they were regarded as the focal figures of the faith community in matters of public worship, specifically for Salvation Army rituals which came to be regarded as substitute sacraments, such as those mentioned above, and for funerals. Lt. Colonel Fred Hoyle wrote, "I believe it is the prerogative of the officer to officiate on the occasion of dedications, weddings and funerals. The officer is also the unifying factor in corps life."[118]

Later, but in linear development, is the custom of "installing" officers in certain positions—particularly corps commanding officers, divisional commanders and territorial commanders—in public gatherings. Whereas once the individual simply arrived, was extended words of welcome, and got on with the job, now a standard church-like liturgy of charge and acceptance may mark the occasion. In the case of territorial commanders, someone with the rank of commissioner is usually brought in to preside at their installation—and their eventual retirement—if necessary, from another country.

Possibly a similar ritualization of initially informal custom contributed to the original elevation of the presbyter's role in the early church; doctrine follows praxis. In due course, unchecked, such customs would affect the Salvation Army's nascent ecclesiology. At the same time, officers in less public roles, behind a desk at headquarters for example, continue to arrive and get on with it, blessed with a welcome cup of tea if at all. All of this also indicates that although sacramental observances are usually taken as the initial catalyst for the process of clericalisation in the church, the Army's clericalisation gathered momentum after their abandonment (apart from the substitute sacraments described above), suggesting that clericalisation is a sociological process independent of a theological base. Schillebeeckx likewise argues that the development of the priesthood was bound up with the Eucharist only because the leader presided.[119] The Army would argue of course that sacramental observances themselves have a similar history.

Taking the sacraments elsewhere

Could a Salvationist still take the sacraments elsewhere? Booth had told Lunn that a Salvationist would still be at liberty to do this. Begbie, who copies out the whole of Booth's exchange with Lunn, prefaces his chapter with the cautionary tale of Lady Henry Somerset. Lady Henry wanted to become a soldier but asked the General if she might still "be allowed to go for Holy Communion to the Church of England. The answer was

---

118. *Officer*, May 1982, 223.
119. Schillebeeckx, *Church with Human Face*, 145.

a negative."[120] (She became a Methodist instead.) Was the contradiction here simply a matter of "horses for courses"? Lady Henry, after all, belonged to what Booth described as "the dangerous classes . . . "[121]

Over the years, this fifth point made by William Booth in his 1883 announcement ("We do not prohibit our own people . . . from taking the Sacraments . . . if this is a matter of conscience . . . the churches and chapels around will welcome you for this.") has provided an option for a small number of Salvationists, individually exercising that option from which the movement as a whole had withdrawn. It would always be a slightly ambiguous stance in that while the Eucharist would normally be regarded as the focus of a community of faith, such Salvationists would usually still see their corps as their spiritual home. The usual commitment to corps activities would seldom leave time or opportunity for "dual citizenship". This liberty became more seriously frowned upon when Pentecostal and charismatic influence came to be a matter of anxiety.

Subsequent arguments offered

Other reasons for discontinuing sacramental practice have been offered subsequently, at various times, and repeated in various later Salvation Army publications.

For example, Sandall claims that "a very practical consideration was that its orthodox administration was a snare to the poor souls who had been slaves to drink." The Christian Mission Conference of 1870 had urged all members to abstain from intoxicating drinks, and prescribed only unfermented wine for the sacrament of the Lord's Supper.[122] But the use of non-alcoholic, wine, even if merely "diluted jellies," was common amongst non-conformist churches of a "temperance" persuasion—presumably the "unintoxicating wine" referred to in the report of the 1878 War Congress, already mentioned.[123] Fairbank cites the cashbook for the Channel Island corps of St Peter Port, where an entry for 1st November 1881 shows an expenditure of 1/6^d on "blackcurrant jelly for wine for the sacrament."[124] According to Owen Chadwick, "the use of unfermented wine is first found about 1873 as part of the temperance campaign."[125] Strangely, the solution of communion in one kind for people with a weakness for strong drink people was not mooted; alcoholism was still generally considered a matter of will-power rather than pathology.

The argument that there were already too many conflicting views about the meaning and practice of the sacraments is sometimes advanced as a reason for the Army's non-observance.[126] The 1906 *Salvation Army Year Book* claimed that, "working alike in

120. Begbie, *William Booth*, I, 459.

121. That is, of higher social status or educational achievement that the normal run of Salvationists. Clarence Hall records that Booth used the expression when warning Brengle that officership would require unwonted obedience and discipline. (Hall, *Brengle*, 72.)

122. Fairbank, *Booth's Boots*, 124.

123. Bramwell Booth refers to the unappealing "diluted jellies" in *Echoes and Memories*, (1977), 203.

124. Fairbank, *Booth's Boots*, 124.

125. Chadwick, *Victorian Church*, II, 327.

126. Sandall *History*, II, 133.

Protestant, Catholic and heathen countries, the Army could not possibly take this or that side in these matters, but desires to avoid all controversies . . . "[127] This seems oblivious to the fact that the Army's position is yet another such conflicting view, rather than the absence of one. Sandall also refers to William Booth's desire to avoid controversy, quoting Booth as writing in the *Contemporary Review* of August 1882 that controversial questions should be avoided as "the poison of hell."[128] While this may seem a bit rich, coming from so controversial a figure as Booth, in fact he was sensitive to issues which might disrupt the unity of his Army—as Eason's research has shown this to be. He did not want Salvationists caught up in the internecine strife between evangelical and high church Anglicans.

The 1923 *Handbook of Doctrine* stated that "for a period of a few years an experiment was tried by the Founders in the use and administration of some of these ceremonials. They were, however, found to be a source of disagreement, and therefore a weakness."[129] This seems a little disingenuous. Does "experiment" suggest rather more deliberation as well as a greater degree of provisionality about the early practices than was probably the case? There is no record of anyone saying, "Let's try this for a while and see how it works . . . " That is not how it happened.

Bramwell Booth recalled that one of the arguments for the discontinuance of the sacraments in the 1880s was the disagreement over who should administer them. "There arose the question whether the Evangelists alone should be the administrators. Great exception was taken in some quarters to the administration by others, even by the principal local officials; indeed in some places the people absented themselves from the service unless the 'bread and wine' were offered by 'the regular preachers.'"[130] The very disagreement suggests that at least sometimes "lay" people, rather than the evangelists, presided. It also suggests that the polarization of views in the ranks about the status of the ministry had already begun. That this relatively minor problem should have weighed against an apostolic practice at all could suggest both the relative unimportance attached to the sacrament, and also perhaps how unwilling the founders were that any distinction between clergy and lay should be institutionalized within the Salvation Army.

A related issue not mentioned publicly at the time but later suggested as significant was whether sacraments required "priests"? George Scott Railton had attempted to persuade William Booth to acquiesce in the abandonment of the sacraments on these grounds. In a paper written for this purpose in 1881 (in Begbie's words, "set forth with a speciousness and a plausibility which are more curious than persuasive") Railton urged that "there must be no Lord's Supper 'administered' by anybody in such a way as to show anything like a priestly superiority of one over another—every saved person being a 'priest unto God.'"[131] This does at least indicate that there was an on-going debate about this matter. Harry Dean included Railton's argument in a list of reasons for discontinuance in a 1960 *Year Book* article: "The sacraments had been linked, in the main, with

127. *Salvation Army Year Book*, 1906.
128. Sandall, *History*, II, 132.
129. *Handbook of Doctrine*, 1923, 168.
130. Bramwell Booth, *Echoes and Memories*, 203.
131. Begbie, *William Booth*, I, 462.

systems necessitating a separate priesthood for their administration; this suggested a double standard for Christians, and contradicted the New Testament emphasis on the 'priesthood of all believers.'"[132]

Bramwell Booth noted that "the idea of women administering the sacraments at that time was almost unthinkable to many good people, in spite of our stand, from the beginning, on the perfect equality of men and women in the Kingdom of Christ."[133] Mrs Carpenter also suggests that one of the reasons for discontinuance was that "William Booth was not willing to surrender the principle of perfect equality of men and women in every activity of the Kingdom of Christ."[134] The evidence is not conclusive: a letter writer to the *Non-Conformist and Independent* of 9th February 1882 drew attention to the fact that in the Salvation Army for the first time in Christian history the sacrament had been administered by women.[135] We do not know if that had occasioned dissension. The commanding officer at St Peter Port, the Channel Island corps already mentioned, in 1881 was Captain Charlotte Jackson—presumably she presided at the sacrament.

The influence and example of the Quakers has sometimes been mentioned as a factor in the Army's decision. It was claimed that a member of the Quaker Fry family had been an influence on Booth in this respect, but I do not know of any contemporary evidence for this.[136] Railton and Catherine Booth may have been influenced by Robert Barclay's "inner light" theology, and they certainly shared the Quaker view that the spiritual reality made the outward observance redundant. However, it is probable that, in Rightmire's words, "the influence of the Society of Friends on the Salvation Army was more implicit than explicit" and that "the Quaker position on the sacraments provided the early Army leaders with a theological precedent for justifying their non-sacramental practice."[137]

For a long while the subject of observances was seldom discussed. The 1906 *Year Book* said that "The Army abstains entirely from the administration of any sacrament, and from any speaking and writing on the subject."[138] A.J. Gilliard, commissioned as an officer in 1922, wrote, "For a good many years the matter was never in the average Salvationist's thinking. I cannot recall ever coming across it until after I was an officer and then only casually."[139] Colonel A.G. Cunningham claimed in *The Staff Review*, 1929, that "It has been our consistent policy as an organization to abstain . . . from any public discussion on

---

132. Dean, "The Founders and the Sacraments," in Salvation Army, *Another Harvest*, 36. See also his *Sacraments—Salvationist Viewpoint*, (1960) 71–75.

133. Bramwell Booth, *Echoes and Memories*, 203.

134. Carpenter, *William Booth*, 78.

135. Sandall, *History*, II, 134.

136. "Henry William Fry, last surviving grandson of Elizabeth Fry, the Quaker Prison Reformer, who recently passed away at San Francisco at the age of ninety-one, was an intimate friend of the Army Founder. It is said that it was largely owing to H. W. Fry's influence that the Founder decided that The Army should be like the Quakers in not outwardly observing the Sacraments." *War Cry*, 5 August 1939, 7, col. 4. Not mentioned at the time, this seems the creation of hindsight.

137. Rightmire, *Sacraments and the Salvation Army*, 117–18.

138. "Churches, Sacraments and Controversies," *Salvation Army Year Book*, 1906, 54.

139. Gilliard, letter to author, 3 May 1963.

the subject."[140] For more than half of the twentieth century, the Army's self-sufficient subculture tended to protect its members from exposure to theological debate.

However, from time to time from the 1920s on, articles defending the Army's position were published, mainly in "private circulation" journals like *The Officer* and *The Staff Review*, possibly to provide support for officers who found themselves having to defend and explain the Army's beliefs to their soldiers or to clergy in ministers' fraternals. The 1923 *Handbook of Doctrine* included an appendix on sacraments, and its successor volumes have followed suit. Bramwell Booth devoted a chapter to the discontinuance of observance in his autobiography.[141] A chapter on the subject from Mrs Carpenter's life of William Booth, published in 1942,[142] was reprinted separately as a pamphlet in 1945 and reprinted again later, and Robert Sandall's official Salvation Army history, as already mentioned, gave an account of the evolution of the Army's position.

The more numerous publications over the past fifty years have indicated that the subject has been back in Salvationists' thinking, and that answers were thought necessary. Short publications have included: Harry Dean, *The Sacraments—the Salvationist's Viewpoint* (1960); William Metcalf, *The Salvationist and the Sacraments* (1965); Clifford Kew, *Closer Communion: The Sacraments in Scripture and Tradition* (1980); Philip Layton, *The Sacraments and the Bible* (2007). Shorter pamphlets have included: *Saints Without Sacraments* by Brian Tuck (Johannesburg: Salvation Army, 1991); *The Sacraments: A Biblical-Historical Perspective*, [no author attribution] issued by the authority of the Territorial Commander, Canada and Bermuda Territory, 1992, and *The Sacraments: The Salvation Army's attitude to the sacraments viewed in the light of the Scriptures and early Church history*, by Commissioner Hillmon Buckingham and published in Sydney about 2002.

Numerous other recent books, by Philip Needham, Roger Green, Shaw Clifton, Allen Satterlee and others have included sections on or references to the Army's sacramental stance. In response to the World Council of Churches' 1984 "Lima" Document on *Baptism, Eucharist and Ministry*, the Salvation Army produced a document setting out the Army's position.[143] The International Spiritual Life Commission also issued statements on Baptism and Holy Communion in February 1998.

As well as revisiting earlier explanations, these have also advanced further arguments, some of which follow.

Brigadier Harry Dean argued that the Army's position represents a prophetic witness to the Church as a whole; that the Salvation Army's dispensing with the sacraments was an indication of its standing in the "prophetic" over against the "priestly" tradition. He made this point central in his booklet, *The Sacraments—the Salvationist's Viewpoint*, published anonymously but "issued by Authority of the General" (an imprimatur indicating an official Salvation Army statement) in 1960. The view that the Army's position provides a witness to the rest of the Church, that spiritual life is not dependent upon

---

140. *Staff Review*, May 1929, 163.

141. Bramwell Booth, *Echoes and Memories* (1925).

142. Carpenter, *Salvationists and Sacraments*.

143. The responses were published as Thurian and Wainwright, *Faith and Order Paper 137—Churches Respond to BEM*; Volume IV, 230–253, which includes the Salvation Army statement. The Army also published its response separately in book form in *One Faith, One Church*, (1990).

outward forms, has often been expressed subsequently. The Army's response to the "Lima" document, *Baptism, Eucharist and Ministry*, stated that

> Gradually, but positively there emerged that conviction, which Salvationists cherish to this day, that the Holy Spirit was confirming this new expression of Christian faith and practice as part of the Body of Christ, His Church, with a distinctive witness and purpose, which included the non-observance of the traditional sacraments on theological as well as practical grounds.[144]

The Salvation Army's response to the 2013 World Council of Churches publication, Faith and Order Paper No. 214, *The Church: Towards a Common Vision*, has reiterated this position, quoting from the Army's doctrine book and ecclesiological statement:

> The Salvation Army is a permanent witness to the Church as to the possibility, and practicability, of sanctification without formal sacraments. . . . We believe that our calling into sanctity without sacraments is not a contradiction of the ways of other churches, but is something beautiful for Christ, to be held in creative tension with the equally beautiful, but very different, practices of other denominations. In the overall economy of God there are no inherent contradictions, but there are creative paradoxes.[145]

This argument is subject to critical analysis by James E. Pedlar in his 2015 book, *Division, Diversity, and Unity*. In exploring the theology of charisms, using the Salvation Army and the Paulist Order as examples, Pedlar comments:

> This argument was . . . a way of attempting to ingraft non-sacramentalism into the Salvationist charism. That is, if not observing sacraments is part of the vocation of the Salvationist, and if charism and vocation are organically linked, such that the charism is implied in the vocation, then a vocation not to observe the sacraments would imply a non-sacramental charism of some sort. The implication of this line of thinking is that Salvationists are called to non-observance, but not others . . .[146]

He argues that this is to confuse a doctrinal position with a charism, and that such an argument could be used equally, and equally inappropriately, to support any other doctrinal position in theological dispute. By claiming this position as a charism, the Salvation Army shuts down the possibility of theological discussion.

A comprehensive account of the Salvationists' approach to the sacraments, and their first academic exposition, was David Rightmire's 1990 work. He places the Army's early theology in the context of Victorian society, the Wesleyan revival and the nineteenth century holiness movement. He makes the point that by the mid-nineteenth century Wesleyanism had lost touch with its founder's sacramental theology, maintaining

---

144. *One Faith, One Church*, 4.

145. "Church: Towards a Common Vision, A Response from The Salvation Army," 6, (http://www.salvationarmy.org/doctrine/thechurchtcv) quoting from *Salvation Army Handbook of Doctrine*, 270–71 and *Salvation Army in the Body of Christ: An Ecclesiological Statement* 13–14. The subject naturally came up in dialogue between the Catholic Church and the Salvation Army, at which time Commissioner William Francis quoted this same passage (Francis, "Salvation Army in the Body of Christ," 31, citing *Salvation Army in the Body of Christ*, 13–14).

146. Pedlar, *Division, Diversity, and Unity*, 233.

the forms but subordinating other means of grace to the Word. William Booth had been taught William Cooke's subjectivist sacramental position while Catherine Booth especially was influenced by her reading of church history by people like John Lorenz Mosheim and Augustus Neander and a range of seventeenth and eighteenth century "radical restorationist" and "spiritualizing" writers like Isaac Newton and Madame Guyon.

The American holiness revival teaching of Caughey, Finney and Phoebe Palmer also "emphasized a pneumatological ecclesiology that needed little continuity with historical institutions." Phoebe Palmer claimed that "the full baptism of the Holy Ghost" is "the act of ordination on the part of God."[147] Rightmire's argument is that once the Booths' "holiness" or "second blessing" theology was fully developed, it provided a spiritualized substitute for sacramental theology.

> The emphasis on sacramental living by the early Army leaders was the result of a dialectic between their pragmatic theology and explicit pneumatological presuppositions. The abandonment of sacramental practice by no means implied a denial of the sacramental aspect of life. For the Army, the emphasis was upon the reality of new life in Christ, experienced spiritually. What was essential was the necessity of spiritual communion with Christ. This was possible only in the experience of entire sanctification.[148]

Rightmire has now published a new edition of his book, *The Sacramental Journey of the Salvation Army*, with additional material. As well as interpreting Booth's "non-sacramental position as involving the subordination of ecclesiological and sacramental concerns to pneumatological priorities," he examines "how the Army has subsequently interpreted its position, and how its developing sacramental self-understanding raises questions of doctrinal continuity that need to be addressed."[149]

General Paul Rader put it simply: "When our hearts are made holy, all of life is a sacrament."[150] This understanding has led to the recent assertion that it is inappropriate to call the Army *non*-sacramental, firstly because it sees the whole of life as sacramental, and secondly it places the proper emphasis on "Christ as the one true sacrament."[151] Or as the International Spiritual Life Commission put it: "Christ is the one true Sacrament, and sacramental living—Christ living in us and through us—is at the heart of Christian holiness and discipleship."[152] The Salvation Army is not alone in using the expression, "Christ is the one true Sacrament." It was used for example in a recent Catholic website which says that "Christ himself is the one, true, ultimately dependable sacrament . . . His life, thereby, becomes the source of all of our sacraments."[153] A similar point was made by Charles Davis, Catholic theologian, in *A Question of Conscience*: " . . . the seven sacraments, including

---

147. Rightmire, *Sacraments and the Salvation Army*, 150, 155, 158.

148. Rightmire, *Sacraments*, 48.

149. Rightmire, *Sacramental Journey*, from the publisher's flyer.

150. Rader, "The Army's Position on the Sacraments."

151. Clifton, *Who are These Salvationists?* 64.

152. Statement reproduced in Street, *Called to Be God's People*, 89.

153. Newman Apologetics Resource: http://zuserver2.star.ucl.ac.uk/~vgg/rc/aplgtc/hahn/m5/sc-mnt1.html downloaded 27 February 2010.

the Eucharist, could not themselves be regarded as fundamental. The fundamental sacrament is the visible church itself. Christ is the Great Sacrament . . . "[154]

An alternative term suggested by Robert Watson for the Army's position has been "Neo-Sacramental."[155] If we do admit that the whole of life is sacramental—that is, that anything can be a means of grace to us—then perhaps we have to ask whether the Army's position is tantamount to saying, "The whole of life is sacramental, and anything can be a means of grace, *except* the use of water for baptism and bread and wine for a re-enactment of the Last Supper." We are saying they *cannot* be, or *must* not be, in order to emphasize and maintain and witness to the truth that anything else *can* be! Is that a sustainable argument?

Perhaps the most frequently quoted expression of Salvationist sacramentalism has been Albert Orsborn's lovely song, "My life must be Christ's broken bread, my love his outpoured wine . . . "[156] Less often acknowledged is the fact that these verses, deeply spiritual though they are, focus more on the sacrifice made by the worshipper rather than that of Christ, which gets a brief mention in the third and final verse. They celebrate the response rather than the grace.

It has been suggested that the Salvation Army's being a nineteenth century, "modern" phenomenon, as distinguished from "post-modern", could have reinforced the tendency to abstraction rather than the use of concrete imagery like sacraments. Against that, John Rhemick argues that the Army did exactly the reverse, catering to a working class preference for imagery and emotion, over against the arid intellectualism of rational religion. The paradoxical situation is that the Army, as part of its rejection of conventional "churchianity" left on one side the traditional concrete sacramental observances and introduced its own new ones. By contrast, high church Anglicans sought to appeal to a working class constituency by elaborating the ritual observances, bringing color and a sense of the numinous into otherwise drab lives in industrial cities.[157]

The sociologist Roland Robertson proposed that Booth wished to "prevent sacramental power from falling into the hands and under the control of lesser officers in the organizational hierarchy." Roger Green points out that "such an assumption is wrong for two reasons. First, it advances a high view of the sacraments and sacramental power, a view which Booth never espoused. Second, it reduces Booth's theological decisions solely to organizational concerns, and that leads to a myopic view of Booth and his theology."[158] Contrary to Bryan Wilson's claim that the sociology of religion is best investigated by those without belief, Robertson's suggestion shows that it is very difficult for people standing outside the forest to understand what is happening under the trees, and that their assumptions can be quite wrong.[159]

---

154. Charles Davis, *Question of Conscience*, 257.

155. Watson, "The Distillery," *The Present Age*, Vol. 7, No. 2 (Fall 1989), quoted by Couchman, "Neo-sacramental theology of the Salvation Army," 4.

156. Song 610 in the 2015 *Salvation Army Songbook*.

157. McLeod, *Class and Religion*, 112.

158. Robertson, "Salvation Army," in Wilson, *Patterns of Sectarianism*, 49–105, cited in Green, *War on Two Fronts*, 57.

159. Wilson, *Religion in Sociological Perspective*, 25.

William Booth's fourth point in his 1883 announcement was that it be wise for us "to postpone any settlement of the question, to leave it over to some future day, when we shall have more light, and see more clearly the way before us". And in 1895 he was still saying, "This is not a settled question with us . . . " This is one of those matters on which viewpoints within the Army have probably become more diversified as the years have gone on. Some have taken a long view and Booth's words have been re-visited many times by those arguing for the re-introduction of the traditional sacraments to the Army.

In recent years, some advocates of change have been thinking Salvationists exploring ecumenical relationships and finding themselves challenged to defend a position regarded as either misguided or heretical by other Christians.

Others have been Salvationists who simply wished to add this dimension to their worship, or who have done so, joining with Christians of other denominations in their worship. Major John Rhemick, reviewing *Salvation Story*, quoted the authors' "beautiful statement describing sacrament: 'It brings the Incarnation to our doorstep, invites us to swing open the door of our intellectual caution and calls us to allow God's incomprehensible grace to enter—and transform—our ordinary lives.' (*Salvation Story*, 113) Holy communion and baptism do this for me and for many other Salvationists."[160]

Others again have represented major areas of Salvation Army work such as Latin America, where, as John Gowans commented, the Army's non-observance has meant the organization is marginalized and not taken seriously as a Christian denomination by other churches.[161] Illustrating General Gowans' concern, one senior officer who suggested the re-introduction of the sacraments was Commissioner Carl S. Eliasen, formerly TC in Brazil and in South America West, and International Secretary for the Americas at IHQ. In the early twenty-first century, having retired in 1997, and perhaps concerned that the Spiritual Life Commission's recommendations had "allowed individual and unilateral decisions . . . which could easily lead to chaos and confusion," he "considered that it would be useful to have a clear, concrete and clearly defined orientation (in writing) concerning the direction to be taken." While convinced that "there should be no turning away from the basic theological truth and fundamental teaching that no sacrament is essential and that spiritual grace does not depend on any signs and symbols," he proposed that "Enrolment [of soldiers] could be made to coincide [with] Baptism (immersion or aspersion)." Further, "If the Corps Council consider that the observance of the Lord's Supper would contribute to the growth of the Local Church . . . such a ceremony could be held twice a year: on Good Friday . . . [and] on the Sunday closest to the day of the Reformation (October 30)." He suggested that "the celebration of either or both sacraments should be optional." He thought a large number of Salvationists would gladly welcome such a clear, concrete and clearly defined orientation on the subject . . . dispelling their sense of uncertainty, lack of direction and confusion" and eliminating "any misgivings regarding a revolution or divisiveness . . . " Noting that "we have faced other delicate and controversial issues which have eventually been accepted: for example, the matter of divorce amongst officers" . . . Eliasen quoted General Wiseman as writing that

---

160. *Word and Deed*, Spring, 2000, 59–60.
161. *Salvationist*, November 28, 2001, 11.

"Precedents are helpful as a basis, but never as immutable laws."[162] Nothing came of these suggestions.

In Scandinavian countries where Salvationists have typically been regarded as members of the state churches (Lutheran) as well as of the Salvation Army, generations of Salvationists have received the sacraments at their parish churches. The rites of passage of birth (Christening), entering adulthood (Confirmation), marriage (marriage ceremony) and death (funeral) have all involved attendance at church, and many added regular Christmas and Easter communion to these observances. For many years the Norwegian translations of the *Handbook of Doctrine* simply omitted the section on non-observance of Sacraments.[163] The fact that prior to the 1969 *Handbook of Doctrine* the Army was not officially described as a church made this arrangement more plausible. The 2011 publication, *A Sacramental Army* explores the significance of this issue in Nordic countries. Concerning the Army in Finland, Antero Puotiniemu writes that "the importance of participating in the sacraments is mainly an issue among the older generation. The younger generation is less attached to the traditional Lutheran culture and more evangelical in mind, attitude and practice."[164]

Some hopeful of re-introduction have been romantics who have failed to take into account the effect of over a century of custom and the deep attachment many Salvationists have for a doctrinal position which has their total support.

Others again have found that new converts, not from any church background but beginning to read the New Testament without Salvationist preconceptions have been puzzled and unconvinced by the usual Salvation Army explanations.

Some, often under charismatic or ecumenical influence, have attempted to introduce sacramental practices unofficially at a local level, usually without lasting effect and often attracting unfavorable and disciplinary attention. Such efforts also led for the first time to specific prohibitions against officers administering the sacraments. In July 1981 the New Zealand Chief Secretary, Lt-Colonel Dinsdale Pender, circulated to all officers short statements which had been provided by International Headquarters for pasting in the back of their copies of the *Handbook of Doctrine*: "The Salvationist and the Sacraments" and "The Salvationist and Speaking in Tongues". In 1983, Colonel Donald Campbell as Chief Secretary forwarded slightly longer versions, described as "Positional Statements," one on the Sacraments and the other on Speaking in Tongues.[165] The former, giving a concise résumé of the Army's reasons for not practicing the sacraments, concluded: "In view of these biblical and historical considerations, therefore, officers will not conduct, or allow to be conducted in Salvation Army meetings, ceremonies of water baptism or communion (the Lord's Supper)." In the 1990s, in USA Western territory, one or two newly "planted" corps are said to have withdrawn from the Salvation Army rather than discontinue sacramental practices which they had adopted.

---

162. Eliasen, "Reflection on how it might be." Privately circulated paper, 2–4.

163. Lydholm, "Save souls, grow saints and serve suffering humanity," 303.

164. Krommenhoek, Kleman, and Puotiniemi, *Sacramental Army*, 25.

165. Campbell to Heads of Departments, Divisional Commanders and Regional Commander Fiji, letter dated 20 October 1983.

General John Gowans was reported as thinking aloud in a 2001 question and answer session with cadets:

> Is there a possibility? There's always a possibility . . . the Founder allowed the possibility . . . I would hate it to happen if it meant that people . . . believed if you didn't have the sacraments, you were a second-class citizen . . . The only thing that's essential to salvation is the Holy Spirit!
>
> The sacraments are part of every Salvation Army discussion, including High Councils. At every leaders' meeting, this question is raised. It's not a dead question. It's an open question. This is a subject that sadly divides The Salvation Army . . . People [in Latin America] where the Catholic influence is great, would like to see them again. The Army works hard to convert people, who then go to another church that has the sacraments . . .
>
> I've been in Holy Communion for years and never touched the bread or wine . . . It's nevertheless true that some people find it helpful to have a specific symbol . . . Maybe we should take account of those things . . . [166]

The Report of the International Spiritual Life Commission in 1998 reviewed the matter of sacraments in a way which some took as an invitation to further experiment. Concerning the enrichment of Salvation Army worship it suggested amongst other things the use of symbolic acts such as the "Love Feast" without turning them into rituals.[167] Some officers and corps took up the challenge. According to Commissioner Gudrun Lydholm, then a member of the International Doctrine Council, "this has opened the door even further for a debate to reintroduce the sacraments or make the administration of them possible in certain parts of the world. The debate has always been there, but it has become world-wide and been intensified."[168] The Commission's report stated:

> William Booth's statement to Salvationists announcing our discontinuation of the Lord's Supper was not intended to stand for all time. He indicated the matter could be revisited in future. The Commission has done so, with the result that it is not thought necessary or appropriate to re-introduce the practice of sacramental observances at this time. However, as the Founder's statement was provisional, we believe that this provisionality should remain in place, and is an expression of the freedom of Salvationists to continue to respond in constant and instant obedience to the light the Holy Spirit sheds upon the word of God.[169]

Others have responded that the "future day" mentioned was long past by the end of the nineteenth century, and that Booth was in any case merely throwing out a conciliatory but empty gesture to head off any potential objections. General Shaw Clifton firmly rejected any suggestion of change as likely to lead to confusion and division within the Army's ranks, saying that "We ought not to take a solitary passing utterance and seek, 123 years later, to build something theologically complex, and potentially divisive out of

---

166. *Salvationist*, November 28, 2001, 11.
167. Street, *Called to be God's People*, 89.
168. Lydholm, "Salvation Army Doctrines," 51.
169. Street, *Called to be God's People*, 115.

it. After all, the person who wrote it (in an irenic spirit of diplomacy and unity) pointedly failed to act upon it for the remaining 30 years of his Generalship . . . "[170]

A more recent statement of an alternative view is by Commissioner Philip Needham, who had "concluded that . . . the original, practical, theological, and missional arguments for discontinuance are either no longer valid or require views of sacramental practice that are too narrow and limiting . . . and come to the conviction that there would be great benefit to the Salvation Army to restore sacramental practice as a medium of grace, blessing, and missional challenge, and as a visual expression of our unity and participation in the Body of Christ."[171] Needham set out a cogent rationale and proposed a process by which the sacraments might be re-introduced into the Salvation Army. At time of writing, the most recent officially sanctioned statement has been Commissioner Robert Street's booklet, *In the Master's Hands*, revisiting the findings of the Spiritual Life Commission, which he had earlier chaired.[172]

In retrospect, it is of interest that this distinctive Salvation Army position did not arise from any one original Biblical or theological insight or conviction, but from a whole range of factors, some quite significant and others of no great importance. It is perhaps for this reason—along with Booth's hint about re-visiting the subject at some future day—that there has continued to be debate and difference of opinion about the Army's non-practice of the sacraments. The Salvation Army is unlikely to emulate the World-Wide Church of God, a sect founded by the American Herbert W. Armstrong and embracing a range of unorthodox views and doctrines. Armstrong's successors brought their organization, now known as Grace Communion International, back to a more main-line evangelical, orthodox, Nicene Creed-endorsing position, even at the cost of widespread defections by loyalists to their founder's heterodoxy. The Salvation Army's abstention from the practice of the traditional Christian sacraments has not been accompanied by heterodox views on other Christian doctrines, but that does not mean that a change would be easier to bring about.

Notwithstanding General Gowans' reference to the matter being regularly revisited in leaders' meetings, and the recommendation of the International Spiritual Life Commission that the "provisionality" of the Founder's decision should "remain in place,"[173] and Commissioner Needham's recent detailed proposal for change, the official attitude on this issue has probably hardened over the years and it is unlikely that any of these arguments or viewpoints will gather sufficient momentum to initiate a change of direction for the Movement in the foreseeable future.

---

170. Clifton, "People of God," 3.

171. Needham, "My life must be Christ's broken bread," in Metrustery, *Saved Sanctified and Serving*, 126–44.

172. Street, *In the Master's Hands*.

173. Street, *Called to be God's People*, 94.

6

Salvation Army Theology 2: Diversity

> The one-mindedness and one-heartedness of The Army is strikingly exemplified in its newspapers and its prayers. It has 61 publications, issued in 49 countries and colonies. In not one of these can be found any recognition of the controversies, which disturb the Christian world. They represent minds always engaged upon one subject—the subjugation of the world to the Dominion of Jesus Christ.[1]
>
> —George Scott Railton

The previous chapter looked at doctrinal matters upon which the majority of Salvationists might be likely to agree, even though there has been some internal discussion around such matters as the best way of expressing the Salvation Army's teaching on holiness, and about its position on sacraments. Sects often arise around some particular, even peculiar, take on the truth and they tend to hold narrowly to that received revelation. The Salvation Army did not fit that pattern, with the exception of what came to be its view on sacraments, because it was initially an evangelical agency with doctrines calculated to win a broad spectrum of church support. Under those circumstances, as Railton argued, theological disputes could only serve to distract from the main business in hand, salvation. Nevertheless, a comparatively small, close-knit, moderately conservative and evangelical movement is likely to guard its doctrinal positions with care and to find too much diversity or vagueness somewhat threatening. Its publications on doctrine or discipline have traditionally borne the Salvation Army's equivalent of the Catholic Church's "Nihil Obstat" and "Imprimatur;" that is, "By Authority of the General." Although this is now used less than was once the case, Salvationist publications would not include material inconsistent with the Army's official line on any matter.

Sectarian groups which "denominationalise" begin to broaden out in the variety of understandings they will live with. There comes about a spectrum of acceptable

---

1. Railton, *The Salvation Army following Christ*, 195, quoted in Pallant, *Keeping Faith*, 109.

belief—not always comfortable, but at least a "live and let live" arrangement so long as no-one insists too strongly on one view or another. The Army not having remained altogether a small, closely controlled sect, such diversity would be only a matter of time and generally rising levels of education. Some individuals begin to feel restless within the confines of the "faith which was once for all handed down from the saints," as St Jude put it. Some people depart for more congenial circumstances but others have a stronger commitment or loyalty to the institution and want either to influence the views of others, or at least to stake out their own corner within it. The Army's gradual loosening up in this respect is discussed helpfully by John Coutts in his book, *The Salvationists*.[2]

The coming of diversity would nevertheless face institutionalized impediments which need to be recognized. The Salvation Army long dealt with controversial matters as far as possible by avoiding them. This practice arose from the belief of the Movement's founders that any such debate would only serve to distract Salvationists from keeping the main thing—evangelism—the main thing.

As already discussed, this aversion to controversy was one of the causes of the breakdown of the Army's negotiations towards possible association with the Church of England in 1882.[3] As quoted at the head of this chapter, in 1907 George Scott Railton rejoiced that the Salvation Army was able to avoid "the controversies, which disturb the Christian world."

An unintended consequence of this policy could have been some degree of "dumbing down" of Salvationists' ability and willingness to think critically about their faith. This did not apply only to theological matters of course. In an address to staff officers at the 1904 congress Booth explained that taking sides in political questions would firstly, alienate some people from hearing what you needed to say about spiritual matters and secondly, discourage donors from contributing to the Army's funds and thirdly, lessen the Army's potential influence for good by getting offside with the political powers that be.[4] With no representative institutions in which such matters might be raised and discussed, and no articles or correspondence about such matters in Salvation Army publications, there would be no internal intellectual opposition or counter-movement to that sociological and cultural shift towards conservative attitudes on political, social and moral issues which often occurs as radical groups mature.

Early in the twentieth century, former Commissioner Alex Nicol had hoped for a more liberalizing trend, and evidently thought that some others may have shared his hopes.

> The great question is that the General of the Salvation Army bound the organization before it was many months old to preach and declare for ever such doctrines as the following is an example of:
> "We believe that our first parents were created in a state of innocence, but by their disobedience they lost their purity and happiness and that in consequence of their fall all men have become sinners totally depraved and as such are justly exposed to the wrath of God."

2. Coutts, *Salvationists*, 3–17.
3. Booth in the *Contemporary Review*, August 1882, quoted in Sandall, *History*, II, 133.
4. Booth, "Politics," in *International Staff Council Addresses*, 148–64.

> The General threw away the book that Dr. Cook [sic], the professor, put into his hands as a student for the ministry.[5] Young Booth tossed it against the wall of his lodgings in disgust. He said he would sooner starve than preach the doctrine of election. He was a rebel in those days. Now that he becomes the High Priest of a new Order he falls into the trap that has destroyed so many noble-hearted leaders of emancipatory movements . . . he puts his name to a set of doctrines that neither the second nor third nor any other General of the Salvation Army can qualify, amend, or end. The Army is committed for all time to this doctrine and many others equally contentious, and *some of which Staff officers no more believe in than they do that Bacon wrote Shakespeare*. [My emphasis]

Really? That seems an amazing assertion for the turn of the twentieth century. Nicol went on to ask:

> Is the formal acceptance of the doctrine necessary to salvation? If not, on what ground did the General bind his successors and the hundreds of thousands of soldiers that follow his Flag to these declarations, all of which have to be signed by them before they can be escorted into the inner councils of the Army?
> . . . While the Constitution is based on this foundation it is useless trying to keep up the pretense that the Salvation Army is not a sect: it is the most exclusive and pronounced sect among all sects.[6]

Nicol feared that the Army's theological conservatism would inhibit its growth and hoped more liberal views would prevail. Had they done so, would that have contributed to the Army's continued expansion, or ensured its earlier demise?

SCRIPTURE

Even as Nicol wrote, a new conservative theological force was gaining ground—fundamentalism. This arose in the United States in the late nineteenth and early twentieth centuries as a reaction against what was termed "modernism," a pejorative term encompassing theology which took into account the findings of contemporary biblical scholarship, known as "Higher Criticism," and against the "Social Gospel," a demythologized development of post-millennialism. Fundamentalism was popularized by a set of volumes by many distinguished conservative scholars on *The Fundamentals*, the first of which were published in 1909, so before the First World War.[7]

During the war years and into the 1920s and beyond, fundamentalism greatly extended its influence. Karen Armstrong has written of the way fundamentalism in any religion is a common defensive reaction to the instability of times of rapid change—as we see even today amongst some factions of Islam. She observed that;

> Protestant fundamentalism came into being in the United States when evangelical Christians pondered the unprecedented slaughter of the First World War.

---

5. Nicol was mistaken here: Dr Cooke was Booth's *Methodist* teacher; it was a *Congregational* text that Booth rejected because of its Calvinist doctrine of election, during his brief period of training for that ministry.
6. Nicol, *General Booth*, 93–95.
7. Torrey and Dixon, *Fundamentals*.

Their apocalyptic vision was simply a religious version of the 'future war' genre that had developed in Europe. Religious fundamentalists and extremists have used the language of faith to express fears that also afflict secularists.[8]

Christian fundamentalism is a dogmatic position on the nature of Scripture. In the words of James Barr, "It does not start from the detailed factual realities of the Bible: it begins as a dogmatic position which was formed in the past and is imposed upon Scripture; the supposed scriptural evidences for it are valid only when this dogmatic position is already accepted."[9] Fundamentalism stresses five doctrines: biblical inspiration and the inerrancy of scripture as a result of this; the virgin birth of Jesus; belief that Christ's death was the atonement for sin; the bodily resurrection of Jesus; the historical reality of the miracles of Jesus. At first sight such a schema appears indistinguishable from the substance of conservative evangelical doctrines like those of the Salvation Army (although the Army's eleven points of doctrine neglected to mention either the virgin birth or the resurrection). William Booth was not, however, a fundamentalist; he stood in the earlier Wesleyan tradition. For example, for him, biblical inspiration and authority did not imply verbal inerrancy—as we have seen, he expressly denied that idea. Nor would fundamentalism have accommodated Booth's understanding of the sacraments or his views on women's ministry.

At the opposite end of the continuum were the liberal, or modernist, scholars accused by fundamentalists of subjecting the Bible to a hermeneutic of suspicion. They might have ranged from those, at one end, who simply tried to bring to bear on sacred texts the best current textual criticism, to those at the other who began from the assumption—as much a stance of faith as that of the fundamentalist—that nothing in Scripture could be relied upon. Probably few of the latter have thrown their lot in with the Salvation Army in any case.

Adrian Hastings has characterized nineteenth century free church theology as "a literalist clinging to Scripture and to the central Evangelical triangle of divine wrath, human sinfulness and substitutionary atonement."[10] Internationally, the mainstream of the Salvation Army has continued in this Evangelical tradition, seemingly without investing significant effort in deepening or reinterpreting that tradition, despite the enlargement of vision which accompanied the extension of social work. Unfortunately, unexamined theological propositions either tend to become gradually more formal and less related to life, or else simply decay into vagueness. Or as Hastings again put it, the rapid decline of the free churches in the early twentieth century, was "in large part because their inner religious life consisted now of little more than institutionalized emotionalism and moralizing." To what extent could that be said of the Salvation Army? Has its theology been influenced by fundamentalist more than by other streams of scholarship and devotion, or has its involvement in issues of social justice served to balance that tendency?

---

8. Armstrong, *Fields of Blood*, 365. Armstrong's chronology for Fundamentalism is slightly inaccurate but her analysis is cogent.

9. Barr, "Fundamentalist Understanding of Scripture," 71.

10. Hastings, *History of English Christianity*, 110.

That some officers at least were wrestling with the challenges of biblical scholarship even in the 1920s is suggested by a question posed in *The Officer* by "Inquirer" of Scotland:

> Does an acceptance of the conclusions arrived at by the majority of "Higher Critics" as to the composite authorship of some of the books of the Old Testament involve the rejection of The Salvation Army teaching on the Inspiration of Scriptures?

The editor's answer poured cold water on the "conjecture and supposition" characterizing the critics, but did not actually answer the question. Instead, it warned that "... the 'conclusions' of the Higher Critics are extremely unlikely to be of any service in soul-winning—and that is our business, is it not?"[11] Another questioner wondered how the discoveries of archaeologists could be reconciled with the marginal dates given in the Bible, particularly those in the opening chapters of the Book of Genesis. (Perhaps the writer owned a Scofield Bible.) The editor's reply pointed out that Bishop Ussher's seventeenth century chronology formed no part of the Biblical text and was clearly not appropriate for the early chapters of Genesis, where incalculably long periods of time were indicated, but that dates pertaining to more historical periods were being confirmed by modern archaeology.[12]

The editor of *The Staff Review*, commenting on councils conducted by General Higgins in London in 1930, commended his recitation of the Army's doctrines, and his invitation to commissioners present to join him and the Chief of the Staff in signing a copy of the Declaration of Faith.

> This was a timely and significant gesture on the part of the General. Cabled throughout the world by the Press within a few hours, this solemn reaffirmation of faith answered in the clearest manner the hope expressed in certain quarters that "under the new regime" The Army would "broaden out theologically," and the assertion already made by others that its Leaders intended to alter the doctrines of The Army.[13]

One wonders who the "others" were, and where the "certain quarters," and for what they hoped, but none of this should have been surprising; second centuries seem to be significant times in the life of movements. A.F. Walls taught patristics in a West African Anglican theological college in the 1950s. Visiting local churches in his district he realized that the things he was teaching about during the week, he could observe actually happening at the weekend. The same kind of consolidation and reflection he described taking place in the second century churches, was in progress in West African churches in *their* second century.[14] The second century seems to have had a similar significance for the Salvation Army. Roger Green, referring to various late twentieth and early twenty-first century initiatives in Salvationist theological discussion, comments that "these are still tenuous efforts for a denomination yet in its primacy. The Army is only now coming

---

11. *Officer*, April, 1923, 285–86.
12. *Officer*, June, 1923, 473–74.
13. *Staff Review*, April 1930, 103.
14. Walls, *Missionary Movement in Christian History*, xiii.

into an understanding of what it means to have a corporate theological life."[15] General Paul A. Rader acknowledged in 1998 that "The Salvation Army is passing through a critical metamorphosis of self-understanding."[16]

The Salvation Army entered its second century in the 1960s. Its first great age of expansion was well and truly over; it was now becoming more self-conscious, and beginning to clarify and rationalize what it had been doing, as well as adjusting to the fact that it was now operating in a world markedly different from that in which it had taken shape. Salvationists were becoming more aware of the rest of the church, and some were more informed about theological issues and more likely therefore to question the Army's own position.

Some tension could be detected between more liberal and the more conservative outlooks. At the 1958 Commissioners' Conference, Lt. Commissioner Alfred J. Gilliard, Principal of the International College for Officers (an advanced training center in London) "spoke of the problems of theological 'idiom' involving officers from various countries." He was obliged to defend his college against claims by "a number of Commissioners that some officers had been disturbed at some teaching which they regarded as 'the infiltration of liberalism.'"[17] Clearly some did not accept the possibility of diverse views on what they regarded as core beliefs.

The Salvation Army Students' Fellowship provided a semi-official but semi-independent forum for slightly radical discussion in these years and spawned a variety of periodicals, usually quarterly: *Magazine* in Great Britain, *Battlepoint* in New Zealand, *New Soldiers* in the USA and *Impact* in Australia. These were mostly short-lived—*Impact* lasted 1971–1975—though *Battlepoint* survived for 25 years, until 1988. The novelty and difficulty of achieving any forum for free discussion is illustrated by the appearance of the February 1963 number of *Magazine* with several pages featuring only the word "censored." However the Students' Fellowship Council, meeting without the official headquarters representative, had the offending articles printed and circulated to subscribers separately.

There have also been occasional underground reform movements or ginger groups. The Salvation Army Renewal Group was stillborn in the late 1960s. An ephemeral broadsheet, *Crossfire*, appeared in London in March 1971, describing itself as "The electric organ of the radical centre." In the mid–1990s a short-lived UK reform movement called the Independent Salvationist Forum, supported by some officers and soldiers and with a retired colonel/territorial commander as spokesman, was dismissed by the UK territorial commander as "subversive and schismatic."[18] No doubt there were others over the years. With the advent of the internet, blog-sites and websites like that of the "Former Officers' Fellowship" and the now defunct "Rubicon" have provided unofficial but influential opportunities for free discussion. An officially-sponsored discussion forum on the IHQ website seemed to attract limited participation however.

---

15. Green, "The Salvation Army and the Evangelical Tradition," 61.

16. *Word and Deed* (Fall 1998) 1.

17. Unpublished Reports and Recommendations of the 1958 International Conference of Commissioners, 21, in Salvation Army International Heritage Centre Archives AD/5/1/6.

18. Pears, "Towards a Theology of Salvation Army Officership," 24–26.

Membership of the World Council of Churches and of local and national ecumenical bodies, helped broaden Salvationist understanding. In the early 1980s when the organization responded to the World Council of Churches' "Lima" Document on *Baptism, Eucharist and Ministry*, territories were asked to set up working parties to contribute to that response. Some did. The Army's relationship with the World Council of Churches was often slightly fraught, as will be discussed in a later chapter.

The election of the scholarly Frederick Coutts as General in 1963 probably encouraged as well as added some cachet of respectability to theological thinking. John Gowans (General 1999–2002) comments in his memoirs that "Frederick Coutts was regarded by some as a dangerous liberal. Some influential American Salvationists sought to dissuade members of the High Council from electing him. When he was elected to the office of General, one leader was overheard to say that this particular High Council's selection heralded the end of The Salvation Army."[19] Conversely, A.J. Gilliard observed of International Headquarters in 1965 that "There is a decided spirit of release and change here, but I get the idea that we do not yet know what to do with the new opportunities thus provided."[20] A few in the Salvation Army were attracted by a new wave of radical, popular theology associated with writers such as John A.T. Robinson, Harvey Cox and Paul Tillich, and so the Army for perhaps the first time began to develop some conscious pluralism of theological outlook. Writers such as Fred Brown, Bernard Mobbs, and Harry Dean took up the task of earlier intellectuals like Alfred G. Cunningham and Carvosso Gauntlett in trying to widen Salvationists' theological horizons. *The Officer*, edited in turn by Eric Coward, William Burrows and William Clark, entered a halcyon period, with a significant educative role.

Very little in it—certainly nothing like a full-scale public liberal-fundamentalist breach, and the administration was long unwilling for major differences of theological opinion to become widely debated in print. Even slightly liberal thinking had long had a difficult and lonely journey—and scholarship was often deemed "liberal" or "modernist." One of the Army's great women, Colonel Catherine Baird who retired as Literary Secretary in 1957, sought to defend officers victimized on this count. A 1958 letter to General Wilfred Kitching made clear "her abhorrence of the idea of anyone who may 'set up within our ranks a witch-hunting attitude." By her definition, "a witch-hunter is one who seeks, by any means, to suppress or even damage and slander those whose honest convictions do not coincide with his (or her) own. We cannot expect young people to forgive it in the Army where men (and women) should be occupied with more lofty pursuits." She went on:

> Surely anyone should be ashamed to have, after 30 years, no deeper, clearer understanding of the atonement, holiness, last things, and other great doctrines, than he had at the beginning. And surely, this deeper knowledge does not mean that he has departed from that which he first knew. Given the alphabet, a child can write simple words and little more. In manhood, he may write a sonnet. But that does not mean that he no longer believes that "c-a-t" spells cat.
>
> The second deplorable attitude of mind is that of worshipping the written Word rather than the living Word. The godly scholars and saints who gave us the

---

19. Gowans, *There's a Boy Here*, 57.
20. Gilliard (then Literary Secretary and Editor-in-Chief), letter to author, 22 February 1965.

Bible in its present form never could have dreamed that we would mistake them for God, or regard their work as infallible. Martin Luther said, "The Bible is the crib wherein our Lord is laid." To disregard this is surely a denial of the "holy writ" mentioned in your letter . . . If we want the sort of young people who care more for truth than for privileges and places, we shall have to consider a matter of such vital importance without fear or prejudice."[21]

Baird's appeal was in vain. The "Fred Brown affair" of 1970, when the well-known British officer was suspended and eventually was either dismissed or felt compelled to resign over the refusal of the hierarchy to approve publication of work deemed too radical, and his own refusal to submit it for such approval knowing that it would suffer amendment if he did, demonstrated that the institution would not bend too far. The case attracted embarrassing public notoriety in Britain and had serious consequences for some of Brown's Salvationist supporters.[22]

Commissioner Norman Marshall, an American officer who served as chairman of the International Doctrine Council in the 1980s, wrote of the "London bias" as a "liberal bias which must be confronted carefully." He attributed this in part to Commissioner Alfred G. Cunningham who "has cast an influence passed down through the Literary Department that has been damaging for many in his train have occupied positions of influence and have been writers of Army literature. Also, there has been an influence of London University cast upon some officers who have studied there."[23] This animadversion against Alfred G. Cunningham, so long after his time, is curious. He was, after all, the editor who had disparaged the "conclusions" of the Higher Critics and applauded General Higgins' affirmation of faith in 1930.

Some of Cunningham's critics' discomfort related to differing emphases on matters like Biblical inerrancy, or what Marshall called the "authenticity of the Scriptures" and views on creationism/evolution. Just sometimes shades of emphasis and indications of polarized assumptions became apparent, as when a British reviewer damned with faint praise ("could have some value . . . ") an American commissioner's book on the Bible, suggesting that "a simplistic view is in danger of creating some pitfalls for the uninitiated reader."[24] Again, as we have seen, there was a perception of differing interpretations of the Wesleyan doctrine of entire sanctification—like the Corinthians, some said "I am of Brengle" and others "I am of Coutts."

To some extent the different emphases have in the past been represented respectively by the British (International Headquarters) Salvationist literary establishment and that of the United States. The International Training College in London would be more

21. Izzard *Pen of Flame*, 112.

22. *Secular Evangelism*, by Fred Brown (1970); See Gordon Batten and others, letter in *Battlepoint* 29 (September 1970) 13–15. Reports were carried by the *Guardian* (18 September, 9, 10, 13, 17 October 1970); *Times* (9 June 1970); *Daily Telegraph* (15 and 19 October 1970); *British Weekly* (17 September, 16 October 1970); Harold Hill, "The Fred Brown Affair," *Battlepoint* 30 (December 1970) 1–6. *The War Cry* did not mention the matter at all.

23. Marshall, unpublished letter dated 13 January 1990, in International Heritage Centre Archives. Perhaps Marshall had read Frederick Coutts's tribute to the value of C. Ryder Smith's evening lectures on the Old Testament at the University of London. Coutts, *No Continuing City*, 49.

24. Hoyle, *Officer*, January 1982, 26.

likely to encourage the use of Biblical commentaries published by SCM and the American Schools for Officer Training to prefer work of more conservative provenance. Major Ian Barr wrote that "the Army is a fairly broad church, with the Atlantic forming a convenient gulf between our liberal and conservative un-extremes."[25] But lest it be thought that this was simply an Atlantic divide, Escott quotes Captain John Read, when senior tutor at Denmark Hill in the early 1990s, as referring to the "liberal woolly tendency" of the educational syllabus before he instituted "a radical revision of the syllabus which is now more recognizably evangelical."[26] And a letter to the American *New Frontier* accused its distinguished editor, Dr Robert Docter, of pursuing a "liberal agenda."

From the 1980s on there were a number of indicators of a deepening Salvation Army interest in theology. This was seen in the literary activity of such officers as John Coutts, John Larsson, Philip Needham, William Clark, Shaw Clifton, John Rhemick and Chick Yuill, who continued to broaden Salvationists' theological horizons with relatively accessible, popular writing. They were joined by non-officer writers, a new generation of Salvationist academics—all North Americans—like Roger Green, David Rightmire, James Read, Jonathan Raymond and Donald Burke. The very fact that a comparative handful of individuals could be named in this way shows that this was hardly a mass-movement, but on the other hand the Salvation Army is, in world terms, a tiny and closely inter-connected constituency.

At the same time there were increasing numbers of tertiary-educated Salvationists and officers obtaining theological qualifications. More extensive biblical and theological training was provided for officers, which in most Western countries and some others has involved formal credentialing relationships between Salvation Army Training Colleges and external, degree-conferring institutions. The Catherine Booth Bible College (now Booth University College) and the Ethics Centre in Canada, and the William Booth University in the Democratic Republic of the Congo were established.

In 2001 an International Conference on Theology and Ethics was held in Winnipeg, Canada, and one of the proposals arising from this was that territories should initiate further theological discussion. This was followed up at least by the UK Territory since an initial conference in 2004, and in Australasia with a tri-territorial theological forum which has met annually since 2003, publishing the papers presented annually since 2005. Registrations having been opened up beyond officially appointed delegates, these "Thought Matters" conferences have drawn attendances of up to a hundred in recent years. A further international symposium was held in Johannesburg in 2006. In the United States the periodical *Word and Deed* has been published since 1998 and Australia published *The Practical Theologian* from 2003 until 2007 when it was decided to support a peer-reviewed non-denominational Wesleyan journal instead.[27] The fact that such conferences are held and publications are issued at least recognizes that there are theological questions to discuss, which implies that people may hold a variety of views.

Most of the above indicated an increasing interest in being able to "give a reason for the hope within us," and a relative openness, perhaps a Salvationist *glasnost*. This is still

---

25. *Word and Deed*, Spring, 2000, 51.
26. Escott, "Church Growth Theories," 145.
27. *Aldersgate Papers*, PO Box N63 Bexley North NSW 2207; http://acwr.edu.au/aldersgate-papers/.

tempered sometimes by the residual sectarian tendency in institutional circles to believe that there is only one truth and that we hold it, and that diversity of viewpoints is suspect and to be discouraged. On theological matters, continuing protectiveness of a fairly tightly monitored orthodoxy might be illustrated by a case where a former Salvationist proposed to edit a volume on Salvation Army theology to be published by an "outside" publisher and the International Headquarters leadership placed an embargo on contributions by any active officers.[28] The book was still published, but with contributions mainly from *retired* officers (including a retired General) and distinguished Salvationist academics.[29] The ring-fencing of some International Heritage Centre records with decades-long embargoes, including, within the past decade, those concerning doctrine, also suggests a degree of insecurity at odds with both transparency and the encouragement of scholarship. It is to be hoped that some future administration will see fit to end this practice.

At the end of the twentieth century, John W. Hazzard was able to write of the American Salvationists he sampled that even though there was some tension between a "traditional orientation" and a "progressive orientation," that "my impression . . . is that these orientations are not manifested in opposing political camps organizationally."[30] If Hazzard had been able to compare American with British opinion he might have found a wider spectrum of views, occasionally aired in print. Although Hazzard had not detected any "political" sequelae so far as internal alignments were concerned, that may not always be entirely the case. Major Stephen Court, welcoming on his "Armybarmy" blog the appointment of an American as Chief of the Staff in 2010, suggested that this would strengthen conservatism, presumably at the expense of more liberal opinion.

> An American as CoS is rare. Americans in general are known to be more theologically conservative than the rest of the developed world SA. That is notable as a sign of the direction the General and the Army are headed.[31]

That Court's hopes were justified might be suggested by a subsequent revision of the *Handbook of Doctrine*, described as a "correction for clarity." It appears to retreat from Booth's position on Scripture, perhaps to accommodate those preferring a more overtly fundamentalist position. The relevant Minute from IHQ read:

Handbook of Doctrine

Rewording of Paragraph 'The Inspiration of Scripture'

"On behalf of the General, I am pleased to announce a change of wording for a paragraph found on page 11 of the Handbook of Doctrine (Chapter 1—'For further exploration'—1.A.3.—page 11).

---

28. Laurie Robertson to Denis Metrustery, email 8 November 2012.
29. Denis Metrustery, *Saved, Sanctified and Serving*.
30. Hazzard, "Marching on the Margins," 138.
31. Court, armybarmy (blog), http://www.armybarmy.com/2009_12_01_archive.html, downloaded 25 February 2010.

"The old wording in question includes:

"The inspiration of the Bible provides a foundation for our understanding of the reliability of the divine revelation in Scripture. It is uniquely inspired in a way that is different from other writings or works of art. However, this does not mean that the Bible is infallible or inerrant, so that it is incapable of misleading and contains no human error. Whereas we believe that the overall message of the Bible is inspired and reliable, each individual passage must be read and interpreted carefully, in context, and with careful reference to the whole of biblical truth.

"Effective immediately, two paragraphs will replace the one above:

"We believe the message of the Bible is inspired and reliable. However, each individual passage must be read and interpreted carefully, in context and with reference to the whole of biblical truth."We affirm that we can rely upon the Scriptures for instruction and guidance in matters of divine truth and the Christian life, because in Scripture we meet the Word of God himself, Jesus Christ. The Holy Spirit who inspired the writers also illumines those who read its pages and leads them to faith."[32]

Those who felt more secure with infallibility and inerrancy could now breathe more freely. On the other hand, this ruling maintains the even-handed approach commended by Major John Rhemick in 2000, welcoming the new doctrine book *Salvation Story* because "Chapter 6 dealing with the fall of mankind has created an umbrella big enough to include those of us who accept Genesis 1–3 as an historical event without opposing those who regard it as myth or legend."[33]

There is occasional discussion on such issues. For example, a regular *Officer* columnist, Captain Grant Sandercock-Brown of Sydney, devoted his page to demolishing liberal theology at the beginning of 2008, and then even-handedly returned to criticize fundamentalism later in the year.[34] In 2009, Major Terry Grey of Sydney carefully deconstructed the assumption that all readers should be able to agree on the "plain meaning" of the text.[35] No protests appear to have been entered. An American officer's 2009 article in *The Officer*, appearing to take it for granted that all Salvationist would endorse certain fairly conservative views on Scripture and creation, drew a rejoinder from an Australian officer in a subsequent number, that this should not be assumed; her opinion was in turn disputed by a UK officer in a later issue.[36]

On the difficulties standing in the way of an accommodation between conservative and liberal points of view on the Scriptures, the Australian Major Dean Smith has asked, "Are Liberals and Evangelicals singing from the same song-sheet?" He regretfully concluded that they are not, because their respective positions "embody competing

32. *War Cry* (New Zealand) 11 August 2012, 17.
33. Rhemick, "Review of *A Salvationist Handbook of Doctrine*," 56.
34. Sandercock-Brown, "On Liberalism," 48; "Fundamentalism," 48.
35. Grey, "Interpretation of Scripture," 41–43.
36. See Munn, "Divine Revelation in Human History," 31–33; letter from Rees, *Officer*, January–February 2009, 24; response from Poxon, *Officer*, March–April 2010, 25.

and incommensurable conceptual schemes." He could therefore only recommend "the difficult task of understanding each other's position so that genuine dialogue can take place."[37] That such dialogue is unlikely to happen very often may be indicated by the fact that Dr Smith's paper was published in a journal of Jesuit provenance rather than a Salvation Army one. Many would nevertheless concur with General Coutts when faced with the somewhat brash question as to whether he was not a "modernist." "Fundamentalist, modernist, the only '-ist' I want to be known by is salvationist," he replied.[38]

This chapter now looks at some further matters on which Salvationists have come to differ, and have not always *agreed* to differ.

THE SALVATION ARMY IN RELATION TO PENTECOSTALISM AND THE CHARISMATIC MOVEMENT

A seismic shift in church history in the twentieth century was the rise of the Pentecostal tradition. From a tiny and despised minority movement at the beginning of that century it has become a major and most rapidly expanding grouping of Christian faith, taking its place alongside the catholic, orthodox and protestant streams, and being particularly strong in the developing world. Where Pentecostal theology and praxis have been adopted within the other streams of the church since about 1960, it is known as the charismatic movement. While this has not impacted on the Salvation Army to an equal extent universally, it has been influential in some territories. In the Scandinavian territories, the United Kingdom, South Africa, New Zealand, and Australia in particular, it has had some influence on Salvationist belief and expression, both positively with renewal and negatively with some strife and numerical losses. The relationship between the Salvation Army and the Pentecostal and charismatic movements provides a case-study of how an earlier renewal movement, like the Salvation Army, can resist and then accommodate to the growth and influence of a later renewal movement.

The Wesleyan holiness revival tradition postulates the need for a distinct second, experiential, work of grace subsequent to conversion, enabling holiness of life. Its linear descendant, the twentieth century Pentecostal movement, inherited that doctrine but differed from the holiness tradition in that glossolalia was considered the essential, initial sign that such a work of grace had taken place.[39] There was also a difference in emphasis between an earlier stress on eradicating sinfulness and a later focus on power to exercise spiritual gifts.

Pentecostal phenomena, including glossolalia, have been recurring features throughout church history. The steps in this particular twentieth century restoration have been described as "waves." Pentecostals of the early twentieth century were a "first wave." These claimed the baptism of the Holy Ghost as a "second blessing" (or third blessing, if they also maintained a holiness blessing) of which tongues as a personal prayer language were the initial sign. No single founder is claimed for Pentecostalism

---

37. Smith, "Are Liberals and Evangelicals singing from the same song sheet?" 1–16.
38. Thomlinson, *Very Private General*, 179.
39. Of Wesleyan provenance, though there are also Calvinist variants of Pentecostalism.

but the modern movement usually acknowledges Charles Parham's Bethel Bible School of Topeka, Kansas in 1901 and William J. Seymour's Azusa Street mission of Los Angeles, California in 1906, although there were other and unconnected "outbreaks," both earlier and contemporary. It spread rapidly and internationally thereafter.

From about 1960 on, charismatic renewal in historic denominations was seen as a "second wave." Those involved tended to accept that all Christians did experience the presence or in-dwelling of the Holy Spirit, but required a special "filling" or realization of this, and tongues were again the expected indication. A new resurgence of church planting (both of new denominations and of independent congregations) and an emphasis on "signs and wonders" typified a "third wave," a name coined by C. Peter Wagner of Fuller Theological Seminary.[40] "Third wavers" often recognize conversion as the time when a person receives the filling of the Spirit, emphasize the ongoing nature of the Christian experience and do not expect all to have the gift of tongues. R.T. Kendall described a late twentieth century *fourth wave*, "the coming together of conservative evangelical teaching with charismatic worship styles and experience" and willingness to be involved in social action.[41]

We look firstly at arguments for regarding the Salvation Army as a proto-charismatic renewal movement, then at the response of the Army to the Pentecostal movement, and thirdly at the Army's involvement in and response to the charismatic movement.

That extraordinary gifts of the Spirit were being discussed in the early days of the Salvation Army (well before Pentecostalism) is indicated by one of William Booth's regular letters to Salvationists, published in *The War Cry*, in March 1885.

> A good deal of attention is being given just now to what are known as the extraordinary "gifts of the Spirit"; that is, the ability to do something which is beyond the power of man to do without the direct operation of God. Such gifts as these were, without doubt, possessed by the Apostles both before and after the death of our Lord. They had the gift of tongues; that is, they received suddenly the power to speak languages which they had never learned. They had the gift of healing; that is, they cured the sick, opened the eyes of the blind, unstopped the ears of the deaf, and restored the dead to life instantaneously without the use of ordinary means. They wrought miracles; they caused events to happen that were contrary to the usual course of nature . . .
>
> These gifts were useful, inasmuch as they called attention to those who possessed them, declared that the mission of these Officers was Divine, and justified men everywhere in believing what they had to say . . . their possession today might be a great blessing to mankind. There is not a word in the Bible which proves that we might not have them at the present time, and there is nothing in experience to show they would not be as useful today as in any previous period of the Church's history. No man, therefore, can be condemned for desiring them, and the recent remarkable signs and wonders wrought amongst us not only demand, but shall have our most profound and sympathetic consideration.[42]

---

40. Wagner, *Third Wave of the Holy Spirit*.

41. Kendall, *The Anointing*, cited by Barr, "Traffic on a less than Calm Sea," 54–55.

42. Booth, "Gifts of the Spirit," *War Cry*, 14 March, 1885; in Waldron, edited, *The Most Excellent Way*, 1.

Booth was no dispensationalist, so one might have expected the rest of the article to expand further on the desirability of possessing such gifts in the present age. Instead, while continuing to encourage such expectations ("I long for them myself. I believe in their necessity, and I believe they are already amongst us"[43]), the rest of the article encouraged Salvationists not to neglect the ordinary gifts with which they had been blessed, and above all, not to neglect the "more excellent way" of love, as urged in 1st Corinthians 12:31. Booth's article in the following week's *War Cry*, on "The Improvement of Gifts," addressed the best use of natural gifts such as making money, "constructiveness" (employed by architects and engineers), artistry and music, which should all be dedicated to God's service, before returning to "the gift of gifts, the capacity to love."[44] Being a consummate pragmatist, Booth had shut the discussion down by bringing the reader back to matters about which he could speak with assurance.

"Slaying in the Spirit" (known as a "glory fit" in the early Army, for its resemblance to a petit mal seizure), "deliverance ministry" (exorcism) and faith healing were all well-documented in the early Salvation Army, and arguably prophecy might be added to this list, although definitions of this gift differ. Glossolalia, however, does not appear to have figured amongst the early Salvationists' gifting, perhaps surprisingly seeing that it was practiced in British enthusiast circles long before the rise of American Pentecostalism.[45] Since "tongues" is regarded as the distinguishing mark of Pentecostalism this would argue against the experience of early Salvationism being described as Pentecostal rather than simply "revivalist" or "enthusiast." Alan Harley comments that, "There are those who point to the type of unusual phenomena described in Bramwell Booth's *Echoes and Memories* as proof that being 'slain in the Spirit' and the like should be evidenced in contemporary Salvationism. This position fails to recognize that whereas for contemporary Charismatics such happenings are evidence of God's blessing and are thus to be encouraged and sought, for early Salvationists the position was 'seek not, forbid not.'"[46]

A number of early Salvationists moved on to Pentecostalism. Arthur Booth-Clibborn, husband of the Booths' eldest daughter Catherine, is generally included in the pantheon of early Pentecostals on account of his involvement with Alexander Dowie, and he was associated with the Pentecostal movement from 1908. Gerrit Polman, founder of Pentecostalism in the Netherlands, was a junior officer under Booth-Clibborn and another Dutch Pentecostal leader and missionary, Pieter Klaver. Carrie Judd (Montgomery), a well-known USA healing evangelist in the early twentieth century was earlier a Salvationist, as was the first Korean Pentecostal, Heong Huh.[47]

---

43. Booth, Ibid., 3.

44. Booth, Ibid., 8.

45. Possibly class and denominational divides made cross-fertilization from Irving and the Catholic Apostolic Church improbable in any case.

46. Harley, "Are We Really a Holiness Movement?" But there were Salvationists who *did* seek, like Major William James Pearson, well-known faith-healer, and Commissioner Wm. Booth Davey, who wrote *Divine Healing and The Salvation Army* in 1939, when Chief Secretary for Scotland and Ireland.

47. Allan Anderson, Professor of Mission and Pentecostal Studies, University of Birmingham, to author, email 20 March 2008.

By the time the reverberations from Topeka and Azusa Street had begun to be felt in Britain and Europe, the Army was more reserved, and tongues were viewed with suspicion. Lt. Colonel Max Ryan, noting that Pentecostal-type phenomena were common in the early Christian Mission and Salvation Army, concluded that the leadership of the movement had deliberately suppressed such tendencies as it institutionalized.[48] Catherine Booth's death from cancer, despite prayers for healing, has also been suggested as contributing to greater caution. Ryan points out that although faith healing continued to be acknowledged in the *Orders and Regulations*, a 1902 directive from Booth "deliberately distanced the Army from the Pentecostal belief that healing is in the atonement and that physical healing is a right for the Christian."[49]

One of the outstanding Pentecostal leaders was Smith Wigglesworth for whom this rejection of tongues was a factor in his leaving the Salvation Army in 1907.[50] Another Salvationist who left was Thomas Hodgson Mundell (1849–1935) who practiced as a solicitor in Carlisle and Bristol before moving to London, where he was a Salvation Army officer 1893–95. In 1908 he became a Pentecostal and was secretary of the Pentecostal Missionary Union 1914–25. His legacy to the Salvation Army includes Songs 574 and 1022 in the 2015 *Song Book*. The numbers and identities of most other such Salvationist converts to the new faith are unknown. It was not something about which the Army kept records or mentioned in the *War Cry*. About all that can be said is that most of them left the Army for other groups, whereas in the later charismatic renewal movement a greater number stayed and influenced the Army itself from within.

There was a split over glossolalia in the Norwegian church, including the Salvation Army, in 1907.[51] Max Ryan adds that the acknowledged leader of this revival in Norway was Albert Gustav Lunde who had been converted in a Salvation Army meeting in Chicago.[52] When Pentecostalism was introduced to Finland around this time, a Norwegian ex-Salvationist, G. O. Smidt, assumed the leadership of the movement.[53] The Booths sent Brengle to Scandinavia to head off threatened schism. His approach was to preach holiness rather than attack Pentecostal teaching. Brengle described the old General as "fearful of it all"[54] and Clarence Wiseman quotes an entry in the Founder's diary, written during 1907: "It appears that two or three corps are divided on this question of 'tongues' and it will be a good thing if abiding evil does not ensue."[55] Significantly, Bramwell Booth and Colonel Pvolsen, the Norwegian Territorial Commander, told Brengle that

> They think it is of Divine origin, but fear that the devil is trying to spread false fire. Our people welcome it as a release from the awful barrenness with which they have been afflicted so long.[56]

48. Ryan, "Signs and Wonders and The Salvation Army." 1–8.
49. Ryan, Ibid., 7.
50. Frodsham, *Smith Wigglesworth*, 14–15.
51. Hall, *Portrait of a Prophet*, 232–36.
52. Orr, *The Flaming Tongue*, 52, cited by Ryan, "Signs and Wonders and The Salvation Army," 4.
53. Orr, Ibid., 162, cited by Ryan, Ibid., 4.
54. Clark, *Dearest Lily*, 3.
55. Wiseman, *Living and Walking in the Spirit*, 6.
56. Clark, *Dearest Lily*, 3.

It would be instructive to know what was meant by "the awful barrenness": a dearth of converts, or perfunctory and joyless worship. The Nordic territories must have retained some Pentecostal flavor however. General Burrows told me that Wilfred Kitching, when territorial commander in Sweden (1948–51), lost respect and influence in the territory by silencing an officer who was giving a message in tongues in a meeting.[57]

Pentecostal influences were felt elsewhere in the Army world. For example, in Jamaica

> [I]n the 1920s W. Raglan Phillips [a pioneer of the Army in the West Indies] attempted to found a breakaway group called the Light Brigade. Later known as the City Mission, it shared the Salvation Army's format of a rank system and uniforms although its faith was more Pentecostal.[58]

Occasional articles dissuasive of Pentecostalism appeared in Army publications. Bramwell Booth, in an article on "The Abiding Gift of Tongues" reprinted in the New Zealand *War Cry* in 1922, was close to a dispensationalist or cessationist approach, saying that the gift of tongues described in Acts 2 was "not long continued." He also rejected the Pentecostal notion of "prayer language" pointing out that in Acts 2, "It was a gift enabling the speaker who received it to convey his meaning to those who could not speak his language."[59]

Samuel Logan Brengle's article on "Speaking with Tongues and the Everlasting Sign," printed in the New Zealand *War Cry* 1923, was more nuanced in its arguments, acknowledging that the gift described in 1st Corinthians 12 was a prayer language—not to be used in public unless interpreted. He denied however the Pentecostal view that tongues are a sign to believers that they have the Holy Spirit. He would not be drawn on the dispensationalist question, saying that "the gift may or may not have ceased . . . " He did however point out that on the basis of 1st Corinthians 13:8, all need for sign gifts would eventually have passed away whereas "Love is the everlasting sign."[60]

In an article, "Unknown Tongues and the Baptism of the Holy Spirit", published in the American *War Cry* in 1930, Brengle wrote:

1. I cannot and do not deny that there was such a gift as this of tongues in apostolic times.

2. I do not deny that if God so wills He can bestow the gift in these days . . .

3. I do deny, however, that there is any proof in Scripture or in the history of the Christian church that speaking in tongues is the invariable and essential proof that one has received the baptism of the Spirit, or that no one has received the baptism if he has not spoken in tongues. Indeed, Paul made plain the contrary . . . [61]

---

57. General Burrows, interview with author, 18 May 2012.

58. Tortello, "Christian Soldiers," http://jamaica-gleaner.com/pages/history/story0075.html, downloaded 24 November 2011.

59. *War Cry* (New Zealand), 30 September 1922, 9.

60. *War Cry* (New Zealand), 10 February 1923, 4. The article was collected in Brengle's *Resurrection Life and Power*.

61. *War Cry* (United States), 1930, reprinted in Waldron, edited, *Most Excellent Way*, 13–16.

Publication of such articles showed that "tongues" were a live issue in these years and perhaps the Salvation Army felt itself under some pressure from Pentecostal proselytizing. Significantly, whereas in the nineteenth century the words "Pentecost" and "Pentecostal" were in very frequent use in the Army's publications, in articles, sermons and announcements and reports of meetings, after the rise of the Pentecostal movement in the first decade of the 1900s, the words almost disappear from Salvationist vocabulary in print for years. In much the same way, the Pentecostal Church of the Nazarene dropped the word from its name in 1919.[62]

Barry Chant records that many early Australian Pentecostals had formerly been Salvationists.[63] Mark Hutchinson points out that whereas Salvationists have tended to regard their deserters as people unwilling to accept the Army's discipline and Pentecostals to believe that people left the Army because it had lost its fire, it would be more useful to consider the actual links which at the time existed between the Army and the Pentecostal movement around the time of its formation. He suggests that the denominational walls may have been more permeable than was later assumed to be the case.[64]

The early Australian Pentecostal journal *Good News* regularly reported Salvation Army officers preaching at "Good News Hall," or providing their testimonies as to conversion, healing or baptism in the Spirit . . . Some frequented Pentecostal meetings, but did not leave the Army. For others such as H. S. Kilpatrick, and Annie Chamberlain in South Australia, the encounter with the Spirit caused them to leave the Army and establish core groups around which Pentecostal churches later grew.[65] Some corps, such as Cessnock, suffered schism because of Pentecostal preaching.[66]

In the Australia Eastern Territory, Erle Ruse recalled that a large corps in Brisbane, Cooparoo—later Carina corps—had a pentecostal officer, Frank Parren, in late 1950s. He had earlier been stationed at Brisbane Temple and associated with Pentecostal Churches and joined in weekends of prayer and fasting. Some soldiers began speaking in tongues, and left the Army because it was not very receptive.[67]

Likewise, the *New Zealand Evangel* (an Assembly of God paper) mentioned Salvationists from time to time. It printed a testimony by Bertha Jorgensen of Eltham who been converted and become a Salvationist fourteen years earlier, and shortly afterwards had been "led into the light of holiness through the teaching of the Salvation Army." Still later she experienced the "Baptism of the Holy Spirit" in a Salvation Army meeting.[68]

Isolated examples show cross-pollination from the Pentecostal movement to the Salvation Army in New Zealand in the 1920s and 30s. Not all Salvationists with Pentecostal views felt obliged to leave the Army and join a Pentecostal congregation, although

---

62. Synan, *Holiness-Pentecostal Tradition*, 49.

63. Chant, *Spirit of Pentecost*.

64. Hutchinson, "Salvationists: a Case Study in Australian Pentecostal Origins." https://pentecostal-heritagecentre.wordpress.com/2011/08/04/salvationists/ downloaded 21 February 2012.

65. Hutchinson, Ibid.

66. Sanz, "Cessnock—Unpublished Notes on History," 1–12. Salvation Army Heritage Centre, Sydney, Australia.

67. Erle Ruse to author, interview 9 May 2012.

68. *New Zealand Evangel*, III: 5, 1927, 39–40.

some did. Owen Ojala was trained in 1934, spent all his officership in field work in New Zealand and acquired a reputation for a healing ministry. Writing about his corps experiences, Ojala did not claim to speak in tongues, although he described healings, exorcisms, and visions. He believed that "The Gifts of the Holy Spirit have been neglected in the Salvation Army world mainly because one of the gifts mentioned is the gift of tongues, but this is only one of the nine mentioned in 1 Corinthians 12 and its use is strictly controlled in Chapter 14."[69] He claimed to be "pentecostal but not with a capital P," but always felt somewhat of an outsider because of his convictions, adapting Jeremiah to explain that "Immediately you are prepared to live in the inspiration of your ideals you will become a speckled bird."[70]

Salvationists whose spiritual journey led them in a Pentecostal direction in the earlier and mid-twentieth century probably trod a lonely road. The Army did not change to accommodate them and so for many the choices were to conform or to leave. Evidence tends to be anecdotal and not readily discoverable in Salvation Army-sourced material.

In 1960 an American Episcopalian priest, Dennis Bennett, startled his congregation with an account of his new spiritual experience, and his book, *Nine O'Clock in the Morning* described what followed. The expression, "Charismatic" was coined by the Lutheran Harald Bredsen a couple of years later for people who remained with "mainline" denominations, rather than joining Pentecostal churches. Like Pentecostals, charismatics looked for such manifestations as miracles, healing, prophecy, and glossolalia as had been experienced in the apostolic age. By the mid–1960s, the charismatic movement had spread to most denominations including the Roman Catholic Church.

Later in the twentieth century, newer Pentecostal groups appeared, such as John Wimber's Vineyard Movement and the British New Church Movement, separate from both the older Pentecostals and the mainline charismatics. For such new charismatic churches, C. Peter Wagner of Fuller Seminary coined the expression "Third Wave."

Within that broad outline there are many subsets, as particular doctrines or emphases promoted by various charismatic leaders gained support. These have included for example the faith movement derived from E.W. Kenyon and later identified with Kenneth Copeland and Kenneth Hagin, the "shepherding" movement, the Church Growth movement and Spiritual Gift Seminars from Fuller Seminary, Life in the Spirit Seminars (of Catholic provenance), the Alpha course from Holy Trinity, Brompton, the Toronto Blessing, or the Pensacola revival. Various phenomena such as tongues, slaying in the spirit, deliverance ministry and prophecy have been ascendant at different times in what were described as new "moves" of the Spirit. The time and place at which Salvationists have been introduced to charismatic ministry has often therefore determined what kind of emphasis has influenced the Salvation Army in their sphere.

It took a few years for this renewal movement to filter through to the Army, but some examples may be offered.

A number of the "Evangelists" Session at the International Training College in London, 1967–1969, were reportedly charismatic, with half the session rumored to have been sent home. In fact, the intake of 136 cadets had been the highest for some years;

---

69. Ojala, *Sound of Abundance*, 48.
70. Ojala, Ibid., 5. (See King James Version of Jeremiah 12:9 for reference.)

112 were commissioned, but not all the others may have left for the same reason.[71] In Britain some individuals who became charismatic left the Army. Captain Bill Davidson of "Joystrings" fame by his own account did not set out to become "charismatic" but found that his style of ministry at Newark Corps became characterized in this way, attracting official disapproval; he subsequently resigned, and later founded a church in New York.[72] Some corps, such as Harrow in north-west London, successfully adopted a distinctly charismatic style of worship.

In September 1994 the UK territory mounted a School of Evangelism at Swanwick. Numerous reports and letters to *The Salvationist* followed, for and against the charismatic manifestations evident at this event. The territorial commander, Commissioner Dinsdale Pender, mixed his metaphors in writing that "Showers are Strong Meat," acknowledging signs as the work of God but in effect urging caution.[73] "Roots" Conferences were inaugurated by Russell Rook and others, and held annually for many years. The Army in the UK is a sufficiently broad church for a range of expressions to co-exist and there are vigorous "charismatic" corps such as Raynes Park in London.

By contrast, charismatic involvement has apparently tended to be "under the radar" in the American Salvation Army. Enquiry from senior leaders has generally brought a denial that it has been a factor in Salvationists' lives. However, there was reportedly a charismatic session of cadets in the Western territory in 1970–71 and in 1975 cadets used to go in the evening to a charismatic church, although the practice was frowned upon. A commissioner told me that she had belonged to a Pentecostal church before joining the Salvation Army at a charismatic corps and it was not until she went to training college that she discovered that this was not the case with all Salvationists. She thought that the movement tended to exist "underground" because of conservative disapproval. Interdenominational charismatic groups like Women's Aglow and Full Gospel Business Men's Fellowship International (FGBMI) were significant factors in introducing Salvationists to charismatic practices.

Another exaggerated rumor may account for the belief that "a whole session" was lost in Australia Southern in the mid-1960s. However it is true that a number of well-known Australian Pentecostal and charismatic pastors started out as Salvation Army officers in this period. Ben Callander (Southern Gateway Community Church, Victor Harbor, South Australia), John Alley (Peace Apostolic Ministries, Rockhampton, Queensland) and Tony Fitzgerald (now resident in USA) are examples.

Various Australian corps were impacted by the movement. For example, Kilkenny corps and Unley corps in South Australia suffered charismatic splits. The Canterbury corps in Melbourne became charismatic under a charismatic officer in the mid-1990s but subsequently closed in 2001. Corey Turner, Youth Group leader at Box Hill corps, Melbourne, took a group of young Salvationists with him when he left to start his own church, Activate Church, in 2004.

---

71. Thompson, "The Candidate Question," 294.

72. Davidson to author, email 28 October 2011. The "Joystrings" were a celebrated Salvationist "pop group" led by Joy Webb, originating at the International Training College in 1963.

73. Pender, Strong Meat," 5–6.

Erle and Beatrice Ruse, commissioned 1961, were asked after their resignation as officers (not for "charismatic" reasons) to oversight an Assembly of God church during a vacancy, eventually spending nearly twelve years with the AOG. Colonel Harry Goffin, then Chief Secretary, invited them to become officers again, and they were appointed to the Bega corps where the previous officers had left and taken all but two of the soldiers to set up their own Pentecostal church in the town. The corps was built up again.[74] Within today's Australian Salvation Army, it is reported that there are pockets of effective and accepted charismatic practice without it becoming particularly "mainstream" or general in the territory.

John Larsson in his autobiography cites New Zealand as a territory where the charismatic movement severely polarized and affected the on-going life of the Salvation Army, for both better and worse. "Corps were tearing themselves apart on these issues," he wrote.[75] The "Jesus Marches" of the mid–1970s were an early inter-church activity which was largely initiated by Pentecostal and charismatic Christians and in which Salvationists became involved because bands were invited to participate. These, along with such non-denominational organizations as the FGBMFI and Women's Aglow, proved portals to charismatic experience for many Salvationists. An early center of charismatic activity was "Kensington House," a hostel for young people run by Envoys John and Sharon Fawcett in Wellington.

Some New Zealand corps became notable for charismatic flavor. Some members of the South Dunedin corps, under Captain Ken Smeaton in the early 1970s, were early-adopters. The Petone corps (the majority of whose large Band had worn FGBMFI badges on their uniform lapels) split in 1985 when Captain and Mrs Brenton Williams took most of the leadership and half the corps with them in setting up an independent charismatic church. Newton Citadel, a large and traditional inner-city corps, became polarized during the leadership of Captain Graeme Webb, who left in 1989 to become an Elim pastor. Charismatic Salvationists tended to leave; the corps was closed several years later.

In some other corps, such as Invercargill and Linwood, charismatic Salvationists formed groups within a less charismatic whole in the 1980s, but Linwood reportedly lost more than fifty charismatic Salvationists to other churches over a four-year period. St Albans was a Christchurch corps with charismatic flavor. A more traditional officer, Captain Terry Heese, sent in to pull it back into line, found himself unexpectedly employing exorcism, words of knowledge, healing and tongues in his own ministry.[76] From the "Westgate" corps in Auckland a charismatically-inclined officer left to start his own congregation in the area. On the other hand some charismatic-*flavored* corps, such as Miramar and Napier, have thrived. An intentionally, officially-approved charismatic corps plant, Kelvin Grove, provided a rallying point for charismatic Salvationists in Palmerston North and prospered for a time, but closed in 2016 after twenty-three years.

Two significant things happened to influence the New Zealand territory as a whole. Firstly, in the late 1970s a group of charismatic Salvationists became officers, which, given their influence in corps leadership, led to a change in direction for some corps, and

74. Erle Ruse to author, interview 9 May 2012.
75. Larsson, *Saying Yes to Life*, 165–69.
76. Heese's paper on his experiences is held by the New Zealand Salvation Army Archives.

polarization in others. Secondly, an unofficial alliance of such officers and corps led to a united corps camp becoming regular, national "Aggressive Christianity Conventions" between 1985 and 1996.[77] These drew large attendances and were eventually endorsed and incorporated into the official Salvation Army territorial calendar. A key role was played by Commissioner Wesley Harris, Territorial Commander in New Zealand 1986 to 1990, in restraining a largely antagonistic hierarchy and channeling the enthusiasm of the charismatic leadership. It is possible that in being thus domesticated, the movement also lost some of its edge, especially where this had drawn on a sense of difference from the mainstream for vitality. Having divisional committees chaired by divisional commanders who were not themselves necessarily charismatically inclined no doubt made a difference. Harris also commissioned a study group to report on the subject—most other New Zealand mainline churches had been through that exercise between ten and twenty years previously. The group did not draw on other churches' experiences at all, though it is not clear whether that was indicative of the Army's insularity or because of the short reporting time-frame given. An interesting footnote to history is that Andy Westrupp, the corps officer who initiated the Aggressive Christianity Conventions more than thirty years previously, became New Zealand's Territorial Commander himself in 2017.

Gordon Moyles suggests that in Newfoundland the Army benefitted from having a lot of fiery Methodists join it in the early days because the Methodist Church was growing cool, and then a lot of Salvationists moved on to the Pentecostal churches when that became the newer and hotter thing. Nevertheless the Army in Canada had a strong revivalist tradition, especially retained in Newfoundland, where the Army was also strongest. Canada has apparently lost few Salvationists to Pentecostal churches since and it has not been a major issue. While the territory has declined and cooled, a recent minority movement has combined the Pentecostal tradition with an emphasis on evangelism and—unlike a common pattern of charismatic Salvationists elsewhere—on traditionally Salvationist distinctive features. Major Stephen Court's on-line *Journal of Aggressive Christianity* has carried numerous articles on charismatic renewal.[78]

Having been the region where Pentecostalism most strongly affected the Army in the early twentieth century, Scandinavia also embraced the charismatic movement. A Norwegian officer quoted to me in 2012 an invitation from a training principal to conduct a spiritual day: "We have ten cadets, all baptized in the Holy Spirit, high spirit in worship—we expect you to speak prophetically when you are with us. The day would without doubt be seen as 'charismatic:' Tongues, interpretation, prophetic messages, people slain in the Spirit . . . "[79]

Others describe a more divisive aspect of the movement:

> The first wave of the charismatic renewal did affect the Army in Denmark with renewal among the young people and officers to a more evangelistic zeal. Tongues were an issue that was dealt with in a relaxed manner . . . The next wave early 80s came to Denmark via Sweden and to the other countries as well. It was very much connected to the prosperity religion. It had an effect on all free

---

77. The name, "Aggressive Christianity," came from a book of that title by Catherine Booth.
78. http://www.armybarmy.com/jac.html.
79. Jostein Nielsen email to author, 3 May 2012, used with permission.

churches . . . It created division as it was so far from Army teaching and practice . . . As this wave was fading out a Swedish Salvationist Roger Larsson started campaigns all over Scandinavia and . . . created the worst division within the Army that I am aware of in all the Scandinavian countries. . . . When it faded out some corps looked like battlefields . . . The long term effect I am uncertain of. I am sure individuals who are still with us can testify to changes in their lives.[80]

In South America, where Pentecostalism now equals the Catholic church in influence, the charismatic movement had some impact on the Salvation Army. Lt. Colonel Ron Manning recalls from the 1980s that from "The Salvation Army in Brazil, because of its doctrinal teaching on both Communion and . . . Baptism, a considerable number of officers and many excellent soldiers throughout the Brazilian territory joined the wave of transfers to the new Charismatic congregations."[81]

Apart from anecdotal evidence and rare statistics, official publications are evidence of an official response. Examples include William Metcalf's 1973 book, *Another Pentecost?* the introduction to which said, "This book is necessary today, because the Christian Church in many parts of the world is experiencing a revival of the importance of the gifts of the Spirit . . . As well as a renewal of joy, power, worship and service entered into by some, there has been confusion for others. This book tries to give guidance to any who are feeling this kind of confusion."[82]

General Clarence Wiseman's 1975 pamphlet, *Living and Walking in the Spirit* was more in the nature of a pastoral letter, quoting Metcalf's opening sentences to provide his own context.[83] From the Southern territory of the United States came Lt-Colonel Wesley Bouterse's excellent little booklet, *Scriptural Light on Speaking in Tongues* in 1978[84] and the following year Commissioner John Waldron's *Most Excellent Way*, collected articles by William Booth and Brengle.[85] In 1983, Lt. Colonel John Larsson's *Spiritual Breakthrough: The Holy Spirit and Ourselves*, placed charismatic renewal within the context of the Wesleyan heritage to which the Army belongs.[86]

Early in the 1980s short statements were provided by International Headquarters for officers to paste in the back of their copies of the *Handbook of Doctrine*: "The Salvationist and the Sacraments" and "The Salvationist and Speaking in Tongues." Another statement, published by the Chief of the Staff in 1983, while reiterating that "speaking in tongues has been discouraged in Army meetings, and this continues to be our approach," went on to say,

> It is acknowledged that some Salvationists enjoy the use of this gift in their private devotions. The Army rejoices in the knowledge that the Lord is pleased to bestow gifts and graces on its members, and all Salvationists should be

---

80. Gudrun Lydholm email to author, 29 May 2012, used with permission.
81. Manning to author, 27 October 2011, used with permission.
82. Metcalf, *Another Pentecost?* 1.
83. Wiseman, *Living and Walking in the Spirit*.
84. Bouterse, *Scriptural Light on Speaking in Tongues*.
85. Waldron, *Most Excellent Way*.
86. Larsson, *Spiritual Breakthrough*.

encouraged to use their gifts effectively, with sensitivity, wisdom and, above all else, with Christian love.[87]

The fact that such statements were being issued at all suggests that charismatic matters were being discussed and were polarizing opinion. Between 1963 and 2013, in articles, letters and book reviews, *The Officer* carried over 175 references to the charismatic movement—perhaps not such a great number over a fifty year period. Captain Peter McGuigan's 1991 book, *Breaking Strongholds: The Dynamics of Spiritual Warfare* with its greater interest in exorcism belongs to the period of the "third wave."[88]

Major Richard Smith, Church Growth Director in the New Zealand territory, attended an international Salvation Army Church Growth Conference in London in 1989 and reported that

> The positive impact of spiritual renewal, which appears to be bringing new life to large parts of the Salvation Army of the Western world, captured our attention. To make this aspect particularly real to us, comrades from Harrow Corps had been invited to come and present an evening showing the worship style of their corps. . . . They also introduced us to many of their converts and to their converts' converts' converts.[89]

Papers presented included one on the "Place and Exercise of Spiritual Gifts in the Salvation Army," by Major Paul Kellner of USA Southern Territory, who discussed the Wagner-Modified Houts Spiritual Gifts Questionnaire used in several territories.[90]

The International Conference of Leaders in August 1991 recommended that a study group be authorized by the General to advise and make recommendations on the relationship of the Salvation Army to the charismatic movement. In response, General Burrows reconstituted the Doctrine Council (with international membership) in 1992.[91] This Council then "provided a fresh appraisal of The Salvation Army's relationship to the charismatic movement and some of the content of that appraisal is contained in appendix eight of *Salvation Story* on 'The use and abuse of spiritual gifts.'"[92]

However, the immediate fruit of the Council's activity was the drafting of a publication, *Empowered by the Spirit: The Salvation Army and the Charismatic Movement*, in response to the Conference's Recommendation 16. This also brought under one cover the Council's response, General Wiseman's 1975 pamphlet, "Living and Walking in the Spirit" and the 1983 International Headquarters "Guidelines" on "Speaking in Tongues."[93]

Recommendation 16 had consisted of four parts, which the Doctrine Council's response dealt with in order.

---

87. Statement by the Chief of the Staff, International Headquarters, 1983.
88. McGuigan, *Breaking Strongholds*.
89. Smith, "Report on Attendance at the International Strategy for Growth Conference," 2.
90. Smith, Ibid., 4.
91. Rivers, Letter to Territorial Commanders, 12 February 1992.
92. Robinson, "History of Salvation Army Doctrine," 41.
93. Salvation Army, International Doctrine Council, *Empowered by the Spirit*.

16(A) was "That the Salvation Army internationally be more willing to identify with those aspects of the charismatic movement which are helpful and spiritually enriching and which do not conflict with the purpose and mission of the Army."

16(B) urged "That a re-emphasis be made on the doctrine of the Holy Spirit, including both the gifts and fruit of the Spirit, and the need to allow the Spirit to move freely in every part of the Army." The Council proposed a much fuller discussion of the Holy Spirit in a proposed new Handbook of Doctrine, with attention to Fruit of the Spirit and Spiritual Gifts.

16(C) called for the Army to "reaffirm its place as a holiness movement." The Doctrine Council agreed, suggesting areas for teaching.

16 (D) broached more contentious matter: "That the present policy on speaking in tongues be reviewed, taking into account developments which have taken place since the last statement was issued." The Council noted that Salvation Army practice derived from both Scripture and the Army's own tradition. The relevant points here were that tongues were not forbidden in Scripture, but were rather provided with guidelines which were compatible with the Army's practice of encouraging participation under the direction of a meeting leader . . . The Council therefore proposed that tongues should be permitted in Salvation Army meetings, and that training should be given to meeting leaders at all levels at the direction of territorial leadership.[94]

The new proposal would have represented a significant departure from previous practice. However, the in-coming General referred the booklet to the Advisory Council to the General, which recommended that it not be published.[95]

The charismatic renewal coincided with a change in popular culture, most strongly reflected in music styles. This freed up worship, which in some cases had degenerated into a stultified straight jacket. New songs and choruses burgeoned, some both singable and sound. At the same time, many old treasures were lost and the range of theology inculcated by the new songs has been fairly limited. "Worship bands" supplemented and often supplanted brass bands. "Worship Wars," familiar in churches, took their toll—this was a clash of cultures rather than of theologies, but people tended to lose sight of the distinction. Culture is probably more significant than theology for a threatened sense of identity; again, doctrine tends to follow praxis!

Small home Bible study groups multiplied, partly because spiritual renewal creates a hunger for Scripture and for fellowship, and it is also fed by these. In preaching, the recurring themes changed but it is impossible to generalize about the quality of exegesis and application. Perhaps understanding of Scripture has subtly narrowed towards fundamentalism, partly inculcated by American models? Penal substitution as the sole view of the atonement, pre-millennialism and creationism are, for some, the new received orthodoxy. Church growth theory—that silver bullet that has often proved to be a blank when fired—began to seem like a reflection of capitalist economics, a kind of spiritual

---

94. International Doctrine Council, *Empowered by the Spirit*, 3–7. Unpublished proof copy in International Heritage Centre Archives.

95. Recollection of Raymond Caddy. David Guy, email to author, 3 November 2011. The author's request for the wording of the Advisory Council's Recommendation was declined by General Bond on grounds of confidentiality.

Ponzi scheme. Perhaps this tends to be the case when people come to rely on the application of external prescriptions rather than what used to be called "heart religion."

Charismatic renewal involved openness to innovation—"adaptation of measures," as Catherine Booth used to put it. Some people recovered a more active faith. The teaching on gifts, at its best, helped unleash that potential for involvement in God's work. The shadow side, paradoxically, was sometimes a loss of stability and commitment, of which Bramwell Booth had complained in some pentecostal Salvationists of a hundred years earlier.[96] Some people, of whatever persuasion, have a tendency to move around, seeking the latest thing. Alas, the claim to any particular spiritual experience has never guaranteed that the professor, or the denier, of such claims necessarily exhibits more or less human fallibility than anyone else in matters of conduct. In this the Salvation Army's experience is no different from that of any other church.

Teaching about spiritual gifts should reinforce the Army's views on the priesthood of all believers, and the mobilization of all soldiers. At the same time, Pentecostal notions of spiritual authority have actually joined hands with the creeping clericalisation reinforced by the advent of "ordained" officership, compounding the existing danger posed by the rank system. The American charismatic movement has flourished in the context of independency or congregationalism as a preferred church polity so has led some officers to take an over-mighty view of their own authority, not only over their corps but also vis-a-vis the authority of those set over them in the Army hierarchy.

Renewal has in many cases helped break up the old clubbiness that had become in-grown in many corps. Sometimes—perhaps inevitably as people clung together for support in the face of opposition—it also fostered a new kind of in-group, of the spiritually elite, the cosiness of those in the know, a new gnosticism.

The Salvation Army gained some new forms and structures and customs, vocabulary and jargon, some new shibboleths and a tendency, having cast off its own distinctive marks, to dress up in others' cast off fashions. In this identity crisis, there has sometimes been a deliberate shedding of the Army "brand" as irrelevant, old-fashioned and counter-cultural, and accommodation to a generic evangelical-Pentecostal-charismatic style. Again, this has been part of a cultural shift as much as a theological one.

For some, renewal has pandered to the self-absorbed individualism of the "me" generation. On the other hand, some have been endowed with a passion for the lost and become fervent evangelists. In common with a trend amongst Pentecostal denominations, a new commitment to social justice has been unleashed in many younger Salvationists, perhaps a genuine restoration of a founding charism of the Salvation Army.[97]

At one end of the continuum there have been incidents putting one in mind of Bishop Joseph Butler's protest to John Wesley: "Sir, the pretending to extraordinary revelations and gifts of the Holy Ghost is a horrid thing sir, a very horrid thing!" At the other,

---

96. Booth, *Echoes and Memories*, 72.

97. Rev. Don Battley, one of the leaders of the charismatic movement in the Anglican Church in New Zealand, said that he was encouraged to note that many people formerly involved in that movement were now engaged in social justice issues. Battley to Hill, 29 November 2008. It is not clear that the same cause and effect has been evident, or that the same people have necessarily been involved in both movements within the Salvation Army's ranks.

there have been miracles, including those whose Christian lives have demonstrated real and lasting renewal. Cyril Bradwell, doyen of local officers in New Zealand, said that although charismatic renewal wasn't his thing he was convinced of its being a genuine move of the Holy Spirit by observing the transformation of one grumpy, curmudgeonly, contrary bandsman into a joyous, gracious Salvationist as a result of his attending an Aggressive Christianity Convention.[98]

But has this been mostly about rearranging the deckchairs on the Titanic? Overall, apart from significantly driving the inevitable evolution of the Salvation Army in New Zealand, for example, as a sub-culture within the evangelical sub-culture within the Christian sub-culture within the wider society, has the renewal movement left the Salvation Army stronger and more effective than might have been the case?

Membership of the Salvation Army has declined relative to the total New Zealand population since hitting its peak of expansion in the 1890s, and in absolute terms for much of the twentieth century. It is claimed that actual attendances at Army meetings were at a record high for a few years recently. That may not be because of the outworking of the charismatic renewal, which has well past its peak influence: the increase appeared to owe more to Recovery Churches associated with the Bridge rehabilitation program, and to growth in Fiji and Tonga. Numerically, renewal has brought both losses and gains in different places at different times, and there is no research available to show which has been greater. The reasons for either growth or decline often have not been to do with renewal itself so much as with particular personalities, and the ability (and at times, inability) of the movement to manage change and ensure continuity.

Kevin Ward has suggested that by rejecting charismatic renewal the Salvation Army entered decline.[99] Looking back over the past forty years or more of the influence of charismatic renewal on the Salvation Army in New Zealand, the results have been both positive and negative, constructive and destructive. Perhaps these can be paralleled elsewhere in the Salvation Army world. To generalize, the movement probably gained traction because of a widespread hunger for spiritual reality and greater depth of teaching—a reaction to the fact that traditional program-based corps life was reaching the end of its sustainability and had become culturally outmoded. Adverse reaction on the other hand was to be expected from others whose sense of identity was tied up with that same traditional pattern, with which they were comfortable and in which they were fulfilled. This could not be other than a recipe for frustration and offense, as some sought to change as much as possible, and others sought to prevent any change at all. Sadly, the loss of a significant proportion of the spiritually-active and innovative members of a generation could only have contributed to the fragility of the remaining part of the organization.

We could leave the last word to General Larsson:

> As I look back, how I wish we as an Army had been more positive in our response to the Holy Spirit renewal. Had we had prophets who taught us to welcome this movement of the Spirit whilst rejecting the wrong teaching that accompanied it, the story could have been so different. But, instead of hoisting our sails and

---

98. Bradwell, in discussion at a meeting of Study Group on the Influence of the Charismatic Renewal on The Salvation Army in New Zealand, early 1989.

99. Ward, "Changing Patterns of Church Life," 9.

setting them to catch the full force of this gale of the Spirit, we as a movement lowered them. Instead of fanning the fire of the Spirit we sometimes quenched it. And all because the explanation of an experience that was so right was so wrong.

It is, of course, easy to have 20/20 vision with hindsight and none of this was clear at the time. It also has to be said that despite our hesitations as a Movement, the Holy Spirit renewal succeeded in bringing about climate change in the Army—in a positive sense. The temperature in our worship has risen markedly since those days, and we are still rejoicing in the new warmth.[100]

ESCHATOLOGY

Belief in the return of Jesus is part of the earliest Christian creeds. Millennialism is not. Millennialism is a particular take on the timing of Christ's return; the belief that while the present age is wicked and unhappy there will be a future period of 1,000 years in which Christ will reign on earth before taking the faithful to heaven with him. It derives from pre-Christian Jewish expectations of the Messianic reign, drawn from Daniel, 2nd Esdras and the Book of Enoch, to which early Christians added their own apocalyptic books, particularly Revelation. Primitive millennialism died by the fifth century but a pre-occupation with end-times is a perennial Christian phenomenon, being stirred up particularly in unsettled times or around certain dates—the year 1,000 was a popular one. Millennialism has never been explicitly rejected by the church but is not "mainstream." As millennial speculation is held to be a sectarian mark—although broader in scope and very popular in the nineteenth century—it is interesting that although William Booth expressed interest in the subject, and saw his Army as having a role to play in ushering in the Kingdom, the Army adopted a stance no more eccentric than that commonly held by many evangelical Christians of his day.[101]

The Booths followed Wesley and were of their time in adopting a post-millennial view of eschatology: that is, things were going to get better and better, and that getting as many people as possible saved would be the best way of ushering in the millennium, after which Christ would return. Wesley's view, prescribing no dogmatic insistence on any interruption of the space-time continuum, is described by Michael Lodahl:

> John Wesley's 1783 sermon "The General Spread of the Gospel" presents an intriguing tension. Wesley both despaired about the state of the world and at the same time expressed a profound hope that can only be adequately characterized as eschatological; he believed that God had begun a work of renewing creation, specifically through his Methodist movement, that represented the first stirrings of a universal redemption. This tension is heightened by Wesley's continuing and characteristic insistence upon a synergistic model of divine activity in creation; he never veered long from his conviction that the manner of God's working was to renew and to heighten human ability (e.g., understanding, affections, liberty) rather than to annul it. A characteristically Wesleyan interpretation of eschatology must, like Wesley, maintain hope in God's labor to redeem creation through

---

100. Quoted by Terry Camsey in http://therubicon.org/category/the rubi-blog/ downloaded 30 August 2010.

101. See Bennett, *Origins of Left-Behind Eschatology*; Oliver, *Prophets and Millennialists*.

Jesus Christ while also acknowledging that such labor neither bypasses nor cancels authentic human responsibility.[102]

Roger Green, in an article on Booth,[103] quotes Roland Robertson as saying that during William Booth's lifetime, millennial teachings were important in the Salvation Army, and "from time to time the question of the millennium was viewed with some degree of urgency."[104] Robertson suggests that

> During the incipient (i.e. Mission) phase the Salvation Army orientation vacillated between three tendencies: (i) an imminent and individualistic conception of heavenly salvation, which could occur at any time—soon, or in the foreseeable future;[105] (ii) a utopian conception of perfect terrestrial happiness, involving assurance of later heavenly salvation;[106] (iii) a more strictly millennialist belief that 'the end of all things is at hand.'"[107]

The 1881 *Doctrines and Disciplines of The Salvation Army* declined to get into specifics:

> **9. But what is the view of The Army on the subject of the Second Coming of Christ TO REIGN PERSONALLY ON THE EARTH?**
>
> It does not pretend to determine a subject upon which there has been, and is still, so much difference of opinion. But we incline to the opinion that He will not come till the last day of judgement, and rejoice to know that, should He come before then, it will be so much better than our expectation.[108]

Robertson says, however, that the utopian element became more prominent in the "mobilization" phase, and that Booth's essentially reformist social scheme aimed at bringing about the abolition of poverty and suffering in this world—a millennialist aspiration. Catherine Booth, farewelling Railton's expedition to the United States in 1880, said:

> The decree has gone forth that the kingdoms of this world shall become the kingdoms of our Lord and of His Christ, and that He shall reign, whose right it is, from the River to the ends of the earth. We shall win. It is only a question of time. I believe that this Movement is to inaugurate the great final conquest of our Lord Jesus Christ.[109]

Ten years later William Booth announced that "We Salvationists expect [the reign of Christ] to be preceded by further and mightier outpourings of the Holy Ghost than

---

102. Lodahl, Abstract of paper "Creative Eschatological."

103. From: *http://wesley.nnu.edu/wesleyan_theology/theojrnl/21-25/25-05.htm* accessed on 22 May 2007.

104. Robertson, "Salvation Army," in Wilson, edited, *Patterns of Sectarianism*, 71.

105. That is, the individual could be Promoted to Glory—see for example. *Christian Mission Magazine* February 1871, 23.

106. For example, *Christian Mission Magazine*, November 1875, 281.

107. For example. *Christian Mission Magazine*, October 1875, 261.

108. *Doctrines and Disciplines*, Section 23:9.

109. Booth, "Invasion of the U.S.," *War Cry*, 21 February 1880, 1, cited by Rhemick, *New People of God*, 202–03. Catherine Booth's reference is to Psalm 72.8.

any yet known, and reckon that the war will, thereby, be carried on with greater vigour". Booth speculated (how seriously?) that London could become the New Jerusalem, with Hyde Park roofed over to become "The World's Great Grand Central Temple."[110] His vision of the millennium looked remarkably like a Salvation Army international congress, writ large. Allen Satterlee quotes a post-millennial vision from an 1895 American *War Cry*, written as from 1995:

> When we consider in our times, and appreciate the fact that we are in the very beginning of the glorious Millennium, we have cause to rejoice . . . It has not been the reconstruction of society and government—the paternal—modelled after Bible times and practiced by General Booth in his early Army—I say it has not been these improvements, although they have helped. The great power, as we are all aware, is the fact that people have been saved and cleansed from all sin by the Blood of Jesus. This is the power that has brought about this reign of unselfishness and love among the people of the earth. This is the reason the entire world speaks the same language, and the word "foreigner" is obsolete . . . It was upon the debris of social ruin that The Salvation army built up a grander civilization—one that honored and served God . . . The Lord was with His Army as He promised (Joel 2:11). In the year 1900 A.D., The Salvation Army numbered 20,000 field officers; In 1925 A.D. 200,000; when every city, village, and hamlet had corps in the entire world. Whole cities had been converted. By this time, every other subject discussed by newspapers had sunk into insignificance. In 1950 the world was about conquered and the devil so discouraged that he gave up the fight.[111]

Philip Davisson in an article on early Salvation Army post-millennialism draws attention to the way this optimistic belief was reflected in and taught by songs, many of them anonymous, in the 1880 *Salvation Soldier's Song Book*, like:

> The Army's on the march to bring to bring the world to God,
> And all the world is wondering
> At our watchword "Fire and Blood,"
> Bring the gospel trumpet and sound the jubilee,
> Jehovah triumphs over sin and sets the captive free,
> And Satan trembles when he hears the shouts of victory,
> While we are marching to glory.[112]

The new 1922 *Handbook of Doctrine*, having outlined what the Bible actually said on the subject, concluded that

> Considerable differences of opinion exist among God's people . . . and among these differing views The Army does not undertake to decide which is true . . . THE ONE CERTAINTY IS THAT CHRIST WILL RETURN: Hence our duty is (a) to be ready ourselves . . . (b) to do our utmost to get others ready also.[113]

---

110. Booth, "The Millennium," 60, 67.
111. *War Cry* (USA) 12 January 1895, 4, cited in Satterlee, *Turning Points*, 79.
112. Davisson, "Sweeping Through the Land," 39–40.
113. *Handbook of Doctrine* (1922) 152.

A reviewer of the new *Handbook* obliquely criticized those too absorbed in the question of the Parousia: "This chapter also supplied simple and practical teaching about the Second Coming, concerning which so many Christians occupy almost the whole of their minds and thoughts."[114]

The aged Commissioner Elijah Cadman, interviewed in 1916, and asked whether he thought the world was growing better or worse, affirmed, "Better! More persons have heard of Christ and accepted him. Soon the nations will realize they are truly of 'one blood' and war is a device to exterminate them on earth."[115] A saying attributed to Cadman probably best summed up the practical Army view however: "I don't know what day the Lord's coming so I'll polish my boots every morning in case."

Nevertheless, with the age of progress collapsing in the disillusionment of the First World War, pre-millennial views began to gain ground with evangelical and Pentecostal believers. Originating in the seventeenth century and incorporated into his "dispensational" system by the founder of the Brethren, John Nelson Darby, in the 1830s, pre-millennialism held that everything would actually get worse and worse, until a time of great tribulation. The faithful would be rescued from this eventuality by being "raptured up," and afterwards Christ would return as Judge *before* inaugurating the Millennium, rather than *after* it. (Proof-texts can always be rearranged in more congenial patterns to suit the taste.)

The *Scofield Reference Bible*, first published in 1909 and advocating pre-millennialism and dispensationalism, became popular with cash-strapped Salvation Army officers in the 1920s and 1930s, partly because it included a commentary with the text. This would have fostered interest in eschatology and perhaps found its way into their sermons, despite Scofield's theology being Calvinist rather than Wesleyan.[116] Clarence Larkin's *Dispensational Truth*, published in 1920 and selling well for forty years or so was also influential. Even today his works are a source for many ideas held by fundamentalist Christians.[117]

The editor of *The Staff Review* in 1930 thought it necessary to remind his readers:

> [T]here are certain aspects of the Second Coming of our Lord—the idea that he will personally reign on earth in bodily form for a thousand years—which, although held by a minority of devout and thoughtful men and women in the church from time to time, have consistently been rejected by the overwhelming majority of equally devout and learned teachers; teaching which, moreover, has never been given a place in the creed of any of the great denominations of the Church at any time in its history. In view of this The Army's Founders wisely forbore to commit The Army to the one view or the other, and forbade that its platforms should be used for teaching controversial aspects of the subject. What *is* clear to all they taught and permitted Officers to teach: That He *is* coming

---

114. *Officer*, May 1923, 424.

115. Wallis, *Happy Warrior*, 178.

116. The *Scofield Reference Bible* also introduced Bishop Ussher's chronology, with its 4004 BC date for creation, more widely to fundamentalist Christians. A Salvation Army bookshop advertisement for the *Schofield* [sic] *Reference Bible* in the New Zealand *War Cry* (19 July 1919, 7) claimed that it had "Helps at all the hard places on the page where they occur."

117. Larkin, *Dispensational Truth, or God's Plan and Purpose in the Ages*.

again; that of that day and hour no man knows, not even the angels in Heaven; and that we should all be ready all the time for His coming, so that at no time shall He find us unprepared. But beyond that they sanctioned no teaching on the subject . . . Any Salvation Army Officer has begun to miss his way and has mistaken the legitimate use of Army platforms who can give time and thought to trying to show that in the books of Daniel and Revelation light is to be found in regard to the present and future conditions of the nations of the world . . .[118]

Commissioner John Cunningham's report on the New Zealand territory for 1934 alludes to this:

> Before passing away from the Field Officers it may be well to say here that there is an inclination for just a few to get making far too much of the Second Coming of Christ, and now and again we have learned of special announcements and special addresses on the subject. It has been popular among a certain class of Christian people in the Dominion, and whether the few have been trying to catch the popular idea, or whether they have been truly prompted by any sincere thoughts of their own, I am at a loss to say. I have not gone so far as to forbid the kind of thing referred to, but have strongly discouraged it, and have said that the business of the Army is to preach Salvation and get souls saved, leaving to The Lord that which He has not deemed wise to reveal to man. A watch on the few is really necessary, or we may have some of our people becoming cranks on the question.[119]

Despite such ideas being in circulation, the Army's official publications made little mention of eschatology at all, and where they did so, upheld the view set out in the 1881 *Handbook*. Bernard Mobbs's 1964 *Eternity Begins Now* provided an accessible but scholarly exposition of traditional Christian teaching on the subject, quoting the 1881 *Doctrines and Disciplines* summary with approval.[120]

While the Army thus never officially adopted pre-millennial views, these have become widely held. The later twentieth century "Left Behind" series of sixteen best-selling novels by Tim LaHaye and Jerry B. Jenkins popularized this position as a kind of new orthodoxy. Philip Davisson observes that "It is almost received wisdom in evangelical circles today to state that the return of Christ will precede an expected millennial period of kingdom reign."[121] Alan Satterlee contends: "While most Salvationists accept that the pre-millennial view of Christ's return has more Biblical merit, when Salvationists truly believed that their work and witness would hasten the day of Christ's reign on earth, there was more urgency to the work."[122] "Most Salvationists" might be read as "Most American Salvationists . . . " were it not for the fact that a British officer, Phil Layton, a member of the International Doctrine Council, wrote a book on *The Rapture*, promoting a dispensational interpretation of history, which was published by the United Kingdom

---

118. *Staff Officer*, April 1930, 106–7.
119. Cunningham, "Report on the New Zealand Territory," 44.
120. Mobbs, *Eternity Begins Now*, 55.
121. Davisson, "Sweeping through the Land," 29.
122. Satterlee, *Turning Points*, 80.

Territory in 2009.[123] That not all Salvationists would agree that the pre-millennial view "has more biblical merit" is evident from Adam Couchman's critical review of Layton's *The Rapture* in *The Officer* of September–October 2009.

In a recent book exploring the way in which religiously and socially conservative groups across a wide range of religions surprisingly maintain a strong commitment to social justice and egalitarianism in economic views, Nancy Davis and Robert Robinson include a chapter entitled, "The Salvation Army USA: Doing Good to Hasten the Second Coming." They evidently supposed that the Wesleyan post-millennial imperative was alive and well, despite this being at odds with American Salvationists' widely-held pre-millennial theology and right-wing political alignment.[124] On the other hand, James Read has urged that it would be better to admit that the post-millennial dream is long over and suggests that a more appropriate biblical and aspirational model for the times would be the First Testament concept of the "Jubilee Year"—perhaps less ambitious but more practical and resonating better with the concept of social justice in these post-modern times.[125]

As a personal aside, I recall my dismay when in a small group discussion on a Christian approach to ecology and responsibility for sustainable development, a young law student who had come from a "charismatic corps" where obviously pre-millennialism was the received gospel, remarked that as the rapture was going to happen soon, it wasn't really necessary to worry about such things as conservation. Doctrine has consequences.

CONTAINING DIVERSITY

How much diversity can The Salvation Army handle? In Anglican circles—struggling to maintain unity amid deep controversies on matters about which the Salvation Army has not even begun to talk, such as the ordination of bishops living in gay relationships—the word "adiaphora" is sometimes used. This biblical word meaning, literally, "not-different things," or things which "don't make a difference," is significant for Paul in Romans 14 and 1st Corinthians 8, 9 and 10, where he discusses matters about which Christians have been disagreeing. As Tom Wright points out, there is still the difficulty of deciding *which* matters *are* in fact *adiaphora*.[126] Paul's point at any rate is that love should continue to bind Christians together even when they disagree, and that the principle on which they should act is concern for others' welfare. Can a movement which began as a tiny sectarian body learn how to extend its tent-pegs to encompass the principle of adiaphora?

The eirenical counsel, "In essentials unity; in inessentials, liberty; in all things, charity," would not be a bad rule of thumb.[127] Richard Hays in his book, *The Moral Vision of the New Testament*, writes of four tasks: the Descriptive Task, the Synthetic Task, the

---

123. Layton, *The Rapture*.
124. Davis and Robertson, *Claiming Society for God*, 113–141.
125. Read, "Socio-Political Holiness," 25.
126. See Wright, "Presidential Address."
127. Attributed to the 17th century German divine, Rupertus Meldenius about 1627.

Hermeneutical Task and the Pragmatic Task.[128] The last of these is concerned with outcomes, or "the fruits," by which of course Jesus said we would be known as good or bad trees. Perhaps that quintessential pragmatist, William Booth, would be satisfied if liberty and diversity in his Army produced good fruit—which he would understand to mean people getting saved and sanctified, with as little impediment to these ends as possible.

128. Hays, *Moral Vision of the New Testament*, 3–7.

7

Salvation Army Theology 3: Worship

Lex orandi, lex credendi

—Attributed to Prosper of Aquitaine (Fifth century)

"Never was there any religious movement which carried on its operations more openly, or with a bolder disregard of conventional usage and precedent..."[1]

—Richard Durnford, Bishop of Chichester, on The Salvation Army, 1882

The law of prayer is the law of belief, or, as we pray, so we believe. It was long held that Salvationists, in good Wesleyan tradition, imbibed their doctrine from their song books. Even the reflection that many Salvationists today would more likely learn their catechism from the data projector continues to impress on us the significance of what takes place in public meetings. The theology inculcated may however have changed somewhat over the years. For the purposes of this exercise, by "worship" we mean corporate worship; what groups of Salvationists do when gathered for religious meetings.

We propose three very general periods or phases in Salvation Army worship style, roughly parallel to a sociological analysis of Salvation Army history—of enthusiasm, routinization and diversification—not sharply defined of course but overlapping and varying according to locality and cultural milieu.

1. 1865—C. 1900: THE PHASE OF ENTHUSIASM

Early private gatherings of the Christian Mission—"cottage meetings" in private homes or conference-type gatherings in larger venues—were not extensively written about;

---

1. Sandall, *History*, 2, 139.

the participants perhaps felt little need to describe them in detail, and outsiders were not interested. We may surmise that they consisted of the usual non-conformist hymn sandwich of prayer, singing, reading and exhortation. The "Ordinances of the Methodist New Connexion," to which William Booth would have been accustomed, provided for the following, the original "hymn sandwich:"

> In the Sabbath Services the following order is usually observed: a hymn—prayer—a chant, when approved—reading the Scriptures—a second hymn—the sermon—another hymn—the concluding prayer and benediction.[2]

The Christian Missioners' exercises would, in addition, have included testimony, monthly celebrations of the Lord's Supper, and love feasts—the latter sometimes on the same occasion. They not uncommonly climaxed in an altar-call; an appeal for greater consecration on the part of those present, evidenced by an outward response. Preaching for decision, or to unleash a usefully manipulated sense of guilt, touches something deeply entrenched in the evangelical psyche. The concluding exercise of the 1878 "War Congress," an all-night of prayer, was described as follows:

> The great object of the meeting was to address God, and it was in prayer and in receiving answers that the meeting was above all distinguished. Round the table in the great central square [concluded the report] Satan was fought and conquered, as it were visibly, by scores.
>
> Evangelists came there, burdened with the consciousness of past failings and unfaithfulnesses, and were so filled with the power of God that they literally danced for joy. Brethren and sisters, who had hesitated to yield themselves to go forth anywhere to preach Jesus, came and were set free from every doubt and fear, and numbers, whose peculiar besetments and difficulties God alone could read, came and washed and made them white in the blood of the Lamb.[3]

However, most of the Mission's early gatherings were public, and not for worship but for witness. The main focus of their activity was directed outwards and deliberately avoided the conventional and churchly. This activity began in the open air, in the streets, and was adapted to the class of people they were attempting to reach: the lower working class and what Karl Marx called the "lumpenproletariat" or those the sociologists term the "residuum" (a class of society that is unemployed and without privileges or opportunities) in the first instance. What they did had to grab and hold the attention of the passers-by, which meant there had to be great variety, spontaneity, inventiveness, brevity, immediacy, and relevance to the people. This meant brief extempore prayer, singing to popular tunes and numerous and brief testimonies, given as much as possible by people of the same type as they were wanting to attract; preferably those previously known as notorious public sinners, drunkards and ne'er-do-wells, but now miraculously changed. Such people were advertised by their nom-de-guerre; the "saved railway guard" or the "converted sweep" or even the "Hallelujah doctor," Dr Reid Morrison, also known as the "Christian Mission Giant." Any reading or speaking had to be short and punchy.

---

2. Baggaly, *Digest of the Minutes*, 230.
3. Sandall, *History* I, 237–38.

As John Coutts points out, this style of Salvation Army worship was clearly descended from the American "Camp Meeting," employed by Booth's models, Finney and Caughey and honed by the Booths during their years of free-lance revivalism in places like Hayle in Cornwall.[4] Preaching would always be for a decision, to bring the hearer to a point of repentance or commitment or faith, and to express that by an outward response by coming forward and kneeling in front of the congregation. To that extent, the mercy seat (or the drum placed on its side in the open air meeting) would have a sacramental role, providing the locus for the outward expression of an inward grace.

A cognate derivation might be Primitive Methodist practice, for which Hugh Bourne's instruction for a "preaching Service" was to

> Let all the exercises, in general, be short. The preaching, whenever it can, should be followed by a prayer meeting. From the beginning of the Service to the end of the sermon should be about three quarters of an hour, and the prayer meeting should continue about half an hour; the whole to conclude in about an hour and a quarter. After the conclusion, prayer must be made for mourners . . . Long preaching generally injures both the preacher's constitution and the cause of religion.[5]

Although this chapter is not the place to discuss the principles which inform worship in general, it is worth bearing in mind that one element in all kinds of religious worship is said to be an attempt to recreate the original theophany, the "God moment" lying at the heart of a particular faith. So, for example, the Eucharist is intentionally a re-enactment, an anamnesis of the "Last Supper" of Jesus with his disciples, or the Temple ritual with loud trumpets and cymbals and clouds of incense was thought to recreate the scene at the giving of the Torah on Mount Sinai, or the glossolalia of a Pentecostal meeting "singing in the Spirit" might recapitulate in some way the experience of Acts chapter two. Does the repeated invitation to the mercy seat or holiness table in the altar call or "appeal" at the conclusion of a Salvation Army meeting likewise give an opportunity for Salvationists to re-live their moments of conversion, consecration and experience of the work of the Holy Spirit? Is the test of such a meeting the degree to which this might be said to have happened, and the depth of the emotional catharsis experienced?

When, after 1879, brass bands made their appearance, they were firstly for attracting attention in the open air, and secondly for drowning out the noise made by the opposition, as well as for helping to carry the singing of hymns and songs. They had the immense advantage of being in the popular working-class musical idiom. Folk-doggerel words were set to popular tunes.

All these characteristics were carried inside, whether they were inside a theatre or music hall or a bricked up railway arch or the loft over a butcher's shop. The style was modelled on the contemporary music hall, the primary place of entertainment for the lower classes. A master of ceremonies introduced a succession of short acts; speech and music alternated. Salvationists also accepted opportunities to appear as acts in genuine

---

4. Coutts, *Salvationists*, 67.
5. Bourne, *History of the Primitive Methodists*, 59.

music hall shows—Bramwell Booth wrote of appearing on stage as "Item No. 12" at a theatre in Plymouth.[6]

We do not have many descriptions of how such meetings ran, but some from the Christian Mission period were recorded. Sandall says:

> *The Revival* printed at this time [1868] a long description of a Sunday afternoon testimony meeting ("free-and-easy") in the East London Theatre, contributed by Gawin Kirkham, Secretary of the Open-air Mission. The testimonies were reported in detail:
>
>> The meeting commenced at three and lasted one hour and a half. During this period forty-three persons gave their experience, parts of eight hymns were sung, and prayer was offered by four persons.
>>
>> Among those who testified was:
>>
>> One of Mr. Booth's helpers, a genuine Yorkshireman named Dinialine, with a strong voice and a hearty manner. Testimonies were given at this meeting by "all sorts and conditions" and many were stories in brief of remarkable conversions. The report concluded:
>>
>> Mr. Booth led the singing by commencing the hymns without even giving them out. But the moment he began, the bulk of the people joined heartily in them. Only one or two verses of each hymn were sung as a rule. Most of them are found in his own admirably compiled hymn book . . . A little boy, one of Mr. Booth's sons, gave a simple and good testimony.[7]

The Nonconformist described a Sunday evening at the Effingham Theatre in the same period:

> The labouring people and the roughs have it—much to their satisfaction—all to themselves. It is astonishing how quiet they are.
>
> There is no one except a stray official to keep order; yet there are nearly two thousand persons belonging to the lowest and least educated classes behaving in a manner which would reflect the highest credit upon the most respectable congregation that ever attended a regular place of worship.
>
> "There is a better world, they say" was sung with intensity and vigour . . . everybody seemed to be joining in the singing. The lines
>
>> "We may be cleansed from every stain,
>> We may be crowned with bliss again,
>> And in that land of pleasure reign!"
>
> were reached with a vigour almost pathetic in the emphasis bestowed upon them. As they reluctantly resumed their seats a happier expression seemed to light up the broad area of pale and careworn features, which were turned with urgent, longing gaze towards the preacher.
>
> Mr. Booth employed very simple language in his comments . . . frequently repeated the same sentence several times as if he was afraid his hearers would forget. It was curious to note the intense, almost painful degree of eagerness with which every sentence of the speaker was listened to. The crowd seemed fearful of losing even a word.

---

6. Booth, *These Fifty Years*, 193.
7. Sandall, *History* I, 114–15.

> It was a wonderful influence, that possessed by the preacher over his hearers. Very unconventional in style, no doubt . . . but it did enable him to reach the hearts of hundreds of those for whom prison and the convicts' settlement have no terrors, of whom even the police stand in fear . . .
>
> The preacher has to do with rough and ready minds upon which subtleties and refined discourse would be lost . . . He implored them, first, to leave their sins, second, to leave them at once, that night, and third, to come to Christ. Not a word was uttered by him that could be misconstrued; not a doctrine was propounded that was beyond the comprehension of those to whom it was addressed.
>
> There was no sign of impatience during the sermon. There was too much dramatic action, too much anecdotal matter to admit of its being considered dull, and when it terminated scarcely a person left his seat, indeed some appeared, to consider it too short, although the discourse had occupied fully an hour in its delivery.[8]

Clearly, William Booth was not himself restricted by the rule that any speaking should be brief, but then again most Victorian sermons were likely to be of this length or even longer.

Similar meetings were described in the *Christian Mission Magazine* in reports on local activities. One from the "Salvation Warehouse" in Leicester in 1878 mentioned "the preliminary portion of proceedings . . . After various hymns had been sung, a chapter read and prayer offered, Mr Corbridge invited any of the converts who liked to give their testimony for Jesus, limiting the number to 30 and the time to 15 minutes, or half a minute each . . . collection taken . . . then the sermon."[9] From the same place later that year, Wm. Fawcett reported an "Experience Meeting for twenty minutes . . . We had some quick, mighty, Holy Ghost speaking, we sang four times, 105 spoke in that short time, then I spoke for half an hour . . . in the prayer meeting which followed, twenty-five precious souls wept their way to the feet of the Bleeding Mercy and found Salvation."[10]

What grew up by trial and error as the most practical way to proceed became in due course the standard as prescribed by regulation. The first *Orders and Regulations* (1878), largely drafted by Railton, directed as follows:

> Be sure to keep up from the first that perfect ease and freedom as to the form of service which always belongs to us.
>
> Drive out of the place within the first five minutes the notion that there is to be anything like an ordinary religious service. A few free and hearty remarks to your helpers, or to persons just entering the building, whom you wish to come forward, such as a *loud* "God bless you, brother; I'm glad to see you," will answer this purpose, astound Christians, and make all the common people feel at home as much as when they enter the same place amidst the laughter and cheers of weekdays.[11]

---

8. Sandall, Ibid., I, 77–78.
9. *Christian Mission Magazine*, March 1878, 72–73.
10. *Christian Mission Magazine*, October 1878, 269.
11. *Orders and Regulations*, 1878, 54–55.

The first *Orders and Regulations* also provided a description of the meetings and activities of the corps as they would appear to a stranger arriving in the town, thereby providing the officer with a template. Extracts convey the flavor:

14. About a quarter to eight he would observe a procession marching along, which as it passed would be joined by several companies.
15. On nearing the hall he would see another procession of equal size approaching from the opposite direction, and both would meet in the presence of a huge mob at the doors.
16. Two strong men would be seen keeping the entrance with smiling faces; but with the most resolute silent determination to keep back the turbulent, and welcome only the well-intentioned.
17. Upon the front he would observe very large placards, "The Salvation Barracks" being prominent above all.
18. The building would be entered through large gates into a yard, and would turn out to be a plain white-washed room on the ground floor, capable of seating—on low unbacked benches—some thousand people.
19. Upon entering he would find a large number of men present, many of them of a very low description, and a general buzz of conversation prevalent. He would be received at the door by a man who would smilingly show him to a seat. Another would offer him a songbook for 1d.
20. At one side of the place he would notice a platform, some two feet high, capable of seating from 50 to 100 people.
21. He would notice the men as they came in from the open air disperse, some sitting at the end of forms, some in seats at the front, and some on the platform.
22. He would hear one standing at the front of the platform call out a number, and upon this, order would generally prevail. But some young men at one side would laugh and make remarks to one another.
    The leader turning upon them, would caution them to be quiet. One of them would reply in a saucy manner—another would laugh aloud.
    They would then be told they must leave the place, and the first verse of a hymn not given would be started. One of the men seated at the end of a form near would then request these two to go out, and upon their refusal would turn towards a man at the door, who would at once come up with three others and the two would be dragged out before the end of the chorus several times repeated. As they were pushed out two of the men would remain at the door to assist in keeping them out, if necessary.
23. The second verse would be given out with an extraordinary remark, and the singing would be of the loudest and wildest description, the chorus repeated many times, but always led off by the leader.
    In the course of singing the next verse many shouts would be heard, and some would stand on forms and wave their arms.

24. After this, all would suddenly kneel down and at once there would be a burst of prayer from one after another, till in a few minutes six or eight had prayed.

25. Another hymn would then be at once struck up by the leader, and whilst it was being sung a very large number of persons kept outside during prayer would stream into the room, making it nearly full . . .

26. The leader would then announce an extraordinary list of speakers, and strike up a verse while they came forward. Each speaker would occupy a few minutes only, eight or nine being heard in the hour.

27. A lad would sing a solo between two of the speeches, and one speaker would announce, amidst many shouts, that he had never spoken before, but meant to do so again.

28. An old woman rising near the front would ask for a word, would be welcomed by the leader, and would then speak in such a way as to move all present to tears.

29. Encouraged by this, a big man, wearing rather flash clothes, would rise and ask a word, but would be informed there was not time tonight by the leader, who would instantly strike up a verse.

30. About the middle of the hour notices of the services of Sunday and Monday would be given out, and everyone urged to buy and read on Sunday some publications, to be had at the door.

31. The leader would then speak after the rest, urging everyone unconverted at once to come forward and seek Christ, and would then call for silent prayer, after a minute or two of which, prayer aloud would begin.

32. The stranger would now rise to leave; but would at once be spoken to by someone who would walk towards the door with him, urging him not to go. He would notice facing him near the door a motto of the most terrible description, others being placed on each wall and along the front of the platform . . . [12]

That was Saturday night—the hypothetical visitor returned and got saved on Sunday.

This prescription is not unlike the description of the Christian Mission meeting of ten or so years earlier, except that huge crowds are envisaged and provided for, and an immense amount of organization assumed. In some places, that was what it was like. And when Booth insisted that people "do mission work on mission lines, or move off," this is what he meant.[13]

A reporter from *The Secular Review* attended an Army meeting at the People's Hall, Whitechapel in 1879. A selection of quotes from his article gives an impression of the people and practices of the early Army:

> The congregation is evidently drawn from the poorer classes, with here and there a young man or woman who may be slightly superior in point of what the world calls respectability . . .

---

12. *Orders and Regulations*, 1878, 112–114.
13. Bramwell-Booth, *Bramwell Booth*, 90.

> These Salvationists are in earnest—plain, vulgar, downright, most unfashionably earnest . . .
>
> The service begins with a hymn sung to the air of "Ye banks and braes o' bonnie Doon." As the hymn proceeds and the oft-repeated chorus gathers strength, arms and hands are raised to beat time with the singing . . .
>
> And now comes a prayer . . . and we are compelled to acknowledge that it is an able one. It moves the hearers' sympathy. Its eucharistic cries arouse . . . cries of "Amen!" "Glory!" "Hallelujah!" from all around.

As for the preacher, Peter Keen, the reporter noted, "He is natural, and undoubtedly is firmly convinced of the truth of the gospel which he declares. With a rude, untutored, but withal moving eloquence, he preaches a sermon upon the inability of man to do aught for himself, and the consequent necessity of 'throwing it all upon Jesus.'"[14]

The 1881 *Doctrines and Discipline of The Salvation Army* urged lively and attractive meetings amongst the duties of an officer.

> He must not only use all the measures employed by his predecessor that are wise and suitable, but he must be constantly *inventing new ones* . . . [Meetings] must *be interesting*—and *attractive* and interesting to the class he wants to get hold of . . . They must be LIVELY. Nothing can be put in the place of life. "A living dog is better than a dead lion." Anything will be pardoned by the mob rather than dullness. The respectabilities and proprieties will some of them pay to be put to sleep, but the unwashed and unshaven will quickly make off and come no more . . .
>
> I. This means *short, sharp speaking*, full of *facts* and *illustrations*, *plenty of attitude*; your mouth *well open*, and the words well *spoken up*.
> II. This means plenty of lively, sharp *singing*, to *plaintive* or *merry* tunes; none better than *song* tunes, because they are always made expressly to meet the taste of the crowd, and only those that hit on that taste survive. Catch those and use them. . . . [15]

Having gone on to urge "*novelty*!—something perpetually n*ew* and *fresh*" and the use of "*all* your people—every soul of them, down to the charwoman saved only last night" and anyone else who could be borrowed from elsewhere, the instructions included, "Never practice nor allow tomfoolery."[16]

Various types of Meetings were prescribed. Apart from prayer meetings (Knee-drill) there were open-air meetings at various times of the day, the main purpose of which, apart from bearing witness and challenging people to be converted on the spot, was to persuade the public to follow the Salvationists back to their Barracks for the indoor meeting. There were generally public indoor gatherings in the afternoon and evening on Sundays, and on every night of the week.

At first it was not usual to have indoor meetings on Sunday morning. This was the time the working class idled about in the streets, drinking and gossiping and wasting their free time. Therefore, non-stop open-air meetings were to be conducted at this time. Later, when morning indoor meetings came to be held, these were at first attended

---

14. http://www.ourchurch.com/view/?pageID=12278 downloaded 21 January, 2014.
15. *Doctrines and Disciplines*, 1881, Section 32.
16. Ibid.

by small numbers, usually only Salvationists, and used for teaching, especially about holiness. However, it was not expected that all Salvationists would attend, because the soldiers, in their brigades or companies, would take turns away from their own inside meeting to work in the open air.

The "holiness meeting" was at first usually a week night event, for soldiers only, with admission strictly controlled by token or pass. The style would be more restrained, there being no need to entertain the masses; those attending were there because they were serious about their religion. Singing, praying and testifying to "the Blessing" would precede the sermon. By 1882, beginning at Coventry and spreading rapidly, the Sunday morning meeting, attended mainly by Salvationists, became known officially as the holiness meeting.[17] There was always a challenge to seek the blessing of holiness, and an invitation to come forward to pray for this.

The outline of the meeting for the "saints" was therefore the same as that for "sinners": all was focused towards the climacteric appeal. This might be contrasted, for example, with the Anglican liturgy where a general confession and absolution (where these are still practiced) fairly early in the order of events relieves the worshippers of any burden of guilt and sets them free to enjoy the rest of the service. In the Army's meeting plan, any guilt is relentlessly pursued—sung, prayed, and preached towards the appeal, heightening the participant's anxiety in order to ensure their capitulation at the end. Those not making the cut may take their guilt home with them to ensure their return.

On the Sunday afternoon there was a "free-and-easy" meeting, like a music hall concert. Both soldiers and the public attended, and the opportunity to preach and testify was not neglected. There was always a challenge to conversion. There was a church fashion for PSA—"Pleasant Sunday Afternoons"—at this time, but they tended to be lecture-based. The Army's were different, and more focused on testimony and conversion. At night was the "Salvation Meeting," when the largest numbers of the public would attend, and all the stops would be pulled out in the battle for converts.

The arrangement of the Barracks followed the lay-out of the music hall and such places, with a stage for the performers. As the number of soldiers grew, and the Army built or bought its own halls, the platform was often tiered; the soldiers sat on the tiers and the public gathered in the body of the Hall. Only later, as the crowds thinned towards the end of the century, did the soldiers start to fill up the hall itself, and the musicians come to occupy the stage. Booth was insistent that the musicians were there for support purposes, not to be seen or heard for their own sake. The Trade Headquarters Band came to an ignominious end in 1896 when the Founder heard them conclude the epilogue at the Army's exhibition at the Agricultural Hall, Islington, with a rousing rendition of "Rule Britannia." They were disbanded.[18]

Booth was also very reluctant to have singing groups as such—his experience as a Methodist minister had left him believing "choirs to be possessed of three devils: the quarrelling devil, the dressing devil and the courting devil."[19] It was some years before "Songster Brigades" were tolerated. Booth preferred the "Singing, Speaking and Praying"

17. Rightmire, "And the Holy Spirit fell on them." In Metrustery, *Saved, Sanctified and Serving*, 77.
18. Boon, *Play the Music, Play!* 41.
19. Sandall, *History* I, 209.

Brigades initiated by his son Herbert, the members being equally willing and able for any of those assignments. A key role of songster brigades, when they appeared after 1898, was to teach the congregation new songs.[20]

While Booth's prescription in the *Orders and Regulations* suggests and assumes a very tightly controlled and directed performance, all under the orders of one person, in practice the early Army's spontaneity was at odds with this picture, owing more to the revivalist camp-meeting. Lillian Taiz quotes the memoirs of Salvationist James Price:

> One Saturday night during the "Hallelujah wind-up" he nearly passed out. "I seemed to be lifted out of myself," he said, "and I think that for a time my spirit left my body." While he did not faint, "mentally, for a time I was not at home." When he regained awareness, he found himself "on the platform among many others singing and praising God." "[S]uddenly finding myself in the midst of a brotherhood with whom I was in complete accord; without the shadow of a doubt regarding its divine mission, and then the great meetings climaxing in scores being converted, all this affected me like wine going to my head."[21]

Taiz also quotes the *National Baptist*'s description of a Salvation Army meeting:

> Many of the soldiers rock[ed] themselves backwards and forwards waving and clapping their hands, sometimes bowing far forward and again lifting their . . . faces, heavenward. The singing was thickly interlarded with ejaculations, shouts [and] sobs.[22]

Taiz's comment is that "Salvationists had created an urban working-class version of the frontier camp-meeting style of religious expression."

All religious revivals produce their own hymnology. The Christian Mission used mainly the great Wesleyan hymns Booth and some of his supporters brought from Methodism—and they had often been set to the popular song tunes of the previous century. Many of what today we hear as "great hymns of the church" were set to tunes sung in pubs in the eighteenth century. Many of these have been carried forward into the Army's modern repertoire. Before long, however, the Army was producing its own doggerel— and much of it was that. It tended to be set to the music hall tunes and popular songs of the day, such as "Champagne Charlie." In the words of John Cleary, "the early Salvation Army captured, cannibalized and redeemed the popular forms of the day, and filled them with messages that spoke of the love of God for ordinary people and the power of God to change the world."[23] Sometimes "the world" returned the compliment. In his First World War memoirs Robert Graves recalled how Welsh soldiers on the march in France would sing words made up for the Salvation Army tune, "Whiter than the snow:"

> Coolness under fire,
> Coolness under fire,
> Mentioned in dispatches

---

20. Holz, "'Let us come before him." In Metrustery, *Saved, Sanctified and Serving*, 162.
21. Price, "Random Reminiscences," 1889–99, 78, quoted by Taiz, *Hallelujah Lads & Lasses*, 76.
22. *War Cry* (London), 10 July 1880, 4, quoted by Taiz, Ibid., 77.
23. Cleary, "Salvationist Worship."

> For pinching the Company rations,
> Coolness under fire . . .²⁴

Which suggests that by the early twentieth century the Salvation Army had been thoroughly assimilated into working-class culture.

"Penny Song Books" were sold at the meetings. The *War Cry* ran song-writing competitions and printed the results. The *War Cry* was also sold to the congregation so that they could sing the new songs produced that week. Because some people could not read, the leader outlined the words of each verse before they were sung. Many of the songs had choruses, so that the congregations could pick up the repetitive refrains and join in—as had long been the custom in the pubs with popular songs as well. The officers were instructed:

> Remember that the people do not know any tunes except popular song tunes and some tunes commonly sung in Sunday Schools, and that unless they sing, the singing will be poor and will not interest them much . . . Choose, therefore, hymns and tunes which are known well, and sing them in such a way as to secure the largest number of singers and the best singing you can . . . ²⁵

John Rhemick in his *New People of God* explores the significance of the Army's "dramatic expression" as a means of reaching working class people. What a more cultured critic chose to call the Army's "coarse, slangy, semi-ludicrous language" was what reached its target, and popular music provided the right vehicle for such language.²⁶ Paul Alexander, writing on Pentecostal worship, quotes Tex Sample on how "Pentecostal worship is an expression of working-class taste because it is in direct contrast to how 'elitist taste legitimizes social inequality.'"²⁷ The early Army's music was the nineteenth century equivalent of such religious expression.

The style and subject matter of the Army's songs majored on personal religion; the experience of the individual and appeals to the individual. "I" and "we" have experienced this; "You" need to. In the words of Cleary again, the "lyrics were critically linked to evangelism. Songs for worship were also songs that spoke to the lost and broken. These were not songs for the elect body of believers but for the whole lost world for whom Jesus came."²⁸ Many of the new songs did not last the distance; we no longer hear

> We shall see the Judge descending,
> On that great day,
> While the heavenly music
> Sounds sweetly through the air.
> 2 We shall hear the thunder rolling.
> 3 We shall see the Saviour coming.
> 4 We shall see our parents coming.

24. Graves, *Goodbye to All That*, 93.
25. *Orders and Regulations*, 1878) 53–54.
26. Rhemick, New People of God, 167.
27. Sample, *White Soul*, 76, quoted in Alexander, *Signs and Wonders*, 32.
28. Cleary, "Salvationist Worship," 2.

> 5 We shall see our children coming.
> 6 Then repentance will be useless.
> 7 For there will be no pardon.
> 8 Oh, you'll wish you'd been converted.
> 9 Oh, you'll wish you'd been a soldier.[29]

Many songs seemed to celebrate the Salvation Army itself, but certainly inculcated loyalty:

> Come, join our Army, to battle we go,
> Jesus will help us to conquer the foe;
> Fighting for right and opposing the wrong,
> The Salvation Army is marching along.
>
> *Marching along, marching along,*
> *The Salvation Army is marching along;*
> *Soldiers of Jesus, be valiant and strong;*
> *The Salvation Army is marching along.*[30]
>
> WILLIAM JAMES PEARSON (1832–1892)

On the other hand, many Army classics by such notables as Herbert Booth, George Scott Railton, Charles Coller, William Pearson, Richard Slater, Thomas Mundell, and Sidney Cox enriched the Army's continuing repertoire. In his memoirs, Bramwell Booth paid particular tribute to his brother.

> Among the men who stand out prominently as makers of Army music I must put in first position my brother, Herbert. He, a natural musician . . . first originated that kind of music which I may call peculiarly ours. It is right that he should have special recognition for the great work he did. He was the creator of melodies which are now known throughout the world, both within and outside the Army . . . His melodies stand unrivalled in their suitability to Army meetings, and they have earned undying popularity . . . [31]

Such a recommendation is borne out by the retention of no fewer than twenty-two of Herbert Booth's songs in the 1986 Song Book, and eighteen in the 2015 book, including the following:

> Blessèd Lord, in thee is refuge,
> Safety for my trembling soul,
> Power to lift my head when drooping
> 'Midst the angry billows' roll.
> I will trust thee,
> All my life thou shalt control.

29. #20, *Salvation Soldiers' Song Book*, New Zealand, circa 1895–98.
30. *Song Book of The Salvation Army* (2015) number 949.
31. Booth, *These Fifty Years*, 229–30.

> In the past too unbelieving
> 'Midst the tempest I have been,
> And my heart has slowly trusted
> What my eyes have never seen.
> Blessèd Jesus,
> Teach me on thy arm to lean.
>
> O for trust that brings the triumph
> When defeat seems strangely near!
> O for faith that changes fighting
> Into victory's ringing cheer;
> Faith triumphant,
> Knowing not defeat or fear![32]

At the same time the older Evangelical and Wesleyan tradition continued alongside the newer Salvationist style, the book containing old favorites by people like Fanny Crosby, Richard Jukes, William Collyer, Henry Alford, and especially by Charles Wesley. Such writers perhaps provided material more suitable for the holiness meetings, perhaps more worshipful, although the subject matter was less often the attributes of God than it was the personal spiritual life and struggles of the worshippers. The emphasis was on joy, triumph and challenge.

William Booth admitted in 1904:

> I think sometimes that The Salvation Army comes short in the matter of worship. I do not think that there is amongst us so much praising God for the wonders He has wrought, so much blessing Him for His every kindness, or so much adoration of His wisdom, power and love as there might, nay, as there ought to be. You will not find too much worship in our public meetings, in our more private gatherings, or in our secret heart experiences. We do not know too much of
>
>> "The sacred awe that dares not move,
>> And all the inward Heaven of love."
>
> ... worship means more than either realization, appreciation, gratitude or praise; it means adoration. The highest, noblest emotion of which the soul is capable. Love worships.[33]

Perhaps the old man was becoming nostalgic for the Wesleyan worship of his youth. If so, he was not alone in desiring a more reflective mode of worship. A little later, the New Zealand *War Cry* editorialized, "Can we plead . . . for greater reverence while in the House of God? If our halls are buildings containing sacred memories of rich blessing, they should be reverently treated."[34] Ironically, some of those "sacred memories" may have been of the more free and easy era of the Army's first fine flush of enthusiasm, when

---

32. *Song Book of the Salvation Army*, 2015, number 244.
33. Booth, "Spirit of Burning Love," 139–40.
34. *War Cry* (New Zealand), 22 May 1915, 4.

reverence was officially discouraged, and the C.O. was advised, in selecting sergeants, to avoid "people with 'house-of-God' notions, who want to make everything like what is in churches or chapels."[35]

2. C. 1900—C. 1980: THE PHASE OF ROUTINIZATION AND INSTITUTIONALIZATION

Sometimes the tendency of revival movements is to see themselves as recreating the original purity of the church. The Salvation Army did not set out to do this—Booth was simply pragmatic—but his Army came to believe this is what had happened. A 1921 article claimed:

> The Salvation Army is, in a word, the modern manifestation of Apostolic religion. For the first 200 years after the death of Jesus, the Christian Assemblies were very like Salvation Army meetings. The reading of the Prophets or the Psalms, and copies of the manuscripts of the Gospels or Pauline letters, extempore prayers, testimonies—in which the women shared—and, speaking generally, unconventional as against a set form of service.[36]

Again ironically, by then the unconventional was setting in the mold of its own conventions. As John Coutts has written, "The history of Christian worship has been a long duel between form and freedom."[37] By the early twentieth century the Salvation Army's first great age of expansion and excitement was over; it was settling down. The period of routinization began. If the history of the Church alternates between the "priestly" tradition, which seeks to secure continuity of an established pattern, and the "prophetic" tradition, which seeks to regain the original impetus and spirit which had created that pattern, at this stage the priestly tradition was asserting its dominance.

Lillian Taiz has examined the change in the Salvation Army culture in the United States, but her findings are equally applicable to the Army in Britain and the old "western" Commonwealth countries. Firstly (seeing that, in the words of the old song, "In the open air, we our Army prepare"[38]) Taiz remarks on the way "at the beginning of the century the Army started to ritualize its expressive and spontaneous street meetings by institutionalizing them and creating carefully scripted performances." This change is illustrated from the Men's Training Garrison curriculum described in the American *War Cry* of 14 March 1896. By this time Joe the Turk's confrontational antics were becoming an embarrassment to the high command, which tried to discourage officers from courting imprisonment and "martyrdom," and urged compromise and accommodation with local authorities. And Taiz notes that by mid-century "Salvationists had largely abandoned their 'open-air heritage' and no longer performed their spirituality in the streets."[39]

---

35. *Orders and Regulations*, 1886, 288; Part VII, Chapter III, 4(b).
36. "Torchbearer," "The Salvation Army and Sacerdotalism," *Salvation Army Year Book*, 1921, 22.
37. Coutts, *Salvationists*, 64.
38. From Fanny Crosby's 1867 hymn, readily adapted by the Army in its 1878 Song Book.
39. Taiz, *Hallelujah Lads & Lasses*, 142.

Taiz's main point however concerns the Army's adaptation to changing culture—both that within which it operated and that found within its own ranks. The spread of middle-class gentility affected what the donating public would tolerate from the Army, and what the gentrifying second-generation Salvationists would tolerate amongst themselves. While earlier Salvationists justified their extreme "uncouth, noisy and disagreeable" informality on the grounds that such methods were necessary to reach the masses, by the turn of the century the leadership "took steps to improve the organization's public image by discouraging noisy, confrontational public performances while at the same time providing the public with alternative images of Salvation Army religious culture."[40] The same was true of the Army's homeland; it was no accident that perceptions of its new-found decorum and professionalism in Saki's short story were associated with Laura Kettleway's references to the Army's good works of social reformation—respectability was important for fund-raising. Taiz draws attention to the influence of the increasingly important social operations on the change in the Army's internal religious culture. "The social work champions soon realized . . . that in a world that enshrined gentility as a standard for public and private behavior, the organization could no longer afford to foster its own marginalization if it meant to achieve its goals."

The Army's regular congregation was by now composed largely of Salvationists and regular attendees. The style of meeting began to change, transmuting from a variety show back into the typical nonconformist hymn-sandwich, but with more fillings, or "items" incorporated because the musical groups had to have their turn. Regulations give a clue: there was one restricting the band to playing only for the first song in the Holiness Meeting, because they were beginning to assert their concert role and play to be noticed. That regulation was not long in being ignored. By the early 1900s, the Founder was ready to concede the point. According to Gordon Moyles, in 1901 Booth sanctioned "'music for its own sake,' allowing Army composers to create hymn-tune arrangements that could be performed as musical selections in Army worship services."[41]

Extempore prayer suffered the stereotyping of word and phrase that accompanies a lack of preparation. Taiz quotes a Californian thesis to the effect that "services took on a "traditional ritual and form . . . consist[ing] of a call to worship, some offertory, band and songster special numbers, and a message followed by an alter [sic] call."[42]

Taiz perceptively notes that

> in addition to the transformation of its religious culture, changes to the Salvation Army by the twentieth century also reconfigured its religious mission [which] in the nineteenth century . . . was "conversion of the lost." In the twentieth century . . . conversion of the heathen masses became the purview of the social work and was no longer rigorously evangelical . . . Salvation Army spiritual work increasingly focused on "those already converted and . . . those who were being nurtured in the faith." As in the late-nineteenth-century holiness camp meetings, Salvationists in the twentieth century began "preaching to the choir."[43]

---

40. Taiz, Ibid., 145.
41. Moyles, *Come Join our Army*, 74.
42. Gilliam, "Salvation Army Theatricalities," 150, quoted by Taiz, *Hallelujah Lads & Lasses*, 157.
43. Taiz, Ibid., 160.

Sermons began to get longer, and testimonies to diminish, and the officer to do more and more of the speaking. From time to time efforts were made to turn the clock back. Even in the 1890s there was concern that some officers were monopolizing the platform:

> It is rumoured that at some corps the soldiers and sergeants never have a chance, except in the open-air, the captain reserving all the indoor meetings to himself. Surely this is an exaggeration. The General is going to deal with this danger in a future number. Let us be awake to it, and do our utmost to avoid the snare.[44]

Thirty-five years on, in 1928, Bramwell Booth wrote to an officer in charge of a corps he had visited, advising him to, "Rope in your own people in so far as it is at all possible to take part in platform [i.e. speaking and preaching] work. If the soldiers and locals felt the responsibility of speaking to the people the words of life and truth they would fit themselves for this work. This would relieve you of some of your platform responsibilities, and thus enable you to tackle other work."[45] And General Edward Higgins wrote, "I am afraid the idea has sometimes got abroad that Officers are intended to be like parsons and preach sermons, to monopolize all the time of a meeting while the people they are supposed to lead in fighting do nothing."[46] Despite regulation and precept, there seemed an inevitable drift towards a semi-formal churchliness, with parsonical performances from the officer, who came to see "the platform" as his special charge and prerogative to be guarded jealously. Alas, as John Coutts says, "The clichés of a third rate mind can be as boring as the Prayer Book you cannot find the place in."[47]

Sadly, the custom of "lining out" the words of songs continued a century after all the people could read and had the words before their eyes—custom once fixed, dies hard. Too many meeting leaders then felt they had to justify the practice by preaching a mini-sermon Midrash on the words they superfluously read aloud to their congregations. In time the afternoon "free and easy" evolved into the "praise meeting" in which, where it survived in larger corps, the band played to the songsters and the songsters sang to the band, and both attempted to entertain the mainly Salvationists and their bored, long-suffering children who attended, with ever more esoteric offerings, including transcriptions from the great masters.

The former Commissioner Alex Nicol, lamenting the Army's loss of its first love in about 1910, gave a depressing picture of an Army meeting in a London corps.

> I visited a Corps in North London a few weeks ago which stands in the first grade . . . It has an excellent brass band, a band of songsters, a well-organized Junior Corps, and the hall in which the meetings are held is situated in the heart of an industrial population on a site that is among the best in the neighborhood. It has an excellent history and is respected by the people as a whole. Few people can be found in the neighborhood to say an unkind word about it, although if the question was put to them if they visit the Corps, the answer would be that they "see

---

44. *Officer*, April 1893, 107.
45. Bramwell-Booth, *Bramwell Booth*, 492.
46. Higgins, *Stewards of God*, 16.
47. Coutts, *Salvationists*, 77.

the Corps pass by with its band, and some years ago, when Captain So-and-so was in charge, I occasionally looked in."

What did I see and hear? A small audience, including officials, of about a hundred people and this Corps has a membership of some four or five hundred, a humdrum service without life in the singing, or originality of method or thought in the leadership, such as would not do credit to an average mission-hall meeting of twenty or thirty years ago. But for the music of the band and the singing of a brigade of twenty songsters the Corps would be defunct. The outside world was conspicuous by its absence. The audience was made up of regular attendants.

Having provided a blow-by-blow account of the depressing proceedings, Nicol concluded:

> And I declare that this spirit of the meeting is the spirit of the Corps in the Salvation Army throughout England and Scotland. It has ceased to be true to itself, and as a consequence, no matter how the Army organizes and disciplines its forces, the future of the movement is black indeed, and will become blacker unless—But that is not my business.[48]

It could be understood that even though the words and music of the earlier era survived in the *Song Book* and usage of this later time, once the spirit had gone out of the concern in the way Nicol described, spontaneity would relapse into formalism in their performance. How far, with 'redemption and lift,' might a gradual distancing from genuine working-class roots have also contributed to this change?

Fortunately the worship of the Army in general evidently did not continue to sink into the morass Nicol described, partly because of some improvement in its musical skills and perhaps with the wider adoption of traditional church hymnody and the production of Army songs of greater merit. The Army's "hymn sandwich plus items" format evolved into an instrument capable of fostering and maintaining its distinctive spirituality, even though this might appear unusual to outside observers. The story is told of a BBC producer who in the late 1960s had recorded a meeting at Regent Hall Corps, London, for broadcast. He remarked afterwards, "That was a very good concert. But tell me, when do you hold your service for worship?" Writing of Salvation Army worship towards the end of this period, Gordon Moyles says:

> The present basis of the Army's evangelical work is its two public worship services, conducted in all corps every Sunday. These too, on the whole, have become predictable, traditionalized and staid.
>
> The predictability of Salvation Army worship, only infrequently thwarted by an imaginative corps officer, lies in the fact that a meeting format—opening song, prayer, choir and band selection, testimony period, sermon, appeal—originally adopted as innovative and lively, is now accepted as sacred and has become ritual. Salvationists have forgotten that the novelty attached to early meetings depended not so much on their format as on their content: lively war songs, sparkling testimonies, sensational conversions, spontaneous demonstrations and unexpected diversions were the attractions that kept the Army barracks filled. This is not to say that revivalistic techniques have disappeared from Salvation Army worship; far from it. Revivalist specials still survive; at Congresses, where charismatic leadership is nearly always evident, one may still witness

48. Nicol, *General Booth*, 336–38.

emotionally-charged scenes of repentance and conversion; and there are corps, particularly in the outports of Newfoundland, where one may still experience the exuberant evangelism characteristic of all corps a few decades ago. On the whole, however, and especially in those corps dominated by middle-class attitudes, routine and the desire for respectability have tempered the Army's exuberant mode of worship. Apart from the peculiar contribution of the band, there is little in a Salvation Army worship service which differs remarkably from what one might encounter in the Sunday services of any other conventional, conservative conversionist sect.

So much in Salvation Army practice has in fact become "tradition," and therefore sacrosanct, that the Army itself has become a bulwark of traditionalism. The improvisation and spontaneity of early Salvationism have been replaced by established ritual, and some of the results of that early improvisation have become sacred institutions, enshrined as effectively as sacerdotalism itself.[49]

John Cleary suggests that,

Salvation Army methods were so successful that the Salvationist culture was soon able to close itself off from the world. By 1912 Army music could be sold only to Salvationists and Salvationists were not permitted to perform non-Army music. Brass bands continued to have a powerful cultural role long after their evangelical influence had waned.

This is due in some part to the fact that group music-making is one of the most creative and cost-effective ways of mobilizing a significant body of people for a purpose that is both personally fulfilling and spiritually uplifting. Additionally the brass band is one of the few group musical activities which is relatively simple to teach, yet allows amateurs access to the best and most sophisticated music of the genre.

While this gave Salvationist culture its international cohesiveness and strength, it turned the culture in on itself. The composer Eric Ball remembered Bramwell Booth speaking to cadets at the International Training College of The Salvation Army [describing the Army] as "A nation within the nations, with its own art and culture and music." The Salvation Army remained largely secure within this culture, insulated from the currents of the world for almost a century.[50]

In this respect, the maturing and institutionalized Army became for a time more, rather than less, sectarian, in the sense that it increasingly offered an all-embracing social milieu for its members, which probably went some way towards justifying Roland Robertson's description of it as an "established sect." Any tendency towards a denominationalizing accommodation to the wider world was delayed by the very strength of its own sub-culture.

This was not all loss, however. The Army's brass band culture provided a vehicle for the pursuit of excellence—at its best, "to the Glory of God"—and helped retain the loyalty and commitment of a greater proportion of men in the ranks than might otherwise have been the case. The *Song Book*s of the twentieth century also provided a widening range of style and theological teaching. John Coutts observes that earlier *Song Book*s

---

49. Moyles, *Blood and Fire in Canada*, 231.
50. Cleary, "Salvationist Worship," 7.

followed a lay-out "reminiscent of Wesley's Hymns . . . The Suffering Saviour—Sinners Invited—Sinners Warned—Death—Judgement—Hell," in other words, getting straight down to the evangelistic business. From 1953, however, a more creedal construction began with "God, His Being and His Praise." The 1953 and even more so the 1986 edition also familiarized Salvationists with more hymns from the rest of the church, some going back to the Middle Ages and earlier. The Army also developed a genre of worship songs of its own, still deeply personal and in fact inward-looking rather than evangelistic as the early Army songs had been, but equal in style and content to anything in any tradition. To mention just one from the 2015 *Song Book*, Albert Orsborn's well-known 1947 poem:

> My life must be Christ's broken bread,
> My love his outpoured wine,
> A cup o'erfilled, a table spread
> Beneath his name and sign,
> That other souls, refreshed and fed,
> May share his life through mine.
>
> My all is in the Master's hands
> For him to bless and break;
> Beyond the brook his winepress stands
> And thence my way I take,
> Resolved the whole of love's demands
> To give, for his dear sake.
>
> Lord, let me share that grace of thine
> Wherewith thou didst sustain
> The burden of the fruitful vine,
> The gift of buried grain.
> Who dies with thee, O Word divine,
> Shall rise and live again.[51]

Many other writers—Doris Rendell, Ruth Tracy, Catherine Baird, Will Brand, Bramwell Coles, and Miriam Richards for example—made their mark.

Besides such song-writers as those mentioned, there were voices attempting to recover some freshness and instill some wisdom even in this period of increasing decadence and routine in worship. In other words, the prophetic tradition which had created the Army style in the first place was re-emerging to critique the pattern into which that style had become set. Of these, Fred Brown's *Salvationist at Worship* was a classic exposition.[52] Frederick Coutts also wrote a series of articles in *The Officer*, and included them in his *In Good Company*, addressing the important elements of meeting

---

51. *Song Book of the Salvation Army*, 2015, number 610. © The General of The Salvation Army. Used by permission.

52. Brown, *Salvationist at Worship*.

leadership: public prayer, the structure of the meeting and the preaching of the word.[53] Would that both Brown's and Coutts's work were prescribed reading for all leaders of Salvation Army worship today.

What did not change with respect to the Army's own hymnody was its tendency to focus on the individual's interior spiritual life. There was a good deal of "I" and not much of "we"; not many of its songs explicitly attempted to express the corporate worshipping life of the community. Nevertheless, at its best the kind of music and verse available this era went a long way towards meeting William Booth's desire for more true "worship" in Salvation Army gatherings and laid down a tradition capable of supporting the spirituality of ordinary Salvationists in a changing world. That "programmatic" corps tradition reached its apogee in the 1950s and 1960s. After that it gradually began to pass its use-by date for many.

While the matter of Salvation Army architecture has not been explicitly addressed in this history, the design of the meeting place—from the earliest co-opted spaces in shops and theatres, to the purpose-built "Barracks," to the increasingly ornate "Citadels" and "Temples," to the diverse creations of modern architecture, some under the influence of the wider liturgical movement in the church—would always have some influence on the kind of gathering which took place in it. The evolution of the penitent form provides graphic illustration. At first a simple form or row of chairs sufficed to kneel at, but despite protestations that the place itself was of no merit, the "mercy seat" became sacred furniture. A 1908 article on "The Proper Use and Care of the Penitent Form," described the new style introduced at the recently opened West Green Citadel in London. "The floor surrounding the Mercy Seat is slightly raised and enclosed by heavy red cords, which are easily removed when the form is in use."[54] Allen Satterlee's essay on "The First World War" in his *Turning Points: How the Salvation Army found a different path*, draws attention to this change in architecture as representing a change of focus in the Army's life.[55] A valuable outline of the evolution of Salvation Army religious architecture was provided by David Blackwell in the 1959 *Salvation Army Year Book*, and a recent study of Salvationist architecture in the United Kingdom is that by Ray Oakley in his *To the Glory of God*.[56]

3. C. 1960 TO THE PRESENT DAY: A PHASE OF DIVERSITY, OR ANOTHER STEREOTYPE?

In the second half of the twentieth century a restlessness crept in upon the established patterns. Some younger Salvationists began to look to more contemporary models for Army music-making. The iconoclastic editor of the Danish *War Cry* and author of that country's territorial history, Brigadier Ketty Røper, in her "Reflections on Denmark's 75th Anniversary, Is it all Jubilation?" regretted that "Jazz is one of the modern powers

---

53. Coutts, *In Good Company*.
54. *Field Officer*, September 1908, 327–28.
55. Satterlee, *Turning Points*, 77–78.
56. Blackwood, "Evolution of Corps Architecture," 30–35; Oakley, *To The Glory of God*.

which we—at any rate in Denmark—stifled at birth and with it many young people whose loss we now pay for dearly." Recounting the story of one such group of musicians, she asked, "Why could we not admit that most of our meetings are boring . . . and that progress has ceased?"[57]

With the advent of Rock'n'Roll and the rise of youth culture, the guitar began to make its appearance in the citadel. The Joy Strings burst upon the astonished Army world in the early 1960s, encouraged by General Coutts. *Punch* was led to observe that, "If the Salvation Army is anything, it is a gay, aggressive, revolutionary, movement not a pathetic body of survivors." John Cleary suggests that, sadly, this was a false dawn because the powerful and reactionary forces of bands and songsters were marshalled for the spate of centenary celebrations from 1965. The rock band remained peripheral to the Army's vision.

Cleary's comment is apt:

> In 1965 the huge edifice that was Salvation Army music publishing had just entered its most mature and sophisticated phase. Both composers and musicians reached levels that put them on a par with the best in the secular world. Ray Steadman-Allen's The Holy War marked the emergence onto the world stage of serious Salvation Army brass music. Eric Ball, Dean Coffin, and Wilfred Heaton, had prepared the way, but in 1965, with the International Staff Band's album The Holy War, featuring Ray Steadman-Allen's Holy War on one side and Christ is the Answer—Fantasia for Band and Piano on the other, Salvationist music had "arrived."
>
> In this holy war the Joystrings were simply blown away. Salvation Army brass musicians around the world welcomed the success of the Joystrings, but regarded them at best as a novelty, perhaps a distraction, and at worst as a satanic influence on true Salvationist culture. Numerous youthful musical aspirations were crushed by the contempt of local bandmasters, and the threat of Headquarters to act against those who had not submitted their work to the Music Board for prior approval.
>
> The Army of the 1960s failed to recognize that brass bands had come to occupy the very same niche that church choirs had in the previous century. Choirs achieved the highest form of musical art with the best composers writing great works of lasting value—men like Elgar, Stanford, and Parry. But though of great merit, they were totally out of touch with the sounds of the music halls and gin palaces, where the early Salvationists found their inspiration. Army bands might have been playing Toccata but it was the Joystrings who touched the public.[58]

It is also true that the Salvation Army of the twentieth century suffered under a disability less problematical in the nineteenth—the matter of copyright. Revivalists of earlier centuries could set new and religious words to whatever popular tunes were being sung by the people they wanted to evangelize; by the 1960s that simply was not possible. From Scott Joplin to John Lennon to Mick Jagger, those melodies were now off limits, even if the copyright fees could have been afforded. A tremendous link with popular

---

57. *Officer*, May–June 1962, 150–52.
58. Cleary, "Salvationist Worship," 8.

culture had been cut off; Christian musicians would have to provide their own and attract attention in a market never more competitive.

In succeeding years the great series of musicals with words by John Gowans and music by John Larsson contributed a score of lasting classics to the Army's hymnology. Indeed, some twenty of Gowans' songs were included in the 1986 book, including.

> If human hearts are often tender,
> And human minds can pity know,
> If human love is touched with splendour,
> And human hands compassion show,
>
> *Then how much more shall God our Father*
> *In love forgive, in love forgive!*
> *Then how much more shall God our Father*
> *Our wants supply, and none deny!*
>
> If sometimes men can live for others,
> And sometimes give where gifts are spurned,
> If sometimes treat their foes as brothers,
> And love where love is not returned,
>
> If men will often share their gladness,
> If men respond when children cry,
> If men can feel each other's sadness
> Each other's tears attempt to dry,[59]

Along with others by such writers as Harry Read, Maureen Jarvis, Iva Lou Samples, and Howard Davies, for example, the songs from those musicals have made a lasting contribution. Unfortunately, these by themselves were apparently insufficient to inspire an indigenous Salvationist renewal of corporate worship. An opportunity seemed to have been missed.

The Salvation Army, having failed to capitalize on the new life which was emerging from its own tradition, eventually bought into what was being offered from a different tradition. It was not until the 1980s that the "Western world" Army began to descend into the "Worship Wars" which were triggered by the rise of the charismatic movement and the burgeoning of new songs for yet another strand of revival. To some extent the Army succumbed to this influence because of the frustration of many Salvationists with an ossified tradition, so that they began looking elsewhere for inspiration—to Pentecostal and charismatic styles.

Spasmodic attempts were made to address the need for some rejuvenation of Salvation Army worship over the years. Colonel (later General) John Larsson of the United Kingdom presented a paper on "New Joy in Worship" at a Church Growth conference

---

59. *Song Book of the Salvation Army*, 2015, number 467. © The General of The Salvation Army. Used by permission.

in London, touching on what was a crucially divisive issue in some corps. New Zealand delegate Richard Smith's Report stated:

> In introducing this topic Colonel Ian Cutmore spoke of the need for "the kind of worship in our meetings that satisfies the people who come and will not stay otherwise." John Larsson's emphasis was on the need for real effort to make Sunday meetings the apex of all we do and so a major priority on the time of officers, musicians and other leaders in the corps situation. Colonel Larsson quite strongly stated that many of our meetings were stereotyped, were uncreative, were unsatisfying spiritually and were often the result of the regular turning of a handle to produce a patterned object. The value of the meeting in actually assisting every person present to lift their heart to God in praise and in obedience was much affected by the proper use of suitable words and music and the creative building of the meeting itself.
>
> He quoted an American CSM who asked, "would we want to spend eternity in a typical Army meeting? The meeting of Christians together for worship, for praise and for challenge should be the nearest thing to heaven we experience on this earth." GOSH! The possibility of larger corps particularly having a small group of qualified leaders as a "worship team" responsible for the planning of the first 40 minutes of a meeting was floated. A major emphasis was the need to adopt styles of worship and communication which clearly spoke to the local cultural needs and expectations. The tragedy of the imposition of a conservative Anglo–Saxon worship and meeting style upon cultures all around the world was something that needed attention. Change would demand considerable openness to allowing liberating changes in terminology, music, and style. There was a strong feeling that in all territories and commands there should be an endorsement of the use of contemporary music in meetings, and the insistence that officers facilitate inspiring meetings through the use of music and other means of communication.[60]

In an attempt to provide some resources for development of worship, in 2003 General Larsson appointed Colonels Robert and Gwenyth Redhead, domiciled in Canada, to an international role as "General's Representatives for the Development of Evangelism and Worship through Music and other Creative Arts." This innovative appointment capitalized on the Redheads' personal giftings but its effectiveness was naturally dependent upon their individual influence and example in the course of their extensive travels conducting meetings and workshops. In 2004 they also convened an international Music and Other Creative Arts Forum in Canada, attended by sixty-one delegates from thirty-four territories and commands, which formulated recommendations to the General and delegates resolved to implement aspects of the program in their own settings. Only so much could be done this way, and in any case the role did not survive the Redheads' retirement in 2005.

Despite such efforts, it was the Pentecostal–charismatic mode, the "worship song," rather than any home-grown Salvationist idiom which tended to be adopted by Corps in some parts of the Western world. As a result, changes of an altogether more sweeping kind have overtaken Salvation Army worship in the last part of the twentieth century

---

60. Smith, "Report on Attendance," 5–6.

(and this is from a New Zealand perspective, and may not be apparent to the same degree elsewhere). And of course those changes were resisted most strongly by those who believed that the tradition they defended was that of the "apostolic age" of the Salvation Army rather than the creation of the 1950s.

In earlier days Sunday meetings at Salvation Army corps had marked "similarities," even internationally. Anyone going to "the Army" knew in general terms what to expect. Increasingly however, from the later 1970s, this became less the case. Meetings were marked now by variety, diversity and non-conformity rather than the uniformity, conformity and predictability into which the original Salvation Army free style had set. Each corps might be very different in its worship expression. In some the traditional song-sandwich, with input from the usual musical sections, would be encountered. In others, an almost Pentecostal style of meeting might be found. An English survey showed a similar pattern emerging: "It seems clear that worship style has changed dramatically from the traditional model to a much more diverse approach . . . Importantly, the diversity was not only between corps; within some individual corps a variety of styles was being integrated."[61]

Over the course of the last twenty or so years of the twentieth century, the balance of probability swung in favor of the newer format, so that many corps meetings now frequently look and feel more like a typical "charismatic" church service. The "song sandwich" has been largely replaced in some corps by a long period of standing and singing choruses, with many people singing with hands raised above their heads, followed by a rather long sermon. In some cases it would appear to be the form rather than the spirit of the charismatic style which has been adopted. Uniformity, conformity and predictability still prevail, though of a different flavor. *Un*predictability tends to be confined to the question of when the repeated last lines of a song will finally peter out, about which the worship leader may keep the congregation guessing as long as possible, or until he or she senses that the majority have disengaged. There also sometimes appears to be a dearth of public testimony and opportunity is less often given for such expression of experience.

In some other corps, worship has not changed to the same extent. Following a lurch towards the charismatic style there is now a better traditional and contemporary balance in these. A period of chorus singing accompanied by a musical group (guitars, drums and electronic keyboard) is inserted into the already rather crowded meeting program, not uncommonly introduced by, "Now we're going to have a time of worship," as though nothing else which has taken place to that point qualifies for that description.

There has been a move away from the use of the Salvation Army *Song Book* and traditional hymns of the church to the use of music and song material from other, though limited, sources. "Songs of Praise" and "Songs of the Kingdom" were in turn superseded by songs of Vineyard and Hillsong provenance, amongst other material. There is a much reduced theological range in the sung material, with more of "me" stuff—as there was in the early Army, though with a different message and often less theological depth. There can be a concentration on "feel good," triumphalist and "prosperity gospel" themes, to the exclusion of the original Army preoccupation with the needs of the lost and disadvantaged. It tends to be music for the self-conceived saints rather than for the sinners.

61. Mitchinson, "A Study of Influential Levers."

What is sung in Sunday worship powerfully communicates doctrine, under the radar as it were, and reinforced through frequent repetition. Some material is sound; some questionable. Much of it is monotonous, both musically and conceptually. It also tends to perpetuate the individualistic focus, to the neglect of the community.

It will be interesting to see how the 2015 *Song Book* is taken up in this new world. In earlier days when almost exclusively the sung material for Sunday worship came from the *Song Book* more doctrinal checks and balances existed. Material to be included in each edition was closely vetted, filtered through the Doctrine Council. Now, apart from *Song Book* material, there is apparently less careful scrutiny or requirement, other than the need for licensing to avoid infringements of copyright.

In some corps, the choice of songs is sometimes less in the hands of the officer and more as selected by "worship leader." William Booth, with his insistence on meetings being under the integrating direction of one person, would not have been pleased. There is less use of the brass band, which used to make a significant contribution in every meeting. In the New Zealand territory, bands are struggling to survive, even in some larger corps. Their number has probably halved in the past thirty years. In many corps there has been an almost complete demise of uniformed music sections—no band, no songsters, no singing company, no junior band or timbrels. In many corps the worship team has replaced the band, songsters, organ and piano, while in others there is a relatively comfortable cooperation between the new and the traditional music groups.

In the early 1960s, when television was introduced to New Zealand, there was within a year or two a change in attendance patterns. Instead of the morning meeting being the smaller and the evening meeting the larger, with greater likelihood of non-Salvationists attending, their attendances were reversed. By the 1990s, the evening meeting had begun to disappear entirely, despite attempts in places to make it a specialized youth meeting. The collapse of intentionally focused "holiness" and "salvation" meetings into one event had implications for what was taught and preached. Traditional Wesleyan holiness teaching largely disappeared, although other reasons have contributed to this change. In a few larger corps, multiple congregations have been attempted, with relatively discrete congregations meeting at separate times, to give opportunity for a variety of styles of worship.

Technology plays a larger part, having moved on from overhead projectors to data projectors, projecting song material, power point sermons, and video clips. Despite more depth in the biblical and theological training of officers, sermons straight off the internet, not invariably taken from doctrinally impeccable sites, may be encountered. The apotheosis of this show-business trend was demonstrated by the carefully choreographed and spectacular sound and light displays in the meetings held at the "Boundless" 150th anniversary international congress in London in 2015. While this was an exceptional occasion with large numbers of people being marshalled under unusually tight security conditions, it represented the opposite pole from the spontaneity and participative worship once thought to characterize Salvationist assemblies.

The whole issue of worship styles and choice of material has been cause of much pain and concern, along traditional/contemporary lines. Some older, more traditional

Salvationists have felt betrayed and abandoned. By that time, however, frustrated early-adopters of the new had sometimes long departed.

This outline has really only referred to the "Western" world—and only to those parts with which I am familiar. Furthermore, some parts of that world might not recognize what I have described. Attending an attractive small corps in Washington DC, USA, in 2002, I felt I had time-travelled back to the corps of my adolescence in 1950s New Zealand.

But 80 percent of Salvationists are to be found today in the "developing world." Indeed, though songs of European provenance have often provided the staple fare in third world contexts, they were usually adapted to local melodic and harmonic preferences in ways which could catch out an inattentive visitor, and the translations sometimes supported idiosyncratic doctrine. In 1932, Salvationist journalist Arthur Copping, encountering an open-air meeting in a part of what was then the Gold Coast of West Africa where the Salvation Army was barely yet officially present, marveled "over the fidelity with which, under widely different conditions of race and culture, the Army reproduced its essential character of letting sincerity find expression in the freest human style, with no aid sought from ceremonial, special intonation or solemnity of manner."[62]

Of Zaire (now Democratic Republic of the Congo), it is reported that "the shift from missionary to national leadership [in the mid-1970s] was received with exuberance among Zairean salvationists. Indigenous worship songs and instruments were reintroduced in Sunday meetings as were other expressions of worship such as dancing which resulted in remarkable corps growth."[63] In the same period in Rhodesia-Zimbabwe there was a world of difference between the relatively decorous singing customary in the largely missionary-led Howard Institute Hall and the altogether more boisterous and *triple forte* celebrations at a rural village corps, where people rarely sang without simultaneously dancing, and there were as many vocal parts as in Tallis's "Spem in Alium," only totally impromptu.

From Zambia in the mid-1980s, Captain David Wells observed that

> It was natural that when Europeans and American missionaries came they brought with them the only forms of worship they knew. It is regrettable that we still try to coerce people into worshipping in ways that move our hearts rather than encouraging them to develop their own styles of worship . . . It is only in the last three years that Chikankata has done some pioneer work in the use of Tonga music in Tonga worship, but little has been done by Headquarters to encourage its use throughout the Command. The Catholic diocese to the south of us has used traditional type music exclusively in its worship for several years now. The Tonga people have a sacred clap using cupped hands that is used exclusively for religious songs and as an accompaniment to prayer to God, and they have a secular clap similar to our fingers-to-palm clap which is used for all non-religious songs. We, thoughtless creatures that we are, introduced into worship our type of clap which is associated with the beerdrink etc., and completely ignored the religious one which always generates a spirit of worship.[64]

62. Copping, *Banners in Africa*, 21.

63. Diakanwa and Dunster, "Congo (Kinshasa) and Angola Territory" in Merritt, edited, *Historical Dictionary*, 109.

64. Wells, "W(h)ither Pilgrims," 10.

While the influence of western officers as missionaries and leaders may have imposed a song-sandwich model and acclimatized versions of European hymns on such territories, some have doubtless long since broken the mold and explored indigenous ways of being Salvationists. Still, as John Coutts comments, "it is easier to call for indigenous music and local theology than to sit down and produce it."[65]

It is probably an unreasonable expectation that the new *Song Book* might accommodate all these sectional and international interests.

John Cleary asks of the way forward:

> How do we bridge the gulf between contemporary style and theological substance? There is in fact a direct link between the lyrical and musical styles of today and the revolutionary message of William Booth and John Wesley. It can be found where evangelicals give hope to the most oppressed . . . The black spirituals spring out of a combination of the heart-felt cry of the oppressed and the world-redeeming hope of Wesley and Finney. It is music that is grounded in the love of God, speaks with the voice of the prophet, shows all the tenderness of Jesus and moves through the power of the spirit. It is no accident that out of this musical form sprang the most popular musical forms of the twentieth century; Blues, Jazz, Rock and Soul. This is music that speaks from heart to heart. It lives with sorrow and pain yet sings of hope.
>
> Black Gospel music is the bedrock of contemporary Christian music. The Salvation Army has missed this connection twice before. Once in the 1910s, when having so successfully embraced the sounds of the secular English Music Hall and the American Minstrel shows of the 1880s, we turned our back on the religiously based Blues and Jazz of the early 1900s. And again in the 1960s, the Joystrings reconnected Salvationists with popular culture at a critical turning point in the modern world. Unfortunately, the movement as a whole was deaf to the message.
>
> The consistent path for the Salvationist is radical engagement. The Salvation Army needs to embrace contemporary Christian music. It needs to learn the lessons of its own history and infuse that music with a comprehensive sense of compassion and care, which belongs to the roots of Gospel music and the origins of The Salvation Army.
>
> It is something of an irony that at the very time some Salvationists are questioning its mission, the evangelical church is rediscovering its need for a theology that engages with the world. Evangelists such as Philip Yancy and Tony Campolo in the United States, magazines like *Christianity Today* and *Christian History* are turning to the great evangelical revival for inspiration. The evangelical churches are recovering the message of William and Catherine Booth and the early Salvation Army.[66]

In conclusion, we look back to our introductory suggestion that we might distinguish three very general periods or phases in Salvation Army worship style, roughly parallel to the sociologists' analysis of Salvation Army history.

We might take the first phase, enthusiasm, as an example of the "prophetic" attempt to recover first principles, in this case of the evangelization of the poor and disadvantaged.

---

65. Coutts, *Salvationists*, 134.
66. Cleary, "Salvationist Worship," 9.

The second phase, of routinization, can be seen as an example of the reassertion of the "priestly" function of stability, the maintenance and preservation of what has been achieved.

In the third phase there is a tension between the "prophetic" and the "priestly" and it is not clear whether they will learn to co-exist or if one will achieve dominance for a period. The newer, charismatically-influenced worship style was itself the product of a revival movement, even as the "old Army" was in its time. However, by the time the charismatic movement came to influence the contemporary Army it was already losing its original momentum and was itself turning into another example of a "priestly" phase of church life. Its music is in the course of becoming as esoteric and out of touch with the world as that of Herbert Howells or Ray Steadman-Allan. (How many non-Christians tune in to "Christian" radio? Or how many Christians, for that matter?) The Salvation Army has been caught both ways; it has been the locus of a struggle between two equally controlling and outdated modes. Perhaps Alice Cooper or Pink Floyd[67] might have been better models than Hillsong of a genuinely original spiritual voice in the contemporary world. A real diversity of source and expression, encompassing traditional Salvation Army classics, music from the charismatic tradition and other "mainstream" contemporary hymns (of which the Army appears largely unaware) would be helpful. For example, one of the most skilled and prolific of modern hymn-writers is Shirley Murray of New Zealand. Her hymns are widely used in mainstream churches and especially popular in the United States and Canada, from Mennonite communities to Catholics and progressive congregations, but are virtually unknown to New Zealand or any other Salvationists.

John Cleary's analysis of the present challenge suggests that the Salvation Army needs to look to its own roots for the inspiration and resources whereby it might renew its mission and worship. We should not assume of course that all Army music must be evangelical and therefore to engage the "world" it must be focused on and stylistically drawn from popular culture. The difficulty with this, as it has been ever since the second and third generations of Salvationists arose, is that the Army also needs to keep its own, home-grown constituency engaged. It may need therefore to maintain somehow a smorgasbord of styles, fostering mutual acceptance and toleration, in order to keep the whole together.

---

67. "And did you exchange A walk on part in the war For a leading role in a cage?" Pink Floyd, "Wish you were here," 1975. https://genius.com/Pink-floyd-wish-you-were-here-lyrics.

8

Social Work 1: In Darkest England

> "You cannot warm the hearts of people with God's love
> if they have an empty stomach and cold feet."[1]
>
> —Attributed to William Booth

William Booth was brought up poor, in the home of an alcoholic who went bankrupt then died. He had to leave school at thirteen; was apprenticed to a pawnbroker to help support his family and was turned out of work on the expiry of his six-year apprenticeship so that his employer could avoid paying him journeyman wages. He spent a year unemployed in the "hungry forties." As a teenage street-preacher, he and his friend Will Sansom picked up a derelict alcoholic woman, and from their slender means provided clothing and food, rented accommodation and bought furniture for her, and got her converted.[2] The origins of Salvation Army social work lie in these experiences. Booth was neither mere objective observer nor charitable benefactor of the poor; he hated poverty and hunger because he had been poor and hungry. He had a heart for the poor.

THE CHRISTIAN MISSION PERIOD

Social work was first undertaken by the Christian Mission when existing poverty was exacerbated by unemployment arising from the collapse of ship-building on the Thames during a "bust."[3] In February 1867 Booth wrote to the *Christian World* that the Mission's soup-kitchen was "supplying 200 quarts of soup and a proportionate amount of bread per day."[4] In July the Mission acquired its own premises, a converted beer shop in

---

1. There are many variations of this saying, but I am not aware of the original source.
2. Coutts, *Bread for My Neighbor*, 28.
3. "Boom" and "bust": expansion and contraction in the capitalist economic cycle.
4. *Christian World*, 15 February 1867, quoted by Fairbank, *Booth's Boots*, 2.

Whitechapel Road, and fitted out part of it as a soup kitchen. Booth's Report of September 1867, under the heading "Relief of the Poor," stated:

> Side by side with the sin and vice and crime which abound in the East of London, as a necessary consequence, the most painful poverty prevails. [Note Booth's view of cause and effect] . . . Since the last commercial panic this destitution has increased tenfold. Great numbers have been reduced from plenty to actual starvation, and at this hour in the richest city the world ever saw there are thousands who literally are pining away for want of bread.
>
> Nine months ago our loving Father plainly indicated that we were to do something for these suffering ones, and since then we have been able to administer relief to the amount of £300. We are now distributing 240 tickets for bread and meat weekly, in addition to which money is given out where needed; sometimes money is lent, situations are sought out, and in various ways a helping hand is extended to the afflicted and suffering poor.
>
> We now have in operation several maternal societies.
>
> During last winter we had a soup kitchen at Poplar from which we supplied 140 quarts of soup with bread daily; this work we hope to resume there immediately, and also in Whitechapel where such assistance will be equally needed.[5]

The Report quoted a Mission visitor as saying,

> How could I hope to impart any spiritual help if I could not do something to alleviate the dreadful poverty? Would they not call it mockery to talk about their souls whilst their bodies were perishing with hunger? But when I give them a loaf of bread or a pound of meat their hearts are opened, and I can preach Christ with some hope of success.[6]

This early raised the issue which would always dog the Army's footsteps: the accusation that the needy were bribed to be converted, or forced to endure preaching in order to receive assistance.[7] Early in 1868 *The Saturday Review* alleged that funds given for relief purposes were being misused to "tempt the poor to worship by the bait of a breakfast and coal ticket."

Railton was unabashed about this:

> Free breakfasts are given now and then on Sunday morning . . . But after soup and after breakfast came prayer, the prayer of men who meant to prevail, together with appeal upon appeal, urging to immediate surrender to God as the only remedy for their miseries, temporal and spiritual . . . "[8]

All Booth could do was "to repeat that never had attendance at any meeting, nor any profession of faith, been required as a prior condition to receiving help . . . "[9] His report listed "The General Poor Fund" as one of four funds kept separate in the Mission's finances, from which "we help the poor, indiscriminately, that is without regard to

---

5. Sandall, *History* I, 90–91.
6. Sandall, Ibid., I, 91.
7. For example, in George Orwell's *Down and Out in Paris and London* (1933) and in the press beat-up "For God's Sake, Pay!" in the United Kingdom (1981).
8. Railton, *Twenty-One Years Salvation Army*, 37–38, quoted in Fairbank, *Booth's Boots*, 2.
9. Coutts, *Bread for My Neighbour*, 34.

whether they belong to the Mission, the only condition being want. Inquiry into need is always made before help is given."[10]

A key figure in all this relief work was James Flawn, formerly a member of the Huguenot "Christian Community" and one of Booth's supporters from the 1865 tent mission days. Having been a starving orphan child himself, he did not forget the poor when he had established a successful cook-shop. (Takeaways are not new; the working poor often had neither time nor facilities to cook their own food.) In 1871, Flawn organized Booth's feeding stations, of which there were four or five dubbed "Food-for-the-Million" shops by the early 1870s, working with fifteen-year-old Bramwell Booth, who kept the books. Flawn later took over catering for the "Training Homes" for Salvation Army officers, dubbed "Commissary Flawn." (He died in his eighties in 1917, still a Salvationist.)

Amongst activities listed in *The East London Evangelist* for February 1868 were sewing classes at various centers, a further poor relief measure which enabled participants to make a little money. An attempt was made to set up a rescue home for women at this time, as converted prostitutes had no option but to go back on the streets, but enough money could not be raised and donations given were handed over to the Rescue Society.[11]

At Christmas 1869 the Mission provided three hundred dinners—four pounds of beef, a plum pudding and one ounce of tea to each of three hundred families, distributed by the Booth family and helpers—a decision arising from Booth's resolution the previous Christmas that having seen the destitute on his way home from preaching on Christmas morning, he would "never have a Christmas day like this [a happy but selfish family celebration] again!"

Poor relief was also undertaken by the Mission's "Sick Poor Visitation Society," of which a prominent member was Miss Jane Short, a lodger and friend of the Booth family. She advertised in the *Christian Mission Magazine* of April 1870 for old clothing, boots and shoes, explaining, "While the chief object and aim of The Christian Mission is to bring sinners to Jesus, we feel it a duty and a privilege to minister to the bodily wants of the necessitous."[12] A "Blanket Loan Society" also operated, and later on "Maternity Bags" were made available.

The People's Mission Hall, opened in Whitechapel Road in April 1870, incorporated a "People's Soup and Coffee House," which offered "Australian Sheep Tongues for 1^d, cooked 1½^d" amongst other delights. With this opening, the existing soup kitchen on the site was transferred to the old Mission Hall at 188 Whitechapel Rd. Charles Mitchell, who had been running this, died suddenly and the Mission Committee wished to dispose of plant and premises. They offered it to William Booth in a private capacity for £140. Being in financial difficulties he decided to take it over as a business, along with the other "Food for the Million" outlets, in order to gain a means of support. (He was not paid by the Mission and there was a shortfall in the donations received from friends for his personal maintenance.) Unfortunately he couldn't devote any attention to

10. Sandall, *History*, I, 92.
11. Sandall, Ibid., I, 100.
12. Fairbank, *Booth's Boots*, 3.

the enterprise himself, and because it was loss-making and difficult to get trustworthy employees, he sold it on in 1875.

In the second half of the 1870s, the Mission's involvement in social action tailed off for various reasons:

Firstly, by 1877 Booth had reluctantly concluded that the Mission could not afford to continue relief work, and wrote to the Charity Organization Society informing them of this. (This body, always critical of Booth, had been formed to prevent duplication of effort and discourage indiscriminate charity as likely to encourage pauperism. Booth later remarked, "The Charity Organization Society believes in the survival of the fit . . . We believe in the survival of the unfit!") This decision did not mean that Booth had ceased to care about poverty: it was simply that he did not have the resources to spare. The Mission, and then the Salvation Army, was entering a period of extremely rapid expansion, with which Booth was always struggling to keep up: fifty stations in 1878, to over five hundred corps in 1883, to more than a thousand by 1886, with work spread to five continents.

Secondly, it could be, as suggested by Coutts, that the Army was also distracted by the onset of vigorous and widespread persecution as a result of this higher profile, although this continued to be even more the case in the 1880s when social work began to be taken up again[13].

Thirdly, there is the possibility that Booth was dissatisfied with the tangible results of work undertaken so far. He had never pretended other than that the purpose of social work was to render the recipients the better able to receive his spiritual message. If that were not happening, then some rethinking was called for. Jenty Fairbank suggests that he therefore "had second thoughts about gratuitous handouts."

> A free tea is certainly a method of gathering together many who could in no other way be induced to come and listen to the gospel of Christ. But we look with great doubt and little hope upon crowds who come to seek the bread that perisheth, and who even when the Master himself dispensed it, generally went away unchanged spiritually.[14]

Booth never persisted with what was not working to his satisfaction; strategic withdrawal was one of his strengths. Although Booth was always ready to respond to urgent need without reserve, when the Army did renew its efforts of this kind, he made it a cardinal principle that there should be an element of self-help involved so that people retained self-respect, valued what they received and were not further pauperized by assistance. In *In Darkest England*, Booth made the point that, "No benefit will be conferred upon any individual except under extraordinary circumstances, without some return being made in labour . . . We shall not have room for a single idler throughout all our borders."[15]

Fairbank quotes Elijah Cadman:

> Our people can smell a man who is really destitute . . . Once a young ex-barrister lieutenant was very near disobeying the orders of his wiser captain and letting

---

13. Coutts, *Bread for My Neighbor*, 38.
14. Railton, *Heathen England*, 107, quoted in Fairbank, *Booth's Boots*, 2.
15. Booth, *Darkest England*, 272.

in a man whose vows of poverty were of an extremely convincing nature; but clinging to the sheet anchor of his instructions, his perseverance was rewarded by seeing the man sit him down on the pavement, pull off his boots, and then from the toe of his stocking extract the requisite four pence![16]

THE SALVATION ARMY IN THE 1880s

It would appear then that a few years of the late 1870s saw a hiatus in the ability and willingness of the Christian Mission to engage in social relief. Yet, within a short time the Mission, transformed into an Army, was back into the field. Despite this official withdrawal from social relief work, unofficial Salvationist involvement, arising from local initiative rather than central direction, gathered momentum. Salvationists were instinctively committed to helping others, as shown by John Gore's invitation, at the conclusion of the first, and entirely unofficial, open-air meeting in Adelaide in 1880, for anyone who hadn't had a meal that day to come home with him and have one. While *caritas* was not the Army's stated "core business," Salvationists simply could not help themselves. This must argue strongly for its being an aspect of the movement's founding charism.

First back into social work seems to have been Mrs Cottrill, a Salvationist in Whitechapel. In 1881 she began taking prostitutes into her own home and then finding them other employment. The work grew beyond her resources and was officially taken over in May 1884, with the provision of a house and with Mrs Bramwell Booth responsible for the work. Florence Booth remained in charge of social work with women until 1919. Similar rescue projects sprang up in many places, often because Salvationists had begun taking women into their own homes for safety. A Rescue Home was set up in Glasgow in May, 1883; a "Fallen Sisters" home was established in Melbourne in May, 1884; in Wellington, New Zealand, Mrs Annie Rudman and Mrs Hawker took the initiative in taking women home from the streets, as did the Brownlie sisters in Dunedin, who then also rented and furnished a house for this purpose and handed it over to the Army.

Arising from rescue home work was a demand for adoptive parents for babies. The Booths had long practiced this. In consequence of the family's involvement in the lives of the poor they also ended up taking children into their home in informal adoption. Of George, there is little known except that "Georgie" participated in meetings with other children of the family and is last mentioned in a letter of 1890, when he is reported as arriving safely in New York. Harry Andrews, born in 1874 and whose mother's dying request was that the Booths should take care of her new-born baby, eventually accompanied Emma and Frederick Booth-Tucker to India. There he subsequently gained fame and qualifications as a Salvation Army officer and doctor, gaining a posthumous Victoria Cross in 1919 when killed attending to wounded on the North West Frontier while seconded to the Indian Army Medical Service.

But the Booth family could not absorb all the waifs and strays available and from 1884 the *War Cry* carried frequent advertisements for adoptive parents. By 1891 an Adoption Department was attached to the Rescue Headquarters, later the Children's

---

16. *All the World*, September 1889, 428, quoted in Fairbank, *Booth's Boots*, 85.

Aid Department. From time to time the need for an orphanage was mentioned—in 1885 the *Daily Chronicle* reported that a gentleman had offered to donate a building for this purpose—but William Booth was not prepared to embark on this work.[17] He had a horror of Victorian workhouse-style orphanages. In 1886 the *War Cry* carried a General Order under the heading "No Orphanages." He also discouraged officers from adopting any more children. His daughter Eva had already adopted three. It was not until 1901 that "The Nest" was opened as a home for little girls.

Once the Army was established in Australia, James Barker teamed up with Dr John Singleton in his ministry to men in prison in Melbourne. Finding that discharged prisoners usually became recidivist because they had nowhere else to go, Barker and the Rev John Horsley took men to their own homes. In December 1883, Barker secured a small house near the Melbourne jail and this became the first "Prison Gate Home." An officer was appointed to meet men at the gate of the prison upon their release. Back in England, Mrs Commissioner Railton was reporting work to assist ex-convicts in 1884 and by July of that year a Prison Gate Home was operating in Hackney. Of the two officers stationed at the prison gates, one had been twenty years a prison warder and the other forty years a prisoner. Wood-chopping and later boot-making enabled the ex-prisoners to earn their keep; the *Liverpool Daily Post* reported that General Booth

> . . . comes to the conclusion that if men are to be Christians they must have food, and if they are to eat they must work. Two things only he insists upon—first, that those who accept his aid shall be willing to work; and next, that they shall obey orders . . . His great rule all through is to be that, if a man will not work, neither shall he eat, and by rigidly adhering to this principle he hopes to ultimately make his scheme self-supporting.[18]

By 1887 there were five Prison-Gate centers in Victoria and similar projects had been initiated in New South Wales, New Zealand, South Africa and Britain. An emissary from home had been sent out to look at Barker's work in Australia, and Barker was transferred back to London to replicate it there. Captain Robert Little, in charge of the Prison Gate work in Auckland, New Zealand, also started a soup kitchen for the destitute in 1886, having discovered "sickly, half-fed men . . . shivering and half-clad," sleeping out in the Domain and cemetery.[19]

In 1884, a group of Sydney Salvationists, concerned for the destitute, opened a home "to house these poor people until they can 'turn around' and get work." In 1887, James Barker in Melbourne formed the first "Samaritan Brigades" attached to Collingwood and Sandhurst corps to visit neighborhoods and give practical aid where found needed.[20]

In Spring of 1884, Emma Booth, in charge of training women cadets, proposed that a group of cadets should be housed in a room in "one of the worst districts" of London and engage in what would now be called "incarnational ministry"—"Let them dress as

---

17. Fairbank, Ibid., 54.
18. *Liverpool Daily Post*, quoted in *War Cry* 11 October 1890, quoted in Fairbank, *Booth's Boots*, 79.
19. Bradwell, *Fight the Good Fight*, 51.
20. Bolton, *Booth's Drum*, 120–21.

the people do (only be clean), visit, sympathize, and put before them the example of a good life."[21] This became known as the "Cellar, Gutter and Garret Brigade." Cadets served on a roster a month at a time. In 1886 this work became part of the London division. By April 1887 there were six slum posts and this work spread to other cities, and other countries: Canada and Denmark that year. Slum Sisters, in various guises, became a world-wide phenomenon.

In the mid-1880s the Salvation Army involved itself in a very public campaign to raise the age of consent, resulting in the Criminal Law Amendment Act of 1885. W.T. Stead, crusading editor of the *Pall Mall Gazette*, had discovered what Florence Booth had also found; that children were being sold into London brothels, a "white-slave trade." The House of Commons had twice failed to raise the age of consent from twelve to sixteen years. Stead, Bramwell Booth and the social campaigner Josephine Butler combined forces to plan an exposé of this trade and force the Government to act. Gordon Moyles suggests that the Army's official accounts of this campaign significantly exaggerated the Army's role and inadequately acknowledged Stead's leading role in the whole affair[22]

Briefly, the Army provided a converted former brothel-keeper, Rebecca Jarrett, who arranged to buy thirteen-year-old Eliza Armstrong from her mother for Stead for "immoral purposes," to show how easily it could be done. Eliza was taken into the care of the Army and, having been certified by a doctor as being *virgo intacta*, taken to friends in France for safety. Stead then led off with a series of articles on "The Maiden Tribute of Modern Babylon" in the *Pall Mall Gazette* beginning on 6th June 1885, creating such a furor that Parliament was eventually prevailed upon to pass the legislation.[23] To urge them to this end, the Army organized a petition, signed by 393,000 people and carried into the House of Commons by eight cadets. It also organized the distribution of Stead's paper from IHQ when W.H. Smith refused to stock it on his railway station bookstalls. George Bernard Shaw was one who acted as a volunteer street newsboy on this occasion.

The sting in the tail came when offended interests and enemies of Stead discovered that Eliza's mother had not consulted her father about the deal, and Stead, Jarrett and Bramwell Booth were thereupon charged with abduction and aiding and abetting an indecent assault upon the girl, who by this time had been returned unharmed to her mother. The relevant 1861 Act had never been used against those actually involved in the "trade" of course. After a travesty of a trial, Booth was acquitted but Stead was sentenced to three months and Jarrett to six months in jail. It was not until ten years later that someone found that Eliza was in fact illegitimate and her putative father had no claim on her, so that the case would have collapsed had this been known at the time.

Following on from the Eliza Armstrong case, the Army launched a "New National Scheme for the Deliverance of Unprotected Girls and the Rescue of the Fallen." Shortly

21. Sandall, *History*, II, 97–98.
22. Moyles, *Exploring Salvation Army History*, 59–66.
23. Criminal Law Amendment Act 1885 (48 & 49 Vic., c. 69, an Act to make further provision for the protection of women and children, the suppression of brothels and other purposes). The new law also allowed police, without obtaining a writ, to enter premises where it was suspected that girls were being held. One of the "other purposes," slipped in on a motion from the maverick MP Henry Labouchere, was the suppression of homosexual acts between consenting males, which was not on the Salvation Army's agenda but which was invoked against Oscar Wilde and many others subsequently until the 1960s.

there were five rescue homes operating in London for the reception of young women and girls leaving prostitution and four others elsewhere in the United Kingdom. By 1886 a "Receiving Home" provided a place of transition to other accommodation. Within the next few years there were rescue homes operating in many parts of the world; four in Australia, three in New Zealand, three in Canada, three in South Africa, one in Ceylon and one in Sweden. In the United States, a beginning was made in social service under the administration of Commissioner Frank Smith with prison work in 1885 and women's social work in 1886—a rescue home for "fallen women" in New York, followed by similar work in California the following year. There were reports of others though the number is now unknown. In the New York slums, a "Garret, Dive and Tenement Brigade" was in action by March 1889, with a day-nursery or crèche in operation by March 1890.[24]

In France, an institution opened in 1885 was closed by the authorities after eighteen months and a woman soldier looked after girls two at a time in her own home for seven years before permission was secured to reopen an institution. The first number of *The Deliverer*, a monthly paper recording this work, was published in July 1889. In 1892 *Orders and Regulations for Rescue Homes* were issued. As a practical extension of the rescue work, a "Maternity home," Ivy House in Hackney, London, was operating by 1889, leading eventually to the establishing of maternity hospitals in many parts of the world.

Some of the "fallen women" of London were being sought by their families at home in the country, and the new scheme included a central office in London where enquiries might be made and the appointment of officers in towns and cities to investigate. The first definite report of a case was mentioned in May 1886. During the first four months of 1888, two hundred and fifty missing girls were sought and sixty found. By the end of 1891, six hundred people had been located in that year.[25] From this "Rescue Work Inquiry Department," the later Missing Persons, now the Family Tracing Service, evolved.

Yet a further spin-off from the rescue work was training of the women in useful and employable arts. Florence Booth was against simply putting the girls to laundry work, the most obvious activity at first. She provided general training for work as servants, and also in bookbinding (practicing on binding Salvation Army penny songbooks), in operating knitting machines, and in upholstery. The sale of goods produced helped to pay for the program. A steam laundry was bought and added to the women's industries in 1891.

In 1887 William Booth, returning late at night from a winter journey, observed that men were sleeping out in the cold in niches on London Bridge. The next morning he demanded that Bramwell "Go and do something!" "Get hold of a warehouse and warm it and find something to cover the poor fellows. But mind, Bramwell, no coddling!"[26] By January 1888 the first shelter, with accommodation for seventy or eighty men, was opened in West India Road, Limehouse. The ubiquitous James Flawn attended to catering arrangements. Before the end of the first week, 2,000 people were being fed daily, 700 of them in one day being children.

Susie Swift, of whom more anon, had been advocating a lodging house a year before Booth's London Bridge epiphany. In a front page *War Cry* article headed "In and Out

---

24. Wisbey, *Soldiers Without Swords*, 63, 99–102.
25. Fairbank, *Booth's Boots*, 43–44.
26. Sandall, *History*, III, 68.

of the Lodging Houses," she asked, "Doesn't somebody else's heart go out towards the scheme of a Salvation Army Lodging House?"[27] The India Dock shelter became known as "The Threepenny Doss." Apparently, "dosser" was derived from "dozer"—someone who could not find anywhere to sleep and therefore had to doze in brief snatches wherever possible. This doss-house was located above Flawn's dining room. The bedsteads were made by placing forms on their sides, enclosing six-foot spaces in which leather-covered mattresses stuffed with wool, or even seaweed, were laid out.

Because women were being turned away from the men's doss-houses, a situation to which Susie Swift drew attention in the *War Cry* of March 10th, 1888, there was a move towards providing them with accommodation as well. This was eventually opened in Hanbury Street, London, in March 1889. A derelict swimming pool was set up to accommodate two hundred and fifty women and fifty children. A crèche next door could accommodate up to one hundred and fifty children.

At the end of 1888, General Booth approached the Home Secretary for a government grant of £15,000 towards the Army's shelters for the homeless, a first attempt to solicit government aid. In Victoria, Australia, the government had been providing this for some years but the British government was not yet ready for this step. However, Booth went ahead with three more London shelters in 1889, adding five more in London plus one in Bristol in 1891.

An early example of the sort of smear campaign which followed the launch of the Darkest England scheme occurred in 1888 when the House of Lords was conducting an enquiry into "sweating." This pernicious system at this time involved the farming out of unfinished goods to home-based workers paid pitiful wages for their completion. Slum officers were encountering families making a shilling a day from rabbit fur pulling, or six shillings a week for paper sorting etc. Evidence was given by the Rev. William Adamson that the Salvation Army was officially engaged in sweating, undercutting poor families subsisting on match-box making, and that male and female members of the Army, living in barracks, had brought down the cost of laundry in the same way. It turned out that Adamson had no personal observations to offer; he had heard this story at a meeting of the Charity Organization Committee. Bramwell Booth appeared before the enquiry to refute the charges, pointing out that no Salvationists lived in barracks. He denied that the Army engaged in either activity mentioned—though it did shortly afterwards get into both industries mentioned, partly in order to *raise* the wages paid.

In August 1889 the London dockers went on strike for a wage of 6^d an hour, the "docker's tanner." Booth opened a subscription fund to provide meals for the dockers and their families. This enabled an average 7,000 meals to be provided daily for the duration of the strike from the East India Dock depot, and later from Whitechapel Road in addition. As Coutts observes, the role of Cardinal Manning in negotiating a successful conclusion to this strike is generally recognized by historians; Booth's role in helping the dockers survive to that point receives less credit.[28] Norman Murdoch records that contemporaries were more forthcoming.

---

27. *War Cry*, 17 July 1884, 3, quoted in Fairbank, *Booth's Boots*, 84.
28. Coutts, *Bread for my Neighbour*, 14.

Strike organizers Ben Tillett and John Burns deemed the Army's work the most practical next to that of the Catholics. Worldly Wiseman wrote in the *Daily News* that the Army was the only church, chapel or mission that came "heart and soul into the strike, sympathizing cordially with the strikers."[29]

Two more projects emerged in 1890. One which had been on Booth's mind for some time was that of an employment agency. Susie Swift mentioned this in a March 1890 *All the World* article entitled "Sociology and Salvation."[30] The General referred to it again in a speech in April and it was launched in July 1890. Commissioner Frank Smith, newly appointed in charge of men's food and shelter depots, reported after one week that of two hundred applications made for jobs, between forty and fifty men had already been placed. It was 1909 before the British Government entered this field. The other idea mooted by Swift was for an "industrial home" and a start had been made with the forming of a "painting, whitewashing and renovating brigade."

The record of relief work attempted in the Christian Mission period, as well as the renewal of such efforts by the Salvation Army during the 1880s, stands against the notion that Booth only turned to social work in 1890 to shore up a failing evangelical mission. This accusation, made at the time and periodically resurfacing in the work of historians and sociologists ever since, is not quite accurate. It is true, as Norman Murdoch's research has shown, that the Army's work in its original patch, the East End of London, was struggling, and in Britain generally was going through doldrums even as it was expanding elsewhere.[31] But that is another matter. What is clear is that during the 1880s the scale of the Army's social and relief work steadily increased. By the end of 1890, Booth presented a summary of work in operation in Great Britain, as follows:

Rescue Homes (fallen women)	33
Slum Posts	33
Prison Gate Brigades	10
Food Depots	4
Shelters for the Destitute	5
Inebriates' Home	1
Factory for the "out of work"	1
Labour Bureaux	2
Officers and others managing these branches	384[32]

All of this shows that the publication of Booth's *In Darkest England and the Way Out* in October 1890, and the rapid expansion of social work that followed, represented no sudden and inexplicable or ulteriorly motivated change in policy. Most of the enterprises which were incorporated into the Darkest England scheme were already in operation to

---

29. Murdoch, *Origins*, 157.

30. *All the World*, March 1890, 113, reprinted in *In Darkest England*, Appendix, [iv], quoted in Fairbank, *Booth's Boots*, 108.

31. Murdoch, *Origins*, 70-87, 120-22, 131-36.

32. Sandall, *History*, III, 74.

some extent before it was launched. The Army's engagement in social relief and reform was consistent with its character from its inception. As Booth's 1867 analysis ("Side by side with the sin and vice and crime which abound in the East of London, *as a necessary consequence*, the most painful poverty prevails.") had shown, he viewed social problems as the consequence of sin, and therefore to be addressed with the message of salvation. However, he did not restrict the application of "salvation" to "spiritual" endeavors alone; physical needs had to be met physically. The *Letter of James* had said as much, nearly two millennia before.

As we have already noted, it is cogently argued by Roger Green that in the course of the late 1880s Booth also entered into a new understanding of the way in which the individual and social gospels were related, and this led to a whole new emphasis on the latter. It was not just that social work was a means to a spiritual end (though it was), but that it *was* a spiritual end in itself, even if not the whole end. There was a deepening of the theological imperative behind the work. But discontinuity between before and after "Darkest England" should not be too greatly stressed; this review of work undertaken during the 1880s shows that the Army was already seriously committed to social action before the scheme was announced, and the scheme incorporated all the existing social operations within its purview. What it did was to give them a greater over-all coherence and provide for them an ideological structure.

THE "DARKEST ENGLAND" SCHEME AND SOCIAL WORK FROM 1890

The title of Booth's 1890 book, *In Darkest England and The Way Out* was a play on Henry Morton Stanley's *In Darkest Africa*, published earlier the same year. Booth sought to show that the condition of Britain's own underclass was every bit as benighted as that of the denizens of the Dark Continent.

Before looking at the book itself we should mention two controversies relating to it: its authorship, and the reasons for Booth's scheme. Both have been written up by, amongst others, the American scholar, Norman H. Murdoch, one of the Army's earlier revisionist historians.[33]

Authorship

Besides William Booth himself, three other people were involved in varying degrees with the preparation of the book: William T. Stead, Frank Smith, and possibly Susie Swift.

William Thomas Stead (1849–1912) was a crusading journalist, editor of the *Pall Mall Gazette* 1883–1889. He introduced the interview, and originated the technique of creating news rather than simply reporting it. He campaigned against child-prostitution, working with Bramwell Booth on the Eliza Armstrong case; brought about the downfall

---

33. Norman H. Murdoch, Professor of History at the University of Cincinnati, Ohio, took a fresh look at the sources of the Salvation Army's well-rehearsed mythology and questioned many long-held assumptions. His conclusions may be disputed (he enjoyed robust debate) and his work was not universally appreciated, but in re-examining received traditions, proposing new approaches and opening up areas for discussion, he made a valuable and lasting contribution to Salvationist historiography.

of the Liberal politician Sir Charles Dilke over his divorce case; and founded the *Review of Reviews* in 1890. He was an imperialist and friend of Cecil Rhodes but fell out with him by opposing the British in the South African War; published a life of Catherine Booth in 1900, as well as numerous other books; became a Spiritualist; was a Pacifist, and was involved in moves that led to the creation of the International Court of Justice. He died on the Titanic when travelling to a peace conference in New York.

In his preface to *In Darkest England*, Booth acknowledged

> . . . valuable literary help from a friend of the poor, who, though not in any way connected with the Salvation Army, has the deepest sympathy with its aims and is to a large extent in harmony with its principles. Without such assistance I should probably have found it—overwhelmed as I already am with the affairs of a world-wide enterprise—extremely difficult, if not impossible, to have presented these proposals in so complete a form, at any rate at this time. I have no doubt that if any substantial part of my plan is successfully carried out he will consider himself more than repaid for the services so ably rendered.

To scotch rumors that Booth hadn't written his own book at all, Stead wrote in a letter to *The Star* in January 1891:

> According to the theory favoured by those who are eager to clutch at every stick with which to beat the General, his Darkest England scheme is not his scheme at all but Smith's and mine. Smith conceived the scheme, and I wrote the book—so the story runs—and the General is a mere man of straw or puppet in the hands of Frank Smith and W. T. Stead. What arrant nonsense all this is! They little know the General who indulge in such speculations . . .
>
> General Booth naturally and properly called upon all those under his command to render whatever assistance they could towards making the new departure a success. That is obvious from the structure and nature of the book. It is composed largely of reports from officers in the field . . . When he got these reports he set to work writing his book. At that time Mrs Booth was dying, but by the aid of diligent dictating and laborious writing he succeeded in preparing a book which in its rough state was about twice or thrice the size of *In Darkest England* . . .
>
> The General asked me to find him a literary hack to help him lick the huge and growing mass of material into shape. I volunteered to hack. I served as scribe temporarily under his orders, and I succeeded with the aid of three zealous and competent stenographers in getting through my journeyman work up to time. But it revolts me to hear people who profess to be friends of mine talking as if the help I was proud to render to General Booth in any way detracts from his claim to be considered author of the whole scheme . . . It is his scheme if ever a scheme was any man's, and although many were glad to help, the sole responsibility and the dominating mind were his and his alone.[34]

A correction never overtakes a good story: Alex Nicol (who should have been in a position to know) wrote in 1910 that "The book itself was written, and to some extent inspired, by a warm friend of the Army, Mr. William T. Stead."[35] St John Ervine writing

---

34. *The Star*, 2 January 1891, quoted in Fairbank, *Booth's Boots*, 133–34 and Coutts, *Bread for My Neighbour*, 77–78.

35. Nicol, *General Booth*, 190.

more than forty years after the event described the book as having been "written from his [Booth's] elaborate notes by William T. Stead" . . . "written in the energetic prose which William Stead so skillfully employed . . . and "in the vigorous prose of William Stead"[36] Norman Murdoch's 1985 suggestion was that "Booth's part in authorship may have been little more than that of proof reader of Smith's proposals."[37] In 2003 he described the writing of the book as follows: "Swift put Smith's plans into a first draft and helped Stead, a journalist friend of the Booths, refine the plan for a popular book, *In Darkest England and the Way Out*, which the Booths altered during the drafting process."[38] At least one recent website refers to the book as "ghost-written by William Stead, editor of the *Pall Mall Gazette*."[39]

All of that ignores Stead's observation that Booth had already prepared material "twice or thrice the size of *In Darkest England*" before handing it over for editing down. Those familiar with William Booth's other writing are sufficiently aware that the General's own prose was nothing if not energetic and vigorous! Bramwell Booth was not an impartial witness, but in his memoirs he recalled of his father (admittedly not with reference to this book) that "It was only in minor things that he was prepared to accept from others. The main thing must be his own. He would hand over to me the bare bones of an address and ask me to give it some garb of flesh [but] if I produced anything of radical importance to the subject his remark would be, 'I asked you to mend this up for me, I did not ask you to make it your own.'"[40] One suspects the same would have applied to the writing of *In Darkest England*.

Frank Smith (1854–1940) joined the Army as an officer in 1881, commanded corps at Liverpool and Bristol for six months each, then in 1882 was appointed divisional commander for London where he was involved in opening rescue homes. When Major Thomas Moore led a secession of a hundred officers from the Salvation Army in the United States in 1884, Smith was dispatched there to sort it out. Taking sixty English officers with him and finding fifty American loyalists with seventy-seven Corps, Smith built this up to 312 corps and 654 mostly American officers, being recalled to London for health reasons in 1887.[41] He had been back in London to speak at a "Purity Rally" in the Maiden Tribute Campaign in 1885. Bernard Watson described him as the first of three American commanders to give "welfare work high priority."[42]

On route to America in 1884 Smith had read one of Henry George's books on solving poverty by having a single tax, on land, and had been converted to socialism. Back in England he took a break from active service; Murdoch suggests that he "engaged in socialist activity, writing and research" and began networking with other social activists. He also occasionally acted as Booth's travelling secretary and reported his trips in *The War Cry*. Stead said in his 1891 letter to *The Star* that in 1887 Smith "was in America attending

---

36. Ervine, *God's Soldier*, I, 690, 697.
37. Murdoch, "William Booth's *In Darkest England*," 97–103.
38. Murdoch, *Frank Smith*, 2.
39. http://www.designinginformation.org/2009_10_01_archive.html, accessed 30 March 2010.
40. Bramwell Booth, *These Fifty Years*, 50.
41. Murdoch, *Frank Smith*, 5.
42. Watson, *Soldier Saint*, 63.

to his own business." He took part in agitation for labor reforms 1887–1890 and Murdoch says he went to prison for leading a street protest during the Trafalgar Square riots.[43] Smith was indeed arrested (as a Commissioner) as the result of a clash with police while leading a Salvationist procession in 1890. He refused to pay the 40 shillings fine and opted for the 21 days confinement, but Booth paid the fine to get him out.[44]

Murdoch's contention is that "between 1874 and 1884 the Christian Mission had virtually no social program" and that Frank Smith's influence on the Booths caused the Army's attitude to social reform to change between 1884 and 1887.[45] Smith had long wanted more social action. Stead says that "two years ago, nay, even one year ago, General Booth did not see his way to the utilization of The Salvation Army as an instrument of social reform. Smith wanted it to be so employed three years ago."[46] We have seen that the Army became more deeply involved in social action between 1884 and 1887, when Smith was out of the country, but it is entirely possible that Smith did influence Booth with his social reform ideas in 1888–1889 when he was in charge of the London's food depots and workshops. Booth was also capable of forming his own opinions.

Murdoch's other suggestion is that Catherine Booth's removal by death and Railton's by "internal exile" meant the loss of two influences which would have held Booth to a "spiritual side only" policy and thus left the way open for Smith's social policies. Catherine was on record as saying in 1881, "What does it matter if a man dies in the workhouse. If he dies on the doorstep, covered with wounds, like Lazarus—what does it matter if his soul is saved?" But that was nearly a decade earlier; there is no reason why Catherine's own views should not have developed, as did her husband's. *In Darkest England* was being written in the house where Catherine was dying; William discussed it all with her and she had read all the manuscript of the book before she died in October 1890. It is as likely that she would have supported William's new direction as that she would have opposed it. Indeed, had she opposed it, that might have made a difference to what happened. She allegedly told Henry George that "privately she would further his ideas as much as she could but that her position made it impossible for her to advocate his views publicly."[47] Railton did fall out with Booth over what he thought of as the commercialization of the Army at the expense of its evangelical zeal, but this was in 1894, long after the publication of *In Darkest England*, and when he had long been supplanted by Bramwell Booth in the role as chief advisor and executive.[48]

With the launching of the scheme in October 1890, Smith was appointed "Commissioner of the Social Reform Wing" but to everyone's consternation he resigned in December. Coutts says that Smith had addressed three questions to Booth: "Was there to

---

43. There was a brief labour riot in Trafalgar Square on 8 February 1886 ("Black Monday") and a more serious clash on 13 November 1887 ("Bloody Sunday"), when three people were killed and over 200 hospitalized. 400 were arrested and 50 detained in custody. Smith could have been present at the second.

44. Fairbank, *Booth's Boots*, 135–36.

45. Murdoch, *Frank Smith*, 7.

46. Fairbank, *Booth's Boots*, 133.

47. Ausubel, *In Hard Times*, 115.

48. Watson, *Soldier Saint*, 126–33.

be a distinct department responsible for implementing the social scheme? Was that department to be the social wing? Was he to be responsible for that department?"[49] At first sight, one would have thought the answer to all three questions was in the affirmative. It would appear though that Smith wanted the social work to be entirely independent of the control of the Army's headquarters, and Booth was not prepared to allow that. The scheme's finances, though kept scrupulously separate from the spiritual wing's accounts, were still administered by IHQ, and that seems to have been the sticking point.

Smith's leaving was made much of in the press, always eager for scandal. But there was none, and Smith did not join with the denouncers. He wrote to Booth:

> You need fear no alarm as to my intentions. I do not contemplate anything along the lines of opposition. While I just as earnestly as ever agree to the end desired, we differ as to the methods of working. Anything I can do outside to bring about the object in view, you can reckon on me.[50]

The Times special correspondent did "not believe that The Salvation Army contains a man capable of taking his place."[51] But the old Christian Missioner, Elijah Cadman was brought in to run Darkest England, and did so for nearly ten years.

Smith joined the Fabian Society and became involved in left-wing politics, published a *Worker's Cry* paper, was a friend of Keir Hardie—when their papers amalgamated he became editor of *The Leader and Worker's Advocate*—and won a seat on the Greater London Council in 1892. But in December 1901 Smith was back as an officer with the rank of Brigadier, as divisional commander for Bolton. He resigned again in 1904 and returned to political life. Amongst other activities he was a member of the London County Council for four terms, and eventually a Labor Member of the House of Commons 1929–1931. People who fell out with the Booths and resigned from the Army usually became "un-persons." Smith resigned three times, but remained a close friend of the family; he appeared before the 1929 High Council in Bramwell Booth's defense and published a book called *The Betrayal of Bramwell Booth*. Florence Booth was at his death-bed when he died aged 86 in 1940 and his adopted daughter, Lt. Colonel Evangeline Britton Smith, lived with the Booth family until her death in 1951.[52]

The American, Susie Forrest Swift (1862–1916), sister of Elizabeth Swift Brengle, worked for the Salvation Army from 1883 to 1897. Beginning with rescue home work in London, she went on to officer training and literary work, being editor of *All the World* and writing for other Army papers. Initially simply "Miss Swift," she was gazetted as a Staff-Captain in 1889. She was a Brigadier at the time of her resignation in order to become a Roman Catholic nun in the United States. Swift's Salvation Army journalism was particularly focused on social work and the promotion of social reforms and it is quite possible that she had some input into the book, and was one of the unnamed Salvationists whom Booth acknowledged in his Preface. In his 1985 article, Murdoch states that

---

49. Coutts, *Bread for My Neighbor*, 106.
50. Fairbank, *Booth's Boots*, 137.
51. Fairbank, Ibid., 137.
52. The biographical outline draws on Murdoch, *Frank Smith*.

Swift "claimed to have assisted Booth in writing *Darkest England*,"[53] but he offers no citation for that claim in either that article or his 2006 book. We do not therefore have hard evidence for Murdoch's statement that "one can reasonably surmise that Frank Smith, who did the research on a reform agenda in North America and Europe, turned his notes over to Swift for her to produce an outline for a possible book," that she "organized Smith's research into Darkest England's first outline" before W. T. Stead "wrote the book from Swift's outline" before "William and Bramwell Booth . . . read the manuscript and put their imprimatur on it."[54] While not denying the involvement of any of these parties in the preparation of book, this scenario goes beyond the evidence.

The reasons for Booth's scheme

The other contentious issue Murdoch raises is the reason for Booth's lurch towards a systematic scheme for social work in 1890. His general argument is that Booth turned to social work because his evangelistic work had stalled and was declining in the 1880s, just as Murdoch also argues that Booth re-invented the Christian Mission as the Salvation Army because the Mission's work was stalled in the late 1870s.[55] His statistical evidence supporting this argument has been presented in our first chapter, the Overview. Murdoch suggests that, "It was at least partially due to these difficulties with the Salvation Army's evangelistic work in the mid–1880's that William Booth was prepared to adopt social reform ideas from Frank Smith and others."[56]

The motivation Murdoch appears to impute to Booth in taking this new direction is that he was both pragmatic and opportunistic, and concerned as much for the viability and survival of his mission as for the poor. While Salvation Army historiography has tended to gild Booth's lily, does this go to the opposite extreme? Booth was pragmatic above all, but was he devious? Murdoch was not alone in his analysis of the Army's situation, however. Roland Robertson, in his contribution to Bryan Wilson's *Patterns of Sectarianism*, has this to say:

> It seems clear that William Booth's Darkest England Scheme was in part prompted by an awareness of a fall in the number of recruits and the belief that this might be compensated for by an extension of the Army's secular influence and a new assertion of its prominence in the public eye.[57]

Robertson does not cite any evidence for this assertion, other than a footnote reference suggesting, "On the process of goal-transformation in organizations and the process whereby people formerly regarded as potential members become potential clients, see Sheldon L. Messinger, 'Organizational Transformation: A Case Study of a Declining Social Movement,' *American Sociological Review*, 20, February 1955, 3–10." Normally one proceeds from the particular to the general; Robertson projects the generalization

53. Murdoch, "William Booth's *In Darkest England . . .* A Reappraisal", 108.
54. Murdoch, *Soldiers of the Cross*, 31–32.
55. Murdoch, *Origins*, 71–87.
56. Murdoch, "William Booth's *In Darkest England . . .* A Reappraisal," 110.
57. Robertson, "The Salvation Army," in Wilson, *Patterns of* Sectarianism, 83.

back to an assumed particular example. While the typological comparison is interesting, and it is quite possible that Booth's motivations were as mixed as any other man's, we might prefer some contemporary evidence for Booth's having thought this way.

However, whatever Booth's motivation, an IHQ insider who worked closely with the Booths expressed a similar view of the Army's situation. Alex Nicol stated:

> As an officer who knew the mind of the field officer, I fearlessly asserted that the Social Scheme, when it was introduced, meant the salvation of the Salvation Army. We hailed it as a relieving force to an army in an awkward situation.[58]

The Book

Part I of the book, "The Darkness," utilized statistics from the work of social writers Henry Mayhew and Charles Booth, but was compiled largely from the findings and testimony of Salvation Army officers already engaged in the field.[59] It showed that a "submerged tenth" of the population of Great Britain, some three million people, lived in abject poverty and misery.

Booth proposed what he called the "Cab Horse Charter." He took the image from Thomas Carlyle, whom he quoted as saying that the four-footed worker has already got all that this two-handed one is clamoring for: "There are not many horses in England, able and willing to work, which have not due food and lodging . . . The human brain, looking at these sleek English horses, refuses to believe in such impossibility for English men."[60] So Booth went on:

> When in the streets of London a Cab Horse, weary or careless or stupid, trips and falls and lies stretched out in the midst of the traffic, there is no question of debating how he came to stumble before we try to get him on his legs again. The Cab Horse is a very real illustration of broken down humanity; he usually falls down because of overwork and underfeeding. If you put him on his feet without altering his conditions, it would only be to give him another dose of agony; but first of all you'll have to pick him up again. It may have been through overwork or underfeeding, or it may have been all his own fault that he has broken his knees and smashed the shafts, but that does not matter. If not for his own sake, then merely in order to prevent an obstruction of the traffic, all attention is concentrated upon the question of how we are to get him on his legs again. The load is taken off, the harness is unbuckled, or, if need be, cut, and everything is done to help him up. Then he is put in the shafts again and once more restored to his regular round of work. That is the first point. The second is that every Cab Horse in London has three things; a shelter for the night, food for its stomach, and work allotted to it by which it can earn its corn.
>
> These are the two points of the Cab Horse's Charter. When he is down he is helped up, and while he lives he has food, shelter and work. That, although

---

58. Nicol, *General Booth*, 192–93.
59. Mayhew, *London Labour and the London Poor*; Charles Booth, *Life and Labour of the People*.
60. Booth, *Darkest England*, 19.

a humble standard, is at present absolutely unattainable by millions—literally millions—of our fellow men and women in this country.[61]

Throughout, Booth's points were illustrated by actual examples provided by officers working with people in trouble, shocking and pathetic stories calculated to arouse indignation and sympathy.

Part II, "Deliverance," suggested what might be done, and what Booth proposed to attempt, given the resources. The principles on which he proposed to act were seven:

1. [The Scheme] must change the man when it is his character and conduct which constitute the reasons for his failure in the battle of life.
2. The remedy . . . must change the circumstances of the individual when they are the cause of his wretched condition, and lie beyond his control.
3. Any remedy . . . must be on a scale commensurate with the evil with which it proposes to deal.
4. Not only must the scheme be large enough, it must be permanent.
5. It must be immediately practicable.
6. The indirect features of the scheme must not be such as to produce injury to the persons whom we seek to benefit.
7. While assisting one class of the community, it must not seriously interfere with the interests of another.

Essentially the scheme dealt with the "Problem of the Unemployed," for which Booth did not see hand-outs as the long-term solution.

> To deal with him effectively you must deal with him immediately, you must provide him in some way or another at once with food, and shelter, and warmth. Next you must find him something to do, something that will test the reality of his desire to work. This test must be more or less temporary, and should be of such a nature as to prepare him for making a permanent livelihood. Then, having trained him, you must provide him wherewithal to start life afresh. All these things I propose to do.[62]

To do these things, Booth's scheme envisaged the formation of

> . . . self-helping and self-sustaining communities, each being a kind of co-operative society, or patriarchal family, governed and disciplined on the principles which have already proved so effective in the Salvation Army. These communities we will call . . . Colonies. There will be—
> (1) The City Colony.
> (2) The Farm Colony.
> (3) The Over-Sea Colony.[63]

---

61. Booth, Ibid., 19–20.
62. Booth, *Darkest England*, 91.
63. Booth, Ibid., 91–92.

The "City Colony" would consist of institutions which would act as "Harbours of Refuge" for the needy. The existing shelters already provided these, and would be augmented as rapidly as funds permitted. Those people who, having had their immediate physical, social and spiritual needs met in these "elevators," and who could be reintegrated into society from this point would be, and those not yet ready would be passed on to the next stage, in the country.

The "Farm Colony" would be an estate in the provinces, in the country—"that is, back to the garden." ("God didn't put Adam and Eve into a factory; he put them into a garden," he said.[64]) With some other reformers of the time, Booth believed that in a large measure the distress of the cities had been caused by rural depopulation and the influx of people into urban settings which could not cope with them. Now some, having been taught useful arts and otherwise restored morally and spiritually in the country again, could be placed in employment at this stage or taken into the "Cooperative Farms which we intend to promote." Most, however, would be passed on to the third stage.

That third stage, the "Over-sea Colony," depended on the availability of "millions of acres of useful land to be obtained almost for the asking, capable of supporting our surplus population in health and comfort . . . " in South Africa, Canada, Western Australia and elsewhere. Booth was not alone in believing that Britain's problem was having too many people, and that emigration would benefit all parties.

> We propose to secure a tract of land in one of these countries, prepare it for settlement, establish in it authority, govern it by equitable laws, assist it in times of necessity, settling it gradually with a prepared people, and so create a home for these destitute multitudes.[65]

Booth sought to overcome any aversion potential colonists might have to going overseas, saying it was "absurd to speak of the colonies as if they were a foreign land. They are simply pieces of Britain distributed about the world, enabling the Britisher to have access to the richest parts of the earth."[66] No wonder Stead told Cecil Rhodes that he had secured Booth not only "for social reform but also for Imperial Unity."[67]

Launching the scheme

In Darkest England was a runaway success—Stead promoted it as the "Book of the Year" in his *Review of Reviews*. It was published on 20th October 1890 and the first printing of 10,000 copies sold out in one day. Second and third editions of 40,000 copies soon followed. A year later *The War Cry* was advertising a fifth edition of 200,000. The General donated the profits of £7,383 to the scheme (equivalent to perhaps £200,000 to £250,000 in today's money).

To begin this work, Booth asked for the public to contribute an initial £100,000, and thereafter he would need £30,000 a year. If one million pounds were found, the

---

64. *The Social News*, 14 November 1891, 7, quoted by Fairbank, *Booth's Boots*, 157.
65. Booth, *Darkest England*, 93.
66. Booth, Ibid., 143–44.
67. Murdoch, *Origins*, 161.

interest on that amount would secure this on-going funding. This was "going for bust." By 30 January 1891, £102,559 1s 2d had been donated, and Booth signed the "Darkest England Trust Deed" in a public meeting. This provided that the General was the legal trustee, that all properties were invested in him as trustee, that the money and property would be kept distinct from those of the Salvation Army, and that the General would be liable in case of breach of the Trust.

The press was largely supportive. *The Star* held that "The Salvation Army has a right to speak in this matter. It is not a mere offshoot of aristocratic or middle class sentiment. It comes from the people." *The Daily Telegraph* hoped "that General Booth's great experiment . . . will have a good start, fair play and eventual success." *The Daily Graphic* believed that on the Army's record of consistent work of mercy, "The General's book may be commended both to those who are interested in the fate of their fellow men and those who are not." Individuals including the Prince of Wales, Cardinal Manning, Keir Hardie, Henry Campbell Bannerman, and Sir John Gorst all offered support. Francis Thompson, who had been down and out himself, urged: "Here at last is a man who has formulated a comprehensive scheme, and dared to take upon himself its execution . . . In God's name, give him the contract! And, except in God's name, it were wanton to try it."[68] An open letter to "the clergy and pastors of British Churches" supporting Booth's call for financial help was signed by twenty-two leading ministers. Others, including Archdeacon Farrar and the lawyer H. J. Greenwood, responded extensively in print in Booth's support against his detractors.

The book's huge success and the scheme's popularity also conjured up a storm of denunciation. As Coutts summarizes it, "Hostile comment . . . could be divided into three parts. There was no such widespread need as William Booth had described. Or, if there was, current public relief, when properly administered, was adequate. This being so, the man was only seeking notoriety or money—possibly both—for himself."[69] Critic-in-chief was Professor Thomas Henry Huxley, who loathed what he called Booth's "corybantic Christianity."[70] He wrote a series of denunciatory letters to *The Times*, and then published them in book form as *Social Diseases and Worse Remedies*, conjuring up the threat of a fanatical religious dictatorship. *Punch* responded with a cartoon of Booth as parliamentary puppet-master.[71] C.S. Loch, Secretary of the London Charity Organization Society and long a foe of the Army, published *An Examination of General Booth's Scheme*, showing that there was no need for it. Others were incensed that Booth gave inadequate recognition to other people who had suggested proposals similar to some found in the book, or insufficient credit to others who were already engaged in trying to help the poor. The social reformer, Mary Jeune, dismissed Booth in 1891 as "a man whose modes of religion and leading have only created amusement and scorn."[72] The Lord Mayor of London, rejecting Booth's appeal for the loan of a

68. Coutts, *Bread for My Neighbor*, 79–80.

69. Coutts, Ibid., 83.

70. Corybant was a priest of the Phrygian worship of Cybele, performed with noisy and extravagant dances.

71. Harry Furniss, cartoon in *Punch, or the London Charivari*, 26 March 1892, 154.

72. Jeune, "General Booth's Scheme," in *National Review*, January 1891, 697, quoted in Haggard,

building for temporary accommodation, denied that a reported one hundred and fifty men were sleeping out on one of the Thames bridges. An investigation then found one hundred and sixty-four men on the bridge in question on the winter's night of the 21st January 1891.

It was not long before a campaign of slander gathered force, including correspondence in *The Times* alleging financial impropriety by the Army, and repeated accusations that it kept or published no accounts, although they had been published annually since 1867. Booth offered to submit to an enquiry into the scheme's finances. The Earl of Onslow was asked to select a committee and he chose Rt. Hon. Sir Henry James QC MP (Chairman); Mr Sidney Buxton MP, Under-Secretary for the Colonies; Mr Walter Long, late Parliamentary Secretary to the Local Government Board; Mr Edwin Waterhouse, President of the Institute of Chartered Accountants; Mr C. E. Hobhouse MP (Secretary). Buxton withdrew on the death of his wife. The others produced their sixty-nine-page report in December 1892, completely exonerating Booth and the Army. It also disclosed that Booth himself had never drawn any salary from either the Salvation Army or the Darkest England scheme, being supported by the interest on an investment made by a friend in Christian Mission days.

Most papers accepted the report, though *The Times* complained that "into many questions connected with the doings of The Salvation Army the committee has carefully abstained from inquiring."[73] They had followed their comprehensive brief, but none of this brought about a cease-fire. Old lies and new continued to be given oxygen as the years went on.

In the meantime, money to continue developing the scheme had to be found. The hoped-for million pounds investment fund never materialized. Instead of the £30,000 needed in the first year's operations, a little over £3,000 had been raised. Nothing daunted, Booth pulled out every stop in search of £65,000 for 1893. By mid-January the total raised was £15,250. In 1895 the Darkest England Fund had a turnover of £151,000, including the income from the sale of goods manufactured in the various institutions. £18,000 came from donations and £9,000 came from "Grace Before Meat" boxes—the half-pennies of the poor Salvationists. The "spiritual wing" of the Army also subsidized the "social wing." All of this is to say that the Army fought an unending war against shortage of resources and that this in itself was sufficient reason why the scheme was never able to be implemented to the extent Booth had hoped, quite apart from any other inherent difficulties.

One measure taken to counter adverse publicity was the publication of *The Darkest England Gazette* in 1893, renamed *The Social Gazette* the next year and published until 1924. This carried a constant stream of reports on successful work accomplished. Meanwhile *The Deliverer* had been boosting the women's rescue work since July 1891.

Persistence of Victorian Liberalism, 74.

73. Sandall, *History*, III, 95.

Implementation

So, how far were the three phases of the scheme implemented?

The "City Colony" had a head start, being built on the institutions already in operation. These were expanded and their number increased; five new shelters were opened in London in 1891. In February a lodging house known as The Ark was opened for those men who had come through the shelter, gained employment, and needed a better class of accommodation, and another, The Lighthouse, intermediate between the two, was shortly inserted into the hierarchy of elevator accommodation at 6^d per night. By the end of 1894 there were 500 beds available for men at 1^d per night, 3,500 beds at 2^d per night and 100 at 3^d. Two further shelters accommodated 1,300 men for 4^d to 6^d per night, in addition to the superior Ark, Lighthouse and Anchor, also at 6^d. Superior lodging houses for similarly upwardly mobile women were also opened in Cardiff, Liverpool and London.[74]

The penniless could earn their accommodation at the cheapest shelters by wood-chopping but four elevators or sheltered workshops offered more regular employment. The salvage wharf at Battersea could employ 300 men for up to three months. By 1893 the City Colonies provided work for 2,700 people in a match factory, a crèche-knitting factory, a book-bindery, a laundry and a text-making and needlework factory. The Army also sponsored eighteen labor bureaus and a registry office for unemployed domestic servants.[75] By 1897, 81,831 unemployed men had registered and 69,119 of them had found employment. 18,039 had entered the Elevator factories—150,000 by 1902.[76]

Detractors of the scheme found a number of weaknesses and the ungrateful authorities were often ready to find fault as well. Registers of occupants were required, and upon examination it was found that the Prince of Wales, Jack the Ripper and most members of Cabinet had availed themselves of the Army's hospitality. The shelters were alleged to be hotbeds of disease. A man with smallpox was discovered admitted to Blackfriars—it was later found that he had already been in and then turned out of a common lodging house by Dr Waldo, the Officer of Public Health for the district, but it was the Army that bore the blame. The death of an old lady in a woman's shelter was blamed on the Army's lack of care, despite the inquest showing that she was debilitated and starved before admission.

Blackfriars hostel was declared overcrowded and Dr Waldo on behalf of the Vestry of Southwark demanded that the number of occupants be reduced. A magistrate therefore directed that 250 men be turned out into the winter's night—despite an expert showing that the men each enjoyed more cubic feet of air than did first-class passengers on an ocean liner. The Army, and the Booths in particular, were accused of running inferior dosshouses for their personal gain. Further legal battle was enjoined over whether the hostels should be registered as common lodging houses—these were by reputation overcrowded and verminous. Booth was charged with keeping an unregistered lodging house for women in Hanbury St, and acquitted, then charged with the same offence

---

74. Coutts, *Bread for My Neighbour*, 119; Fairbank, *Booth's Boots*, 90–92.
75. Haggard, *Persistence of Victorian Liberalism*, 72.
76. Sandall, *History*, III, 134.

in respect of a men's shelter in Whitechapel Rd and found guilty. The conviction was overturned on appeal. Prosecutions tended to be motivated more by prejudice against the Army than by concern for the welfare of its clients. But mud sticks.

Periodic accusations of sweating were levelled against the Army concerning the work undertaken by its clients. As the Army had from time to time denounced sweated labor in such varied forms as artificial flower-making, chain-making, paper bag and cardboard box-making, match-making, sack-making, dress-making and walnut peeling, it was seen as hoist on its own petard. In particular the Army was accused of undercutting other tradesmen and manufacturers by using the cheap labor of men and women in its care, as well as undermining trade unions' efforts to gain fair wages for employees. For example in 1895 it was alleged that the Army underpaid its printing employees. The Printers' Laborers' Union was invited to examine the wage sheets and found that the wages paid were already higher than the Trade Union proposed.

On another occasion the Parliamentary Committee of the Trades Union Congress investigated claims of sweating at the Army's Hanbury Street elevator, and cleared the Army of any wrong-doing. Accusations that the workers were starved as well as sweated were met by publishing the current menu. It was also shown that the "sheltered workshops" ran at a loss to the Army because their purpose was rehabilitation and training rather than profit. Men or women in the early stages of recovery from destitution were seldom able to put in a fully productive day's work.[77]

Booth always sought to make the work as self-supporting as possible, and so the products of the various elevator factories were marketed. The women's work centers usually had an officer attached as a "peddler," whose full-time job was to sell goods door to door. Goods were advertised in Army publications amongst other places.

The most celebrated enterprise the Army embarked upon was the scheme for match-making. In 1888 the Army had supported Mrs Annie Besant's match-girls' agitation against sweating in that industry, but in May 1891 took on the industry itself by setting up a match factory. It attacked two evils with this: underpayment of labor and the use of yellow phosphorus in manufacture, the fumes from which led to "phossy jaw" or necrosis of the bones of the face. A hundred workers were paid 4^d a gross rather than the industry standard of $2¼^d$ or $2½^d$, to make the product safely with red phosphorus rather than yellow. These "Lights in Darkest England" matches were more expensive but a campaign saw them adopted by Mr Gladstone at 10 Downing Street and by many other prominent citizens. Public opinion forced the big manufacturers to follow suit and the Army sold its factory in 1901; yellow phosphorus was made illegal in Britain in 1908—long after many other countries had done so.

The existing social work with women, under the direction of Mrs Florence Booth, whom the General had made a commissioner in 1888, remained a separate entity administratively even though it was reckoned as part of the Darkest England scheme. Nicol

---

77. Nicol admitted there *had* been sweating in the case of the "Notorious Harbury [sic] Street carpenters' shop. It was alleged that sweating was practiced there—I know it was. The Army officials argued to the contrary, and I am rather ashamed that I was among the number. But the facts proved too stubborn for the leaders of the Army, and an arrangement was come to by which both the men and the Army will, I think, eventually be the better." Nicol, *General Booth*, 202.

says the women's work was much more successful and better organized than the men's work. Florence headed it for thirty-five years, and her daughter, Catherine Bramwell Booth, was also leader from 1926 to 1946, with a couple of years leave to write her father's biography in the early 1930s. This separation of men's and women's work became standard throughout the world, even in countries where originally all work had been under the direction of one person—in New Zealand initially under a woman, Ensign Annette Paul, appointed to this responsibility in 1891. Lillian Taiz draws attention to the fact that the development of social work with rigidly gender-specific programs and administration, was in marked contrast to the Army's usual principle and practice.[78] With Florence Booth's appointment in charge of "rescue" work in the mid-1880s, this began before the "Darkest England" scheme got under way, and lasted into the third quarter of the twentieth century—until 1978 in Britain. This gender-demarcated social work was well-established before the advent of the "Home League" in the early 1900s led to the adoption of the "women's work" concept on the field side of the Army. Perhaps it influenced that development.

The second stage of the program, the "Farm Colony," was launched with the purchase of 800 acres (almost 324 hectares) for £1,200 in Essex in March 1891. This was later expanded to 3,200 acres. The remains of the thirteenth-century Hadleigh Castle were on the property so it was named the Hadleigh Farm Colony. Cowsheds, piggeries, sheepfolds and stables were constructed, along with a dairy, mill, factories to process farm produce, offices, stores, along with five dormitories accommodating fifty colonists each, a dining room for 300, laundry, reading room, hospital and eight staff houses, in addition to the existing farm cottages and buildings. Produce from fields and orchards was sent into London either for consumption at the various Army institutions or for sale. The colony diversified into other industries, such as brick-making—one million bricks were sent off on Thames barges in 1894.

Colonists received from the elevators and shelters signed an agreement to work for shelter and maintenance, without wages. However, after a trial month they could be allowed grants of a shilling a week, or 1/6^d, or 2/6^d—for third class, second class and first class colonists respectively—depending on their ability and enthusiasm. After 1894 some local body Boards of Guardians began to send their able-bodied workhouse inmates to Hadleigh for training and the opportunity to get jobs in the country. Despite the variety of income-producing operations, the colony operated at a deficit—£5,900 in 1895 and £3,000 in 1901, with a roll of 250 residents. In 1912 it was found that in its first twenty-one years, Hadleigh had received 6,870 men, of whom 4,297 had gone to jobs and 407 had emigrated since 1904.

Associated with the Farm Colony phase of the scheme were experiments in industrial villages, agricultural villages and cooperative farms. The most notable in Britain was the Boxted small holdings experiment, opened in 1910, using a private grant from a Mr Herring. Forty-six small-holders were settled on five-acre holdings, provided with cottages, seed and stock and supported until the holdings were able to support them and their families. The £100,000 grant was to be repaid by the Army in annual instalments of £4,000 to the King Edward Hospital Fund. Most settlers made good; some did not,

---

78. Taiz, *Hallelujah Lads & Lasses*, 127–28.

and refused to vacate their plots as agreed, causing considerable bad publicity for the Army when they were forcibly evicted. Though a public inquiry vindicated the Army's conduct, it was glad to hand over responsibility to a Small-Holders Limited Company a few years later.

The third stage, "The Oversea Colony," was most frustrating for Booth. He spent a great deal of time and energy over the next eighteen years, seeking for a site for this around the world without success.

In 1891 Booth visited the antipodes, and in New Zealand was given some hopes that land would be made available. Despite support from the Premier and Governor and their expressed willingness to set aside 10,000 acres for lease in perpetuity at low rentals, nothing eventuated. He fared no better in Australia. Bradwell says that in both countries there was "agitation against the scheme by Trades and Labour Councils . . . on the grounds that living standards of workers would be depressed by this introduction into the colonies of what they termed 'undesirable persons, the pauper and criminal scum of the alleys and byways of Great Britain.'"[79] Sandall notes that in New Zealand in 1892 "a scare was raised that 5,000 of the 'submerged' were to be embarked for that country." The London *War Cry* reported that "both islands seem to have been alternatively rocked between fervid wrath at the prospect of an 'invasion' and determination to smash up the Cabinet for hoodwinking the public!"[80] Frustrated, Booth informed the Australians before leaving,

> It seems to me that immediately a man lands on these shores he sticks up a placard and shouts: "Australia for the Australians." A nation cannot be true to the great principles which have to do with human happiness and welfare, without suffering, any more than the individual; and selfishness, if it is hateful in the individual, must be deplorable in the nation.[81]

Nicol records an extended address on the same theme in Adelaide. Alas, rebuke was unlikely to succeed where persuasion had failed. The Army did establish farms in Australia—but not for the British colonists.

In mid–1892 Major Clibborn was sent off to look for property in South Africa, but returned empty-handed. While *The Social Gazette* the following year first suggested that lack of money was the main problem, it was later admitted that even though land had been offered in some thirty-eight countries, there was a lack of *suitable* land. By 1894 it was becoming clear that in fact the colonies were reluctant to accept "the sweepings of the London slums." In early 1895 Booth had meetings with government officials in Canada and asked for a large tract of land in the north-west; encouraging noises were offered, but no land. By 1896 Booth was discouraged:

> I have . . . still one bold generous offer awaiting further enquiry which is not likely to be defeated by selfish and ignorant prejudice. This, at the moment appears to be my last hope of realizing my purpose as it regards the overseas colony under the British flag, to which I have hitherto tenaciously clung. Should that

---

79. Bradwell, *Fight the Good Fight*, 53–54.
80. Sandall, *History*, III, 152.
81. *Adelaide Observer*, 28 November 1891, 33, quoted by Bolton, *Booth's Drum*, 228.

prove another disappointment, I must reconsider some of the generous offers that have been made elsewhere.[82]

The 1891 gift of land near Mazowe in Rhodesia by the British South Africa Company and Cecil Rhodes' interest in the Hadleigh farm encouraged Booth to look to Southern Africa again. In 1906 he was promised further support from the British South Africa Company, but after a year in which he was given the run-around from politician to politician it transpired that the Company was insolvent and no more was to be expected in that direction. That did not stop him from going back to Rhodesia to look in 1908. A further approach to Canada eventually foundered on the Canadians' stipulation that the British government would bear the expense. Again, a fruitless round of visits to politicians finally convinced Booth that his oversea colonies were not to be.

Meanwhile, there was another way; the Army could sponsor emigration to the colonies even if it did not have its own domain amongst them. It had been doing this in a small way for some years. Under Cadman the Social Wing started pushing emigration more intentionally in early 1891 and by November that year it had dealt with seven hundred applicants and dispatched ninety-five emigrants with letters of introduction to colonial officers. The first batch of men sent from Hadleigh left in 1901. The pace stepped up; the 1907 *Year Book* reported that 15,000 had emigrated through the Army's agency in the previous three years.

The key figure in this new push was David Lamb, who took charge of emigration in 1903. Lamb, an apprentice pharmacist, had become an officer in Aberdeen in 1884 at the age of 18. He was made a captain without any training and was involved in administrative work his entire career. In 1889 he went to work in property and finance at IHQ in London and two years later to South Africa as chief secretary. By the end of 1891 the Lambs (he married Minnie Clinton in 1888) were back in London and he became chief secretary to Elijah Cadman in the social scheme. In 1892 he became Bramwell Booth's secretary for social affairs. After spending 1897 as director of the trade department, he was back in social work in 1898 as governor of Hadleigh farm colony and chief secretary of the city colonies until 1903 when he was appointed to run a migration program. He spent the rest of his life in this work, serving as international social commissioner 1912–1929 and as social work consultant until his retirement ten years later at the age of 73. He continued working in retirement, touring the world, collecting honors as he went—Order of the Founder, CMG, Hon. LLD from Aberdeen, Fellow of the Royal Empire Society—until his death in 1951 at 84.

By 1905 the Army had chartered a steamship to take over 1,000 migrants to Canada, 600 of them being wage-earners. All had jobs before disembarking. In 1906, there were four voyages taking 1,250 migrants each time. By 1910, 50,000 people had been helped to leave Britain. A source of anxiety to H. Rider Haggard was that so many were able-bodied single men, so that many British women—already numbering a million more than men—would lose the opportunity to marry. Lamb felt that with the excess of men

---

82. Fairbank, *Booth's Boots*, 170.

over women in the British Dominions, some of the 45,000 British widows, with their 120,000 dependent children, should also emigrate.[83]

A. M. Nicol, writing in 1910, also had doubts about the success of the scheme to that point, though not holding Lamb entirely to blame:

> He was appointed by the General to organize the Emigration Department, in which, however, he has been a failure; that is, so far as carrying out the General's ideal of emigration is concerned. Originally that department was intended to be a method for transferring people in adverse circumstances from this country, where they were being crowded out of the labor market, to places such as Canada and America, where there existed a more general demand for labor. This branch of the Army's operations for some reason or other has not attracted subscriptions, and yet the agency has sent tens of thousands of people to Canada, and the publications of the Army have boasted that in some instances the parties that have been sent under the aegis of the Army have carried with them as much as £30,000 & somewhat different financial reputation from what the General expected to belong to the people that should accept his hand of help in this way. The department has grown to be a miniature Cook's Agency. It simply meets the need of a class that prefer to sail to a new shore under the guidance of the Army's officials; otherwise it has practically failed to grapple with a fraction of the social problem which it was hoped by its originator it would partially solve.
>
> The worst aspects of its operations, however, are confined to the Canadian side of the case. The Army has no special facilities to offer their clients. Colonel Lamb is the officer who has had the shaping of this department largely in his hands, and it may be placed to his credit that if he had had a freer hand he probably would have done something opposed to the general interests of the Army, but calculated to introduce a first class stream of labor to the Dominion from the ranks of those unable to pay their own ocean fare. He is nothing if not original in many of his suggestions for taking the underdog up out of his extremity, and for fearlessly going in the teeth of the conventional; but like all societies that have to consider not one aspect of the question, but how one department will affect another, he has been handicapped in measures for raising money to aid the thousands who have applied to the Army and have been refused, on the ground that there were no available funds. Colonel Lamb has paid many visits to Canada and has done much to teach Government officials how to do emigration work on a cheap line.[84]

In New Zealand a government department of immigration was set up in 1920 and in its first two years the Salvation Army found accommodation for 3,901 and jobs for 982 people.[85] Boys aged fourteen to eighteen were given a short course at Hadleigh and then passed through the Army's Hodderville training farm near Putaruru in New Zealand and on to farming jobs. The immigration secretary, Major Alf Greene, was their legal guardian until they turned twenty-one. With the 1922 Empire Settlement Act, schemes like the Army's received further support and the British government made use of the Army's migration and settlement department. The liner "Vedic" was chartered for

83. Fairbank, Ibid., 180.
84. Nicol, *General Booth*, 366–67.
85. Bradwell, *Fight the Good Fight*, 96.

emigrants to Australia in 1927, 1928 and 1929, with officers accompanying the migrants and arranging accommodation and employment.[86] Boys were trained in farm work for three or four months at the Army's Riverview farm in Queensland; girls were housed at a hostel in Perth and employment as domestic helps was sought. Unfortunately the onset of the world-wide depression made settling in harder for the migrants.[87]

It is estimated that between 250,000 and 300,000 people were assisted to emigrate from Britain under the schemes Lamb originated.[88] All up, the Army provided a useful service but the "oversea colony" failed to fulfil Booth's vision; it did not take Britain's submerged tenth off its hands.

Evaluation

In retrospect, how did the Darkest England Scheme work out?

Statistics give part of the answer. The Army was always punctilious about keeping statistics—though this has often seemed more from publicity and fund-raising considerations and the need to maintain accountability than for any analytical use that might be made of them. However this has meant that periodic reports enable the progress of the scheme to be tracked.

In an appendix to *In Darkest England*, Booth had given a summary of social work undertaken as in October 1890, including a total of eighty-nine institutions or social enterprises, managed by 384 officers and others. It is not made clear, but that number probably included both British and overseas work since other statistics in the appendix were inclusive.

In his preface to Bramwell Booth's 1899 book, *Social Reparation*, reporting on the Darkest England scheme, William Booth cited the following figures:[89]

	1896	1898	Increase
No. of Institutions	341	450	109
No. Officers employed	1,445	1,832	387
No. Submerged dealt with daily	12,600	18,000	5,400
No. received nightly into Shelters	10,000	15,000	5,000
No. Women passing through Homes per annum	3,000	4,600	1,600
Accommodation for Ex-Criminals	381	———	———
No. Elevators and Labour Factories	41	53	11
No. Land Colonies	10	14	4
No. National and Municipal Governments subsidizing the work	17	24	7

While the Army was a highly centralized organization and the movement was always ready to advertise its overseas activities, which were included in the above tables, social work in other countries was entirely separate from the British work, and the Army

---

86. Coutts, *Bread for My Neighbour*, 161.
87. Bolton, *Booth's Drum*, 229.
88. Sandall, *History*, III, 158; Murdoch, *Soldiers of the Cross*, 261.
89. Booth, in Bramwell Booth, *Social Reparation*, 5.

was always careful to point this out in connection with fund-raising: "No funds given for The Darkest England Scheme are used for the work in other Countries."[90]

When Booth came to review the results of the scheme as a whole after sixteen years, he could set them out as follows: in 1890 the following ideas were mooted and those marked with an asterisk were actually carried out.

* Food depots	Travelling hospital
* Night shelters	* Inebriate homes
* Workshops and labor yards	* Rescue homes
* Labor bureaux	* Preventive homes
The household salvage brigade	* Inquiry office
* The farm colony	Refuges for street children
The industrial village	* Industrial schools
* Agricultural villages	Asylums for moral lunatics
The oversea colony	* Improved lodgings
Universal emigration	Workmen's cottages
* The salvation ship	* The poor man's bank
* Slum visitation and nursing	* The poor man's lawyer
* Prisongate brigade and ex-criminals homes	* The intelligence department
Matrimonial bureau	Whitechapel-by-the-Sea

By 1906 the following branches of work, not named in the original proposals, had been added to the scheme:[91]

Wood yards	Midnight soup kitchens
Shoe blacking brigades	Street cleaning brigades
Express brigades	Knitting and needle workrooms
Laundries	Police-court visitation
Midnight work amongst women	Special training home for social officers
Maternity homes	Farthing breakfasts for children
Hospitals	Servants' homes.

In sum: it made a difference. It did not solve the problem of the "submerged tenth," but other social, political, and economic forces also came to bear on that problem over the years.

Not all the Darkest England schemes took off or could be sustained. "Booth's Beer," a non-alcoholic beverage, produced at the Limehouse shelter, was advertised in the *War Cry* in 1891–1892 but does not seem to have found favor. Some pioneering activities presaged much later developments: tree-planting and road working gangs in 1893 reappeared as job-creation projects in the late twentieth century. Some were proposed but took a while to appear; Susie Swift was talking up the need for accommodation for elderly women in *The Deliverer* in 1891 but it was 1910 before the first Salvation Army homes for the aged were commissioned in Britain.

Besides the Army's institutional work, it also promoted or campaigned for other social reforms arising from its involvement in social work. Women's needs and women's rights were themes to which the Army papers often returned. Even in 1876 *The Christian*

---

90. Bramwell Booth, Ibid, 99.
91. *Sketches of Salvation Army Social Work* (1906) quoted by Fairbank, *Booth's Boots*, 149.

Mission Magazine had campaigned for shops to provide chairs for shop-girls to rest on when not serving customers; an 1895 issue of *The Social Gazette* was designated "The Shop Assistants' Number." When legislation in 1900 made the provision of seating compulsory the *Gazette* attacked employers who obeyed the letter of the law by providing the seats but would not let the girls sit on them. In 1891 *The Deliverer* tried to put "The Women's Side of the Labour Question" on behalf of working mothers who had no bread-winning partner, and the first issue of the *Gazette* proposed a "Servant Girls' Charter." While Catherine Booth was never a suffragette, she was on record as saying in a public meeting in 1882 that "it is time we women had some sort of voice in choosing our law-makers!"[92]

Alex Nicol's 1911 summary of the successes and failures of the "scheme" after twenty years' operation still repays consideration:

> Ever since the Army started social work I have been a constant and sympathetic student of its developments in all lands, and this is my deliberate verdict upon the whole scheme of social salvation reform:
>
> 1. That the Salvation Army by taking up social work conferred a distinct boon upon the community. It has lifted the study of sociology into a warmer atmosphere.
>
> 2. That the Salvation Army, by introducing social auxiliaries to its campaigns for the salvation of the sunken masses of the people, has awakened the Churches of Christendom to a more practical conception of its mission in this century . . . Till the book *In Darkest England and the Way Out* appeared, the Churches generally were asleep on social questions.
>
> 3. That the Salvation Army has been unwittingly the best argument in support of State Socialism. It has accentuated discontent, confirmed the wail of the exponents of Socialism, and by failing to secure the co-operation that the leader desired by which he asserted he could deal a death-blow at pauperism the Army has supplied the Socialists with a powerful weapon in favour of their program.
>
> 4. That in departing from his individualistic theories, and going in for the wholesale management of submerged humanity by means of shelters, metropoles, and colonies, General Booth has forced the pace of State interference with the general social conditions of the poorer classes of the people.
>
> 5. That the Social Scheme has forcibly illustrated the utter helplessness of present methods to rid society of the evils which foster destitution, vice, and idleness. The official organ of the Army admitted, at the opening of the year 1911, that despite better trade and the decline of unemployment, as registered at labour exchanges and verified by trade-union returns, the distress in London was as great and as acute as ever.
>
> 6. That the Army has not faced the logical conclusion of the experience that it has gained in dealing with the submerged masses, with the result that it is perpetuating failures, and deceiving people with the idea that all it does for the poor is beneficial, whereas much that it does is injurious to the poor.
>
> 7. That the proportion of men socially and permanently redeemed from destitution is infinitesimal when compared with the time, labor, and money expended upon their reformation. If the Army were to alter its return forms so as to tabulate the number helped, and the number permanently restored as the

---

92. Bramwell-Booth, *Catherine Booth*, 395.

outcome of that help, the results disclosed would prove to be disappointingly small. The Scheme as a social restorative is, indeed, a failure. As an ameliorative agency it is a success.

8. That the religion of the Salvation Army is a greater failure, if tested by results, among the men's social agencies than in any other branch of its operations. The general idea about the Salvation Army is that the nearer that it gets to the most abandoned classes the more wonderful and the more numerous are the converts. It is a sad admission to pass on to the world that the opposite is really the case. The results are fewer. General Booth would almost break his heart if he knew the proportion of men who have been "saved," in the sense that he most values, through his social scheme.

9. That the Women's Social Work is, on the contrary, as great a success in this respect as the Men's is a failure. The moral, social, and spiritual value of that work can scarcely be over-estimated. It reflects undying credit upon all associated with Mrs. Bramwell Booth in the management of rescue homes, shelters, hospitals, and inebriate institutions.

10. That the colonization experiments are too costly, too cumbrous, and have not to any appreciable extent been utilized for the purpose for which they were organized. It is admitted by the General, if I am not mistaken, that he committed a serious mistake in opening the Hadleigh Farm Colony before he was sure of the location of the Colony Over the Sea. Up to the present that section of the Army's social program has not been given effect to . . . This was most unfortunate, inasmuch as the success of the General's scheme can never be considered complete till he has had an opportunity of showing what can be done with rejuvenated city labour in a colony managed, as it would be, in a country away from the surroundings and temptations of squalid dwellings and low ale shops. If the money sunk, for instance, in establishing the Farm Colony at Hadleigh had been devoted to the work of the City Colony, the results would probably have been 1000 per cent more encouraging . . . The Hadleigh Colony has been of real aid to a number of able-bodied paupers, who have passed a period of probation at market gardening previous to being transferred to Canada. Still it has been much exaggerated by those not familiar with the relationship of the Colony to the scheme as outlined in the General's book.

11. That while the Army colonies can no longer be charged with insanitation and overcrowding, and the general administration has considerably improved, there is force in what some critics have pointed out again and again, namely, the commercial spirit has seriously nullified the power of the social and reformative. The officer in charge of a shelter is actuated by a compound influence. He has to make the shelter pay its way, in fact, he has to improve its income. He has to work hard to do so. He is up early and late, is at the beck and call of all concerned, and, as a rule, he has no leisure for qualifying himself for the most arduous of all his tasks, personal dealing with the inmates of the shelter. The majority of officers fall under the temptation of the commercial spirit . . . When, therefore, the shelter officer's figures are examined, and he finds, as he does, that more attention is paid to the financial side of the account than to the spiritual, it is small wonder that the shelters and elevators degenerate into shoppy or lodging-house affairs.

It seems, therefore, to be fair to conclude, if these propositions are correct, that the effort, worthily and nobly conceived, and extended to its present dimensions, is still in an unsatisfactory stage. It has attacked many, but solved no single problem. It has drawn into its many nets of mercy thousands of the ghosts of our social underworld and inspired them with cheer and some little hope; but the march of poverty still goes on. Lazarus, with all his sores, is still at the gates. The horrors on the Embankment show no sign of dying out. Thirty thousand men at least are out of work in London. The nomads of our civilization wander past us in their fringy, dirty attire by night and by day. If a man stops us in the street and tells us he is starving, and we offer him a ticket to a labour home or a night shelter, he will tell you that the chances are one out of ten if he will procure admission. The better class of submerged, or those who use the provision for the submerged in order to gratify their own selfishness, have taken possession of the vacancies, and so they wander on. If a man applies for temporary work, the choice of industry is disappointingly limited. One is tempted to think that the whole superstructure of cheap and free shelters has tended to the standardization of a low order of existence in this nether world that attracted the versatile philanthropist at the head of the Salvation Army twenty years ago. If we look to the land as the solution of one-half of our social problems, all that General Booth can point to is a colony of casual labourers at work on his colony at Hadleigh and to a handful of small holders learning petit culture under favourable conditions.

But, unlike the evangelist of earlier days, the leader of the Salvation Army would appear to have gathered very little new light upon the problems on which he is at work. He stands by a somewhat antiquated laissez faire, and seems incapable of seeing the rise of new forces in the world. In dealing with the objections that he anticipated when he launched his scheme, he argued that if the work upon which he was to embark would be better done by the State, he would let them try, and leave it alone himself. Now all that has changed. The State has started shelters, swept aside miles of insanitary dwellings, brought the lodging houses of the metropolis under vigorous inspection, established public baths and laundries, assumed a master control of a thousand and one things that concern the food and housing of the people, and recently ensured, by the application of the Children's Free Meals Act, that the education of the children of the metropolis shall be carried on under reasonable conditions. The National Administration of affairs has not been idle. The Local Government Board have multiplied their ramifications, and the Old Age Pensions Act has at least chased some of the horrors away from the aged poor of the land. Labour Exchanges have worked a small revolution, and if developed on the lines that are suggested at the Imperial Conference, may do more to solve some of the problems that General Booth and the Church and other Armies are engaged upon than anything else. The Prison Commissioners have resolved upon the abolition of the ticket-of-leave system, and the substitution of notification to Discharged Prisoners' Societies, in which figure the Salvation Army, the establishment of a central association for giving effect to this and other provisions, more or less in the direction of bringing voluntary agencies under the ultimate control of the State.

And yet there is one gleam of hope in what the General and his brave army of officers have brought on to the arena of social endeavour. He has shown what sanctified passion is capable of doing and undoing. It is still the paramount power when the task is the regeneration of the individual. If that fails, then nothing in heaven or earth can succeed. An officer in the Salvation Army, whom the General was questioning as to the failure of his Corps, had tried everything and failed. "Did you ever try tears?" said the old man. The young man had not.

But officers as a rule know how to weep and work, and man for man they are a wonderful combination of devotion, compassion, and practicality.[93]

Nicol's final paragraph labelled the Scheme a "failure":

THE FAILURE OF THE SOCIAL SCHEME. From an economic standpoint the social experiment of the Salvation Army stands condemned almost root and branch. "So much the worse for economics," the average Salvation Army officer will reply. Perhaps. But at the end of twenty years the Army cannot point to one single cause of social distress that it has removed or to one single Act which it has promoted that has dealt a death-blow at one social evil. Its work has been purely of the nature of the ambulance, and God forbid that I should raise so much as a little finger against all that it has done and is doing in that respect. I have lost a considerable amount of faith since I ceased to be a Salvationist in the value of voluntary effort. Prevention is better than cure. The amazing revelations of the Royal Commission on the Poor Law demonstrate that fact in a negative manner, and until a good part of the Minority Report is given fair play in actual practice, we shall not be able to adequately realize the full force of the old saw that prevention is better than cure. We are still babes at the business of saving men, women, and children. We have stamped out certain diseases which periodically turned London into a mortuary, and we have done much to awaken the public conscience to the science of moral salvation (and the Army has done more in this respect than any other Christian organization). But the General would show himself the true statesman if he manfully told the world that his social scheme has not got to close quarters with the evils which he set out to demolish. By doing so he will eventually raise himself higher in the public estimation, and what is of far more consequence, clear the atmosphere of a lot of maudlin sentiment as to the character of the work upon which he and others are engaged, and help to point the way to another and more effective treatment of the social disease.[94]

Perhaps Booth's great scheme must be adjudged a failure in terms of his high hopes and ambitions for changing the face of Britain, and even of the world. Booth's vision was always longer than his reach, but that does not mean that his vision was mistaken. To transform human society into heaven on earth, and he desired nothing less, was always going to be beyond the power of the Salvation Army. Another hundred years of governmental and non-governmental effort have not achieved that ideal. Booth and his Army can at least be given credit for trying, and for the degree of success accorded what was after all a small, poor, ill-equipped religious sect.

93. Nicol, *General Booth*, 203–11.
94. Nicol, Ibid., 375–76.

9

Social Work 2: Out of Darkest England

"Why all this apparatus of temples and meeting houses to save men from perdition in a world which is to come, while never . . . stretching out to save them from the inferno of their present life?"[1]

—William Booth

SOCIAL WORK OUTSIDE BRITAIN

Social work in a number of overseas territories pre-dated the Darkest England scheme, so the work in other countries had a momentum of its own. Nevertheless, there were flow-on effects internationally, with some cross-pollination of ideas and personnel, and consequently, in most countries where the Salvation Army operated, it rapidly became known as a social work agency as well as an evangelical mission. The field is too large for detailed reporting, but examples may be cited simply to demonstrate its scope.

The winter of 1890–1891 was particularly severe on continental Europe so a number of facilities were established to meet exceptional need. In France shelters and kitchens cared for thousands. Shelters were opened in Holland when it was found that tramps had frozen to death in the parks. In Sweden, an existing shelter for men was joined in 1892 by two more food and shelter depots in Stockholm—one equipped with a Turkish bath also used by the local police. Wood-chopping provided work. In 1905 the Army took over an old prison at Göteborg. In Norway similar work began in 1893, in Belgium in 1894, in Denmark in 1895 and in Germany in 1904.[2]

In the United States of America, "low-cost lodging houses" for men and women were opened in New York in 1891, followed shortly by others across the country. Commander and Mrs Booth-Tucker pushed social work from their appointment in 1896.

---

1. Booth, *In Darkest England*, 16.
2. Sandall, *History*, III, 114–17.

Industrial homes and household salvage schemes set up at that time set a pattern still in operation in the States. Land colonies were also established in several places in the mid-west in 1898. H. Rider Haggard, an advocate for the "back to the land" movement, was asked by the British government to report on these in 1905 and found them successful and the colonists happy.[3] Unfortunately the Army suffered considerable financial losses with high interest rates on borrowed money and drought years, and the three settlements were closed down soon afterwards. Shelters in Canada began in 1893, before which the basement of Toronto Temple Corps provided food and lodging for vagrants.

In South Africa the Army set up a city colony "Social Reform Brigade" in 1894 with rescue homes for white women and in 1896 a shelter for white men in Cape Town, and in five other centers by 1899. A social farm was opened at Rondebosch in 1893 and one at Driefontein in 1898, and later a prison-gate home and farm at Fairview. These were not for British Colonists—or for Africans.[4]

Australia was in severe depression in the 1890s; the Army opened a free labor bureau next to the prison-gate home in Melbourne in 1890, and fed unemployed men—552 meals on the first day. Similar facilities were provided in Sydney and Adelaide. As the situation grew worse, people from the country flocked to the city for help, and those from the city were heading into the country (rail passes provided by the government), or to the goldfields. Families were dispersed, women turned to prostitution, and babies were abandoned.[5] Model farms were set up in Victoria, New South Wales and Queensland. The basement of the Sydney barracks was opened for accommodation in 1893. Shelters were opened in Sydney, Melbourne and Brisbane. Hostels, Metropoles, and People's Palaces (cheap family hotels) followed. The same pattern took place in New Zealand.

In Java, Dutch East Indies, the Army was asked to take over responsibility for shelters set up after devastating floods in Semarang in 1902. With others established elsewhere, these became "beggars' colonies" in which the inmates undertook industries such as making coconut matting and preparing bamboo for building material.

In Colombo, Ceylon, the government and city council asked the Army to provide accommodation, healthcare and work for a beggar-population of about 1,200 in 1913. Success with this led to the scheme being extended to Bombay in 1920.[6] In the Punjab a project for helping dispossessed farm-laborers was initiated by Booth-Tucker when he acquired 2,000 acres of derelict land from the government and set up "Shantinagar" (Village of Peace) in 1916. The agreement was that when the Army had finished paying off the land over thirty years it would become the property of the colonists. This was finally achieved in 1948, by which time 3,000 people lived there. Other farm colonies were established in other parts of India.

Harry Andrews (already mentioned as an adoptee of Emma Booth) began an amateur dispensary in a bathroom in Nagercoil in 1893, later taking a medical degree in Chicago. He was also instrumental in attracting to India another medically qualified officer, Percy Turner who served twenty-one years at Nagercoil from 1900, while Andrews

---

3. Haggard also wrote up a report on the Army's social work in Great Britain in 1910, *Regeneration*.
4. Murdoch, *Soldiers of the Cross*, 131.
5. Bolton, *Booth's Drum*, 122–26.
6. Sandall, *History*, III, 130–31.

established hospitals at Anand and Moradabad. Eventually there were twenty-three Salvation Army hospitals and clinics in India. Other general hospitals were established by the Army in Australia, Canada, the USA, and Japan, what is now Indonesia, and later again in Central Africa. Maternity hospitals were set up in many other countries.

In more recent years the Army's involvement in medical work has come under extreme pressure. In western countries—Britain, North America and Australasia—the Army's hospitals have nearly all closed down or been sold. In developing nations the cost of keeping up with technology and maintaining the supply of qualified personnel has become prohibitive. As help for the poorer patients was dependent on making some profit from tending the richer, inability to keep up with the latest medical technology affected the viability of hospitals because those who could afford it went elsewhere. Some years ago the decision was taken in principle that the Salvation Army would concentrate on primary health care, which would be at grass-roots level and cost less. Whatever the virtues of this policy, it has met, as might be expected, with local resistance and distress, most notoriously in the case of Howard Hospital in Zimbabwe. There, in eighteen years' service, a Canadian officer-doctor, Paul Thistle, had successfully attracted sustainable financial support to maintain a surgical practice along with an extensive community health service. Unfortunately, after protracted disagreement with headquarters over the treatment of donations the Thistles were given two days to leave the country, and dismissed from their officership by their home territory, with serious repercussions for local health care.[7] They continue to be Salvationists and to work in Zimbabwe, but for another mission.

The magnitude and variety of Salvation Army social work internationally rapidly became too great to describe within these pages. An international social work conference was convened in London in 1911 and its papers published in 1912 as "Principles of Social Work."[8] To give an idea of the range of operations, papers were read on Unity of Operations; Indian Criminal Tribes; Savage Babies [the babies referred to were *British*]; Canadian Prison Work; Small Holdings; Hospital Finance; Saving Young Australia; American City Nurseries; Child Emigration; Sweaters and Sweated; Javan Leper Cleansing; God's Searchlight Work [personal interviewing]; Homing English Women; Restoring the Inebriate; Catching London Boys; Inspiring Outcasts; Filling Up Canada; The After-Care of Women; English Long-Timers (recidivist criminals); Norway's Aged Poor; Slum Mothers; Caring for Slum Babies; Spiritual Standards; Women Convicts; Salvation in the Shelter.

Another such conference, in 1921, was attended by representatives from twenty-six countries. Papers were read on Training; Prohibition in the USA; Co-operation with Governments and other organizations; Spiritual aims and results in social work; the development of character in young officers; Spiritual work in the People's Palace; Social work amongst the natives of South Africa; Seasonal Social Work; Children's Shelters; Prison populations; Relationship with the Press; the Criminal Tribes of India; Social

---

7. http://www.newzimbabwe.com/news-10621-Protests+doctor+finds+new+job,+church/news.aspx. 20 March 2013. See also Tina Ivany, *Cry for Chiweshe* (2017), available on Amazon.

8. A further collection of the papers from the 1911 International Social Conference was published in 1917.

problems in China; Lepers and Leper Work; Children of the East; Relief work for the blind in India; Agriculture and the training of boys and girls; Juvenile Offenders and Detention Homes; Work amongst boys in Australia; Social Finance; Tuberculosis—the fight in Japan; the Widow's Counsellor; Hospital Work; Colony for Inebriates; Prison Work and After-Care; work amongst girls; Prisoners in Canada; Candidates and Social Work; Discharged Prisoners in Switzerland; Migration Work.[9]

To pick up on one or two examples from the 1921 conference topics, however:

The "Criminal Tribes of India" provide a fascinating case study. These groups were originally nomadic traders but finding themselves under increasing pressure in a depressed economy and amongst closer settlement arising from the extension of roads and railways, some allegedly turned to crime. The Criminal Tribes Act of 1871 branded them collectively as criminals and gave the authorities power to place them in reformatory settlements. On his two visits to India in the early and mid–1890s, William Booth lobbied Indian government officials to approve and fund Salvation Army settlements for these people. It was not until 1908 that the government of the United Provinces suggested the Army might begin working with the tribe known as the Doms. In subsequent years numerous other settlements were established for various groups, in Madras, South India, and Bengal.

Booth-Tucker's presentation on this subject was perhaps cast in the most favorable light, with the initial hesitations of the tribes-people large overcome by the kindness of the Salvationists—apart from the recalcitrance of a tribe "of Mohammedans of a very bigoted type"—and in one place a group "of 1,800 people, all calling themselves Salvationists . . . a happy, God-fearing community," refused to leave the Army's care when legally their supervision was no longer required.[10] Eason's research and papers by some Indian academics have indicated that everything did not always go so smoothly and a good deal of coercion was involved at times though less so than in the government's own establishments.[11] Eason concludes

> While The Salvation Army, along with the LMS, the SPG and the Wesleyan Methodists, may have forged a cozy relationship with governments in the reclamation of the criminal tribes, they paid a price for their involvement in this kind of work . . . tribes people not only resented their confinement but often resisted the efforts of Salvationists to evangelize them. These circumstances led more than one officer to question the spiritual possibilities of such an enterprise . . . In the process . . . they became agents of an imperial regime, helping to enforce legislation that was both repressive and Draconian.[12]

The "Colony for Inebriates" described in *Social Problems in Solution* was the island of Kurön, near Stockholm, Sweden, bought by the Army for this purpose in 1911. The article quoted the island's medical officer as ascribing its success to four factors: (1) its isolation; (2) the Salvation Army organization, discipline and trained staff; (3) its Christian spirit (although there is no attempt at proselytizing); (4) the leadership of one man

---

9. Salvation Army, *Social Problems in Solution*.
10. *Social Problems in Solution*, 129, 133.
11. Eason, "Christianity in a Colonial Age," 313–31.
12. Eason, Ibid., 330–31.

rather than a committee. It operated at a loss, because although the government contributed two kroner per day per man, the Army had declined registration under which the authorities would pay much more but would also sentence men to it for a fixed period.

In this the Swedish experiment differed from the New Zealand model, on Pakatoa and Rotoroa islands in the Hauraki Gulf, reported on at the 1911 conference. Pakatoa came first in 1907, and was reserved for women inebriates after the men were moved to the larger Rotoroa nearby in 1908. In New Zealand the Army was asked by the government to provide accommodation after the passage of the Habitual Drunkards Act in 1906 provided the machinery but no place for incarceration.[13] While the four factors mentioned in connection with Kurön island also applied in the case of Rotoroa, there was therefore a coercive element involved from the beginning, with greater government funding to make the place sustainable. Administration was by the Salvation Army but on behalf of the Justice department. As in Sweden, and in fact everywhere at the time, alcoholism was perceived as a moral and spiritual failing rather than a physical illness, so isolation and the gospel were the only treatment available.

With increasing recognition of the pathology of alcoholism in the post-World War Two era, New Zealand was fortunate to have as chief secretary for nine years Colonel Bramwell Cook, who had served as chief medical officer of the Emery hospital, Anand, India from 1932 to 1953. In the late 1950s, he instituted a new medical and spiritual model of treatment, initiating the "Bridge" program into which Rotoroa Island work was absorbed in 1980. Appointed to Sydney as Territorial Commander in 1963, Cook brought about similar changes in the Australia Eastern Territory's work.[14]

In some territories, local circumstances led to the Salvation Army's entering such specialized fields as education. In Newfoundland (at that time not yet a province of Canada) the difficulties met by Salvationists trying to enroll their children at existing schools, all church-run, led to the Army's setting up its own school system in 1898. It maintained up to a peak of ninety schools until integrating with those of other protestant churches in 1969. The encouragement of colonial governments led to the Army's establishing schools in some other countries—a peak of 226 schools in Rhodesia in 1965 (and still sixty-five in Zimbabwe today after changes in government policy led to many being taken over by local councils) and 50 in Zambia. Many other African territories also maintain schools and some are significant providers in the field: Kenya West had 466 and Kenya East 346 schools in 2015. The Army in the Democratic Republic of the Congo has 366 and the six Indian territories between them run nearly 200 schools. Internationally the movement claims 963 kindergartens, 2,015 primary schools, 1,114 secondary schools, seventy vocational training centers and eleven colleges and universities.[15] As with the Army's medical services, its schools have contributed significantly

---

13. Hutson, *Set Free*, 29.

14. Bramwell Cook OF, K-i-H, CMG, BA, MD, FRCS, MRCP, FRACS, DTM&H was probably unique in retiring as a TC and Lieut. Commissioner after a career comprising just three appointments. He then took up medicine again, retiring for a second time in 1983 at the age of 80. Cook, *White Gujaratis*, 212.

15. *Salvation Army Year Book*, 2016, 30.

to the expansion of its membership in Africa and Asia as their alumni have taken their places in the growing middle classes of developing nations.

It is now almost a foregone conclusion that in the case of emergency or disaster, the Salvation Army will fly in a team for relief work, for example after the earthquake in El Salvador in 1986, or after the Rwandan genocide in 1994, or the Bosnian conflict in the mid-1990s, or after the invasion of Iraq in 2003, and the Indian Ocean tsunami in 2004, to mention but a few. An international emergency services coordinator is based at IHQ.

Of course, these few examples of "salvation with its sleeves rolled up" cannot do justice to the great range and depth of work still undertaken by what is in world terms a relatively small organization, chronically underfunded in most areas of its activity, and made possible by the continuing sacrifice and devotion of many of its workers.

THE EFFECT OF THE 'DARKEST ENGLAND' SCHEME ON THE SALVATION ARMY ITSELF

We are changed by what we do, a principle underlying a number of therapeutic models, or as Louis Sullivan's classic design formula has it, "form follows function." The same is true for movements and institutions. In addition to the impact of *In Darkest England* on its intended targets, on the denizens of the submerged tenth and on wider society, the scheme's effect on the Salvation Army itself was perhaps as significant and long-lasting. This section looks at six areas in which that effect is still felt.

A New Lease of Life and Reputation

Firstly, it gave the Salvation Army a new lease of life and a new reputation. Norman Murdoch, in examining the background and influences which led William Booth to promote his Darkest England scheme, pointed out that "Each time Booth made a new beginning it came as a result of a block to advancement, seldom admitted, but always apparent to an astute observer. Progress for him was never a straight line. In his march to glory, glory was often less his goal than personal or organizational survival."[16] While not imputing any devious motive to the Founder, or proposing that it was a desperate measure to save the day, we can acknowledge Darkest England as an example of that leading principle enunciated by Catherine Booth—the "adaptation of measures."[17] Indeed, former Commissioner Alexander Nicol, who worked at the center of the Army's counsels during these years, recalled that

> The fact is, the organization was beginning to stagnate. The interest in its methods had begun to wane. The cessation of persecution had left it without a theme for exciting public sympathy. Attendance was down. Soul-saving was down. The membership was a most fluctuating quantity, and the Army was hampered financially. The dramatic introduction of a new policy with the bold challenge that the Army Chief would, if the money were forthcoming, eventually rid England

---

16. Murdoch, "William Booth's Darkest England: A Reappraisal," 109.
17. Catherine Booth, "Adaptation of Measures," in *Papers on Aggressive Christianity*, 43–60.

of pauperism, and establish a system that would stamp out the evils of the casual ward and drain our social morass of its pestilential parasites, was seriously accepted by a section of the public. The Army itself was wildly enthusiastic about it. It revived the spirits of the organization.[18]

That new lease of life derived in part from the whole new respect and appreciation the Salvation Army began to enjoy as a result of the new scheme. Of course the Movement had been "serving suffering humanity" before this. Social redemption was part of its DNA, as far back as the teen-age Booth's efforts to rehabilitate an old beggar-woman in Nottingham, and the Army was already engaged in a range of social work long before the scheme's announcement. The sheer scale of the new proposals captured the public imagination however and, despite inevitable criticism, the Army never looked back. Its reputation henceforth would derive more from this than from any other aspect of its ministry. Indeed, it has become commonplace for Salvationists in some places to bemoan the fact that the Army is recognized only as a social agency rather than as a "Church"—and some have the grace to be embarrassed by the appreciation with which their vicarious good works are acknowledged.

Booth himself was perceptive on this point. When addressing delegates to the International Social Council of 1911, he reflected on how things had gone: "We have not realized all our expectations, nor fulfilled all our dreams. It was not to be expected that we should. This is an imperfect world . . . "

> Nevertheless, and not withstanding all our shortcomings, the position now occupied by our social operations, and the influenced exercised by them . . . is in evidence in every continent and on every hand.
>
> There is no doubt that the world, as a whole, feels much of the admiration and gratitude which the press lavished upon me on my recent birthday [his 82nd]—admiration which was assuredly intended not only for myself, but for the Army as a whole, and not only for the Army as a whole, but for its social workers in particular . . . [19]

A New Structure: the Social Wing

Secondly, in "saving" it, and making its name great, the scheme also altered the structure of the Salvation Army, establishing a new entity within its ranks. In part, this was occasioned by the need for public accountability; with the creation of the Darkest England Trust in January 1891 so that donors could be assured that their money was doing that for which they had given it. This, along with the multiplication of institutions for social work, created a whole new "wing" of the movement. Instead of social work being a minor operation on the side, it became equal in scope to the field work. While there was naturally already a degree of separation in the administration of the evangelical and the limited social work of the organization before 1890, the expansion of the latter consolidated and entrenched this demarcation. With the greatly increased number of

---

18. Nicol, *General Booth*, 192–93.
19. Booth, *International Social Council Addresses*, 20.

officers engaged (of whom several hundred were soon transferred to "social"), social work became virtually a separate career path with, in some cases, separate training. The majority of officers would spend much or in many cases all of their careers in either field or social service—and sometimes "social" bore a second-class officer stigma.

This was not perhaps what had been hoped for originally. According to Alex Nicol, Bramwell Booth's own earlier vision for the Army's social work had been an integrated, soldier-based activity, an incarnational ministry:

> He [Bramwell Booth] formed the idea in those days of subduing black patches of our city life by the sheer moral and sweetening influences of clean, happy, self-denying Christians who should voluntarily come out of their ordinary homes and go down and actually live amongst the poor and degraded.
>
> In company with the writer he wandered about the slums of South London night after night studying the habits, customs, and character of the occupiers of squalid and overcrowded tenements, dilapidated rookeries, and blind, dismal alleys. An article followed in the *War Cry*, giving a word-vision of this neglected London, and calling for the consecration of the followers of the Friend of Sinners to save the people.
>
> He dreamed of a nether London honeycombed with sanctified fathers and mothers, living the Christ life among the hovels of the poor and the black localities of vice by day, and preaching the Gospel at night. A beautiful dream, inspired by an idealism far, far beyond the matter-of-fact Christianity of modern days and even the predisposition of the Salvationist to suffer for Christ's sake.
>
> . . . it is interesting that at a period in the evolution of the social idea of the Army and before the Darkest England Scheme was as much as dreamt of, Mr. Bramwell Booth, the Chief of the Staff, was endeavoring to grapple with that problem of all problems, how to Christianize the heathen of England by the force of moral example, and by holy and self-sacrificing men and women living, not occasionally visiting, but actually living in the slums.[20]

Apart from the setting up of "Slum Posts" (which were superseded by other measures), Bramwell Booth's original vision of an integrated mission did not eventuate; other voices carried the day. Any alternative to a more institutional approach would in any case have been very difficult to bring about at that time when institutional structures were the expected norm and sheer logistics would have overwhelmed the available help.

The tension between models of service is hinted at in a letter to *The Times* written on 29th December after the resignation of Commissioner Frank Smith and reprinted in *The War Cry* of 3rd January 1891. William Booth indicated that "Smith had not been left so free and independent in his actions as he wished . . . it is remembered that this department would have to work in harmony with divisional commands throughout the country . . . "[21] The immediate source of disagreement was over where the accounts should be kept—within the social headquarters or by the general headquarters—and Smith realized that the hand holding the purse-strings also decided the policies. Here was to be discerned a cloud no larger than a man's hand. The way the scheme eventually developed nevertheless led to almost separate Armies or parallel universes; field and

---

20. Nicol, *General Booth*, 295–97.
21. Fairbank, *Booth's Boots*, 137.

social departments in every territory worked almost independently until administrative changes almost a century later enabled their re-integration.

The changing relationship can be illustrated from the United States where the Booth-Tuckers began implementing the social scheme more vigorously in the later 1890s. Lillian Taiz quotes 1898 correspondence from the national social secretary Colonel R. E. Holz complaining that he was "merely a 'figurehead,' ignored by both the district and NHQ [National Headquarters]." "Every Divisional Officer looks upon the Social Work in his Division as his own affair, and resents any interference on the part of the National Social Secretary." However, in 1904 the United States Salvation Army "strengthened centralized authority, shifting responsibility from the CDOs [Chief Divisional officers] to the hands of social officers who answered directly to NHQ." Resentment now flowed the opposite direction: Colonel French, leader of the Pacific Coast Province for example, complained that the "relieving of the Provincial Officer of the responsibility of the Social means his being totally ignored by the officers of the Social Department" and also threatened the financial stability of the province.[22] That last comment suggests that whatever the intention, social finances were difficult to corral under a joint command.

Over the years, the Salvation Army has oscillated between these two solutions to the administrative relationship between evangelism and welfare. Its headquarters in most territories in the later twentieth century were restructured firstly by integrating men's and women's social departments and then by replacing separate field and social administrations with a tri-partite personnel, program, business–administration structure. This finally dismantled the system set in place internationally by the Darkest England scheme. The falling out of fashion of institutional care except for a few specialist areas, at least in most Western societies, has also contributed to the beginnings of a re-integration of social and field work. In New Zealand the majority of corps now exercise what is dubbed a "community and family ministry," often including such services as food banks and budgeting services. The task of truly integrating the "church" community and the "client" community is, however, an on-going challenge, especially where professional expertise is required in serving the latter group.

Some specialist areas, such as addiction rehabilitation programs, retain a separate national management. In territories where social work is answerable to divisional commanders, headquarters national "consultants" for that work sometimes struggle to establish and maintain consistent policies and professional practices in social services across a territory, while having to carry the judgement of the divisional commanders. Conversely, in the case of "nationally managed" specialist programs not answerable to divisional commanders, the work is less integrated and unified in approach, and there can be problems inherent in overlapping authorities. The administrative pendulum in the Australia Eastern territory swung back again in 2015, with all social work being removed from divisional jurisdiction and entrusted to a team based at territorial headquarters.

Irrespective of the system of governance adopted, there is also the matter of what happens at the grass roots. William Booth nevertheless long entertained hopes that

---

22. Taiz, *Hallelujah Lads & Lasses*, 125.

Salvationists in general might embrace his vision, becoming not only soul-winners but social workers as well.

> In this great expedition, though I am starting for territory which is familiar enough, I am, in a sense, entering an unknown land. My people will be new at it. We have trained our soldiers to the saving of souls, we have taught them Knee-drill, we have instructed them in the art and mystery of dealing with the consciences and hearts of men; and that will ever continue the main business of their lives ... But the new sphere on which we are entering will call for faculties other than those which we have hitherto cultivated, and for knowledge of a different character; and those who have these gifts, and who are possessed of this practical information, will be sorely needed.[23]

Even in 1904, he was still casting that vision:

> And I see that Citadel (Corps) is not only a house of prayer and a Battery of Salvation, but a centre of every conceivable humanizing and spiritualizing influence and activity ... [24]

However, the Salvation Army has struggled to coordinate its evangelical and social outreach, not only at administrative level but also at delivery level. With social work left to the specialists, and increasingly institutionalized with the Darkest England scheme, it became ever more remote from the lives and experience of the rank-and-file soldiers and officers engaged in corps work. There were always those who resisted this tendency and sought to preserve Booth's integrated vision. Lt. Colonel Alida Bosshardt, who ran the Amsterdam Goodwill Centre 1948–78, would have "no social work without the involvement of Soldier Volunteers for in Bosshardt's view they were the bearers of the Army's identity as they embodied both sides of its mission." "If we don't preach the gospel anymore," she said, "we might as well hand over the lot to an undenominational organization."[25]

Differing responses are found in various contexts. Vassili Joannides recorded an officer addressing young people gathered in Youth Councils in Sweden: "As a soldier of the Salvation Army, you must be involved in our social work. How can you pretend that you are a faithful soldier and that you love your neighbor if you do not participate in soup distribution?"[26] He also described his corps commanding officer at Paris Coeur de Vey asking him to report on his social work volunteering (it had involved assisting a teenager with home-work) while the officer's spouse recorded his answers in an official log. Discussion with the French territorial commander, however, revealed that it was evidently a problem that white French Salvationists were reluctant contributors to social; programs: "They separate their everyday life and their religious life. They do not want to be involved in the social work of the church."[27]

---

23. Booth, *Darkest England*, 283–84.
24. Quoted by Wiseman, "Call to Renewal and Change," in Waldron, *Creed and Deed*, 284–85.
25. Harm and Polman, "Leger des Heils" in *Vrij Nederland*, 25 December 1982, 39, quoted by Bollinger in "A Dynamic Courtship," 342.
26. Joannides, "Accountability and Ethnicity," 243.
27. Joannides, Ibid, 248, 290.

As Salvationists rose in the social scale, they sometimes became less interested in attempting, and less able to attempt, to integrate the clients from social work into their communities of faith. This contributed to the phenomenon of "Goodwill Corps" in Britain (now re-absorbed into the Field), ARC (Adult Rehabilitation Centre), Harbor Light (addiction services) and now Kroc Centre corps in the United States, or the Bridge Recovery Churches (linked to addiction services) in New Zealand, in some cases quite separate from the ordinary Salvation Army "church" communities.

Such initiatives have at times actually brought the Army round full circle to Booth's early comment that when he referred his converts to the churches, (1) they didn't want to go; (2) the churches wouldn't have them; (3) he needed them himself.[28] Only now, it was the "citadels" and "fortresses" which took on the role of the "churches" and the social centers the task of the "Army." I recall a New Zealand Salvationist expressing disquiet at the number of "social cases" beginning to attend her large, traditional corps: "——— corps is supposed to be a "Good-Will Corps" isn't it? Why don't these people go there and leave the citadel to us?"[29] Booth once commented that he wanted to stretch his arms around both rich and poor, but found it difficult to reach far enough; perhaps sometimes his Army has a similar problem. Fortunately others still shared Booth's vision.

Over the course of some eighteen years to 2007, Dr Ian Campbell, initially coordinating the Salvation Army's response to the international AIDS/HIV epidemic and working as IHQ medical advisor and later as international health program consultant, inspired, recruited and helped resource people committed to integrated mission in all parts of the globe, and especially in the developing world. Counter-intuitively for a "top-down," hierarchical organization, this corps-based work was premised on the need to listen first to what local communities said about their needs, the solutions they proposed, and then at what further assistance could be offered. Endorsing a document on "exploring the theological roots to integrated mission" in 2005, the then international secretary for program resources, Commissioner Donald Odegaard, referred to this as a "call to return to our roots as a movement of faith, whilst embracing some of the relatively new practices that our current and future 'mission in community' requires."[30]

In a recent book, Dean Pallant explores developments in what used to be called "medical missionary" work, of which the flagships were once large hospitals.[31] He outlines how Salvation Army health services in the developing world have been forced by financial, technological, clinical, and personnel constraints to move increasingly from the institutional, hospital model to a community-based primary-care clinic model. Pallant makes a strong plea that this be intentionally faith-based, linked with and provided for by corps, with local Salvationists involved in ministry. He warns against the condescending, "instrumental" attitude "which manifests itself in congregations wanting to 'do something' about the plight of 'the poor' rather than commit to deep relationships

---

28. Booth, "How We Began," in Railton, *Twenty-One Years Salvation Army*, 22–23.

29. This was a curious allusion, in that "Good-Will Corps" were not a phenomenon found in New Zealand but the speaker was evidently familiar with the concept and would have preferred that "social cases" attended a corps other than her own.

30. Odegaard, letter dated 12 January 2006.

31. Pallant, *Keeping Faith in Faith-Based Organizations*.

with people."[32] Of course, integrating this work with corps does not, alas, ensure that those involved in providing services will be free from "instrumental" and patronizing attitudes, but it must be hoped that training and oversight help avert these difficulties. Ideally, this recaptures the vision of the integrated ministry of soul-winners-cum-social workers, living where they minister, proposed by Bramwell Booth in the 1880s and enunciated by William Booth in 1890 and 1904, but effectively negated by the separatist, institutional model which emerged from In Darkest England. International Salvation Army policy now promotes integrated ministry to the extent that the success of "strategies to connect and integrate spiritual and social ministry" is included amongst areas for mandatory triennial reporting by territories to International Headquarters.[33]

Fund-Raising: the triumph of Public Relations

Thirdly, the setting up of a capital-intensive program meant greatly expanded appeals for public support required to maintain it—fund-raising, or "Public Relations," on an unprecedented scale. This also influenced the ethos and practices of the Salvation Army in ways still evident. The Army's relationship with funding providers—individual, commercial, institutional and governmental—remains fraught with both opportunities and hazards.

Eason comments on the fact that the Army re-invented itself after 1890—being no longer at odds with the establishment, but rather cultivating it, partly in order to gain publicity and donations to its funds. From being a figure of mockery or derision, William Booth became in his old age a revered elder statesman. This happened abroad even before it became true of England. In Australia, the Army received huge official and public support from the mid–1880s. In New Zealand, Booth's visits were greeted with great crowds in the streets; he was accorded meetings with the Premier and was hosted by the Chief Justice in the early 1890s and on his subsequent visits.[34] It was 1904 before Booth was invited to Buckingham Palace for an audience with King Edward VII.

"Beware when all men speak well of you" was applicable to the Army by the turn of the century. In her address to the 1921 international social conference, Commissioner Adelaide Cox spoke on "Co-operation with Governments and Other Organizations." While alert to the advantages, she drew attention to the dangers involved in accepting support and financial aid:

1. *Having a say.* Sometimes when people give us grants, they expect to have a voice in the management of the work for which the grant is given . . .

2. *Having a bigger say.* Sometimes those who offer us a grant desire to come into our private councils . . . to the point of telling us . . . to what extent we may influence them in spiritual things . . .[35]

32. Pallant, Ibid., 165.
33. Territorial Annual Report and Triennial Review Document.
34. Booth also sought to reconcile those two estranged dignitaries: Bradwell, *Fight the Good Fight*, 64–66.
35. *Social Problems in Solution*, 39–41. Ironically, General André Cox's reforms of governance now propose the intentional invitation to non-Salvationists "to have a say."

Such concerns were even then in their infancy; Cox might have added the danger of contributing to them even by wanting the "best" for the Army. I remember a public relations secretary justifying a misleading statement in a video prepared for fundraising on television by saying, "Well, that's what the public think we do, so that's what we're telling them." The need for funding always lays siege to strict truthfulness; even back in 1911 Nicol was pleading for more integrity in the presentation of the Army's statistics.[36] The slippery slope steepens imperceptibly. Much depends upon who are the gate-keepers for promotion; the spin-doctors or the practitioners at the coal face.

Inseparable from fund-raising is advertising. Arnold Brown and KMP's brilliant and successful "For God's sake care, give us a pound" campaign in Britain in the late 1960s was ground-breaking, but still subject to hostile media comment and analysis long after, as in Chris Wolmar's "For God's Sake Pay" article in the *New Statesman* more than a decade later.[37] Interestingly, Evangeline Booth had penned the precursor of KMP's 1967 slogan back in 1914: "Pity all you like, but for God's sake give!"[38] Her memorable line, "There is no reward equal to that of doing the most good to the most people in the most need," in its more recent truncation to simply "Doing the most good!" has been represented as charitable one-upmanship and invited accusations of hubris by critics. However, Winston Churchill's "Where there's a need, there's the Salvation Army" was adopted with great success, as was "The Army of the Helping Hand," attributed to King George V.[39] Not all Salvation Army advertising has the flair of these examples and sometimes graphically depicts the relationship between provider and recipient of services as one of patronage and dependency. At the worst, this represents a disempowering reality.

A major long-term consequence of the Darkest England scheme is that in some countries the greatest part of the Salvation Army's funding comes from government, although the Army's financial reporting and public relations spin have not always been frank in this regard. This was far from what Booth envisaged. While alive to both benefits and dangers of government grants, he was careful to say that

> No Social Work must be undertaken (except under very extraordinary circumstances, and then only with the consent of International Headquarters) which has to be sustained by any Government grant, the continuance of which is uncertain. If this principle is departed from, you will be likely to find yourselves left with enterprises upon your hands involving large expenditure of money, for which the income which led you to their initiation has been withdrawn.
>
> It is not enough to say that the obligation is such that you can abandon the effort should the income be withdrawn. In many cases the probable result will be that a real work of mercy is in progress, in which instance although your arrangement will allow you to withdraw from it, your heart will rebel against it. Therefore you must look carefully ahead when any offers of this description are made to you.[40]

36. Nicol, *General Booth*, 195.
37. Wolmar, "For God's Sake, Pay," 20–21.
38. *War Cry* (USA) October 31, 1914, cited by Norris and Beverly Magnuson, *Salvation in the Slums*, 264.
39. *Horsham Times*, 3 September 1935, 4.
40. Booth, "The Relation of Social Work to Governments," 85–86.

June Milligan's 1982 analysis of the situation in the United Kingdom summed up the change:

> From the situation in William Booth's day when he criticized the State's provision of care, such as it was, and sought to organize a complete welfare system based on Salvation Army principles, the Salvation Army has become, in terms of its social services, little more than an adjunct to the State system.[41]

While this may be too sweeping a generalization it is true that as the state in many jurisdictions began to intervene more intentionally to mitigate poverty and avert the dangers inherent in social and economic inequalities by developing various forms of "welfare state," the role of the voluntary sector including the Salvation Army, became one of plugging gaps. Some wondered whether charities would become redundant under these circumstances. General Orsborn, responding to this trend in the 1940s, rejected that assumption:

> It is a fallacy to assume that in a socially highly developed society there would be no room left for the Salvation Army. The contrary is proved. In countries where governments have implemented far-reaching social measures, the supplementary services of the Army are appreciated all the more. The Army asks itself: what is necessary, what has to be done; how can the Army place itself in the service of society and the country in which it operates, and depending on the answer the social services will be organized and performed.[42]

The American Donald Kettl has characterized groups which have become default public service organizations to government as "proxy-organizations" or "proxies," enjoying preferential status when it comes to appropriating government resources, but running the risk of competing policy goals and putting their own identities at risk.[43] Dennis Garland, then Salvation Army Consultant on Homeless Persons, Employment and Youth Ministries in Sydney, echoed Adelaide Cox's 1921 warning in his thesis on the "apparent colonization of the Army's policy positions" . . . "by government and society at the expense of its own Christian beliefs and internal rhetoric."[44] His point was that we are shaped by the discourse we adopt. The temptation is to adopt the discourse of our funders—he who pays the piper calls the tune. General Clarence Wiseman once warned:

> It is conceivable that the Army might be pressured to get involved with well-funded new forms of social service, notwithstanding the fact that others might be better equipped to handle the job, and even more important, that the new demand might drain off personnel and/or other resources from already over-taxed services for the poor, the handicapped, the alienated and the fallen.[45]

Where the bulk of the Army's funding for addictions treatment for example is from the government, as it is in New Zealand, that reality can have implications for what we

---

41. Milligan, "The Persistence of The Salvation Army," 229.
42. Spaan, *De Vreedzame Strijd*, 100–101, cited in Bollinger, "Dynamic Courtship," 105.
43. Kettl, *Government by Proxy*, 1–19, cited in Bollinger, Ibid., 28–29.
44. Garland, "The Salvation Army and the State of Welfare," iii.
45. Wiseman, "Call to Renewal and Change," in Waldron, *Creed and Deed*, 280.

are prepared to do: there can be an unwillingness to undertake services which will not attract such funding. For example, where government policy is to encourage short-term, non-residential treatment for addicts, and that is what it will fund, accommodation for older, chronic-relapsing alcoholics needing "time out" can be allowed to fall into disrepair and eventually close, although the need for such a service remains. On a happier note, the Army's addiction services in New Zealand have responded magnificently to an appeal from a notorious gang to help its members with methamphetamine addiction, when no other agency would accept the challenge.[46] And, mercifully, financial vulnerability has not inhibited the Salvation Army's social policy and parliamentary unit in the same country from speaking out on public and government policy when necessary, so that government, media and public tend to pay attention when it speaks.

Commentators on charity in the United States speculated on the likely impact of the huge Kroc donation (totaling $1.8 billion) on the Salvation Army itself; whether it could staff and service the community centers projected without suffering major changes to its own ethos. Certainly the new mega-institutions, twenty-six of them by late 2014, are going well, but the Army is inevitably different because of their advent. A recent report noted the economic halo effect of the centers, indicating that the largest economic effect in the community is catalyzed by the centers' spending.[47] To date, no similar studies have been undertaken to measure the number of conversions or new soldiers or the reduction of poverty in the designated communities, and it is too early to determine what kind of measurable outcomes will result from the massive investment of resources in these centers.

Just as the Darkest England Trust of 1891 was called into being in order to demonstrate that no donations for social work had been diverted to maintaining evangelical work, the same need has in more recent years led to the entire restructuring of Salvation Army operations in some countries to ensure that government money is not subsidizing the preaching of the Gospel. In the Netherlands the legal division of the various facets of Salvation Army operations into six "foundations," held together by a shared mission statement rather than by linked governance, dates from 1990. This solution resolved very long-standing constitutional ambiguities, which had culminated in a decade-long internal debate within the Leger des Heils in the Netherlands as to whether it was primarily a Church or a "Foundation."[48] In France the Salvation Army Congregation also has its own Board, distinct from that of the Salvation Army Foundation which has administered social programs since 2002.

At a local level, in many countries it would be difficult to separate evangelical and social income and spending. In New Zealand, most corps run "family stores" to sell donated goods, and many corps would probably not survive without their income. The quid quo pro is that corps need to provide social services as well as religious meetings. In smaller centers this is simply encompassed by the corps officer's own community

46. http://www.salvationarmy.org.nz/research-media/media-centre/local-news/notorious-whanau-continues-to-fight-the-p; http://www.salvationarmy.org.nz/our-community/faith-in-life/our-people-our-stories/journeying-together; accessed 25 October 2016.

47. http://www.salvationarmyusa.org/usn/kroc-centers, accessed 26 September 2015.

48. Outlined in Bollinger, *Dynamic Courtship*.

engagement although elsewhere quite extensive services are offered by employed staff. Likewise in the USA, it is suggested that if funds raised in the name of social services were totally separated from those for the church component of the work, the vast majority of the corps would be forced to close.

Elsewhere the difficulty has been manifest in other ways. In parts of the USA, the Salvation Army's dependence upon public funding for its services has allegedly meant restraints on its ability to preach the gospel. Here is a 2010 report:

> Several New York government agencies have adopted new standards to ensure the Salvation Army cannot use public funds to proselytize.
>
> The new policy is part of a settlement agreement in *Lown v. The Salvation Army*. In 2004, the New York Civil Liberties Union filed a lawsuit after learning that the Salvation Army required social workers and other employees in its government-funded social services programs to identify their church affiliation, the frequency of their church attendance and to sign an endorsement of the ministry's mission to "preach the Gospel of Jesus" . . .
>
> "When the Salvation Army's religious mission was made mandatory in our work place, it changed the climate in a way that caused us fear and concern about our ability to ethically deliver services," said Marina Obermaier, a social worker administrator who worked for eight years with Salvation Army foster families in New York City and on Long Island. "Our ethical commitment as social workers means that we may not be judgmental or refuse to offer services to our clients that are beneficial to them."
>
> Under the two-year settlement agreement, every government agency listed in the lawsuit must ensure that the money they provide to the Salvation Army does not subsidize religious activities . . . the NYCLU will receive regular reports from these government agencies, and a federal court will ensure that the agreement is enforced.[49]

That announcement evoked an impassioned response from retired Commissioner Joe Noland, formerly the USA eastern territorial commander:

> "An agreement has been reached . . . " that The Salvation Army "not" preach Christianity—a principle so many sacrificed and some even died for? The article goes on to say the SA "Agreed to be monitored." What! Other agencies to monitor the non-fulfilment of its mission statement: " . . . to preach the gospel of Jesus Christ and to meet human needs in His name without discrimination." It's not about losing $50 million in government contracts is it? It's not about preserving the bureaucracy is it? It's not about partnering, secularly, to enhance a broken down, bureaucratically protected foster care system is it? It's not about survival is it? It's not about compromise is it? . . . Getting involved with government contracts in this country always requires compromise, one way or another . . . [50]

Corporate funders may now look for partners to do work of *their* choice, sometimes presumably because there appear to be commercial advantages in being seen to be doing

---

49. Americans United for a Separation of Church and State: April 2010 AU Bulletin, http://www.au.org/media/church-and-state/archives/2010/04/salvation-army-in-ny-cant.html, downloaded 11 April 2010.

50. theRubi-Blog http://therubicon.org/category/therubi-blog/page/2/, 23 February, 2010, accessed 15 April, 2010.

such work, rather than adopting a particular charity's mission. The Army may end up not doing its own mission. Any such involvement, whether with government or with other funders is also likely to come with strings attached and to leave the movement open to criticism by those perhaps not well-disposed to the funder itself. For example in Australia the Army's attempts to assist with the care of refugees on Nauru and Manus Islands in 2012–2013 brought upon it in May 2013 the accusation of being "a branch of government."[51] Weighing the advantages and risks to the mission itself is a challenging task.

Social Welfare or Social Justice?

Fourthly, although William Booth does not seem to have invented the metaphor of an *ambulance* at the foot of the precipice of human failure, and the need to erect a *fence* at the *top*, he had the same idea.[52] He aimed to transform society. While most of the Salvation Army's social work would be ambulance at the bottom activity, picking up the losers in the competition for survival, it has from time to time sought to construct fences at the top as well. Some of this work could be described as social justice activity, in the sense that it has sought to bring about structural change in order to achieve a more just society. Indeed, one of the purposes of the In Darkest England scheme itself was to bring about structural change, since Booth was one of those Victorian reformers who believed that over-population was the root cause of the long depression from the early 1870s to the late 1890s, and that mass emigration was part of the answer to this problem.[53]

It has been suggested that the Darkest England scheme saved the Salvation Army from suffering the fate of so many other British evangelical missions which burned out and faded away by the end of the nineteenth century. By 1890, however, the Army had already spread well beyond Britain and had gathered a momentum which probably would have saved it from that fate, at least for much longer. What Darkest England and the expansion of social work probably did though was to save the Salvation Army from what in Evangelical circles has been called "the Great Reversal."[54] Whereas nineteenth century evangelicals had a lively interest in a contemporary expression of the Kingdom of God—converts of Booth's mentor, Finney, were expected to sign up for either the anti-slavery or the women's suffrage campaigns—many post–World War One evangelicals turned their backs on social activism and became more "other-worldly," under the influence of fundamentalist pre-millennial and dispensational teaching. While it took to the end of the century before many evangelicals again began to take seriously the "already" as well as the "not yet" of the Kingdom, the Army had remained committed to social action throughout.

Such activity is always likely to cross into political action, which has always been a problem for the Salvation Army. There has always been within the Army a degree

---

51. Haigh, "The Salvation Army is a Branch of Government," On-Line Opinion, 16 May 2013.

52. Found in poem by Joseph Malins, 'A Fence or an Ambulance,' 1895. The cliff-ambulance-fence figure is often attributed to Booth, as by Henry Gariepy in *Christianity in Action*, 58, but I have not found it in Booth's writing.

53. Ausubel, *In Hard Times*, 180.

54. Moberg, *The Great Reversal*.

of tension between these two complementary endeavors. Booth had been attracted by Chartism in his youth, going to hear Feargus O'Connor speak in Nottingham when he was thirteen. He was dissuaded from this allegiance by James Caughey, who denounced Chartism as destructive of social order and argued that the wrongs of the world needed to be righted by individual conversion.[55] John Rhemick points out that abstention from political agitation was also the official policy of the Methodist New Connexion to which Booth belonged:

> As a religious community, we neither have interfered, nor do we profess to interfere, with political concerns; like the kingdom of our Lord and Master, the Methodist New Connexion has no relation to the political affairs of this world.[56]

In Christian Mission days, trying to relieve dire poverty and starvation in the East End, Booth was still of the opinion that

> Legislation may do much to counteract the mischief but the spread of religious feeling will do more. The true Christian is a real self-helper. In bringing the truths of religion before the suffering masses we are also assisting in the great work of social reform . . . When we have taught people to be religious, half the battle has been won.[57]

William Booth spoke to the point in addressing the 1904 International Staff Conference, admitting that "there may be some Officers amongst us today . . . who may not feel free to accept my advice as to a total abstinence from politics in the wide sense . . . " but warned that were they to "proclaim ourselves as taking any particular side on political questions agitating this or any other country . . . would be to stem the flowing tide of our soul-saving efforts, and create discussion and strife where now peace and unity reign."[58] He supported his argument with the example of Christ, who confined his attentions to making men good rather than getting involved in political agitation against the Romans.

Frederick Coutts quoted approvingly Charles Williams' reflection that such bodies as the Poor Clares and the Salvation Army were exceptional in that unlike the "organization of the Christian churches" they did not remain "in the eyes of the masses of men the great support of the dominant social order."[59] Others, however, have seen the Army as precisely that. Comparatively early in the Salvation Army's life, Catherine Booth solicited the support of the political and financial establishment for the Army on the grounds that it would help save Britain from anarchy and revolution, invoking the specters of "the steady advance of socialist opinions" which in France and Germany "threatens all orderly government, and menaces the existence of any government at all," even citing "the discovery of the Black Hand Associations in Spain, which openly avow the most terrible principles of the socialist theory . . . "[60] Clearly the Salvation Army did not aim

---

55. Green, *Life and Ministry of William Booth*, 17.

56. Salt, *Memorial of the Wesleyan Methodist New Connexion)* 252, quoted in Rhemick, *New People of* God, 29.

57. Booth in *The East London Evangelist*, January 1869, quoted in Sandall, *History* I, 119.

58. Booth, "Politics" in *International Staff Council Addresses*, 148–64.

59. Coutts, *Bread for my Neighbour*, 171, citing Williams, *Descent of the Dove*, 205.

60. Booth, "The Salvation Army, and its Relation to the State," in *Salvation Army in Relation to the*

to turn the world upside down. Granted an audience with King Edward VII in 1904, William Booth checked that the King would be happy for him to tell Salvationists that his Majesty "regards its [the Salvation Army's] success as important to the well-being of the Empire."[61] Harald Fischer-Tiné likewise quotes a *War Cry* article asking, "In what do the imperial services of the Army consist?" and providing the assurance that it was

> In its endeavors to soften and remove the effect of extreme poverty, to raise the fallen, to succor the needy and assist the distressed, the products of a civilization which turns out an appalling proportion of waste products—paupers, prostitutes, criminals and lunatics in every class of society, and by this means to soften the conflict between the 'haves' and the 'have-nots' which constitute a fertile soil for the seeds of rebellion that threaten the mother country.[62]

Fischer-Tiné draws attention to "the Salvation Army's transformation from a Home Mission Movement, based on traditions of lower middle-class and upper working-class religiosity, and often viewed as disturbing by the authorities, into a world-wide service business for social control . . . This transformation happened almost simultaneously in India [with custody of 'criminal tribes'] and Great Britain and the developments on both sides influenced the other." He also cites the recognition of the Army in Meiji Japan, with Booth's 1907 audience with the emperor, as a "useful handmaiden of the state." Structural change was not the Salvation Army's purpose; rather, to protect the status quo by making it more bearable. George Bernard Shaw similarly observed that the Salvation Army had become "a sort of auxiliary police . . . taking off the insurrectionary edge of poverty," and "thus preserv[ing] the country from mob violence and revolution."[63] The oft-quoted Halévy thesis attributed the same role to Methodism in the eighteenth century, saving England from a revolution like that in France.[64]

Quite apart from theoretical and theological justifications for a non-political stance, overt political action would always run the danger of polarizing the Army's own adherents, as well as of offending actual and potential supporters and donors amongst the public. However, the line between what is political and what is not is not easily drawn, and the fight against poverty has always attracted some Salvationists into seeking more direct action. A number of Labor party and generally left-wing politicians got their start in the Salvation Army, and then decided to take a more direct route in ushering in the Kingdom of God on earth. Frank Smith was the outstanding example in the United Kingdom but there were others, like his friend George Lansbury, Labor luminary and leader who had belonged to the Army in his youth.[65] Unlike Smith and Lansbury, most, however, left religion for politics. Rare later examples of politically active Salvationists

---

Church and State, 2.

61. Begbie, *William Booth*, II, 325.

62. *War Cry* article from January 1911 quoted by Fischer-Tiné, "Global Civil Society and the Forces of Empire," in Conrad and Sachsenaier (edited), *Competing Visions of World Order*, 51.

63. Fischer-Tiné, "Global Civil Society," 36, sources Shaw's observations from Radhkrishna, *Dishonored by History*, 78, and cites Bailey, "Salvation Army Riots," 231–53, 236–37.

64. The argument that Methodism saved England from revolution by diverting energies from politics to religion, in Halévy, *England in 1815*, 387, 424–25.

65. Lansbury, *My Life*, 85.

in the UK were the Edinburgh Socialist local body politician James Crichton, Sir John Boyd, chairman of the Labor Party in 1967 and general secretary of the Amalgamated Engineering Union 1975–1982, and Derek Foster, a Labor MP 1979–2005.

Elsewhere in the world, there were not many. Vere Cornwall Bird of the West Indies was one Salvationist who gave up officership to fight for land reform, formed the Antiguan Labor Party and served as prime minister 1981–1994. Of antipodean examples, J. H. G. Chapple, born in Rockhampton in 1865, was a Salvation Army officer 1890–98, appointed to New Zealand in 1893, editor of the *War Cry* in 1897, joined the Presbyterian Church in 1898 and became a minister, joined the pioneer Socialist Party in 1905 and resigned the ministry because of opposition to his radical views within his church. According to Manning Clark, John Curtin, prime minister of Australia for three years in the Second World War, had in his youth been "a desperate pilgrim for the means of salvation. He had tried Catholicism, the Salvation Army (playing the cornet for a brief time at street corners), Rationalism . . . and Socialism."[66] Curtin's alcoholism as well as his thirst for social justice may have played a part in his association with the Army.

The first leader of the New Zealand Labor Party, the Australian-born Harry Holland, had been a Salvationist in his youth and left after reading Henry George, Edward Bellamy and Karl Marx while unemployed for several years from 1888. Lee Martin, a member of the first Labor Cabinet in New Zealand and minister of agriculture 1935–41 had been a Salvation Army officer 1891–1896. Salvationist William Denham from Invercargill was also a Labor MP 1935–46 and Mel Brooks of Blenheim in the 1970s. Norman Kirk, prime minister of New Zealand's third Labor government from 1972 until his early death in 1974, described himself as "coming from a long line of bandmasters and backsliders."[67] A New Zealand Labor politician who avoided backsliding was Bill Coleman of Gisborne, who managed from the late 1920s to his death in 1951 to combine Salvation Army local officership at various times with mayoral and parliamentary and even junior ministerial roles, at great personal cost.

The general Salvation Army view of deserters to the political army may be seen in this comment on the resignation of Colonel Boon in 1894:

> We regret to report the resignation of Colonel Boon. He has left the Army with a view to joining the Independent Labor Party, in the hopes of securing by direct political agitation and law reform the results which we believe can best and indeed *only* be achieved by salvation. We can only say that we believe our comrade has made a fatal mistake, which he will regret both in time and in eternity . . . Who can doubt that a drunkard-saving, slum-visiting, people-converting F.O. ranks far higher in the *Heavenly* scales than any M.P. in the land.[68]

Frank Smith got off very lightly by comparison. And Boon, unlike Smith, stayed on once he had come back a year or so later.

66. Clark, *History of Australia*, VI, 10.

67. Kirk, as Leader of the Opposition, 13 March 1966, speaking at a Sunday afternoon "Citizen's Rally," once a feature of the annual Salvation Army Congresses in New Zealand. (The *War Cry* report refrained from quoting him verbatim.)

68. *Officer*, August 1894, 232. Boon was soon back in the fold; he was Staff Secretary at IHQ when Albert Orsborn was an office boy there in the early 1900s. (Orsborn, *House of My Pilgrimage*, 32.)

Roland Robertson suggests some possible background to why some Salvationists migrated to labor movements. The Army had drawn on working class adherents because it had provided a vehicle for protestant religious expression in contradistinction from the middle and upper classes; it provided a religion of other-worldly compensation for deprivation in this world; and its style was unabashedly working-class. However, in the 1880s, "the dissolution of the religious context of socio-political discussion and decision was near and the Labor Church movement and ephemeral working-class allegiance to the Salvation Army were two of the major collective responses to this relatively normless situation."[69] . . . with the rapid development of trade unions of unskilled and skilled manual workers, and of the socialist parties . . . the probability of working class aspiration being expressed through religious media declined considerably."[70]

The Salvation Army's determination to remain above politics and not identify with any political parties has come full circle to perhaps the majority of Salvationists being generally right-wing, supporting conservative parties. The Army has often believed that it was maintaining a non-political stance when in fact its very abstention from political expression has amounted to support for an oppressive status quo. A case in point could be its avoidance of confrontation with racist regimes in South Africa and Rhodesia in the later twentieth century, seen by nationalists as support for those regimes.

What were the reasons for this swing to conservatism? The tendency to "redemption and lift," whereby the sobriety, thrift and diligence of converts brought an improvement in their socio-economic standing might also have contributed to their moving towards the conservative end of the political spectrum.[71] Charles Booth quoted a Salvation Army officer from Peckham at the turn of the century as saying that "Conversion has a wonderful effect on a man; he is very soon decently clothed, his home becomes better, and though he remains a working man, outwardly he might pass with the clerks."[72] Elizabeth Milligan suggested that

> For those involved in Salvation Army activity respect for the societal order is an integral part of their nomos. Political involvement is not forbidden, nor is any particular political viewpoint prescribed, but it is assumed that this area of life will, like every other, be ruled by Salvationist principles. The Salvationist may be politically active but he must be a Salvationist first and foremost and as such extra-Salvation Army activity becomes marginal . . . Empirically this perspective shows itself by a dearth of public figures who are affiliated to the Salvation Army.[73]

Or is it that a hierarchical, controlling polity is naturally more in sympathy with social and political conservatism? Again, moral conservatism is also often associated with political conservatism. Or is it a reluctance to alienate wealthy donors by calling

---

69. The "Labor Church" movement, which flourished from about 1891 to around 1910, was supposed to provide an expression of religion for the labor movement. It left theological beliefs to the personal preference of its members.

70. Robertson, "Salvation Army," in Wilson, *Patterns of Sectarianism*, 93–94.

71. The phrase "redemption and lift" is attributed to the missiologist Donald MacGavran, who saw it as an deterrent to evangelistic endeavour. MacGavran, *Understanding Church Growth*, 209.

72. Charles Booth, *Life and Labour*, Third Series, VI, 78, quoted by Bailey, "In Darkest England," 139.

73. Milligan, "Persistence of the Salvation Army," 354–55.

for structural change which could disadvantage them? Booth said that had he gone with Chartism and embraced radical politics, "Should I . . . at this moment have had the open door to the hearts of Conservative as well as Radical people that is mine at this hour? I do not think I should."[74]

Booth himself was politically conservative.[75] Given Catherine Booth's 1883 argument, quoted above, that the Salvation Army should be supported because it stood between society and the forces of disorder, it would be too much to argue that it was simply the Darkest England scheme that swung the Army from being a revolutionary, counter-cultural phenomenon and made it a hand-maiden of the establishment. That tendency was clearly already in the Booth's and in the Army's Methodist evangelical DNA. However, the Darkest England scheme did confirm and set that disposition in concrete. Because the Army needed public support and funds, both public and private, in order to carry out its works of social amelioration, it was tied irrevocably and permanently to the chariot wheels of conservatism. And the sense that this was the case may have contributed to the disillusionment and departure of some of those left-wing Salvationists who chose the "shorter way" to bringing in the Kingdom of God apparently offered by political activity.

Despite that reluctance to become involved, the Army has nevertheless sometimes initiated social action which has addressed economic, social or legal injustices, sometimes spilling over into political action at various times in its history.

- The "Maiden Tribute Campaign" against child prostitution was certainly overtly political, seeking a change in legislation.
- The "Lights in Darkest England" matches were a successful attempt to bring about changes in the economic structure, undertaking a commercial venture in order to force manufacturers to change their practices.
- In 1897 the Salvation Army had its own brand of tea, named 'Hamodava,' the Singhalese word for salvation. It was imported from Ceylon and blended in Melbourne by Salvationists. Unlike modern fair trade organizations, the Army's Tea League was not formed purely to assist farmers; its aim was to raise money for Salvationist missionaries. Nevertheless, the Army's dealings with tea growers were purportedly just and ethical in a world where these people were all too often exploited.[76]
- In Japan, where the Army had been operating for only five years in 1900, the Army joined forces with an American Methodist missionary, U. G. Murphy, to tackle the three-century old system of prostitution which bound women to brothels by debt. An 1872 imperial ordinance forbidding the practice was being ignored and court orders resisted by the police. A three-month highly publicized campaign marked by violence against the Salvationists was ended when the Emperor signed a new

---

74. Booth, *International Staff Council Addresses*, 159.

75. Green, *William Booth*, 17. In his private correspondence, offended by charges that the Army used sweated labor, Booth referred to "the lying, jealous, God-hating crowd who have so senselessly attacked us," this evidently including "the Labor Party—both Socialistic and Trade Union Wings—" on whom he hoped to "turn the tables." Quoted in Murdoch, *Christian Warfare*, 86.

76. *On Fire*, 28 March 2008, 4.

ordinance enforcing the rule that any girl who wanted to be freed, and stated so at a police station, could be free irrespective of any indebtedness to the brothel-keepers. In the first year, 12,000 young women obtained their freedom.[77]

- Because of German submarine action early in the First World War, there was a shortage of grain in Britain and in one town the bakers fixed price of bread at levels which disadvantaged the poor. General Bramwell Booth wrote to the bakers requesting them to lower the prices, but was ignored. When he announced that the Salvation Army would open a bakery and charge pre-war prices, the price of bread came down and that action did not have to be taken.[78]

- In France, the Army fought a campaign to end the practice of transportation of felons to Devil's Island in French Guiana, from which few were ever able to return. Commissioner Albin Peyron sent Ensign Charles Péan to inspect and report in 1928 and in 1933 Péan was able to return there to establish a Salvation Army post. He wrote three books on the evils of the system of "doublage" whereby convicts had to remain in exile for a period equivalent to their original sentence, but had no means of earning a living—or of getting back to France. Between 1933 and 1949 twelve officers cared for prisoners and exiles while Péan agitated for reform. Eventually the island prison was closed and all the men were repatriated.[79]

- The Salvation Army is deeply involved in developmental work in the third world, both using its own funds and channeling funds from government and other sources, in order to empower people to find and achieve their own solutions to local problems.

- In recent years, the whole concept of social justice and the need to set up more fences at the tops of cliffs, and even to level the cliffs themselves, has gained increasing currency and support within the Salvation Army, especially amongst younger Salvationists. In New Zealand Major Campbell Roberts OF, now retired Secretary for Social Program, has been involved in various forms of social action for many years. One of his interventions, for example, was to turn up at an auction where a house was to be sold because the owners couldn't afford the extortionate interest charged by a loan shark. He told the gathered crowd of the circumstances and as a result no-one was prepared to bid for the house. He was then able to negotiate terms for the people to save their home. He is an acknowledged authority on housing and has been a member of various Government task forces (set up by political parties of both left and right) on the subject. He established and was the first Director of the Salvation Army's Social Policy and Parliamentary Unit which interfaces with the public and with politicians on social and social justice issues, producing reports which are very influential. Campbell Roberts also helped initiate and is still involved in regular meetings of the prime minister or deputy with heads of churches on social issues, which have continued under successive governments since 2000.

77. Sandall, *History*, III, 197–99.

78. Clifton, http://www.newfrontierchronicle.org/seeking-justice-together/, accessed 25 November 2016.

79. Sandall, *History*, III, 302–05.

Despite these and other forays across the border into what might be called social justice action, the Army has remained a reluctant player, ever since Booth wrote to his son, Bramwell:

> I cannot go in for any more "campaigns" against evils. My hands and heart are full enough. And moreover these reformers of society have no sympathy with The Salvation Army nor with Salvation from worldliness and sin. Our campaign is against sin! . . . The Christ people who are not for a religion of deliverance from sinning are God's great enemies.[80]

Campbell Roberts and Danielle Strickland comment:

> Booth seems to have had difficulty in consistently integrating the three aspects of the biblical triangle of faith, mercy and justice. Viewing the totality of his ministry, they were all present, but at particular times he found difficulty in giving *balance* to these three aspects of biblical truth. As well, Booth tended to see mercy and justice flowing from personal faith and this led him to be suspicious of social reformers like W.T. Stead and Frank Smith, who wanted to redeem the present world.
>
> This theological ambivalence to the biblical call to justice has continued to plague our movement to the present day. Our theological pragmatism and involvement with people has ensured a consistent and outstanding ministry of spontaneous and organized mercy to the needy of the world, but in areas of justice the Army has been less surefooted. And where we have become involved, it has tended to be around areas of personal morality rather than structural evil.[81]

A landmark development was General Clifton's setting up of the International Social Justice Commission in New York in 2007. Handily sited near the United Nations Headquarters, although reporting to the Administration Department at IHQ, the ISCJ advises the General and senior IHQ staff on matters of social justice, and resources interterritorial action on such matters as people-trafficking. Its strategic plan includes the following objectives:

- Raise strategic voices to advocate with the world's poor and oppressed.
- Be a recognized center of research and critical thinking on issues of global social justice.
- Collaborate with like-minded organizations to advance the global cause of social justice.
- Exercise leadership in determining social justice policies and practices of The Salvation Army.
- Live by principles of justice and compassion and inspire others to do likewise.[82]

---

80. Begbie, *William Booth*, II, 169.
81. Roberts and Strickland, *Just Imagine*, 43.
82. *The Salvation Army Year Book*, 2013, 33.

A Saving Work?

Fifthly, questions may be asked about how a revivalist mission, like the earlier Salvation Army, was able to maintain its evangelical fervor in this new iteration. A waning of fervor is normal by the second and subsequent generations of evangelical movements but the question is whether the deliberate broadening of objective, along with its concomitant administrative burdens, contributed to that process.

Booth had no time for those who said that the body didn't matter. In *In Darkest England*, he dismissed as "religious cant, which rids itself of all the importunity of suffering humanity by drawing unnegotiable bills payable on the other side of the grave," the view of "conventional religious people who relieve themselves of all anxiety for the welfare of the poor by saying that in the next world all will be put right."[83] But by the same token he never disguised his view that for a man to be saved spiritually was the highest good: "I must assert in the most unqualified way that it is primarily and mainly for the sake of saving the soul that I seek the salvation of the body."[84] Roger Green's work on the change in Booth's theology shows that whereas previously he had thought of social action as merely a way of making it possible for people to hear the Gospel, by 1890 he came to see it as an expression of the Gospel.[85] In "Salvation for Both Worlds," Booth wrote,

> I saw that when the Bible said, 'He that believeth shall be saved,' it meant not only saved from the miseries of the future world, but from the miseries of this [world] also. That it came from the promise of salvation here and now; from hell and sin and vice and crime and idleness and extravagance, and consequently very largely from poverty and disease, and the majority of kindred woes.[86]

Not long before his death, addressing the 1911 international social council, Booth said,

> By Social Work, I mean those operations of the Salvation Army which have to do with the alleviation, *or removal* [my italics], of the moral and temporal evils which cause the misery of the submerged classes, and which so greatly hinder their Salvation. Our Social Operations, as thus defined, are the natural outcome of Salvationism, or, I might say, of Christianity, as instituted, described, proclaimed and exemplified in the life and teaching and sacrifice of Jesus Christ.[87]

Nevertheless, William Booth remained conflicted on this score; the General sometimes fretted that the commitment to social work had been undertaken at the expense of evangelical work. After twenty years, he was anxious about whether his officers were still up to it: with perhaps a rueful frankness he listed the following amongst reasons for shortcomings in the Darkest England program:

---

83. Booth, *Darkest England*, 80.
84. Booth, Ibid., 45.
85. Green, *War on Two Fronts*.
86. Booth, "Salvation for Both Worlds," in Eason and Green, *Boundless Salvation*, 53–54.
87. Booth, *International Social Council Addresses*, 1.

1. There has been a great lack of direct aim at the true goal of our social work on the part of officers who have been engaged in its direction . . .

2. Another cause of our short-comings has been the lamentable fact that some of our officers have been deficient in personal religion . . .

3. Another of our difficulties has been the scarcity of suitable people for carrying the work on . . . [88]

Booth was not alone in fearing that the main thing had not been kept the main thing; I have already referred to A.M. Nicol's equally pessimistic evaluation of the situation:

> General Booth would almost break his heart if he knew the proportion of men who have been "saved," in the sense that he most values, through his social scheme . . . I will make bold to say that the officials cannot put their hands on the names of a thousand MEN in all parts of the world who are to-day members of the Army who were converted at the penitent forms of shelters and elevators, and who are now earning a living outside the control of the Army's social work.[89]

Trying to account for this melancholy state of affairs, Nicol pointed out that the social work officers carried huge physical and administrative burdens, leaving little time or energy for the spiritual side of their work. This is not to deny that an incalculable amount of spiritual work and soul-saving has been achieved, despite such difficulties, by a host of dedicated Salvationists engaged in social work over the years since *In Darkest England* was published. The question of whether social workers can also be soul-winners is even more acute in the present era, when so much of the Army's specialist social work is done by professionals who are not themselves members of the Salvation Army, and, though their employment contracts may require them to work within the parameters of Salvation Army beliefs, they may not be Christians either. When I learned that, at the time, the senior clinician at an Army addiction rehabilitation center was a practicing Hindu, I found myself wondering what William Booth would have thought about that.

Professionalization has been a fraught area for the Salvation Army. As government requirements and public expectations have gradually raised the bar for training and qualifications, the Army has attempted to equip its officers to meet the need. In New Zealand in the mid–1950s a policy of enabling officers to enroll for university social work qualifications was initiated but for various reasons—sometimes perhaps a lack of adequate pastoral care and supervision at a time when an individual was immersed in a wholly new secular and academic environment—an unfortunately high proportion of seconded officers, who tended to be thought the more able of their peers, ceased to be involved in the Army even though embarked on new social work careers thanks to its support. Some other territories suffered similarly. Stijn Bollinger notes of the Netherlands too that

> The demand for professionalization by education had resulted in an unforeseen development. Former policy adviser of the Army's probation department, Maris

---

88. Booth, Ibid., 18–19.

89. Nicol, *General Booth*, 205. Nicol's capitalization of MEN relates to his observation that the "Women's Social" led by Mrs Florence Booth had been much more successful in soul-saving as well as general rehabilitation of its clients.

recalls that many officers that had followed higher education were "a loss to the Army":

> "Even though they came from a family of officers, they distanced themselves from it . . . They could absolutely not relate with the Army any longer. The officers in particular—they hurried out. And they especially disappeared completely outside the organization. Thus the organization became more secularized."[90]

William Booth's inner tension between "saving" and "serving" has been inherited by his Movement. There is now a continuum of thought on this subject within the Salvation Army, from one extreme view that anything other than getting people "saved" is fudging the Gospel and selling people short, to the other extreme that merely giving a cup of water in Christ's name is in itself a sharing of the Gospel. As Martin Fletcher's 2015 *New Statesman* article observed,

> Army officers say they are loath to exploit the vulnerable people they help. "We don't run our night shelter as a recruiting tool. We run it because it's flipping cold outside and we don't want people to die," said Lieutenant John Clifton, whose corps in Ilford, east London, provides winter dormitory accommodation for 25 homeless men and women. "I don't think it's ethical to take advantage of their physical need."[91]

This is also saying the gospel is to the whole person, not to their "soul" alone. An earlier Salvationist commentator on this theme was Fred Brown, in his 1970 book, *Secular Evangelism*. Referring to the growth of "over-sixty" clubs associated with corps in Britain, he remarked on the opposition they also aroused:

> This development was not, however, universally popular with Salvation Army officers. Some of them argued that it represented yet another unfortunate diversion from their main task of evangelism. Others justified the vast expenditure of strength, time and money involved in running the clubs with the comforting thought that converts might result. One fiery evangelist, sincere, dedicated and industrious, summed up the attitude of a small minority when he refused to establish a club on the grounds that God had called him to build an Army, not act as nursemaid to people with one foot in the grave . . . He turned from a ministry of meeting human need in the name of building first the Kingdom of God. He put converts before people. He thought more of saving souls than serving sinners.
>
> The basic trouble was that . . . he was not committed to people for their own intrinsic value. He was committed to them as a means to an end.[92]

The other end of the continuum is expressed by Stephen Court in a 2010 blog:

> We are The SALVATION Army. We are all about Salvation. But salvation is not all about everything and anything. Some get mistaken on this point. Some might

---

90. Interview with Maris, September 2, 2011, in Bollinger, *Dynamic Courtship*, 160.
91. Fletcher, "The Salvation Army turns 150."
92. Brown, *Secular Evangelism*, 30.

suggest that when we serve a cup of cold water we SAVE them from thirst; when we feed them we SAVE them from hunger; when we clothe them we SAVE them from cold/embarrassment; when we house them we SAVE them from indigence; when we find them a job we SAVE them from unemployment; when we make friends with them we SAVE them from loneliness; when we greet them nicely we SAVE them from silence; when we teach them we SAVE them from ignorance; when we . . .

Fair enough. But The Salvation Army is not about saving people from thirst. It is about saving them from sin and hell. "Salvation" in our name is all about salvation from sin through the blood of Jesus Christ via repentance and faith and from hell; through continuance in a state of salvation via continued obedience faith in the Lord Jesus Christ.

It is good and nice to save people from thirst, hunger, cold, embarrassment, indigence, unemployment, loneliness, silence, and ignorance. But such a 'salvation' is but a human imitation of the divine salvation that we are really all about. Only divine salvation lasts beyond the grave. Human helps are merely that. Don't settle for a cheap imitation.[93]

The argument is sometimes expressed in the dichotomy of whether we are "saved to save," as William Booth actually put it, or "saved to serve."

Stijn Bollinger, in his thesis on the relationship between the Salvation Army and the state in the Netherlands, notes that this dual mission is not a unique feature of the Salvation Army.

In his work on the Dutch diaconate, Erik Sengers acknowledged that such a double objective was present in many charitable organizations in both the Catholic and the Protestant segments of Dutch society. Furthermore, Sengers made a plea to reintroduce the original Latin term caritas (charity) instead of diaconate, for caritas emphasizes the connecting force between the biblical expressions 'love' and 'doing good deeds,' whereas the word diaconate had come to focus merely on the latter. Charity means both 'word and deed' and, according to Sengers, thus is the most appropriate term for the combining force between the two parts of the dual mission of many charitable organizations.[94]

Given the likeness Jesus discerned between the greatest and the second greatest commandments (Matthew 22. 37–39), the dual mission would seem to most faithfully represent the gospel. General Frederick Coutts expressed the same comprehensive view that

Our evangelical work and social work . . . are but two activities of the one and the same salvation which is concerned with the total redemption of man. Both rely on the same divine grace. Both are inspired by the same motive. Both have the same end in mind. And, as the Gospel has joined them together we do not propose to put them asunder.[95]

This section has looked so far at the consequences the Darkest England scheme has had for the Salvation Army's reputation, structure, overseas missions, fund-raising,

---

93. http://www.armybarmy.com/blog.html, Thursday, 6 May, 2010.
94. Sengers, *Caritas*, 30–33, cited by Bollinger, "Dynamic Courtship, 32.
95. Coutts, quoted by Dean, "The Dynamic Centrality," 357.

mission-focus and evangelism. The Army's contemporary debate on these areas is indeed "out of Darkest England," with its origins in the Darkest England scheme which continues to shape, and challenge, the Army's thinking as well as its structures.

Moral and Social Issues

The Army's thinking on these areas is also expressed in what it says about those conjoined twins, moral and social issues. Precept and practice tend to walk hand-in-hand; orthodoxy and orthopraxis are closely identified in churches, whether of conservative or liberal persuasion. Since such early initiatives as the "Maiden Tribute" campaign in the 1880s, the Salvation Army's interventions in public affairs have usually been when they seem to have impinged on matters of personal morality. Of these the longest-running would have been about "temperance" and "prohibition." The Salvation Army joined forces with other groups, not only religious, to attack the liquor trade in the name of public morality. Issues of the *War Cry* in many countries for many decades featured articles and cartoons attacking the Demon Drink and its purveyors.

When the Salvation Army began instituting Public Questions Boards at some territorial headquarters in the 1950s, in order to formulate responses and offer guidance to Army leadership on matters of public interest, there would probably have been a degree of unanimity amongst Salvationists over the kinds of issues dealt with—such matters as liquor licensing legislation loomed large on the agenda, but general welfare legislation was also dealt with. As the "permissive society" gathered momentum in the 1960s, the Army tended to identify with morally conservative opinion on such matters as sexuality and censorship, participating in the "Festival of Light" in Britain in the early 1970s for example and supporting campaigners for stricter public morality and broadcasting standards in various jurisdictions.

In 1980 International Headquarters issued a collection of "positional statements," prepared initially as a result of the discussions at the 1979 international conference of leaders meeting in Toronto.[96] In the ensuing years these statements were extended and revised and began to range more widely on issues such as nuclear disarmament. A Moral and Social Issues Council was formed at IHQ in 1987, becoming a function of the UK Territory upon the separation of those entities in 1990. A social and moral issues desk was established at IHQ in 1998. Some territories began to issue their own versions of these statements, tailored to local consumption or accommodating local interests, although all had to be approved by the Chief of the Staff in London to ensure international consistency on such matters. Such positions are not binding on Salvationists individually but represent the organization's official attitude and are offered as a guide. In time, agreement on some contentious matters was becoming harder to reach. I recall the New Zealand moral and social issues council in the early 2000s being unable to agree on the revision of a statement on "war and peace" because it was evenly split between proponents of the "just war" and conscientious objectors to any war. Likewise, I sat in on a meeting of the combined Australia Southern and Eastern territories' MASICs when they

---

96. "Positional Statements" issued by Authority of the General, International Headquarters, 1980.

addressed the issue of homosexual behavior (at the behest of a territorial commander who wanted his hand strengthened in anticipation of a gay candidate for officer-training). While one member stated that he saw no difference between a faithful heterosexual relationship and a faithful same-sex relationship, another member opined that the latter "would burn in hell." A meeting of minds, there was not.

Less strictly monitored than positional statements were less formal discussion papers ("guidelines" in Australia and "discussion documents" in New Zealand) developed in some territories to assist Salvationists in considering contentious issues. For a period IHQ ceased publication of international positional statements but central direction was subsequently re-established with the setting up of the International Moral and Social Issues Council (IMASIC) in 2007.

Of all those positions currently maintained, the Salvation Army's stance on homosexuality has caused it possibly most public discomfort in recent years. Most notoriously, in 1986 the territorial commander in New Zealand (against the advice of most of his heads of departments and against the recommendation of international headquarters) committed the Army to supporting a petition against proposed legislation decriminalizing homosexual acts. A counter-petition supporting decriminalization was presented to the parliamentary select committee by a group of Salvationists led by Max Cresswell, professor of philosophy at Victoria University, and the now Major Campbell Roberts O.F. The legislation passed, but the Army's reputation was dealt lasting damage, not wholly repaired by public apology made by a later territorial commander twenty years on.[97] Over the years, and increasingly, some Salvationists have spoken out against the adoption of discriminatory attitudes in the Army and their views would be held more widely today. In a survey conducted by the Moral and Social Issues Council in New Zealand in 2014, a little over half of respondents held to a traditional view of same-sex relationships. Just under half were either uncertain or had moved to a more accepting view of same-sex relationships. The traditional viewpoint was more strongly represented among soldiers (58 percent) than officers (51 percent).[98]

In the USA, agreement by the Western territory to recognize health insurance benefits for the partners of gay employees in 2001 came under sustained attack by James Dobson and the Focus on the Family organization, so that the national commissioners' conference buckled and countermanded the Western territory leadership's decision, with ongoing public relations consequences, both for and against.[99] Such decisions have left long-lasting, perhaps ineradicable, impressions, despite the Army's track record for delivering services to all without discrimination.

---

97. http://www.salvationarmy.org.nz/uploads/TSA_and_Homosexual_Law_Reform_Bill.pdf, downloaded 23 June 2016. Rapprochement with the Army was initiated from the Wellington Rainbow Board, because younger members of the gay community thought that older members of their community needed to move on from 1986 attitudes and felt it was important to recognise the Army's leading role as a social justice advocate. It took 18 months of negotiations to sign-off. Email, Campbell Roberts to author, 27 March 2017.

98. http://www.salvationarmy.org.nz/our-community/faith-in-life/christian-ethics/same-sex-attitudes-survey, downloaded 23 June 2016.

99. http://www.christianitytoday.com/ct/2002/january7/11.18.html, accessed 23 June 2016.

The Salvation Army's positional statements have reflected changing attitudes. Acceptance of the fact that being gay is not simply a matter of personal choice but is of far more complex derivation has led the Army to distinguish between orientation and activity, the former not considered blameworthy but the latter incompatible, at present, with soldiership in the Army. This half-way-house solution is of course still discriminatory and internationally a "salvos for an inclusive church" movement maintains a closed facebook page, supports gay Salvationists and urges further change. Given the endemic homophobia in many territories where the Salvation Army is now strongest numerically, this promises to be a long and uphill battle. The spectacle of the Anglican communion dismembering itself on the same issue gives leaders reason for anxiety.

On such matters doctrine becomes quite difficult to disentangle from discipline—those twins whose union was announced in the title of the first Salvationist instruction manual on belief, *The Doctrines and Discipline of The Salvation Army*. Internationally there are fault-lines which are also culturally determined, and these are under the seismic pressure of globalization. For the church there is the added complication that morality may be seen as derived from the scriptures, especially when "they only constitute the Divine rule of Christian faith and practice," as stated by the Army's first doctrine. It may have been assumptions of biblical literalism and inerrancy which allowed an unfortunate Australian officer in 2012 to be manipulated during a hostile radio interview into unintentionally giving the impression (it was not his personal view) that the Salvation Army supported the death penalty for gays because that is what the book of Leviticus decreed.[100] In this electronic age, corrections never overtake a story too good for someone not to use and embroider, again and again. A gay Salvationist in New Zealand observed on the thirtieth anniversary of the decriminalization of homosexual acts, an event marked by renewed criticism by some of the Salvation Army's role at the time, that we just have to "suck it up" as the price of our loyalty to the Army.

Regarding the disputes breaking apart the world-wide Anglican communion, a retired bishop, Brian Castle, has observed that "the real issue is not sexuality but the interpretation of Scripture." Citing earlier questions over which the church has finally agreed on a consensus, including such core issues as the person of Christ 1,500 years ago, Castle asked for a "searching out, relating, and engaging with those with whom we strongly disagree, and listening respectfully to the way that God is speaking to them through the Scriptures."[101] Can Salvationists do that?

Changes in Salvationist Social Services over the past forty years.

We have noted that one legacy of Darkest England is that for much of the twentieth century, Salvation Army social work in many "western" countries at least, was largely institutional, officer-staffed, and separate from the corps (field) work, while men's and women's social programs were also administered separately. For example, in 1939 the

---

100. http://www.huffingtonpost.com/2012/06/26/andrew-craibe-salvation-army-official-gays-put-to-death_n_1628135.html, accessed 23 June 2016.

101. Brian Castle, "Can the Communion stay together?" 13.

Army ran thirty-nine institutions in New Zealand, including nine children's homes, twelve hostels, five aged care homes, six maternity hospitals, three hotels, one farm, one sanatorium for alcoholics, and two "labor yards." In addition to these, there were police court officers and "samaritan" officers providing poor relief in main centers, and corps officers supplied local relief in provincial towns and more rural areas. That pattern, really largely derived from the "Darkest England" scenario, remained the norm until the last quarter of the twentieth century.

From that time changes began to be introduced, in part in response to changing government policies and expectations as well as because of the Army's internal reflection, the decline in the number of its officers, and its financial needs. There was less institutional and residential care, and more community-based work; greater government regulation and more need for trained professionals. More non-officer staff and not just fewer officers but also fewer Salvationists were therefore employed. Men's and women's social work became integrated, as increasingly were "field" work and social work—now many social work centers were more closely associated with corps and many corps became involved in some social work. Some areas of work largely disappeared in many territories—maternity hospitals, children's homes and even aged care in Australia southern and New Zealand territories. On the other hand, some fields of work such as addiction services have greatly expanded. Some new fields became established (or old fields were rediscovered), such as employment training.

Challenges

Introducing a publication containing papers presented at a symposium on "The Theology of Social Services" held at the Catherine Booth Bible College in Canada in 1985, Earl Robinson summed up the issues facing Salvation Army Social Services:

1. Should The Salvation Army's emphasis be that of a balanced ministry between evangelism and social responsibility, the whole gospel to the total human personality? If so, is it possible for that balanced ministry to involve an equal partnership between evangelism and social responsibility, or is prioritization inevitable as the Church Growth Movement would suggest?

2. Should The Salvation Army expand into socio-political action concerning social ethics instead of relegating itself to evangelism and social service, even at the possible risk of a diminishing church growth?

3. With many areas of social work now passing into secular or government hands or funding, should The Salvation Army maintain involvement in those areas in fulfilment of the cultural mandate, or withdraw from areas of ministry in which there is little or no room for fulfilling the evangelistic mandate because of government or secular restrictions?

4. Is it possible to maintain a Christian social services program without the bulk of the workers in that program being persons who have experienced an individualistic

reconciling conversion? In other words, what is the relevance to The Salvation Army today of the Social Gospel/Fundamentalist controversy of the 1920s and 1930s?

5. More explicitly and perhaps in summary, is it possible to develop a theology of social service which goes beyond Christocentric examples to something more developed, something which does approach theological rationale and a theological world-view?[102]

The issues identified by Robinson remain at the heart of debate on Salvation Army social work more than thirty years later.

---

102. Robinson, "The Whole Gospel," in Waldron, *Creed and Deed*, 4.

10

To the Ends of the Earth

On we march with the blood and the fire,
To the ends of the earth we will go;
And the Savior's love will be the theme of our song
Because we love him so.[1]
—Charles Mehling

THE INTERNATIONAL EXPANSION OF THE SALVATION ARMY

Booth's London headquarters became an "international headquarters" in 1880, and the words were soon emblazoned on the front of the Queen Victoria Street buildings like a HOLLYWOOD sign. Booth himself wished that the word "foreign" should be banished from Salvationists' vocabulary; Robert Sandall refers to his saying so in 1886 and quotes him saying in 1889 that he would like to abolish the distinction between "Christian countries" and "heathen lands" and "just divide mankind into two classes—the friends or the enemies of his Saviour Lord."[2] However, the IHQ appointment of "Foreign Secretary" was not superseded by "International Secretaries" until after 1908 and the "Foreign Office" became the "Overseas Department" in 1927.

The first chapter mentioned briefly some examples of the Salvation Army's early expansion overseas and the way its social work was taken up internationally has also been mentioned, but this chapter attempts a more systematic analysis of the Army's spread. It would not be useful to try to condense the story of the Salvation Army in all its territories into a chapter. Many territories have produced full-length histories—some more than one—and the bibliography includes many of these. Entries in *The Salvation Army*

---

1. *Song Book of The Salvation Army*, 2015, No. 932.
2. Sandall, *History*, II, 226.

Year Book also include a sentence or two of historical introduction, and John Merritt's admirable *Historical Dictionary of The Salvation Army* provides a summary of the history of each territory and command.[3]

As an aside at this point, it may be noted that at time of writing one significant territory had not yet been accorded a volume of its own; that is the original one, of the British Isles. This may be because all international Salvation Army histories inevitably start with Britain, and all thematic material naturally refers to Britain as well, so it seems as though the ground is already covered. Another reason may be that the British territory was until 1990 under the direct authority of International Headquarters and its administrative head was the General. The British Commissioner was in charge of evangelical work, while Britain's social work (for many years separately men's and women's) and the International Training College, along with several other departments, all reported independently to IHQ. All this has meant that the on-going life of the Army in Britain has remained to some extent under the radar of historians. Britain's own Salvationist history, written particularly to explore the Army's story in the land of its origin and disentangled so far as that might be appropriate or practicable from what Norman Murdoch used to call "the Salvationist Imperium," is yet to be written, and it would be a worthwhile project.

For the present purpose however, I have rather sought to adduce certain themes from the Army's world-wide history, and illustrate them with reference to particular countries.

Before addressing that purpose, however, a brief overview of the Army's spread is in order, even though an outline chronological account has already been included in the first chapter and does not need to be repeated here. In summary, by decades, it can be seen that after the initial scramble expansion was at times as strongly influenced by international events and trends as by the Army's internal mission imperative. In the 1940s and 1950s, not only were few new countries entered but in a number of places the Salvation Army succumbed to war and then to cold war pressures. Following the fall of the Soviet Union some of these countries were re-entered, and recent decades have seen wider expansion again.

1880–1889	24 countries entered	1950–1959	2
1890–1899	14	1960–1969	3
1900–1909	13	1970–1979	7
1910–1919	12	1980–1989	8
1920–1929	11	1990–1999	5 + 5 re-opened
1930–1939	11	2000–2009	10
1940–1949	0, and at least 7 suppressed	2010–2015	8

The immediate local triggers for the Salvation Army's spread around the world are not easily categorized country by country, because the initial impetus was often from more than one direction. To take just one example, in 1894 two officers were sent from the Netherlands, with riding instructions from the Salvation Army's Foreign Secretary

---

3. Merritt (ed.), *Historical Dictionary*.

in London, to raise the flag in the Dutch East Indies, now Indonesia. In the background however, some Netherlands Indies clergy and friends in Holland had been urging the Army to act; a Dutch Salvationist living in Surabaya had been witnessing and looking forward to the coming of the Army; a Sumatran lady, converted in England by the Christian Mission, had written to the Army in Australia offering to build a hall and quarters for officers and give £1,000 to their support; a Chinese lady in Semarang had had a dream of preachers wearing red tunics (they did) and told people about it; a group of Javanese "spiritual orphans"—converts of a departed preacher—was waiting in Central Java in the place the pioneer officers settled.[4] Sometimes again there was a series of false starts before permanent success was achieved in a new locality, as in Italy between 1887 and 1889, making it more difficult to place a finger on a firm date.

Recognizing therefore that most stories were far from simple, and there may be differing views on some of the following, we might still attempt to categorize some of the reasons for the Army's spread, with examples, in this doubtless incomplete list as follows:

- Invitations from people who wanted the Army to come to their country: (2)

    New Zealand, 1883: Arabella Valpy wrote to Booth requesting the Army, and sent money. *Caribbean, Jamaica*, 1887: Former slave Agnes Foster, and W. Raglan Phillips, an English resident of Jamaica, both of whom had been converted to Salvationism at different times and had both started their own missions, wrote to William Booth in 1885. In 1887, Booth sent out his pioneer Caribbean party. The rest of the West Indies/Caribbean territory was added at intervals up to 2011.

- Emigrants taking the Army with them to their new country unofficially, and writing back for reinforcements: (3)

    USA 1879: the Shirley family. *Australia* 1880: Gore and Saunders. *Canada* 1882: Mr and Mrs William Freer, Mrs Shaw, Annie Maxwell, Jack Addie, and Joe Ludgate.

- Someone coming to Britain (or elsewhere) from another country to join the Army and then taking it back home with them: (4)

    India, 1882: Frederick Tucker. *Sweden*, 1882: Hannah Ouchterlony. *Netherlands*, 1887: Gerritt Govaars. *Finland*, 1889: several Finns sent to London to become officers, (Constantin Boije af Gennäs, Hedvig von Haartman and Alva Forsius) on the initiative of Baroness Louise af Forselles.

- Someone joining the Army elsewhere and then taking it home: (1)

    Germany, 1886: Fritz Schaaff.

- Migrant workers starting the Army at home after meeting it elsewhere and then asking for officers to be sent: (4)

    The Philippines, 1937; *Zambia (Northern Rhodesia)*, 1924; *Mozambique*, 1916; *Malawi*, 1967 from Rhodesia.

- Migrant workers starting the Army in their country of employment after belonging to it at home and then asking for officers to be sent: (1)

    Middle East, 2008.

---

4. Brouwer, *Salvation Army in Indonesia*, 4.

- A group of Christians start a mission, or an unofficial branch of the Army, and ask the Army to take it over: (6)

    Norway, 1887; *Nigeria*, variously from 1902 *and then officially* 1920; *Latvia*, 1923; *Mexico*, 1934; *Portugal*, 1964–1971; *Liberia*, 1978–1988.

- The Army provides relief in emergency and stays on: (3)

    Bangladesh, 1970 after a cyclone; *El Salvador*, 1989 after an earthquake; *Rwanda*, 1994 after genocide and civil war.

- The Army is requested by a Government to do some specific task, leading to wider work: (1)

    Hong Kong, 1930.

- Limited work under special circumstances like Red Shield war services to troops or with refugees followed by withdrawal: (2)

    Egypt, 1915–19 and from 1936–49 at Port Said to cater for sea-farers, and in the Second World War for troops; *Vietnam* 1999; *Curaçao*, Mission to Seamen, 1927–early 1980s.

- Advance initiated by IHQ: (17)

    France 1881; *South Africa* 1883; *Italy* 1887–89; *Argentina* 1890; *Japan* 1895; *Korea* 1908; *Chile* 1909; *China* 1915; *Kenya* 1921; *Brazil* 1922; *Belgian Congo* 1934; *Singapore* 1935; *Yugoslavia* 1933–1948; *Spain* 1971; *Russia* re-opened 1991; *Poland* 2005; *Mali* 2007.

- Advance initiated by a THQ in a neighboring or other country: (33)

    Switzerland, 1882 from France; *Sri Lanka (Ceylon)*, 1883 from India; *Denmark*, 1887 from Sweden; *Uruguay*, 1891 from Argentina; *Rhodesia*, later *Zimbabwe*, 1891 from South Africa; *Dutch East Indies*, later *Indonesia*, 1894 from Holland; *Iceland*, 1895 from Denmark; *Peru*, 1910 from Chile; *Cuba*, 1912 from USA; *Myanmar (Burma)*, 1915 from India; *Russia*, 1915 from Finland; *Belize*, 1915 from Barbados; *Bolivia*, 1921 from Chile; *Hungary*, 1924 from Germany; *Austria*, 1925 from Switzerland; *Estonia*, 1927 from Finland; *Taiwan*, 1928 from Japan, and re-established 1965; *Manchuria*, 1930 from North China; *Uganda*, 1931 from Kenya; *Tanganyika*, later *Tanzania*, 1933 from Kenya; *Congo Brazzaville*, 1937 spread from Leopoldville (Belgian Congo) to *French Equatorial Africa*; *Philippines*, 1937 from USA Western territory, but also as result of migrant workers meeting Salvation Army elsewhere; *Papua New Guinea*, 1956 from Australia; *Fiji*, 1973 from New Zealand; *Angola*, two Angolan officers, trained and serving in Congo Kinshasa, started in *Angola* 1974, others in 1978, officially recognized 1985; *Colombia*, 1985 from Panama; *Tonga*, 1986 from Fiji; *Romania*, 1999, from Russia/CIS; *Mongolia*, 2008 from Korea; *Nepal*, 2009 from India East, *Cambodia*, 2012 a Korean soldier's initiative, taken over officially by Korean Territory; *Greenland*, 2012 from Denmark.

Of course that is not the full story, because ultimately IHQ has always to give permission for an international extension of the Salvation Army's work. Further, behind many of the seventeen or so advances categorized as made on IHQ initiative, and the thirty-three attributed to some other territorial initiative, there may well have been stories similar to others already mentioned. It is striking, however, how many ventures followed up an invitation, or have been initiated by the Salvationists or headquarters of neighboring or other related countries. All this is to say that the expansion of the Army was never centrally directed upon a master-plan, but usually followed upon the perception of God's opening of a door and some person's initiative to go through it.

Primary recognition is therefore given to the theological and spiritual drivers for expansion; what Dr Lightfoot described in 1882 as "the universal compulsion for the souls of men."[5] We could mention here the post-millennial conviction that the Army was to the fore in ushering in the universal reign of Christ. Concerning this, Commissioner Erik Wickberg speculated in a 1965 article on "The International Salvationist and His Citizenship," that William Booth hoped that he might be instrumental in converting the whole world. He quoted Begbie to this effect, citing Booth's 1903 comment that "it was possible to bring men and women of every degree and temperament into the fold of The Salvation Army, and he even dared, in certain moments of enthusiasm, to think that he himself might live to accomplish this consummation." Begbie thought that the fact that Booth's travels in his old age, his being greeted with universal respect and appreciation, and his constantly seeing and hearing of "the most astonishing, the most dramatic, and also the most pathetic stories of individual conversions . . . must surely have been an inspiration of irresistible power . . . In a certain measure it may be said that he looked for a Second Advent."[6]

Early Salvationists' post-millennial optimism has already been mentioned in the section on eschatology, including Catherine Booth's conviction that "this Movement is to inaugurate the great final conquest of our Lord Jesus Christ."[7] This was also a pronounced theme in Salvation Army song-writing and some songs of this kind are still to be found in the 2015 *Salvation Army Song Book*:

From Song 953:

> With Salvation for every nation,
> To the ends of the earth we will go
> With a free and a full salvation,
> All the power of the cross we'll show.
> We'll tear Hell's throne to pieces,
> And win the world for Jesus,
> We'll be conquerors for ever,
> For we never will give in.
>
> WILLIAM JAMES PEARSON (1832–92)

---

5. Joseph Barber Lightfoot, Bishop of Durham, in an 1882 sermon on the Salvation Army, quoted by Bramwell Booth, *Echoes and Memories*, 76.

6. Begbie, *William Booth*, II, 274–75, quoted by Wickberg, 1965 *Year Book*, 17.

7. Booth, "Invasion of the U.S.," quoted by Rhemick, *New People of God*, 202–03.

From Song 963:

Joy! joy! joy! there is joy in The Salvation Army,
Joy! joy! joy! in the Army of the Lord.
We will sing, we will sing, till the world is full of joy;
We will shout, we will shout, till glad voices rend the sky
With a thousand bands and a thousand drums
We will praise the Lord in bright, happy homes,
We will sing and shout till the Master comes,
We will ever praise the Lord.

WILLIAM JAMES PEARSON (1832–92)

From Song 967:

Though some would try to crush us,
We're rising every day,
And soon o'er every land and sea
Our flag shall have the sway;
Salvation free to all men
Shall be our battle cry,
For the day of victory's coming by and by.

JAMES CONNER BATEMAN (1855–88)

It could also be mentioned here that the Army's early expansion was also facilitated by inventions such as railways, telegraph, and steam navigation. The technological advances of the late nineteenth century might be compared with the Roman roads and Roman peace which enabled the spread of Christianity in the first century. Modern transport and communications made the expansion of the Salvation Army much more rapid than it might have been, and ensured tighter control from the center than might have been possible a few years earlier. Officers could be dispatched and transferred at shorter notice than ever before. IHQ and subsidiary headquarters even employed a telegraphic code book so that dispositions of the salvation war could be conveyed at greater length, more quickly, more cheaply and in greater secrecy than by open telegram or cable, even though occasionally there were problems with decoding information.[8] Booth himself celebrated the value of technology:

> The world has grown much smaller since the electric telegraph was discovered and side by side with the shrinkage of this planet under the influence of steam

---

8. Such a misunderstanding between William and Bramwell is mentioned in letters from South Africa on 9 September and 7 October 1908, cited by Murdoch in *Christian Warfare*, 71, 86.

and electricity there has come a sense of brotherhood and a consciousness of community of interest and nationality on the part of the English-speaking peoples throughout the world.[9]

Certainly modern transport networks meant that William Booth could have claimed that "all the world is my parish" even more aptly than John Wesley since he was enabled to travel more miles in more countries, and preach to more people, and perhaps see more conversions than anyone before his time. In his last decade, the Founder's early twentieth-century motorized preaching tours in England were justly celebrated as thoroughly modern and innovative, despite the discomfort he endured—and the dust and grit in his eyes which precipitated his final blindness.

The influence of technology did not cease with the Founder's departure from the scene. Radio and television have long been exploited for communicating the gospel—and for advertising—and in California the Army runs an innovative television production arm, SAVN-TV. Some of the present expansion in India and Africa is facilitated by the internet and the mobile phone.

Beyond those factors, the Salvation Army's 150-year history has been played out on a world stage set by imperialism, nationalism, internationalism and globalization. It is the interplay of such movements with the Salvation Army's expansion that I want to review in more detail; in particular the tension between the Army's claim to internationalism and the realities of its emanating from an imperial center and in consequence developing what in some respects might be called an imperial culture. To tease out the definitions a little here, internationalism involves the idea of cooperation for the benefit of all, across national, political, cultural, racial, and class boundaries. Imperialism tends to denote the advocacy of imperial or sovereign interests over the interests of the dependent states. Globalization refers to that process of international integration arising from the sharing of world-views, ideas, products, and other aspects of culture; in Robertson's words, "the compression of the world and the intensification of consciousness of the world as a whole."[10]

IMPERIALISM: THE SALVATION ARMY'S IMPERIAL CULTURE

It will be obvious that the evangelical and social work of the Salvation Army can be said to be internationalist in character. This has been enthusiastically celebrated throughout its history. On the Army's centenary in 1965, Alfred Gilliard forecast "in the next century a richness of internationalism which only William Booth and a few of his intimates distantly glimpsed, a fulfilment of the momentary promise of the early days, when William Booth's young men and women went out like a swift ocean wave out into the unknown, there to touch young men and women of other races and cultures in the glory of a Pentecostal brotherhood."[11] In her 2012 presentation to the joint Roman Catholic and Salvation Army dialogue, Karen Shakespeare cited Robert Sandall's celebration of

---

9. Booth, *Darkest England*, 143.
10. Robertson, *Globalization*, 8.
11. Gilliard, "Catching up with William Booth," 10.

the fact that "there has never been a Salvation Army missionary society, rather there are expressions of The Salvation Army in various countries which seek to be relevant to the local culture, so the interaction between the context and the tradition of the movement leads to adaptations of Salvationism that are culturally relative and culturally produced. At the same time, expressions of Salvationism have been shared throughout the world, so that some traditions have become almost universal and are encountered far from their natural place of origin. Thus any discussion of the mode of Salvation Army mission must take into account both our unity and our diversity."[12]

More contentious is the suggestion that the Army's own character and culture has an imperial aspect. To be clear, I am referring to the imperial aspect of the Salvation Army itself, rather than its being an agency for specifically British imperialism. Nevertheless, the ground for this was laid culturally as well as politically by the British imperialist enthusiasm fostered by Disraeli and encouraged by the Conservative party in the fourth quarter of the nineteenth century. British imperialism was thus part of the context in which the Salvation Army arose and spread, and for many Salvationists it was inevitably part of their mind-set. Such an attitude was not the sole prerogative of the British of course, but also informed the late nineteenth-century "scramble for Africa" by European powers as well as the sense of "manifest destiny" which marked the continental expansion of the United States. Some saw in all this the hand of God and proof of divine favor; others, less religiously inclined, celebrated the survival—and dominance—of the fittest. Harald Fischer-Tiné observes that "even organizations and historical actors like the Salvationists who, at the outset viewed themselves as distinctly apolitical and sometimes even antigovernment, were marked by the imperial rhetoric and modes of knowledge production that were regarded as authoritative at the time: the imperial social formation heavily influenced the ways to look at and make sense of the world."[13]

While Booth did not go in for the wackier theological constructs of empire such as British Israelitism, he was pragmatic enough to ride on imperialism's coat-tails when that was helpful to his mission. In 1886 he said, "I do not care how far the British flag floats, nor over how much it floats, so long as it waves there righteously, because under the British flag the Salvation Army has a good chance of working out its principles with success."[14]

A difficulty was that while he was willing to make use of the Empire, the Empire also sought to make use of him, and he could not guarantee its righteousness. Ann Woodall says that

> Booth's immigration scheme turned him, in a practical sense, into a social imperialist. From his writing it would be possible to make a strong argument that Booth became such because he saw it as a virtuous way to ease the problems of poverty in the East End. However, in seeking to implement his plans he became

---

12. Shakespeare, "Forms of Mission Today—a Salvation Army Perspective," in *Conversations*, 260–261, referring to Sandall, *History*, II, 225.

13. Fischer-Tiné, "Global Civil Society and the Forces of Empire," 52.

14. Booth, "Great Exhibition Address by the General," in *War Cry*, 8 August, 1896, quoted by Eason, "Christianity in a Colonial Age," 377.

involved with others of whom two in particular . . . were quite definitely imperialists, namely W.T. Stead and Cecil Rhodes.[15]

Woodall quotes a letter Stead wrote to Alfred Milner on 23rd October 1890: "You will be delighted to see that we have got the Salvation Army solid not only for Social Reform but also for Imperial Unity."[16] Booth may not have conceded Stead's claim here, had he known of it, but might not have objected too strongly either. Teasing out the Army's claim to internationalism from these imperial origins and influences is not always simple, whatever the aspirations and ideals of the Army's Founders and their successors. Rebecca Carter-Chand suggests that

> it was not the ideals of cultural internationalism (i.e., the hope that international identities and international contact would lead to a more peaceful world order) that carried it through dark times. [The Salvation Army's] internationalist identity was based on a multi-national structure (i.e., it existed globally as one international organization, divided along national lines but reporting to the International Headquarters in London). This multi-national structure was inspired by British imperialism, and later celebrated as evidence of the flowering of cultural internationalism.[17]

Thomas Hobbes wrote in his *Leviathan* that "The Papacy is not other than the Ghost of the deceased Roman Empire, sitting crowned upon the grave thereof."[18] Like Hobbes' papacy, the Salvation Army came to resemble the ghost of the (eventually) deceased British Empire lingering, crowned, and seated upon its grave. In fact, emancipating its internationalism from those imperial roots in practice has been a work requiring more than a century, and there were both political and cultural implications to be disentangled. As Fischer-Tiné observes, the Salvation Army consciously sought to avoid political statements or involvement, but multi-national organizations can seldom stand so aloof from realpolitik.

We might see the Salvation Army's own culture as in some ways like a religious or spiritual equivalent of imperial culture, a sort of "ghost in the machine" to borrow Gilbert Ryle's phrase.[19] It has helped to knit the movement's far-flung territories together. A number of strategies and characteristics have helped establish the identity and self-image of the Army as a kind of international sub-culture, and to maintain its coherence. Among them might be included:

- Identity cues like the uniform, ranks and terminology, flag, crest and other badges, including later the Red Shield.
- Salvationists' doctrines and beliefs held in common, along with a common evangelical enthusiasm.

---

15. Woodall, *What Price the Poor?* 197.
16. Whyte, *Life of Stead*, II, 13, quoted by Woodall, Ibid., 197–98.
17. Carter-Chand, "Doing Good in Bad Times," 7.
18. Thomas Hobbes, *Leviathan or The Matter, Forme and Power of a Common Wealth Ecclesiasticall and Civil* published in 1665. The name derives from the Biblical Leviathan, as in Job 40 and 41.
19. Ryle, *The Concept of the Mind*.

- Commitments to a common life-style and discipline in the soldiers' covenant and officers' undertakings.
- The hierarchical polity and structures, expressed in *Orders and Regulations* and minutes emanating from IHQ.
- Leadership tours overseas by William Booth, his successor-Generals and other leaders sent to inspect the work and rouse the troops in the Army's far-flung territories.
- Cross-pollenation brought about by the international transfer of leadership and other officers, along with the practice of bringing officers to London to the International Training College and International Staff College (later, International College for Officers, and now, International College for Officers and Center for Spiritual Life Development).
- The reprinting of material from the British (or "international") *War Cry* in the papers of overseas territories, and the publication of periodicals like *All the World, The Warrior, Vanguard, International Company Orders* (Sunday School lessons) and Corps Cadet lesson manuals, brass band Journals and the internationally-circulated English-language journal for officers, *The Officer*.
- The common use of many songs and choruses, both melodies and words (even if in various translations), and common liturgical characteristics like its informal worship or meeting format, testimony and extemporary prayer.
- Participation in various imperial exhibitions held in Great Britain from the 1880s to the 1930s.
- The holding of international events such as the international congresses of 1886, 1894, 1904, 1914, 1965, 1978, 1990, 2000, 2012 and 2015; and other conferences and commissions. The objects of the first international war congress, held in London in June 1886, were announced as being:

    1. That the leaders and soldiers of the movement might become better acquainted with each other.
    2. That there might be a great increase of that brotherly love and mutual sympathy which largely prevailed, but which it was very desirable should be deepened.
    3. That new methods and plans of action might be laid down, explained, understood and acted upon.
    4. That there might be a great Pentecostal baptism of the fire of the Holy Ghost upon the multitudes who would assemble together, purifying from sin and inflaming all with the pure love of God and pitying compassion for perishing men, that should spread salvation to the uttermost parts of the earth.[20]

All these strategies contributed to the binding of all together in a common subculture with a sense of belonging to a world-wide fellowship. A non-Salvationist French scholar, Dr. G. Swarts, spoke of the "profound unity" of this "completely internationalized

---

20. Sandall, *History*, II, 298–99.

organization," declaring that "a French Salvation Army officer certainly in every respect resembles one of his Indian or American colleagues more than he does a French non-Salvationist."[21] Note that Swarts specifically mentioned officers; I have referred to that distinction in Chapter 3: "The conditions of officers' service would constitute their professional milieu in a way that could not be true of non-officer, volunteer Salvationists . . . giving officership a character which could be described as clerical compared with that of the rank and file." It is difficult to avoid making a comparison with a Catholic order in this respect. However, the sense of "belonging" is felt to some degree by most Salvationists and not only by officers. Joan Hutson was writing of ordinary New Zealand Salvationists in a provincial corps, but her comments could be extrapolated much further afield:

> The feeling of "family," with all its ups and downs, extended way beyond the borders of Gisborne. A Salvationist could walk into any corps throughout the country, indeed throughout the world, and feel welcome. There was even a distinctive Army whistle used primarily in New Zealand from about the time of the Great War. Thought to have been the opening bars of a once popular march, it was used to attract the attention of a fellow Salvationist whether in a military canteen, across the street or at a rugby match—all immensely tribal. The strong Army culture meant that the uniforms, the belief system, the rituals, the jargon and, yes, even the whistle all loudly declared that Salvationists were "at home" even if they knew not one person present. At the deepest level of consciousness, they belonged.[22]

IN TIME OF WAR

Mention of that whistle in time of war reminds us that such times of conflict raise most obviously the tensions which might emerge between imperial or national loyalties and the Army's commitment to internationalism—the unity of peoples across national, political or cultural divides. The go-to source for the story of the Salvation Army in war time is General Shaw Clifton's *Crown of Glory, Crown of Thorns*, based on his doctoral thesis.[23] His title is aptly taken from Frederick Coutts' words, "The Army's internationalism is its crown of glory in peacetime, but in time of war it becomes its crown of thorns."[24] Here too one of the themes is the tension between true internationalism and imperial or national and local loyalties; between a commitment to peace and the desire to serve one's own community engaged in war.

Ironically, given that he founded an "Army," William Booth and most of his family, most of whom held senior positions in the organization, were pacifists to varying

---

21. Swarts, *Le Banc des Pénitents* (Paris, Librarie Philosophique J. Vrin), a course of lectures given at the Sorbonne in 1931 on the soul-saving methods of The Salvation Army, quoted by Gauntlett, *International Army*, 6.

22. Hutson, *As for Me and My House*, 227.

23. Clifton, *Crown of Glory, Crown of Thorns*; Clifton, "The Salvation Army's Attitudes and Actions."

24. Coutts, *Portrait of a Salvationist*, 18, quoted by Clifton, *Crown of Glory*, 509.

degrees—although not pacifists for pacifism's sake, unalloyed. His biographer, Harold Begbie, recalled Booth's priorities. In short, war was a distraction from saving souls:

> It was not only the dreadful and inhuman hatreds roused by war which distressed William Booth. The moral earnestness which it occasions always seemed to him a waste of the human spirit. He saw with bewilderment and pain a nation which tolerates sin and suffering in its own midst roused by war to an almost incredible condition of moral energy and spiritual enthusiasm. Why, he asked himself, would not people give to the war against evil—which is the root cause of poverty and pain—something of this same energy and enthusiasm?[25]

Thus, the first issue of the private magazine for officers in 1893 laid down its editorial policy: "No bloody war spirit, no pandering to the brutal craving for wholesale slaughter, has polluted our pages. We hate war, and all its paraphernalia . . . Let us beware, even in our illustrations, lest we pander to, or tolerate, the cruel taste for blood."[26] On the outbreak of the second Anglo-Boer war in 1899 William Booth had written, "No matter who wins . . . I lose, for there are Salvationists fighting on both sides."[27] His instructions to Salvationists at that time were reprinted in the *War Cry* of 5 August 1916: "Live in the spirit of intercession. Plead for a speedy termination of the horrid strife. Pray for your comrades . . . on the British side, and pray also for your comrades, the Salvationists, who are on the other."[28]

Bramwell Booth, succeeding his father as General in 1912, made a similar appeal in 1914.[29] He forbade Salvation Army officers to enlist as combatants unless they were compelled by law to do so.[30] Booth is said to have forbidden the use of the word "enemy" in Salvation Army publications and in his 1915 Christmas message echoed Tertullian's claim that "Every land is my Fatherland for all lands are my Father's!"[31] Florence Booth, the General's wife, wrote that to pray for victory was not an option open to Christians since "victory must equally mean defeat for others."[32] The British *War Cry* printed reports of the Army inside Germany and told stories of "good Germans" to counter the prevailing Germanophobia, and colonial versions of the *War Cry* reprinted these articles. Soon after the end of hostilities Bramwell Booth invited a German officer to speak at a Salvationist rally in London.

At the same time as these pacific statements and gestures, there was some ambiguity about the Army's position—both with respect to war itself, and in its relationship with

25. Begbie, *William Booth*, II, 237–38.

26. *Officer*, January 1893, 4.

27. Reprinted in (NZ) *War Cry*, 19 September 1914, 4.

28. (NZ) *War Cry*, 5 August 1916, 4.

29. (NZ) *War Cry*, 26 September 1914, 5.

30. (NZ) *War Cry*, 7 November 1914, 2. Twenty New Zealand Salvation Army officers either resigned or were given leave to enlist.

31. Collier, *General Next to God*, 250; Bramwell-Booth, *Bramwell Booth*, 353. Carter-Chand points out that although reference is often made to the embargo on the word "enemy," and it is not implausible, no original source for the claim has been evinced.

32. *War Cry* (UK), 24 October 1914, 6, quoted in Clifton, "The Salvation Army's Attitudes and Actions," 124.

Germany. While refusing to apportion blame for the South African war, William Booth had initiated welfare services amongst British troops serving there, under the direction of Staff-Captain Mary Murray, herself the daughter of a British Army General. Similar support was provided from 1914, with ambulance and nursing services, "comforts" for the troops, hostels and welfare services of many kinds, along with military chaplaincies in due course. The Salvation Army thus supported the combatants if not the combat. Perhaps cannily reading the likely response of his own troops, Bramwell Booth did not attempt to bind upon Salvationists his own pacifism, rejecting any suggestion that he should forbid soldiers of the Salvation Army to take up arms or proclaim that all war was murder.

Nor could all Salvationists muster the same commitment to international goodwill as the General proposed. He himself could not always abstain from patriotic sentiment, as when at a service in the London Opera House to commemorate Salvationist servicemen killed in the war, the national anthem having been sung and the Union Jack and the Army flag waving side by side, "The General declared that those who had fallen had done so in 'the cause of righteousness.'"[33] In his 1919 Report on the Army's War Services, Commissioner Henry C. Hodder, territorial commander of the Salvation Army in New Zealand, who had two sons serving in the Canadian forces, could not resist stating his conviction that Germany had "forced war upon the world," and that the "Salvation Army flag followed the Union Jack."[34]

The fact is that the Salvation Army in all theatres of the First World War and in subsequent conflicts as well, has usually offered with alacrity any support possible and consistent with its principles, to the authorities of each combatant nation state, and thereby often secured public and governmental good-will, and financial support which lasted into the post-war years.

Perhaps symbolizing the two poles of the Army's allegiances, at least two of Booth's successors as General, George Carpenter (Australian, 1939–46) and Frederick Coutts (British, 1963–69) became avowed pacifists (although Coutts had served in the Royal Air Force late in the First World War); while Clarence Wiseman (1974–77, Canadian) and Jarl Wahlström (1981–86, Finnish) served as military chaplains in the Second World War.

Notwithstanding this ambivalence of loyalties, the Salvation Army has been a force for international peace and goodwill even at such times. Innumerable stories have been told of the international fellowship facilitated across national and cultural lines, particularly significant in times of war. Carvosso Gauntlett's 1945 pamphlet, *An International Army*, recounted a number of such stories of Salvationist soldiers on warring sides being able to transcend national divisions, before, during and after the war. One such poignant event was the funeral of a Belgian Salvationist killed in a Brussels air-raid where the four Salvationist pall-bearers were two Belgians, a British airman in hiding and a German soldier of the occupation troops. Another was the story of a Japanese guard in a prisoner of war camp, a Salvation Army officer in peace-time, seeking out British Salvationists to sing and pray with them.[35] Melattie Brouwer also tells how an Indonesian Salvation

33. Clifton, *Crown of Glory*, 117.
34. Quoted in Clifton, "The Salvation Army's Attitudes and Actions," 274.
35. Gauntlett, *International Army*, 3, 4.

Army officer, Captain Wuarlela, was trying to re-establish contact with Salvation Army outposts in Sumatra during the chaotic days following Japanese invasion in early 1942. Arrested as a suspected spy, his life was saved by a Japanese officer, Miyahira, a Salvation Army lieutenant in Java before the war, who recognized him.[36]

More recently, Commissioner Don Ødegaard has described how his officer-parents in occupied Norway were dismayed by the knocking at their door by a member of the Wehrmacht in combat uniform. Alarm was allayed when the German soldier unbuttoned his uniform tunic to reveal a Salvation Army guernsey beneath; he was also a Salvation Army officer.[37] After the war, the young Ødegaard was able to holiday with the visitor and his family in Germany. A darker story was told by Commissioner A.J. Gilliard, Principal of the International College for Officers in London in the 1950s. He recalled seeing at the opening of one session a look of shock and dismayed recognition pass between two delegates. Asking to see them privately, he learned that the German officer had been in command of an occupation unit in Norway during the war, and in that capacity had been responsible for the execution of hostages including the sister of the Norwegian officer, at that time in the underground resistance. Fifteen or so years later, after the war, both were Salvation Army officers in their respective countries and attended the ICO.

During the Second World War, when IHQ was cut off from direct contact with Salvationists in Axis-controlled countries, some contact was maintained through officers of neutral powers, both in Europe and in the Far East. The Swedish territorial commander, Karl Larsson, took the step of declaring the Salvation Army in Sweden as independent of IHQ for the duration of hostilities in order to keep in touch with, support and encourage spiritually the Army in Germany and occupied Europe without arousing Axis suspicions of British subversion. Swede Eric Wickberg (General 1969–74) was seconded from IHQ as liaison officer, travelling through Europe for this purpose. Wickberg described how

> During a visit to Prague in 1940 [I] conducted a meeting . . . I spoke in German and was translated into Czech. There were a dozen seekers at the Mercy Seat and they were joined by a young German soldier of the Wehrmacht in full uniform. I shall never forget how I watched a Czech Salvation Army officer go down from the platform, kneel beside the German youth, put his arm around him and pray with him.[38]

Not all Salvationists could muster up charitable feelings towards the occupiers and not all stories had happy endings. One story from the Second World War in the Netherlands told how "At the start of the occupation, before The Salvation Army was prohibited, a German Salvationist, in his military uniform attended Sunday meetings at the corps taking his place on the platform with the band. This was something one Salvationist could not cope with. He could not accept the presence of, nor worship alongside his brother in Christ, a fellow Salvationist who was a member of the occupying forces. He resigned his soldiership and never returned to the corps." Of the same man, however, my

36. Brouwer, *Salvation Army in Indonesia*, 128.
37. *Officer*, March–April 2016, 7.
38. Wickberg, *Salvation Army Year Book*, 1965, 19–20.

informant wrote that "During the years which followed he hid Jewish children from the occupier and was later honoured by the state of Israel for his courage . . . After the war, the same man also intervened, at great personal risk, to save the daughter of the town's mayor, a Dutchman who had been a member of the Nazi party. Whilst the angry crowd was baying for the ex-mayor's blood the former Salvationist intervened to save the child from some terrible physical reprisals. It has to be acknowledged that there were also Salvationists who had joined the National Socialist party and their shame was inherited by later generations."[39]

NATIONALISM: SALVATIONIST CULTURE AND LOCAL CULTURE

The counterpoint to imperialism is nationalism and the story of International Headquarters' relationship with its overseas territories has often reflected the tension between these forces; at times creative and constructive, at other times not. With all the unifying, international factors described in the preceding pages, the Salvation Army has faced, firstly, the task of making the Gospel indigenous (a task shared with the rest of the church) and secondly, of making the Salvation Army indigenous. Carrying with it such a strong imperial culture of its own, it has been conflicted in consequence, sometimes identifying with local culture and aspirations, and sometimes, often unwittingly, attempting to impose an alien character upon them.

To take what may be thought a comparatively minor example, Brindley Boon remarked of the Army in Argentina, that "Although the guitar is the most popular instrument in South America, stringed instruments have not been used a great deal in Salvation Army service. Brass bands did not make instant appeal." Admittedly Boon's theme was bands—which officially included "stringed bands"—but he went on to describe the various and not overly successful efforts made to foster brass bands there, without reflecting further on the cultural impropriety and failure to capitalize more intentionally on the local idiom.[40] A much happier story on the same theme is found in Misheck Nyandoro's history of the Army in Zimbabwe, where he describes the huge enthusiasm and success which followed on from the adoption of the use of hoshos and big drums, hitherto more customarily employed by spirit mediums in tribal dances:

> When the officers stood and began rattling their hoshos to the accompaniment of the big-bodied drums, the interest and emotions of old and young alike were quickly stimulated, and the high-pitched ululations could hardly be stopped. . . . the agreeable sound of the hoshos produced a common bond of familiarity for the African people, and gave the officers a chance to appeal to their minds and spirits. Now when the Bible message was presented it found amazingly receptive hearts and minds.[41]

---

39. Correspondent (prefering anonymity) to author, 11 April 2014.

40. Boon, *Play the Music*, 62.

41. Nyandoro, *Flame of Sacred Love*, 153. A "hosho" is a dried gourd with seeds in it, used as a rattle to accompany singing and dancing.

The only sad reflection is that this did not take place until 1967, whereas the Salvation Army had been in Mashonaland since 1891.

People from other cultures are not always sensitive to local symbolism. When Salvation Army work was pioneered in Russia during the First World War, some Orthodox practices such as making the sign of the cross and standing for prayer were utilized by Salvationists, and the Salvation Army crest incorporated the traditional Orthodox three-bar cross (also known as the Suppedaneum cross).[42] When the Army re-entered Russia nearly 70 years later, in 1991, the pioneer officers, Sven and Katie Ljungholm, chose to use the earlier Salvation Army crest as a mark of respect to Russian spirituality but a later expatriate commander unilaterally replaced this with the Latin cross used in the rest of the Army world.

The church has long struggled to differentiate between culture and faith but has also had a distinguished history of cultural adaptation, particularly associated with the work of Catholic pioneers like Raymond Lull (1235 to 1315), missionary to the Saracens; Francis Xavier (1506 to 1552), in India and Japan; Alessandri Valignano (1537 to 1606), in Japan; Matthew Ricci (1552 to 1610) in China; and Robert de Nobili (1577 to 1656), in India. All of these Catholic missionaries opposed the prevailing notion that Christianity should be accompanied by the replacement of indigenous culture with that of Europe and sought to make the Gospel as nearly Indian, Japanese or Chinese as possible. The lesson has to be relearned in every age; the twentieth century Methodist and ecumenical leader Daniel T. Niles from Ceylon used to say the seeds of the Gospel were planted out in cultural flower-pots, but that the pots needed to be broken for the plants to flourish.[43]

In his 1965 article on "The International Salvationist and His Citizenship," already mentioned, Commissioner Erik Wickberg set out to describe how the international character of the Army developed, and its contemporary trend. In the first place, he said, "William Booth intended to let his soldiers in other lands be 'Jews to the Jews' and 'Greeks to the Greeks,' while retaining a rigid administrative control from London." He was sure that the decision to send a Swedish woman to pioneer the work in Sweden and then leave her in control there for ten years was "one of the reasons why the Army in that land became the strongest expression of Salvationism in Europe."[44] It is unfortunate that such commitment to indigeneity and continuity has not been common; more usually, rapid changes of senior leadership, often from other cultures and "doing time" on the promotional ladder, with ever-changing policies and commensurate loss of institutional memory, have been the norm.

Wickberg quoted A.P. Clasen's *Der Salutismus*, for his view on the Army's durability as an international movement: there were two reasons, one "interior" and the other "exterior."[45] The first was its joyful religion, the second, "the process of anglicizing the

---

42. Besides the cross bar to which Christ's hands were nailed, the sign placed on the cross by Pilate and the foot-rest are also depicted.

43. Quoted by Michael Hawn in http://www.umcdiscipleship.org/resources/history-of-hymns-saranam-saranam. (Accessed 12 December 2016). I also remember hearing Niles use this image at an Ecumenical Youth Conference in New Zealand in 1966.

44. Wickberg, "The International Salvationist and his Citizenship," 16.

45. Clasen, "Der Salutismus," in Wickberg, Ibid., 16.

world . . . It will last as long as these reasons remain valid." While agreeing that the rise of English as a *lingua franca* was significant, Wickberg suggested that the Army took hold in Europe *in spite of* rather than because of its British origin.

Former Commissioner Alex Nicol, writing in 1911, would have agreed with that conclusion:

> In this position [Foreign Secretary] for three years I witnessed remarkable demonstrations of the application of the Army's methods of evangelization to the continent of Europe. The conclusions that I arrived at then I adhere to still. In Latin-speaking communities the Army's methods failed. They were too English, too vulgar, too much of an outrage upon the generally accepted idea of the worship of God, and the confession and absolution of sin. People at first came in crowds to the gatherings of the Army, and not a few were drawn to the penitent form and attracted for a season to the service of the Army. But the Army had nothing, and still has nothing, to offer the lapsed children of the Roman Catholic Church who were or are restored to faith in God by means of its services. A meeting of the Army in Italy or France, for instance, is the same in spirit, character, and method as it is in Drury Lane or Newcastle. The leaders of the Army not including the General have an innate aversion and prejudice to Roman Catholicism, and it is therefore not surprising that after twenty years' work in France the Army is in a worse condition numerically than it was at the end of its first ten years.
>
> The explanation is simple. It took General Booth twelve years in London to find an answer to the cry "How to reach the masses?" But neither he nor his officers spent ten days in France studying the same question from the standpoint of the Frenchman. "The Army was a success in England, and it must be in France!" So they concluded, and having commissioned its best officers to apply an English ritual to the people of a Catholic-minded nation, and one which these same officers could not alter without obtaining the consent of Headquarters, it is not surprising that the result, so far, is failure. Where the Army succeeds in France the recruits are generally gained from people who have been influenced by Protestant teaching. The Army will have to learn Latin before it understands the magnitude of its task, and to unlearn its creed and code of discipline, if it is to lift, religiously, the masses of the people out of their metaphysical and materialistic apostasy from the faith of their mothers and fathers . . . In the same capacity of Foreign Secretary I visited other parts of the Continent, such as Scandinavia, Germany, and the Netherlands, and found that where the Army operated upon a Protestant stratum its officers met with a response similar to that in England.[46]

Particularly in its earlier years, notwithstanding Nicol's impressions of the work in Europe, the Salvation Army made serious attempts to relate to non-European indigenous cultures. They were not always well-advised. David Rightmire recounts how pioneers in Japan aroused only hilarity when parading in clothing they had bought in Hong Kong on their way to Japan, under the impression they were in Japanese "native dress." Unfortunately, they were wearing night attire.[47] However, other attempts proved more successful.

---

46. Nicol, *General Booth*, xii–xvi.
47. Rightmire, *Salvationist Samurai*, 16–17.

Reading of Francis Xavier's exploits was an influence on Frederick Tucker, later Booth-Tucker, who became the Salvation Army pioneer of this cultural accommodation in India.[48] Having been a magistrate in the Indian Civil Service, Tucker went to Britain to see Booth and join the Army after being sent a copy of *The War Cry* in 1881. Appointed to lead the Army's invasion of India—which he had persuaded Booth to order—in September 1882, Tucker and his officers assumed Indian names, worked at language study and adopted fakir dress and life-style, begging for their daily food. This was a significant factor in the Army's gaining acceptance on the sub-continent, and meant that Tucker was able to attract to his ranks some significant and able leaders like Arnolis Weerasooriya, Yesu Dasen, Mhusa Bhai and Narayana Muthiah.

Booth's letter to would-be reinforcement personnel in 1886 is a masterpiece of cross-cultural adaptation.[49] Booth-Tucker's own instructions to his English officers are even more salutary:

> Service will be a matter not merely of being willing to go anywhere, but of wishing to live and die for the particular race to which you are sent. You will be absolutely alone and under close scrutiny. It will be essential to learn at least one Indian language. You must leave entirely and forever behind you all your English dress and habits. Officers will be barefoot.
>
> You will avoid the English quarter, but will always live among natives—sometimes in a cave, a shady tree, or someone's veranda—or in a mud hut 16 by 10 feet. You will cook as they do, and wash your clothes in the stream with them. You have nothing to fear from the climate. The people are different and intensely religious. Find out what their thoughts are before you share yours. And if you are planning to return, don't go. We would not think of sending anyone out who did not plan to make it a life work.[50]

Becoming itinerant fakirs, waves of English and other European officers (including Tucker's first wife) paid the price with their lives. For this reason, however, the policy was eventually changed. One element in the mix was no doubt the increasing reluctance of successive waves of missionaries from the home country to commit to the dangers and hardships involved in adaptation to native customs and conditions, as well as a renewed sense of racial and cultural superiority in some cases.

Booth-Tucker, recalling the difficulties in maintaining his Indian policy, said that

> The Founder, who gave much personal time and consideration to these questions, was anxious to maintain a careful balance between the two contrary currents of opinion which now existed—the one being the tendency to extreme fakirism, while the other ... to equally extreme Europeanism.
>
> There was also the very real danger that the gulf which had long existed between Indians and Europeans, even in Missionary circles, might creep into our own ranks. It was only to be expected that relaxations, which had been granted to European Officers, should be claimed on similar grounds by their Indian comrades, resulting ultimately in the separation of the Indian Officer from his Soldiers, who would be unable to provide him with the comforts and advantages

---

48. Williams, *Booth-Tucker*, 40.
49. Reproduced in Booth-Tucker, *Muktifauj*, xv–xix.
50. Downloaded from http://www.armybarmy.com/blog.html on 22 February 2012.

which they did not themselves possess. This would mean the creation of Indian, as well as European, Officers, who would be more or less "foreign" in their way of living, and dependent upon "foreign" funds for their support.[51]

Nicol, the Army's Foreign Secretary at the time, recalled the story behind the story:

> In the name of self-sacrifice and a death-consecration for the salvation of India, delicate European ladies were subjected to degrading conditions of life. Not a few suffered martyrdom or became incapacitated for continuous labors among the lower castes where the great bulk of the Army's work is carried on; some died from enteric, cholera, and other Oriental diseases . . . It was a critical period in the Army's history . . .
>
> In this crisis the General acted with great astuteness . . . He debated the question with his advisers, temporized, minimized and immortalized the losses of officers, and exalted the gains to the Army arising out of the undoubted fact that a certain entrance to native thought had been obtained by the tribute the Army paid to India in discarding the names and dress and food of the mighty Sahib. And then he promised that he would go out to India and study the subject for himself on the spot. This proved a master move. From that very moment all dissatisfaction in England came to an end . . . They felt sure that when he got to India he would denounce the begging of rice from natives, living in huts, and the adoption of social practices that were both insulting and degrading to the tastes of white men and women. He did so . . . So one by one the system was either modified or abandoned.[52]

The Army's mission in India is one of the examples used by Andrew Mark Eason in his exploration of a marked change in the Salvation Army's dealings with indigenous peoples in the later nineteenth century.[53] He extrapolates from the way in which the Army departed from its original simple revivalist mission, conducted in Britain by "the earliest officers, drawn mainly from the lower working classes" during the 1880s. The Darkest England scheme of 1890 instituted what might be described as "a more conventional civilizing mission of social and educational uplift" of the urban poor in Britain. The Army's mission became "for the poor" rather than "of the poor."

Eason proposes and explores the outworking of this change upon the Army's missionary enterprise. Originally, the early missionary officers in the 1880s had adopted a deliberate policy of accommodation to national cultural norms. The missionaries were there to save souls, not to turn them into Englishmen. This was most strongly evident in India in the early years under the leadership of Tucker. To a lesser extent but in the same way in South Africa under Henry Thurman, the second leader of the Army in that territory from 1886 to 1889, there was a policy of adapting as much as possible to Zulu culture. With riding instructions from London to accommodate their life-style to those of their target group and "become as a native to the natives," officers led by Jim Osborne attempted to do this.[54] Although Eason does not include it in his study, Ernest Hold-

---

51. Booth-Tucker, *Muktifauj*, 95.
52. Nicol, *General Booth*, 164–66.
53. Eason, "Christianity in a Colonial Age," iii.
54. Osborne," *All the World*, March 1897, 7, cited by Eason, Ibid., 165.

away's mission to New Zealand Maori from 1888 followed a similar pattern, working chiefly in rural areas and utilizing the indigenous language. Holdaway was quoted as saying by the following year, "I always think in Maori," and made language study a priority for officers sent to join him.[55]

After this enlightened beginning, the policy of cultural adaptation and accommodation was reversed in these three mission fields in the 1890s, and a more deliberately "civilizing" mission was adopted, certainly in India and Africa, where the overseas officers reverted to European habits and style. The policy of cultural adaptation was replaced by a greater emphasis on "social salvation," an assimilationist model which in effect saw indigenous culture as something to be left behind. It could be argued that the effect of this was similar to that change from "of the people" to "for the people" seen with the introduction of the Darkest England scheme.

The force of Eason's argument is perhaps diminished only a little by the fact that no general order emanating from International Headquarters decreed such a universal policy reversal; the reasons were more local to each situation. For India there was indeed a change of policy, but as we have seen it was occasioned by the need to stem the unsustainable mortality rate amongst expatriate officers living as Indians.[56] In South Africa the reason is not so clear but the change of approach may simply have been the preference of a new officer in charge, the yet-to-become famous Allister Smith. In New Zealand, the decision to disband the Maori Division in 1894 (and again in 1898 after a second attempt) was taken at the Colony Headquarters in Christchurch and there is no evidence that the new policy was dictated from the Territorial Headquarters in Melbourne or from London. In practice it proposed to treat the indigenous Maori in the same way as "Pakeha" (people of European origin and culture) and for a variety of reasons that did not work. Shortage of money and personnel, not to mention a lack of understanding by expatriate senior officers, appear to have lain behind the change of policy.[57]

Nevertheless, the fact that these developments happened about the same time suggests at least a common mind-set involved, perhaps an attitude to the "heathen" which Eason identifies, alike to that evident in the "Darkest England" approach to the poor, even if a common policy determination may not be found. While willingness to accommodate to the host culture on one hand, and a tendency to see it as something to be left behind on the other, have been variously demonstrated by individual missionaries over the years, it is the latter attitude which seems more often to have informed official policy and determined structural provisions.

It would be nice to think that the Salvation Army has always been color-blind; in practice that has not always been the case. Besides his careful examination of the Army's work on the ground in India and South Africa, Eason also explores the way its overseas mission was presented at home between the 1880s and 1920s, particularly through its periodicals and its representation at international congresses and exhibitions. Whereas in the 1880s, the word "heathen" was applied indiscriminately to the unsaved whether at

---

55. *War Cry* (New Zealand) 16 November 1889, 7.
56. Nicol, *General Booth*, 164–66.
57. Eason, "Christianity in a Colonial Age," 215; Hill, *Te Ope Whakaora*, 264–66.

home or abroad (as in Railton's 1877 publication, *Heathen England*), by the mid-1890s the word was reserved for a racially and culturally condescending description of the "dark races" to which the Army was bringing the light of the gospel. African and Indian displays and participating personnel tended to be offered for the curiosity, entertainment and education of British visitors to these events rather than to underline their common identity as Christians and fellow-soldiers.

William Booth himself was naturally a man of his time and age: pursuing his dream of an overseas colony for the regeneration of Britain's poor, it did not occur to him that such lands were not "empty" simply because unsettled by Europeans, that they might already be occupied and cherished by indigenous peoples. Accepting from Cecil Rhodes' British South Africa Company the gift of what became "Pearson Farm" at Mazowe in Rhodesia, he did not enquire about the subjugation and expulsion of the Hwata clan of the Shona nation which had occupied that land for centuries. Writing to Bramwell from South Africa in 1908 when seeking land for his Salvation Army settlement, "he was less concerned about whether the Dutch or British would prevail, since in a few years the question would not be what Nation of Whites shall have the mastery, but whether the Whites will have any mastery at all. Not whether it shall be Dutch land or British land, but whether it shall be a white man's land . . . William argued that to keep 'mineral production' and 'mastery of the country in general' from falling into the hands of non-whites, the 'white man' must 'add to his numbers such as will join him.'"[58] Such racist views could then co-exist with his vision of salvation for the lost and the universality of the Gospel without any sense of incongruity, in a way inconceivable a century later.

Racial prejudice has always been a danger when missionaries, with the best of intentions, have taken their own culture with them to foreign shores, sometimes expressed in patronizing attitudes and firm social boundaries. While the majority have had the grace to overcome such tendencies, it seems to have been more difficult when the host country has had institutionalized racial divisions. Attitudes of some missionaries, and of some Salvationist immigrants, in southern Africa for example, identifying with apparent ease with the apparatus of apartheid, could shock the idealistic newcomer. Even the revered South African prophet of holiness teaching, Senior-Major Allister Smith, son of the great missionary, strongly defended white minority regimes—as a bulwark against communism and as more beneficial to all than majority rule.[59] Indeed, Henry Gariepy's *Christianity in Action* describes how the Salvation Army had "thrown down the gauntlet on the evils of Apartheid" under General Eva Burrows in the 1980s but fails to mention its decades-long complicity with those evils or Commissioner Paul Du Plessis's significant nostra culpa and submission to the South African Truth and Reconciliation Commission on behalf of the South African territory in 1997.[60]

Unconscious racial prejudice could also underlie an apparently benevolent paternalism, expressed for example by the distinguished Salvationist journalist Arthur

---

58. Murdoch, *Christian Warfare*, 69–70.

59. Allister Smith, letters to *Battlepoint*, December 1974, 11–15; September 1975, 16.

60. Gariepy, *Christianity in Action*, 169. For Du Plessis, see www.justice.gov.za/trc/media/1997/9706/s970603f.htm, downloaded 11 April 2010.

Copping in his early 1930s account of officers in West Africa, no doubt reflecting the opinions of missionary officers he had encountered:

> Many of the African officers were new not only to Christianity but also to civilization—two totally different things of course, if hopelessly confused in the popular mind. Their work as Army officers is rooted in the one as in the other. Thus that work had its spiritual, God-inspired side, with getting people converted and keeping them so; in which department, it would appear, those African officers attained for the most part to a splendid efficiency. Then there was the social, man-inspired side, concerned with keeping accounts, conforming to regulations, and maintaining certain standards of personal conduct; and it was here the African officer was apt to tax the patience of his European superiors.[61]

The Salvation Army was in its tenth year on the Gold Coast when Copping visited, and expanding like a bush fire, so it could be understood that the administrative capacities of those new officers were still developing. It was another twenty years, however, before the first Ghanaian divisional leaders would be appointed; nearly thirty years after Copping's visit the first indigenous general secretary took office; it was more than sixty years later, in 1996, that the first Ghanaian became territorial commander in his own land. While Ghana may have been a comparatively late starter in the indigenous leadership stakes, the pattern was observable elsewhere and we might wonder how long colonial assumptions endured, demonstrated by a reluctance to trust indigenous leadership or to provide specific training for such responsibilities, a practice adopted by some other denominations somewhat earlier. Such attitudes were noticed by local Salvationists.

Despite the best of intentions, because of lack of insight and understanding even such staff training and regional development programs as the Army has provided, sometimes have run the danger of serving the purposes of imperialism and domestication rather than becoming tools to upskill and create vision. Ideally, as A.J. Gilliard proposed, the Army's hymnology and theology may "be deepened and enriched by the contributions of many nations. We have glimpsed this at the International College for Officers when the African voice told us what the African eye saw in the Scriptures and the Chinese mind interpreted Christ for us."[62] Forty years later however, a delegate's reminiscence suggested that "the ICO has become more a college that inducts the officers into a prevailing culture of leadership."

REASSERTION OF LOCAL IDENTITY

Newton's third law, "For every action, an equal and opposite reaction," may be discerned at work in the Salvationist world. Despite the strength of the international culture, local feeling was inevitably expressed in opposition at times and some examples may be given.

Such a nationalist reaction was encountered earliest in the United States of America, the Salvation Army's first mission-field. Major Thomas E. Moore, second leader of the Army in the United States, found that for legal reasons he needed to have the

---

61. Copping, *Banners in Africa*, 17.
62. Gilliard, "Catching up with William Booth," 10.

Salvation Army incorporated in the United States. Problems arose with the purchase of property, because by Army regulation Booth held all property as "General for the time being"—something difficult to ensure in some states of the USA where an alien could not hold property. Moore was forced to hold property in his own name and this left him personally liable so for two years he sought to have the Army registered as a religious and charitable organization in the United States. Booth resisted this, and when international auditors found Moore's books in disarray, ordered him to transfer to South Africa. Instead, Moore seceded in 1884, taking most of the forces and all the property with him, his group emphasizing their American credentials, in contrast to the "Britishness" of the other Salvation Army. Herbert Wisbey notes that "anti-English feeling was not difficult to arouse in the 1880s, and the Salvation Army was primarily 'English' to many Americans."[63] After many schisms, a remnant of Moore's American Salvation Army still exists as the American Rescue Workers. After control from international headquarters was re-established by Frank Smith later in 1884, Booth was forced to agree to incorporation in the United States anyway.

Moore was in fact an Englishman himself, but had quickly identified with the American cause. The same could be said of Ballington and Maude Booth, commanders of the Salvation Army in America from 1887 until 1896, when they refused to accept farewell orders. Thwarted in their attempt to retain control of the troops by the dramatic intervention of the younger sister, Evangeline Booth, they established their own organization, the Volunteers of America, which still exists as a social service provider. Evangeline herself, taking command of the United States Salvation Army in 1904, also identified strongly as an American and took American citizenship. During the First World War she threw her influence behind the war effort and her "doughnut girls" became famous with American troops, by this means gaining the permanent affections of the American people for the Salvation Army and securing its financial future. She was not infrequently at odds with her brother, the General, and her *War Cry* happily spoke ill of the enemy, against international editorial policy.[64] Resisting Bramwell Booth's attempts to re-appoint her elsewhere in the post-war years, in part by mustering influential American support and raising the specter of yet another independence movement, she eventually completed thirty years as commander of the American forces before her own election as General.

Those mentioned above were English Salvation Army leaders, taking on American roles—though all were supported by American followers. Underneath the leadership canopy, the ground-level Army inevitably underwent some cultural transformation as it Americanized. However, according to Lillian Taiz, the really significant changes that took place for the American Army in the late nineteenth and early twentieth centuries paralleled those affecting the Army elsewhere, to possibly an even greater degree than in its homeland. In all territories, the social scheme helped make the Army respectable, both in its internal effects and its external reputation. With its partition into field and social wings, its grassroots working-class exuberance was progressively toned down and brought under control, partly to avoid alienating the donors and partly as the second

---

63. Wisbey, *Soldiers Without Swords*, 80.
64. Clifton, "The Salvation Army's Attitudes and Actions in War Time," 258–61.

generation of Salvationists aspired to middle-class status. The unwashed could be left to the social workers while the task of corps leadership progressively focused on retaining the existing adherents and their families. Meanwhile the torch of American working class evangelism was passed to the new Pentecostal enthusiasts.[65] Such developments however owed little to nationalist sentiment vis-à-vis internationalism; apart from occasional visits from the General the average American Salvationist may have had little reason to be aware of the wider Salvation Army; the United States was a world in itself.

North of the border, dissatisfaction with "foreign dominance" contributed to the 1892 Philpott secession in Canada. Led by Brigadier Peter Philpott, this split was fed by Canadian resentment of English control as much as by reaction to Herbert Booth's dictatorial manner. To be fair, Booth inherited a confrontation set up by his predecessor, David Rees, who had rejected requests to examine complaints about extravagances by senior (British) officers while ordinary (Canadian-born) officers suffered privations. Forced to resign, Philpott was joined by almost sixty officers and over four hundred soldiers. They set up "Christian Workers" churches in Toronto, with Salvation Army-like methods and doctrines, though these groups did not endure.[66]

As members of the British Empire and perhaps of less diverse origins than the North Americans, Australasian Salvationists were much closer in loyalty to Britain—their local editions of the *War Cry* happily referring to the "Motherland" and "Home"—so tensions of a nationalist kind do not seem to have been marked, despite the colonial personality from time to time tending to demonstrate both colonial arrogance and its reverse, "colonial cringe," in relation to Britain. Some inter-colonial rivalry existed however, partly arising from the fact that New Zealand was subordinated to headquarters in Melbourne from 1894 to 1912. Cyril Bradwell found "some evidence to suggest that New Zealand Salvationists were not entirely happy about the new command structure" in the 1890s.[67] A lingering resentment may be discerned in the advice given to his successor by a farewelling territorial commander as late as 1934, that "N.Z. in the days of her connection with the Australian command, did not always receive the consideration to which she was entitled, and in some cases hardly secured fair play . . . It is therefore never wise to speak or write of 'Australasia,' with thoughts of thus including New Zealand."[68]

As already noted, both the Australian and New Zealand public, as distinct from the Salvationists, tended to react adversely to their countries being regarded as a destination for resettlement of the Salvation Army's British poor. The reason that unionists and others objected to Booth's immigration scheme was that because of depression, unemployment was already high. More competition for jobs was not desired. As Macintyre notes of Australia, "Immigration came to a halt after 1891: there was a net increase of just 7000 during the rest of the decade."[69] Booth's attempts to find land in Southern Africa encountered similar opposition from some.[70] However, as we have scant evidence of

---

65. Taiz, *Hallelujah Lads and Lasses*, 166–67.
66. Moyles, *Blood and Fire in Canada*, 123–28.
67. Bradwell, Fight the Good Fight, 60.
68. Cunningham, "Farewell Brief," 1935, 1. Salvation Army Archives, New Zealand. (Plus ça change . . .)
69. Mcintyre, *Concise History of Australia*, 130.
70. Murdoch, *Christian Warfare*, 47–48.

what ordinary Salvationists, or their leaders, thought about such matters, this casts little light on relations between these colonial territories and the international Army. There were of course only enthusiastic reports of participation in international congresses by those fortunate enough to attend such events.

Nationalist feeling became more evident in European territories, however, partly as they felt the need to identify themselves as truly national in character rather than simply as branches of an English organisation, and also as leading figures in the Salvation Army in these countries sometimes began to resent IHQ's control.

In Germany as in other countries the process of the Army's acclimatization went hand in hand with social work and respectability, and it could claim to be contributing to the well-being of the Fatherland. According to Carter-Chand, the German Heilsarmee began to emphasize its theological affinity with the German Reformation and Radical Pietism, whereas the Anglophone world rather traced its spiritual heritage to the transatlantic "Great Awakenings."[71] With the outbreak of war in 1914, the Heilsarmee naturally identified more strongly with its German nationality, with *Der Krugsruf*'s masthead emblazoned "Mit Gott für Kaiser und Reich" from 1915. A sensible and overdue measure was the substitution of "H" for the "S" previously used as uniform insignia. At least a hundred German Salvation Army officers were called up to military service, more than twenty being killed in the course of the war.

In 1915, the German leadership drew up "Terms and Conditions for the General," requiring some changes in their relationship with IHQ to take account of changing circumstances. Carter-Chand reproduces these from German Archives:

1. GGmbH—the GGmbH is exclusively in German hands.[72] It is acknowledged that the members of the Heilsarmee will answer to the General.

2. The Junker Assets—These should be invested in Germany. Since this property is German, it should be possible to transfer it, even during the war, on neutral territory.

3. Finances—In the future, the Heilsarmee in Germany cannot send any more money to England for any purpose. This allows us the financial position to save money in Germany for mission purposes, so that this can only be used in German colonies.

4. Leadership—One of the top two leaders can be a neutral, who must absolutely speak German. The neutral cannot go against the will of the majority of the staff officers to hold his office.

5. Foreigners in Germany—The overall situation in Germany forbids any English to hold positions in the Heilsarmee. In addition, no foreigner can hold an executive position. The finance secretary must be German.

---

71. Carter-Chand, "Doing Good in Bad Times," 117–18.

72. GGmbH: Gemeinnützige Gesellschaft mit beschränkter Haftung signified the legal entity of the Salvation Army as a limited liability non-profit organization.

> We declare our loyalty to the General and leader of the Heilsarmee and will not tolerate any split.
>
> Furthermore, we remain spiritually connected to the entire Heilsarmee and acknowledge the existing Rules and Regulations of the Salvation Army.[73]

Although he met with Bramwell Booth in neutral Sweden in 1916, the acting territorial commander, Lieut. Colonel Carl Treite, was largely cut off from international headquarters by the war. Treite eventually sought to secede from the international organization, although unsuccessful in achieving this before the war's end, after which Der Heilsarmee re-affirmed its affinity with the parent body and benefitted from the influx of relief and aid.[74]

Equally unsuccessful were the efforts by a group of senior German officers to wrest control of Der Heilsarmee in 1933 and negotiate with Reich Bishop Ludwig Muller for its subordination to the Nazi-controlled "German Protestant Church." Even though a majority of the socially and politically conservative Salvationists probably tended to support the Nazi government, this might have been a bridge too far. Territorial leadership discovered the plot, restructured the territory, dismissed the ringleader, and reappointed the others to positions of less influence. Under Franz Stankuweit, territorial commander from 1934 until his death in 1941, and his successor Johannes Büsing, Der Heilsarmee managed to survive the war, progressively restricted but not totally suppressed as in some occupied countries.

Carter-Chand also mentions restlessness with British control in several other European territories: "There were separatist movements in the 1920s within the Czech, Finnish, and Swiss Salvation Army branches; other national territories like Sweden and Holland experienced tensions with the London International Headquarters."[75]

A breakaway group seceded from Frälsningsamén in Sweden in 1905. A group of Salvation Army officers led by Brigadier Kaleb Svensson demanded reforms of the Salvation Army's administration and a reduction of foreign influence over the Salvation Army in Sweden. Not succeeding in these objectives, they formed the Svenska Frälsningsarmén (Swedish Salvation Army) which in the mid-1980s became a non-territorial district of the Mission Covenant Church.[76] In the Netherlands, Gustaaf Maste, the first head of social work for men in the territory (a post he had held from 1906–1921) resigned to form a Dutch Salvation Army in 1921, partly because he believed there was need for a more democratic constitution for the Salvation Army. His Nederlandsch Leger des Heils still exists although it has remained quite small.[77]

---

73. Carter-Chand, "Doing Good in Bad Times," 147. Terms and Conditions to the General. 9 July, 1915. BA Berlin, R 5101, Heilsarmee. The "Junker assets" were the estate of the late Colonel Jacob Junker, bequeathed to the Salvation Army.

74. Carter-Chand, "Doing Good in Bad Times," 147–48.

75. Ochsner, Homberger, and Schiffmann, *Die Schweizerische Reformbewegung in der Heilsarmee*, cited by Carter-Chand, Ibid., 226.

76. https://www.fralsningsarmen.se/Sidor/Skolmaterial/Historia/Tidslinje/, accessed 14 December 2016.

77. Bollinger, "Dynamic Courtship," 175–76.

Nationalist feeling was also expressed in Asian territories, with strongly critical demonstrations in two meetings held during General Bramwell Booth's visit to Korea in 1926. On 14th November 1926 a Seoul daily newspaper, *Dong A Ilbo*, carried an extensive list of grievances, which ranged from concern at the differential living standards of Korean and expatriate officers, to the lack of executive appointments for Korean officers, to quite specific complaints as to the attitudes and behavior of some western missionaries—although the document also acknowledged the commendable qualities of some others. Some thirty officers were dismissed following these events, although some were subsequently re-engaged. No other official acknowledgement of the protests was made until General Paul Rader, having earlier served in Korea for 22 years, made an official apology on behalf of International Headquarters some 70 years later, and the story was first told in print by Commissioner Peter Chang in 2007.[78] After the liberation of Korea from Japan in 1945, a group of officers agitated for the Korean Salvation Army to become independent of the international movement, but that did not happen.[79] The first Korean-born territorial commander took office in 1973.

Japan achieved indigenous leadership somewhat earlier than Korea, thanks to the stature of Gunpei Yamamuro (1872–1940), who became the first national officer in 1895 and territorial commander in 1926 after a period as chief secretary. His *Common People's Gospel* (*Heimin no Fukuin*) published in 1899 is still regarded as a classic work. Strongly patriotic as well as a devoted Salvationist internationalist, Yamamuro served at a time when local nationalist feeling had significant political ramifications. As a coincidental example of the center's occasional unawareness of local feeling, A. J. Gilliard, editor of the London, or "International," *War Cry* for many years, described how he had received a wake-up call when he wrote an editorial strongly critical of the Japanese invasion of Manchuria in 1931. Within twenty-four hours, Commissioner Yamamuro was under (fortunately temporary) house-arrest in Tokyo. Of the Army in Japan, Albert Edward Baggs wrote:

> This study probes the causes and effects of the Japanese Salvation Army's deep commitment to the cause of nationalism. It explores the Salvation Army's English origins and its basically conservative nature, presents a biographical study of the Salvation Army's first native Japanese officer, Yamamura Gumpei [sic], explains how and why the Salvation Army in the space of twelve years rose from obscurity to national renown and gained recognition from the state. The Army's social service work is explored in depth by describing its relief program at the time of the Kanto earthquake of 1923, and by dissecting the various aspects and purposes of its work during the height of Japan's economic depression (1931–32). The final chapter analyses the struggle of the Japanese branch of the Salvation Army for a greater degree of autonomy within the Army's world-wide structure.[80]

After Japan's entry into war in 1941, the Army was proscribed. The 1940 *Year Book* gave figures of 434 officers, 252 employees, 133 Corps and 20 institutions for Japan; the

---

78. Chang, *Salvation Army in Korea*, 46–55.
79. Rader, Review of Chang, *Officer*, July–August 2008, 35.
80. Baggs, "Social evangel as nationalism," cited in Shulman, *Japan and Korea*, 73.

1947 *Year Book* reported 220 officers, 65 Corps and 20 institutions. Jack Nelson suggests that the decline from the Army's pre-war "glory days" was because, although the Army's humanitarian work was respected, Christianity "is generally considered a foreign (i.e. deviant) religion" in Japan. Further, "Brass bands, school-like uniforms, military regimentation, and strict moral codes do not attract young people into the movement."[81] They may once have done so when they were more the cultural norm.

De-colonization in the years following the Second World War found the Army in many places unprepared, with indigenous officers untrained for senior administrative roles though there were expectations by some that these would be forthcoming. In the Netherlands East Indies during the Japanese occupation, responsibility for directing the Army's operations in many places had been taken over by Indonesian officers after the internment of most European missionaries and the work was held together in exceedingly difficult circumstances. The Salvation Army was proscribed and went underground. After the defeat of Japan, another three years of struggle followed before the Dutch conceded independence to Indonesia. During this period, as Melattie Brouwer notes, "experienced Indonesian officers were now taking over positions of responsibility which had been relinquished by their overseas colleagues." Some were frustrated at the slowness of indigenization of leadership—a group of younger officers mounted an abortive coup d'etat, with a lieutenant promoting himself to colonel[82]—but it was not until 1965 that Commissioner Jacobus Corputty became Indonesia's first indigenous territorial commander.[83]

Sometimes special circumstances gave rise to unanticipated local tensions. When Adjutant Henri Becquet began working in the Belgian Congo in 1934, an influx of recruits resulted from the misapprehension that he was the reincarnation of the prophet Simon Kimbangu. Later, realization that this was not the case led to an exodus and the establishment of Army-like independent churches which grew strongly in the 1950s and 60s.[84] Former Captain Simon Mpadi set up his own Eglise des Noirs movement in 1939, at first doctrinally and organizationally derived from the Salvation Army and wearing khaki uniforms, but later emphasizing the traditional beliefs and history of past African prophets and warriors.

One of the numerous independent church bodies in Zimbabwe is the Christian Marching Church, based on Salvation Army forms and started by a former Salvation Army officer, Petros Katsande, in 1956, perhaps more closely adapted to Shona culture than could be managed by the original Salvation Army. A less successful venture was the Soldiers of God Church, commenced by another former officer, Bernard Mangizi Makone. Having attended an extended training course in England in 1950–1951, Makone was disappointed in his leadership ambitions within the Army and eventually broke away to form his own organization, recruiting some other Salvationists. This did not prosper

---

81. Nelson, "Moral Entrepreneuring in Japan," 51.

82. Kia Ora Tyler, a New Zealand officer serving in Indonesia in immediate post-war years, to author.

83. Brouwer, *Salvation Army in Indonesia*, 164. Corputty twice declined the hereditary Regency of Rumahkai in Ceram in order to remain an officer. *War Cry* (Canada) 6 April 1953, 6.

84. Lanternari, *Religions of the Oppressed*, 31–32.

and eventually most of the members rejoined the Salvation Army.[85] These movements represented a growing frustration at the Army's slowness to promote African leaders, especially at a time when nationalist expectations were beginning to rise.

Wherever there has been contact between an imperial or colonial power and a traditional society, and there has been a degree of social, economic, or cultural oppression in consequence, the responding religious expressions have ranged from the breaking away of alternative independent Christian churches, to the emergence of syncretistic amalgams of Christian and traditional beliefs. The Salvation Army inevitably has been affected by such circumstances. The residue of racial oppression has also contributed eventually to a degree of reverse racism at times in some places.

PATTERNS OF GROWTH AND DECLINE, AND INDIGENIZATION OF LEADERSHIP

As leadership issues reflect local aspirations, it is useful to explore a little further how this has worked out over the years.

For many years now the trend has been for European territories to diminish in numbers of soldiers while African and Indian territories have grown. The Salvation Army is not alone in such growth in these countries; in fact, by comparison with other faith traditions, and in particular with the newer Pentecostal stream, it lags behind in many. The question of why Christianity has "taken off" in the "global south" from the later twentieth century has been addressed in many studies and some of the answers suggested may illuminate the Salvation Army's history as well.

One argument is that the poorest nations, those which have been subjected to colonial exploitation and have suffered most deprivation, are also the most religious. This is not simply a re-run of Marx's "religion is the opiate of the people" contention, because the statistics for Christian expansion confirm the argument. Highly successful societies in terms of economic and social development tend to be less religious but where people are anxious about survival they are more likely to seek spiritual support. This is such a broad generalization and subject to so many caveats and exceptions that it cannot be the whole explanation, but religion in general, the Christian church in particular, and the Salvation Army with it, obviously flourishes in such communities. The Salvation Army began in the slums and has always claimed to be especially concerned for the well-being of the poor and marginalized, so the connection is not improbable.

It is also worth considering that the Salvation Army's strongest growth in Africa and Asia has followed decolonization, independence and majority rule. Is it that the Army has been able to capitalize on the sense of freedom and ride on the coat-tails of national and cultural assertiveness? If so, perhaps the persistence of international and expatriate control lies behind the fact that the Army has benefitted less from this factor than some other denominations and less than the new independent churches, while it has expanded more significantly since indigenous leadership and cultural adaptation of the Army have become more general.

---

85. Nyandoro, *Flame of Sacred Love*, 41–42.

The "global south" is too diverse for such arguments to be applied everywhere. The Salvation Army has not grown so significantly in Latin America as in Africa for example. Independence from Europe came long before the Salvation Army to that continent so the Army's boat has not floated on that particular tide. Neither has the Army's concern for the poor been reflected in its growth there even though there is economic and social inequality in these communities. Pentecostalism has proved much the stronger new growth there, and it is likely, as argued by some South American Salvationists, that the Army's non-sacramental position has disadvantaged it in societies with strongly Catholic roots.

However, African and Asian expansion in particular point up the decline in European territories. Some European commands have no more soldiers than a single corps might in other territories: Italy and Greece have 228 between them, Spain and Portugal have 383 (2017 *Year Book*). Until recently, some commands in developing countries had more soldiers than some territories elsewhere: the Uganda territory while still classified as a command in 2010 had 5,646 soldiers compared with France-Belgium territory with 919 or Finland-Estonia with 794 soldiers, or even New Zealand with 5,565.

The whole of Europe, excluding the United Kingdom, had 25,274 soldiers in 2010, down to 19,998 in the 2017 *Year Book*: it could become one territory, able to bear comparison with USA Western (17,306) or Congo Brazzaville (20,250). By contrast Zimbabwe has 126,861 soldiers. Kenya was formerly the largest territory, but in 2008 was divided into Kenya West (then 113,722; 126,472 in the 2017 *Year Book*) and Kenya East (then 70,665; now 84,066).

If we compare the 2000 and the 2017 *Year Book*s, we see the following:

2000	
Africa	377,236
South Asia	263,360
East Asia	76,559
	717,155
North America	110,442
Central and South America	16,434
Australasia	28,290
Europe	32,369
UK	41,240
	228,775

2017	
Africa	519,720
South Asia	370,861
East Asia	103,580
	994,161
North America	101,411
Central and South America	25,557
Australasia	19,784
Europe	19,998
UK	23,573
	180,323

In 2000, African, South Asian and East Asian territories contributed 75.81% of the Salvation Army's total number of soldiers. By 2017, they supplied 84.64% of the total. Statistics depend upon where and where they are taken, at the beginning of the year or the end; and whether, for example, the growing territory of Papua New Guinea is counted with Australia (as it used to be) or with East Asia (as it is in this table). Within these groups, some results will be atypical of their group: the Japanese soldiers' roll, included in East Asia, has fallen by a third in the period covered, while much of the growth in Central and South America can be attributed to the Caribbean and South America West territories. However, the general picture of growth and decline is clear. The age-demographics of membership in the western territories suggest that such a decline will continue. It is salutary that criteria set in 1986 for the upgrading of a command to a territory (1,000 soldiers, 100 officers, 40 percent of budget to be raised locally, 90 percent of officers to be nationals, 60 percent of HQ officers to be nationals) have been under review since 2013, though no agreed solution has yet emerged.[86] Not all existing European or other territories would meet all those criteria.

A comparison between the number of active and retired officers in a territory usually indicates demographic trends which have been in place for some time: the Sweden-Latvia territory has 137 active and 187 retired officers; Finland-Estonia, 48 active and 93 retired; the United Kingdom, 1,042 active and 1,380 retired. By comparison, Korea has 627 active and 195 retired; Pakistan has 240 active, 94 retired; Kenya East 535 active and 69 retired. Relative life-expectancy no doubt plays a role, but such demographics are almost certainly reflected in soldiers' rolls as well as in the number of officers.

As far as leadership is concerned, the internationalism of the Army has always been claimed as a leading principle but perhaps has been honored in the breach. Despite its rapid international advance and the pioneering appointments to high rank of a very few Asian leaders, the high command of the Army remained largely European, if not British, in character until late in the twentieth century.[87]

The majority of senior commands were for many years monopolized by British officers. The Army took forty-one years to appoint an Australian territorial commander for an Australian territory. It took longer in New Zealand. Despite the farewelling TC in 1946, J. Evan Smith, recommending the appointment of a New Zealander, it took eighty-nine years before a New Zealand officer, Ernest Elliot, was trusted to lead his home territory, in 1972. To date only five of Elliot's thirteen successors as territorial commander have been New Zealanders. We might compare the series of mainly British territorial commanders with the succession of titled Englishmen who long filled the roles of governor and governor-general in and over self-governing members of the British Commonwealth, in the manner of the pro-consuls who once administered the uncivilized outposts of the Roman Empire. Hobbes was right!

Only at the first High Council of the twenty-first century did non-Europeans comprise as many as a third of its members, although by then four-fifths of soldiers came from non-European majority territories. For many years the leadership of the Army at all but local levels in the developing world was in the hands of expatriate European, "Old Commonwealth" and North American officers. Many of these had committed their lives to particular countries or continents and served there for all or most of their active officership, often becoming deeply familiar with local cultures. By the later twentieth century such officers were thinner on the ground; there were fewer expatriates in total and most spent a few years as "reinforcement officers" and then returned to their home

---

86. Roberts, "Self-Denial and Self Support," 29.

87. For example, Weerasooriya as Chief Secretary in India in the 1880s until his early death as a consequence of his nursing an English officer with cholera; Muthiah in India and Yamamuro in Japan as Territorial Commanders in the 1920s and 30s.

territories.[88] The generations of missionaries' children who grew up with a foreign nationality or spent their formative years in boarding school do not have so many successors.[89] By the 1960s, an increasing number of non-officer Salvationists also began to give shorter-term (one to three years) service overseas.

Dearth of indigenous third world leadership arose partly from colonialist attitudes and inadequate personnel strategies and training. Some missionary organizations intentionally prepared local leadership by giving them advanced educational opportunities in Western countries—the Catholic Church in particular has done this. In Rhodesia the United Methodist Church, for example, gave Abel Muzorewa (later bishop, and briefly prime minister), amongst others, a university education in the USA. The Salvation Army thought it sufficient to send a captain on the Rhodesian Training College staff to sit in on classes with cadets for a few months at the International Training College in London. Still, a university education was not always considered particularly advantageous for a European officer either except as a means of accessing government subsidies.

It is difficult to avoid the conclusion that in some cases change has been forced upon the Army by political considerations and the non-availability of visas as much as by progressively enlightened attitudes. Commissioner Paul du Plessis notes that "Both Methodism and The Salvation Army have been committed to the deployment of national full-time workers and leadership. But the extent to which the Army has retained central control militates against this ideal."[90] However, in recent decades the promotion of national officers to leadership has become much more intentional.

The following table traces the advance of non-European territorial leadership:

	1965	1990	2017
Number of Territories & Commands	45	50	62
Number of Territories and commands of majority European ethnicity	24	27	26
Number of Territories & Commands of majority non-European ethnicity	21	23	36
Number of ethnic Europeans leading non-European territories and Commands	19	10	11
Number of Non-Europeans leading commands of majority European ethnicity	0	0	1

There is a further twist to the policy of international appointments. It has been a longstanding practice (especially since the advent of indigenous officers in such senior roles) that wherever possible one or other of the territorial commander and chief

---

88. Examples for comparison: Commissioner Frederick Adlam spent forty-six years' service in Africa. Arriving in 1972, the year before Adlam retired, I spent just six years in Rhodesia/Zimbabwe.

89. In recent years the Army has taken note of the fact that cross-cultural experiences may entail significant difficulties for both parents and children and most contributing territories now take advantage of externally facilitated courses to debrief returning missionaries and their families. At the end of the twentieth century a book was made available for returning reinforcement personnel: Burt and Farthing, *Crossing Cultures*.

90. Du Plessis, "Echoes of Methodism," *Word and Deed*, November 2004, 9.

secretary appointments will be held by a national of the country and the other by an officer from a different territory. This has meant that where a national of a "developing" country has been appointed in charge, his second-in-command will be usually an appointee from a "developed" country, and vice versa. At the time when more national officers were beginning to be appointed as territorial commanders in developing countries, in the 1970s and 80s, some "joint territorial commanders" were appointed, with the intention that the foreign (generally European or American) "joint" would mentor the national "joint" to prepare for their assumption of sole eminence. At its best this worked well, even though it was sometimes viewed by national officers as yet another example of paternalism and reluctance to trust national officers. The appointment of Commissioner David Moyo as the first national leader in Zimbabwe was described by a contemporary as "just thrust upon him," and "a heavy load, shouldered without adequate preparation or practical experience"—and he had been for two years previously a "joint" commander.[91] Even less happy was the experience of a "joint" in another African country, who was simply unable to cope with his extremely controlling European colleague and went AWOL. In the Indian sub-continent it eventually proved impossible to get visas for overseas administrative officers, and the problem is solved by having one of the two top posts filled by an Indian officer from a different Indian territory. In that vast and diverse country that can often mean an Indian officer of a different race and culture from that of the territory. It was usual, and is still not uncommon to have an overseas, often Western, officer appointed as financial secretary in developing countries.

In 2010 there was only one "third-world" officer commanding a "first-world" territory, the Indonesian Roy Frans as TC in the Netherlands—an ironical reversal of history in that his home country used to be the Dutch East Indies (although that was before Frans was born). Both Peter Chang (from Korea) and David Edwards (from Guyana) have also served as TCs in USA Western in the past. At time of writing, the sole example is South African Clive Adams as TC in the United Kingdom. Stephen Court in his *Armybarmy* blog regularly campaigns for more such appointments on the grounds that leadership from new or growing territories would inject new life into old and declining ones. That is an untested assumption: the degree to which short-term senior leadership in itself actually influences growth or decline is debatable, and no doubt varies. On the other hand, while cultural misunderstanding and maladroitness have been largely one way in the past they could become a two-way street in such regimes without careful attention.

Stephen Court has applied these trends to the Salvation Army's administrative arrangements by using the newly consolidated Australian Territory's combined 15,000 soldiers as a baseline. Thus India, with nearly 320,000 senior soldiers could legitimately comprise twenty-two territories rather than the six into which it is currently divided. Kenya alone, with over 408,000 soldiers in its two territories, could form about twenty-five territories. By the same token, many existing territories would be reclassified as commands or divisions, or lesser entities. The implications for future High Councils would be obvious; the consequences for future international governance less predictable.[92]

91. Nyandoro, *Flame of Sacred Love*, 192.

92. http://armybarmyblog.blogspot.co.nz/2017_01_01_archive.html#5165989816717960570, accessed 10 January 2017.

FINANCE AND FUNDING

Another rubbing point between the local and the international can be that of resources. The principle of tithing, whereby corps tithe to their division and their division tithes to their territory, also helps maintain international headquarters. Although the principle of self-support has been upheld as the ideal from the earliest days of the Salvation Army, it is often impossible to attain. Just as some corps need to receive larger grants from their division than the value of the tithes they contribute, the same happens in respect of territories. Since overseas expansion began, some poorer territories, commands and regions have needed to be assisted financially by richer territories. A paper read to the 1904 International Staff Conference addressed the question, "Ought Strong Territories to Help Those Which Are Weak?"

> [A]ssistance should be given at such a time and in such a way as not to increase the helplessness of the territory which it is desired to help . . . We are not called upon to bear the infirmities of the weak simply for the sake of bearing them, but that he may shortly walk alone and be helpful to others . . . [A]ssistance ought to be given so that it does not unduly weaken the one rendering help.[93]

The intention was willing, the practice was weak; it did not happen. As the Army expanded increasingly in developing countries, the work became a burgeoning charge on its homelands and for the first half of the Army's history, the primary source of such funding was the British territory, supported also by the Self Denial offerings of other territories. After the Second World War the balance of financial power shifted, and before the second half of the twentieth century the United States of America had become the major funding provider—a point tersely underlined by an American contributor to an on-line discussion in 2012 with "IHQ needs to remember where its funding comes from," although this point had been gratefully acknowledged by General Orsborn sixty years earlier.[94] The occasional bout of arm-wrestling between Anglo and American variants of imperialism may have taken place behind the scenes at times. With the separation of International Headquarters from the United Kingdom territory in the 1990s a clear demarcation was drawn between their funds as well, so that Britain ceased to subsidize the international center in any way differently from the way other territories contributed.

At the end of the twentieth century the then International Secretary for Finance, Commissioner Brian Taylor, issued a serious warning that the Army's international funding had "reached a turning point." While money could be found for social services, community development programs, and emergency relief, because government, public and donor funding was readily accessible for all these purposes, support for the Army's core purpose, evangelical mission, was less forthcoming. World-wide, a small minority of corps were self-supporting, and a minority of territories likewise. Within territories this meant that funds raised by public subscription were being used to support evangelical work, and increasingly countries were putting in place legal impediments to such a practice. In the past grant-aided territories had been helped by the international self-denial

---

93. Roberts, "Self-Denial and Self Support," 26.

94. http://fsaof.blogspot.co.nz/2012/01/positional-clashing-of-cymbles.html; Orsborn, *House of My Pilgrimage*, 181–82.

fund but demand was increasingly exceeding income. He concluded that "[w]e need our Salvationists . . . to have vision of support for the evangelical mission of the Army."[95]

In September 1999, Commissioner John Larsson, then Chief of the Staff, in a presentation to the IHQ international development consultants group, stated that "the reality is that we cannot continue to expand into other countries. We must consolidate and see how to go forward, marrying needs and resources."[96] Such practicalities probably lay behind the decision to withdraw from Vietnam after initial work with refugees there, for example, in 1999. In that year the Salvation Army was working in one hundred and four countries. Either the line has proved impossible to hold or else additional funding has been found; by 2016 the Army was working in one hundred and twenty-eight countries, the additional areas all being in need of external funding. Over the intervening years, the Army's strength in countries which have traditionally supplied the "sinews of war" has continued to decline (with the exception of that of the United States) while exponential growth has taken place in the neediest parts of the globe.

Each year the *Salvation Army Year Book* now publishes the income and expenditure of the overseas service funds. Each territory, no matter how poor, makes some contribution through its self-denial fund to the international self-denial fund. Very few territories however do not also draw on it for funds. From 1998 until 2013 these few were known as the FIT, or financially independent territories; the others were the GAT, or grant aided territories. FIT territories in the 2008–2009 year were the four United States territories, Canada, the two Australian territories, the United Kingdom, Switzerland, New Zealand, Japan, Korea, the Netherlands and the Scandinavian territories: Norway, Sweden, and Denmark, and Finland. In 2012 the four US territories provided 60 percent of the total international self-denial fund (which that year amounted to £18.2 million), while 69 percent of the Army's adult membership resides in the Africa and South Asian territories, which are all supported.

Following the abolition the FIT/GAT nomenclature, a distinction is now made between "implementing" and "facilitating" territories, as part of a strategy to reduce dependency and encourage accountability and self-support with a renewed spiritual emphasis on giving in self-denial.[97] Nevertheless the basic imbalance of responsibility between developed and developing nations remains and the international financial situation is clearly fraught with the continuing dangers of dependency. It also has to be admitted that restraining leadership from excessive expenditure on "vanity projects" in both developed and developing nations remains a challenge for international supervision.[98]

In a 2016 article General Cox criticized the assumption and expectation that ample funding is required and would be forthcoming to underwrite any forward move, citing a number of historical examples of great work growing from meagre resources: " . . . it

---

95. Taylor, "At a Turning Point," *Officer*, December 1999, 30–31.

96. Larsson, quoted by Allan Bacon, (then a member of the international development consultants group), in "The Salvation Army: The International Situation 2016," 2.

97. Roberts, "Self-Denial and Self Support," 26–29.

98. "Vanity projects" can range from inappropriately grandiose buildings to lavish celebrations, in either case conceived of as memorialising the achievements of senior officers.

does not always take great sums of money and other resources in order to grow the Kingdom. It does require true Salvation Army soldiers . . . "⁹⁹

The most recent reforms of governance are also intended to encourage self-sufficiency. A 2016 update by Commissioner John Wainwright, International Secretary for Business Administration, referred to the way in which ten territories are working towards no longer requiring support from the international self-denial fund within ten years and a further twenty are committed to reducing their dependency on this funding. International support in areas of accounting systems, property and information technology is being enhanced in order to facilitate such efforts.¹⁰⁰ At the same time, new financial standards known as international financial and accounting standards (IFAS) are bring rolled out to bring the Army's international book-keeping into the electronic age and better support developing territories.¹⁰¹ It is to be hoped that such measures will help ensure the sustainability of the Salvation Army's operations.

GLOBALIZATION: UNITY IN DIVERSITY

A final reflection on our theme of local and international: while cultures remain diverse, elements of "global culture" are increasingly present in all. The process has been going on for centuries—really, ever since Neanderthals encountered homo sapiens, whenever there have been differing cultures in touch with each other—but is accelerating and now global in reach. We sometimes think of this simply in terms of the rest of the world becoming "westernized." For example, even fifty years ago, beside a road in the Zambezi Valley used only by a store-owner, the local school teacher and the Salvation Army mobile clinic staff, the sole advertising hoarding represented Coca Cola—the best known brand in the world. In some parts of Africa, all street signs and most shop signs are courtesy of Coca Cola. Smart-phones and the world-wide-web now enable people in the most isolated places to follow blow-by-blow the personal lives of American celebrities. All languages are absorbing loan words from American English at an increasing rate.

But globalization has not been a one-way street; it is a two-way process. The local and native have fought back, making deep inroads into the languages, economies, cultures and spiritualties of the West. There has been, in Roland Robertson's words, both "homogenization" and "heterogenization." The local has contributed to the global and the global to the local.¹⁰² If the analogy is not too forced, elements of culture inter-act and change one another like particles in a hadron particle collider. The term "glocalization" ("global" and "local") has been coined to describe this process, which grows increasingly complex.¹⁰³

99. Cox, "Year of Total Mobilization," 6.

100. Wainwright, "Reducing the Gap," 24–27.

101. Carpenter, "Compliance, Integrity and Trust," 10–11.

102. Robertson, "Glocalization: Time—Space and Homogeneity—Heterogeneity," in Featherston, Lash and Robertson, *Global Modernities*, 25–44.

103. Robertson writes that the Japanese term for glocalization, "dochakuka," literally means "to indigenize." Robertson, "Beyond the Discourse of Globalization," 4.

From a broader perspective, the interaction between imperialism and nationalism was in itself a manifestation of the globalization process. Its impact on the Salvation Army could be said to include such elements as the eventual consensus on the need to appoint indigenous leadership as a matter of course—although the fact that in 2017 a third of non-European-majority entities were still led by people of European ethnicity suggests that there is some way to go with that project. To make comparisons, it would be interesting to know what the equivalent Catholic arch-diocesan ratio might be. The inter-active way this give-and-take process is at work within the wider church may be illustrated by a complaint made by Dr Josiah Idowu-Fearon, secretary-general of the Anglican communion, that "the importance that African church leaders attach to the question of same-sex relationships is the result of interference by conservatives in the United States."[104] Of course, Anglicans are comparatively used to having their dirty linen washed in public, whereas the Salvation Army would usually prefer not to have it washed at all, except when compelled to as in recent years by the Australian Royal Commission into Sexual Abuse.[105] It would therefore be difficult to produce a Salvation Army equivalent of Idowu-Fearon's observation. Opportunities for the robust exchange of ideas are more limited in the Army except at the highest level, with, until General Cox's reforms are more generally effected, few structural processes for helping arrive at the kind of consensus the Movement believes should characterize its decision-making. Influences in either direction are therefore more difficult to observe, and are as likely to be personal as ideological, but they will be active nevertheless.

The world is, in some ways then, becoming more uniform—while at the same time, paradoxically, local diversity is reinforced by its involvement in the process. Within its own sphere, the Salvation Army has both contributed to that process and also operates within it. The same global economic and political pressures impact on all territories, though to varying degrees. In these days of electronic communications, international social media and more frequent travel, the connections between Salvation Army territories and headquarters are more immediate than ever, binding the Army ever more closely together. That has not meant uniformity, however.

THE SALVATION ARMY AND THE ECUMENICAL MOVEMENT

Roland Robertson includes amongst the late nineteenth century manifestations of globalization, "the beginning of the modern religious ecumenical movement which at one and the same time celebrated difference and searched for commonality within the framework of an emergent culture for 'doing' the relationship between the particular and the . . . universal."[106] It seems appropriate therefore to deal with the Salvation Army's ecumenical experience within the context of globalization. The "glocalization" process, as Robertson described it, can be seen in how, in reaching out to other Christian faith communities,

---

104. *Church Times*, 16 December 2016, 14.

105. For example, http://www.abc.net.au/news/2016-09-12/salvation-army-failed-to-protect-children-royal-commission-finds/7835784, accessed 9 February 2017.

106. Robertson, "Glocalization," 36–37.

the Salvation Army has been obliged to define more carefully its own faith and order. In becoming more aware of the wider ecumenical context, it has inevitably absorbed elements of the wider church practice and belief into its own systems. When King Edward VII asked William Booth what the churches thought of him now, the Founder replied, "Sir, they imitate me!"[107] More than a century later we have seen from changes in the Army's ecclesiology and worship that this has not been a one-way street either.

In local contexts the Army has related in a wide range of ways to other Christian and other religious bodies, but the governing principles from the Army's point of view was laid down by the Founder in the *Orders and Regulations* (1886). These were eirenical, enjoining that

5. The F.O. must not, either in public or in private, pull to pieces the creed or denounce the practices of any other religious organization . . .

6. Instead of trying to discover those points in which Christians differ from him . . . he should seek for those upon which they may agree with him, and dwell upon these . . .

8. . . . the F.O. must not only refrain from any attempt to bring them over to his views, but wish them God-speed . . .

9. The F.O. must not hold any controversy about the doctrines, sacraments, ceremonials or practices of any religious sect . . .

10. The F.O. must never allow himself to say anything . . . reflecting on ministers or religious teachers, which is calculated to lessen their influence or power to do good . . .

11. The F. O. must never neglect the duties of his own Corps to join in the services of any denomination . . .

12. The F.O. must not allow any services, processions or other operations that he may conduct, to interfere with the comfort and efficiency of the services of any other religious organizations . . . never allow his band to play . . . in marching past any church . . . during the hours of Divine Service.

15. When Catholics ask the F.O. if he is a Protestant, let him reply that he is a Salvation Soldier . . .

For good measure, the Regulations also laid down principles for interfaith relations.

16. . . . when . . . the F.O. is brought into contact with Mohammedans, he should never begin by attacking Mohammed as a false prophet or otherwise attacking the notions or practices of their religion. On the contrary, the F.O. should commence by enquiring whether they really pray to God as they profess to do . . . and whether they are as careful as the Koran . . . tells them to be, about praying and living so as to be ready for judgement day.

17. When the F.O. meets with a Jew, he should always decline any dispute about Jesus Christ or the New Testament. Instead, he should press the Jew as to whether he keeps the commandments; and whether he realizes that communion with God and

107. Begbie, *William Booth*, I, 113.

that experience of victory over sin which is described in the Psalms and other parts of the Old Testament, and which was undoubtedly enjoyed by those who wrote those Sacred Books.

In all these conversations of course the officer was enjoined to share his own testimony as to his experience of God in the hope that this would attract interest and attention:

18. In short, the F.O. must, without any sacrifice of principle, or any hiding of his light under a bushel, be all things to all men, and he will be sure thereby to gain some.[108]

Booth was evidently without prejudice in religious matters, having spent his early years conducting revivals for anyone who invited him, and he was also aware that he needed the good-will of a wide range of church adherents in order to finance his operations and achieve his goals. Railton, of course, was happy worshipping with anyone from Catholics to Quakers, and did so.

In the mission field, in keeping with these principles, the Army has operated on the principle of "comity" where possible. This refers to the practice in some countries (for example in Rhodesia, now Zimbabwe) of missionary organizations dividing up a territory into spheres of influence so that they would not be in direct competition with one another for proselytes or for school pupils. Competition for converts was always a possibility however, and accusations of "sheep-stealing" were not unknown, especially when the Army's expansion took it into areas already "missionized." Eason quotes examples from India:

> . . . the organization initially met its teacher shortage by poaching those belonging to other missions. As expected, such a strategy only heightened the existing tension between the Army and other missionary societies. Writing to the editor of *The Harvest Field* in 1894, James Duthie, a missionary with the LMS, complained that a number of native teachers in Travancore had left his mission to run rival schools set up by the Army. The same pattern was apparent in Gujerat, where Salvationists began to establish village schools in the mid–1890s. Situating themselves in areas serviced by American Methodists, officers managed to draw away teachers and pupils from the Methodist mission . . . [109]

Salvation Army officers generally however attempted to maintain co-operative relationships with other denominations, taking part in inter-church activities, including those of the Wesleyan family of churches. Commissioner Thomas Coombs represented the Founder and spoke at the Third Ecumenical Methodist Conference held in London in September 1901.[110] Officers were likely to belong to local ministers' fraternals by the time of the First World War,[111] and possibly earlier, although the editor of *The Officer* told a correspondent in 1928 that although regulations did not actually forbid officers to

---

108. *Orders and Regulations*, 1886, 529–33.
109. Eason, "Christianity in a Colonial Age," 289.
110. Coombs, "Representing the Salvation Army," 344–47.
111. Edward Joy, "Share More Memories, Please!" 103.

belong to local free church councils in Great Britain, headquarters disapproved of such attendance as a distraction from the officer's real work.[112]

The Army had declined an invitation to attend an ecumenical missionary conference in 1888 but was involved in the 1910 World Missionary Conference in Edinburgh.[113] Attending subsequent ecumenical meetings, the Salvation Army was a founding member of the World Council of Churches in 1948. Some elements within the Salvation Army have always been wary of this association. General Albert Orsborn was reluctant to be involved when the World Council was formed. In an address on the Salvation Army in relation to ecumenism, given to the 1969 commissioners' conference, Commissioner Hubert Westcott quoted Orsborn's memorandum to the Advisory Council in 1947 as concluding with, "I do not wish my period of leadership to be associated with the gravitation of the Salvation Army nearer to church life in faith and order." Having received the Advisory Council's recommendation to join, Orsborn commented, "It occurs to me to wonder why we should participate in the Assembly . . . but the majority of our leaders think that we should be represented and therefore I have told the Chief to arrange it."

However, Orsborn subsequently failed to replace the retiring Commissioner A. G. Cunningham on the executive council of the WCC central committee.[114] His successor, Wilfred Kitching, wrote concerning the WCC that "we may have at times lost something by seeking to withhold interest in the affairs of the Church."[115] Successive Generals or other leading Army figures involved in the ecumenical movement have been at pains to explain the nature and limits of this association over the years, especially at times of WCC general assemblies.[116]

For some Salvationists there was possibly a fear of absorption into some generic super-church, espousing modernist or possibly Roman doctrines (depending on the individual phobia), and the loss of identity and mission. At the extreme end some sympathized with the views of Dr Carl McIntire, an American Presbyterian minister vehemently opposed to the WCC, who established an "International Council of Christian Churches" in 1948 and in his journal the *Christian Beacon* was wont to charge the WCC with being a Catholic-modernist-Communist conspiracy.[117] Commissioner Reginald Woods,

---

112. *Officer*, May 1928, 371–72.

113. Johnston, edited, *Report of the Centenary Conference*, quoted by Rowdon, "Edinburgh 1910," *Vox Evangelica* 5 (1967) 54.

114. Orsborn, *Officer* (March–April 1954) 73–8; Brown, *Gate and Light*, 232; Westcott, "The Salvation Army in Relation to Ecumenism."

115. *Magazine* (December, 1961) 5.

116. Orsborn, "World Council of Churches," 73–78; Kitching, "The Army and the World Council of Churches, Part I, 289–90; Woods, "Some Questions Answered," 291–94, 323–34; Kitching, "The Army and the World Council of Churches, Part II, , 361–65; Woods, "And it Came to Pass," 109–13; May–June 1962, 167–72; July–August 1962, 257–60; September– October 1962, 289–94; "New Delhi Speaks, 1," March 1963, 125–28; "New Delhi Speaks, 2,"April 1963, 161–64, 167; Williams, "Personal Reflections," 150–54, 178.

117. See http://www.ptsem.edu/grow/Library/collections/McIntire.htm. Accessed 3 November 2005. One is reminded of the lady in a 1942 Second World War *Punch* cartoon, begging her newspaper-thumping husband to calm himself, since even Hitler could not be *both* dregs *and* scum!

the Army's representative on the WCC central committee in the 1960s, evidently took his influence sufficiently seriously to rebut some of his allegations in an article in *The Officer*.[118]

The meta-narrative of cold war and chiefly American fears of Communism as well as regard for the sensibilities of donors were certainly factors contributing to the Army's withdrawal (suspension of membership pending discussions) from the central committee of the WCC in 1979 over the issue of aid to liberation movements in Africa.[119] Letters in Salvation Army archives in USA support this allegation, and letters in London archives show that leaders in London had tried unsuccessfully to mollify the American leaders' opposition to the World Council of Churches. The deaths of Army personnel in a 1978 guerrilla attack on the Usher Secondary School in Rhodesia-Zimbabwe helped precipitate the issue.[120]

The Army's concerns were not solely political however. The 1980 report of a commission also referred to a "change of emphasis," if not a change of policy, in the council's approach to ecumenism. "The WCC has undoubtedly become more active in recent years in its quest for church union." Referring to the influence of the Faith and Order Commission's 1975 study booklet, *One Baptism, One Eucharist and a Mutually Recognized Ministry*, the report says that "the emphasis on a 'mutually agreed ministry' has made it necessary for The Salvation Army to define more clearly the position of an officer in relationship to other ministers and in relationship to the soldiery . . . It would be fair to say that the Army takes 'the priesthood of all believers' more literally than most member churches and therefore gives its laity—at least theologically—a more important role than that accorded by most other churches . . . this is a position which the Army wishes to safeguard." The report suggested that "the Army will have to be prepared to find itself increasingly 'out of step' with other denominations, even to the extent of becoming a permanent irritation to them."[121] This special pleading was probably an over-reaction, if not a little paranoid, given that the Army did not in fact give its laity a role any more prominent than did many churches.

The Army eventually settled on maintaining its association by adopting non-voting "fraternal" status in 1981.[122] This relationship derived from the Army's new status as a "Christian World Communion," which it shared with such bodies as the Roman Catholic Church, the Conference of Seventh Day Adventists, the World Methodist Council, the Lutheran World Federation and the Baptist World Alliance. This reflects the Army's international polity as distinct from membership of the Council by separate national churches of each denomination.[123] This association is now referred to as "advisor" status, a category shared by all participants in the Conference of Secretaries of World

---

118. Wood, "New Delhi Speaks, 2," *Officer*, April 1963, 162.

119. Murdoch, "In Darkest Africa," 9.

120. Gariepy, *History of The Salvation Army*, VIII, 20.

121. "Findings of the Commission Appointed to Review the Relationship of The Salvation Army with the World Council of Churches," 32–33.

122. Arnold Brown, letter dated 31 July 1981 to Philip Potter of WCC, in Brown, *Gate and Light*, 239.

123. *One Faith, One Church*, 1.

Communions. This means they are invited to participate in central committee meetings and general assemblies of the World Council of Churches but do not have a vote.[124]

The North American Salvation Army remained suspicious of the WCC. Commissioner Victor Keanie's report on the sixth world assembly (Toronto, 1983) commented, "We were aware of a lack of interest and in some cases antipathy regarding the WCC on the part of Canadian Salvationists (in common with their USA neighbors) . . . It seems obvious that our North American friends have not understood the relationship of the Army to the WCC and in general seem to be adversely influenced by the media interpretation of the Council's activities."[125]

The WCC produced its Faith and Order Paper 111, the "Lima" document on *Baptism, Eucharist and Ministry*, in 1982. This end-product of many years of discussion by the Faith and Order Commission represented the areas of "theological convergence" among the major confessional groups as the conferences brought together not only the WCC member bodies but also representatives of the Roman Catholic Church and some other non-members. The document was transmitted to churches with a request for their official response. While the intention had been that churches would look for areas of agreement, the majority ended up by drawing lines around their own particular distinctives and the result pleased no-one. Catholics (in the broad sense) felt the document was protestant in emphasis; protestants felt "left out."[126]

To prepare a response, International Headquarters asked all territories to set up study groups "composed of theologically and experientially qualified Salvationists, ordained and lay."[127] Probably some did so. The resulting paper contained the first extensive official statement on the Army's doctrine of ministry, even though it was necessarily reactive, taking its cues from the Lima document. The responses were published as *Faith and Order Paper 137—Churches Respond to BEM*; pages 230–53 of Volume IV contain the Salvation Army statement. Copies of the Army's response were distributed to officers in some territories at least, as it became available.[128] The Army also published its response separately in book form as *One Faith, One Church* in 1990. The Salvation Army continues to be involved in this kind of ecumenical relationship. Although the World Council of Churches has been running out of steam as the old main-line liberal denominations of the West, formerly its main drivers, have diminished, churches in the developing world continue to support it.

An alternative way forward in recent years has been the holding of bilateral theological discussions between denominations. So far the Salvation Army has talked with the General Conference of Seventh Day Adventists, the World Methodist Council and the Catholic Church on an international level, not in order to initiate union or united action so much as to enable greater understanding and explore commonalities.[129]

---

124. Earl Robinson to author, email, 2 April 2005.
125. Victor Keanie, Unpublished Report, 1983, 2.
126. Compare Collins, *Diakonia*, 256–57, and Volf, *After Our Likeness*, 20.
127. Thurian and Wainwright, edited, *Churches Respond to BEM*, 232.
128. Lt.-Colonel Trevor Standen, letter to all officers in New Zealand, dated June 1987.
129. Robinson, "Bilateral Theological Dialogues," 5–13.

Conversations with the Catholic Church, published by IHQ in 2014, is a record of papers presented and recommendations arising in discussions between 2007 and 2012.

Another direction, proposed by Cardinal Walter Kasper, has been "receptive ecumenism," whereby church communities agree to share their weaknesses and problems together in the expectation that they will be able to help one another in their common task. Such willing vulnerability seems perhaps more Christ-like in approach than the defensive posturing which can be associated with some ecumenical "show-and-tell" gatherings.[130] Promoted by Paul Murray of the Centre for Catholic Studies at Durham University, a comparative research project in "Receptive Ecumenism and the Local Church" was entered into by the UK territory's northern division from 2007.[131] In New Zealand the Salvation Army was involved in discussions of this kind with partner churches in the National Dialogue for Christian Unity in 2015, discussing issues of common interest such as handling of abuse complaints and maintaining youth work.

UNITY AND DIVERSITY

Kasper conceived the principles of "receptive ecumenism" as he recognized that the old ecumenical dream of organic unity was in fact receding. The world is, in some ways, becoming more uniform, but in others less so. Likewise, the Salvation Army is perhaps growing steadily less uniform, as its own sub-cultures develop and diverge and as the hold of central control over opinion and conduct is gradually weakened. To take one simple example, responses to General John Gowans' unprecedented world-wide survey of officer opinion on the International Commission on Officership's 1999 report, threw into stark relief contrasting attitudes held by different parts of the Army world. Responses from the UK territory and the three Australasian territories were strongly in favor of abolishing all ranks other than those of captain and general; by contrast, responses from the developing world and from the United States of America were strongly supportive of retaining the present multi-rank hierarchical structure. It was the latter which carried the day.

The international diversity of the Army is now such that one size no longer fits all. General Wickberg noted many years ago that "Over the years there has been a steady increase of local self-government, and there is no desire on the part of International Headquarters to halt or retard this trend."[132] It was remarked on by Commissioner Earle Maxwell, Chief of the Staff, at the 1998 international conference of leaders, when he said that "it is becoming increasingly difficult, from an IHQ point of view, to formulate international decisions, with their implied global relevance, that can then be comfortably implemented in every territory or command."[133] It is interesting to read this alongside Avery Dulles' 1978 prediction concerning the post-Vatican II Catholic Church: "The internal pluralism in the church itself will be such that directives from on high will be

130. Murray, *Receptive Ecumenism*.

131. http://community.dur.ac.uk/m.j.p.pound/Phase_2/Phase%20II%20-%20Governance%20and%20Finance%20-%20Salvation%20Army.pdf.

132. Wickberg, "International Salvationist," 18.

133. Maxwell, "Shaping the Army of the Future," 5.

variously applied in different regions, so that the top officers will not be able to control in detail what goes on at the local level."[134]

That does not mean that the Salvation Army has reached the condition described in W.B. Yeats' lines: "Things fall apart, the centre cannot hold, Mere anarchy is loosed upon the world."[135] Or that the central administration is any less willing to exercise control, even though General Larsson wrote in 2004 of the constant challenge to maintain international unity "in this era of increased 'territorial discretion.'"[136] All "reserved appointments" anywhere in the world and all promotions to the rank of lieutenant-colonel and above must be personally approved by the General.[137] General Burrows told me that she had made a practice of committing to memory relevant information about all officers of that rank in order to be able to review with integrity proposals for promotion.

In fact the pendulum has been swung back in some areas. Whereas earlier in the twenty-first century the decision had been taken to cease issuing "Moral and Social Issues" statements internationally, leaving it up to each territory to frame such definitions and prescriptions according to local conditions and cultural norms, an International Moral and Social Issues Council was again constituted (with international personnel), for the purpose, inter alia, of laying down such guidance on matters of behavior.[138] Likewise, although, or perhaps because, there is wider discussion of the Army's position on the sacraments than ever before, it appears that the official position is being more firmly reinforced than hitherto. General Bond's "One Army, One Mission, One Message" slogan, introduced upon her election in 2011, also conveyed the message of unity. Electronic media also permit the General and international leadership to be much more accessible and Salvationists internationally to be much more immediately aware of the world-wide fellowship to which they belong than ever before.

In the face of centrifugal tendencies, opportunities are taken to reinforce the moral authority of the traditional structure. Not long ago a Canadian territorial commander welcomed the visiting General on behalf of his territory with the assurance:

> I want to remind you that it takes Spirit power and Spirit anointing and Spirit choosing to have men and women able to lead the Salvation Army in 126 countries around the world . . . I'm going to take the liberty on your behalf to assure them that we in the Canadian & Bermuda Territory wish to support the International Salvation Army. We will do so by being attentive to the messaging that comes out of IHQ on occasions where we are called to support particular thinking and actions points. We will do that by respecting them as our **spiritual authority here on earth.** They are God-ordained people established to lead us in the days in which we face many challenges and more importantly this Territory will support our international leaders with our prayers.[139]

---

134. Dulles, *Models of the Church*, 208.
135. Yeats, "The Second Coming," *Collected Poems*, 211.
136. Larsson, "Being True to Ourselves," 2.
137. "Reserved appointments" include senior leadership positions in a Territory or Command.
138. Read, "Developing a Cohesive Opinion," 38–39.
139. Commissioner Brian Peddle, 22 June 2014, http://salvationist.ca/2014/06/territorial-congress-2014-videos/.

The Legal Section at International Headquarters also keeps a watching brief on those formal mechanisms which maintain the international integrity of the Salvation Army. Given the great variety of legal instruments under which the Army operates in its many territorial jurisdictions, the Legal Section has to ensure that the purposes of the Salvation Army: "the advancement of the Christian religion as promulgated in [its] religious doctrines, and pursuant thereto, the advancement of education, the relief of poverty, and other charitable objects . . . " are referenced in any constitutional documents. Further, such instruments need to reference the Orders and Regulations under which the entire organization operates, and finally, "the role of the General as the Army's ecclesiastical leader" has to be preserved.[140]

What works in the opposite direction? The Catholic Church, to which the Salvation Army's structure bears close resemblance, embraces the concept of "subsidiarity," the principle that a central authority should have a subsidiary function, performing only those tasks which cannot be performed at a more local level. In a centralized, hierarchical bureaucracy, as maintained by both the Catholic Church and the Salvation Army, this is always an ideal easier to enunciate than to practice, but as we have already observed, the tide has been flowing that direction in many ways. Efforts to reinforce standards of financial probity, for example through positional statements on "corruption," will continue to meet resistance where the acceptance of "gifts" is deeply engrained in a culture, and endemic poverty reinforces the temptation to supplement inadequate incomes. In many countries there are also strong cultural expectations that family members will be supported and helped when their relation has access to influence or resources. It also has to be said that instances of corruption, nepotism, cronyism, bullying, and abuse of power have not been confined to "developing countries."[141]

From his taking office in 2013 General André Cox undertook to address these and related issues and his "Accountability Movement" is well into the stage of implementation. One aspect of this reform movement seeks to strengthen central control in the sense that it looks for a more general adherence to the same standards of probity and integrity throughout the organization. Another aspect however supports international diversification in that local legislative requirements for governance are to be more strictly recognized and observed. All these factors serve to reinforce the globalization, or glocalization, of the Salvation Army—that dialectic between the local and the universal.

Reforms within the Salvation Army face the same kind of opposition as encountered by Francis I as a reforming Pope, and for the same reasons. Apart from individuals' self-interest and reluctance to divest themselves of power and control, one of the downstream effects of globalization is that societies and individuals begin to feel their identity under threat and under these circumstances religious traditions may tend to become more important. In particular, nostalgia for the way things used to be in times thought of as more settled and less threatened can support the tendency towards conservative

---

140. Hodder, "International Headquarters Legal Section," 17.

141. Complaints should not always be taken at face value, but for the record it was an American officer who commented thus on a blog: "I see many officers leaving because they get disenfranchised with blatant examples of favoritism, nepotism and sometimes even racism from upper leadership." http://matchfactory.org/2017/05/salvation-army-officership-why-no-one-wants-our-job/. Accessed 14 May 2017.

and even fundamentalist thinking. With the increasing representation of the developing world in the Army's senior ranks and decision-making bodies, and the tendency for "developing world" opinion in theological, moral and ecclesiological matters to be conservative, like that of the financially powerful North American territories, it might be anticipated that the application of any greater centralized control will tend to be in this direction. Third world voices have not been heard very often for much of the Salvation Army's history—there has been no great documentary resource for historians to research in the past—but this is changing rapidly in the twenty-first century as Salvationists from Asia and Africa are beginning to contribute more to the Army's internal debates. In a world becoming more polarized, in which fundamentalist opinions seem to be more widely and firmly held, it will be interesting to see how diversity of opinion and liberal views might fare within the Army's ranks in the future. It will be a test of leadership to manage the next period of transition without alienating some at either end of the Army's continuum.

Conclusion

Looking Back

In the earlier part of this survey of the Salvation Army's history and its distinctive features, we looked at these in terms of a sociological model proposed by Max Weber at the beginning of the twentieth century. Deriving from this schema, Roland Robertson's analysis considered the Salvation Army's development through the incipient phase, its enthusiastic mobilization, its necessary organization for permanence and its consolidation as an institution. Towards the end of this work, considering the Army's international expansion, again drawing on Robertson's more recent sociological analysis, we have looked, although more briefly and superficially, at the interplay of global and local elements in the process variously described as "globalization" and "glocalization" which provide a another framework for considering how the organization exists in a very different world today.

Such a review and analysis takes nothing away from the truly remarkable record of a tiny East End mission which has grown to become a respected world-wide philanthropic and religious institution of something like one and a half million people, still vigorously extending its influence in many places, and still making a difference for good for the lives of millions of others. Hardly the smallest part of what could have been said about that has been said, but the ability to stand back and see the Salvation Army in the context of its times and a willingness to let the past inform the present—to "stop, look back, *often*"—can only enhance its capacity to do better in the future.

Appendix One

Ranks of The Salvation Army 1878–2017

Current ranks shown in **bold.** Arrows show promotion routes at various times.

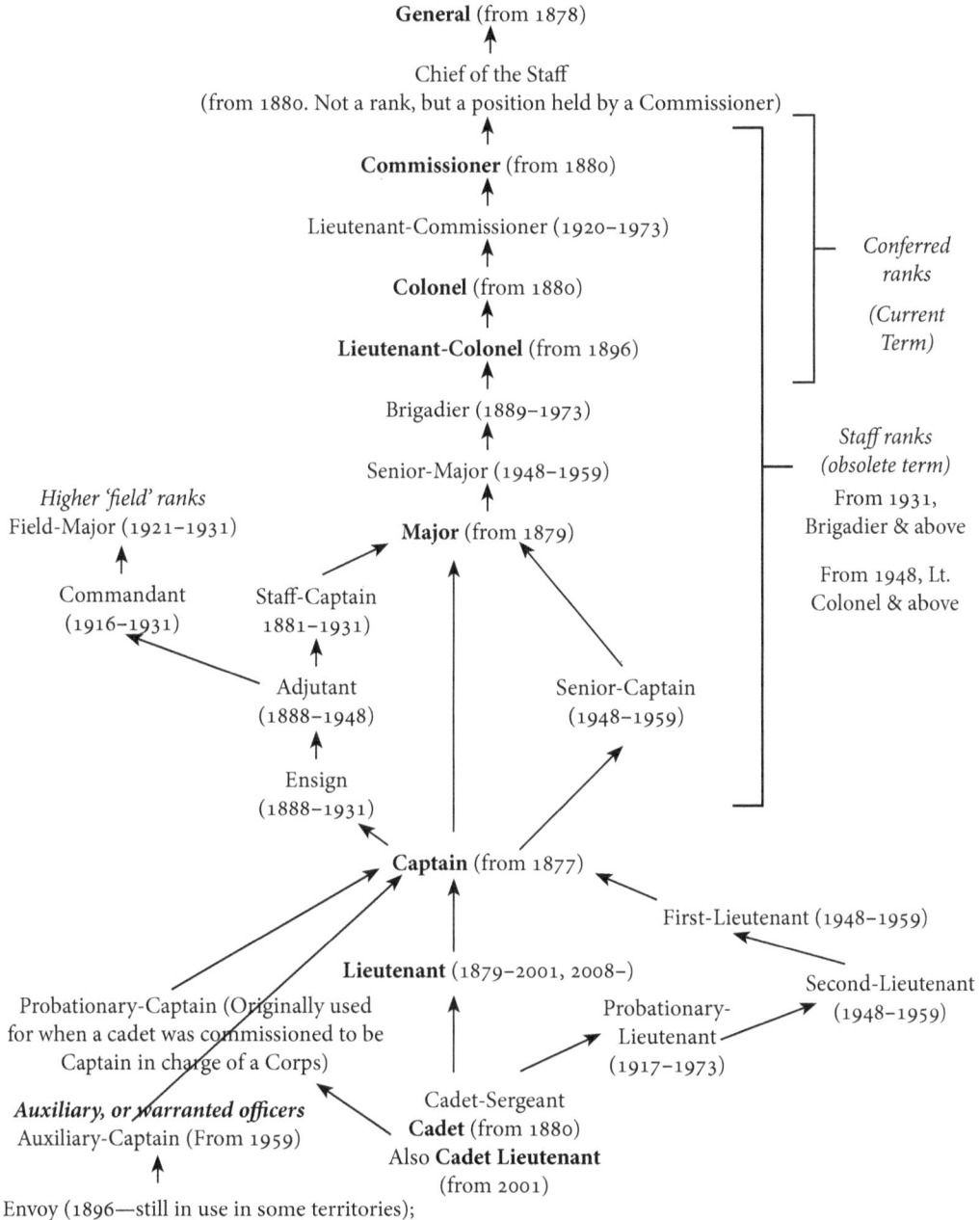

Appendix One: Ranks of The Salvation Army 1878–2017

From early days, any rank above that of Captain was described as a "staff rank." As officers in field (including "social") appointments were progressively admitted to higher ranks, the lowest rank of "staff" was progressively raised. Promotion to ranks below "staff" or "conferred" level depends on years of service. "Commissioner" was not originally a rank but a role representing the General, which could be exercised by an officer of a rank such as Major or Colonel. Lieut.-Commissioner was therefore a curious amalgam of military and civil service titles.

Appendix Two

The Booth Dynasty

(Showing family members who were officers)

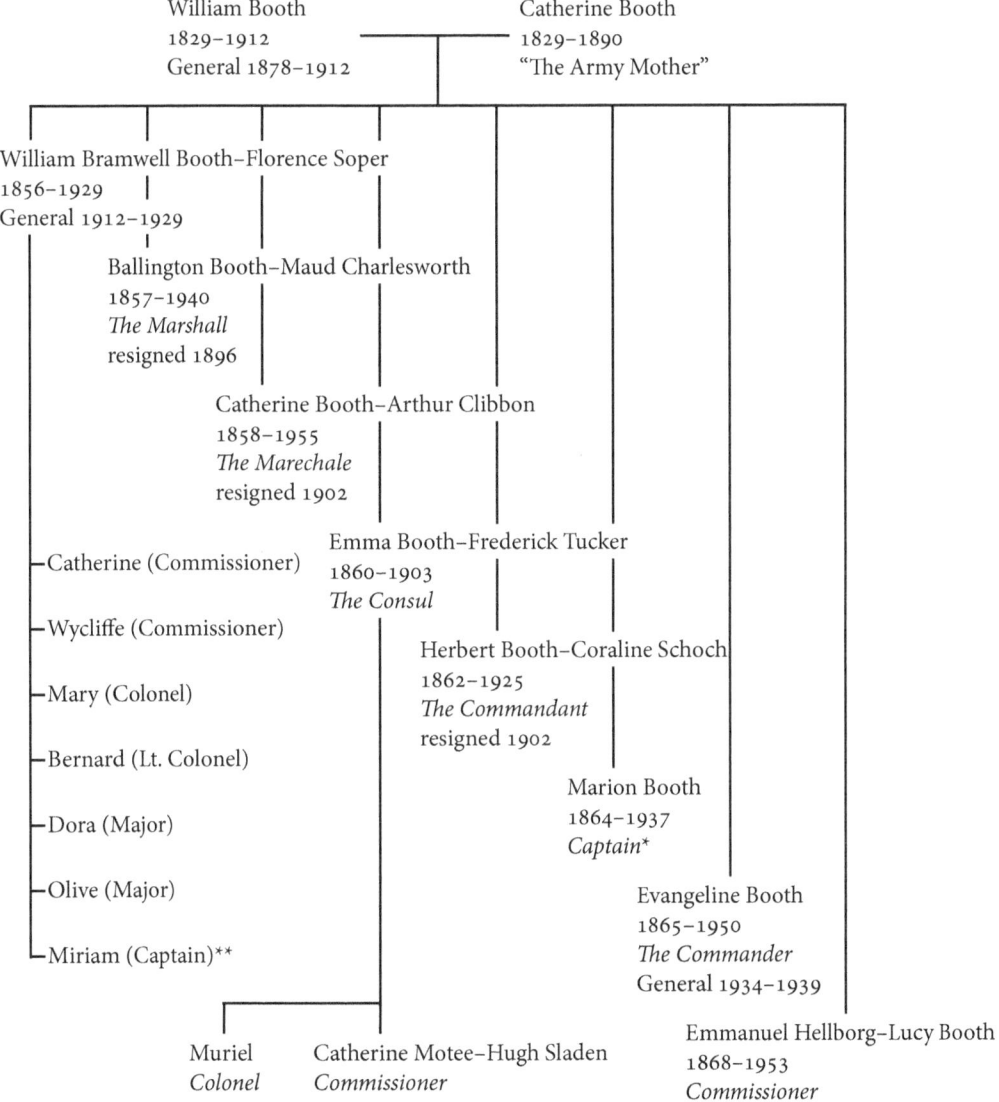

* Marion, an invalid, held the honorary rank of Captain
** Miriam, also an invalid, was commissioned but did not serve in an appointment.

Appendix Three

Glossary

Adherent Member: A person who wishes to regard the Salvation Army as their "church," and making a confession of faith, but without taking upon themselves the life-style commitments involved in being a "Soldier."

Advisory Council to the General: Body established in 1947 to advise the General on policy and senior appointments. Replaced by General's Consultative Council in 2001.

Articles of Faith: The "11 points" of Salvation Army Doctrine, professed by all soldiers.

Articles of War: Now known as the "Soldier's Covenant," signed by soldiers when enrolled, or "sworn in," confessing personal salvation, adherence to Salvation Army beliefs, and committing to a Salvation Army life-style.

Cadet: Person in training for Salvation Army officership.

Candidate: A soldier who has been accepted for training as an officer.

Census Board: The body of senior "local officers" of a Corps, charged with maintaining the rolls. Now "Pastoral Care Council."

Chief of the Staff: Second in command to the General.

Chief Secretary: (CS) Officer second in command of a Territory.

Command: Salvation Army term for a distinct geographical area reporting to IHQ, usually a country, with fewer than about 40 Corps, although there are historically-derived inconsistencies.

Commanding Officer: (CO) Usually the officer in charge of a Corps.

Commissioner: Senior commissioned rank usually held by Territorial Commander or Head of Department at IHQ.

APPENDIX THREE: GLOSSARY

Corps: Local Salvation Army mission unit, analogous to a parish or congregation.

Corps Council: Advisory group of senior local officers and other people in a Corps, advising the Corps Commanding Officer on local policy and programme.

Corps Sergeant Major: (CSM) senior local officer, principal volunteer assistant to the Commanding Officer.

Dedication: Equivalent to infant baptism or christening, without use of water. Does not denote reception into the church but is regarded as occasion for thanksgiving and opportunity for parents to make commitments regarding the child's upbringing in the faith.

Division: Geographical area comprising a number of Corps. Equivalent of diocese in episcopal church polity. Smaller units, comprising fewer Corps than a Division, may be Districts led by a District Officer

Divisional Commander: (DC) Officer in charge of a Division. Originally known as "Divisional Officer" (DO).

Field: Generic term for evangelical operations, including Corps. Sometimes inclusive of the "social work," and sometimes used as exclusive of or distinct from social or welfare operations.

General: International leader of The Salvation Army.

General's Consultative Council: Council comprising Commissioners and Territorial Leaders, advising the General on matters of mission strategy and policy. Operates through an electronic database, with selected members also meeting quarterly at IHQ with the General in the chair.

Hall: Salvation Army meeting place. Often termed a Barracks in early days; later many terms such as Citadel, Fortress, Temple.

High Council: Gathering of all active Commissioners, along with all Territorial Commanders and Territorial Presidents of Women's Organizations for the purpose of electing the General. Convened upon the General's retirement, or if a number of Commissioners requisition a High Council to determine the General's fitness for office.

International Headquarters: (IHQ) London-sited head office of the Army.

Junior Corps: Sunday School, also known as Young People's Corps, under direction of the Young People's Sergeant Major, or YPSM.

Junior Soldier: Young person, from age of 9 upward, who signs a pledge, affirming faith and making promises regarding life-style.

Local Officer: (LO) Non-commissioned, volunteer official of a Corps.

Meeting: A religious service. The Army employs no set form of liturgy, and extempore prayer and testimony are valued.

Minute: The Army's legislative instrument. Administrative order issued by or on the authority of Territorial Commander or Chief of the Staff.

Officer: Full-time, commissioned (since 1978, "ordained") worker in the Army. Regarded as analogous to clergy.

Orders and Regulations: Rules governing Salvation Army operations.

Outpost: Small centre of work, subsidiary to a Corps.

Promoted to Glory: Deceased.

Recruit: A person who has professed conversion and is undergoing instruction to prepare for enrolment as a soldier.

Region: Small administrative grouping, comprising a number of Corps, often pertaining to a national political unit. (Tonga is a Region of the New Zealand, Fiji and Tonga Territory.) Led by a Regional Commander.

Salvationist: A generic term for a member of The Salvation Army.

Soldier: A person who has signed the Soldier's Covenant (Articles of War) and been enrolled as a member of The Salvation Army. Must have professed conversion and accepted Salvation Army doctrines, and committed to a distinctive lifestyle involving not only normal Christian ethical standards but also abstention from alcohol, tobacco, gambling and other than medically prescribed use of drugs.

Territorial Commander: (TC) Officer in charge of a Territory.

Territorial Headquarters: (THQ) Administrative office from which a Territory is directed.

Territory: Major geographical unit of command, which may comprise a country (such as Indonesia), part of a country (such as the USA Western) or several countries (such as New Zealand, Fiji and Tonga).

The Movement: One of the Salvation Army's self-descriptors.

The War: War against sin, the Army's mission.

The Work: Salvation Army ministry and service.

Bibliography

In this Bibliography, works published by the Salvation Army without the acknowledgement of individual authors or editors are grouped in alphabetical order of title under the corporate entry of "Salvation Army."

Abbott, Andrew. *The System of Professions: An Essay on the Division of Expert Labor.* Chicago: University of Chicago Press, 1988.
Agnew, Milton S. *Manual of Salvationism.* New York: Salvation Army, 1968.
———. *Holy Spirit, Friend and Counselor.* Kansas City: Beacon Hill, 1980.
Aitken, Tom. *Blood and Fire, Tsar and Commissar: The Salvation Army in Russia,* 1907–1923. Milton Keynes: Paternoster, 2007.
Alexander, Paul. *Signs and Wonders.* San Francisco: Jossey-Bass, 2009.
Anderson, Ray. S. "Theology of Ministry." In *Theological Foundations for Ministry: Selected Readings for a Theology of the Church in Ministry,* edited by Ray Anderson, 6–21. Edinburgh: T&T Clark, 1979.
Anon. ed. *Life of General Booth.* London: Nelson, [1912].
Aragon, Lorraine V. "Making a Male God and Female Careers: The Salvation Army and Gender in Central Sulawesi, Indonesia." Abstract of Paper given at American Association of Sociologists Annual Meeting, March 1999. http://www.aasianst.org/absts/1999abst/SE/se-115.htm.
Armstrong, Karen. *Fields of Blood: Religion and the History of Violence.* London: Bodley Head, 2014.
Ausubel, Herman. *In Hard Times: Reformers among the Late Victorians.* New York: Columbia University Press, 1960.
Bacon, Allan. "The Salvation Army: the International Situation 2016." Privately circulated paper.
Baggaly, William. *Digest of the Minutes, Institutes, Polity, Doctrines, Ordinances and Literature of the Methodist New Connexion.* London: Methodist New Connexion Bookroom, 1862. http://books.google.co.nz/books?id=H-ICAAAAQAAJ&printsec=frontcover&dq=William+Baggaly,+A+Digest+of+the+Minutes,+Institutes,+Polity,+Doctrines,+Ordinances+and+Literature+of+the+Methodist+New+Connexion&source=bl&ots=gcKaQ4OTjv&sig=O_bCQ6nVFH2m-pJBApfvrBAzs0&hl=en&ei=QSTSS475BorUtgOq8ZX-CQ&sa=X&oi=book_result&ct=result&resnum=1&ved=0CAYQ6AEwAA#v=onepage&q&f=false.
Baggs, Albert Edward. "Social Evangel as Nationalism: a Study of the Salvation Army in Japan, 1895–1940." PhD diss., New York State University, 1966.
Bailey, Victor. "'In Darkest England and the Way Out,' The Salvation Army, Social Reform and the Labour Movement, 1885–1910." *International Review of Social History* 29 (1984) 133–77. http://kuscholarworks.ku.edu/dspace/bitstream/1808/8331/1/Bailey_SalvationArmy.pdf.
———. "Salvation Army Riots: The 'Skeleton Army' and Legal Authority in a Provincial Town." In *Social Control in Nineteenth Century Britain,* edited by A.P. Donajgrodzkij, 231–53, 236–37. Totowa, New Jersey: Rowman and Littlefield, 1977.
Barbour, Nigel. "The Salvation Army and Migration." *Hallelujah!* 2 no. 4 (2009) 35–36.

Bibliography

———. "Salvation and the Sea." *Hallelujah!* 2 no. 4 (2009) 55–60.

Barr, Ian. "Traffic on a less than Calm Sea." Paper given at Brengle Fellowship, Australia Southern Territory, 2009. In *Boston Common: Salvationist Perspectives on Holiness*, edited by Stephen Court, 51–58. Melbourne: Salvo, 2010.

Barr, James. "The Fundamentalist Understanding of Scripture." In *Conflicting Ways of Interpreting the Bible*, edited by Hans Küng et al. *Concilium* 13 (October 1980) 70–74.

Beckford, James A. *Social Theory and Religion*. Cambridge: Cambridge University Press, 2003.

Begbie, Harold. *William Booth, Founder of The Salvation Army* (London: Macmillan, 1920).

Benedict XVI: see under Ratzinger.

Bennett, David Malcolm. *The Origins of Left-Behind Eschatology* (Maitland, Florida: Xulon, 2010).

Berger, Peter L. *The Social Reality of Religion*. Baltimore, MB: Penguin, 1967, 113, quoted by Jean-Daniel Plüs, "Globalization of Pentecostalism or Globalization of Individualism? A European Perspective." In *The Globalization of Pentecostalism: A Religion Made To Travel*, edited by Murray W. Dempster et al. 170–82. Oxford: Regnum, 1999.

Bishop, Gary. *Darkest England & The Way Back In*. Leicester: Matador, 2007.

Blackwell, David, "Evolution of Corps Architecture in the United Kingdom," *Salvation Army Year Book*, 1959, 30–35.

Blackwell, Miriam. *The Open Door: The Salvation Army Re-entry into Russia*. London: Salvation Army, 2004.

Boardman, Hubert. "Officership—a Functional Ministry." *The Officer* (November 1972) 516–19, 522.

Boon, Brindley. *Play the Music, Play! The Story of Salvation Army Bands*. London: Salvation Army, 1966.

———. *Sing the Happy Song*. London: Salvation Army, 1978.

Booth, Charles. *The Life and Labor of the People*. London: Williams and Norgate, 1889. *Life and Labor of the People in London*, London: MacMillan, second edition published in nine volumes between 1892 and 1897. A third edition in seventeen volumes, London: MacMillan, 1902–03. https://archive.org/details/lifelabourofpeop07bootiala.

Booth, Catherine. "The Invasion of the U.S." *The War Cry* (21 February 1880) 1.

———. *Papers on Aggressive Christianity*. London: Salvation Army, [1880] 1891.

———. *Popular Christianity*. London: Salvation Army, 1887.

———. *Practical Religion*. London: Salvation Army, 4th edn 1891.

———. *The Salvation Army in Relation to Church & State*. London: Salvation Army, 1889.

Booth, Florence. "The Place and Power of Women in The Salvation Army." *The Field Officer* (August 1914) 509–13.

Booth, Ken. "Something about Ordination." Paper read at seminar arranged by Ministry and Training Division of the Christchurch Diocese, held at Bishop Julius Hall, 31 July 1999.

Booth, Maud B. *Beneath Two Flags*. New York: Funk and Wagnalls, 1889.

Booth, William. "Holiness. An Address at the Conference." *The Christian Mission Magazine* (August 1877) 193–98.

———. *In Darkest England and the Way Out*. London: Salvation Army, 1890. http://thesalvationarmyng.org/ebboks/booth_darkest_england.pdf.

———. *International Staff Council Addresses*. London: Salvation Army, 1904.

———. *Letter to Commissioners and Territorial Commanders*. London: Salvation Army, 1900.

———. *Letters to Salvationists on Religion for Every Day*. London: Salvation Army [n.d.].

———. "Salvation for Both Worlds [A Retrospect]." *All the World* (January 1889) 1–6.

———. "The Millennium; or, The Ultimate Triumph of the Salvation Army Principles." *All the World* (August 1890) 337–43. Reprinted in *Boundless Salvation: The Shorter Writings of William Booth*, edited by Andrew Eason and Roger Green. New York: Peter Lang, 2012, 60–71.

———. "The Relation of Social Work to Governments." In *International Social Council Addresses, Part I, Principles*. London: Salvation Army, 1911.

———. "What is The Salvation Army?" *The Contemporary Review* 42 (August 1882) 175–82.

———. comp. *The Salvation War: Under the Generalship of William Booth*. London: Salvation Army, published annually 1882-1886.

———. "The Spirit of Burning Love." In *International Congress Addresses*, 1904. London: Salvation Army, 1904, 136–48.

———. "'Woman is Equal to Man.' General Booth's Manifesto to The Salvation Army." *Leeds Evening Post* 24 August 1908. International Heritage Centre Archives, PWB/7/1.

———. and Alfred J. Cunningham. *The Bible: Its Divine Revelation, Inspiration and Authority*. London: Salvation Army, 1961.

Booth, W. Bramwell. *Echoes and Memories*. London: Hodder and Stoughton, [1925] 2nd edn 1977.

———. *Servants of All*. London: Salvation Army, 1899.

———. *Social Reparation, or, Personal Impressions of Work for Darkest England*. London: Salvation Army, 1899.

———. *Talks with Officers*. London: Salvation Army, 1921.

———. *These Fifty Years*. London: Cassell, 1929.

Booth-Tucker, Frederick. *Muktifauj, or Forty Years with The Salvation Army in India and Ceylon*. London: Marshall Bros, [1923].

Bollinger, Stijn. "A Dynamic Courtship: The Salvation Army and the Welfare State." PhD diss., Vrijie University, Amsterdam, 2013.

Bolton, Barbara. *Booth's Drum*. Sydney: Hodder and Stoughton, 1980.

Bourne, Hugh. *The History of the Primitive Methodists, Giving an Account of Their Rise and Progress up to the Year 1823*. Bemersley: printed for the Author, at the Office of the Primitive Methodist Connexion, by J. Bourne, 1823. Sourced from Jamespedlar.wordpress.com/2017/02/24/a-window-on-early-primitive-methodist-meetings.

Bouterse, Wesley. *Scriptural Light on Speaking in Tongues*. Atlanta: Salvation Army, 1978.

Bramwell-Booth, Catherine. *Bramwell Booth*. London: Rich & Cowen, 1932.

———. *Catherine Booth: the Story of her Loves*. London: Hodder and Stoughton, 1970.

Bradwell, Cyril R. *Fight the Good Fight: the Story of The Salvation Army in New Zealand 1883–1983*. Wellington: Reed, 1982.

———. *Touched with Splendour*. Wellington: Flag, 2003.

Brengle, Samuel Logan. *Heart Talks on Holiness*. London: Salvation Army, 1897.

———. *Resurrection Life and Power*. London: Salvation Army, 1925.

———. *The Soul Winner's Secret*. London: Salvation Army, 1903.

Bringans, Grace. *Seeds of Faith: 100 years of History. The Salvation Army—Burma/Myanmar*. Singapore: Salvation Army, 2015.

Brouwer, Melattie. *The History of the Salvation Army in Indonesia, Volume 1, 1894–1949*. Melbourne: Citadel, 1996.

Brown, Arnold. *The Gate and the Light: Recollections of Another Pilgrim*. Toronto: Bookwright, 1984.

Brown, Fred. *Secular Evangelism*. London: SCM: 1970.

———. *The Salvationist at Worship*. London: Salvation Army, 1964.

Brunner, Emil. *Dogmatics III, The Christian Doctrine of the Church, Faith, and the Consummation*. London: Lutterworth, 1962.

———. *The Word and the World*. London: SCM, 1931.

Bulley, Colin. *The Priesthood of Some Believers: Developments from the General to the Special Priesthood in Christian Literature in the First Three Centuries*. Carlisle: Paternoster, 2000.

Burt, Margaret and Peter Farthing. *Crossing Cultures: How to Manage the Stress of Re-entry*. Sydney: Salvation Army, 1996.

Cairns, Philip. "Is the Salvation Army Pentecostal?" COFE Association Lecture, 18 May 2006. *The Practical Theologian* 4 no. 2 (September 2006) 45–55.

Calvert, Graham, ed. *Health, Healing and Wholeness: Salvationist Perspectives*. London: The Salvation Army, 1997.

Cameron, Helen. "Let it Not Be So Among You: Women and Men in Ministry, Leadership and Governance." Paper presented to the Salvation Army International Theology Symposium, Johannesburg, 2006. Also published as:

———. "Women and Men in Ministry, Leadership and Governance." *Word and Deed* 9 no. 2 (May 2007) 63–81.

———. "Make Love, Not War: the Impact of the 1960s on The Salvation Army in the UK." A paper for the Voluntary Action History Society, London, 17 March 2007. http://www.vahs.org.uk/wp-content/uploads/2007/09/make_love_not_war.pdf.

Campbell, Craig. "The Use of Scripture in The Salvation Army." MTh thesis, Melbourne College of Divinity, 1995. http://books.google.co.nz/books/about/The_Uses_of_Scripture_in_the_Salvation_A.html?id=qb6gNwAACAAJ&redir_esc=y.

Carpenter, Matthew. "Compliance, Integrity and Trust." *The Salvation Army Yearbook*, 2017, 10–11.

Carpenter, Minnie Lindsay. *Commissioner Lawley*. London: Salvation Army, 1924.

———. *Miriam Booth, A Sketch*. London: Salvation Army, 1918.

———. *The Salvationists and the Sacraments—A Doctrinal Statement*. London: Salvation Army, 1945.

Carpenter, Stella. *A Man of Peace in a World of War*. Montville, Queensland: Privately published, 1993.

Carter-Chand, Rebecca. "Doing Good in Bad Times: The Salvation Army in Germany 1886-1946." PhD diss., University of Toronto, 2016.

Castle, Brian. "Can the Communion stay together?" *Church Times* (1 April 2016) 13.

Chadwick, Owen. *The Victorian Church*. London: Adam and Charles Black. [1966] 2nd ed., 1970. Vol. 1.

Chang, Peter H. *The Salvation Army in Korea*. Seoul: Salvation Army, 2007.

Chant, Barry. *The Spirit of Pentecost: The Origins and Development of the Pentecostal Movement in Australia, 1870–1939*. Lexington, Kentucky: Emeth, 2011.

Chesham, Sallie. *Born to Battle: The Salvation Army in America*. Chicago: Rand McNally, 1965.

Clark, Manning. *The History of Australia*. Melbourne: University of Melbourne Press, 1978. 6 volumes.

Clark, William, ed. *Dearest Lily: a Selection of the Brengle Correspondence*. London: Salvation Army, 1985.

———. "Divinely Called." *The Officer* (July 1976) 289–90.

Clasen, Peter Adolf. "Der Salutismus. Eine sozialwissenschaftliche Monographie über General Booth und seine Heilsarmee". Schriften zur Soziologie der Kultur, Band 2. Jena, Diederichs, 1913. XX 331 S., gr.okt., Kt., unbeschn. #21970. PhD Diss., Heidelberg, 1913.

Cleary, John. "Chosen to be a Soldier." Unpublished paper presented March 2002 at the Salvation Army College of Further Education, Sydney.

———. "Salvationist Worship—A Historical Perspective." *eJournal of Aggressive Christianity* 42 (April–May 2006) 2. http://www.armybarmy.com/pdf/JAC_Issue_042.pdf.

Clifton, Shaw. *Crown of Glory, Crown of Thorns: The Salvation Army in War Time*. London: Salvation Army, 2015.

———. *New Love: Thinking Aloud about Practical Holiness*. Wellington: Flag, 2004.

———. "People of God—Salvationist Ecclesiology, Part Two: Our God-given position on sacraments—a Candid Reflection." *The Officer* (March–April 2007) 2–7.

———. *Strong Doctrine, Strong Mercy*. London: Salvation Army, 1985.

———. "The Salvation Army's Attitudes and Actions in War Time, 1889–1945." PhD diss., King's College, London, 1989.

———. *Who Are These Salvationists? An Analysis for the 21st Century*. Alexandria, Virginia: Crest, 1999.

Coates, Thomas F.G. *Prophet of the Poor: The Life Story of General Booth*. London: Hodder & Stoughton, 1905.

Collier, Richard. *The General Next to God*. London: Collins, 1965.

Collins, John. *Diakonia*. Oxford: Oxford University Press, 1990.

Conrad, Sebastian, and Dominic Sachsenaier, eds. *Competing Visions of World Order: Global Moments and Movements, 1880s–1930s*. New York: Palgrave Macmillan, 2007.

Cook, H. Bramwell. *White Gujaratis: Bramwell and Dorothy Cook*. Christchurch: Privately published, 2007.

Coombs, Thomas B. "Representing the Salvation Army." In *Proceedings of the Third Oecumenical Methodist Conference*. New York: Eaton and Mains, 1901, 344–47. https://archive.org/stream/10784643.emory.edu/10784643#page/n3/mode/2up.

Copping, Arthur E. *Banners in Africa*. London: Hodder and Stoughton, 1933.

Couchman, Adam. "The Neo-sacramental Theology of the Salvation Army." B Theol Hons diss., Charles Sturt University, Sydney, 2007.

———. "The Rapture—a Response." *The Officer* (September–October 2009) 38–41. Also found at http://www.setapartinchrist.com/2010/08/rapture-response.html.

Court, Stephen, ed. *Boston Common: Salvationist Perspectives on Holiness*. Melbourne: Salvo, 2010.

Cousineau, Madeleine, ed. *Religion in a Changing World: Comparative Studies in Sociology*. Westport, Connecticut: Praeger, 1998.

Bibliography

Coutts, Frederick. "Are We Great Enough to Move Towards One Another as Christ Moved Toward Us?" Pamphlet published by Salvation Army International Headquarters, 1967.
———. *Bread for My Neighbour: The Social Influence of William Booth*. London: Hodder and Stoughton, 1978.
———. *In Good Company*. London: Salvation Army, 1980.
———. *No Continuing City*. London: Salvation Army, 1976.
———. *The Better Fight: History of The Salvation Army* VI, 1914–1946. London: Hodder & Stoughton, 1973.
———. *The Salvation Army in relation to the Church*. London: Salvation Army, 1978.
———. "The Smallest of Knapsacks." *The Officer* (November 1981) 503–04.
———. *The Weapons of Goodwill: History of The Salvation Army* VII, 1946–1977. London: Hodder & Stoughton, 1986.
Coutts, John. *The Salvationists*. London: Mowbrays, 1977.
Cox, André. "Immeasurably More." *The Officer* (November–December 2013) 4–5.
———. "Year of Total Mobilization." *The Officer* (January–February 2017) 4–6.
Cox, Gordon. *Musical Salvationist: The World of Richard Slater (1854–1939)*. Woodbridge, Suffolk: Boydell, 2011.
Cox, Helen. "Defining the War: Salvation Army Social-Welfare Participation in Australia, 1881–1902." PhD diss., University of Melbourne, 2012.
Cox, Hilda. "Married Women's Officer Role Within the Salvation Army." *The Officer* (September 1990) 408–12, 415.
Cresswell, Max. "Laos—The Whole People of God." *Magazine* (June 1962) 3–7.
Crow, Kenneth E. "The Church of the Nazarene and O'Dea's Dilemma of Mixed Motivation." http://nazarene.org/files/docs/The%20Church%20of%20the%20Nazarene%20and%20ODeas%20Dilemma%20of%20Mixed.pdf.
Cunningham, John. "Report on the New Zealand Territory." July 1934. Salvation Army Archives, New Zealand.
Dale, Percival. *Salvation Chariot: A Review of the First Seventy-One Years of The Salvation Army in Australia 1880–1951*. Melbourne: Salvation Army, 1952.
Darbyshire, Bramwell. Letter. *The Salvationist* (18 April 1998) 6.
Davie, Grace. *Religion in Britain Since 1945: Believing Without Belonging*. Oxford: Blackwell, 1994.
Davis, Charles. *A Question of Conscience*. London: Hodder and Stoughton, 1967.
Davis, Christin. "The Equality Paradox." *Caring* (Fall 2012) 24–30.
Davis, Nancy J., and Robert V. Robertson. *Claiming Society for God: Religious Movements and Social Welfare*. Bloomington, Indiana: University of Indiana Press, 2012.
Davisson, Philip W. "Sweeping Through the Land: Postmillennialism and the Early Salvation Army." *Word and Deed* 5 no. 2 (May 2003) 29–50. http://hebrews412.com/wp-content/uploads/2013/07/WD_2003_May_3_Sweeping_Through_the_Land.pdf.
Dean, Harry. "Dynamic Centrality." *The Officer* (August 1972) 353–57, 359.
———. "The Founders and the Sacraments." In *Another Harvest of the Years*, 35–40. London: Salvation Army, 1975.
———. *Reason to Believe*. London: Hodder and Stoughton, 1970.
[———.] *The Sacraments—a Salvationist Viewpoint*. London: Salvation Army, 1960.
Dempster, Murray W., et al., eds. *The Globalization of Pentecostalism: A Religion Made To Travel*. Oxford: Regnum, 1999.
Dennis, Margo. "In Her Own Right: Women Officers and Equality in The Salvation Army." MA Thesis, Deakin University, Melbourne, 1998.
DeRego, Frank R. Jnr. and James D. Davidson. "Catholic Deacons: A Lesson in Role Conflict and Ambiguity." In *Religion in a Changing World: Comparative Studies in Sociology*, edited by Madeleine Cousineau. 89–98. Westport, Connecticut: Praeger, 1998.
Diakanwa, Daniel and Robin Dunster. "Congo (Kinshasa) and Angola Territory." In *Historical Dictionary of The Salvation Army*, edited by John Merritt, 109. Lanham, Maryland: Scarecrow, 2006.
Disraeli, Benjamin. *Sybil, or the Two Nations*. London: Coulburn, 1845. Vol 1.
Driver, Geoffrey. "Booth's Boots." *New Christian* (24 August 1967) 9–10.
Duff, Mildred. *Hedwig Von Haartman*. London: Salvation Army, 1904.

Dulles, Avery. *Models of the Church*. New York: Doubleday, 1978.
du Plessis, Paul. "Echoes of Methodism in The Salvation Army's Commitment to World Mission." *Word and Deed* 7 no. 1 (November 2004) 5–16.
Eason, Andrew Mark. "Christianity in a Colonial Age: Salvation Army Foreign Missions from Britain to India and South Africa, 1882–1929." PhD diss., University of Calgary, 2005.
———. "The Salvation Army and the Sacraments in Victorian Britain: Retracing the Steps to Non-observance." *Fides et Historia* 41 no. 2 (June 2009) 51–71. http://www.thefreelibrary.com/The+Salvation+Army+and+the+sacraments+in+Victorian+Britain:+retracing . . .-a0218882622.
———. "The Salvation Army in Late-Victorian Britain: The Convergence of Sect and Church." *Word and Deed* 5 no. 2 (May 2003) 3–27.
———. *Women in God's Army: Gender and Equality in the Early Salvation Army*. Waterloo, Ontario: Wilfred Laurier University Press, 2003.
Eason, Andrew M. and Roger J. Green, eds. *Boundless Salvation: The Shorter Writings of William Booth*. New York: Peter Lang, 2012.
Eliasen, Carl. "Reflection on how it might be, Baptism and the Lord's Supper in The Salvation Army, to satisfy the unease of many Salvationists regarding the matter." Privately circulated paper.
Ervine, St. John. *God's Soldier, General William Booth*. London: Heinemann, 1936.
Escott, Philip. "Church Growth Theories and The Salvation Army in the United Kingdom." PhD diss., University of Stirling, 1996.
Fairbank, Jenty. "And Then There Were None." *The Officer* (October 1988) 408–11.
———. "Angles on Salvation Army History." *The Salvationist* (14 October 1995) 8–10.
———. *Booth's Boots*. London: Salvation Army, 1983.
Featherston, Mike, et al. *Global Modernities*. London: Sage, 1995.
Finke, Roger, and Rodney Stark. *The Churching of America 1776–1990*. New Brunswick New Jersey: Rutgers University Press, 1992.
Fischer-Tiné, Harald. "Global Civil Society and the Forces of Empire: The Salvation Army, British Imperialism, and the 'Prehistory' of NGOs (ca. 1880–1920)." In *Competing Visions of World Order: Global Moments and Movements, 1880s–1930s*, edited by Sebastian Conrad and Dominic Sachsenmaier, 29–67. New York: Palgrave Macmillan, 2007.
Flagg, Deborah. "Softly Eclipsed." *New Frontier* (30 April 1997) 6–7; *The Officer* (October 1997) 12–17.
Flannery, Austin. *Vatican Council II: The Conciliar and Post-Conciliar Documents*. Collegeville, Minnesota: Liturgical, 1975.
Fletcher, Martin. "The Salvation Army turns 150." *New Statesman* (12–18 June 2015) 34. http://www.newstatesman.com/politics/2015/06/salvation-army-turns-150-what-role-does-it-have-play-secular-society.
Fookes, James. "Gymnastic Equipment in our Young People's Corps." *The Officer* (October 1923) 322–24.
Francis, William. "The Salvation Army in the Body of Christ." In *Conversations with the Catholic Church: A Record of the Informal Conversations Between The Catholic Church and The Salvation Army*, [no editor given] 25–36. London: Salvation Army, 2014.
Friederichs, Hulda. *The Romance of The Salvation Army*. London: Cassell, 1907.
Frodsham, Stanley Howard. *Smith Wigglesworth, Apostle of Faith*. Springfield, Missouri: Gospel, 1948.
Gardiner, Alfred George. "Bramwell Booth and the Future of his Movement." By the Editor of the *Daily News and Leader*, and reprinted in *The Salvation Army Year Book*, 1915, 2.
Gariepy, Henry. *Christianity in Action: The International History of The Salvation Army*. Grand Rapids, Michigan: Eerdmans, 2009.
———. *General of God's Army*. Wheaton, Illinois: Victor Books, 1993.
———. *The History of The Salvation Army: Mobilized for God*, VIII 1977–1984. Atlanta, Georgia: Salvation Army, 2000.
Garland, Dennis. "The Salvation Army and the State of Welfare: An analysis of Text and Narrative." MA (Hons) thesis, University of Western Sydney, 2004. http://arrow.uws.edu.au:8080/vital/access/manager/Repository/uws:582.
Garland, Elizabeth. "Impact Measurement." *The Salvation Army Yearbook*, 2017, 8–9.
de Gasparin, Comtesse Agenor. *Read and Judge The (So-Called) Salvation Army*. London: Griffiths and Farran, 1883.

Gates, Donald Keith. *Altruism in the Context of Economic Ideologies and Systems of Healthcare and Welfare Delivery: A Multi-Disciplinary Examination*. Sydney: Lulu.com., 2006.
Gauntlett, S. Carvosso. *International Army*. London: Salvation Army, 1945.
Gilbert, Alan D. *Religion and Society in Industrial England: Church, Chapel and Social Change 1740–1914*. London: Longman, 1976.
Gilliam, Jobie. "Salvation Army Theatricalities." MA thesis, California State University, 1989.
Gilliard, Alfred James. "Catching up with William Booth." *War Cry* (UK) (12 June 1965) 10–12.
Gowans, John. *There's a Boy Here*. London: Salvation Army, 2002.
———. "Short Service Commissions." *The Officer* (March 1971) 189–90, 193; *Impact* (1973) 3 no. 1.
Graves, Robert. *Goodbye to All That*. Harmondsworth, UK: Penguin [1929] 1960.
Green, Roger J. "The Call to the Inner Life." *Pipeline* (February 2009) 13 no. 2, 6–7.
———. *Catherine Booth: A Biography of the Cofounder of The Salvation Army*. Grand Rapids, Michigan: Baker, 1996.
———. *The Life and Ministry of William Booth, Founder of The Salvation Army*. Nashville: Abingdon, 2005.
———. "The Salvation Army and the Evangelical Tradition." *Word and Deed* 5 no. 2 (May, 2003) 51–69.
———. *War on Two Fronts: the Redemptive Theology of William Booth*. Atlanta: The Salvation Army, 1989.
———. "Why Social Holiness?" Paper presented at the Speak Out Online Conference of the International Social Justice Commission, 22–28 March 2010. Reprinted on http://www1.salvationarmy.org/IHQ/www_ihq_isjc.nsf/vw-dynamic-index/8C9DFA482DB00419802578AF004AB201?openDocument.
Grey, Terry. "The Interpretation of Scripture." *The Officer* (January–February 2009) 41–43.
Grinsted, Stephen. "Christian Mission to Salvation Army." *The Officer* (March–April 2010) 14–16.
Haggard, H. Rider. *Regeneration: Being an Account of the Social Work of The Salvation Army in Great Britain*. London: Longmans Green, 1910.
Haggard, Robert F. *The Persistence of Victorian Liberalism: The Politics of Social Reform in Britain 1870–1900*. Westport, Connecticut: Greenwood, 2001.
Haigh, Bruce. "The Salvation Army is a Branch of Government." On-Line Opinion, 16 May 2013. http://www.onlineopinion.com.au/view.asp?article=15013.
Halévy, Élie. *Histoire du Peuple Anglais au XIXe Siecle*, first published 1913. English translation: *History of the English people in the Nineteenth Century, I, England in 1815*. London: Ernest Benn, 1960.
Hall, Clarence. *Samuel Logan Brengle: Portrait of a Prophet*. Chicago: The Salvation Army, 1933.
Harley, Alan. "Are We Really a Holiness Movement?" In *eJournal of Aggressive Christianity* (April–May 2009). http://www.armybarmy.com/JAC/jac60.html.
———. "The Wesleyan Understanding of Holiness of Life." *Practical Theologian* 2 no. 2 (2004) 23–28.
Harris, Wesley. "Officership is Availability." *The Officer* (June 1979) 243–45.
Harvey, Paul. "Booth, William." In *Oxford Companion to English Literature*, edited by Paul Harvey, 99. Oxford: Oxford University Press, Third edition, [1946] 1960.
Hastings, Adrian. *The History of English Christianity 1920–1985*. London: Collins, 1986.
Hattersley, Roy. *Blood & Fire: William and Catherine Booth and Their Salvation Army*. London: Little, Brown, 1999.
Hay, James. *Aggressive Salvationism: Achievement for God and Souls*. Melbourne: Gordon Hay, 1951.
Hay, Margaret. "Holy Leadership? A Historical Case Study of Brigadier Florence Birks." Paper read to the 2013 "Thought Matters" Conference in Melbourne. In *Perfect Love, Imperfect people: Holiness in Leadership and the Church*, edited by David Janssen and Christina Tyson, 19–25. Melbourne: Salvation Army, 2014.
———. "Married Women-Officers." *The Officer*, February 1991, 70–71.
Hay, Michael. "Onward Christian Soldiers: the Salvation Army in Milton, 1884–1894." In *Building God's Own Country: Historical Essays on Religions in New Zealand*, edited by John Stenhouse and Jane Thomson, 113–23. Dunedin: Otago University Press, 2004.
Hays, Richard. *The Moral Vision of the New Testament*. New York: Harper Collins, 1996.
Hazzard, John W. "Marching on the Margins: An Analysis of The Salvation Army in the United States." *Review of Religious Research* 40 no. 2 (December 1998) 121–41. http://www.jstor.org/discover/10.2307/3512298?uid=3738776&uid=2&uid=4&sid=21103065419457.
Heathcote, Wyndham S. *My Salvation Army Experience*. London: Marshall Bros, 1891.

Hein, Jennifer. "More Inspirational than Penetrating: The Salvation Army's Use of History." *Aldersgate Papers* 8 (September 2010) 27–45.

Hentzschel, Garth. "Hidden Turmoil of the Army's Early Days." *Pipeline* (October 2013) 16–18.

Hiebert, Paul. *Mission and Renewal of the Church*. Pasadena, California: Fuller, 1983.

Higgins, Edward J. *Stewards of God*. London: Salvation Army, undated but early 1930s.

Hill, Harold. "Four Anchors from the Stern: The Salvation Army as Church—A Dissuasive." *The Practical Theologian* 5 no.1 (November 2007) 26–41. http://salvos.org.au/scribe/sites/boothcollege/files/publications/Pract-Theo11o7%20.pdf.

———. *Leadership in The Salvation Army: A Case Study in Clericalisation*. Milton Keynes, UK: Paternoster, 2007.

———. ed. *Te Ope Whakaora, The Army that Brings Life: A collection of documents on The Salvation and Maori 1884–2007*. Wellington: Flag, 2007, 2017.

Hill, Michael. *The Religious Order: A Study of Virtuoso Religion and its Legitimation in the Nineteen-century Church of England*. London, Heinemann, 1973.

Hobbs, Doreen. *Jewels of the Caribbean: The Salvation Army in the Caribbean Territory*. London: Salvation Army, 1986.

Hodder, Kenneth. "Let's Use Soldiers." *The Officer* (October 1993) 435–36.

———. "The Development and Use of Lay Leaders Within the Decision-Making Processes of The Salvation Army." Paper given at the 1995 International Conference of Leaders. Salvation Army International Heritage Centre Archives.

Hodder, Kenneth G. "The International Headquarters Legal Section: One Body and One Spirit." *The Officer* (May–June 2011) 16–17.

Hollins, John. "A Note of Warning." *Contemporary Review* 74 (September1898) 436–445. Reproduced in *eJournal of Aggressive Christianity* 70 (December 2010–January 2011) 46–53. http://www.armybarmy.com/JAC/article7-70.html.

Holz, Ronald W. *Brass Bands of the Salvation Army: Their Mission and Music*. Richmond: Streets, 2007.

———. *History, Harmony and Humanity: Ray Steadman Allen*. London: Salvation Army, 2012.

———. "'Let us Come before Him . . . with Music and Song: Communicating the Gospel Message through Music in 'Traditional' Salvationist Worship." In *Saved, Sanctified and Serving*, by Denis Metrustery, 155–72. Milton Keynes, UK: Paternoster, 2016.

———. Two articles on the history of Salvation Army music in Norman Murdoch, ed. *Christian History* 26 (May 1990) "The Story Behind Salvation Army Music," and "Major Events in Salvation Army Music." Available on https://www.christianhistoryinstitute.org/uploaded/50cf7a06bfbfa4.38571468.pdf.

Horrell, David. "Leadership Patterns and the Development of Ideology in Early Christianity." *Sociology of Religion* 58 no. 4 (Winter 1997) 323–41.

Horridge, Glenn K. *The Salvation Army, Origins and Early Days, 1865–1900*. Godalming: Ammonite, 1993.

Howe, Norman. "The International Commission on Officership, a Report." *Officer* (August 1999) 18–20.

Howe, Renate. "Five Conquering Years: The Leadership of Commandant and Mrs H. Booth of the Salvation Army in Victoria 1896–1901." *Journal of Religious History* 6 no. 2 (December 1970) 177–98.

Hubbard, Thomas. "The Army a Church?" *The Officer* (November 1978) 516–17.

Hull, Walter, edited by Lindsay Cox. *That Peculiar Body: The Salvation Army's Social Work Beginnings in Australia 1883–1887*. Melbourne: Salvation Army, 2004.

Hunt, Carroll Ferguson. *If Two Shall Agree*. Kansas City, Missouri: Beacon Hill, 2001.

Hunter, Denis. *While the Light Lingers*. Sunderland: Glendale, 2005.

Hutchinson, Mark. "Salvationists: a Case Study in Australian Pentecostal Origins." Paper for the Australasian Pentecostal Heritage Centre, Alphacrucis College, Sydney. https://pentecostalheritagecentre.wordpress.com/2011/08/04/salvationists/.

Hutson, Joan. *As for Me and My House: A Salute to early Salvation Army families of Gisborne, 1886 to 1952*. Wellington: Flag, 2004.

Hutson, Don and Joan. *Set Free: One Hundred Years of Salvation Army Addiction Treatment in New Zealand 1907–2006*. Wellington: Flag, 2013.

Izzard, John C. edited by Henry Gariepy. *Pen of Flame: the Life and Poetry of Catherine Baird*. Alexandria, Virginia: Crest, 2002.

Jamieson, Penny. *Living at the Edge: Sacrament and Solidarity in Leadership*. London: Mowbray, 1997.

Joannides, Vassili, "Accountability and Ethnicity in a Religious Setting: the Salvation Army in France, Switzerland, the United Kingdom, and Sweden." DSc diss., L'University Paris Dauphine, 2009.

Johnson, Benton. "A Critical Appraisal of the Church-Sect Typology." *American Sociological Review* 22 no. 1 (February 1957) 88–92.

———. "On Church and Sect." *American Sociological Review* 28 no. 4 (August 1963) 539–49.

———. "Church and Sect Revisited." *Journal for the Scientific Study of Religion* 10 (1971) 124–37.

Johnston, J., edited. *Report of the Centenary Conference on the Protestant Missions of the World*. 2 vols., 1888, i. x, xi. http://www.biblicalstudies.org.uk/pdf/vox/vol05/edinburgh-1910_rowdon.pdf.

Joy, Edward H. "Share More Memories, Please!" *The Officers' Review* (April–June, 1944) 103–06.

Kasper, Walter. "Still a Place for Optimism: Ecumenical Dialogue Symposium." *The Tablet* (13 February 2010) 8–9. http://www.thetablet.co.uk/article/14286.

Keanie, Victor. Report on World Council of Churches Sixth General Assembly, unpublished, Salvation Army International Heritage Centre Archives.

Kelly, Dean M. *Why Conservative Churches are Growing*. New York: Harper and Row, 1972.

Kendall, R.T. *Anointing: Yesterday, Today, Tomorrow*. Lake Mary, Florida: Charisma, 2003.

Kettl, Donald F. *Government by Proxy, (Miss?)Managing Federal programs*. Washington DC: CQ, 1988.

Kew, Clifford. *Closer Communion: The Sacraments in Scripture and Tradition*. London: Salvation Army, 1980. pdf http://www.salvationarmy.org.uk/uki/Library.

Kipling, Rudyard. *Something of Myself, For my Friends, Known and Unknown*. Cambridge: Cambridge University Press, 1991 [Macmillan 1937].

Kitching, Wilfred. "The Army and the World Council of Churches, Part I." *The Officer* (September–October 1961) 289–90; "The Army and the World Council of Churches, Part II." *The Officer* (November–December 1961) 361–65.

Knox, Ronald. *Enthusiasm: A Chapter in the History of Religion*. Oxford: Oxford University Press, 1950.

Krommenhoek, Vibeke, et al. *A Sacramental Army: A Salvationist View of Sacramental Living in a Nordic Context*. Helsinki: Salvation Army, 2011.

Küng, Hans. *Structures of the Church*. London: Burns & Oates, 1965.

Küng, Hans, Jürgen Moltman, and Marcus Lefebure, eds. *Concilium* 138: *Conflicting Ways of Interpreting the Bible* (October 1980).

Kunz, Victor. "The Salvation Army—Its Origin, Spirit, Work." Unpublished paper, 1947, The Salvation Army International Heritage Centre Archives.

Lansbury, George. *My Life*. London: Constable, 1928.

Lanternari, Vittorio. *Religions of the Oppressed: A Study of Modern Messianic Cults*. New York: Mentor, 1965.

Larkin, Clarence. *Dispensational Truth, or God's Plan and Purpose in the Ages*. Glenside, Pennsylvania: Larkin, 1918, revised 1920.

Larsson, Flora. *My Best Men are Women*. London: Hodder, 1974.

Larsson, John. *1929: A Crisis that Shaped the Salvation Army's Future*. London: Salvation Army, 2009. See also a video on the first High Council, introduced by General Larsson, at http://www.youtube.com/watch?v=iBEvYfWEbfI.

———. "Being True to Ourselves." *The Officer* (November–December 2004) 2–3.

———. *Doctrine Without Tears*. London: Salvation Army, 1974.

———. "Salvationist Theology and Ethics for the New Millennium." Opening address to the International Theology and Ethics Symposium, Winnipeg, Canada, May 2001. *Word and Deed* 4 no. 1 (Fall 2001) 10–23.

———. *Saying Yes to Life*. London: Salvation Army, 2007.

———. *Spiritual Breakthrough: The Holy Spirit and Ourselves*. London: Salvation Army, 1983.

Layton, Philip. *The Rapture*. London: Salvation Army, 2009.

———. *The Sacraments and the Bible*. London: Salvation Army, 2007.

Lewis, Clive Staples. "De Descriptione Temporum." *Selected Literary Essays*. Cambridge: Cambridge University Press, 1969, 1–14.

Ljungholm, Sven-Erik. *Return to Battle: in Russia and Beyond*, 1, 1913–1923. Powys, UK: Aberant, 2017.

———. and Kathleen Bearcroft. *Return to Battle: in Russia and Beyond*, 2. Powys, UK: Aberant, 2017.

Lydholm, Gudrun Maria. *Lutheran Salvationists? The Development Towards Registration as a Faith Community in The Salvation Army in Norway with a Focus on the Period 1975-2005*. Eugene, Oregon: Wipf and Stock, 2017.

———. "Salvation Army Doctrines." *Word and Deed* 8 no. 1 (November 2005) 33-54.

———. "Save Souls, Grow Saints and Serve Suffering Humanity: The Development Towards Registration as a Faith Community in The Salvation Army in Norway with a Focus on the Period 1975-2005." PhD diss., University of Oslo, 2015.

Michael Lodahl. "Creative Eschatological Tension in John Wesley's Sermon 'The General Spread of the Gospel.'" Abstract of paper presented at 2011 Wesleyan Studies Group at the American Academy of Religion, Point Loma Nazarene University. https://www.aarweb.org/sites/default/files/pdfs/Annual_Meeting/2011/2011Abstracts.pdf.

Macchia, Frank D. "The Struggle for Global Witness: Shifting Paradigms in Pentecostal Theology." In *The Globalization of Pentecostalism*, edited by Murray Dempster, et al, 8–29. Oxford: Regnum, 1999.

MacGavran, Donald. *Understanding Church Growth*. Grand Rapids, Michigan: Eerdmans, 3rd edition 1990.

McGuigan, Peter. *Breaking Strongholds: The Dynamics of Spiritual Warfare*. Sydney: Salvation Army, 1991.

McInnes, Beverley. *Flag Across the Zambezi: A History of The Salvation Army in the Zambia and Malawi Territory 1922–1977*. Lusaka: Salvation Army, 1997.

Mcintyre, Stuart. *A Concise History of Australia*. Cambridge: Cambridge University Press, 1999.

McLeod, Hugh. *Class and Religion in the Late Victorian City*. London: Croom Helm, 1974.

Magnuson, Norris and Beverly. *Salvation in the Slums: Evangelical Social Work 1865–1920*. Eugene, Oregon: Wipf and Stock, [1977] 2005.

Marshall, Gordon. "Sect." in *Dictionary of Sociology*, 1988. Encyclopaedia.com:http://www.encyclopedia.com/doc/1O88-sect.html.

Martin, David. *Pacifism*. London, Routledge and Kegan Paul, 1965.

Mayhew, Henry. *London Labour and the London Poor*. London: Penguin, [1851] 1985.

Maxwell, Earle. "Shaping the Army of the Future." *The Officer* (August 1998) 4–7.

Merritt, John, ed. *Historical Dictionary of The Salvation Army*. Lanham, Maryland: Scarecrow, 2006.

Metcalf, William. *Another Pentecost?* London: Salvation Army, 1973.

———. *The Salvationist and the Sacraments*. London: Salvation Army, 1965.

Metrustery, Denis, ed. *Saved, Sanctified and Serving: Reflections on Salvation Army Theology and Practice for the 21st Century*. Milton Keynes: Paternoster Press, 2016.

Mews, Stuart. "The General and the Bishops: Alternative Responses to Dechristianisation." In *Later Victorian Britain, 1867–1900*, edited by Terence R. Gourvish and Alan O'Day, 209–28. London: Macmillan, 1988.

Michels, Robert. *Political Parties: A Sociological Study of the Oligarchical Tendencies of Modern Democracy*. Translated by Eden and Cedar Paul. New York: Hearst, [1911] 1915. https://archive.org/stream/politicalpartiesoomich#page/n7/mode/2up.

Milligan, June Elizabeth. "The Persistence of The Salvation Army: a Challenge to the 'Sociology of Sectarianism.'" PhD diss., University of Glasgow, 1982. http://theses.gla.ac.uk/4038/1/1982MilliganPhD.pdf.

Mitchinson, Norman John. "A Study of Influential Levers used by The Salvation Army in the United Kingdom to Secure Local Centre Outcomes in Conurbations Consistent with its Mission and Objectives." DBA diss., Heriot-Watt University, Edinburgh, 2012.

Mobbs, Bernard. *Eternity Begins Now*. London: Salvation Army, 1964.

Moberg, David O. *The Great Reversal: Evangelism Versus Social Concern*. Philadelphia, Pennsylvania: Lippincott, 1972.

Monahan, Susanne C., ed. *The Sociology of Religion, A Reader*. Upper Saddle River NJ: Prentice-Hall, 2001.

Morris, Mary. "Female Ministry, Equality and the Salvation Army." Diss. (degree not recorded), Oak Hill Theological College, London. Undated but accessed by the Salvation Army International Heritage Centre Archives on 6 April 1998. THESES/106.

Moyles, R. Gordon. *Blood and Fire in Canada: The History of The Salvation Army in the Dominion 1882–1976*. Toronto: Peter Martin Associates, 1977.

———. *Come Join Our Army*. Alexandria, Virginia: Crest, 2007.
———. *Exploring Salvation Army History: Essays of Discovery*. Edmonton, Alberta: AGM, 2009.
———. *Farewell to the Founder*. Alexandria, Virginia: Crest, 2012.
———. *The Salvation Army in Newfoundland: Its History and Essence*. Toronto: Salvation Army, 1997.
Munn, Janet. *The Theory and Practice of Gender Equality in The Salvation Army*. Ashland Ohio: Gracednotes, 2015.
Munn, Olivia, and Stephen Court. *Uprising: a Holy Revolution*. Melbourne: Credo, 2007.
Munn, Richard J. "Divine Revelation in Human History: a Salvationist perspective." *The Officer* (September–October 2009) 31–33.
———. "Married Officer Leadership." *The Officer* (July–August 2004) 10–11.
———. "Salvation Army Married Officer Leadership: For Such a Time as This." DMin diss., Gordon-Conwell Theological Seminary, North Carolina, 2004.
Munro, H.H. ("Saki"). *Short Stories of Saki*. London: John Lane The Bodley Head, 1930.
Murdoch, Norman. *Christian Warfare in Rhodesia-Zimbabwe: The Salvation Army and African Liberation 1891–1991*. Eugene, Oregon: Wipf and Stock, 2015.
———. "In Darkest Africa: Martyrdom and Resistance to Colonialism in Rhodesia." *Journal of Third World Studies* 22 no. 1 (Spring 2005) 211–32.
———. *Origins of The Salvation Army*. Knoxville: University of Tennessee Press, 1994.
———. *Soldiers of the Cross: Susie Swift and David Lamb, Pioneers of Social Change*. Alexandria, Virginia: Crest, 2006.
———. "William Booth's *In Darkest England . . . A Reappraisal*." *Wesleyan Theological Journal* 25 no. 1 (Spring 1990) 107–17. http://wesley.nnu.edu/fileadmin/imported_site/wesleyjournal/1990-wtj-25-1.pdf.
———. "Female Ministry in the Thought and Work of Catherine Booth." *Church History* 53 no. 3 (September 1984) 348–62.
———. *Frank Smith: Salvationist Socialist (1854–1940)*. Prepared for the National Salvation Army Social Services Conference, Orlando, Florida, 2003.
Murray, Paul. *Receptive Ecumenism and the Call to Catholic Learning*. Oxford: Oxford University Press, 2008.
Needham, Philip. *Community in Mission: A Salvationist Ecclesiology*. London: Salvation Army, 1987. pdf from http://www.salvationarmy.org.uk/uki/Library.
———. "Leadership in the Holy Catholic Church." *The Practical Theologian* 5 no. 1 (November 2007) 6–25. http://salvos.org.au/scribe/sites/boothcollege/files/publications/Pract-Theo1107%20.pdf.
———. "Redemption and Social Reformation: A Theological Study of William Booth and His Movement." MTh thesis, Princeton Theological Seminary, 1967.
———. "Some Thoughts on Jeremiah's Editorial." *New Soldiers* (Spring 1965) 40–44a.
Neely, Thomas B. *The History of the Origin and Development of the Governing Conference in Methodism*. New York: Hunt & Eaton, 1892, 9–10, quoted in James Kirby et al., *The Methodists*. Westport, Connecticut: Greenwood, 1996, 78.
Nelson, Jack E. "Moral Entrepreneuring in Japan: a labeling theory analysis of the Salvation Army's efforts." *Review of Religious Research* 40 no. 1 (September 1998) 35–54.
Nicol, Alexander M. *General Booth and The Salvation Army*. London: Herbert and Daniel, 1911.
Niebuhr, H. Richard. *The Social Sources of Denominationalism*. New York: Meridian, [1929] 1957.
Nyandoro, Misheck. *Flame of Sacred Love: The Salvation Army in Zimbabwe 1890–1991*. Harare: Salvation Army, 1993.
Oakley, Ray. *To the Glory of God: History of the Development of The Salvation Army in the British Isles as Expressed, Illustrated and Symbolised through its Buildings and some Paintings*. Leamington Spa: Privately published, 2011.
O'Brien, Glen. "Why Brengle? Why Coutts? Why Not?" In Mal Davies, ed., *Love Divine—Excelling in Love: The Salvation Army's place in the Wesleyan Holiness Tradition*, 49–66. Windows of Opportunity 5 (2009). Proceedings of the Australasian Tri-Territorial Theological Forum.
Ochsner, Karl, Hugo Homberger, and Paul Schiffmann. *Schweizerische Reformbewegung in der Heilsarmee 1926–1930*. St. Gallen: self-published pamphlet, 1930. Evangelisches Zentralarchiv, 1/2975.
O'Dea, Thomas F. "Five Dilemmas in the Institutionalisation of Religion." *Journal for the Scientific Study of Religion* 1 no. 1 (October 1961) 30–41.

———. *The Sociology of Religion.* Englewood Cliffs, New Jersey: Prentice-Hall, 1966.
Ojala, Owen L. *Sound of Abundance: The Holy Spirit at Work in the Salvation Army in New Zealand.* Privately published, 1991.
Oliver, W. H. *Prophets and Millennialists: The Uses of Biblical Prophecy in England from the 1790s to the 1840s.* Auckland: Auckland University Press, 1978.
Ormerod, Neil. "Mission and Ministry in the Wake of Vatican II." *Australian Ejournal of Theology.* 1 (August 2003). Downloaded 23 February 2004 from http//:://dlibrary.acu.edu.au/research/theology/ejournal/aet_Ormerod.htm.
Orr, J. Edwin. *The Second Evangelical Awakening in Britain.* London: Marshall, Morgan and Scott, 1949.
Orsborn, Albert. *The House of My Pilgrimage.* London: Salvation Army, 1958.
———. "The World Council of Churches." *The Officer* (March–April 1954) 73–78.
Ottman, Ford C. *Herbert Booth: A Biography.* New York, Doubleday, Doran, 1928.
Packer, J.I. "A Stunted Ecclesiology? The Theory and Practice of Evangelical Churchliness." *Touchstone* 15 no. 10 (December 2002). http://www.touchstonemag.com/archives/article.php?id=15-10-037-f.
Pallant, Dean. *Keeping Faith in Faith-Based Organizations: A Practical Theology of Salvation Army Health Ministry.* Eugene, Oregon: Wipf & Stock, 2012.
Palmer, Martin. *The Sacred History of Britain. Landscape Myth and Power: the Forces that have shaped Britain's Spirituality.* London: Piatkus, 2002.
Pears, Richard. "Towards a Theology of Salvation Army Officership: An Examination of Officer Ministry in the United Kingdom." MTh thesis, Oxford University, 1996.
Pearson, Hesketh. *Bernard Shaw: His Life and Personality.* London: Collins, 1944.
Pedlar, James E. *Division, Diversity, and Unity: A Theology of Ecclesial Charisms.* New York: Peter Lang, 2015.
Pender, Dinsdale. "Showers are Strong Meat." *The Salvationist* (UK) (29 October 1994) 5–6.
Plumb, J.H. *England in the Eighteenth Century.* Harmondsworth: Penguin, 1950.
Plüs, Jean-Daniel. "The Globalization of Pentecostalism or Globalization of Individualism? A European Perspective." In *The Globalization of Pentecostalism: A Religion Made To Travel,* edited by Murray W. Dempster, et al. Oxford: Regnum, 1999.
Pollock, J.C. *Moody Without Sankey.* London: Hodder & Stoughton, 1963.
Power, Bruce. "Towards a Sociology of Salvationism." *Word and Deed* 2 no. 1 (November 1999) 17–33.
———. "Revisiting the Sociology of Salvationism." *Word and Deed* 18 no. 2 (May 2016) 47–69.
Price, James W. "Random Reminiscences," 1889–99, RG 20.27, Salvation Army American Archives, quoted by Taize, *Hallelujah Lads & Lasses: Remaking the Salvation Army in America* 1880–1930, 99. Chapel Hill: University of North Carolina Press, 2001.
Price, Peter. "Vatican II: End of a Clerical Church (1)." *Australian Ejournal of Theology* (August 2003). http://dlibrary.acu.edu.au/research/theology/ejournal/aet_1Price.htm.
Rader, Kay. "Keeping the Dream Alive," in *Terms of Empowerment: Salvation Army Women in Ministry.* New York: Salvation Army, 2001.
———. "Women in Ministry." Address to the International Council of Leaders, Melbourne, 12–20 March 1998. Salvation Army International Heritage Centre and Archives.
Rader, Paul. "Holiness and Mission, A Salvationist Perspective." Address to 2016 Asbury University-Salvation Army Growing Saints Conference, January 2016, in *Word and Deed* 19 no. 1 (November 2016) 5–16.
———. "The Army's Position on the Sacraments." Paper for The Salvation Army's USA Western Territory's Hispanic Ministries Seminar, San Pedro, California. May 9, 1994. Cited in Clifton, *Who Are These Salvationists?* 61
Radhkrishna, Meena. *Dishonored by History: "Criminal Tribes" and British Colonial Policy.* New Delhi: Orient Longman, 2001.
Railton, George Scott. *General Booth.* London: Hodder & Stoughton, 1913.
———. *Heathen England.* London: Partridge, 2nd edn, 1878.
———. *Twenty-one Years Salvation Army.* London: Salvation Army, 1886.
Ratzinger, Joseph [later Pope Benedict XVI] with Vittorio Messori. *The Ratzinger Report: An Exclusive Interview on the State of the Church.* San Francisco: Ignatius Press, 1985.

———. Pope Benedict XVI. "Responses to Some Questions Regarding Certain Aspects of the Doctrine on the Church." Document issued July 10, 2007. http://www.vatican.va/roman_curia/congregations/cfaith/documents/rc_con_cfaith_doc_20070629_responsa-quaestiones_en.html.

Read, James E. "Developing a Cohesive Opinion." *Caring* 16 no. 1 (Spring 2010) 38–39.

———. "Socio-Political Holiness 'in the world'." Paper presented at the Salvation Army's 3rd International Symposium on Theology and Ethics, London, 2010. *Word and Deed* 13 no. 2 (May 2011) 19–37; and in Matthew Seaman, ed. *Darkness and Deliverance: 125 years of the Darkest England Scheme*, 166–79. Nambour, Queensland: Chaordic Creative, 2016.

Read, John. *Catherine Booth: Laying the Theological Foundations of a Radical Movement*. Eugene, Oregon: Wipf and Stock, 2013.

Rhemick, John. *A New People of God*. Des Plaines, Illinois: Salvation Army, 1984.

———. "Review of "*A Salvationist Handbook of Doctrine*." *Word and Deed* 2 no. 2 (Spring 2000) 56–60.

Richards, Miriam. *It Began with Andrews: The Saga of a Medical Mission*. London: Salvation Army, 1971.

Rightmire, R. David. "'And the Holy Spirit fell on them . . . ' Transitions in Salvation Army Holiness Teaching: A Historical Assessment." In *Saved, Sanctified and Serving: Reflections on Salvation Army Theology and Practice for the 21st Century*, edited by Denis Metrustery, 73–88. Milton Keynes, UK: Paternoster Press, 2016.

———. *Sacraments and the Salvation Army: Pneumatological Foundations*. Metuchen, New Jersey: Scarecrow, 1990.

———. *Salvationist Samurai: Gunpei Yamamuro and the Rise of The Salvation Army in Japan*. Lanham, Maryland: Scarecrow, 1997.

———. *Sanctified Sanity: The Life and Teaching of Samuel Logan Brengle*. Alexandria, Virginia: Crest, 2003.

———. *The Sacramental Journey of the Salvation Army: Studies in Holiness Foundations*. Alexandria, Virginia: Crest Academic, 2016.

Rivers, Julian. *The Law of Organized Religions: Between Establishment and Secularism*. Oxford: Oxford University Press, 2010.

Roberts, Campbell, and Danielle Strickland. *Just Imagine*. Melbourne: Salvation Army, 2008.

Roberts, William A. "Self-Denial and Self-Support." *The Officer* (September–October 2013) 26–29.

Robertson, Roland. "Beyond the Discourse of Globalization." *Glocalism: Journal of Culture, Politics and Innovation*, 2015, 1. DOI: 10.12893/gjcpi.2015.1.6.

———. *Globalization: Social Theory and Global Culture*. London: Sage, 1992.

———. "Glocalization: Time—Space and Homogeneity—Heterogeneity." In *Global Modernities*, edited by Mike Featherston, et al., 25–44. London: Sage, 1995.

———. "The Salvation Army: The Persistence of Sectarianism." In *Patterns of Sectarianism*, edited by Bryan Wilson, 49–105. London: Heinemann, 1967.

———. *The Sociological Interpretation of Religion*. Oxford: Basil Blackwell, 1970.

Robinson, Earl. "Bilateral Theological Dialogues." *Word and Deed* 8 no. 1 (November 2005) 5–13.

———. "People of God: Salvationist Ecclesiology." *Word and Deed* 9 no. 1 (November 2006) 13–17, 28–31.

———. "The History of Salvation Army Doctrine." *Word and Deed* 2 no. 2 (Spring 2000) 31–45.

———. "The Salvation Army—*Ecclesia?*" *Word and Deed* 2 no.1 (November 1999) 9–42.

———. "Wesleyan Distinctives in Salvation Army Theology." *Word and Deed* 6 no. 2 (May 2004) 5–21. https://www.salvationist.org/extranet_main.nsf/vw_sublinks/9685F44B8B9A9D9D80256F16006BB313?openDocument.

Rowdon, Harold H. "Edinburgh 1910, Evangelicals and the Ecumenical Movement." *Vox Evangelica* 5 (1967) 49–71. http://www.biblicalstudies.org.uk/pdf/vox/vol05/edinburgh-1910_rowdon.pdf.

Ryan, Max. "Signs and Wonders and The Salvation Army." *Past is Present* 1, no. 1 (Spring 2000) 1–8. Reprinted in *eJournal of Aggressive Christianity* 11 (February–March) 2001. http://www.armybarmy.com/pdf/JAC_Issue_011.pdf , 10–24.

Ryle, Gilbert. *The Concept of the Mind*. Chicago: Chicago University Press, 1949.

Salt, W. *Memorial of the Wesleyan Methodist New Connexion: Containing a Short Account of the Circuit Preachers Who Have Died; and a General Statement of the Leading Transactions of the Connexion from its Formations in 1797 to the Present Time*. Nottingham: Sutton & Son, 1823.

Salvation Army. *Another Harvest of the Years*. London: Salvation Army, 1975.

Bibliography

———. *Aspects of Social Work in The Salvation Army*. London: Salvation Army, 1917.
———. "The Church: Towards a Common Vision, A Response from The Salvation Army," Paper prepared by the International Theological Council in 2016. a33bb181-9797-44a2-bf8b-529efb591649_The%20Church%20-%20TSA%20response.pdf.
———. *The Doctrines and Discipline of The Salvation Army*. London: Salvation Army, 1881.
———. "Findings of the Commission Appointed to Review the Relationship of The Salvation Army with the World Council of Churches," Unpublished Report, January, 1980, in International Heritage Centre Archives *ACG/5/6* and *WBC/1/1/2*.
———. *Handbook of Doctrine*. London: Salvation Army, 1923.
———. *Handbook of Doctrine*. London: Salvation Army, 1969.
———. *Holiness Readings: A Selection of Papers on the Doctrine, Experience and Practice of Holiness, reprinted from The War Cry*. London: Salvation Army, 1883.
———. International Doctrine Council. *Empowered by the Spirit: The Salvation Army and the Charismatic Movement*. Unpublished. Proof copy dated 7 January 1993. Salvation Army International Heritage Centre, file IDC/5/3.
———. *International Social Council Addresses Part One, Principles of Social Work*. London: Salvation Army, 1911, 19-20.
———. *Journey of Renewal: The Accountability Movement of The Salvation Army*. London: Salvation Books, 2016.
———. *Manual of Guidance for Staff Officers*. London: Salvation Army, Undated. Copies in the New Zealand Salvation Army Archives were issued, over the signature of the General, in 1969 and 1971.
———. *One Faith, One Church: The Salvation Army's Response to Baptism, Eucharist and Ministry*. London: Salvation Army, 1990.
———. *Orders and Regulations for Officers of The Salvation Army*. London: Salvation Army, 1930.
———. *Orders and Regulations for Officers of The Salvation Army*. London: Salvation Army, 1974.
———. *Orders and Regulations for The Salvation Army*. London: Salvation Army, 1878.
———. *Orders and Regulations for Field Officers*. London: Salvation Army, 1886.
———. *Orders and Regulations for Field Officers*. London: Salvation Army, 1888.
———. *Orders and Regulations for Staff Officers of The Salvation Army in the United Kingdom*. London: Salvation Army, 1895.
———. "Report and Recommendations of Gender Issues Commission, 2004." Salvation Army UK Territory.
———. *Salvation Story: Salvationist Handbook of Doctrine*. London: Salvation Army, 1998.
———. *Servants Together*. London: Salvation Army, 2002, 2nd edn. 2008.
———. *Social Problems in Solution: Papers read at the International Social Council, London, Conducted by the General, 1921*. London: Salvation Army, 1923.
———. *Spiritual Conflict: A Glance at the Every Day Work of The Salvation Army*. London: Salvation Army, 1902. http://www.salvationarmy.org/doctrine/thechurchtcv.
———. *The Salvation Army Directory, No II*. London: Salvation Army, 1900.
———. *The Salvation Army Handbook of Doctrine*. London: Salvation Army, 2010.
———. *The Salvation Army in the Body of Christ: An Ecclesiological Statement*. London: Salvation Books, 2008. http://www1.salvationarmy.org/ihq/documents/Ecclesiological-Statement.pdf.
———. *The Salvation Soldiers' Song Book*, Colony Headquarters, New Zealand. Undated, but the back cover names Brigadier Hoskin, New Zealand Colony Commander 1895-98.
———. "Torchbearer." "The Salvation Army and Sacerdotalism." *The Salvation Army Year Book*, 1921, 22.
———. *The Why and Wherefore of The Salvation Army Orders and Regulations*. London: Salvation Army, [1886] 1922.
Sample, Tex. *White Soul: Country Music, the Church and Working Americans*. Nashville, Tennessee: Abingdon, 1996.
Sandall, Robert. *The History of The Salvation Army* I, 1865-1878. London: Nelson, 1947.
———. *The History of The Salvation Army* II, 1878-1886. London: Nelson, 1950.
———. *The History of The Salvation Army* III, Social Reform and Welfare Work. London: Nelson, 1955.
Sandercock-Brown, Grant. "On Liberalism." *The Officer* (January-February 2008) 48.
———. "Fundamentalism." *The Officer* (July-August 2008) 48.

Sanz, Ken. "Cessnock—Unpublished Notes on History." 1–12. Salvation Army Heritage Centre, Sydney, Australia.
Sarbin, Theodore, ed. *Narrative Psychology: The Storied Nature of Human Conduct*. London: Praeger 1986.
Sarbin, Theodore and Vernon L. Allen. "Role Theory." In *Handbook of Social Psychology*, edited by Gardner Lindsey and Elliot Aronson, 488–567. Reading, Massachusetts: Addison-Wesley, 2nd ed. 1968.
Satterlee, Allen. *Turning Points: How the Salvation Army Found a Different Path*. Alexandria, Virginia: Crest, 2004.
———. *Salvation Assault: the History of the Salvation Army in Papua New Guinea*. Port Moresby: Salvation Army, 2006.
Schaef, Anne Wilson, and Diane Fassel. *The Addictive Organization*. New York: Harper Collins, 1988.
Schillebeeckx, Edward. *Ministry: A Case for Change*. London: SCM, 1981.
———. *The Church with a Human Face*. New York: Crossroad, 1985.
Schoenherr, Richard A. "Power and Authority in Organized Religion: Disaggregating the Phenomenological Core." *Sociological Analysis* 47 (March 1987) 52–71.
Scofield, Cyrus O. Annotated, *Scofield Reference Bible*. London: Oxford University Press, 1909, revised 1917.
Scotney, Hubert. "The Salvation Army is a Christian Mission." *The Officer* (July 1969) 452–54.
Seaman, Matthew, ed. *Darkness and Deliverance: 125 years of the Darkest England Scheme*. Nambour, Queensland: Chaordic Creative, 2016.
———. "In Darkest Creation? Broadening Deliverance to the Whole Oikos," and "Grounding in Darkest England: Personal, Social and Ecological Regeneration." In *Darkness and Deliverance*, edited by Matthew Seaman, 194–234 and 235–72. Nambour, Queensland: Chaordic Creative, 2016.
Sengers, Erik. *Caritas. Naastenliefde en Liefdadigheid in Diakonia van de Kerk*. Delft: Eburon, 2012.
Shade, JoAnn. *Seasons—A Woman's Calling to Ministry*. London: Salvation Army, 2007.
Shakespeare, Karen. "Forms of Mission Today—a Salvation Army Perspective." In *Conversations with the Catholic Church: A Record of the Informal Conversations Between The Catholic Church and The Salvation Army*, [no editor given] 260–70. London: Salvation Army, 2014.
Shaw, George Bernard. Preface to "Major Barbara" in *Complete Prefaces*. London: Paul Hamlyn, 1965, 115–37.
Shulman, Frank J. *Japan and Korea: An Annotated Bibliography of Doctoral Dissertations in Western Languages, 1877–1969*. Abingdon: Frank Cass, 1970.
Smith, Dean. "Are Liberals and Evangelicals singing from the same song sheet?" *Heythrop Journal* 51 no. 5 (2010) 831–46.
Smith, Frank. *All About the Salvation Army*. New York: Salvation Army, 1885.
Smith, Margaret (compiled). *Fighting for God and Eternity: The Diaries of Colonel William Murray*. Powys: Abernant, 2012.
Smith, Richard. "Report on Attendance at the International Strategy for Growth Conference, London." 16 August 1989. New Zealand Salvation Army Archives.
Smith, Solveig. *By Love Compelled: The Story of 100 Years of The Salvation Army in India and Adjacent Countries*. London: Salvation Army, 1981.
Spaan, J. *Vreedzame Strijd. 60 jaar Leger des Heils in Nederland*. Den Haag: Voorhoeve, 1947.
Stark, Rodney, and Roger Fink. *Acts of Faith: Explaining the Human Side of Religion*. Berkeley: University of California Press, 2000.
Stark, Werner. *The Sociology of Religion, Vol. II: Sectarian Religion*. London: Routledge and Kegan Paul, 1967.
Street, Robert. *Called to Be God's People*. London: Salvation Army, [1999] 2nd edn. 2008. http://www1.salvationarmy.org/ihq/documents/called-to-be-gods-people.pdf. (With William Booth's 1883 statement and contributions by Shaw Clifton and John Read).
———. *In the Master's Hands: Each Life Sacramental*. London: Salvation Army, 2016.
Strickland, Danielle. "Infinitum." http://www.daniellestrickland.com/projects/infinium/. Downloaded 7 June 2016.
———. "Married Women's Ghetto Rant." *Journal of Aggressive Christianity Online* 41 (February–March 2006) 5–10. 2006)likely to be believed.)vide alternative accounts and answers to all the complaints listed by Mary. This problem is th http://www.armybarmy.com/pdf/JAC_Issue_041.pdf.

BIBLIOGRAPHY

[Sumner, Abner] "An ex-staff officer, A.S." *The New Papacy: Behind the Scenes in the Salvation Army.* Toronto: Albert Britnell, 1889.

Swatos, W.H. "Church-Sect and Cult: Bringing Mysticism Back In." *Sociological Analysis* 42 no. 1 (1981) 17–26.

Swift, Susan. "The Conversion of Susan Swift." Unpublished manuscript, 1897, quoted in Norman Murdoch, *Soldiers of the Cross: Susie Swift and David Lamb, Pioneers of Social Change,* 101. Alexandria, Virginia: Crest, 2006.

Synan, Vinson. *The Holiness-Pentecostal Tradition: Charismatic Movements in the Twentieth Century.* Grand Rapids, Michigan: Eerdmans, 2nd edition, 1997.

Taiz, Lilian. *Hallelujah Lads& Lasses: Remaking the Salvation Army in America 1880–1930.* Chapel Hill: University of North Carolina Press, 2001.

Taylor, Brian. "At a Turning Point." *The Officer* (December 1999) 30–31.

Taylor, David. *Like a Mighty Army: The Salvation Army, the Church and the Churches.* Eugene, Oregon: Wipf and Stock, 2014.

———. "Army, Order or Church? An Attempt to Locate The Salvation Army Within the Wider Family of Churches and to Consider the Implications of this Position." Paper read to the United Kingdom Territory Theological Symposium, July 2004.

Thomlinson, Ronald. *A Very Private General: Biography of General Frederick Coutts CBE, Hon DD (Aberdeen).* London: Salvation Army, 1990.

Thompson, Arthur. "Candidate Question." *The Officer* (July 1974) 292–97, 304.

Thurian, Max, and Geoffrey Wainwright, eds. *Churches Respond to BEM: Faith and Order Paper* 137. Geneva: World Council of Churches, 1986.

Tillsley, Bramwell. *This Mind in You.* Atlanta, Georgia: Salvation Army, 1990.

Torrey, Reuben A., and Amzi C. Dixon, eds. *The Fundamentals: A Testimony to the Truth.* Chicago: Testimony, 1909–1915.

Tortello, Rebecca. "Christian Soldiers: The History of The Salvation Army in Jamaica." http://jamaica-gleaner.com/pages/history/story0075.html.

Townsend, W.J., A.B. Workman, and G. Eayrs. *A New History of Methodism.* London: Hodder and Stoughton, 1909.

Troutt, Margaret. *The General Was a Lady.* Nashville: Holman, 1980.

Tuck, Brian. *Salvation Safari: A Brief History of the Origins of the Salvation Army in Southern Africa 1883–1993.* Johannesburg: Salvation Army [1985] 2nd edn.1993.

Volf, Miroslav. *After Our Likeness.* Grand Rapids: Eerdmans, 1998.

Wagner, C. Peter. *The Third Wave of the Holy Spirit: Encountering the Power of Signs and Wonders Today.* Ann Arbor, Michigan: Vine, 1988.

Wahlström, Jarl. *Autobiography of General Wahlström, A Pilgrim's Song.* London: Salvation Army [1989] 2012.

Wahlström, Marie. "The Place and Position of the Woman Officer in The Salvation Army." Paper read at the 1984 International Conference of Leaders, Berlin. Salvation Army International Heritage Centre Archives *AD/5/1/12/3*.

Wahlström, Tor ("Aristion"). "The Gift of Humility." *The Officer* (November–December 1967) 412–13.

———. "More Sociology and Salvationism." *The Officer* (December 1974) 550–51, 556.

———. "Salvationism and the Sociologists." *The Officer* (November 1974) 490–91, 524.

Wainwright, John. "Reducing the Gap." *The Officer* (May–June 2016) 24–27.

Waldron, John D. ed. *Creed and Deed: Towards a Christian Theology of Social Services in The Salvation Army.* Toronto: Salvation Army, 1986.

———. ed. *The Most Excellent Way.* Toronto: Salvation Army, 1978.

———. ed. *The Privilege of All Believers.* Toronto: The Salvation Army, 1981.

———. ed. *The Salvationist and the Atonement.* Toronto: Salvation Army, 1982.

———. ed. *The Salvation Army and the Churches.* New York: Salvation Army, 1986.

———. ed. *The Salvationist and the Scriptures.* New York: Salvation Army, 1988.

Walker, Pamela J. "Proclaiming Women's Right to Preach." *Harvard Divinity Bulletin* 23 no. 3/4 (1994) 20–23, 35.

Wallis, Humphrey. *The Happy Warrior: Elijah Cadman.* London: Salvation Army, 1928.

Walls, Andrew F. *Missionary Movements in Christian History: Studies in the Transmission of Faith.* Maryknoll, New York: Orbis, 1996.

Ward, Kevin, "Changing Patterns of Church Life in Christchurch from 1960 to 1999." Paper presented at the Society for the Scientific Study of Religion held in Kansas City, October 2004. https://kevinrward.files.wordpress.com/2012/03/changing-patterns-of-congregational-life-in-nz-1960-2000.pdf.

Ware, William. "Saturday Afternoon Cinema Matinees for Children: Suggestions for Counter Attractions." *The Officer* (September 1925) 243–46.

Waters, Cecil. "Us and Them!" *The Officer* (July 1992) 317–18.

Watson, Bernard. "Contemporary Framework (2) Amidst the Workers." *The Officer* (April 1970) 261–65.

———. *Soldier Saint: George Scott Railton, William Booth's First Lieutenant.* London: Hodder & Stoughton, 1970.

Webb, Geoff and Kalie. *Authentic "fair dinkum" Holiness for Ordinary Christians.* Melbourne: Salvation Army, 2007.

Webster, Francis S. "Personal Reminiscences." In *Life of General Booth*, 153–69. London: Nelson, [1912].

Wells, David. "W(h)ither Pilgrims: the religious work of the Salvation Army in Zambia—an assessment." *Battlepoint* (September 1975) 10–13.

Wesley, John. *Journal.* New York: Mason, 1837.

———. *The Works of the Reverend John Wesley A.M.* New York: Waugh and Mason, 1835. 7 volumes.

———. "A Plain Account of Christian Perfection." in *The Works of the Rev John Wesley*, 1831, VI, 500. http://books.google.co.nz/books?id=Jns9AAAAYAAJ&pg=PA500&lpg=PA500&dq=1.

———. *Sermons*: "Scripture Way of Salvation." 3, http://wesley.nnu.edu/john-wesley/the-sermons-of-john-wesley-1872-edition/sermon-43-the-scripture-way-of-salvation/.

Westcott, Hubert. "The Salvation Army in Relation to Ecumenism." Proceedings of 1969 Commissioners' Conference, International Heritage Centre Archives *AD/5/1/8 File 1*.

Whyte, Frederic. *The Life of W.T. Stead.* London: Jonathan Cape, 1927.

Wickberg, Eric. "The International Salvationist and his Citizenship," *Salvation Army Year Book*, 1965, 15–21.

———. "Movements for Reform." Address at the 1971 International Conference of Leaders. Minutes in Salvation Army International Heritage Centre.

Wiggins, Arch R. *The Father of Salvation Army Music: Richard Slater.* London: Salvation Army, 1945.

———. *The History of The Salvation Army* IV, 1886–1904. London: Nelson, 1964.

———. *The History of The Salvation Army* V, 1904–1914. London: Nelson, 1968.

Williams, Charles. *The Descent of the Dove: A Short History of the Holy Spirit in the Church.* London: Fontana [1939] 1963.

Williams, Harry. *An Army Needs an Ambulance Corps: A History of The Salvation Army's Medical Services.* London: Salvation Army, 2009.

———. *Booth-Tucker: William Booth's First Gentleman.* London: Hodder & Stoughton, 1980.

———. "Personal Reflections on the Central Committee Meeting of the World Council of Churches." *The Officer* (April 1979) 150–54, 178.

Williams, J. Rodman. *Renewal Theology: Systematic Theology from a Charismatic Perspective*, 3, *The Church, The Kingdom and Last Things.* Grand Rapids, Michigan: Zondervan, 1992.

Wilson, Bryan R. "Analysis of Sect Development." *American Sociological Review* 24 (February 1959) 3–15.

———. *Patterns of Sectarianism: Patterns and Ideology in Social and Religious Movements.* London: Heinemann, 1967.

———. *Religion in Sociological Perspective.* Oxford: Oxford University Press, 1982.

———. "The Persistence of Sects." *DISKUS* 1 no. 2 (1993) 1–12. http: //www.uni-marburg.de/religionswissenschaft/journal/diskus/wilson.html.

Winston, Dianne. *Red Hot and Righteous: The Urban Religion of The Salvation Army.* Cambridge, Massachusetts: Harvard University Press, 1999.

Wisbey, Herbert A. Jnr. *Soldiers Without Swords: A History of the Salvation Army in the United States.* New York: Macmillan, 1955.

Wiseman, Clarence. *A Burning in My Bones.* Toronto: McGraw-Hill Ryerson, 1979.

———. "Are We A Church?" *The Officer* (October 1976) 435–39, 441.

———. "Call to Renewal and Change." In Waldron, ed. *Creed and Deed: Towards a Christian Theology of Social Services in The Salvation Army*, 271–86. Toronto: Salvation Army, 1986.

Bibliography

———. "Coming of Age: A Study of Salvation Army Soldiership in the Latter Twentieth Century." *The Officer* (September 1969) 586–90.

———. *Living and Walking in the Spirit*. London: Salvation Army, 1975.

Wolmar, Chris. "For God's Sake, Pay." *New Statesman* (22 May 1981). Reprinted in *Battlepoint* 20, no. 3 (September 1981) 20–21.

Woodall, Ann M. *What Price the Poor? William Booth, Karl Marx and the London Residuum*. London: Ashgate, 2005.

Woodbury, David, ed. *Hallelujah! The Story of The Salvation Army in the Western South Pacific*. Sydney: Salvation Army, 12 issues 2007–2011.

Woods, Reginald. "Some Questions Answered." *The Officer* (September–October 1961) 291–94, 323–34.

———. "And it Came to Pass." *The Officer* (March–April 1962) 109–13; (May–June 1962) 167–72; (July–August 1962) 257–60; (September–October 1962) 289–94.

———. "New Delhi Speaks, 1." *The Officer* (March 1963) 125–28; "New Delhi Speaks, 2." *The Officer* (April 1963) 161–64, 167.

World Council of Churches. *Church: Towards a Common Vision; Faith and Order Paper No. 214*. Geneva: World Council of Churches, 2013.

Wright, Tom. Presidential Address to Synod of Durham, 2010, http://ntwrightpage.com/2016/04/05/diocese-of-durham-diocesan-synod-may-21-2010/.

Yeats, William Butler. *Collected Poems*. London: Macmillan, 1958.

Yee, Check Hung. *Good Morning China*. Alexandria, Virginia: Crest, 2005.

Yon, Patricia. "Areas of Stress and Conflict in the Lives of Married Women in Ministry Within The Salvation Army." MA thesis, University of Keele, 1993.

Yuill, Chick. "Matters Arising." *The Officer* (October 1985) 438–40.

———. "Nettles and Wineskins." Frederick Coutts Memorial Lecture for 2004 at the College for Further Education, Sydney; published in *Practical Theologian* 2 no. 2 (September 2004) 1–22.

Index

A

Abbott, Andrew, 92
Accountability reforms, 122–23, 366, 375–76
Adams, Clive, 363
Adlam, Frederick, 362n88
Advisory Boards, 119–20
Advisory Council of Salvation Army Laymen, 120–21
Advisory Council to the General, 85
Agar, Rachel and Louise, 14, 128, 140
Agnew, Milton, 182
Aggressive Christianity Conferences, 224, 229
Alexander, Paul, 247
Alford, Henry, 249
Alley, John, 222

Ames, Donna, 136
Anderson, Ray, 93
Anderson, William, 273
Andrews, Harry, 269, 299–300
Aragon, Lorraine V., 136
Architecture, 256
Armstrong, Eliza, 271
Armstrong, Herbert W., 203
Armstrong, Karen, 206–7
Ashton, Polly, 129
Asquith, Herbert, 80
Ausubel, Herman, 3
Auxiliary captains, 107–9

B

Bacon, Allan, 365n96
Baden-Powell movement, 40
Baird, Catherine, 44, 210–11, 255
Ball, Eric, 254, 257
Baggs, Albert Edward, 357
Barclay, Robert, 195
Barclay, William, 169
Barker, James, 21, 270
Barnardo, Thomas, 5
Barnes, Cyril, 12, 182
Barr, Ian, 212
Barr, James, 207
Bateman, James Conner, 336
Battley, Don, 228n97
Beatty, Susannah, 19
Becquet, Henri, 358
Begbie, Harold, 159, 192, 194, 335, 341
Bellamy, Edward, 317

Benedict XVI (Pope), *see* Ratzinger
Bennett, David, 12
Bennett, Dennis, 221
Bennett, Jean, 39
Benson, Edward White, 75, 77
Berger, Peter, 49–50, 55
Besant, Annie, 287
Bhai, Musa, 348
Bible, 206–8, 213–15
Bible Christians, 137
Bingham, Gordon, 113
Bird, Vere Cornwall, 317
Birks, Florence, 132
Blackstone, William, 139
Blackwell, David, 256
Boardman, Hubert, 137n72
Bollinger, Stijn, 323–25
Bond, Linda, 49, 132, 374

Index

Boon, Brindley (grandson), 345
Boon, Brindley (grandfather), 317
Booth family, 33–35, 381
Booth, Ballington, 20, 34, 62, 79–80, 186, 353
Booth, Catherine, 1, 4–6, 8–9, 13–14, 28, 31, 33, 61, 63, 65, 68, 105, 335
    On politics, 278, 294, 315, 319
    On social work, 278, 294, 303, 315, 319
    On theology, 160, 169, 173, 177, 179, 181, 190, 195, 198, 218, 228, 231
    On women, 126, 128, 138
Booth, Charles, 281, 318
Booth-Clibborn, Arthur, 217, 289
Booth (Booth-Clibborn), Catherine, 21, 34, 79–80, 129, 178, 217
Booth, Cornelie, 80
Booth (Booth-Tucker), Emma, 34, 269–70
Booth, Evangeline, 23, 35, 44–45, 79–80, 82, 85, 130, 132–33, 270, 310, 353
Booth, Florence, 82, 125–26, 131, 140, 147, 269, 271–72, 279, 287–88, 295, 342
Booth, George, 33, 269
Booth, Herbert, 26, 34, 80, 246, 248, 354
Booth, Ken, 91
Booth (Booth-Helborg), Lucy, 35
Booth, Marion, 34
Booth, Maud, 34, 57, 79
Booth, Miriam, 35
Booth, Wickliffe, 82
Booth, William, xiv, 4–6, 8–9, 12–18, 23–25, 28, 31–36, 38
    On doctrine, 157, 159–60, 164–65, 171–75, 177–78, 184–86, 188–95, 198–200, 202, 205, 207, 213, 216–18, 230–32, 235
    On ecclesiology, 51, 56–71, 73–83, 87, 94–95, 104, 112, 117, 119
    On inter-faith relations, 368–69
    On international expansion, 331, 335–42, 346–49, 351, 354
    On politics, 314–19
    On social work, 265–68, 270, 272–98, 301, 304–11, 314–16, 319, 321–25
    On women, 124, 127–30, 139–40
    On worship, 238, 240–41, 243, 245–47, 249, 251, 256, 261
Booth, William Bramwell, 5, 9, 13, 16, 23–24, 26–27, 31, 33–34, 36–37, 40
    On doctrine, 158–59, 165, 178–80, 183, 190, 194–96, 217–19
    On ecclesiology, 66, 72–76, 78–84, 87, 96, 102, 106–7, 111–12
    On international expansion, 342–43, 351, 353, 357
    On social work, 267, 271–73, 277–78, 280, 290, 292, 305, 309
    On women, 125, 129–30, 132–33, 140
    On worship, 240, 248, 252, 254
Booth-Tucker, Frederick, 17, 21, 79, 82, 178, 269, 298–99, 301, 306, 348–49
Borthwick, George, 113
Bosshardt, Alida, 307
Bourne, Hugh, 239
Bouterse, Wesley, 225
Boyd, John, 317
Bradwell, Cyril, 120–21, 133, 229, 289, 354
Bramwell-Booth, Catherine, 82, 84–85, 133, 177, 288
Brand, Will J., 255
Bredsen, Harald, 221
Brengle, Samuel Logan, 39, 78–79, 179–82, 187, 193n121, 218–20
Brewer, Ruth, 134
British South Africa Company, 290, 351
Broadbent, Sarah, 20
Brooks, Mel, 317
Brouwer, Melattie, 343, 358
Brown, Arnold, 47, 97–98, 211, 310
Brown, Fred, 210, 255–56, 324
Bruggemann, Walter, 188
Brunner, Emil, 71, 189
Buckingham, Hillmon, 196
Burke, Donald, 212
Burrell, Honor, 128
Burrows, Eva, 47, 86, 99, 132, 135–36, 150, 219, 226, 351, 374
Burt, Margaret, 362n89
Büsing, Johannes, 356
Butler, Joseph, 228
Butler, Josephine, 3
Buxton, Sidney, 285

C

Caddy, Raymond, 227n99
Cadman, Elijah, 13, 18, 20, 41, 233, 268–69, 279, 290
Callander, Ben, 222
Campbell, Donald, 201
Campbell, Ian, 308
Campbell Bannerman, Henry, 284
Campolo, Tony, 263
Carey, Edward, 121
Carlile, Wilson, 58

Carlyle, Thomas, 281
Carpenter, George, 35, 45, 82, 85, 147, 165, 343
Carpenter, Minnie Lindsay, 133, 147, 195–96
Carter-Chand, Rebecca, 339, 355–56
Castle, Brian, 328
Caughey, James, 62, 160, 177–78, 239, 315
Chadwick, Owen, 1, 3, 193
Chalmers, James, 5
Chamberlain, Annie, 220
Chang, Peter, 357, 363
Chant, Barry, 220
Chapple, H.G., 317
Charismatic and Pentecostal movements, 215–30, 259–60
Charity Organization Society, 268, 273, 284
Chartism, 2, 315
Chavasse, Francis, 5
China Inland Mission, 5
Christian Mission, 8, 10, 16, 64–65, 94, 137, 158, 161, 173, 182–83, 193, 237, 240–41, 265–68, 285, 293–94, 315
Church Growth, 221, 226–27
Church of England (negotiations with Salvation Army in 1882), 75–77
Churchill, Winston, 310
Clark, Manning, 17, 317
Clark, William, 97, 210
Clasen, A.P., 346
Cleary, John, 115–17, 246–47, 254, 257, 263–64
Clement, Christine, 135
Clericalism and clericalisation, 91–92
Clifford, John, 33
Clifton, John, 324
Clifton, Shaw, 21, 48, 88, 98, 155, 196, 202, 212, 321, 341
Coleman, Alice, 16
Coleman, Bill, 317
Coles, Bramwell, 255
Coller, Charles, 248
Collingridge, Eliza, 66, 128
Collyer, William, 249
Comity, principle of, 369
Condie, Alan, xiii
Consultative structures, 119–23
Coombs, Thomas, 369
Cook, A. Bramwell, 135, 302
Cooke, William, 159
Cooper, Alice, 264
Cooper, William, 44
Copeland, Kenneth, 221
Copping, Arthur, 262, 352
Corbridge, William, 241
Corps Councils, 120
Corputty, Jacobus, 358
Cottrill, Elizabeth, 269
Couchman, Adam, 235
Court, Stephen, 182, 213, 224, 324–25, 363
Coutts, John, 31, 122, 142, 149, 153, 165, 205, 212, 239, 250, 252, 254–55, 263
Coutts, Frederick Lee, 39, 44, 87, 141, 157, 169, 171, 180–81, 210, 215, 255–57, 268, 273, 278–79, 284, 315, 325, 341, 343
Coward, Eric, 210
Cox, Adelaide, 131, 309–11
Cox, André, 49, 69, 104, 114, 120, 122, 155, 156, 309n35, 365–66, 375
Cox, Harvey, 210
Cox, Hilda, 140
Cox, Sidney, 248
Cozens-Hardy, Herbert, 68
Cresswell, Max, 120, 327
Crichton, James, 317
Criminal Tribes, 300–301
Crosby, Fanny, 249
Crow, Kenneth E., 103
Cunningham, Alfred G., 165, 195, 210–11, 370
Cunningham, John, 234
Curtin, John, 317
Cutmore, Ian, 259

D

Darby, John Nelson, 233
Darbyshire, Bramwell, 97–98
Dasen, Yesu, 348
Davey, William Booth, 217n46
Davidson, Bill, 222
Davidson, James, 108
Davidson, Randall, 57, 75–77, 184
Davie, Grace, 50
Davies, Howard, 143, 149, 258
Davis, Annie, 9, 128
Davis, Charles, 198
Davis, Nancy, 235
Davisson, Philip, 232
Dean, Harry, 169, 194, 196, 210
Deed Poll, 9 (definition, 9n10), 13, 32, 67, 80–81, 83
Denham, William, 317
Denominationalism, the Salvation Army as a church denomination, 56–60, 86–90
De Rego, Frank, 108
Devil's Island, 320
Diakanwa, Daniel, 262n63

Index

Dickens, Charles, 2
Disraeli, Benjamin, 2, 338
Dobson, James, 327
Docter, Robert, 212
Doctrines, 157–75
Dodd, C.H., 181
Donaldson, Robert and Janine, 154
Doré, Gustave, 2

Dowdle, James, 28, 66
Dowie, Alexander, 79
Driver, Geoffrey, 119
Dulles, Avery, 373
Dunster, Robin, 262n63
Du Plessis, Allister, 136
Du Plessis, Paul, 351, 362
Durnford, Richard, 237

E

Eason, Andrew Mark, 76, 154, 185–86, 194, 301, 349–50, 369
East London Christian Revival Society, 8, 161–63
East London Special Services Committee, 5, 7
Ebdon, William, 140
Ecumenical movement, 367–73
Edmonds, Henry, 24–25, 35, 128, 184
Edward VII, King (also as Prince of Wales), 284, 309, 316, 368
Edwards, David, 363

Eliasen, Carl S., 200
Elliot, Ernest, 361
Elvin, Mary, 144
Emmons, Joy, 147
Envoys, 106–7
Ervine, St John, 41, 61, 96, 276–77
Eschatology, 230–35
Evangelical Alliance, 164
Evangelization Society, 8
Evans, Rachel, 16

F

Fairbank, Frank, 44
Fairbank, Jenty, 124, 131, 193, 268
Farrar, Frederic William, 178, 190, 284
Farthing, Peter, 362n89
Fawcett, John and Sharon, 223
Field, Benjamin, 165
Finke, Roger, 87
Finney, Charles, 62, 160, 177, 239, 314
Fischer-Tiné, Harald, 316, 338–39
Fitzgerald, Tony, 222
Flagg, Deborah, 153
Flawn, James, 267, 272–73
Fletcher, John, 177
Fletcher, Martin, 324

Ford, Gladys, 146
Foster, Derek, 317
Fowler, James W., 176
Francis I, Pope, 375
Frans, Roy, 363
Fredericksen, Miriam, 144
French, George, 306
Fritz, Emily, 144
Fry, Henry William, 195n136
Fullerton, Rosemarie, 151
Full Gospel Business Men's Fellowship International (FGBMFI) 222–23
Fundamentalism, 164, 206–7

G

Garabed, Joseph, 21, 250
Gariepy, Henry, 351
Garland, Dennis, 311
Gauntlett, Carvosso, 44, 210, 343
Gauntlett, Marjorie, 125
General's Consultative Council, 85
George V, King, 83, 310
George, Henry, 277–78, 317
Gilliard, Alfred James, 44, 117, 120, 195, 209–10, 337, 344, 352, 357
Gladstone, William Ewart, 80, 287

Globalization, 337, 366–67, 375–77
Goffin, Dean, 257
Goffin, Harry, 223
Gore, John, 16, 269
Gorst, John, 284
Gowans, John, 48, 59, 84–85, 98, 108, 146, 200, 202–3, 258, 373
Graves, Robert, 246
Green, Roger, 12, 61, 160, 170, 172–75, 196, 199, 208, 212, 231, 275, 322
Greene, Alfred, 291

Greenwood, H.J., 284
Grey, Terry, 214
Grice, Edna, 132–33

H

Haartmann, Hedwig, 140
Haggard, H. Rider, 56, 290, 299
Hagin, Kenneth, 221
Haldane, Richard, 80
Hall, Clarence, 180, 193n121
Hallelujah Bands, 5, 63
Hamel, Gary, 122
Hamodava tea, 319
Hampton, Ruth, 146
Hardie, Keir, 279, 284
Harley, Alan, 182, 217
Harris, Ray, 189
Harris, Wesley, 93, 224
Harvey, Paul, 157
Hastings, Adrian, 187, 207
Hattersley, Roy, 119
Hawker, Mrs, 269
Hay, James, 14, 35, 39n94
Hay, Laurence, 138
Hay, Margaret, 142–43, 149, 151
Hays, Richard, 235
Hazzard, John W., 213
Hazell, George, 184
Heathcote, Wyndham S., 70
Heaton, Wilfred, 257
Heese, Terry, 223
Halévy, Élie, 316
Henderson, Sir Edmund, 20
Heong, Huh, 217

Grinsted, Stephen, 12
Groothius, Rebecca Merrill, 139
Guy, David, 227n95

Hiebert, Paul, 118
Higgins, Edward J., 37, 43, 84, 208, 252
High Council, 81–84, 131–32, 361, 363
Hillsong, 260, 264
Hobbes, Thomas, 339, 361
Hobhouse, C.E., 285
Hodder, Henry C., 343
Hodder, Kenneth, 113–14
Hodder, Marjorie, 126
Holdaway, Ernest, 349–50
Holiness, 175–82
Holland, Harry, 317
Holland, May, 146
Hollins, John, 60, 119
Holz, Ernest, 150
Holz, Richard E., 306
Homosexuality, 326–27
Hopkins, Evan, 5
Horrell, David, 92
Horridge, Glenn, 11, 19, 35, 120, 139, 184
Horsley, John, 270
Hostetler, Arvilla, 146
Howells, Herbert, 264
Hoyle, Fred, 192
Hughes, Hugh Price, 5
Hutchinson, Mark, 220
Hutson, Joan, 40, 341
Hutson, Lynette, 152
Huxley, Thomas Henry, 24, 284

I

Idowu-Fearon, Josiah, 367
Infinitum, 117
International Commission on Officership, 100–101
International Doctrine Council, International Theology Council, 99–101, 159, 211, 226–27

International expansion, 16–18, 331–41
International Management Council, 86
International Social Justice Commission, 321
International Spiritual Life Commission, 196, 198, 202–3
Irving, Henry, 33

J

Jackson, Charlotte, 195
Jagger, Mick, 257
James, Henry, 285
Jamieson, Penny, 135, 136n65
Jarrett, Rebecca, 27, 271

Jarvis, Maureen, 258
Jeffries, Charles, 20
Jenkins, Jerry B., 234
Jeune, Mary, 284
Joe the Turk, *see* Garabed, Joseph

407

INDEX

Johannides, Vassili, 307
John Paul II, Pope, 118
Johnson, Benton, 54
Johnson, Luke Timothy, 189
Joplin, Scott, 257

Jorgensen, Bertha, 220
Joystrings, 222, 257
Judd, Carrie, 217
Jukes, Richard, 249

K

Kasper, Walter, Cardinal, 51–52, 373
Katsande, Petros, 358
Keanie, Victor, 372
Kelly, Dean M., 39
Kellner, Paul, 226
Kendall, R.T., 216
Kendrick, Kathleen, 150
Kenyon, E.W., 221
Kettl, Donald, 311
Kew, Clifford, 196
Kilpatrick, H.S., 220

Kimbangu, Simon, 358
Kipling, Rudyard, 15
Kirk, Norman, 317
Kitching, Wilfred, 46, 52, 210, 219, 370
Klaver, Peter, 217
Knox, Ronald, 53, 59
Kraemer, Hendrik, 112
Kroc donation, 312
Krupa Das, P.D., 144
Küng, Hans, 71
Kunz, Victor, 58

L

Labor Party, 2, 316–17, 319n75
Labor Church movement, 318n69
Labouchere, Henry, 271n23
La Haye, Tim, 234
Lamb, Abram, 128
Lamb, David, 84–85, 290–92
Lansbury, George, 316
Larkin, Clarence, 233
Larsson, John, xi, 48, 82, 87–88, 169, 212, 223, 225, 229, 258–59, 365, 374
Larsson, Karl, 58, 140, 344
Larsson, Roger, 225
Lawley, Harriet, 128
Lawley, John, 128
Layton, Philip, 189, 196, 234
Lennon, John, 257
Lesworthy, G. W., 112
Lewis, C. S., 53n7

Lewis, Fay, 135
Lightfoot, Joseph Barber, 75, 335
Lima document, 98, 196–97, 210, 372
Lindsay, Vachel, 56
Little, Robert, 270
Ljungholm, Sven and Katie, 346
Loch, C.S., 284
Lock, Louisa, 15, 20
Lodahl, Michael, 230
Long, Walter, 285
Lovatt, Roy, 134
Love Feast, 192,
Lull, Raymond, 346
Lunde, Albert Gustav, 218
Lunn, Henry, 57, 188, 190, 192
Luther, Martin, 211
Lydholm, Gudrun, 202, 225n80

M

Macchia, Frank D., 168
MacFarlane, Mary, 126, 131, 133–34
McGuigan, Peter, 226
McIntyre, Carl, 370
Macintyre, Stuart, 354
McLeod, Hugh, 10, 28–30
Maiden Tribute Campaign, 271, 319, 326
Makone, Bernard Mangizi, 358
Manning, Henry Edward, Cardinal, 24, 59, 273, 284

Manning, Ron, 110, 225
Mapp, Henry, 44
Marshall, Gordon, 53
Marshall, Norman, 211
Martin, David, 116
Martin, Lee, 317
Marx, Karl, 2, 238, 317, 359
Maste, Gustaaf, 356
Match Factory, Lights in Darkest England, 287, 319

Maxwell, Earle, 114, 373
Mayhew, Henry, 281
Mehling, Charles, 331
Messinger, Sheldon L., 280
Metcalf, William, 196, 225
Methodism, 59–62, 64, 67, 77, 90, 92, 94, 96, 106, 115, 119, 159, 161, 180, 184, 187, 316, 362, 369
Methodist New Connexion, 5, 94, 158, 161–64, 186–87, 238, 315
Methodist Reform Movement, 61
Michels, Robert, 91
Millennialism, post-millennialism, pre-millennialism, 230–31, 335–36
Milligan, Elizabeth, 55, 311, 318
Milner, Alfred, 339
Mitchell, Gordon, 182
Miyahira, Lieutenant, 344
Mobbs, Bernard, 210, 234
Moody, Dwight L., 8, 62
Moore, Thomas, 186, 277, 352
Moral and Social Issues Councils, 122, 326–27
Moravian Brethren, 182

Morris, Emma Elizabeth Florence, 16
Morrison, Ann, 130
Morrison, Reid, 238
Moule, Handley, 5
Moyles, R. Gordon, 10, 26, 42–43, 54, 59, 109, 165, 171, 224, 251, 253–54
Moyo, David, 363
Mpadi, Simon, 358
Müller, Ludwig, 356
Mumford, Catherine, *see* Booth, Catherine
Mundell, Thomas Hodgson, 218, 248
Munn, Olivia, 182
Munn, Richard, 155
Munro, Hector ("Saki"), 37–38, 251
Murdoch, Norman H., 10–12, 18, 25, 29–30, 119, 160, 273–75, 277–80, 303, 332
Murphy, U.G., 319
Murray, Mary, 343
Murray, Paul, 373
Murray, Shirley, 264
Murray, William, 14–15
Muthiah, Narayana, 41, 348
Muzorewa, Abel, 362

N

Ndoda, David, 111
Needham, Philip, 88, 99, 112, 120, 165, 196, 203
Neill, Stephen, 181
Nelson, Jack, 358
New York Civil Liberties Union, 313
Nicol, Alexander M., 17, 26, 28, 30, 205–6, 252–53, 276, 281, 287n77, 289, 291, 294–97, 303, 305, 310, 323, 347–49

Niebuhr, H. Richard, 38
Nielsen, Jostein, 224n79
Nielsen, Julius, 133
Niles, Daniel T., 346
Nobili, Robert de, 346
Noland, Joe, 313
Non-commissioned officers, 105–9
Nyandoro, Misheck, 345

O

Oakley, Ray, 256
O'Brian, William, 137
O'Conner, Fergus, 315
O'Dea, Thomas, 42, 92, 110
Odegaard, Donald, 308, 344
Officership, 93–104
Ojala, Owen, 221
Oliphant, Elwin, 187

Onslow, William, Earl of, 285
Opposition and persecution, 18–27, 284–87
Order, the Salvation Army as an Order, 116–18
Orr, J. Edwin, 5–6
Orsborn, Albert W. T., 45–46, 59, 85, 87, 102, 103n44, 199, 255, 311, 364, 370
Osborne, Jim, 349
Ouchterlony, Hannah, 129

P

Packer, James, 64
Pallant, Dean, 308
Palmer, Martin, 90
Palmer, Phoebe, 62–63, 126–27, 160, 177, 198
Parham, Charles, 216

Parker, Edward J., 85
Parkin, Geoffrey, 143
Parkinson, Mrs Harry, 144
Parkyn, Marianne (*see* Marianne Railton)
Paul, Annette, 288

Péan, Charles, 320
Pears, Richard, 132–33, 136
Pearson, Elizabeth, 16
Pearson, William James, 217n46, 248, 335–36
Peck, Jesse Truesdale, 178
Peddle, Brian, 374
Pedlar, James, 55, 197
Pender, Dinsdale, 201, 222
Pentecostal and Charismatic movements, 215–30, 260, 264, 354
Persecution and opposition, 18–27, 284–87
Petrie, Laura, 102, 131
Peyron, Albin, 320
Phillips, W. Raglan, 219
Philpott, Peter, 26, 354
Pink Floyd, 264

Pius X, Pope, 114
Politics, 314–19
Pollard, George, 17
Polman, Gerrit, 217
Poor Clares, 315
Povlsen, Agnes, 131
Povlsen, Jens, 218
Power, Bruce, 55
Price, Clara, 16
Price, James, 246
Price, Peter, 121
Primitive Methodism, 137, 184, 192, 239
Prosper of Aquitaine, 237
Public Questions Boards, 121, 326
Puotiniemi, Antero, 201

Q

Quakers, 195

R

Rabbitts, Edward, 5
Radcliffe, Reginald, 65
Rader, Kay, 136, 139, 151–52
Rader, Paul, 31, 47, 100, 122, 151, 153, 182, 198, 209, 357
Railton, George Scott, 4, 9, 16, 19, 21, 34, 51, 56, 65, 69, 72–73, 117, 128, 137, 168, 178, 190, 194, 204–5, 231, 241, 248, 266, 278, 351, 369
Railton, Marianne, 137, 270
Rajakumari, Mary, 144
Ranks of officers, 379–80
Ratzinger, Joseph, Cardinal (Pope Benedict XVI), 52, 90
Raymond, Jonathan, 212
Read, Edward, 182
Read, Harry, 258
Read, James, 212, 235
Read, John, 71n95, 160–61, 169, 177, 212
Redhead, Gwenyth, 147, 259
Redhead, Robert, 259
Rees, Arthur, 127
Rees, David, 354
Rendell, Doris, 255
Reynolds, Captain Mrs, 20, 129

Rhemick, John, 22n53–57, 23n58, 161, 170–72, 199–200, 212, 214, 247, 315
Rhodes, Cecil John, 276, 283, 290, 339, 351
Ricci, Matthew, 346
Richards, Miriam, 255
Rightmire, R. David, 195, 197–98, 212, 347
Roberts, Campbell, 320–21, 327
Roberts, William A., 364n93
Robertson, Roland, xv, 3, 7, 11, 13, 31, 42, 50, 54–55, 96, 199, 231, 254, 280, 318, 337, 366–67, 377
Robinson, Barbara, 154
Robinson, Earl, 60, 87, 89, 329–30
Robinson, John A.T., 210
Robinson, Robert, 235
Rodwell, Heather, 132
Role theory, 91–92
Rook, Russell, 222
Roots conferences, 222
Røper, Ketty, 256–57
Rowell, Minnie, (*see* Minnie Lindsay Carpenter)
Rudman, Annie, 269
Rupp, Gordon, 59
Ruse, Earle and Beatrice, 220, 223
Ryan, Max, 218
Ryle, Gilbert, 339

S

Sacraments, 182–203
Salvation Army Students' Fellowship, 41, 209
Sample, Tex, 247
Samples, Iva Lou, 258
Sandall, Robert, 65–66, 75, 184, 193, 289, 331, 337
Sandercock-Brown, Grant, 214
Sanwick, 222
Sarbin, Theodore, 91–92
Saki, *see* Hector Munro
Satterlee, Allen, 39, 196, 232, 234, 256
Saunders, Edward, 16
Saunders, Ruth, 146
Savage, Raeline, 132
Sayers, Sarah, 128
Schillebeeckx, Edmund, 186, 192
Schoenherr, Richard, 92
Scofield Reference Bible, 233
Scotney, Hubert, 97
Scripture, 206–8, 213–15
Seaman, Matthew, 175
Second Evangelical Awakening, 5–6
Secularization, 49–50
Sengers, Erik, 325
Sergeant, Charles, 80
Seymour, William J., 216
Shaftesbury, 7th Earl of (Anthony Ashley-Cooper), 23, 172
Shakespeare, Karen, 149, 154, 337
Shaw, Annie, 16
Shaw, George Bernard, 41, 271, 316
Shepherd, Kate, 15
Shirley, Eliza, 16
Short, Jane, 267

Simmonds, Francis and Rose, 140
Singleton, John, 270
Skeleton army, 19–21
Slater, Richard, 248
Smeaton, Ken, 223
Smidt, G.O., 218
Smith, Allister (father), 72, 350
Smith, Allister (son), 182, 351
Smith, David, 60
Smith, Dean, 214–15
Smith, Ellen, 132
Smith, Frank, 272, 274–80, 305, 316–17, 353
Smith, J. Evan, 361
Smith, Richard, 226, 259
Soldiers, 109–16
Social justice, 314–21
Somerset, Lady Henry, 192–93
Stanley, Henry Morton, 275
Stankuweit, Franz, 356
Stark, Rodney, 87, 117
Stark, Werner, 40, 43
Stead, William T., 3, 27, 271, 275–80, 283, 339
Steadman-Allen, Ray, 257, 264
Steele, Daniel, 178–79
Stobart, Violet, 144
Street, Robert, 203
Strickland, Danielle, 117, 145, 149, 155, 321
Sullivan, Louis, 303
Sutherland, Thomas, 17
Svensson, Kaleb, 356
Swansbury, Gordon, 148
Swarts, G., 340–41
Swatos, William, 59
Swift, Susan, 58, 272–75, 277–80, 293

T

Tait, Campbell, 75, 77
Taiz, Lilian, 179–80, 246, 250–51, 288, 306, 353
Tanedo, Noveminda, 152
Tavel, Franz von, 140
Taylor, Brian, 364
Taylor, David, 116–17
Taylor, Gordon, 115
Terry, Roy, 112
Thistle, Paul, 300
Thomas, David, 127
Thomas, Katrina, 146
Thompson, Arthur, 143

Thompson, Francis, 284
Thompson, William, 75
Thurman, Henry, 349
Tillich, Paul, 210
Tillsley, Bramwell H., 47, 53, 151, 182
Tracy, Ruth, 255
Treite, Carl, 356
Troeltsch, Ernst, 53
Tuck, Brian, 196
Tucker, Frederick, *see* Booth-Tucker
Turner, Corey, 222
Turner, Percy, 299

V

Valignano, Alessandri, 346
Valpy, Arabella, 17
Vatican Council II, 73, 109
Victoria, Queen, 1

Vinti, Miriam, 143, 153
Vineyard, 221, 260
Volunteers of America, 34, 79, 353

W

Wagner, C. Peter, 216, 221
Wahlström, Jarl, 47, 58n33, 86, 343
Wahlström, Marie, 125, 142
Wahlström, Tor, xv, 102, 117
Wainwright, John, 366
Waldensians, 92
Waldron, John D., 165, 169, 225
Wall, Phil, 117
Walls, Andrew Finlay, 208
Ward, Kevin, 229
War, 341–45
Waterhouse, Edwin, 285
Waters, Cecil, 98, 136
Watson, Bernard, 9n9, 110, 277
Watson, Robert, 199
Watt, Lynda, 149
Webb, Geoff and Kylie, 182
Webb, Graeme, 223
Weber, Max, 53, 377
Webster, Francis S., 58
Weerasooriya, Arnolis, 348, 361n87
Weggery, Lawrence, 143
Wells, David, 262
Werken, Johanna van den, 135
Wesley, Charles, 249
Wesley, John, 5, 37, 56, 60–62, 67–68, 70, 72, 76, 126, 159, 175–77, 180, 187, 228, 230
Westbrook, Emma, 16
Westcott, Brooke Foss, 75, 190

Westcott, Hubert, 370
Westrupp, Andy, 224
Whiller, James, 138
Whyte, Alexander, 5
Wickberg, Eric, 46, 335, 344, 346, 373
Wigglesworth, Smith, 218
Wilkinson, Charles Allix, 75–76
Williams, Brenton, 223
Williams, Charles, 315
Williams, Eileen, 150
Williams, H. Rodman, 73
Wilson, Bryan R., 7, 40–43, 54–55, 83, 199
Wimber, John, 221
Wisbey, Herbert, 353
Wiseman, Clarence, 47, 86, 88, 120–21, 200–201, 218, 225–26, 311, 343
Wolmar, Chris, 310
Wolseley, Garnet, 73
Women's Aglow, 222–23
Wood, J.A., 178
Woodall, Ann, 338–39
Woods, Reginald, 370
Wordsworth, William, 14
World Council of Churches, 98, 109, 196–97, 210, 370–72
Wright, Edward, 17
Wright, Tom, 235
Wuarlela, Captain, 344

X

Xavier, Francis, 346, 348

Y

Yamamuro, Gunpei, 357
Yancy, Philip, 263
Yeats, W.B., 374

Yinger, John Milton, 4
Yon, Patricia, 144, 148
Yuill, Chick, 97, 182, 212

Z

Zinzendorf, Count Nicolaus, 59

www.ingramcontent.com/pod-product-compliance
Lightning Source LLC
Chambersburg PA
CBHW081147290426
44108CB00018B/2461